Contents

PART II HISTORICAL CONTEXT   127

CHAPTER 6 Fault Lines   129

CHAPTER 7 The Nature and End of the Cold War   155

Preface

On January 20, 2009, the United States inaugurated the first post-9/11 president. Barack Obama became not only the country's 44th chief executive, he inherited a situation of enormous economic crisis and peril and a foreign and national security environment that had undergone considerable trauma and faced enormous dangers and uncertainties. The economic crisis clearly dominated the early Obama agenda, but the energetic new president quickly placed high priorities on national security legacies from the past eight years and challenges and opportunities for the future. The purpose of this fourth edition is to try to identify, analyze, and place in perspective the influences and dynamics of this emerging post-9/11 national security world.

This new edition represents the current point in an odyssey both for the author and for the subject matter, American national security policy. My first excursion into this subject matter came with the publication of the first edition of the predecessor of this text, *National Security*, in 1985. That text reflected the situation at the time, which remained fixated on deterring a nuclear third world war with the Soviet Union. How far the world has come since then! When the first edition of *National Security for a New Era* appeared in 2003, there were new influences to add, notably the impact of international religious terrorism and nontraditional influences like globalization. The impact of U.S. involvement in wars in Afghanistan and Iraq have, at least for a time, become the overriding influence and the context in which American security policy will evolve and in which it can most fully be understood for the upcoming years.

Some of the discussion about the impact of Afghanistan and Iraq on the future must, of course, be conditioned by the fact that neither war has yet ended for the United States. From the perspective of early 2010, when these words are written, two things about that ending seem clear: One is that both are examples of the kinds of open-ended, inconclusive, and controversial conflicts that dominate the contemporary landscape of violence into which the United States sometimes finds itself drawn. The other is an increasing ambivalence toward engaging scarce American resources in such wars, especially in times of economic stress. Because residual involvement in each case still could stretch out for several years, the result will almost certainly be politically poisonous and probably accentuate the negative impacts suggested in these pages. In the inimitable words of former Secretary of Defense Donald Rumsfeld, the United States is likely to move from the realm of "knowing what we do not know" to the realm of "not knowing what we do not know." It will certainly be an adventure.

NEW TO THIS EDITION

Like its predecessor, this text has evolved as well. The first edition appeared in 2003, as the events of September 11, 2001, had cast an increasingly encompassing cloud over the relatively tranquil (at least in retrospect) 1990s. That decade had been dominated by the forces of growing economic globalization, which was then overshadowed by the new geopolitics of combating international religious terrorism. Because both forces remained prominent aspects of the global mix, the first edition was subtitled *Globalization and Geopolitics*. The subtitle was meant to suggest a competition between these two mostly dissimilar approaches as the dominant paradigm for national security, and the subtitle remained unchanged for the second edition.

The subtitle—and with it, much of the thematic emphasis—changed for the third edition to *Globalization and Geopolitics After Iraq*, reflecting the extraordinary impact the author believes the Iraq War will have on American thinking about and actions on matters of national security for the next five to ten years or even possibly beyond. As American combat participation in Iraq continues to diminish toward the final withdrawal of combat troops specified in the December 2008 Status of Forces Agreement with Iraq, other parts of the national security environment will become relatively more prominent. The war in Afghanistan has already eclipsed Iraq in important ways in the public attention, as have related concerns in Pakistan. These changes, in turn, represent continuations and permutations of the global war on terror (GWOT) inherited from the Bush years. Exactly how these tangled aspects of U.S. national security policy in the Middle East are worked out will vitally affect how the country views its national security future. The new dynamics help explain the absence of a subtitle; the system is in sufficient limbo that it is difficult to characterize in one phrase.

Domestically, there will be a great debate about how to rebuild American armed forces (especially the Army, Marines, and Reserves), stressed to or beyond the breaking point by Iraq, as well as a debate about the kinds of circumstances in which those rejuvenated forces will be used in the future. A major aspect of that debate will be how much—or how little—the United States can afford to expend on national security and remain safe (a concern reflected in Chapter 3) American forces and to avoid what the American public has overwhelmingly decided was the promiscuous use of force in Iraq. A major outcome of the "lessons learned" from Iraq will be "No More Iraqs" and the question will be what that means and whether that lesson is more enduring than it was after Vietnam.

The substantive changes in this edition can be briefly summarized as follows:

- The order of chapters has been extensively revised so that all conceptual and historical chapters are in a more logical flow than in previous editions.
- Sections have been rearranged to accommodate the changes in chapter ordering.
- One new chapter (Chapter 10) has been added to reflect the greater emphasis on Afghanistan in this edition.
- Major revisions have been made in Chapters 6, 9, 11, and 13 to reflect changing priorities in the national security environment.
- There is a more systematic historical review of the evolution of national security thinking and actions since the end of the Cold War than before.
- The likely impact of the new Obama administration on national security concerns has been added in appropriate sections of various chapters and particularly in Chapter 14.

These summary observations can be elaborated more fully. A major emphasis of the fourth edition is a reorganization of materials into a more coherent conceptual ordering than in previous editions. Those who are familiar with earlier editions will find that the chapters that have been reorganized remain familiar if updated. Their reordering is intended to create a more logical flow of the ideas and arguments developed throughout the book.

The new flow of this edition reflects those intentions. It is divided into three parts. The first part, Conceptual Context, lays the formation for thinking about American national security. It begins with a discussion of the changing nature of the national security problem (Chapter 1), sets the realist conceptual grounding of how policy makers have thought about national security (Chapter 2), examines the most important concepts of the realist paradigm (Chapter 3), fits national security into the historical American experience (Chapter 4), and places national security into the domestic political context (Chapter 5).

Part II, the Historical Context, consists of five chapters that develop national security's evolution since World War II/It begins with the idea of critical points (or fault lines) in that development (Chapter 6), moves to an examination of the Cold War (Chapter 7), analyzes forces during the 1990s (Chapter 8), looks at the new dynamics created by 9/11 (Chapter 9), and concludes with surviving, transcending policy problems (Chapter 10).

Part III, New Challenges, addresses more directly the theme identified in the new subtitle. It begins with the problem of asymmetrical warfare—the dominant dynamic of much contemporary violence—in Chapter 11, applies those dynamics in Afghanistan and Iraq (Chapter12), examines terrorism and solutions to underlying sources of instability (Chapter 13), and concludes by examining traditional and nontraditional challenges confronting the Obama administration (Chapter 14).

FEATURES

This book has been organized, as its predecessor editions have been, in three parts designed to provide comprehensive introductions to national security topics and thus to function as a core text in national security courses. The table of contents is discussed in the next section, but the organization moves from Part I, which provides the conceptual context for the study of U.S. national security, to Part II's concerns with historical and current political and military realities, to Part III's emphasis on ongoing security issues and the application of the discussion to likely futures.

An effort has been made to make the text as reader-friendly and easy to follow as possible. Each part, for instance, begins with a brief discussion and rationale of the chapters in that part of the book, and each chapter begins with a preview that provides a glimpse of the material in that particular chapter. Each individual chapter also contains recurring features: a set of Amplification and Challenge! boxes that expand on materials discussed and raises question for reader consideration; a set of Study/Discussion questions drawn from the text; and a Selected Bibliography of materials the author considers relevant and understandable for undergraduate readers.

SUPPLEMENTS

Longman is pleased to offer several resources to qualified adopters of *National Security for a New Era* and their students that will make teaching and learning from this book even more effective and enjoyable.

For Instructors

MyPoliSciKit Video Case Studies.   Featuring video from major news sources and providing reporting and insight on recent world affairs, this DVD series helps instructors integrate current events into their courses by letting them use the clips as lecture launchers or discussion starters.

For Students

MySearchLab.   Need help with a paper? MySearchLab saves time and improves results by offering start-to-finish guidance on the research/writing process and full-text access to academic journals and periodicals. To learn more, please visit www.mysearchlab.com or contact your Pearson representative. To order MySearchLab with this book, use ISBN 0205798659.

Longman Atlas of World Issues **(0-321-22465-5).** Introduced and selected by Robert J. Art of Brandeis University and excerpted from the acclaimed Penguin Atlas Series, the *Longman Atlas of World Issues* is designed to help students understand the geography and major issues facing the world today, such as terrorism, debt, and HIV/AIDS. These thematic, full-color maps examine forces shaping politics today at a global level. Explanatory information accompanies each map to help students better grasp the concepts being shown and how they affect our world today. Available at no additional charge when packaged with this book.

ACKNOWLEDGMENTS

No work of this magnitude is accomplished alone. During the drafting and redrafting of this text, I have benefited from the useful comments and suggestions of a number of reviewers whose suggestions strengthened the effort. They include Valentine J. Belfiglio, *Texas Women's University*; David Benjamin, *University of Bridgeport*; Charles Cushman, *George Washington University*; Gary L. Guertner, *University of Arizona*; Joe D. Hagan, *West Virginia University*; Patrick Haney, *Miami University*; Christopher Jones, *Northern Illinois University*; Richard J. Kilroy Jr., *East Carolina University*; Lawrence Korb, *Center for American Progress*; Edward G. Moore, *University of Texas at Brownsville*; Linda Petrou, *High Point University*; J. Patrick Plumlee, *University of North Florida*; Philip Schrodt, *University of Kansas*; Michael E. Smith, *Georgia State University*; and Chris Van Aller, *Winthrop University*. Any remaining errors are, of course, my own.

Donald M. Snow
Professor Emeritus, University of Alabama

PART

I

CONCEPTUAL CONTEXT

Part I consists of five chapters, each of which provides some perspective, or context, for understanding the national security situation. Chapter 1 looks at some basic dynamics of the system, including the idea of fault lines and their impact on change, the basic idea of change and its impact on thinking about national security, and the problems of change for the Obama administration. The discussion then turns to the operating rules of international politics since the peace of Westphalia, the so-called realist paradigm that defines the geopolitical approach, in Chapter 2. That paradigm was under fire during the 1990s as an adequate description of a globalizing world; it was revived with the campaign against terrorism and the U.S. wars in Afghanistan and Iraq as a way to evaluate those experiences. Regardless of challenges to realism, however, its basic concepts remain relevant to analyzing national security, and these concepts are amplified in Chapter 3. The United States has had a unique historical experience in matters of national security. The evolution of that experience and how current realities have affected those historical and physical influences are the chief topics of Chapter 4. Among the elements of that experience has been a feeling of security based in the impregnability of the country—a feeling that has now been effectively deflated. The operation of the American political system adds a further set of opportunities and constraints to thinking about and acting on national security, and these influences are examined in Chapter 5.

CHAPTER 1

The Changing Problem of National Security

PREVIEW

The United States is arguably at a crossroads about national security as the increasingly unpopular Iraq War is moving slowly toward an uncertain conclusion, the war effort in Afghanistan continues to occupy the country's attention, and international religious terrorism remains an unresolved problem. In this situation, it is natural to ask questions about the amount of change that has occurred in the national security environment and what those changes mean for the United States. This chapter introduces these concerns and how the Obama administration thinks about and implements national security policy.

The past two decades have been trying for American national security policy and for those who make, implement, and study that policy and the strategies and plans that carry it out. Two special and largely unpredicted and unprecedented events have served as the benchmarks of change from what now seems (but certainly did not at the time) to have been the relative stability, even tranquility, of the Cold War to the current imbroglio. The first of these was the end of the Cold War, which, in retrospect, began with the succession of Mikhail S. Gorbachev in the former Soviet Union in 1984 and culminated with the formal demise of that state with the last tick of the clock in Moscow at the end of 1991. The balance of the 1990s would witness the remarkably peaceful disappearance of the Soviet-led Communist half of the bipolar politico-military competition that was the touchstone of the four decades of the Cold War competition that defined the American national security problem. The Soviet implosion would be followed by the adjustment to a world with only one standing military superpower.

The second event, of course, was the attacks of September 11, 2001 and the introduction of international religious terrorism as a continuing anchor of U.S.

security concern. It is instructive that the Cold War is now referred to as the "long peace," signifying the absence of systemwide military trauma on the scale of the world wars that distinguish humankind's most violent century, the twentieth. It is also instructive that national security practitioners and analysts increasingly refer to the post–September 11 period as the "long war," suggesting a long-term endurance of the competition with international religious terrorism. The Iraq War has been one controversial punctuation point in this "long war." Afghanistan has been another.

Since the tragic events of September 11, 2001, American concern for national security has been almost totally focused on—some might argue transfixed by—the problem of international terrorism and its likely recurrence on American soil. In the immediate wake of the airplane hijackings that ended with those airplanes being used as missiles against highly visible and symbolic American economic (the World Trade Center towers) and military (the Pentagon) targets, the reaction was of an astonished world fundamentally transformed by the acts of Usama bin Laden and his terrorist organization, Al Qaeda. The United States launched a military campaign to overthrow the Afghani government, which had provided the terrorists sanctuary, and began a manhunt for the elusive bin Laden and his cohorts that continues to this day. The national security establishment reoriented itself to a primary emphasis on suppressing terrorism and preventing its recurrence. The invasion and conquest of Iraq by the United States and its "coalition partners" in 2003 was largely justified as part of the terrorist campaign as well.

The transition was difficult. Partly, the reason had to do with the nature of the new challenge: *terrorism*. Although terrorism is certainly nothing very new, its application by foreigners on American soil is novel. Domestic terrorist acts have certainly occurred sporadically during American history—the assassination of American presidents, for instance, and the bombing of the Murrah Federal Building in Oklahoma City in 1995 come to mind. Although not widely recognized at the time, the first attack on the World Trade Center in 1993 was indeed an opening gambit of international religious terrorism punctuated by September 11. At the same time, Americans overseas have been victims of terrorist attacks: during the 1990s, the same Al Qaeda network that committed the September 11 acts was implicated in attacks against the American embassies in Dar es Salaam, Tanzania, and Nairobi, Kenya, in 1998 and against an American warship, the USS *Cole*, moored in a Yemeni port in 2000, for instance. The September 11 attacks dwarfed these previous actions physically and conceptually: nearly three thousand people were killed in the shocking events, which were committed by foreigners acting on our own soil.

Part of the ensuing confusion was conceptual as well. Although a small community of analysts (some of whom are noted in the readings at the end of this chapter) has studied the problem and likelihood of terrorist activity for years, the subject of terrorism had not previously caught the public's attention. The attacks on 9/11, of course, changed that focus dramatically. Terrorism quickly became the primary threat facing the United States, and national security concerns worked their way up or down the defense agenda in large measure in relation to the extent they could be associated with the national response to terrorism. The global war on terrorism (GWOT) became the shibboleth of the Bush administration approach to national security.

The Iraq War is one prominent example of an action related to the trauma of September 11. As an event, it is conceptually of a lower order of importance than either the end of the Cold War or the terrorist attacks, but its impact has eroded the public perceptions of the uses of American force in ways not seen since the reaction to the Vietnam War in the latter half of the 1970s. American military involvement in Iraq is winding down, and the Obama administration is struggling to bring closure to the parallel effort in Afghanistan. How the United States responds to the end of the Iraq and Afghanistan military experiences will, at a minimum, help shape the future of the American national security debate, whether it concerns how American military forces are rebuilt or the ways in which those forces are employed to wage the war against terrorism or to realize other and unrelated national ends. Conceptually, Iraq occupies a position within the "long war" similar to that occupied by Vietnam within the Cold War: essentially a sideshow to the central competition but justified by its arguable contribution to that central competition. Exactly how Iraq and Afghanistan will be remembered remains an open question that only time can answer. To look at the national security problem—to begin thinking about national security—two directions, outlined here, recur as primary emphases in the chapters that follow. One of these emphases is the theme of change, and it has two aspects in light of the September 11 events. The first is the extent and depth of change that the terrorist attacks introduced into the calculus of national security. The second regards changed dynamics of the environment in light of critical events in the past decade or more. Chief among those influences is the changing nature and profundity of threat. The other emphasis is on the basic nature of the national security environment, and this book introduces and examines two fundamental depictions: an environment dominated by, among other things, international economic growth and expansion (globalization) and related nontraditional security concerns and one dominated by military threats and what to do about them. How these and other factors will be arranged, or rearranged, in the post–9/11 environment will serve as a recurring theme in the pages that follow.

THE NATURE OF CHANGE

The question of change and how to adapt to it successfully is a more-or-less constant part of the national security debate, and it really consists of two questions. One is, How much has the environment truly been altered by events such as those of September 11? The other is, What dominant characteristics of the national security environment have been altered as a result of those changes? Because of the proximity of events, there is no consensus on either of these matters at any particular point in time, and the contemporary situation is no exception. Having said that, this chapter introduces perspectives about the contemporary situation that will be elaborated in the rest of the text and is intended to assist readers in reaching personal judgments on these matters and their implications.

How Much Has Changed?

Immediately after the trauma of September 11, the almost universal reaction of Americans and many of those overseas was that the change wreaked by the suicide air bombers was profound: that everything (at least figuratively) had changed. But was such a radical interpretation accurate? The other way to think about September 11 was that the roots of change so dramatically demonstrated by 9/11 were present before the bombers struck and that those influences remain as prominent aspects of the environment. From this perspective, the underlying dynamics had not so much changed as had the vivid demonstrations of some of the most dramatic, traumatic implications of those dynamics. In other words, did 9/11 signal a dramatic change, or did it provide an indelible example of ongoing dynamics? Each perspective deserves at least brief elaboration.

The popular view of the impact of September 11 on the national security environment at the time was that it represented a fundamental, encompassing alteration of the problems facing the United States in the world and how these problems had to be confronted. Partially born of the sheer magnitude and audacity of the attacks on the World Trade Center and the Pentagon and their vivid, relentless depiction on television, the initial reaction was that everything had changed, a perception largely reinforced both by the volume and the emphasis of the news media and by political figures. The terrorist acts were so dramatic that it was easy to view this as a "new kind of war," one that Americans had difficulty understanding and placing into context.

Two related elements stood out from the initial shock. The first was the realization of physical vulnerability facing Americans. As pointed out in Chapter 4, one of the unique and favorable parts of the American historical experience has been the virtual invulnerability of American soil to foreign attack. The last time there was an organized physical assault on American soil was during the War of 1812. While Soviet nuclear forces were capable of destroying the United States physically during the Cold War (see Chapter 7), American soil has seldom been threatened, and the integrity of the American homeland has rarely been a source of major concern. The terrorist breach of American invulnerability was thus particularly shocking. Although international terrorists did not (and do not) threaten American existence in the way that Soviet rockets did, American vulnerability to harm (if not extinction) was established by the events of September 11.

The second, related aspect was the continuing nature of vulnerability and the realization that the problem would not dissipate soon. This "new kind of war" would not be climactically decided on some major battlefield where the perpetrators would be decisively vanquished. Rather, the "war on terrorism" would be a long and difficult *campaign* (to borrow the description of French President Jacques Chirac) that would take considerable time and vigilance—a long war, in contemporary language.

The contending interpretation suggested that less had really changed than was presumed immediately after the tragedy. The assertion that not a great deal has changed emphasizes continuities in the pre– and post–September 11 environments. It suggests, for instance, that the basic sources of instability in the international system, before the event, came from the most unstable countries of the developing world and that they still do. During the 1990s, this instability was manifested largely in chaotic civil conflicts, where the policy question for the United States was whether these were important enough for American involvement. Contemporary conflicts continue in some of these states, and the locations (Sudan, for instance) are the same kinds of places that provide the apparent breeding grounds for terrorism, the eradication of which is the current underlying policy rationale. In the 1990s, the United States joined an international humanitarian effort in Kosovo; in 2001, the United States assisted in the overthrow of the Taliban government of Afghanistan on the grounds of denying sanctuary for terrorists, followed by "regime change" in Iraq in 2003. In the 1990s, the rationale was relieving humanitarian disasters, while in the 2000s, many of the same kinds of actions in the same kinds of places were justified as responses to terrorism.

At the same time, terrorism was a problem before September 11, and it continues to be a problem. Usama bin Laden had attacked Americans before his most spectacular foray (for instance, the Trade Towers in 1993), and he remains a menace. The antiterrorism community had been warning of possible terrorist attacks directly against the United States for years, but their warnings had largely gone unheeded (at least partly because those previous warnings had proven false). While it is true that essentially no one had predicted the scale, exact nature, or audacity of the attacks that did occur, it is equally true that terrorism did not come into existence on September 11.

New Dynamics in the Environment?

The years since 1991 have been an especially dynamic period in the evolution of American national security. As argued primarily in Chapter 4, the first two hundred years of the republic were marked by two major periods in national security terms. The first is what I call the formative period, lasting from the birth of the republic through World War II. This period was distinguished by a relatively low order of priority for national security concerns and relatively small commitments to defense matters, with "spikes" of concern when the country was thrust into war situations, followed by a return to the demilitarized normalcy of peacetime. The second is the Cold War, from the latter 1940s until the implosion of Soviet Communism in 1991. This period was distinguished from its predecessor because it was the first major American sustained involvement in national security affairs, when the United States developed and maintained large standing armed forces in peacetime and when the prevailing paradigm was the national security state (the situation in which preserving the integrity of the state is the major defining purpose of government). It was also the first time the existence of the United States became a matter of concern because Soviet nuclear weapons could physically destroy the United States as a functioning society, admittedly with terrible likely consequences for the Soviet Union as well.

The period from the beginning of the downfall of Communist regimes in Europe in 1989 until the terrorist events of 2001 produced large changes in the American national security problems. Two major events—fault lines—have largely defined those perceived changes. As a result of the second change in particular, there has also been a growing belief that the nature of warfare itself may be changing. A major question addressed in the pages that follow is the continuing dominance of the effects of those traumatic events on the future and how the country and individuals adapt to change.

Fault Lines. What is a *fault line* as used in this text? The main idea of the analogy is that fault lines represent traumatic events—akin to the rupture of physical fault lines on the earth's surface accompanying earthquakes—that alter the environment and require an adjustment in the posttraumatic period. The notion is fundamentally compatible with the concept of tectonic shifts that Graham T. Allison, Jr., introduced over a decade ago to describe the impact of the implosion of Communist rule.

Two of these fault lines emerged in the decade and a half after 1989 and altered the national security environment in more or less fundamental ways. Both are discussed extensively in Chapter 6 and elsewhere throughout the text but can be briefly introduced here. The first fault line was the end of the Cold War, symbolized by the peaceful demise of the Soviet Union and the fall, in most cases peacefully, of Communist regimes there and elsewhere. The net result was the end of both the military and the ideological competition between the Communist states, led by the Soviet Union and to some extent China, and the West, led by the United States. Only four states in the world remain technically Communist today, and two of those—China and Vietnam—have renounced Marxist economics, a major underpinning of the ideology. (Only North Korea and Cuba remain staunchly Communist, and Cuba's continuing allegiance to the ideology will likely be challenged with the passing of Fidel Castro.) In systemic terms, this fault line was the more consequential of the two because it affected the very nature of the operation of the international system and the basic threats to that system's existence.

The second fault line, of course, was the emergence of international terrorism through the events of September 11, 2001. As noted, those events and their aftermath have had their main impact on the United States (many other states had already experienced this phenomenon and made whatever adjustments they could to it). The impact of this traumatic event has been to raise awareness of vulnerabilities not previously acknowledged and to mobilize government and society to try to reduce that vulnerability.

It is useful to compare and contrast the two fault lines and their impacts. The end of the Cold War completed a period of stress and challenge, and the reaction to it involved undoing the structure of confrontation and creating a new structure to replace it. With some exceptions (see Chapter 7), that adjustment has largely been made. By contrast, 9/11 created a new period of conflict and tension, one that since has been consumed by the effort to respond to and control or eliminate the resulting threats. Whether the environment of 2010 and beyond will still fundamentally resemble 2001 is a matter of debate, but the legacies of 9/11 remain a vivid part of the landscape.

The impact of Iraq fits into this conceptual structure. The U.S. invasion, conquest, occupation, and eventual withdrawal from Iraq almost certainly would not have occurred had there been no 9/11. The aftermath of Iraq will primarily affect how the United States conceptualizes and uses force in the foreseeable future; it will likely have derivative systemic impacts to the extent that American use of force is either promoted or constrained by its process of self-examination. Unlike September 11, Iraq was not an unanticipated event that shocked and, in some ways, transformed the international system. Rather, it was the result of a conscious policy decision by the Bush administration that, it was argued, was an integral part of the response to terrorism—a corollary of 9/11.

Within the framework of the fault lines (or Allison's tectonic plates) analogy, the Iraq and Afghanistan experiences can be thought of as aftershocks, upsetting occurrences related to the original earthquake created by the September 11 fault line shift. How well this analogy holds up depends in some large measure on the extent to which the Iraq decision was the result of actual circumstances set in motion by the GWOT (the position of war supporters) or to which the relationship was non-existent and manufactured (the position of critics).

National security environments and the impact of the fault lines can also usefully be categorized in terms of threats, a concept developed in more detail in Chapter 3. During the Cold War, the stakes were exceedingly high because the potential consequences of war between the superpowers and their allies (planning for which was the central national security problem of the era) included an all-out nuclear exchange that could culminate such a war. That the Cold War could escalate to a nuclear hot war was plausible in an environment of ideological and political competition for predominance in the world.

As the Cold War evolved, however, those very potential consequences contributed to a gradually lowering likelihood of war. As time passed and arsenal sizes and deadliness increased, both sides increasingly realized that a hot war could effectively destroy them both, leaving no winner. The result was a *necessary peace* (the title of a 1987 book by the author) in which both sides avoided war not because of any mutual empathy but because of fear of the consequences of war. That realization contributed to the perceptions leading to the end of the Cold War.

The end of the Cold War (the first fault line) obviously changed the nature of the threat environment. Russia, as the major successor state of the defunct Soviet Union, maintained the nuclear power to destroy the United States, but the death of Communism left it without any plausible ideological reason to use such weapons against a former adversary that was gradually becoming a friend and even an ally. Although the arsenal sizes remain formidable, arms control agreements culminating in 2002 have reduced their size on both sides. Thus, the period ushered in by the end of the Cold War (roughly the 1990s) saw both a reduction in the likelihood of major threats being carried out and a gradual lowering of the consequences. Actions by the Putin and Medvedev regimes in Russia in recent years have suggested some return to authoritarian rule and at least the possibility of renewed rivalry (see the discussion in Chapter 7).

Exposure of the second fault line further changed the threat calculus in different ways. Al Qaeda, and probably other groups in the future, shows a very high level of willingness to carry out threats that, as argued in Chapter 13, probably cannot all be eliminated in advance: some will succeed. Thus, the likelihood of threats being carried out, in this case by international terrorists, has increased from the Cold War and post–Cold War periods. While the drama and scope of the September 11 attacks serve as stark testimony to the willingness to do as much harm as possible, the consequences of terrorist threats are considerably less great than would have been the case had the Soviet Union launched a nuclear strike during the Cold War. The threat posed by terrorists, in other words, is to do harm, not to threaten the basic integrity of the American state. Should terrorists come into possession of some of the weapons of mass destruction (WMD, including nuclear, biological, and chemical weapons), as many fear and predict, the amount of harm they could do would increase; it is hard to imagine their development of a capability that would threaten the integrity of the United States.

The quality of the threat environment has thus evolved. The Cold War posed a very deadly threat environment (enormous consequences of war) but one that became less dangerous (lower likelihood threats would be carried out) as time passed. The end of the Cold War gradually reduced the deadliness of threats both psychologically (the reduction of motivation) and physically (arms control reductions of arsenal sizes) and reduced dangerousness as well, since threats gradually dissipated. Usama bin Laden and his Al Qaeda adherents, on the other hand, issue plausible threats (ones they are willing and able to carry out in some circumstances), but unless their capacity to do physical harm increases dramatically, such threats will remain at a much lower level of deadliness than was the case during the Cold War. These dynamics suggest several other changes in the environment as well.

The Changing Nature of War? Reaction to the terrorist attacks and subsequent analyses, which include the American campaigns in Afghanistan and Iraq, have raised a popular notion that warfare may be changing, in the sense both that the terrorists are practicing a new kind of war and that, in the future, traditional, conventional forms of warfare may have to be altered or may become obsolete. Traditional warfare, also known as symmetrical warfare, may be replaced by its opposite, asymmetrical warfare, as the dominant form of fighting the United States will face in the future. That prospect was likely even before American involvement in Afghanistan and Iraq. The experience of American opponents in both those theaters reinforces and makes even more likely that prospect.

The term *asymmetrical warfare* has previously been used more or less interchangeably with several other terms to describe irregular warfare and is newer than the dynamic it purports to capture. In fact, the term refers to a form of and an approach to warfare as old as war itself. At its base, asymmetrical warfare is defined as the situation in which both (or all) sides do not accept or practice the same methods of warfare. Asymmetry can extend both to the methods which opposing sides use to conduct military operations and to the rules of warfare to which they adhere. Guerrilla warfare, which the United States encountered in Vietnam when irregular enemy soldiers engaged in tactics such as ambushes, is one form of asymmetrical warfare. Terrorism is another. What is common about asymmetrical approaches is their rejection of whatever conventions of war are practiced by their opponents. Those fighting asymmetrically thus reject the rules of war favored by their opponents; consciously targeting civilians is an example.

The concept of asymmetrical warfare implies its opposite, symmetrical warfare. Symmetrical warfare occurs when both sides adopt and fight in the same basic ways and follow the same basic rules. In the contemporary environment, symmetrical warfare generally refers to fighting between traditional, European-style armed forces (armies, navies, air forces) where both sides agree to be bound by the same rules of engagement, basically as specified in the various Geneva Conventions on war. A synonym for symmetrical warfare is *traditional western war* (western in the sense that it is warfare fought along the lines of European-style combat that evolved over time). World War II was the epitome of symmetrical warfare (even if some isolated combatants fought asymmetrically). In the American and European tradition, it is the acceptable, "honorable" way of war.

Why would someone in effect break the accepted conventions and rules on war and fight asymmetrically (a synonym for which is *dishonorably* to some)? The historical answer is clear: what is now called asymmetrical warfare is the approach of a weaker foe trying to overcome the advantages of a force that is superior in whatever the accepted, conventional forms of warfare of the time prescribe. If one side knows that it will lose if it plays by the opponent's rules, it only makes sense to reject those rules in ways that may turn its weakness into strength and negate the opponent's strengths. There is certainly nothing new or novel about this; in fact, it may be the only thing that makes sense for a weaker party.

Those who are advantaged by conventional standards will always decry the resort to asymmetrical means. The U.S. Army would always prefer that its opponents face it in massed formations on conventional battlefields where overwhelming American firepower can be brought to bear to destroy the opponent, a tradition of warfare that some date back to Ulysses S. Grant during the American Civil War. An inferior opponent would be foolhardy to cooperate in its own destruction by fighting the way the Americans prefer to fight. Thus, they adopt other means.

Those who argue that asymmetrical warfare is becoming the norm may have a point, although they seldom acknowledge the irony of why they are correct. Since the end of the Cold War, the gap between American conventional (symmetrical) military capability and that of any conceivable foes has progressively widened. This gap was first demonstrated in the Persian Gulf War of 1990–1991, and it has since then increased. In 2002, for instance, the defense budget of the United States stood at about $350 billion out of a worldwide total of about $800 billion (including the American total). American military expenditures for 2002 were greater than the expenditures of the next fourteen largest-spending states combined. The budget increases for 2003 pushed the U.S. portion to over one-half of the global total, meaning the United States spent more on defense *than the rest of the world combined*, where it has remained since then.

The result is a conventional, symmetrical military situation in which, effectively, *no state or probable combination of states can successfully confront and fight the United States symmetrically*, using conventional methods and rules. The very success of the American military machine has had the effect of negating its own advantage. Any potential adversaries contemplating fighting the Americans can only conclude that the only chance they have of winning is to change the rules to negate the American advantage. In an act that amounts to an unconscious self-fulfilling prophecy, the United States has created the situation in which its future will almost certainly be in opposition to opponents fighting asymmetrically.

The American experiences in Afghanistan and Iraq reinforce this situation. Both involvements have pitted American (and allied) conventional forces against opponents who are much weaker in conventional terms. In 2003, the United States faced an Iraqi conventional force it had defeated decisively twelve years earlier. In the ensuing years, the capability gap between the two had increased enormously to the point that the Iraqis had (and knew they had) no realistic chance in symmetrical warfare against the United States. As a result, after a token conventional defense, they accepted the inevitable symmetrical defeat and reverted to asymmetrical means of resistance discussed in Chapter 12. The Afghans, on the other hand, possessed essentially no conventional army in the first place and could only combat the latest round of foreign intrusion on their soil asymmetrically. Whether these situations are harbingers of the future is a major part of the discussion in Part IV of this book.

The Homeland Security Emphasis and Beyond. The changed environment induced by September 11 has also produced institutional change within the U.S. government. The trauma of the terrorist onslaught created an atmosphere ripe for proactive approaches to the apparently changed environment, and revelations that the government was not organized optimally to deal with the crisis only added to the clamor for change. The outgrowth of these factors was the institutionalization of homeland security.

A concern for homeland security is, of course, much older than its current dressing. Keeping the homeland secure from foreign enemies is a basic part of national security and has always been implicit in the problem of national security. For almost two centuries before September 11, however, the need to directly secure the homeland had not been an immediate, pressing matter because the United States was effectively immune (or invulnerable) to attack, a point elaborated in Chapter 4. Al Qaeda burst the myth of invulnerability and sent us scurrying for ways to protect ourselves from evidently capable violators of our safety.

The result has been an institutionalization of and emphasis on homeland security as a prominent aspect of American national security. It began within weeks of the disaster when, by executive order, President George W. Bush created the Homeland Security Council and appointed former Pennsylvania Governor Tom Ridge as its director. In 2002, the Homeland Security Act was passed, creating the Department of Homeland Security (DHS) as a Cabinet-level agency and attempting to bring a number of functions related to dealing with threats to security (notably terrorism) under one governmental roof.

The national security effort has also been broadened to include nontraditional concerns. While military security remains the bedrock concern, other items are now considered integral aspects of security. Energy security is now widely considered on the national security agenda, and the economic crisis of 2008 has added economic security as well. Both these are introduced in the next section and elaborated in Chapter 14.

Adaptation to Change. Changing times require observers to evaluate and react to the possibilities change presents. As Americans face the post–9/11 world and an administration apparently dedicated to major adjustments away from immediate post–9/11 policies, the question is whether one agrees or disagrees with the changes being proposed.

The first temptation is to use labels and categories that are familiar, like "liberal" or "conservative," to evaluate change, but are these convenient designations adequate to allow sensible adaptations? If not, is it possible to create a more complex set of distinctions that will be more helpful in making adequate judgments? This discussion suggests a five-point set of criteria that may be helpful in understanding how one feels about national security issues.

The first category is basic worldview. It refers to the generalized view that a person has toward the international system; the acceptability, desirability, and immutability of how the system works; and how or whether one could act to change the arrangements that do exist. The basic orientations that dominate discussions in national security debates are realism and idealism.

Realism is the historically dominant philosophy and the underlying belief system for the realist paradigm developed in the next chapter. Roughly speaking, realism (as the name implies) seeks to describe the world the way it is. Its central tenet is that world politics is a geopolitical struggle among sovereign states in an international system of anarchy (absence of government), in which states are the central units that compete to maximize their national interests. Inherent in the description is the maintenance of and occasional resort to organized armed force as one way that states achieve their interests.

Realists intend both to describe the world and to provide a set of methods to survive and succeed in the world. Realists do not place a value on the "goodness" of the order they describe; rather, they argue the sensible approach for policy makers is to determine how to adapt to and make the best of the world as it is.

Idealism sees the world differently. Most idealists accept the realist description of the world as basically accurate (if somewhat overdrawn). They differ on the question of immutability of the present condition and whether one should work to improve that condition. Idealists, in a general sense, believe that the world is imperfect and in need of reform and that positive change is positive. For many idealists, the major imperfection of current international politics is its normalization of force as an acceptable method for bringing about change.

Both realism and idealism are part of the American tradition. Realism tends to dominate among policy makers because it does offer a description of the structure and workings of the system. Rhetorically, it is often thought to be better to be "realistic" rather than the alternative.

Idealism, however, also has its place in the United States. Americans have always possessed a sense of moral and other superiority that is accompanied by an evangelical desire to share that vision with the rest of the world. Idealists often disagree on the method of achieving change. The Bill Clinton and George W. Bush administrations, for instance, both had the idealistic goal of spreading democracy to places where it does not exist. They disagreed on how to go about that promotion: Clinton's goal was to spread American soft power through globalization, as opposed to the neoconservative credo of "regime change" (including the resort to force) of the Bush terms.

The second dimension is political orientation. In the contemporary political debate, this is the most emotional and, in many cases, most misleading dimension. It is often manifested in the dichotomy between liberalism and conservatism, but these terms have become so emotionally laden that it is hard to determine their meaning outside of some specific context. Both terms can and are often used to convey either praise or condemnation.

It is helpful to examine both categories and to define them. The basic liberal–conservative dichotomy omits too many other possibilities or requires placing people and their ideas into categories that do not truly fit them. Political orientation can more usefully be divided into five orientations that form a continuum.

Starting at the far "left" is radicalism. Radicals generally support substantial, even fundamental, change in political relationships, normally toward some currently non-existing condition. Often, radicals display a willingness to resort to force. Next comes liberalism. Classic liberalism has two major characteristics. First, it emphasizes tolerance of the views and opinions of others (indeed, one classic meaning of being liberal is that one is tolerant of others). Second, liberals are positively oriented toward political change and have a generally positive view of the role of government in promoting that change.

In the middle of the spectrum is pragmatism. Pragmatists do not espouse a predisposition on the question of political change and the positive or negative role of government. Rather, they tend to be moderate on issues and take positions on particular questions based on their assessments of the individual merits in particular situations. Pragmatism and moderation have traditionally been highly revered characteristics, but in an ideologically charged era, pragmatism has a bland image that seems to pale in the face of stronger, more ideologically driven positions.

To the right of center are conservatism and reactionism. Conservatism, in its literal sense, means support for the status quo: conservatives seek to "conserve" relationships that exist. Thus, conservatives are generally opposed to or suspicious of political change, and since most change is associated with government activity, traditional conservatives favor a small and restricted role for government. The major operational difference between conservatives and liberals indeed comes down to the question of how active government should be in promoting change or regulating behavior. Reactionism, on the other hand, is the advocacy of change to some past state of political affairs. Because such change generally includes a reduction of government activity and thus a reversion to some past set of relationships, reactionaries are more extreme than conservatives are.

Placing someone (including oneself) on this continuum is difficult. The boundaries between the categories are not sharp and clear. People do not always (even usually) consistently act from the premises of one position or another: a person may be quite liberal on some issues and conservative on others. Also, many people hold different philosophies when it comes to domestic and international issues. So-called Kennedy Democrats (supporters of the late President John F. Kennedy) were generally liberal on domestic issues but conservative on foreign policy matters. Similarly, contemporary traditional and social conservatives may take very activist, including idealistic, positions on international issues.

The third dimension is approaches to involvement and refers to how active the United States should be in world affairs. The two major positions on American involvement are internationalism and neo-isolationism. Internationalists generally feel that the United States should take a prominent, activist position in the world and that acting as a world leader best serves the national interest. Neo-isolationists, on the other hand, are less inclined toward such activism. Instead, neo-isolationists believe that the United States should limit its participation in world affairs whenever and to the extent possible and should concentrate its energies on domestic American concerns. Most Americans consider themselves to be internationalist in general terms, although the degree of international activism that they advocate varies.

The fourth dimension is participation preference. Regardless of how one feels about the extent to which the United States should involve itself in the world, a further question is the quality and nature of that participation. The concern centers around whether the United States should prefer to act in concert with as much of the international community as possible when it interacts with the world or whether it instead should be willing to act on its own, even when such action puts it at odds with friends and opponents, when it feels its interests are served by going it alone.

The two basic positions on this dimension are multilateralism and unilateralism. Multilateralists believe that American policy and actions should generally be developed and coordinated with the policies of others, and especially American friends and allies. The underlying assumptions are that American interests include keeping friends and that the wisest policies often reflect the development on international consensus on issues. Unilateralists believe that U.S. interests should override international concerns and that the United States must be willing to go against international consensus when international views would harm American interests. The positions are not mutually exclusive. Multilateralists would, for instance, agree that there are occasions when the United States must ignore international views and act alone, and unilateralists would agree that developing an international consensus is preferable if possible. The difference in operation is more a matter of preference and predilection than inviolate dogma.

The final distinction, efficacy of force, is how to promote American interests, and it hinges on the question of the proclivity of resorting to the use of force as the means to solve problems. One way to state this distinction uses the terms hawks and doves. The names are conventional. Hawks have a generally positive view of the utility of force over a range of situations and thus believe that the possible resort to "hard power" should be considered in a range of situations. Doves generally oppose the use of military force except in extreme situations and prefer to use "soft power" (e.g., economic instruments) to achieve national goals. In the American realist

Challenge!

YOUR OWN PERSONAL INVENTORY

To clarify how you feel about national security affairs, develop a personal inventory on the five dimensions. The central question about each dimension may help you categorize yourself.

1. *Basic Worldview:* Should the basic mission of policy makers be to adapt to and make the best of the world situation as it is (realism), or should they try to change world conditions (idealism)?
2. *Political Orientation:* Should government seek to induce change through any means available (radicalism); promote change through moderate, tolerant reform action (liberalism); view situations and the desirability of change solely on their individual merits (pragmatism); seek to preserve existing relationships within a limited form of government (conservatism); or seek to remove or roll back existing conditions (reactionism)?
3. *Approaches to Involvement:* Should the United States play a generally activist leadership role in the world (internationalism), or should it seek to avoid international involvement whenever possible (neo-isolationism)?
4. *Participation Preference:* Should the United Sates generally try to build international consensus before acting (multilateralism) or look at its own interests first with less regard to international preferences (unilateralism)?
5. *Efficacy of Force:* Is force useful in a wide range of situations (hawk) or only in a narrow range of circumstances (dove)?

tradition, however, both hawks and doves have traditionally believed that force should be employed only as a method of last resort, when all other methods fail. Hawks are, however, more likely to believe military solutions constitute the appropriate last resort than are doves.

The five dimensions can be combined to create profiles that are useful in distinguishing individuals and their national security orientations. Moreover, developing one's own personal inventory and comparing it to others (those of political candidates, for instance) can also provide a way to see if one agrees or disagrees with the positions or sides of others in any particular debate. The purpose of the *Challenge!* Box is to facilitate constructing such an inventory.

OBAMA'S (POTENTIAL) DRAMAS

The forty-fourth president entered office with a very full agenda with which to deal. As already noted, the deep economic recession was the single most compelling item on that agenda. But he quickly made the challenge more complex by conflating other complex, controversial, and expensive domestic programs like energy, education, and health care with economic recovery. National security concerns crowded onto the president's plate. President Barack Obama inherited two ongoing hot wars in Afghanistan and Iraq and the less well-defined metaphorical war on terror from his predecessor, and his own domestic priorities created budget deficit prospects that begged for some kind of remediation. Reduced spending on inherited, problematical national security crises seemed one way to reconcile competing priorities for a president whose aides sometimes referred to him (particularly during the presidential campaign) as "No Drama" Obama.

The new post–9/11 security agenda is complicated by two broad forces that are becoming more prominent than in the past. One of these is the impact of *nontraditional* security threats. Challenges to national security that are not wholly or even predominantly military in nature have been part of the equation for some time under the guises of concerns such as environmental, energy, and even economic security, but they have become more prominent than in recent years and particularly with the incumbency of Obama.

Why has this nontraditional agenda become a more important concern? Partly, it is because these issues have become more central to the American and world debates. The effects of global climate change are now a familiar part of the political debate, for instance, and the volatility of petroleum prices has made energy a more encompassing concern. In addition, there has been a growing tendency to consider these issues as *security* concerns—matters that affect the safety and sense of safety and well-being of people. The spike in petroleum prices in mid-2008, for instance, energized a growing perception of the need for energy independence—the absence of dependence on foreign sources of energy—as a major security issue. Finally, these issues, which are discussed more fully in Chapters 8 and 14, have become more prominent because more traditional, military-based security concerns have receded on the agenda. The United States still faces foreign enemies that would do it harm by recourse to armed violence, but these threats are certainly less deadly than the threat posed by Soviet Communism, for instance. The major traditional threat to the United States comes from international religious terrorism, but to anticipate the discussion in Chapter 13, that threat is not military in a traditional sense and may gradually decline.

The economic crisis that seized the United States and most of the rest of the world in 2008 represented a second major force affecting the national security environment. A legacy of the Cold War was the notion that national security concerns—once again, largely defined in military terms—were so basic and incapable of compromise that they needed to be tended to virtually regardless of their economic costs and consequences. Virtually alone amongst post–World War II presidents, only Dwight D. Eisenhower (himself a retired general) argued forcefully that the bedrock of national security was a healthy economy and that overspending on national security could be injurious to, rather than supportive of, American national security.

The weakness of the American economy revealed in 2009, and the very expensive programs designed to revive it have returned the debate to Eisenhower's concerns, if not his context. Traditional demands associated with national security will likely no longer enjoy a carte blanche level of access to public funds as demands for fiscal restraint beyond recovery muscle their way to the top of the agenda. As an example, President Obama identified savings associated with winding down the wars in Afghanistan and Iraq as a major source of deficit reduction in early 2009, and the Pentagon undertook a far-reaching review aimed at reducing spending on questionably necessary "big ticket" (i.e., expensive) military projects such as the F-22 fighter aircraft. As a reassessment of the Afghanistan commitment began to occur in Washington in late 2009, the economic impact of a long continuing war there has become one salient factor in assessing the future American role there.

Conclusion: Where From Here?

Change is an endemic characteristic of the political environment. Within the realm of national security concerns, the most important problems center on the changing nature of threats and appropriate responses to those threats. Change in both aspects of national security—threats and responses—are part of the contemporary situation.

The change environment was jolted by the fault line of 9/11, which spawned the global war on terror and provided the justification for American involvement in Afghanistan and Iraq. These responses to terrorism provided the leitmotif for a very militarily activist, expensive, and in some cases controversial (e.g., Abu Ghraib, Guantanamo) national security policy during the Bush years.

Barack Obama entered office with different proclivities and facing an altered environment. He had been a consistent opponent of the Iraq War and had deplored GWOT extensions such as allegations of illegal treatment of prisoners at detention facilities, and promising to rectify what he perceived as the mistakes of the GWOT-driven actions of his predecessor helped propel him to the Oval Office. At the same time, the "ammunition" he had available to attack these problems was constrained by the dictates of the economic crisis at home.

The threat environment facing the Obama administration is not so much reduced as it is changed. Terrorism is still at the center of the agenda, but questions remain about whether it, too, has changed and whether the terrorism policies of the past, to cite the most obvious example, are the most appropriate guidelines for the future. Assessing the risks and navigating through them toward the future dominate the national security debate in the pages that follow.

Study/Discussion Questions

1. Why have the last twenty-five years been described as particularly trying for American security policy? What events have contributed to that change? How?
2. What are fault lines? How do they contribute to a changed international environment for security policy? How does the Iraq War fit into this framework? Rate the fault lines in terms of their impact.
3. How has warfare changed? What is asymmetrical warfare, and why has it become the dominant form of violence the United States faces? How does Iraq reinforce this change?

4.   What new sources of change have entered the calculus of national security? What new areas of concern have arisen? How?
5.   Is the national security environment facing the Obama administration different from that faced by the Bush administration? If so, how?

SELECTED BIBLIOGRAPHY

Allison, Graham T., Jr. "Testing Gorbachev." *Foreign Affairs* 67, no. 1 (Fall 1998): 18–32.

Bloom, Mia. *Dying to Kill: The Allure of Suicide Terror*. New York: Columbia University Press, 2005.

Brooks, Stephen G., and William C. Wohlforth. "Reshaping the World Order." *Foreign Affairs* 88, no. 2 (March/April 2009): 49–63.

Byford, Grenville. "The Wrong War." *Foreign Affairs* 81, no. 4 (July/August 2002): 34–43.

Campbell, Kurt M. "Globalization's First War?" *Washington Quarterly* 25, no. 1 (Winter 2002): 7–14.

Carafano, James J., and Paul Rosenzweig. *Winning the Long War: Lessons from the Cold War for Defeating Terrorism and Preserving Freedom*. Washington, DC: Heritage Books, 2005.

Clarke, Richard. *Against All Enemies: Inside America's War on Terror*. New York: Free Press, 2004.

Feguson, Niall. "The Axis of Upheaval." *Foreign Policy*, March/April 2009, 55–60.

Fromkin, David. "The Strategy of Terrorism." *Foreign Affairs* 53, no. 3 (July 1975): 683–698.

Gates, Robert. "A Balanced Strategy." *Foreign Affairs* 88, no. 1 (January/February 2009): 28–39.

Haass, Richard N. "Regime Change and Its Limits." *Foreign Affairs* 84, no. 1 (January/February 2005): 66–78.

Hoffman, Bruce. *Inside Terrorism*. 2nd ed. New York: Columbia University Press, 2006.

Hoffmann, Stanley. "Clash of Civilizations." *Foreign Affairs* 81, no. 4 (July/August 2002): 104–115.

Howard, Michael. "What's in a Name?" *Foreign Affairs* 81, no. 1 (January/February 2002): 8–13.

Kagan, Robert, and William Kristol, eds. *Present Dangers: Crisis and Opportunities in American Foreign and Defense Policy*. San Francisco: Encounter Books, 2000.

McFaul, Michael. "Democracy Promotion as a World Value." *Washington Quarterly* 28, no. 1 (Winter 2004/2005): 147–164.

Miller, Steven E. "The End of Unilateralism or Unilateralism Redux?" *Washington Quarterly* 25, no. 1 (Winter 2001/2002): 15–30.

Nacos, Brigette L. *Terrorism and Counterterrorism: Understanding Threats and Responses in the Post–9/11 World*. 2nd ed. New York: Penguin Classics, 2006.

Nye, Joseph S., Jr. "Transformational Leadership and U.S. Grand Strategy." *Foreign Affairs* 84, no. 4 (July/August 2006): 139–149.

O'Hanlon, Michael. "A Flawed Masterpiece." *Foreign Affairs* 81, no. 3 (May/June 2003): 47–63.

Pillar, Paul D. *Terrorism and U.S. Foreign Policy*. Washington, DC: Brookings Institution Press, 2003.

Shambaugh, David. "The New Strategic Triangle: U.S. and European Reaction to China's Rise." *Washington Quarterly* 28, no. 3 (Summer 2005): 7–26.

Snow, Donald M. *The Necessary Peace: Nuclear Weapons and Superpower Relations*. Lexington, MA: Lexington Press, 1987.

———. *What After Iraq?* New York: Pearson Longman, 2009.

Stern, Jessica. *Terrorism in the Name of God: Why Religious Militants Kill*. New York: HarperCollins, 2003.

Tucker, Robert W., and David C. Hendrickson. "The Sources of American Legitimacy." *Foreign Affairs* 83, no. 6 (November/December 2004): 18–32.

Walt, Stephen M. "Taming American Power." *Foreign Affairs* 84, no. 5 (September/October 2005): 105–120.

Watanabe, Akio. "A Continuum of Change." *Washington Quarterly* 27, no. 4 (Autumn 2004): 137–146.

Zakaria, Fareed. *The Post-American World*. New York: Current Affairs Press, 2008.

CHAPTER 2

The Realist Paradigm

PREVIEW

Realism and the realist paradigm have been central to the operation of the international system and American attitudes toward the world. Moreover, geopolitics, one of the two competing themes around which this book is organized, finds its philosophical and operational basis in realism and the realist paradigm. Because of these factors, the chapter lays out the realist argument, its implications in a geopolitical world, and the controversy about its continuing relevance to understanding the contemporary national security environment. Many opponents of realism question the validity of the paradigm and its consequences, and their objections are discussed. The chapter concludes with a discussion of the future applicability of the realist paradigm in the contemporary environment.

When attempting to deal with a reality as complex, changing, and bewildering as the international environment that is the setting for national security, it is necessary to adopt some intellectual framework to help order and understand the meaning and context of events, their causes and effects, and how one must and wants to respond to and influence those occurrences. The failure to adopt some way to order and simplify understanding can leave one simply paralyzed and unable to respond to the environment.

This framework can be thought of as a tool to comprehend the "rules of the game" of whatever reality one confronts. The function of a framework can be understood by analogy. Imagine attending and watching a baseball game with no idea what the rules or objectives of the game are. In that situation, what one would see are two sets of people in contrasting uniforms on a field with odd markings alternately throwing, catching, or chasing a round ball that others swing at with a wooden (or aluminum) stick that sometimes they manage to hit, causing people to run around in some manner. Ultimately, one group is declared the winners and one the losers for reasons that are not apparent. It is all utterly confusing—unless one knows the rules.

The baseball analogy may seem frivolous, but understanding the actions of states and groups within states can be equally frustrating and incomprehensible unless or until one understands what "rules" underlay the "game" of international politics and, for present purposes, those aspects of actions that affect one's personal and national security. The idea that has dominated the way practitioners and scholars have understood international relations for centuries has been something called realism, and the framework it provides for organizing the "rules of the game" of national security affairs is often referred to as the realist paradigm.

This chapter introduces the realist paradigm, the elements of that paradigm, and some critiques and limitations ascribed to realism. Because Americans are relatively latecomers to the "game" of realist politics, however, many Americans retain a sense of unease about realism. Because of this, it is helpful briefly to explore some of the sources of this ambivalence before analyzing the realist paradigm.

The United States has been a leading member of the international system only since the end of World War II. It has occupied a position as a major international force for the entire lifetime of most present Americans, but not for most of the period the modern state system has existed. Most Americans have never known a time when the United States was not a major player on the world scene, and this fact has the potential to distort perceptions about global geopolitics and the American role within the national security arena in which geopolitics is acted out.

American preeminence has thus not always been the case. The simple fact is that geopolitical participation, and especially leadership, has been the historical exception rather than the rule for the United States. For most of its history, Americans sought to be above what they viewed as the corrupting influence of power politics, and the result has been a historical ambivalence about the American role in international politics. As a consequence of this, the United States struggled through its first total immersion in power politics during the Cold War and continues to have ambivalence about the proper role of the country on the world scene.

Why is this the case? And what are its sources? Any list of influences will be subject to criticism both for what it includes and for what it omits. However, at least three factors can be identified that form what might be called the American strategic culture and that capture the essence of typical American views of the world of geopolitics.

The first factor is what some analysts have called *American exceptionalism*. Rightly or wrongly, Americans have always thought of this country as a special place, one that is qualitatively better than other places. The United States was, after all, the first country in the world to adopt political democracy, and it has long provided a refuge from the tyranny of political ideologies (e.g., fascism, Communism) and practices (e.g., involuntary military service) elsewhere in the world. As a result, Americans think of themselves as a kind of chosen people, a self-image captured in symbols as diverse as the Statue of Liberty's invitation to bring us "your huddled masses" seeking freedom and Ronald Reagan's image of the United States as the "shining house on the hill."

The perception of being exceptional leads to a second strain in the United States' historical view of itself: *isolationism*. Because contact with and participation in the international system are potentially tainting, there is a residual sentiment to limit the degree of American participation in an essentially corrupt and potentially corrupting enterprise. In its most extreme form between the world wars, this sentiment manifested itself in a virtual withdrawal from international politics (although not international economics) under the banner of "splendid isolation." In a more contemporary sense, neo-isolationism argues for sharp limits on the degree of American interaction with and leadership in the world. This sentiment finds substantive voice in policy areas as disparate as American misgivings about participation in United Nations–sponsored peacekeeping missions and opposition to economic globalization. To many foreign and domestic critics of American policy, this tendency manifests itself as American *unilateralism*, the inclination to ignore the sentiments and advice of others and to act alone in international affairs.

There is another factor, which is what might be called American *ambivalence* about the effects of geopolitical participation. Very few Americans would describe themselves as isolationists or maintain that the United States has no leadership role in the world. Pure isolationism ended effectively with the Japanese attack on Pearl Harbor, and neo-isolationism was largely discredited by September 11, 2001. Nonetheless, ambivalence remains. The consequence of involvement often is to ensnare the country in a web of international rules and regulations (what are sometimes called regimes) that limit American independence in ways about which many have second thoughts because such involvement can preclude some actions the country might prefer to take.

American attitudes toward its sovereignty stand out as examples of national ambivalence. Sovereignty, which means supreme authority, is central to the realist paradigm and is discussed more fully in the next section of this chapter. For present purposes, suffice it to say that the United States is among the strongest defenders of state sovereignty because strict sovereignty minimizes the extent to which the judgments or standards of outsiders can be imposed on the country or individual Americans. Thus, for instance, the United States is one of only a handful of states that has refused to ratify the statute of the International Criminal Court (ICC), which has the jurisdiction to try people accused of committing war crimes. The reason for the American government's refusal to accede to the statute is its reluctance to permit Americans to be tried by foreign judges if they are accused of committing war crimes.

This reluctance to dilute authority puts the United States at odds with much of the international community on a number of matters, and American ambivalence toward participation results in anomalies and inconsistencies in the country's relations with the world, some of which will be explored in the pages that follow.

These examples are simply illustrative of the tension, ambivalence, and complexity with which the United States fits itself into the geopolitics of the contemporary system. These problems have been accentuated as the United States adjusts its policies in light of the response to international terrorism, and these policies will continue to evolve in the future. To understand this evolution more fully, the discussion first looks at the geopolitical system that was inherited from the Cold War—the realist paradigm—and objections to it as the operating principle of international politics.

REALISM AND THE REALIST PARADIGM

Realism has traditionally served two functions. It has been both a leading theoretical approach to the study of international relations and a practical guide for political leaders as they conduct foreign policy. Realism has thus served as an intellectual tool and a set of guidelines for policy makers. Whether it can continue to serve these purposes as well in the future as it has in the past is part of the contemporary critique of realism.

These dual functions are not coincidental. The academic basis of realism came from the study of international relations by scholars whose first interest was in physical observation of how world leaders, diplomats, soldiers, and the like actually carried on their activities. Developed and ordered into a coherent explanation of international relations during and after World War II, the content of theoretical realism roughly coincided with the actual conduct of international affairs at least through the Cold War. One of the reasons the approach is called realism is that it is said to reflect reality.

Realism is controversial, largely because many people—and especially a number of international relations scholars—dispute the reality the realists portray and seek to reform or reverse some of the basic dynamics that the realists portray. Among the phenomena that realists describe and reformers wish to change is the "normalization" of the recourse to force—in other words, war. Additionally, some notoriety has been attached to realism because the name has been essentially "highjacked" by actors who portray themselves as realist but who support policies that are decidedly nonrealist. The impact is to blur what is and is not truly realist.

As a basic approach, realism is as old as observation about the relations between independent political units. Many believe that Thucydides' *History of the Peloponnesian Wars*, written in the fifth century B.C., is the original statement of the philosophy of realism and would add sixteenth-century Italian diplomat and advisor Niccolò Machiavelli's *The Prince* to the roster of realist classics.

Realism became a dominant approach to understanding international relations in the period surrounding World War II. At the end of World War I, a group of scholars known as "idealists" came to dominate the study of the international system. Given the enormous carnage of the Great War, there was considerable sentiment to reform a system whose rules—based in implicit realism—had allowed the first great conflagration of the twentieth century to occur. They based their reform on the institutionalization of peace around the League of Nations and grounded their scholarship in ways to improve the peace system by improving the effectiveness of the League in reinforcing and preserving the peace.

Unfortunately, their advocacy (what they sought to accomplish) colored their observation of the actual international politics of the interwar period (what was actually occurring). The idealists either did not see World War II coming or felt it could be avoided, but the League-based institutional framework they had built proved entirely inadequate to slow the rush to war in the 1930s. This failure was most dramatically stated by the English scholar E. H. Carr in his critique of idealism published in 1939, *The Twenty Years' Crisis, 1919–1939*.

Realism emerged from World War II as the dominant explanation of and approach to international politics. In 1947, Hans Morgenthau published the first edition of his landmark exposition, *Politics Among Nations*, in which he laid out in detail the realist position. Emphasizing the roles of things like power, conflict, and war, the resulting realist paradigm seemed particularly well suited for describing and organizing the policy response to the emerging Cold War competition between the Communist and non-Communist worlds.

Even at the height of the Cold War confrontation, realism never lacked for critics. Part of that criticism comes from the conjunction of the academic and practical aspects of realism: it is not only an academic "theory" for understanding the world but also a set of rules of the road for conducting international affairs that includes at least a partial, implicit endorsement of its principles. The alternative to thinking about or acting outside the bounds of realism became thought of as unrealistic. Those who do not like the implications of a realist-run world generally do not like the academic approach either. In some cases, this intellectual objection is stated in terms of questioning the conceptual adequacy of the realist paradigm for describing and explaining international relations; in others, the objections are rooted in opposition to the effects of conceptualizing the world through the prism of the realist paradigm.

Resolving the theoretical debate about whether realism is the best approach to understanding international politics goes beyond present purposes. As they relate to questions about the actual conduct of foreign and national security affairs, the basic concepts of realism have formed the framework within which national security decisions have been made at least since the 1940s. As a result, the pattern of historical and contemporary national security concerns cannot adequately be understood without understanding (but not necessarily embracing) the realist paradigm. Operating or reforming the operation of the international system, and particularly those dynamics central to national security, begins with understanding the realist paradigm.

BASIC CONCEPTS AND RELATIONSHIPS

The basic dynamics of the realist paradigm can be reduced to a series of six propositions about the international system that can be arranged deductively in syllogistic order. Each individual statement contains one or more of the key concepts, and collectively, they define the realist perspective. Numerous observers object to and contest the implications of some of the observations that make up the paradigm. Because the paradigm has been such an important part of international reality, however, its content is important.

The six propositions composing the realist paradigm are as follows:

1. The international system is composed of sovereign states as the primary units in both a political and a legal sense.
2. Sovereign states possess vital interests and are the only units in the system entitled to vital interests.

3. Vital interests become matters of international concern when conditions of scarcity exist and are pressed by competing state actors.
4. When issues involving scarce resources are present in the relations between sovereign states, then power must be used to resolve the difference.
5. The exercise of power is the political means of conflict resolution in international relations.
6. One political instrument of power is military force, which is one option for resolving differences between states.

Following the syllogism from the first to the sixth proposition, a conclusion must be reached that in a system of sovereign states, states must possess, and from time to time use, military force to resolve problems that arise for them in the system. The realist paradigm therefore justifies a concern with national security defined, at least in part, by military force. It is not surprising, then, that the realist paradigm finds considerably more intellectual favor among most students and practitioners of military affairs and varying levels of disregard and disdain among people opposed to the use of military force as a "legitimate" tool for resolving differences among states. (Some military thinkers, of course, share the critique of various parts of realism.)

As stated in terms of these propositions, the realist paradigm is only a skeleton of concepts and relationships. It gains meaning when the basic concepts that compose it are examined and put together in the logical sequence of their presentation in that set of propositions.

Sovereignty

The most basic and critical principle of international relations and building block of realism is *state sovereignty*. The idea was originally articulated by a sixteenth-century Frenchman named Jean Bodin as a way to justify concentrating the authority of the French monarch by asserting his supreme authority over lesser French nobles. Sovereignty was enshrined as the basic operating principle of international relations through the series of agreements ending the Thirty Years War (1618–1648) known as the *Peace of Westphalia*. The Thirty Years War had, in some measure, been about whether the church or the state would be the principal holder of political authority in the future. Those supporting the notion of state authority prevailed, and they seized upon state sovereignty as the institutional and legal basis for institutionalizing their secular triumph over sectarian authority.

Sovereignty means *supreme authority*. Within a system in which sovereignty is the basic value, no entity can have authority superior to that of the sovereign. When Bodin coined the term and it was adopted by others, such as the English philosopher Thomas Hobbes, sovereignty was thought to be a quality that primarily applied to the domestic relations among individuals and groups within states rather than the relations between states. In the early days of the modern state system, that domestic sovereignty was considered to rest with the monarchy. In fact, Bodin never considered the effects on the relations between sovereign entities.

The extension of the concept to the international level occurred over the next century and is usually associated with the seventeenth-century legal scholar Hugo Grotius. It has been the principal operating rule underlying international politics ever since.

Both the domestic and the international ramifications of sovereignty remain largely in force, although with quite opposite effects. Domestic sovereignty remains the basis of the authority of the state over its territory, although sovereignty is now thought of as residing with the people (who confer part of their sovereignty on the government) rather than with a person—the monarch. The result of sovereignty applied domestically is to create the legal and philosophical basis for political *order*, since authority to act rests with the state.

The effect of sovereignty on international politics is to create *anarchy* (absence of government) as the basis of the relations between states. In the international arena, state sovereignty literally means no state can have any jurisdiction over what goes on within another state. Thus, all relations among states are among equals wherein no state has the authority to compel any other state to do anything, at least in a legal sense that does not always conform to actual practice. There is no authority above those with supreme authority, meaning there is no basis for governance in international relations. A formal state of anarchy therefore exists in the international realm. Jurisdiction over disputes resides with the parties to the dispute, who must figure out how to decide their differences on their own, usually without recourse to an outside authority. While the inviolability of state sovereignty has never been as absolute as the definition implies (states violate other states' sovereignty routinely), it remains the major organizational tool for defining relationships within the international system.

On the face of it, this seems an odd way for the international system to conduct its business. The practical outcome is that there is no equivalent of the judicial branch of government to settle disputes, and the parties are left to fend for themselves when differences among them arise. There is a reason for this state of affairs, however. States have matters of such importance to them that they are unwilling to have them left to the judgment of outsiders. As a consequence, states demand as total control over those matters as they can enforce. This leads us to the second major concept of the realist paradigm.

Vital Interests

The main reason sovereign states are generally unwilling to compromise on some matters is because states, unlike other entities in the Westphalian system, have what are called vital interests. Indeed, Morgenthau argued the centrality of "vital interests defined as power" to the entire realist theory. Vital interests are defined as properties and conditions on which states will not willingly compromise and which are thus too important to be submitted to any superior authority. Such interests are to be guarded to the fullest extent of state capability. Some analysts would add that a vital interest is any interest that is sufficiently important that the state will use force to ensure its realization.

Table 2.1: National Interest Matrix

	Intensity of Interest			
Basic Interest at Stake	Survival	Vital	Major	Peripheral
Homeland Defense				
Economic Well-Being				
Favorable World Order				
Values Promotion				

Generally, states formally or informally rank their interests in a hierarchical fashion that denotes how important a particular interest is and hence what measures it will undertake to realize the condition or property in question. Donald Nuechterlein provides a useful way to categorize these interests in the form of the national interest matrix (Table 2.1). Both dimensions of the matrix are hierarchical. Clearly, the most intense interest a state has is its physical survival, followed by those interests on which the state will not willingly compromise (vital interests). Major interests are matters that would inconvenience or harm the state if unrealized but that can be tolerated, and peripheral interests are, as the label implies, matters more of inconvenience than harm. Similarly, the most important basic interest a state has is in defending itself, followed by promoting its economic well-being, its view of the world order, and its own values.

The critical point in national security terms is the boundary between vital and major interests because it is generally agreed that vital interests are ones the state will use force to guarantee, and major interests fall below that threshold. The location of that boundary between when force will and will not be used is a matter of disagreement.

The disagreement over whether the United States should have gone to war with Iraq can be thought of in these terms. For most traditional realists, the idea that vital interests are those important enough to use military force to achieve has the corollary that force should be used *only* when vital interests are involved. This latter assertion forms the basis for disagreement over Iraq. To critics who argue the United States should not have gone to war in this instance, there were no factual outcomes of the Iraq–U.S. relationship that were sufficiently negative for the United States to justify using force to resolve them. For instance, there was agreement that the removal of Saddam Hussein was desirable, but critics of the war argued that his removal was not sufficiently important *to the United States* (as opposed to *Iraqis*) to justify forcibly overthrowing his regime. Supporters of the decision argued that the worst-case outcome—Hussein's providing terrorists with weapons of mass destruction (WMD)—violated vital interests or was sufficiently intolerable to the United States to make the invasion necessary. Much of the same debate surrounds the ongoing war in Afghanistan.

The boundary between vital and less-than-vital interests is and will always be an important point of contention within the domestic and international security debate, as illustrated in Amplification 2.1. Looking at the basic interests at stake,

Amplification 2.1

FINDING THE BOUNDARY BETWEEN VITAL AND LESS-THAN-VITAL INTERESTS IN IRAN

One of the major alternatives to the definition used here for vital interests is to say that vital interests are any interests worth fighting over. The danger of this definition is that, when reversed, it implies that any time a country is fighting, its vital interests must be engaged. This is a dubious proposition because it denies that countries ever fight over less than basic differences. But since people employ the distinction, it does mean the boundary between vital and less-than-vital interests is an important one in the study of national security.

Unfortunately, the boundary does not exist in any literal sense, either in the abstract or regarding specific situations. The reason for this is psychological and subjective. What is an intolerable circumstance for some people may or may not be intolerable for others. One dictionary definition of security, for instance, is "safety or a feeling of safety." Beyond direct physical threats (e.g., a Russian missile or terrorist attack against the American homeland), most threats to security—or situations in which interests are at risk—fall within the psychological range of what makes people feel insecure and what interests are imperiled. People can and do honestly disagree on these matters, and as a result, the location of the boundary between vital and less-than-vital interests and when it is necessary to use force become matters of honest disagreement.

One way to make this boundary determination in any given situation is to ask, How intolerable would the worst possible outcome be? If the answer is that the worst possible outcome would be absolutely intolerable, then a vital interest may be involved, and force may be contemplated to avoid that outcome. If, however, the worst possible outcome would be tolerable, although annoying or inconveniencing, then a vital interest may not be involved.

Take the case of Iranian acquisition of nuclear weapons as an example. The United States has declared that possibility intolerable, implying that Iran getting nuclear weapons violates U.S. vital interests. How so? Presumably, such weapons are intolerable if they permit Iran to threaten to attack the United States with nuclear weapons or if Iran might provide those weapons to terrorists. But is that outcome possible or likely? Depending on how one answers that question, the prospect of using armed force to avoid Iran nuclear attainment becomes realistic or unrealistic.

for instance, there is little disagreement that defending the homeland is vital to the state, and hence, challenges to that interest will be met by force. Responding to the September 11 attacks clearly followed from this interest. As one goes down the list of basic interests, the question of their vital nature becomes more debatable. In the Persian Gulf War, for instance, the American interests involved were clearly economic (access to petroleum energy that literally fuels the American economy). Interestingly, control of or guaranteed access to Iraqi oil (to which the United States had been denied access since 1972) may be an outcome in Iraq that would qualify as fulfilling a U.S. vital interest.

Two final concepts about vital interests and sovereignty bear mention: because vital interests are so important, the state is unwilling to accept contrary judgments about its interests when it can avoid them. As a result, the state is unwilling to submit disputes to a higher authority (a sovereign above the state) for fear such an authority might rule against the state in an unacceptable manner that would have to be disobeyed or ignored in order to ensure an acceptable outcome. Vital interests, in other words, are matters that are too important to relinquish control over the outcomes. Having said that, the word *willingly* is part of the definition of vital interests because when vital interests come into conflict, somebody wins and somebody loses. Usually, it is the weaker party who must unwillingly accept an unacceptable outcome, with the upshot that the interplay of vital interests in a realist world is an exercise in power politics.

Power Politics

International relations is an inherently political enterprise in which the principal political actors are states seeking to maximize their advantage in an environment where all cannot be equally successful. Who gets what is the essence of the political process in this arena. For this purpose, a variation of political scientist David Easton's definition of politics will be used: *politics is the ways in which conflicts of interest over scarce resources are resolved.*

This definition contains two related elements. The first is procedural: "the ways in which conflicts . . . are resolved." The second is substantive: what "scarce resources" have to be allocated and who gets those resources. The two dimensions are intimately related: the nature and importance of the resource may determine the procedures that are employed to decide the outcome; and the procedures may influence or prejudice the substantive outcome. Generally, the less important the issue (a major or peripheral interest, for instance), the more likely a state will be either to submit the matter to some outside authority for judgment of the outcome or to accept a less-than-optimal outcome. When a matter is of the highest importance to the state (a survival or vital interest), then the state is likely to invoke its own sovereign authority to maintain as much control over the outcome as it can.

The unique possession by states of vital interests produces a political structure in which state sovereignty is the central feature in determining political outcomes. As already noted, sovereignty precludes the formation of political processes that can authoritatively allocate values in areas deemed vital by the sovereign states. The result is international anarchy in dealing with matters of interests vital to the state. As long as states retain vital interests, this essential anarchy will remain the central procedural aspect of international politics.

In the situation of anarchical international relations, states achieve their interests to the extent they have the ability to do so—through a process sometimes known as *self-help*. Since the need to resolve important international political problems generally occurs when vital interests are involved and scarcity exists, the outcome is, by definition, likely to be that one or all parties must accept less of a condition or property than they previously deemed vital. Determining outcomes becomes an exercise in the application of power.

Power is an elusive and highly controversial concept, but it is central to the realist paradigm. Its elusiveness comes from trying to operationalize and measure power in order to predict who will prevail when states clash in the international arena. This difficulty is discussed in Amplification 2.2.

Power is also a controversial concept because one of the most obvious and prominent forms that power takes in the international arena (and within some states) is military force. Those who oppose the use of military force thus find themselves in opposition to a system in which power, including military power, is a central, even normal, way to resolve differences. In this case, the key to a more tranquil, peaceful world lies in the abrogation of power as the basis of politics.

Amplification 2.2

MEASURING POWER

Although the concept of power is pervasive as a means to describe international relations, ways to measure it have remained largely elusive. As noted in the main text, finding ways adequately to measure and thus to be able to compare the power that different states possess would be highly desirable because it would make the outcomes of interactions between states much more predictable than they are in fact.

There are two difficulties involved. The first is finding physical measures that adequately describe the abilities of states to influence one another. A concerted effort has been to try to find concrete, physical measures, such as the size or sophistication of countries' armed forces or the productivity of states' industrial bases, to indicate which is the more powerful country in any head-to-head confrontation. The problem is that such measures work only part of the time. There is, for instance, no physical measurement to compare national capabilities that would lead to the conclusion that North Vietnam had any chance of defeating the United States in a war, but it certainly did.

The second problem is that concrete measures of capability have difficulty getting at the psychological dimension of will and commitment that people may possess. How can an outside observer determine, for instance, when a clash of interests is clearly more important to one party to a dispute than it is to the other (at least before the fact)? Once again, the Vietnam War is illustrative. The outcome of that war—unification of the country—was clearly more important to the North Vietnamese and their southern allies than its avoidance was to the United States and the population of South Vietnam. This is clear in retrospect; it was not at all clear before and even during the conduct of hostilities. Being able to see clearly after the fact is of very little comfort to the policy maker.

Part of the controversy is definitional as well. Although some analysts would say the definition used here really describes influence rather than power, it is possible to adopt a common and straightforward definition of power: *the ability to get someone to do something he or she would not otherwise do.* The definition skirts the controversy over measurement of power by not specifying what power *is* so much as describing the *effects* of the application of power.

The definition highlights two major characteristics of a power situation. First, it says that power is not an attribute possessed by parties so much as it is a relationship between an entity seeking to exercise power and another entity seeking to resist the application of that power. A power relationship is commonly applied through the issuance of a threat (a promise to do something harmful unless what is demanded is complied with) by one party against the other. The outcome depends on the action of the threatened party. If the threatened party believes that the threatening party can (has the capability to) and will (has the credibility to) carry out the threat in the face of noncompliance, the threatened party may comply. If, however, the threatened party doubts either the will or the ability of the threatening party to carry out the threat, it may conclude differently. Whether power is successfully applied is thus a mutual matter in the interaction between the parties, not something simple and concrete like a comparison of the sizes of military machines or industrial capacities (although these are clearly relevant when deciding if the threatening party has the wherewithal to carry out the threat).

The other characteristic of a power relationship is that it is situation-specific. What this means is that the application of power occurs not in an abstract sense but within very specific situations. It is important to recognize this fact because the vagaries and special circumstances surrounding any particular relationship may influence how a power relationship plays out, sometimes in unpredictable ways.

An example helps illustrate these characteristics. In the early 1970s, the African country of Uganda was ruled by a particularly harsh and objectionable ruler, Idi Amin Dada. Amin was a sergeant in the British colonial force who declared himself a general when Uganda achieved independence in 1962 and who seized power from the postcolonial government in 1971. He had as many as three hundred thousand Ugandans of tribal origins other than his own killed, and in 1972, forty-five thousand Asian residents, who had formed the backbone of the country's commercial system, were expelled. As Uganda drifted toward chaos, the United States withdrew its diplomatic personnel in 1973.

The United States—as well as a number of other countries—wanted Amin removed from the Ugandan presidency. Amin was not about to leave, so power would have to be applied to get Amin to do something he clearly would not otherwise do. The problem was, What kind of power did the United States have over the dictator? By any objective measure, the United States was overwhelmingly more powerful than Uganda, but was that power relevant to the specific situation of overthrowing him? Was there some form of leverage the United States could apply to remove Amin? Was American power relevant in this case?

The answer was that it was not. To try to achieve its goal, the United States threatened and implemented an embargo on the importation of Ugandan coffee into the United States (a prohibition ignored by the American firms that bought Ugandan coffee until they were caught violating the sanctions), but the embargo did not have enough impact to cause Amin to step down. In the end, Ugandan rebels, assisted by neighboring Tanzanian armed forces, which possessed far less absolute but much more proximate and believable power than the Americans, finally managed to drive Amin out of power and into exile in April 1979.

It is the combination of capability and will that makes power effective in individual situations. In the Ugandan example, the United States clearly had the military capability to overthrow the Ugandan regime (or for that matter, obliterate it with nuclear weapons). What it lacked was the credible will to apply that force in a situation that was at most annoying but clearly did not affect American vital interests.

In order to exercise power, of course, the state must be capable of carrying out threats. Doing this requires possessing the *instruments of power*. In traditional terms, these instruments are divided into three categories: diplomatic (or political), economic, and military power. Diplomatic power encompasses qualities such as the persuasiveness of a country's diplomatic corps, the attractiveness of the country's political profile, and the country's ability to use the other implements to back up political rhetoric. Economic power is the use of economic rewards and deprivations to obtain compliance with a country's demands. Military power is the threat or actual use of military threats or applications to achieve a country's goals.

Some authors believe the list of instruments should be extended in the contemporary environment. A leading candidate is informational power, the ability to control and manipulate the amount and quality of information an adversary has in a power situation. Elements of this power include information-gathering ability (obtaining intelligence) and manipulation (interrupting information sources and transmission or distorting that flow). Information is so important that some analysts argue that intelligence should be considered an independent instrument of power. An exotic form, *cyberwar* attempts to disrupt and control computer systems and their ability to collect, analyze, disseminate, or even retain information.

In an anarchical system, power and politics are intimately related. Politics, after all, is about who gets what in terms of scarce resources, and by definition, scarcity means that some parties will have to do what they otherwise prefer not to do. In the absence of authorities who can decide on allocations, the parties must help themselves through the application of power, including the use of military force on occasion.

PARADIGM IMPLICATIONS

What does the realist paradigm mean for the actual operation of the international system and its national security aspects? Is an understanding of the basic concepts simply an intellectual enterprise without practical application to the real world, or is the paradigm a kind of rule book or road map that guides policy makers and thus allows students to understand how the system works? For better or worse, the latter is most clearly the case, and summarizing the paradigm's implications helps move the discussion forward.

The realist paradigm begins with state sovereignty as its basic value, meaning there can ultimately be no higher authority than the state in determining what happens to the state. The absence of a higher authority is not coincidental but is the direct result of the possession of vital interests by states (but not other political entities). These vital interests are so important to the state that it will not willingly compromise on them and will use all means available, up to and including military force, to ensure that they are honored. The two concepts, sovereignty and vital interests, require and reinforce one another. The prosecution of vital interests in an anarchical system precludes the possibility that a superior authority could—possibly capriciously—compromise a vital interest of the state. Sovereignty provides the conceptual bedrock to deny that possibility. The government of the United States has been and continues to be among the world's staunchest defenders of state sovereignty, and at the bottom of almost all its defenses of the concept is its insistence that no outside power should be allowed to create conditions to which Americans do not want to and should not be subjected.

In a world of plenty, the state of international anarchy would not be a particular problem because states would rarely come into direct conflict with one another over who gets what. In the real world, of course, scarcity, not abundance, is often the case, necessitating political processes to determine outcomes of disagreements. Sometimes conflicts can be resolved peacefully and cooperatively, and sometimes not. When situations involve the vital interests of states, those states are generally unwilling to submit them to bodies that could exercise jurisdiction and instead rely on more informal means of conflict resolution to settle differences. Settlements in conditions of scarcity mean that some or all of the parties to a given dispute must accept less than they would have preferred—in other words, do something they would prefer not to do. Because of this, international politics inevitably is power politics.

In a world of sovereign states interacting through power politics, the state succeeds to the extent it can through self-help. In order for one state to get others to do what it wants but the others do not, that state must possess the ability, in specific situations, to convince or compel other states to act in ways that serve its national interests. A state must, in other words, possess power to succeed.

Power comes in a variety of guises. The most common, but not only, forms are political or diplomatic power, economic power, and military power. The applicability of any particular form of power will vary depending on the situation and both the ability and the willingness of a state to use its power to gain compliance with its positions. Generally speaking, the more power a state has, the more successful it will be in achieving its ends. In the anarchical situation of international politics, among the forms of power that must be available is military force. Thus, the international system ultimately is an environment in which the threat of or recourse to force is a "normal" activity some of the time and in which states that succeed must possess, and sometimes use, armed forces.

CRITIQUES AND ANOMALIES OF
THE REALIST PARADIGM

Many analysts decry the sets of conditions produced by the realist paradigm and point both to anomalies that it produces in the interactions among states and to questions about its continuing empirical adequacy in describing international reality. To the critics, there is simply too much that occurs in the world that cannot be explained by realism, and thus, the day-to-day debate about national security policy must be expanded beyond realism.

An exhaustive criticism of the realist paradigm goes beyond present intent. For present purposes, the criticisms can be viewed from two perspectives. One of these argues that the principles underlying the realist paradigm, and especially state sovereignty, have never been as strictly adhered to in fact as they are in principle—in other words, the paradigm is only partially accurate in describing the operation of the world system. The other perspective maintains that adherence to the paradigm produces a flawed international system—in other words, the paradigm's effects are pernicious. Ironically, realism is blamed for creating a system in which the resource to force is too easy and too hard.

Critiques

State sovereignty is the realist concept that draws the greatest negative attention because it creates an international institutional setting of purposive anarchy that necessitates a world of power politics and guarantees that international relations will emphasize conflict rather than cooperation. The critics maintain that state sovereignty has never been as absolute as its extreme representation would suggest. However, the more closely one supports the practice of absolute sovereignty, the more opposition one encounters. The basic underlying theme of this critique is that realism is *empirically* inadequate to describe the world, a position increasingly held in academic and policy circles.

Early political theorists like Hobbes and Bodin favored something like the absolute sovereign powers of the state to justify the power of monarchs. The suggestion that the principle of sovereignty results in an impenetrable state authority unaffected or unlimited by outside forces is not, and never has been, more than a fiction. States interfere in the political lives of other states all the time, and the behavior of states is limited by international regulations (usually ones that they have explicitly agreed to be limited by) on a regular basis. Moreover, contemporary forces such as economic globalization and the impact of the telecommunications revolution are making state boundaries increasingly porous and state control over everything that happens within its jurisdiction increasingly difficult to maintain. Critics argue that it is empirically false to maintain otherwise and that important trends in international relations suggest sovereignty will continue to erode in fact, if not in principle. The staunch defense of absolute sovereignty is, in other words, a losing battle.

As sovereignty erodes, so does the salience of some of the operating principles of the paradigm, and this is nowhere truer than in areas related to national security and the use of force. It is, for instance, not at all clear that some uses of military force to achieve national interests are as acceptable today as they were a century or even a decade ago. Wars between states have virtually ceased. (The American invasion of Iraq was a notable exception.) All members of the United Nations renounced their right to declare war as part of their conditions for joining the world body, and although that does not mean that force has disappeared, no state has formally declared war on another state since World War II. As the international response to Iraq's 1990 invasion and conquest of Kuwait clearly demonstrated, the aggressive use of force across borders is no longer acceptable behavior. The issue of acceptability is, of course, not universal and is related to power. Iraq's action was deemed an unacceptable act of aggression against Kuwaiti sovereignty and was reversed.

The other major manifestation of the realist paradigm that is under question is the use of vital interests as the benchmark against which to measure when force should and should not be employed. This assault is largely the result of changes in the international threat environment since the end of the Cold War, and particularly the result of what I call the *interest–threat mismatch*—the situation in which important interests and threats do not coincide—and the neoconservative challenge.

During the Cold War, when the realist paradigm was clearly the dominant worldview of policy makers on both sides of the conflict, there was no mismatch: vital interests (national survival, for instance) were threatened, and thus, the idea that force would be threatened or used in East–West confrontations provided clear guidance for the development, deployment, and potential employment of force. Interests, and threats to those interests, were clearly aligned and coincided with one another.

The situation changed radically after the implosion of the Communist half of the Cold War. The important interests of the United States remain what they were before: American homeland security and a free and democratic Western Europe and Northeast Asia with which the United States can engage in commerce and political relations, for instance. What changed was that those vital interests were essentially no longer threatened. There is no Communist menace hanging over Western Europe; the West Europeans move steadily to incorporate more and more of formerly Communist Europe into institutions such as the European Union. Thus, where there were American vital interests, there was no meaningful threat that would justify the use of force—important interests and threats were misaligned

The interest–threat mismatch takes form from this assessment of the post–Cold War environment: *the most important American interests in the world are hardly threatened, and the threats that do exist are largely tangential (are hardly interesting).* International religious terrorism, of course, is the obvious exception to this observation. In these circumstances, if the realist paradigm is used as the sole (or main) criterion to determine when or if the United States will employ force in the world, the result will be paralytic because hardly any situation will meet the criterion of engaging vital interests and thus justifying force. During the Cold War, the realist paradigm was the hawk's standard because it counseled large and robust forces to deal with real threats to vital interests. In the post–Cold War world, that same paradigm turned the hawks into doves, since the paradigm directs non-involvement with military force when vital interests are not threatened. The post–September 11 response to international terrorism, of course, realigns interests and threats in that area of concern. The main problem is not the existence of the threat but how to counter and remove it.

What this suggests is that the implications of the realist paradigm can be used to promote or discourage the use of force, depending on the situation. The key, of course, is the realist criterion of vital interest engagement as the activating justification for employing force. Under any strict interpretation of the paradigm, force is an appropriate instrument of policy only when vital interests are engaged; when they are not, then force is not justifiable.

This implication has been important since the end of the Cold War and the beginning of the interest–threat mismatch. In the 1990s, in particular, there were relatively few situations where U.S. vital interests were unambiguously threatened by international situations. As a result, realist justifications for forceful responses were problematical.

While the terrorist threat of the early 2000s appeared to realign threats and interests, an additional element was added: the ascendancy of the so-called neoconservatives into positions of power and influence in the U.S. government. These neoconservatives share with traditional realists a support for the legitimacy of force as an instrument of power to gain compliance with demands. They differ from realists about the range of situations in which force is appropriate and about the efficacy of force as a change agent. Neoconservatives believe that the realist restrictions on the use of force are too restrictive. Rather, they implicitly expand the range of situations in which force can be used to include situations realists would argue involve major or even peripheral interests and thus fall below the threshold of invoking force. Disagreement about the American invasion of Iraq, discussed in Amplification 2.3, illustrates this disagreement.

The influence of the neoconservatives has substantially disappeared with the passing of the Bush administration, which embraced their philosophy. Whether the salience of the paradigm based in the neoconservative revision will return is uncertain, but it is not the only source of opposition by critics. To a large number of interested observers, the paradigm is objectionable both because of the activities it legitimizes and because of the kinds of viewpoints it deemphasizes. The most obvious objectionable activity is the acceptance, even promotion, of military force as a normal form of state action in some instances; the most obvious example of what it does not emphasize is cooperative behavior among states.

The realist paradigm legitimizes the recourse to armed violence as a means to achieve state interests by acknowledging military force as one of the normal instruments of power. In addition, the approach's emphasis on observation of "reality" (actual behavior of states) notes that states (and groups within states) do in fact occasionally resort to the use of force to achieve their ends and that in some cases they succeed in achieving their ends by doing so—the ends justify the means. Many realists would contend, for instance, that the attempt by the idealists to downplay and even ignore the role of military forces between the world wars contributed to the destabilization of the 1930s that ended with World War II. Moreover, given the

Amplification 2.3

REALISTS, NEOCONSERVATIVES, AND THE IRAQ WAR

A seemingly strange disagreement about American involvement in Iraq developed between a number of retired general officers and the Bush administration over whether the United States was justified in making war on Iraq. The discord seemed strange because of the general affinity between an avowedly conservative military establishment and a professedly conservative Bush administration.

Although not always phrased in these terms, the disagreement boiled down to differences arising from the realist paradigm. Most of the retired officers who came to oppose the war were traditional realists who firmly believed that American vital interests were not threatened in Iraq, that force was thus not justified, and that the war could not be supported. Those in the administration who counseled war were, by and large, neoconservatives who believed that the paradigm's entreaty was too restrictive and that force was justifiable even if traditional vital interests were not involved. In this case, recourse to the realist paradigm would have made the recourse to violence less, rather than more, likely.

predatory nature of some states, the absence of force is a virtual invitation for states to take advantage of the militarily disadvantaged.

Opponents of realism contend that it is the very structure of an international system based in the realist paradigm that creates—even promotes—an emphasis on military force and the recourse to war. The villain, of course, is sovereignty-induced anarchy that leaves international politics a Hobbesian "war of all against all." In this view, the solution to the "problem" of war is institutional reform of the international system to create orderliness through institutions that can enforce the peace and remove the vigilantism of a realist order. In order to accomplish this, the conceptual victim must be state sovereignty, replaced with ultimate authority either in the hands of a superior entity (e.g., a world government or the like) or returned to the people (popular sovereignty). At any rate, the object is the sovereign state, which the opponents of war argue must be fundamentally reformed before peace can be instituted and enforced.

In addition to its alleged warlike implications, other critics point out, the principle of state sovereignty tends to emphasize noncooperative rather than cooperative behavior in the relations among states more generally by erecting barriers to interaction across state boundaries. For instance, the sovereign independence of states, it is argued, runs counter to the growing globalization of the world's economy by erecting physical barriers to the movement of people and goods across sovereign boundaries. Because examples of international cooperation are numerous and growing, the inability of strict realism to explain these exceptions to its anarchical, conflictual description of the world raises questions about its adequacy as an intellectual ordering device.

This line of objection can be put in a more general and theoretical form. Realism tends to emphasize the conflictual elements of international relations and to downplay evidence of international cooperation. While conflict is clearly an important element of international relations, so too is international cooperation. There are certainly aspects of international interactions that are zero-sum (one party loses what the other party gains), but there are also positive-sum situations (where both parties can gain). Critics of realism argue that realists dismiss the cooperative aspects too often and that an approach placing great emphasis on cooperation not only results in a more accurate description of international relations but also leads to the promotion of a greater level of cooperation and thus enhanced international tranquility.

In some ways, this difference goes back to the disagreement in the philosophies of Thomas Hobbes and John Locke (among others) about the nature of man and society. The realists portray a more Hobbesian world (indeed, some of the early realists explicitly included their assessment of man's base nature as flawed as part of the philosophical underpinning of their theorizing), whereas those who emphasize cooperation are manifesting a more Lockean philosophy (wherein people enter into society out of a positive desire for association with their fellows). In more contemporary terms, the debate can be couched in terms of which is the dominant international reality, globalization (cooperation) or geopolitics (conflict), or some combination—which, of course, is an underlying theme of this book.

Anomalies

There are also anomalies in an international system that is built on the philosophical basis of realism but that, in practice, does not precisely conform in its operation to the realist mold. Two examples, one American and one Russian, illustrate both the paradigm and its inconsistencies and difficulties.

As noted earlier, the United States joins the People's Republic of China as one of the staunchest defenders of the principle of state sovereignty in the world. The political and philosophical base of this strongly held position is the belief that individual Americans and the country more generally should not be subject to imposition or control by foreigners and that, as a result, the United States should resist international attempts to place the United States under regimes that would impose international norms on Americans.

Regardless of its merits, this position often forces the United States into a politically uncomfortable position in the world—often in opposition to the vast majority of other states and in the company of states with which it does not particularly like to be associated. Invariably, these situations involve American resistance to or refusal to join international agreements that limit the right of signatories to engage in certain behavior (and are most ominous when the treaty includes provisions for international enforcement—a direct abrogation of sovereignty). Ironically, the agreements to which the United States objects are often proposed by the U.S. government itself (either by the permanent bureaucracy or by a previous administration), indicating substantial disagreement within the United States itself on the sovereignty issue.

One of the most obvious examples is American nonparticipation in and nonacceptance of the International Criminal Court (ICC). This body was created in the 1990s partly as a response to the commission of war crimes in places like Yugoslavia and Rwanda, with the idea that the ICC would provide a permanent forum within which to prosecute allegations of war crimes and other internationally prohibited behaviors. The Clinton administration was a supporter of the ICC, and the president signed it but did not forcefully push for its ratification by the Senate before leaving office. The Bush administration opposed the treaty and withdrew it from Senate consideration, leaving the United States as one of the few major powers not part of the ICC and not covered by its jurisdiction.

On March 4, 2009, the ICC handed down a multipart indictment of Sudanese President Omar Hassan Ahmad Al-Bashir for crimes against humanity (including murder, extermination, rape, forcible transfer, and torture) for actions in Darfur. The Obama administration supported the indictment behind the scenes but was constrained in its response because the United States is not a member (Sudan is not, either) and because members of the Bush administration might also be charged under provisions of the ICC statute. Although the Bush administration itself charged the Sudanese government with genocide over Darfur (a charge not included in the indictment), the United States was limited in its condemnation because its concern with sovereignty was partly responsible for putting it in the anomalous position of being restrained in its response to this issue. The Challenge! Box extends these implications.

Challenge!

OBAMA, THE ICC, AND BUSH "WAR CRIMES"?

The Obama administration will be under pressure to submit the ICC statute for ratification, an action that it is philosophically inclined to do. But will it? Or should it?

The issue is clouded by the prospect that American accession to the ICC could make it vulnerable to enforcing potential warrants against members of the Bush administration, including the former president himself, on grounds of crimes against humanity—specifically torture as defined in the United Nations Convention Against Torture (UNCAT), of which the United States is a signatory and enforcement of which falls within the aegis of the ICC. As long as the United States is not a member of the ICC, it can arguably deny its jurisdiction and ignore its actions (which is the Sudanese position on Bashir). If it joins the ICC, such a position becomes untenable.

What should the United States do? Quite apart from the merits of the cases against Bush officials, should Americans—especially a former president—be subject to non-American international justice? What is more important: justice against international transgressions or the inviolate control of the United States over its citizens?

The United States is not alone in being party to anomalies in the current system. Russia, which has acceded to the ICC, has for over a decade been waging an arguably genocidal campaign in the renegade province of Chechnya, which has been actively attempting to secede from the Russian Federation since the middle 1990s. The Russians have brutally repressed this movement, and war crimes have clearly been committed under orders that possibly go all the way to the top of the Russian political leadership. Yet there have been no serious calls for an investigation of the situation by the international war crimes apparatus. Why? One reason is that Russia maintains the situation in Chechnya is purely an internal matter within the sovereign jurisdiction of the Russian government (and thus arguably beyond the purview of any other authority). For another, Russia maintains its Muslim Chechen opponents are terrorists, since many of the "freedom fighters" waging the war allegedly are associated with the training regime in Afghanistan that produced Al Qaeda terrorists (thus giving the Russians status as participants in the war against terrorism). Finally, Russia is also a large and powerful country that no one wishes to antagonize unnecessarily, so the position goes officially unchallenged.

The staunch American defense of sovereignty and the ambivalence Americans display when anomalous issues arise from its defense often confuse and mystify other countries, including both American friends and foes. Defying international norms in the name of defending American freedom of action is often equated with American unilateralism—a kind of disregard for the rest of the world. This was clearly the case in the early George W. Bush administration. Beyond reaction to the Kyoto convention on global warming, this was evident in 2001 regarding the administration's obdurately defended intention to field a national missile defense in the face of essentially universal opposition from abroad (a problem made moot when the Obama administration abandoned the Bush-proposed system in October 2009), in addition to opposition to the ICC and the land mines convention.

Defense of sovereign prerogative is also a politically partisan position in the United States, adding to international confusion. Although there are exceptions, the strongest advocates of protecting American sovereignty have tended to be conservative and Republican, whereas those who exhibit a willingness to subject the United States to sovereignty-restricting provisions of international agreements have tended to be more liberal and Democratic. On other than trade matters, the Democratic Party has been more internationalist than the Republican Party, meaning there is a likelihood that the transition in control between the parties will continue to have a real impact on attitudes toward international issues with ramifications for American state sovereignty across time.

CONCLUSION: THE REALIST PARADIGM TODAY

Despite its limitations and mounting criticism of it, realism remains the dominant organizational device by which the governments of sovereign states organize their approach to dealing with the world. The criticisms are, without doubt, growing. During the Cold War, these criticisms tended to be isolated within groups outside national governments—academics, liberal commentators, and members and advocates of nongovernmental organizations (NGOs), for example. Given the gravity of the task of managing international affairs in a world where the Soviet opponent was thoroughly committed to realist power politics, advocacies of ideas such as reducing the influence of sovereignty fell on mostly deaf ears, particularly among political decision makers responsible for protecting national interests in a dangerous world where the Soviet opponents were the ultimate realists. Communism could be opposed only in kind, according to the prevailing wisdom.

A less threatening, apparently more globalizing environment in the 1990s saw critical, less realist views become more acceptable in practice and in principle. At one level, the series of interventions in peacekeeping roles by U.N.-deputized forces represented an indirect assault on the notion of total sovereign control of territory. International agreements like the ban on land mines and the establishment of the permanent war crimes tribunal are more direct assaults, as they subjugate the rights of states to act unilaterally in the face of international norms. Some see this trend as a healthy maturing of international relations. Others see grave dangers in these erosions of state sovereignty and assaults on the structure of the Westphalian order. The Clinton administration was more receptive to change; the Bush administration proved to be less so, a predilection reinforced after the terrorist incident of 2001 and responses to it. The Obama administration has moved back toward the Clinton position.

Does the realist paradigm fit the new, evolving international order? Any direct, categorical answer will, of course, oversimplify a more complicated world order in which yes–no answers exclude the middle ground between them and result in a distortion of reality. Cold War realism may not be the perfect paradigm for a post–Cold War and post–September 11 world, but its basic structure has not disappeared. The fault line that began to emerge in 1989 raised questions about the continuing relevance of the paradigm; such criticism has been much less evident since 2001.

A remarkable example may illustrate the evolution of the realist paradigm. On June 29, 2001, the late Slobadan Milosevic, the former president of Yugoslavia, was extradited from Belgrade to The Hague in the Netherlands, where he faced charges of crimes against humanity as specified in the statute of the ICC, which had issued the indictment under which his extradition was carried out (since the ICC statute had not been ratified by enough states to come into permanent being at the time, the indictment came from the tribunal established specifically for Yugoslavia).

The extradition was the remarkable aspect of the event. Milosevic had been indicted in 1999 for his alleged participation in crimes against humanity committed against Albanian Kosovars in Kosovo in 1999. Although Milosevic was defeated in 2000 in his bid for reelection, it was widely believed that the indictment was symbolic and that any trial of Milosevic would have to be carried out in his absence (*in absentia*) because the Yugoslav government, which was not a signatory of the ICC statute, would protect him on the grounds that any attempt to arrest and extradite him would be a violation of Yugoslav sovereignty. This obstinacy flew in the face of widespread world opinion, which regarded Milosevic as a war criminal—or at least believed he should face the charges against him. International economic sanctions against the country were put in place in 2000 to pressure the government into honoring the indictment.

So what changed the minds of members of the successor Yugoslav government of Vojislav Kostunica and caused them to turn over the former dictator to international authorities? The answer is that several factors, two of which bear mention, were involved and demonstrate the continuity and change of the new order.

The first was domestic and had the effect of eroding resistance to international demands for his surrender to international authorities. While many ethnic Serbs had denied the early charges of atrocities against the Kosovars ordered by the Milosevic government, evidence emerged in 2001 clearly showing that mass murders had been committed that could be linked only to the government in power at the time. Defense of Milosevic became much harder to sustain, and the defense of his freedom based in national sovereignty gradually eroded. In the end, fully 60 percent of the Serbian population of Yugoslavia favored extradition.

The other factor was international, the effect of the sanctions imposed by the international community because of the Yugoslav campaign in Kosovo. The people of Yugoslavia became more intolerant of the physical deprivation they were enduring as a result of the sanctions than they were committed to their sovereign control and protection of the former leader. The North Atlantic Treaty Organization (NATO) allies promised the Kostunica government that economic penalties would be lifted as soon as Milosevic was turned over to authorities; it was hardly a day after he reached The Hague that economic assistance began to flow to Belgrade.

So which principle prevailed? The answer is clearly both. The international norm was strengthened by the fact that Yugoslavia relented and allowed the dilution of some of its sovereign jurisdiction over a distinguished citizen, hardly a vindication of the realist paradigm. At the same time, what caused the international norm to succeed was the application of the economic instrument of power in a way that would make the most hardened realist proud. Regarding Milosevic personally, he died of natural causes a week before his trial was scheduled to be completed in 2006.

Study/Discussion Questions

1. How do American exceptionalism, isolationism, and ambivalence toward the international system influence the American view of national security? Elaborate.
2. What is realism? What is the realist paradigm, and how does it serve as both a theory of international relations and a guide to action for policy makers?
3. What are the key concepts in the realist paradigm? How do they form a syllogism that dictates that states must possess and occasionally use armed force?
4. Define and discuss the primary concepts of realism: sovereignty, vital interests, and power politics. Why is the boundary between vital and less-than-vital interests so critical in the area of national security?
5. What are the principal objections to the realist paradigm? Discuss each. What anomalies does strict defense of the realist paradigm create for U.S. policy?
6. Using the realist paradigm as your organizational tool, construct arguments for and against the Iraq War. Compare them. Which do you find most convincing? Why?

SELECTED BIBLIOGRAPHY

Art, Robert A., and Kenneth N. Waltz. *The Use of Force: Military Power and International Politics.* Lanham, MD: Rowman and Littlefield, 2004.

Bodin, Jean. *Six Books on the Commonwealth.* Oxford, England: Basil Blackwell, 1955.

Brodie, Bernard. *War and Politics.* New York: Macmillan, 1973.

Carr, E. H. *The Twenty Years' Crisis, 1919–1939.* London: Macmillan, 1939.

Cusimano, Mary Ann, ed. *Beyond Sovereignty.* New York: Bedford/St. Martin's, 1999.

Fromkin, David. *The Independence of Nations.* New York: Praeger Special Studies, 1981.

Grotius, Hugo. *The Rights of War and Peace: Including the Law of Nature and Nations.* New York: M. W. Dunne, 1981.

Hashemi, Sohail H., ed. *State Sovereignty: Change and Persistence in International Relations.* University Park: Pennsylvania State University Press, 1997.

Hobbes, Thomas. *Leviathan.* Oxford, England: Clarendon, 1989.

Kegley, Charles W., Jr., and Gregory A. Raymond. *Exorcising the Ghost of Westphalia: Building World Order in the New Millennium.* Upper Saddle River, NJ: Prentice Hall, 2002.

Locke, John. *Two Treatises on Government.* New York: Cambridge University Press, 1988.

Lyons, Gene M., and Michael Mastanduno, eds. *Beyond Westphalia: State Sovereignty and International Relations.* Baltimore, MD: Johns Hopkins University Press, 1995.

Machiavelli, Niccolò. *The Prince.* Irving, TX: University of Dallas Press, 1984.

Mills, Kurt. *Human Rights in the Emerging Global Order: A New Sovereignty.* New York: St. Martin's Press, 1998.

Morgenthau, Hans J. *Politics Among Nations.* 6th ed. Revised by: Kenneth W. Thompson. New York: Alfred A. Knopf, 1985.

Nuechterlein, Donald E. *America Recommitted: United States National Interests in a Reconstructed World.* Lexington: University of Kentucky Press, 1991.

Schelling, Thomas. *Arms and Influence.* New Haven, CT: Yale University Press, 1966.

Snow, Donald M., and Eugene Brown. *International Relations: The Changing Contours of Power.* New York: Longman, 2000.

Snyder, Jack. "One World, Rival Theories." *Foreign Policy,* November/December 2004, 52–62.

Thucydides. *The History of the Peloponnesian Wars.* New York: Penguin Books, 1954.

Waltz, Kenneth. *Man, the State, and War: A Theoretical Analysis.* New York: Columbia University Press, 1959.

CHAPTER 3

Security, Interests, and Power

PREVIEW

Arguably, the most basic purpose of the state is to provide for the physical safety—or security—of itself and its people, and the state is clearly the designated political element for doing so in the state-centered international system organized around the realist paradigm. Realizing security requires applying the rules of the paradigm to an ongoing and changing reality. To better understand how this application occurs, this chapter analyzes the impact of change on four basic categories of ongoing importance. First, what is the nature of security? Second, how have the nature and extent of risk been affected? Third, what impact has change had on basic interests? Fourth, what is the changing nature of effective power in the present and the future?

The realist paradigm depicts a global condition where states must compete to realize their most basic wants and needs in a situation where scarcity is not unusual. In the Westphalian system, the governments of states (sometimes called nation-states) are entrusted with basic functions of conducting that competition on behalf of their citizenries. The most basic service that governments attempts to provide is the safety—or security—of itself and its inhabitants.

The realist paradigm suggests this competition is waged primarily over the hierarchy of interests that the state maintains—usually on behalf of its citizens. The range and importance of those interests were presented in the last chapter, as was the notion of scarcity—the inability of all aspirants simultaneously to have all of a resource they desire. Security itself can be a scarce resource, and when scarcity exists in an anarchical setting, power in its various guises becomes the means by which conflicts of interest over scarce resources are resolved (the definition of politics).

This whole series of dynamics would be complex and bewildering enough if it played out in a relatively static and unchanging environment, but it does not.

Instead, that environment is marked by a constant tendency toward change. The notion of fault lines describes the contemporary theme of change.

National security analysis tries to determine what it is in the environment that may provide concern for the security and well-being of Americans and citizens of the world generally and to determine what, if anything, can be done to attenuate or eliminate the sources of disturbance. The same questions are asked today that were asked fifty or a hundred years ago; it is the answers that change to a greater or lesser extent, based upon the flow of events.

The United States is clearly still in the process of reassessing the national security problem for a new century. International terrorism introduced a force not previously confronted and certainly not resolved by the Afghanistan and Iraq Wars. Before that introduction, the environment seemed less negative than it did during the Cold War. As the responses unleashed by the fault line of 9/11 have evolved, people have begun questioning the amount of effort that should be devoted to the national security enterprise and, at a more personal level, the amount of personal effort or sacrifice that should be expected. Those commercial airliners slamming into their targets removed the complacency about security that had developed in the tranquil 1990s. "Everything has changed" became the mantra after September 11, 2001; "nothing will ever be the same again." Dormant security concerns were revived and now seem permanent parts of an environment that has been unalterably changed. Or, has it?

As noted earlier, the period leading to September 11 has been called the "long peace." If the first half of the twentieth century was arguably the bloodiest period in human history, the second half was relatively benign in terms of the toll of war. The hypothetical consequences of general war may have been great during the Cold War, but the reality was that bloodshed was basically confined to the peripheries—the developing world—where the major powers became involved only when they chose to become involved, as the Americans did in Vietnam and the Soviets did in Afghanistan. After 1991, breaches of the peace were basically isolated to internal war in parts of the world outside the normal range of important American interests. The terrorist attacks that killed nearly three thousand Americans and other nationals darkened that sunny horizon and presented a new national security imperative, the beginning of the "long war." But is it a temporary interruption of the long peace or something more permanent and ominous?

The Obama administration came into office in January 2009, nearly 7½ years after 9/11 had cast its long shadow on national security and at a time when residual conflicts continued to rage in Afghanistan and Iraq. Part of the Obama legacy has been the need to reassess that environment and the continuing applicability of a chain of responses begun in 2001. The purpose of this and the other chapters in Part I is to lay some of the conceptual groundwork for that appraisal.

In this chapter, the discussion proceeds through four sequential steps. Keeping the United States and Americans safe from harm—or secure—is the basic value of national security policy, so the discussion begins by exploring what makes people secure. Because safety is potentially imperiled from a variety of sources that may exceed resources, it looks at the question of how to decide what to protect and what to accept as risk. Deciding where to nullify risk and where to accept it is a matter of what the country's most important interests are, so the discussion returns to the matter of determining levels of interest. This assessment leads to a concern about how the United States can use its powers to the service of its security in the future.

THINKING ABOUT SECURITY

Security is a variable. One dictionary definition of security is what makes people safe or *feel* safe. This definition suggests that security has both a physical and a psychological dimension and that both dimensions assume different values, or vary. The most obvious source of variability is factors that threaten the things people value. The most objective of these are physical threats such as the ability of Russia to destroy the United States with nuclear weapons. Psychological threats—what makes people feel secure or insecure—are often less tangible and are subject to individual interpretation: different people feel secure or insecure in the same situation. In either case, the degree of security that is experienced can vary depending on the individual and the situation.

This leads to the second variable quality of security, which is the interpretation of the environment. Does the environment make one feel secure or insecure? If the latter, what actions might be contemplated to change the environment and make it less threatening (increase a sense of security)? Clearly, a hostile physical environment will diminish the psychological feeling of security more than a benign environment and thus produce greater feelings of insecurity in people.

The discussion about these aspects of security can be divided into two related concerns. The first is the changing balance between military and nonmilitary sources of security concern. This leads to and is conditioned by the second concern: the various levels of security that affect different actors in international politics and an assessment of how concepts of security may be changing.

Military and Nonmilitary Elements of Security

Historically, national security and military security have been largely synonymous. Although other matters might threaten the well-being of the country, those threats about which policy makers and analysts were principally worried and which fell most obviously into the category of national security dealt with military threats. Military elements were certainly the predominant form of security threats during the Cold War.

The inclusion of nonmilitary elements into what was considered national security began to occur during the Cold War, particularly in the area of economic security, raised in Chapter 6. There have been previous occasions when economic and other concerns entered the national security arena—trade matters with Great Britain, for instance, had been an important part of the conduct of the American Civil War, and a major threat to the United States from a German victory in World War I was the possible exclusion of American manufactures from the European continent. To cite a different kind of example, suppression of the Barbary Pirates in the early 1800s may have been the first time that responding to what are now called nonstate actors became a national security concern.

Nonmilitary and semimilitary elements have been added to contemporary concepts of security. Among the nonmilitary aspects (threats with no military component), "economic security" has been broadened to encompass environmental security, for instance. Other added security concerns are partly military and partly nonmilitary. A primary example of these *semimilitary* aspects of security and responses to them is the problem of international terrorism. As the campaign against the Taliban and Al Qaeda in Afghanistan has demonstrated, these problems can have a clearly military component, but significant aspects of terrorism and its suppression are also political and law enforcement concerns for which military responses are ineffective (see Chapter 12).

Military, semimilitary, and nonmilitary elements have melded in the post–Cold War period, in part because the purely traditional military elements of security are clearly less extensive and less intense than they were before. The virtually total absence of the danger of a major, system-threatening military conflict like the world wars is a major characteristic of the contemporary system, even after September 11. In some sense, the long peace continues to get longer.

The nonmilitary and semimilitary elements of security have risen in relative importance as military threats have receded. In the contemporary system, there is a series of smaller military threats, some of which existed during the Cold War but received less attention then and some of which have emerged since then. What they have in common is that none provides a direct, general threat to the United States physically in the way a potential Soviet nuclear attack did. The 2001 terrorist threat against the United States demonstrated that the American homeland has become vulnerable to harm that can kill many Americans, but these attacks do not currently place the integrity of the United States at direct risk (see the *Challenge!* box).

Other than terrorism, the remaining security threats are at a lower level of urgency and importance, placing them squarely within the psychological dimension of security, where people can and do disagree the most about the importance of the threat. Some threats existed during the Cold War but paled by comparison to the larger problem. The danger and threat of the proliferation of weapons of mass destruction (WMD) to countries in the Second Tier (see Chapter 10) was a problem then and now, for instance.

The military and nonmilitary elements of security come together in concrete ways. The situation between the United States and China is an example. China was, of course, a Cold War military adversary of the United States, even if the threat it posed was somewhat ambiguous after the split between China and the Soviet Union and the opening of Sino-American relations in 1972. Still, national security planners during the 1960s planned for two simultaneous major wars, one with the Soviets and the other with the Chinese (the two-war strategy). The focus of Sino-American military rivalry was and is over the Nationalist Chinese government of Taiwan, which China periodically threatens.

After Deng Xiao-peng's announcement of the "Four Modernizations" in 1979 and their implementation during the 1980s and 1990s, an economic relationship emerged that began to lessen the intensity of the military rivalry. A major pillar of the modernizations was to allow the development of private enterprises in the

Challenge!

DEFINING TERRORISM AS A SECURITY THREAT

What kind of a threat does international terrorism pose to the United States? Much of the discussion described the post–September 11, 2001, efforts by the United States to quell this problem as constituting a "war," which suggests the problem is a military one with a military solution. The Bush administration initially labeled the effort the "global war on terrorism" (GWOT), and that designation was picked up and repeated to the point that it is now the common designation for the effort.

Much of the initial effort seemed to justify this designation. The insertion of American forces into Afghanistan, first to help topple the Taliban government and then to try to round up and destroy remaining pockets of Al Qaeda and Taliban resistance, was clearly military in content. When the U.S. government decided to invade Iraq in 2003, part of the rationale was to defeat terrorism.

But does countering terrorism fall within the category of military dimensions of security? Clearly, suppressing terrorism has a military element, as demonstrated by initial actions, and terrorism experts like Stephen Sloan specifically include military responses as part of dealing with terrorism. Thus, the response to terrorism clearly does not fall within the nonmilitary dimension either.

It is possible to place terrorism in the category of semimilitary responses. The basic argument is that suppressing terrorism has some elements that involve various uses of military force but that the effort also clearly includes elements that are either nonmilitary or quasi-military. Gathering intelligence information on terrorist plans and activities to frustrate the terrorists and arresting and prosecuting those who engage in or plot to commit terrorist acts are also important parts of dealing with the problem, and they are not military actions.

Is the distinction of dealing with terrorism within the semimilitary dimension of security important or just a matter of splitting hairs? If the problem is only partially military in origin and solution, put another way, does the analogy with "war" hold? If it does, that helps frame the public debate—for instance, justifying greater defense expenditures. If the effort is only partly military, on the other hand, then the rhetoric of war—questioning the loyalty of those who question the effort as unpatriotic because the country is "at war"—may be excessive and run counter to democratic rule. What do you think?

Special Economic Zones (SEZs) in the southeastern part of China. When the Cold War ended and the age of globalization came into full bloom, a burgeoning trade between the two countries developed and largely replaced the military rivalry.

Is China currently a national security threat to the United States? From a purely military viewpoint, one can make a small case for a "Chinese threat" in the form of a small, primitive nuclear capability and large conventional armed forces that cannot be projected far from China's shore. Taiwanese rumblings about declaring its independence regularly bring Chinese saber rattling, and Chinese modernization and expansion of its military capabilities in recent years are a matter of some concern. Balanced against those problems, Beijing hosted the 2008 Olympics (a major achievement that had China on its best behavior), and the Chinese Communist Party announced in August 2001 that capitalists would be permitted to join the Communist Party (a seeming oxymoron). China continues to be a major provider of consumer goods for Americans and has been further integrated into the world economy as a member of the World Trade Organization (WTO). Thus, calculating Sino-American military threats is no longer an easy or clear-cut matter as the relationship evolves to one of so-called complex interdependence. Whether there is also a potential threat imbedded in the relationship remains a matter of debate (see Snow, "Rising Powers: China as Friend, Enemy or Frenemy").

The Chinese example is not the only one in which the intersection of military and nonmilitary aspects of security become blurred, of course, and not all are directly American. One source of insecurity is and always has been access to important resources. Among these issues, access to water could provide a similar dynamic in the relatively near future, as Amplification 3.1 suggests.

Amplification 3.1

ISRAEL, SYRIA, THE GOLAN HEIGHTS, AND WATER

One contemporary source of concerns over security is the expansion of situations and conditions about which states may feel insecure and thus feel the need to take action to enhance their security. Military security has, in other words, been augmented by economic security, environmental security, energy security, and a variety of other concerns (discussed extensively in Chapter 14).

One scarce resource that has ascended to the top of the agenda of security concerns in some places is access to adequate supplies of potable water. Nowhere in the world is this concern more evident than in the arid Middle East, where very few states have adequate supplies, particularly to service their growing populations (Turkey is the exception to this rule). In particular, the problem of water has been a major barrier to the ability of Israel to reach an accord with the last of the countries that have opposed it in war, Syria.

The major remaining issue between the Israelis and the Syrians is the return of the Golan Heights to Syria. Before the 1967 Six Days' War, Syria had used the Heights, a series of low mountains that border on northern Israel, to launch mortar and artillery attacks on the Israeli settlements in the valley below. As a result, when Israel was occupying territories of its neighbors, it also occupied the Golan Heights to assure that Syria could not physically resume its attacks.

The Golan Heights are also important because of water. Much of the water that Israel (and Jordan) uses comes from the Jordan River, the source of which is the Sea of Galilee. As the map shows, the eastern shore of the Sea of Galilee forms the border between

Israel and Syria where Syria possesses the Golan Heights, thereby affording the Syrians the physical ability to interfere with that source of Israeli water. The problem is moot with Israel occupying the Heights, since the Syrians are physically kept away from the seashore. Return of the Golan Heights to Syria is the *sine qua non* for a peace settlement between the two countries. Before Israel agrees to transfer the territory back, however, it must have an iron-clad agreement covering military attacks from the Golan Heights and, perhaps more important, assuring that Syria will not interfere with Israel's water supply.

Levels of Security

The discussion to this point has centered on the idea of state security, which is the primary focus of concern in a system where the realist paradigm predominates. This focus is one of the more controversial consequences of a realist paradigm world and has caused many reformers to suggest that there should be a more balanced approach to legitimate security concerns both below and above the level of the state.

Competing levels of security arguments run closely parallel to the debate about sovereignty. The idea that there could be a source of superior authority to the state was, of course, a major issue in the Thirty Years War in the clash between sectarian authorities claiming the primacy of the supranational church and secular authority claiming the supremacy of territories ruled by secular regimes. There are parallels within the contemporary assertion that the security of subnational groups and individuals should be a primary consideration superior to the primacy of the state. This assertion reflects the notion of popular sovereignty that was first put forward by political thinkers such as Locke and Rousseau and that also heavily influenced the writers of the American Declaration of Independence and Constitution. It is at least implicit in the rationale of other democratic systems (minimally, the idea that power and authority flow from the people).

The arguments are more than academic. Some of them, of course, reflect assaults on the sovereign base of the state system and tend to emphasize the negative consequences of a state-centered system with state security as its underlying first principle. Others assert the need for and positive consequences of a reorientation of security around the individual or supranational concerns.

One line of reasoning questions the consequences of states acting principally out of their own security concerns, while ignoring other levels. A most basic formulation of this concern is something known as the *security dilemma*. In this construct, states may act in ways to increase their security against real or potential adversaries—such as building up levels of armaments—regardless of the effect on the larger international system. The response of those targeted by the original action may be to respond in kind (building their levels of arms), which may result in an arms spiral wherein, in the end, all parties are left feeling less secure than in the beginning. Security dilemma situations represent the perspective of *international security*, the security of the overall system.

The security dilemma is not an abstract problem but can be seen in ongoing, concrete situations. Currently, the debate over American construction of a missile defense system shows the dynamic in action. The Obama administration inherited a proposed U.S. deployment of a "light" missile shield (one capable of intercepting a small missile launch) in Eastern Europe (Poland and the Czech Republic). Russia vehemently opposed the shield on the grounds that it was justified by a non-existent threat (Iranian nuclear weapons) and posed a threat to Russian nuclear forces. In response, Russia threatened to retaliate by building additional offensive weapons that could overwhelm the defense. If carried out, the resulting arms buildup could have triggered a new arms race that would leave the international system more dangerous—the security dilemma. The abandonment of the European-based system by the Obama administration in September 2009 has reduced this problem considerably by allaying Russian misgivings.

The American terrorism campaign also raises levels of security concerns. The American military response in Afghanistan has been clearly framed in terms of American state security—removing the source of a threat to the American homeland.

Very few people in the world argued with this rationale for the campaign. When the United States threatened to widen the campaign to other sources of potential threat—notably Pakistan—the prospects were inevitably raised that such actions based on American national security concerns might increase Pakistani instability and thus detract from international stability.

The other level of concern is that of *individual security*, a primary orientation of security around individuals and groups. This emphasis is most often associated with the protection of the safety of people within states. The problem arises from traditional interpretations of the absolute power state sovereignty provides for the state over its population. The consequences of this power have become an international concern in the post–Cold War environment of internal wars that involve atrocities against victim populations and groups within populations.

Traditional definitions of sovereignty give the state total control over its territorial base, including the treatment of individual citizens and groups, and make illegitimate any outside efforts to affect that treatment. In the cases of particularly tyrannical regimes, the result has often been state-sponsored or state-conducted campaigns against their own citizens, which the international community technically cannot prevent or alleviate; it is none of anybody else's business how a state treats its citizens. The conditions in the Darfur province of the Sudan are a stark case in point of this position taken to its extremes.

An assertion of the validity of individual security challenges that assumption. It is related to the assertion of popular sovereignty, since presumably no one would delegate to the state the right to abuse them. The history of individual security, however, is relatively recent and based in two post–World War II phenomena: reaction to the Holocaust and the emergence of notions of individual, enforceable human rights.

The Holocaust was a terribly traumatic event for the international community and gave a black eye to advocates of the notion of total sovereign control. Among other things, it revealed the lengths to which unrestrained governments might go in mistreating their citizens—state sovereignty had run amok. Yet, in the early war crimes trials at Nuremberg, a prominent participating American jurist opined that Nazis could be tried for killing non-German Jews and Gypsies (among others), but not German Jews or Gypsies, since they had sovereign authority over their own populations.

Reaction to the Holocaust boosted advocacies of universal human rights after the war and helped result in a number of international treaties asserting that individuals everywhere had certain rights that could not be denied by governments. Since nondemocratic governments existed and routinely denied and repressed these rights, individual rights and a concept such as individual security reinforced one another.

As noted, the situation in the Darfur region of Sudan is the currently most flagrant case of abuse of individuals by their government, a situation raised in Chapter 14. Sudan has denied claims of atrocities, of course, but it also denies international authorities the right to inspect or intervene to alleviate suffering on the grounds of state sovereignty.

RISK AND RISK MANAGEMENT

In an ideal world, means would be available to remove all our sources of insecurity at all levels. In the real world, however, threats—or potential threats—always outnumber the resources available to negate those threats to safety. The gap between the threats and the resources to nullify those threats is *risk*, and it can be depicted in the suggestive formula: risk equals threat minus capability (risk = threat – capability).

Since risk is calculated on the basis of threats to security, it is also a variable quantity. How much threat must be endured is, according to the formula, the result of two factors, each of which can vary. The first and most elastic of these quantities is threat. As already explained, the degree of threat experienced is the result of physical and psychological aspects of security. Primarily, this means that the amount of potential risk people face is the result of what makes them *feel* secure or insecure, and people differ on what frightens them and must thus be countered to reduce insecurity. For instance, almost all agree that international terrorism threatens the United States but may disagree on what potential aspects of the terrorism problem are most dangerous and immediate and thus threatening.

Threat can also vary depending on the amount of exposure one has to potentially threatening forces, and this element of threat is partially controllable depending on how one deals with actual or potential threats. A global power like the United States will have more potential and real threats to its security than will a smaller state with more parochial interests, for instance, and the extent of threat that must be countered is potentially great. To increase or decrease the amount of actual threat, the way potentially threatening opponents are treated can increase or decrease the threat that must be nullified. If one wants to reduce risk, one way to do so is to reduce the threat, either by denying that a particular situation represents a threat (does Cuba, for instance, still provide any meaningful threat to the United States?) or by trying to remove conditions that may result in threat. The ongoing relationship between the United States and North Korea, discussed in Amplification 3.2, is an example.

Amplification 3.2

WHAT SHOULD THE UNITED STATES DO ABOUT NORTH KOREA?

For the past several years, the United States has been involved in a direct confrontation with the government of the Democratic People's Republic of Korea (DPRK or North Korea). It is, of course, not the first time the two countries have been at odds: the United States' first major military conflict of the Cold War occurred in 1950, when the

North Koreans invaded the Republic of Korea (South Korea) and the United States intervened to restore South Korean sovereignty in a war that lasted over three years and cost over 37,000 American lives.

The DPRK is one of the most destitute, remote countries in the world. It shares with Cuba the distinction of being one of the two remaining countries practicing Communist ideology both politically and economically (the other Communist states, China and Vietnam, have effectively renounced socialist economics). Politically, the country has had only two leaders, the late Kim Il Sung and, since the self-designated "Great Leader" died in 1994, his son Kim Jung Il. The country is among the poorest in the world and suffers periodically from harsh famines because it does not produce enough farm products to feed itself.

The long-standing source of controversy between the United States and the DPRK is the North Korean nuclear program. Although North Korea is a party to the Nuclear Non-Proliferation Treaty (NPT)—whose signatories vow not to develop nuclear weapons—Pyongyang has maintained an active nuclear research program, has the material to build nuclear weapons, and has actually admitted fabricating a nuclear device. Additionally, it has an active missile program, which could become a delivery capability should North Korea produce nuclear weapons.

During the 1990s, relations between the two countries had reduced tensions. In 1993, the DPRK became the first country to announce its intentions to withdraw from the NPT, which produced a flurry of activity. In 1994, the North Koreans suspended their withdrawal in an interim agreement with the United States that called for American assistance to the regime, and in 1999, a further agreement reduced, among other things, travel restrictions between North Korea and the world. This was followed by the first open relations between North and South Korea and with Japan. North Korea was viewed as a relatively minor risk.

That changed with the election of George W. Bush. In addition to designating North Korea a member of the "axis of evil" (along with Iran and Iraq), the administration suspended bilateral contacts with the Kim Jung Il regime. Slighted by these actions, North Korea angrily announced its resumption of efforts to produce nuclear weapons. At American initiative, six-power talks (North and South Korea, China, Japan, Russia, and the United States) have attempted to quell this development but with only limited success. In 2007, the DPRK agreed to dismantle its nuclear program in return for assistance from outside powers very similar to that negotiated in 1994.

What should the United States do about North Korea? One answer is to go back to bilateral diplomacy, which proponents of current policy say was demeaning and ineffective. Another is to continue the six-party talks, which the North Koreans do not like because they prefer bilateral negotiations. A third alternative is for the United States to use military force to deprive North Korea of the ability to make nuclear weapons, an action that could provoke another war on the peninsula that no one wants. The final option is for the United States to ignore the situation and leave it to regional solution. None is an overwhelmingly obvious solution. What do you think?

The other variable in determining risk is capability, defined as the capacity to take actions that nullify threats. Capability is generally defined in terms of various kinds of power available to ensure that threats cannot be successfully carried out against a threatened party. In the simplest terms, for instance, the existence and structure of the U.S. armed forces are designed to ensure that any foreign military invader will be repulsed, thereby nullifying the threat of invasion and conquest of the United States. The semimilitary threat of harm posed by terrorists, on the other hand, is so diverse and diffuse that it is not clear what resources are needed to nullify entirely the risks posed by terrorist threats to do harm to the country.

In general terms, it is almost always true that threats will exceed the capability to nullify them, and this observation is particularly true in the current context of international terrorism and the economic crisis that constrains the United States. There are so many potential targets for terrorist attacks on American soil and overseas that removing all of them from harm's way is, as a practical matter, impossible. This means that choices must be made about which threats to nullify and which targets to leave at risk. Since the potential list of what makes people feel safe or unsafe is subjective, it is always more expansible than the capabilities one might marshal to protect everything.

Those threats that cannot be nullified constitute risk. Determining what risks will and will not be nullified is the job of policy makers, who regularly engage in what amounts to the triage of risk reduction and risk management. Risk reduction, as the name implies, consists of those actions that maximize to the extent threats are nullified. Which threats will be nullified and which will remain risks lie in the realm of risk management.

Risk can be modulated by manipulating either element of the formula. One way to reduce risk is to redefine those things that are considered threatening. Illegal immigration poses a threat that needs to be addressed only if one defines such immigration as a problem. If immigration is declared no longer to be a problem, then the threat is reduced and so is the risk. This particularly controversial example is cited purposely, since any attempt to define away risks will almost always be highly controversial.

The other way to reduce risk is to increase the capability to address and attack threats. In political terms, this means increasing the resources allocated to the particular problem. To continue the illegal immigrant example, if continued illegal immigration is defined as an intolerable threat to the United States, the obvious risk-reducing response is to make the borders more impermeable—for instance, by hiring additional border guards or immigration and Border Patrol employees. That solution would cost money, opening political debates on taxes, deficits, and the reallocation of resources from some other functions that are particularly difficult, given the global economic crisis.

THINKING ABOUT INTERESTS

Where risk is accepted and where it is not depends on the hierarchy of things that are valued (interests). Questions about the role and implications of interests mirror differences over what constitutes security in the contemporary order. The interplay of interests—whose are realized and whose are not—is central to the dynamics of international relations organized around the realist paradigm. The interests at the base of these calculations are invariably state interests. Constructed in this manner, the military aspects of security are prominent because force is one of the options available to achieve the state's most important (or vital) interests.

For better or worse, interest-driven calculations remain the criteria by which states operate in the anarchical international system. When the interests of states come into conflict, the question of which states' interests will prevail also arises, and this leads to trying to determine how important interests are, where and how they are threatened , and thus what means will be employed to attempt to achieve them. Thus, the question of levels of interest must be addressed, although within a somewhat different context than the question of security. These levels, in turn, suggest different national security and military and nonmilitary implications, including economic implications connected to the theme of globalization. Finally, the challenge to traditional concepts of national interest in the form of broader variants of what constitute vital interests is addressed.

Levels of Interests

The various levels and intensities of interest have been introduced in Chapter 2 and need not be repeated here. The heart of that discussion, however, was over the critical traditional national security question of the boundary between *vital* interests and those that are deemed less than vital. The salience of that boundary is, of course, that it is theoretically the demarcation point at which the state will contemplate the use of military force to realize its goals. Interests failing the test of vitality (major or peripheral interests) imply the use of means of lesser intensity than for those that are vital.

This conjunction between interests and security can be depicted in matrix form, as is done in Table 3.1. Analyzing the table, cells 1 and 6 are the easiest to describe. It is the heart of the realist formulation that when vital interests are threatened, force may become an option if the situation is solvable by using force (military security, as depicted in cell 1). At the same time, when less-than-vital interests come into conflict, they are normally solved nonmilitarily because military force is either inappropriate or more drastic than the situation dictates (cell 6). An imminent attack on one's territory would be a clear cell 1 situation; a dispute over tariff schedules would clearly fall in cell 6. When vital interests are involved,

Table 3.1: Interest Levels and Security Means Dimensions

		Interest Level	
		Vital	Less Than Vital
Security	Military	Cell 1	Cell 2
Means	Semimilitary	Cell 3	Cell 4
Dimension	Nonmilitary	Cell 5	Cell 6

the first inclination is to try to use nonmilitary means to resolve the differences—maintaining force as a "last resort" if all else fails (cell 5). Applying economic sanctions would be an example.

The real debate is over the situation in which vital interests are not engaged but military aspects of security may be contemplated because they are the only means that may bring about a satisfactory resolution (cell 2). A strict interpretation of the realist paradigm is very prohibitive in this situation: if American vital interests are not threatened, for instance, the paradigm suggests American use of force should not be contemplated. This was the basic stance taken by the Bush campaign in 2000 when it argued that the United States should not be the "world's 911"; that stance was arguably reversed when the United States invaded Iraq in 2003.

The continued controversy over applying realist criteria for using force rages in cell 2 with strong national security and military implications. Because the United States possesses such an overwhelming amount of force, there is some temptation to apply it to a variety of situations. As Clinton Secretary of State Madeleine Albright once said, "What is the point of having armed forces if you never use them?" The retort from the realist paradigm is that one uses them only when the situation is really important (vital interests) and when force is appropriate. Whether the removal of Saddam Hussein was important enough to justify invading Iraq is a cell 1–cell 2 dispute.

The role of force is more complicated in cells 3 and 4 (semimilitary dimensions). Where vital interests are at stake, force is justified to the extent it can be effective. The military aspects of the war on terrorism are a clear cell 3 application. The questions revolve around how much of a role force plays when it may be a necessary, but not sufficient, condition for success. The war on drugs arguably represents cell 4, since drug use is an important but probably not system-threatening (vital interest) problem. In this case, questions can be raised about whether the problem is severe enough to invoke force and whether the use of force is appropriate for dealing with the problem.

The boundary between military and nonmilitary dimensions of security (vital and major interests) is not a fixed line. It is more like a movable confidence interval of changing widths and locations. Where the line should be and just how wide the interval around it ought to be are the heart of the national security debate about using force. It is a highly political debate in which reasonable people can and do disagree over specific situations and in which location changes as time passes and circumstances change. There will always be high levels of consensus on what situations represent vital interests, but there will equally always be disagreement about the exact location of the intellectual barrier separating those situations that do and do not justify the employment of American armed forces. The existence of semimilitary situations emphasizes this problem.

The debate within cell 2 and in cells 3 and 4 can thus be seen as a question about how much the change in the international environment of the post–Cold War world has moved the width of the band surrounding what is and is not vital and the extent and role of force in semimilitary situations. During the Cold War period, the location was relatively clear. The United States could and would use force when

Soviet-inspired or Soviet-directed Communist movements threatened to come to power at the expense of American friends and allies. The clearest cases were those in which the United States had clearly important interests—Western Europe and Northeast Asia (Japan and Korea)—and, of course, cases in which the Soviets could threaten the United States directly with nuclear weapons. In cases that put the physical survival or independence of the American homeland or the territory of its closest friends at stake (the physical dimension of security), it was clear that military security was at stake and that force would be used (cell 1).

Even during the Cold War, the demarcation was an interval, not a line, and this was most clearly seen in places that might be of interest to the United States in Communist versus non-Communist terms but where otherwise the United States had few interests. Those situations occurred most often in developing world areas such as Africa and much of Asia, and the American assessment became more debatable, falling within the psychological dimension of what makes the country feel secure and about which reasonable people can disagree. These are the instances that fall into cell 2.

Two potentially similar situations on which opposite conclusions were reached illustrate this relationship between interests and security. The first is the American involvement in Vietnam. When the United States replaced France as the principal barrier to Communist victory there after the Geneva Conference of 1954, there was relatively little debate about American direct interests in the outcome of that conflict. Rather, the prevailing criterion for some level of involvement was opposition to Communist expansion globally, of which Southeast Asia happened to be the then most current example. Opposition to Communism as a general proposition led policy makers to conclude that the worst possible outcome (the unification of the country under Communist control) was sufficiently dire to justify military intervention.

In retrospect, it is probably unfortunate that the vitality question was not fully considered at the time because quite possibly the assessment would have been negative. In the end, the worst possible outcome did occur; nevertheless, except for the self-inflicted angst the United States experienced because it "lost" the war, American interests otherwise were hardly affected at all—the answer to how interests were affected was "not very much." What looked at the time like a cell 1 situation looks much more like a cell 2 or even a cell 6 situation in retrospect. This same analysis can be applied to Afghanistan, as is done in Amplification 3.3.

The other example is Nicaragua in the 1980s. How important Sandinista rule was to the interests of the United States was argued both as a matter of the competition between Communist and non-Communist rule and on the basis of geography. At one level, a Marxist Nicaragua would provide a foothold for Communism on the mainland of the Americas, allowing Soviet assistance to be funneled through Cuba into Nicaragua and on to destinations such as El Salvador, where the pro-American government was facing a Marxist insurgency. At another level, an activist Nicaragua might stir up trouble generally in the region, possibly eventually threatening control of the Panama Canal and even destabilizing the southern part of Mexico, where there was an incipient antigovernment insurgent movement active.

Amplification 3.3

VITAL AND LESS-THAN-VITAL INTERESTS AND AFGHANISTAN

One of the critiques of the American decision to maintain forces in Afghanistan has been that the situation there does not constitute a threat to American vital interests and that, by applying the realist paradigm, the use of force was unjustified. Put in terms presented here, critics have essentially argued the situation did not fall into cell 1 of Figure 3.1, but more probably it was a cell 4 situation wherein semimilitary responses would have been more appropriate.

On which side of the vital–less-than-vital divide Afghanistan falls is complicated by the nature of the war. The original (and continuing) rationale has been to defeat Al Qaeda and prevent the return of the terrorists to Afghan sanctuaries. As part of the war on terror, it is arguably a cell 1 application.

Operationally, however, the military effort is more complicated. Virtually all of Al Qaeda is physically in Pakistan and thus beyond the reach of American forces operating in Afghanistan. Rather, the actions of U.S. forces primarily have an impact on the outcome of the civil war between the Afghan government and the Taliban. Whether the United States has enough interest in that conflict to justify force or not is debatable. In other words, is the outcome of the civil war vital to U.S. interests? Should Afghanistan be a cell 1 or a cell 2 example?

Did the Nicaraguan situation rise to a threat to a vital interest, justifying a military response (cell 1), or were the interests less than vital, in which case a military response might or might not be appropriate? There was disagreement between the White House and the Congress on this question, and the ultimate decision was to treat it as either a cell 2 or a cell 6 situation, one not requiring the employment of American military forces—a determination vindicated when the Nicaraguans voted the Sandinistas out of office in 1990.

Why engage in such a lengthy discussion of the relationship between security dimensions and interest levels? For one thing, it illustrates that in the real world, such determinations are difficult and ambiguous. Were the world made up exclusively of clearly cell 1 or cell 6 situations, making and implementing national security policy would be simple. In fact, one source of nostalgia about the Cold War is that the central confrontation between the United States and the Soviet Union was such a precisely cell 1 instance. Building security policy from that central construct was intellectually straightforward and relatively noncontroversial. Having said that, the United States never used military force during the Cold War in an unambiguously cell 1 situation (the closest possible exception may have been Korea); rather, it *deployed* forces to deal with cell 1 contingencies (North Atlantic Treaty

Organization [NATO] forces in Europe), but it *employed* forces in situations more closely associated with cell 2.

The post–Cold War world consists almost exclusively of situations that raise the debate about where the boundary between vital and less-than-vital interests should be placed and what kinds of responses—military, semimilitary, or nonmilitary—are most appropriate. In this case, where the interest–threat mismatch so often holds, there are hardly any clear cell 1 situations for which to prepare and around which to ground planning. If international religious terrorism truly threatened the physical integrity of the United States and was a force appropriate for military eradication, it might rise to cell 1, but it is the exception, not the rule.

Security and Interests in the Contemporary Environment

It is an old saw that basic national interests rarely change but threats to those interests change. A stable, free Western Europe, for instance, is just as important to the United States today as it was a half-century ago; what is different today is that there are no realistic threats to the security of the countries of Western Europe. At the same time, new (or apparently new) threats to long-term interests may emerge, as the terrorist threat to American territory exhibits.

This situation is intellectually difficult for those who think about and plan for national security, especially the military dimension of that security. While there may be a variety of situations that potentially engage American vital interests in the contemporary world, the only one that has activated American interest has been the alleged vital interests in Afghanistan and Iraq. Saddam Hussein's invasion and conquest of Kuwait in 1990 threatened American guaranteed access to Middle Eastern oil, a clear American vital interest. His alleged stockpiling of WMD and consorting with terrorists in 2002 raised questions of vital interests again, a more debatable proposition.

The ongoing effort against terrorism most clearly represents a response to a threat to a vital American interest, but the questionable appropriateness and effectiveness of traditional military action to overcome it muddy the situation. The Afghanistan war illustrates the confusion. As already noted, a traditional military response failed to alleviate the problem in 2001 (Al Qaeda escaped to Pakistan), and subsequent military actions have mostly had their impacts on the international situation in Afghanistan, not on Al Qaeda. It is at least arguable that military action cannot overcome this threat under any circumstances, a possibility explored in Chapter 12.

What defines terrorist acts is their size and responses to them. The African embassy attacks of 1998 killed around two dozen Americans (as well as hundreds of Kenyans and Tanzanians), and seventeen sailors died in 2000 on the USS *Cole*. While these losses were tragic, they were not on a scale that threatens the basic integrity of the United States. It is also not clear how to respond to these kinds of acts. The United States retaliated for the embassy bombings by launching cruise missiles against suspected terrorist training camps in Afghanistan run by bin Laden, but they failed either to kill the Saudi expatriate (which officials later said was their intent) or to slow down his activities. A major conceptual problem, part of the difficulty in the Afghanistan situation, arises because Al Qaeda lacks a territorial base that can be attacked, which is a main use of conventional force in symmetrical war situations.

How to use armed forces when the kinds of situations for which they have traditionally been employed (securing vital interests) are basically absent or partially appropriate is a major agenda item in the current debate about national security. Clearly, many of the actual threats to American national interests arguably fall on the less-than-vital side of the demarcation line. The clear implication is that there is not clear guidance about what military forces, and especially conventional forces, should do in these situations.

How does one deal with such circumstances? One way is to enforce the realist paradigm and accept the decreased saliency of regular military force in the current milieu. If American forces are to be used only when vital interests are at stake, then they will be used relatively infrequently in the near future, or they will be only a variable part of responses to worthy threats. The other solution is to broaden the criteria under which force employment is allowable. This amounts to moving the line between vital and less-than-vital interests more into the less-than-vital category of actions. This was, in the terms used here, the primary change in thinking about the use of force introduced by the neoconservatives during the Bush years. Whether how far or in which direction the Obama administration attempts to move the line will be an important indicator of change or continuity about national security affairs.

APPLYING INSTRUMENTS OF POWER

As noted in Chapter 2, the anarchical nature of international relations requires that states engage in self-help to realize their interests. A recourse to some superior source of authority before which they could adjudicate conflicts of their interests with those of others does not exist. There is no such authority, of course, because states have vital interests that might not prevail if some outside authority decided the outcomes of conflicts of interests. Since, by definition, a state will not willingly accept denial of its most important interests, the solution is to avoid having any body that can make adverse rulings that would probably have to be disobeyed.

This depiction is at the heart of the operation of the realist paradigm. In such a system, states achieve their goals to the extent of their ability to coerce or convince others to comply with their goals or interests (self-help). One can applaud or decry that situation, but it is the dynamic that energizes the system in the absence of some fundamental reform.

Using the Instruments

The instruments of power gain their meaning in terms of whether their application accomplishes the purposes for which they are used. For any instrument to be potentially effective, it must possess two traditionally defined characteristics, to which an implied third can be added. First, a state must possess the physical wherewithal to take the actions it proposes, which is known as *capability*. The absence of capability renders a threat ineffectual if the threatened party recognizes the deficiency. A Chinese threat to close the strategic Straits of Malacca by interdicting ships transiting the straits would be ignored because China has traditionally lacked the long-range aircraft (and refueling capability) or navy to sustain such action. Second, objects of threats must believe that the threatening state would actually employ those capabilities in the ways it says it would in order to accomplish its ends, which is known as *credibility*. Based upon his perceptions of post-Vietnam unwillingness to use force, Saddam Hussein wrongly believed the United States would not use force to reverse his conquest of Kuwait in 1990. Beyond capability and credibility is the ability to apply the instrument in a manner that achieves the sought-after goal, which can be called *efficacy*. During the Cold War, the United States could always have leveled the Soviet Union with nuclear weapons in the event of some transgression, but such an action would have resulted in a Soviet response that would have destroyed the United States and thus would have served no useful purpose.

These characteristics are clearly interrelated. Capability and credibility are linked. At the most obvious level, no state is going to believe a threat based on a capability the threatening state does not possess. Nicaragua, for instance, cannot threaten to invade Mexico because it lacks the military capability to do so. Conversely, however, the ability to carry out a threat does not imply the willingness to use that power. The United States becomes annoyed with France frequently over France's attempts to keep symbols of American culture, such as American popular music and films, out of the country (to limit the amount of penetration of French culture). While it is physically possible for the United States to threaten a nuclear attack against France to force it to lift these restrictions, no one would believe such a threat, meaning it lacks credibility. At the same time, not all instruments are effective in achieving the goals their application is supposed to achieve. The American economic boycott against Cuba for the past nearly fifty years has not succeeded in removing Fidel Castro from power or in lifting Communist rule from the island state.

Orchestrating the uses of the instruments of power is a delicate activity that involves considerable uncertainties arising from the fact that the effective application of power is largely a psychological exercise. At one level, it is a duel between the state threatening to employ an instrument and the state receiving the threat. Assuming the threatened party knows whether the threatener has the capability to do what is proposed (which the threatening party may seek to obscure), it then has to assess whether the threat is credible, which is an exercise in mind reading. There may be some evidence based upon how the threatening state has acted in similar circumstances in the past to provide an indication of the threatener's will, but since no two situations are identical, that evidence may or may not be conclusive: Will he or will he not?

The threatening partner must also make a psychological assessment of the party against whom it is seeking to apply power in a situation of less-than-perfect knowledge of the other party's mental state. Will the other party believe the threatener would carry out the threat or call his/her bluff? At the same time, will the threat gain compliance without having to be carried out (the best possible outcome, since carrying out threats normally involves some harm for all parties)? If not, will carrying out the threat convince the other party to do what the threatening party wanted done in the first place, or will it fail?

During the Cold War, much of this calculation had been successfully worked out, and the dynamics were reasonably clearly defined. Among the instruments of power, the military instrument was conceded to be of the greatest importance, at least in the relations among the contending superpowers. The economic instrument was clearly more important in the relations within the developed countries headed by the United States, but economic sanctions and rewards had virtually no impact on the East–West relations. The greatest ambiguities about which instruments had efficacy were in the developing world, both in the extension of the East–West confrontation and in relations over matters like political and economic development.

The Contemporary Balance of Instruments of Power

Whether there is a real change in how international relations occur today is largely a matter of the state of the third criterion identified for applying instruments: efficacy. The question of change can be rephrased to ask whether other, nonmilitary forces induce change in the post–Cold War world more than did those (normally military) in the Cold War era. Assertions of dramatic change will almost inevitably overshoot the truth, but there may be some discernible differences.

The efficacy of the traditional military instrument has clearly become more restricted. Military threats or actions among the major powers of the developed world absolutely lack credibility. This is really not a change, however, because it was equally unlikely that the western allies (including the market democracies of Asia) would have fought one another during the Cold War. If there is a difference, it is that what President Bill Clinton called the "circle of market democracies", which has been gradually enlarging, to include former authoritarian foes from the old Communist world. In these cases, positive military inducements may have supplanted threats as the instrument to advance American interests in spreading market democracy. Actions such as military arms sales, training programs, and membership and participation in military alliances like NATO are other means to induce formerly nondemocratic countries into the general peace.

The use of military force in the developing world has similarly undergone only modest, peripheral change. Most of the violence in the world occurs within (as opposed to between) developing world states, as was generally the case during the Cold War. What has changed is the incentives for outside involvement in these conflicts. During the Cold War, the American motivation was to prevent the victory of Communist elements, and the calculus included the likelihood and intolerability of Communist success. In the environment prior to 2001, the incentives tended to cluster around humanitarian concerns. The calculus involved whether any lasting good could be achieved by physical involvement and what levels of sacrifice are tolerable to accomplish various levels of good. Blunting and suppressing terrorism has provided a firmer basis for applying the military instrument; as a semimilitary concern, striking a balance between the use of military and nonmilitary instruments is the problem.

The major contraction in the efficacy of military force surrounds the avoidance of major war with potent and threatening adversaries. Only the utter failure of market democracy in a major state such as China or Russia (both possibilities) could produce the underlying animosities necessary to produce a new peer competitor for the United States. Such a transformation would, of course, be carefully monitored from the beginning, and actions would certainly be taken to reduce or contain such developments. More recently, the possibility of a general economic meltdown with unknown international effects has become a less than entirely theoretical source of potential conflict.

The traditional military instrument of power has a different and probably diminished efficacy in these circumstances. If that is the case and the likelihood of a returned equivalent threat to that of the Cold War is unlikely, then those facts should have major implications for the capability component of the capability/credibility/efficacy equation that energizes the instruments of power.

It is easy to overstate how much the economic instrument has undergone change. Globalization clearly expanded the arsenal of economic instruments of power. The emphasis on trade and the removal of trade barriers create opportunities for countries with large markets such as the United States to obtain leverage among those who wish to compete in the American domestic market. Membership in the various universal and regional trading associations can provide the ability to influence economic decisions in various countries, and the ability of the International Monetary Fund (IMF) and other international monitors to guide the development of developing economies has clearly been enhanced as well. These dynamics, of course, operate more positively in an economic climate of expanding global prosperity than they do in economically troubled times.

New forms of power may blossom in the future. The telecommunications revolution has been a particularly potent force in economic expansion, information explosion, and a variety of other areas. The positive expansion of the information age to nonparticipants is an enormous positive inducement to influence behavior. This positive aspect, however, has a darker side in the form of threats to disrupt the very fragile systems on which the telecommunications revolution rests. Cyber terrorism may become an all-too-familiar instrument of power, given the increasing electronic dependency of the international system. The possibilities are bounded only by human imagination.

CONCLUSION: THE CHANGING NATURE OF INFLUENCE

This chapter has raised and examined four related concerns about contemporary international politics that flow from the realist paradigm and its application to the present and the future. The first concern was with security and how a changed environment affects American national security in both a physical and a psychological sense. Is American security enhanced by or detracted from changes that have occurred? The second concern was how the changed security environment affects the kind and amount of risk the country must endure and the problem of risk reduction and risk management. Is the world a riskier place? The third concern was with national interests, phrased in terms of whether the most important interests were more imperiled or reinforced today. Can the United States better realize its interests today than previously? The fourth concern was with how those interests are realized in the form of changes in the effectiveness of the various instruments of power. Are different instruments more efficacious than they were before for realizing interests?

Overall, the major conclusion one must reach is that, despite the intrusion of international religious terrorism, the post–Cold War world is a more secure, less threatening place than before for the United States, and one in which the country is basically better able to realize its interests. One can easily overstate both the pervasiveness of change and the improvement of the situation, but at least in a marginal sense, the generalizations seem to hold, even if one factors in the major source of insecurity that terrorism represents.

The chief cause of improvement is, of course, the end of the Cold War and thus the removal of the largest challenge to security, the possibility of a general systemic war in which the nuclear-armed superpowers confront one another on the battlefield with the fate of civilization in the balance. The vulnerability of American territory to terrorist attacks remains a significant threat but not on the scale of a potential World War III during the Cold War.

What could cause a deterioration of the current situation and the American place in it? A continuing, even worsening cataclysmic turn of the global economy like the Great Depression of the 1930s would certainly represent the worst possible case. One of the fears surrounding the emergence of international terrorism is the prospect that it might trigger a general economic downturn, and while hardly anyone attributes much of the economic crisis of 2008 to terrorists, economic unrest does present a major challenge to the global system.

The United States faces a period of introspection and readjustment that will affect all four of the concerns raised in this chapter. Will the United States have to redefine what makes it feel secure in light of the trauma of an arguable misrepresentation and misapplication of security concerns in Afghanistan and Iraq? Will the new environment be a more or less secure place, and how will the United States respond to that judgment? On the second question of risk, will the United Sates pull back from an aggressive pursuit of risk reduction framed primarily in military terms that typified responses in the immediate post-9/11 environment? Or, will risk be redefined to accept some contemporary situations as less threatening? The third concern surrounds what constitutes vital interests and how they are protected. The aggressive actions taken by the Bush administration represented the expansive view of what constitutes vital interests. Will that vision be sustained, or will the country return to a more restrictive vision of what is worth pursuing with armed forces? Finally, there is the question of applying instruments of power. Will the first post-9/11 administration rely more or less on military force to achieve its goals? Or, will it pursue other paths to reach desired ends?

All the questions raised in this chapter are evolving and are subject to change based both on changing circumstances in the world and on how the international environment responds to changes in the American response. In addition, how the

United States is predisposed to act in the environment is conditioned by distinctly American perceptions of itself and its place in the world. The American experience in national security represents another element in the context of how the United States operates in the world and is the subject of the next chapter.

STUDY/DISCUSSION QUESTIONS

1. What are the major elements that compose security? At what levels does security exist? How are conceptions changing relative to one another? Discuss.
2. What is risk? How does one deal with the problem of risk? What are the chief means by which risk can be managed? Elaborate.
3. Relate levels of interest—focusing on the vital and less-than-vital levels—and means to realize them. In what combinations of interest and means do the most controversial situations arise? Which combinations are most frequent in the contemporary environment?
4. Define the idea and content of instruments of power. Discuss how the uses of different instruments have changed and are likely to change in the future.
5. Is the international environment more dangerous (less secure) for the United States now, or was it during the Cold War? How does the text answer this question? Do you agree or disagree? Why?

SELECTED BIBLIOGRAPHY

Art, Robert J., and Kenneth N. Waltz. *The Use of Force: Military Power and International Politics.* 5th ed. London: Rowman and Littlefield, 2003.

Bauman, Zygmut. *Globalization: The Human Consequences.* New York: Columbia University Press, 1998.

Berkowitz, Bruce. *The New Face of War: How War Will Be Fought in the 21st Century.* New York: Free Press, 2003.

Burton, Daniel F., Victor Gotbaum, and Felix Rohatyn, eds. *Visions of the 1990s: U.S. Strategy and the Global Economy.* Cambridge, MA: Ballinger, 1989.

Cusimano, Maryann, ed. *Beyond Sovereignty.* Boston: Bedford/St. Martin's Press, 1999.

Djerejian, Edward P. "From Conflict Management to Conflict Resolution." *Foreign Affairs* 85, no. 6 (November/December 2006): 41–48.

Drew, Dennis M., and Donald M. Snow. *Making Twenty-First Century Strategy: An Introduction to Modern Nation Security Processes and Problems.* Montgomery, AL: Air University Press, 2008.

Etzioni, Amitai. *Security First: For a Muscular, Moral Foreign Policy.* New Haven, CT: Yale University Press, 2007.

Flanagan, Stephen J., Ellen L. Frost, and Richard Kugler. *Challenges of the Global Century: Report of the Project on Globalization and National Security.* Washington, DC: Institute for National Strategic Studies (National Defense University), 2001.

Florida, Richard. "How the Crash Will Reshape America." *The Atlantic* 303, no. 2 (March 2009): 44–56.

Friedman, Thomas L. "The First Law of Petropolitics." *Foreign Policy*, May/June 2006, 36–42.

Kaplan, Robert D. *The Coming Anarchy: Shattering the Dreams of the Post–Cold War.* New York: Random House, 2000.

————. "Center Stage for the Twenty-First Century." *Foreign Affairs* 88, no. 2 (March/April 2009): 16–31.

Luttwak, Edward N. *Strategy: The Logic of War and Peace*. Cambridge, MA: Belknap, 1987.

Nuechterlein, Donald. *America Recommitted: United States National Interests in a Reconstructed World*. Lexington: University of Kentucky Press, 1991.

Pfaff, William. "Invitation to War." *Foreign Affairs* 72, no. 3 (Summer 1993): 97–109.

Pilat, Joseph F. "Reassessing Security Assurances in a Unipolar World." *Washington Quarterly* 28, no. 2 (Spring 2005): 159–167.

Rogov, Sergei. "International Security and the Collapse of the Soviet Union." *Washington Quarterly* 15, no. 2 (Spring 1992): 16–28.

Sloan, Stephen. *Beating International Terrorism: An Action Strategy for Preemption and Punishment*. Rev. ed. Montgomery, AL: Air University Press, 2000.

Smith, W. Y. "U.S. National Security After the Cold War." *Washington Quarterly* 15, no. 4 (Winter 1992): 21–35.

Snow, Donald M. *When America Fights: The Uses of U.S. Military Power*. Washington, DC: CQ Press, 2000.

————. "Rising Powers" and "Sovereignty and Intervention," in *Cases in International Relations: Portraits of the Future*. 4th ed. New York: Pearson Longman, 2010.

Wolf, Martin. *Why Globalization Works*. New Haven, CT: Yale University Press, 2004.

CHAPTER 4

The American Experience

PREVIEW

The extent to which a country embraces a realist or some alternative orientation toward the world is influenced by its generalized historical experience and other conditioning factors that influence how it sees the world. For most of American history, that experience has been primarily positive, with low levels and qualities of threat that make the current high-threat environment all the more distinct. This chapter begins by identifying general influences on the American experience and then looks at the question historically, designating and describing three historical parts of the national security experience. The chapter concludes with suggestions of how the past may influence the present and future and how recent experience may have affected the impact of historical patterns and legacies.

The way different countries view the world, their place in it, and patterns of threat and opportunity is in part the result of unique factors that help shape the national worldview. Historical experience and geographical accident are part of this endowment that informs attitudes on, among other things, national security. For some countries, the experience has been harsh. It is, for instance, impossible for the citizens of any country on the northern European plain not to have some historically based fear of a possible invasion of their territory from one direction or another and to view matters of national security threats very seriously as a result. At the other end of the spectrum, a country like Japan that successfully isolated itself physically from the rest of the world for hundreds of years has an equally distinctive worldview and perception of what constitutes security.

The relatively benign American historical experience meant the United States was relatively insulated from world power politics certainly until the end of the nineteenth century and arguably until World War II. This respite allowed the United States to delay coming to grips with its own interpretation of the realist paradigm until the last half-century or so. As a latecomer to the international center stage, historical American experience fashioned outside the realist construct has been especially vulnerable to assault.

The United States is no exception to the effects of history. Although the American experience is shorter than that of the traditional European and Asian powers, it has been conditioned by a series of factors that are both historical and physical. The result of American history has been a generally positive view of the world and the security of the American place in it that did not require a great deal of emphasis or continuing effort on matters of national security until World War II and its aftermath. Americans have felt secure for most of their history as a country. This general sense of tranquility has certainly accentuated the sense of insecurity most Americans have experienced since September 11, 2001. Insecurity represents more of a discontinuity for the United States than it does for most other countries.

The American experience with national security concerns can be divided into three basic periods. Following a discussion of basic, underlying, conditioning factors that help shape the American worldview, the text begins with the formative period, from the beginning of the republic in the eighteenth century through World War II, a period of relatively low, episodic American involvement in international affairs, including concerns over national security. The second period encompasses the Cold War, when the United States was thrown literally into the middle of the geopolitical fray as one of the two major actors in the international system and had to learn to act in that environment. The chapter concludes with a discussion of the third period, the contemporary system, and the impact of the two major fault lines on American perceptions about the world.

CONDITIONING FACTORS IN THE AMERICAN TRADITION

At least three conditioning factors stand out as important influences on the way Americans have come to view questions of defense and national security. Alternative lists could undoubtedly be constructed, but these influences are the essential American lack of a sense of shared history; the unique American geographical endowment, which both isolated the United States from hostile others and provided the country with abundant resources that nurtured and permitted its isolation; and the country's Anglo-Saxon heritage, which affected Americans' earliest political attitudes.

American Ahistoricism

It is not unfair to typify the American people as lacking basic, shared historical views of the United States and its place in the world. This ahistoricism has several bases. One is that the American experience is fairly brief when compared to the historical experience of the major European and Asian counterparts. While the territory occupied by the United States was inhabited for thousands of years by Native Americans, most of those Indians did not keep a systematic history, and most Americans do not share a sense of ethnicity or history with these natives. Rather, American history, as most Americans perceive it, is about four hundred years old (dating to the English arrival in Virginia in 1607), and it is not even a history shared by most current Americans or their ancestors. The pattern of American population settlement has been in immigrant waves, and this means relatively few Americans can trace their own roots back to the beginnings of the American experience. It is, for instance, no coincidence that there are no Vietnamese Americans who are members of the Daughters of the American Revolution, and the same can be said for many other Americans whose ancestors had not immigrated to these shores when the "shot heard round the world" was fired in Massachusetts in April 1775.

This lack of historical experience and interaction has not been an altogether bad thing. Most Americans came to the United States either to escape some form of tyranny or calamity in their native lands or with the hope of becoming part of the greater prosperity that the United States appeared to offer, a trend that continues to this day. As Fareed Zakaria noted in a 2007 *Newsweek* analysis, more people immigrate annually to the United States than to all other countries in the world combined, generally because they view the United States as a place of hope and opportunity. As a result, there has been a greater sense of optimism in this country than is present in many more-established cultures where the historical record offers a greater balance of positive and negative legacies. More pointedly, with the exception of some aspects of the Civil War, the United States has no national tragedy that mars the national consciousness and tempers our optimism in the way, for instance, that the Battle of Kosovo in 1389 has tainted Serbian history (after losing the battle to the Ottoman Turks, Serbia fell under foreign control until the early twentieth century).

American ahistoricism contributes to the American sense of exceptionalism and thus to American attitudes toward national security in a couple of ways. When combined with the fact and perception of American physical isolation from the world, the result has been a positive self-image about the United States that has extended to its military experience. Americans have historically viewed themselves as winners both at war and at peace. The contemporary revival of interest in the United States' most successful—and cherished—military experience, World War II (the "greatest generation"), is emblematic of this attitude. The general ahistoricism also allows Americans to ignore less glorious aspects of the military experience, such as its performance in the War of 1812 (in which the United States won decisively exactly one land battle, at New Orleans, fought two weeks after the peace treaty was signed). This general attitude of success has made acceptance of the outcome of the Vietnam and Iraq conflicts all the more difficult, just as the territorial attacks by the September 11 terrorists have assaulted the American sense of isolation and invulnerability.

Americans have also liked to portray themselves as an essentially pacific people, slow to anger but capable of vanquishing any foe once aroused. The premise underlying this belief is the idea that peace is the normal and preferred condition and war is an abnormality that is thrust upon Americans when they are attacked by hostile others. The Japanese sneak attack at Pearl Harbor that dragged a reluctant United States into World War II is symbolic of this conviction, as has been the introduction of terrorism to our shores.

Many outsiders, as well as Native Americans, would, of course, contest both the notion of American passivity and the need to be provoked into violence. It is hard, for instance, to argue that most of the wars against the Indians of the plains and American West were "thrust" upon the United States, and the Spanish, who had already agreed to all of our terms when the United States declared war on them in 1898, would certainly question the reactive nature of Americans in that situation, and so do most Iraqis. The notion of American passivity, as well, can be maintained only with a very selective view of the American experience. While the current American simultaneous involvement in two wars may be somewhat unusually bellicose, it is not unprecedented.

Accident of Geography

Geography blessed the United States in at least two distinctly benign ways. First, the physical location of the United States between two of the world's great oceans made it virtually an island, at least as far as potential foreign incursions from Europe or Asia were concerned. When combined with comparatively weak or friendly countries on the northern or southern borders of the country, the result has been a condition of effective physical invulnerability for much of American history. With the exception of Pancho Villa's raids into the Southwest in the second decade of the twentieth century and a few submarine incursions during World War II along the West Coast, the forty-eight contiguous states (the continental United States or CONUS) were safe from the danger of physical harm from 1814, when the British left at the end of the War of 1812, until 1957, when the successful testing of a Soviet intercontinental ballistic missile (ICBM) made the United States vulnerable to nuclear missile attacks. The only other sources of American physical vulnerability have come when the United States has expanded beyond the continental mass (e.g., Hawaii) or added foreign colonies (e.g., the Philippines).

The other part of the geographic legacy is resource abundance. The American continental land mass was blessed in two ways. First, the farmland in the central United States—some of the best in the world—allowed the United States to produce enough food for itself (and surpluses for export) without any necessary recourse to foreign sources. Second, the United States also possessed adequate supplies of both mineral wealth (e.g., iron ore, copper) and energy (e.g., coal, petroleum, natural gas) to allow it to proceed through most of the industrialization process without the need to rely on foreign sources for natural resources.

The result of both these geographic factors was to produce, as part of the American worldview, an essential independence and sense of invulnerability that set the country apart from most other countries of the world, the majority of which were physically vulnerable, foreign resource dependent, or both. The United States thus had to spend little time or effort framing fulfillment of its basic needs in national security terms. Absent the need to defend American territory from invading enemies, most uses of American force have been expeditionary, sending forces overseas either to defend some American interest (e.g., U.S. colonies) or to aid a besieged country somewhere in the world. At the same time, there was no need to prepare to protect access to natural resources or food supplies from vulnerable foreign sources. Effectively, the result was that the United States had, for most of its history, no compelling need to form a national security strategy to protect it from the vagaries of a world that it could largely ignore if it chose to do so.

These unique geographic advantages began to diminish by the middle of the twentieth century. The Pearl Harbor attack and the Japanese conquest of the Philippines demonstrated that an extended United States was no longer physically invulnerable. Soviet missile capability made that vulnerability more dramatic, and advances in telecommunications and transportation have produced arguable American vulnerabilities to things such as terrorist attacks or cyberwar, a vulnerability dramatically brought home in 2001 and continuing as a source of concern. Economic globalization has tied together the world's economies and reduced American independence in that realm as well.

American resource independence has also been eroded dramatically. Increased demand for energy resources such as petroleum at low prices has made the United States dependent on foreign supplies, with strong and controversial national security consequences in places such as the Persian Gulf, as discussed in Amplification 4.1 and in Chapter 14. At the same time, the development and use of more exotic materials that are unavailable in the United States, such as titanium for jet engines, has also reduced resource independence. The desire for exotic foodstuffs, such as year-round access to fresh fruits and vegetables, has made the United States an agricultural importer as well. The reversal of American longtime isolation has made exposure to vulnerabilities more traumatic than it might otherwise have been.

The Anglo-Saxon Heritage

Although the country has greatly diversified ethnically and nationally and much of the original American culture has changed as a result, the United States was, of course, originally a British colony. Most of the original settlers in the United States were of British extraction, and they brought with them many of the customs and predilections of the mother country.

The Anglo-Saxon heritage affected the early American experience in a couple of obvious and enduring ways. First, it created an aversion to and suspicion of the military, and more specifically the army, in peacetime. This aversion was largely the result of the British experience during the seventeenth century. During the Cromwellian period in the 1640s and beyond, the Commonwealth's armies were used to suppress political opposition to the regime at home. When the monarchy was restored in 1688, one of the provisions of the settlement of the Glorious Revolution was to forbid a standing army on British soil during peacetime to avoid a recurrence of military intrusion into civilian life. The British insistence on stationing elements of the British army in the American colonies after the French and Indian Wars became a serious issue that helped produce the American Revolution. (Americans resented being subjected to a condition that citizens of the mother country would have found intolerable.) This aversion manifested itself throughout the formative period of the American national security experience (see the next section) in the tendency to essentially disarm after

Amplification 4.1

DEALING WITH DEPENDENCE ON PERSIAN GULF OIL

The Persian Gulf littoral, under which two-thirds of the world's known reserves of petroleum are located, has been a major concern and problem for the United States since 1979. Prior to 1979, American interests in the region—almost exclusively based in uninterrupted access to reasonably priced oil—were ensured by the United States' closest regional ally, and the strongest power in the region, Shah Reza Pahlevi's Iran. In 1979, the Shah was overthrown by a violently anti-American revolution that catapulted Ayotollah Ruhollah Khomeini into effective power and resulted in the capture of the American embassy in Teheran and the holding of its personnel for the duration of the Iran hostage crisis. It also removed the enforcer of American policy in the region from power and thus called into question the continuing security of American access to the region's oil.

The Persian Gulf has been a source of major foreign and national security concern ever since. In 1980, President Jimmy Carter issued the Carter Doctrine, declaring access to Gulf oil to be a vital American interest. In 1990 and 1991, the United States led the coalition that evicted Iraq from Kuwait, an action taken in part to prevent Iraq's Saddam Hussein from gaining a stranglehold on Gulf petroleum reserves. Usama bin Laden's ordered terrorist attack on the United States in 2001 was, by his own profession, carried out to help convince the United States to leave Saudi soil. The result is a continuing presence in Afghanistan. Some argue that guaranteed access to Iraqi oil was an important factor leading to war there.

American policy in the Persian Gulf derives directly from U.S. dependence on petroleum from the region. There are alternative sources of oil, but they are inadequate, inaccessible, or more expensive than Persian Gulf oil. In the case of Russian reserves, there is the ongoing question of political stability and geopolitical effects, raised in Chapter 7. Assuming the United States would prefer to be less dependent on oil from the region—and thus more independent in its policy options—what are the alternatives?

As framed in the partisan American debates on the subject, there are two alternatives. One alternative, largely associated with Democrats, calls for an emphasis on conservation, thereby reducing the amount of Persian Gulf and other foreign oil needed by actions such as improving fuel economy in transportation, moving to other sources of energy, and the like. The other alternative, more favored by Republicans, features the development of alternate sources of petroleum and other energy sources plus some conservation, such as opening the Caspian Sea reserves or sources in places such as Alaska. When these questions are combined with the impact of the oil crisis of the summer of 2008, the global economic crisis that began in September 2008, and increasing concern over global warming triggered by fossil fuel burning, the result is a lively debate with significant national security overtones.

major wars and to rely disproportionately on part-time citizen–soldiers for the country's defense. The prohibition on the use of American armed forces in a law enforcement role on American soil enacted in 1868 (known as *posse comitatus*) further reflects the fear of military abuse that has been invoked when some officials proposed an expanded military role for patrolling the Mexican border, for instance. As noted later in the chapter, much of this aversion has been diluted in recent decades.

The other Anglo-Saxon legacy is a strong commitment to constitutional rule, especially to the guarantee of individual rights and liberties. Since military service, especially when it is the result of conscription, is a clear intrusion on individual liberty, there has always been a political reluctance to compel Americans into service. The only exceptions to this have occurred during American involvement in major conflicts requiring the raising of large forces, such as in the world wars, and during the Cold War, when it was accepted that a large "force in being" (standing active-duty armed force) was necessary to deter the menace of expansionist Communism. This aversion reappeared when American opinion turned decisively against the war in Vietnam, which, in its latter stages, was fought mostly by draftees. The fact that no American has been involuntarily inducted into service since the end of 1972 partially reflects attitudes that go back to the formation of the republic but also raises questions about that experience, since the all-volunteer concept results in a force that is both a professional and a citizen force.

The fear of incursion on individual liberties has had a more complicated history and arose with particular clarity regarding actions by the Bush administration (notably the USA PATRIOT Act, discussed in Chapter 5) in support of the global war on terrorism (GWOT) (see Chapter 13) and the war in Iraq (see Chapter 12). In essence, there has been an ongoing debate about the extent (if any) to which strict adherence to individual rights can or must be relaxed in wartime in the name of national security. As a general rule, the court system has allowed some relaxation of these rights during times of war, as in President Lincoln's suspension of habeas corpus during the Civil War and the government's forcible internment of Japanese Americans in camps during World War II. These actions have been controversial in the past and have been particularly questioned in the contemporary context, and the Obama administration moved quickly to vacate a number of Iraq-driven Bush policies that arguably violated civil liberties.

EVOLUTION OF THE AMERICAN EXPERIENCE

The American military tradition has evolved over time and with different experiences the country has undergone. As noted earlier, that experience can be divided into three historical periods: a formative period from the beginning of the republic to the end of World War II, the Cold War experience, and the contemporary, ongoing period. The two earlier historical periods were distinct from one another in two clear ways. In terms of the levels of threats posed to the United States and the American role in the world, the longer, formative period was one of low security threats and commitments, and the Cold War featured high threats and commitments.

Neither historical combination fits the contemporary environment perfectly. On one hand, the level of American involvement in the world since 1989 has never been higher. At the same time, the degree of threat to the United States was greatly reduced during the period between the fault lines (1989–2001), but threats appeared to intensify greatly after September 11, 2001. Because history includes adaptation to changing circumstances a major question is how changes in the environment have altered or amended fundamental American attitudes toward national security.

THE FORMATIVE PERIOD, 1789–1945

The period following the birth of the American republic was obviously formative in developing what would become the American military tradition and how Americans would look at military force. The period was heavily influenced by the events surrounding the Revolution itself and why it had come about. In retrospect (and certainly in comparison to the nature of modern revolutions), the American Revolution was a rather low-key affair in terms of both its motivations and its conduct. As Dennis Drew and I have argued in *From Lexington to Baghdad and Beyond,* it might not have occurred at all had the British government acceded to the American demands to be treated not as colonial subjects but as British citizens, including not stationing British forces on American territory. After the fighting began more or less accidentally at Lexington and Concord in April 1775, it took the colonials almost 15 months to declare they were in fact revolting by issuing the Declaration of Independence on July 4, 1776. The war itself was, by current standards, a fairly low-intensity conflict fought between relatively small armed forces mostly when the weather was good. Although the style of linear warfare fought at the time could produce sizable casualties in pitched, "set piece" battles, bloodshed was also modest by contemporary standards.

A series of "lessons" about military force arose from the revolutionary experience and were, by and large, reinforced during the next century and a half before the United States was thrust into World War II and could no longer remain aloof from world politics. Five elements of the American military tradition were born during this formative period. The first four—an antimilitary bias, the belief in the efficacy of the citizen–soldier, the myth of invincibility, and the preference for rapid mobilization and demobilization—can be directly attributed to the revolutionary experience. The fifth, a preference for total war, was more a product of the Civil War and the events that followed than of conflict in the international system generally. All of these elements collectively reinforced a general sort of disdain for things military that manifested itself, until the Korean War, in an American military establishment that was, except during wartime, small, physically isolated, and generally held in low regard. Clearly, the Cold War and post–Cold War experience has eroded these influences. The question is, How much?

At first glance, one may wonder about whether these influences remain important in the contemporary world. Clearly, the antimilitary bias has faded (largely the result of the greater status accorded the military due to its role in the Cold War), and the near-disaster of Korea (where demobilization after World War II had left the ranks so depleted that only the remobilization of World War II veterans in the Reserves prevented the complete conquest of the Korean peninsula by North Korea) deflated the demobilization effect. At the same time, the role of Reservist citizen–soldiers has clearly been raised by Iraq and will need to be reexamined, the myth of U.S. military invincibility has once again been questioned in ways not seen since Vietnam, and appropriate post-Iraq force levels (an aspect of mobilization) are part of the debate as well. The meanings of victory and defeat are contentious in an era devoid of the historical conceptual simplicity of total war.

Two broad factors have served to place limits on the applicability of these formative-period influences on contemporary perceptions. One has been the increasing salience of military forces in confronting the world since 1945. Put simply, a heightened threat environment has meant Americans need military force more than they did in the early days of the republic and have come to appreciate its contribution more than previously. The other influence has been the transformation of the military itself, since the Vietnam War, from a true citizen force composed of members some of whom were products of conscription to an all-volunteer, professional force. The result, explored in the pages that follow, is a military that is both more professional and more competent but also more removed from its popular roots.

Antimilitary Bias

It may sound strange to assert today, when public opinion polls regularly rate military service as one of the more prestigious professions, but prior to the Cold War, military service was not universally held in high regard in the United States. The peacetime military was generally a small, skeletal body whose purpose was to be ready to train a civilian force for military duty when the need arose. For the most part, the professional military (especially the Army) was consigned to military posts in remote areas of the country, where the general population's day-to-day exposure to it was fairly limited. Moreover, outside the ranks of the professional military itself, soldiering was not thought of as a particularly prestigious occupation. As is the case today, there were regional differences in the extent of this bias, with Southerners more generally supportive of the military than their Northern counterparts.

Much of this sentiment has its origins in the Anglo-Saxon tradition and the issue of British military presence in the colonies prior to the American Revolution. As in England under Cromwell, Crown forces had acted to suppress colonists, and many new Americans wanted to protect against the same possibility in the new republic.

In addition to creating a predilection toward keeping the military as small and nonthreatening as possible, this antimilitary bias favored keeping the military apolitical, and hence politically nonthreatening, as well. The U.S. Military Academy at West Point, for instance, was designed essentially as an engineering school to teach the science of war but not the reasons for war (a precedent primarily followed in the other service academies). The leading work detailing the relationship between war and its political purposes, Carl von Clausewitz's *On War*, was originally published in 1832 but was not translated into English and entered into the

West Point curriculum until 1876. Moreover, professional members of the military were effectively disenfranchised until 1944, when legislation permitting absentee balloting was enacted. Prior to that, military personnel could vote only if they happened to be physically in their hometowns on election day, which rarely happened. Keeping the military apolitical was thought to be important enough that disenfranchisement was not abrogated until the heat of World War II.

The Citizen–Soldier

How could a disdain and distrust for the military be reconciled with the occasional need for military forces to prosecute the wars foisted on the United States? Part of the answer, of course, was to keep the military as small and unthreatening as possible during peacetime. In addition to keeping the military as small and apolitical as possible, the other element was to develop a part-time military whose members were also integral parts of the civilian society from which they came, citizen–soldiers who were more citizens than soldiers. The result was to reinforce and glorify the militia tradition that was part of the colonial experience.

Militia members were part-time soldiers. As the lineal forefathers of the National Guard and Reserves, members served in the militia for fixed terms and with limited commitments as members. Just as contemporary Guard and Reserve units have historically served actively for limited periods each year (e.g., a weekend a month, two weeks in summer camp), militia units would drill periodically, often for short periods (some as little as a few days per year). The idea was that such limited commitment would not "infect" these citizen–soldiers with military values to the point they would lose their primary attachment to the civilian community. The activation of Guard and Reserve units for extended (including involuntary extended) deployments in Iraq is a direct violation of this tradition that has effectively made members more soldiers than citizens, at least temporarily. Whether and how the Guard and Reserves can be returned to their historical status and the implication of changes in their status will be one of the post-Iraq points of controversy where military tradition clashes with contemporary trends.

This arrangement was satisfactory if one could assume the militias were competent to carry out the country's military needs. From the revolutionary period, a myth was developed that this was indeed the case. To some measure, this belief was little more than wishful thinking, but militia units were involved in enough successful operations (Lexington and Concord, Breed's Hill, Saratoga, Cowpens) that their performance could be embellished and instances when militia units dissolved and ran when confronted with regular British Army opponents (Camden) could be ignored. When the country was not at war, the question was largely moot because militias were rarely called upon to demonstrate their strictly military competence.

The argument over the efficacy of the militia has never disappeared and remains an active part of the debate over current and future forces. Reserve and Guard units remain an integral part of the U.S. armed forces, although they are assigned generally noncombatant roles; however, Reserve units have been increasingly placed in combat roles in Afghanistan and Iraq due to shortages of full-time, active-duty personnel. The virtues of Reservists are that they are less expensive than active-duty soldiers and represent an additional reservoir of personnel when active-duty members are inadequate for a given task. The regular armed forces have a generally lower opinion of these successors of the militia men, emphasizing that the citizen component makes them less effective soldiers and thus of lesser value in military operations than full-time, active-duty forces.

Myth of Invincibility

The myth of invincibility asserts the indomitable nature of the American military and is the product of a selective reading of American military history. Its core is the idea that regardless of the circumstances, when the United States is forced to fight, it prevails. The general truth value of this belief is, of course, debatable. While it is true that the United States has generally been successful in war, American triumphs are liberally interspersed with episodes in which the country was less than successful. A more precise statement of the myth would probably be that when the United States becomes involved in long, total wars in which superior American physical resources can be brought to bear to wear out an opponent, fighting according to prevailing rules and American preferences (in other words, symmetrically), it generally prevails. But even that generalization does not apply to all warfare; in Vietnam, the opponent refused to wear out or to fight according to established norms (it fought asymmetrically), and the result was certainly not victory. The same has arguably proven true in Iraq and Afghanistan.

This generally positive assessment of the American military experience has two corollaries. The first is the "can do" syndrome, the idea that no military task is too difficult to overcome if Americans truly apply themselves to surmounting it. The syndrome can be a major impediment to objective assessment of potential missions for which American military forces might be employed, suggesting the possibility of prevailing in situations where a more sober assessment might counsel otherwise. There is, for instance, little on the public record to suggest that any appropriate military officials considered in advance the prospect that the United States might not be able to prevail in Vietnam; no one in the appropriate position to do so effectively said " *can't* do," a more accurate assessment and one held by many midlevel professional military and civilian analysts at the time. This failure is described with regard to Vietnam in McMaster's *Dereliction of Duty* and with regard to Iraq in Yingling's "A Failure in Generalship." It may also apply to the American military effort in Afghanistan.

The other corollary is that Americans prevail because of the brilliance and skill with which they fight. The facts fly largely in the face of such an assertion. The United States has, for instance, produced no major strategist of land warfare, although it has produced exceptional battlefield generals like George S. Patton and strategists who have contributed in other media (sea and air). Moreover, although American fighting forces have acquitted themselves well, the United States entered all its wars prior to Vietnam almost absolutely unprepared to fight them, meaning that in the early stages of those wars, American forces did not excel.

Mobilization and Demobilization

Through most of American history, the pattern of mobilization and demobilization has dominated the American military experience: when war seemed imminent or was thrust upon the country, it would raise and train a force to fight it, but as soon as the fighting ended, it would decommission that force and return it to the normalcy of civilian life. This preference reflected numerous elements of the American culture, from a belief in the abnormality of war to the fear of a standing military in peacetime. It also meant that after every major war until Korea, the United States returned its armed forces to the skeletal form that had existed before the war.

The tradition was sustainable throughout the formative period because the United States was never confronted with an enemy that could pose a direct and imminent threat to American territory—the accident of American geography prevented that occurrence. The luxury of forming a force only when necessary was always available as a policy option. The experience in World War II and the Cold War that followed changed that conclusion. Following the attack on Pearl Harbor (see Amplification 4.2), American forces in the Pacific were nearly overrun and defeated to the extent that it would have been difficult to regain the initiative, and only the heroic efforts of Americans at places like the Battle of Midway and Guadalcanal allowed the United States to recover while it rapidly mobilized an adequate force to meet the emergency. The absence of preparedness was the problem then, and when a similar circumstance nearly prevailed in Korea, the luxury of not having forces in existence was revealed as unacceptable.

Total War Preference

While the impact of the first four elements of the American tradition is generally to limit thinking about the use of military force, these influences are juxtaposed by a preference for involvement in total wars that apparently contrasts with the rest of the tradition. At one level, this development reflected changes in the international environment between the eighteenth and the middle of the twentieth centuries regarding the purposes of war. At the same time, it also was the result of an American perception that if the United States was to go to war, it should be for grand, righteous purposes that made it worthwhile.

The period between the mid–nineteenth and mid–twentieth centuries witnessed an expansion in both the means and the purposes for which war was conducted. The expansion of means was largely the result of the progressive application of the innovations of the Industrial Revolution to warfare. Gradually, it became possible to expand the extent of warfare by increasing the deadly effects of weapons and by increasing the places in which war could be fought. In 1789, warfare was largely limited to ground combat where armies could march and organize their linear formations (essentially large, open fields) and the surface of the ocean; by 1945, the only place war could not be conducted was in space (a deficiency overcome since then). War became larger in terms of where and to what effect it could be fought, and thus why it could be fought.

Amplification 4.2

READINESS AND PEARL HARBOR

The Japanese air attack on American naval and other military facilities at Pearl Harbor was one of the most traumatic events in American military history. Despite a variety of warning signs (e.g., intercepted intelligence reports, suspicious ship movements, growing strains in relations between the two countries), the United States was totally unprepared for the attack when it came early in the morning on Sunday, December 7, 1941. None of the bases on Oahu were on alert status—in fact, most of the personnel at Pearl Harbor had been out at social events the night before and had not yet reported for duty when the Japanese arrived. Virtually no one was even looking for evidence of an imminent attack, which added to the tragedy and destruction when it occurred.

It was partly the fault of the American military tradition that the attack came as such a complete surprise. To most Americans, nearly a century and a third of virtual invincibility had left them complacent, not mindful that such an attack could occur. Despite a war that had been raging for over two years in Europe and the growing expansion of the Japanese Empire into the South Pacific and East Asia, where it would inevitably collide with American interests, there had not been significant movement toward a mobilization of the military by the United States. Prominent Americans like Charles Lindbergh and his fellow members of America First argued that the war was none of the United States' business and should be avoided at all costs. American isolationism, prominently a part of the tradition in the formative stage, was still in full bloom before Pearl Harbor.

The American military tradition to that point facilitated the lack of preparedness exposed at Pearl Harbor. There had been no mobilization prior to the attack because the Roosevelt administration believed the American people would not accept a buildup during peacetime, and so the force at hand was small. It would require a shocked population to respond to the "day of infamy" in order to create the rage necessary to overcome American resistance to taking up arms. Once activated, however, that anger translated into a demand for a total war effort against the Japanese.

This expansion in means coincided with and reinforced an expansion in the reasons for fighting. The triggering events in the expansion of purposes were the American and (especially) French revolutions, which reintroduced political ideology into the causes of war. In the period after the end of the Thirty Years War in 1648, the system had been dominated by more-or-less absolutist monarchies that did not disagree on political matters and generally limited their fighting to small purposes. The French Revolution's evangelical period, when it spread its ideas across Europe, erased those limits; and as the means to conduct war expanded, so too did the reasons for fighting.

The purpose of war became the overthrow of enemy governments, which is the definition of total war. Although it was scarcely realized as such at the time, the prototype was probably the latter stages of the American Civil War, when the destruction of the Confederate Army and the overthrow of the government of the Confederacy were accepted as the necessary preconditions for reunion. The overthrow of the German government became the ultimate goal in World War I, and the epitome of total war was reached in the commitment to the unconditional surrender of Germany and Japan in World War II.

Total war fit the American worldview. American exceptionalism has always had an evangelical component that suggests the virtue of sharing the American ideal with others, and that evangelism could be extended to provide an adequate moral justification to breach the normalcy of peace and go to war. The epitome of this zeal is captured in Woodrow Wilson's address to Congress proposing an American declaration of war in 1917: "The day has come when America is privileged to spend her blood and her might for the principles that gave her birth and happiness. God helping her, she can do no other."

Total wars are much simpler to understand than the limited wars since 1945. In total war, the enemy is considered to be totally reprehensible to the point that only the overthrow of its government is acceptable, and military force is raised and employed with the unified purpose of crushing resistance to the overthrow of that government. Once this goal is achieved, however, the war is over and normalcy (peace) is restored. Because the enemy was depicted as evil, its toppling is morally satisfying as well.

Modern war is not so simple. Because the ultimate contemporary total war is an all-out nuclear exchange (the horror scenario of the Cold War), wars are now limited. The object is not to overthrow the opponent's government (Iraq is an exception) but rather to force the government to stop doing something (supporting terrorists, for instance). The opposition often consists of so-called nonstate actors lacking territory or a population to attack, and there is no sharp and definitive point at which war ends and peace is restored (a particularly painful lesson in Iraq). Some critics of the U.S. military effort in Iraq argue that the American military in particular remains conceptually wedded to traditional concepts of war and that the failure to adapt is, in Yingling's words, "a crisis in an entire institution."

THE COLD WAR, 1945–1989

The end of World War II radically changed the place of the United States in the world and the way in which it had to consider matters of national security. As the wartime collaboration with the Soviet Union gradually deteriorated into the confrontation that would be the key reality in the Cold War, the question of national security moved to center stage in the political constellation. When North Korea invaded South Korea on June 25, 1950, and the United States responded (through the United Nations) by coming to the aid of the southerners, any doubt about the changed nature of international politics and the American role in it disappeared.

The Cold War made military affairs—national security defined in largely military terms—a central reality of American peacetime life. Geopolitics and the realist paradigm were clearly dominant for the first time in U.S. history. The Korean experience demonstrated that a demobilized United States could not compete with a heavily armed Soviet opponent. Thus, the traditional practices of the formative period could no longer be afforded.

The Cold War presented the United States an apparently permanent military enemy for the first time since the military rivalry with Great Britain abated after the War of 1812. The Soviets posed primarily a military threat through the challenge of expansionist Communism, and American policy had to respond militarily. The result was the emergence of a *national security state* in which matters of national defense took on a coequal footing with other foreign policy considerations, and a large, permanent military establishment became an equally permanent part of the landscape.

The military culture changed because of several new conditioning factors in the environment, especially after the Korean conflict. Each factor represented a direct change and even, in some cases, a contradiction with the previous American experience, yet the nature of the Cold War caused these changes to be accepted without fundamental challenges from most Americans.

The Korean War created the recognition that the Cold War would require the United States to maintain a large active-duty force all of the time. Part of the reason for this was the nearly disastrous Korean experience. At the same time, the Soviets did not demobilize after World War II, and they and their allies maintained large, offensive forces. Should the Soviets decide to invade Western Europe, as was widely feared, there would be no time to mobilize, train, and transport a force to the war zone. Instead, a permanent "force in being" composed of both volunteers and conscripts would have to be available on the scene at all times. The need for a large standing force meant that the United States would be in a permanent state of mobilization. A peacetime force of this size could be sustained only by the existence of a national conscription system, the first time an involuntary draft system had actually been used in peacetime in American history. As well, this state of perpetual mobilization meant that defense budgets had to be greatly expanded to support the defense effort.

This expanded role and prominence of the military resulted in much greater prestige being bestowed on members of the military profession than before. With a constant threat against which to protect, the work of the military now seemed more vital than it had previously. The respect that Americans had bestowed on the World War II military was extended to the Cold Warriors as well. Military service and even military careers now became attractive to growing numbers of Americans who would probably not have considered such a career before, a fortuitous phenomenon, given the need for more military members.

The advent and expansion of thermonuclear weapons and the development and deployment of intercontinental range missiles by both sides made military concerns much more important by making the consequences of war potentially personally devastating to all Americans. At the height of the Cold War competition, the two sides faced one another with arsenals of between ten thousand and twelve thousand thermonuclear warheads capable of attacking targets in the other country and against which there were no defenses. An all-out nuclear war between the two would clearly destroy both as functioning societies and would have unknown but possibly catastrophic consequences for the rest of the world. The successful management of the nuclear balance in such a way that nuclear war was avoided—nuclear deterrence—became the country's most crucial business (a literal survival interest). This life-and-death struggle added to the prestige and importance of the national security establishment that designed, developed, and deployed strategies for deterrence. The Cold War world was a potentially very deadly place.

There was also general acceptance that the Cold War confrontation was a protracted competition from which no one could project a peaceful ending. In the minds of almost all analysts, the only alternatives were Cold War and hot war, and since the latter would probably be nuclear, it had to be avoided at virtually all costs. This added a sense of grim vigilance to the entire national security enterprise. It also contributed to the absolute surprise of nearly all observers when the Communist world began to disintegrate in 1989. The possibility that one side or the other would simply collapse and that the competition would end with a whimper rather than a bang had not even been considered by most students of the Cold War, nearly all of whom would have dismissed the possibility as fuzzy-headed idealism.

These factors represent circumstances that directly contradicted the American experience to that point. The idea of permanent mobilization of large standing forces, for instance, would have absolutely appalled the founding fathers, many of whom equated standing armed forces with the potential for Cromwellian-style tyranny. A world of perpetual and potentially disastrous military conflict requiring constant vigilance and extensive preparation and spending was entirely foreign to a country whose broad oceans had provided a barrier that permitted the leisure and luxury of a general mobilization. The idea that a military career would bring great prestige would never have occurred to most of the champions of the militia tradition.

Given the historical precedent, it is remarkable how readily these changes were accepted. Americans who had never been willing to (or had the need to) allow themselves to be taxed specifically to support a large standing peacetime military and who would previously have been fundamentally opposed to the existence of a draft during peacetime accepted both with virtually no complaint. The main reason for this changed acceptance, of course, was a threat that was real and ominous enough to justify greater sacrifices than during the formative period of the American experience.

During the Cold War period, two additional elements of the American military tradition rose in prominence to become permanent parts of the military environment. Both the news media and democratic institutions had, of course, been present throughout American history. In the period surrounding the Vietnam conflict, however, their roles became more defined and influential. At the same time, the "seed" was sown for another influence, professionalization of the military, a factor the implications of which are still evolving.

The Role of the Media

The relationship between the media and the military has changed over time. At times, the media have championed acts of war (e.g., the Spanish-American War); at other times, they have opposed it (e.g., Vietnam). It has always been a complex and contentious relationship, with the two institutions eyeing one another with some distrust and occasionally disdain that was worsened by the very sour experience of the Vietnam conflict and coverage of it. The relationship has arguably become even more complex since the end of the Cold War.

There have always been concerns about the relationship of the media to national security matters. One has to do with what is reported, a concern that centers especially but not exclusively on combat operations. The positions are diametrically opposed. The press believes coverage should be as complete and unfettered as possible, including access to combat operations (whether they have a right to protection in combat zones is another controversial matter) and the right to report what they observe. The media's position is based on the public's right to know what its government's representatives (in this case its military) are doing.

The military disagrees on two grounds. One is that unfettered coverage will provide information that, in the hands of the enemy, could compromise the integrity of military operations and even put soldiers at additional risk. Reporting the locations and outcomes of battles or the directions of troop or other movements is an example. The other concern is that reportage, particularly of less-than-successful military actions, can have a negative impact on public morale and give solace to an enemy. As an example, pictures of American Marines raising the flag on Mount Suribachi at Iwo Jima during World War II were a morale booster that became an important symbol for the Marines. Photographs of the bodies of Americans floating in the surf where they were killed assaulting the beaches at Iwo Jima (which were not published at the time) would have had quite a different impact.

The solution to this dilemma historically has been military censorship. Reporters at the front could get their stories to their media outlets only by using military means of communications, thereby allowing the military to inspect outgoing material and remove anything it viewed as objectionable. This arrangement depended on two underlying dynamics. The first was a relative degree of trust between the soldier–censor and the reporter. The reporter had to believe the censor was acting out of legitimate security concerns and not trying to hide evidence of military ineptitude; the censor basically had to believe the reporter was acting out of good faith in the stories he or she filed. That relationship always had some adversarial content, but it worked adequately until the Vietnam conflict. The other dynamic was the dependence of the media on government means of transmission of their stories from the battleground to home. That dependence has been broken by the invention of the video camcorder and the telecommunications satellite. In combination, these two technologies allow the reporter to witness, record, and transmit material without any assistance (or interference) from military censors.

The interaction between the media and the military in Vietnam transformed the relationship to one of much greater animosity. Early in the war, the relationship was tranquil because reportage was passive: the military would tell the press its version of what happened in the fighting, and the press would dutifully report that information. The picture portrayed was uniformly positive and suggested not only that progress toward winning the war was occurring but also that victory was imminent.

That tranquility was destroyed by the Tet offensive by the North Vietnamese and Viet Cong in January 1968. The enemy launched a general attack throughout the country, and especially against the cities, including the South Vietnamese capital of Saigon, an attack too extensive for the enemy to have conducted if casualty figures provided by the military were correct. Members of the media concluded that they had been lied to, that both they and their audiences had been duped, and that they should be much more critical in the future. Trust between the military and the media was the victim.

In that atmosphere, the ability of the media to bypass military censorship electronically became a major factor. The military's response to the inability to edit coverage before its release was to restrict media access to military operations. The intended effect was to restrict what the media could report (or misreport). This approach, predictably condemned by the media, was demonstrated in the Persian Gulf War, when only a few press members were allowed to accompany military forays, and then only carefully selected actions. Although media criticism of the military has been muted by patriotic concerns in the Afghan campaign, reporters rarely witnessed military operations either in that theater or in Iraq (see Amplification 4.3).

The existence of electronic media and 24-hour-a-day cable television news networks have changed the role of the media in another way. The coverage of war in all its nuances is much more public now than it was in years past. Not only does one know, for instance, the status of fighting and casualty figures in places like Iraq and Afghanistan. In addition, reporters on the scene describe the reactions of Iraqi or Afghan citizens to military actions and political events, including critical coverage of how natives view the American presence. From studios back in the United States, experts on military affairs and area specialists offer detailed and often critical instant analyses of events and trends.

The result is mass public exposure to war—and particularly controversy surrounding it—unknown in the past. At one level, it makes uncritical support for military affairs more difficult to sustain than earlier—imagine, for instance, the difficulty of sustaining support for the Union in the American Civil War during the early years of continuous military setbacks had an aggressive media publicized widely the apparent futility of the effort. Vietnam provided a harbinger of the effects detailed media coverage can produce; the maturation of these trends is being witnessed in Iraq and Afghanistan, with uncertain results.

The Impact of Democratic Institutions

Within a political democracy, popular will is, of course, always a matter of concern in an area such as national security, where the ultimate expression of that policy can be war and the placing of citizens at physical risk. Having said that, the "democratization" of national security affairs is largely a post–World War II phenomenon that,

Amplification 4.3

THE MEDIA AND THE IRAQ WAR

Coverage of the Iraq War illustrates vividly the ever-changing relationship between the media and the U.S. military and the tensions that surround coverage of war. The military's solution to this problem in Iraq was to "imbed" reporters with individual units. Under this arrangement, a few selected reporters have been allowed to accompany military operations in Iraq, but they were highly restricted in what they were allowed to observe and report. The military argued the restrictions were necessary to avoid reporting things that might compromise military operations and to ensure the physical safety of the reporters. The media generally accepted this arrangement because it allowed them to be part of the "action" more than had been the case in Desert Storm a long decade earlier, and many more reporters were allowed some access than were allowed twelve years earlier. The major criticism of the arrangement was that it fostered narrow, myopic reporting because it restricted reporters to observation only of narrow aspects of the war.

That the media accepted the restrictions placed upon them in Iraq has itself been the cause of additional controversy. Many have argued that the imposed myopia created by narrow access to isolated aspects of the war has produced bland, unanalytical coverage that has been generally uncritical as well. Moreover, many conservatives inside and outside the military have come to equate critical coverage with a lack of patriotism and have in some cases impugned the motives of critical reporters. The debate that centers on but ultimately transcends Iraq is whether timid, even cowed, reporting serves the national interest.

Two additional factors have influenced coverage. One is the existence of foreign media forms like Al Jazeera, whose coverage cannot be censored. The other is amateur recordings of events, such as videotapes of abuses at Abu Ghraib prison. Both limit the ability of the U.S. government to restrict information flow.

like so many other influences on contemporary affairs, was accentuated by American participation in Vietnam. During most of the formative period of the American republic, there was little concern with military affairs, and most wars either were highly popular (the world wars, the Spanish-American War) or affected relatively few Americans because of their small size or length. A partial exception to this depiction was selective Northern resistance to the Union cause in the American Civil War, which was the first massive American war and the first to involve large-scale involuntary service—the draft.

The Cold War heightened concerns over national security. Suddenly, national security affairs quite literally became matters of potential life and death, and how well those matters were conducted became very serious and very personal business for the entire population, especially for those young Americans who might be involuntarily conscripted into military service. This first became a concern in 1950 when thousands of World War II veterans had to be recalled to active duty and an army of draftees was assembled to defend South Korea. It became particularly a concern as the Vietnam conflict dragged on and the American conscript force fought a war the public, including many of those inducted, opposed.

The sour taste of the Vietnam experience for many Americans helped elevate the role of popular control over the democratic institutions making decisions about war and peace. In the wake of Vietnam War, the military itself engaged in a good deal of self-examination of what went wrong, and a large part of its conclusion was that the war effort was undermined by public support and opinion that evaporated around them as the war dragged on (Vietnam was the longest war in American history, a distinction endangered by the wars in Afghanistan and Iraq). To the military, the war violated the Clausewitzian trinity, which posited that war can be successfully waged only when there is a bond among the people, the military, and the government. Reasoning that the political authority had never explicitly solicited popular support for the Vietnam conflict (for a discussion, see Snow and Drew), the armed forces (especially the Army) vowed that this would not happen again.

A major consequence of public unhappiness with the Vietnam War was suspension of the draft at the end of 1972, and no American has faced involuntary military service since then. The draft system was replaced by the all-volunteer force (AVF) mostly to alleviate criticism of Vietnam based in sending the sons of American voters to fight and die in that unpopular war. The concept of an entirely voluntary, and thus professional, force is now the accepted standard for organizing American arms and American forces. It has been a gradually successful addition to the American experience that is now imbedded in the American military tradition. Its impact on the American attitude toward force remains a matter of evolution.

Professionalization of the Military

The initial virtue of the AVF was that it responded to dissonance arising from Vietnam and thus repaired the Clausewitzian link between the military and the people. Once the war was over, it also provided an avenue to staff the "force in being" with soldiers and sailors and airmen who chose to perform that role rather than with politically troublesome conscripts. As time has passed, the effect has been to create a more professional, competent military force but one not as intimately tied to its civilian base.

The professional military heartily endorses the change because it has produced a much more disciplined, proficient force than its predecessor, which included members who did not want to be serving, and the military itself is among the strongest detractors of returning to any form of conscription. The professional military of the 2000s performs at substantially higher levels of proficiency than did the Vietnam era military, has substantially fewer disciplinary problems, can be deployed in a wide variety of situations without member dissent, and presents few political problems for civilian authorities. An illustrative point of contrast is the virtual absence of objections to deploying substantial American forces to Afghanistan and

Iraq compared to the Vietnam experience. The obvious major difference is that there has been no involuntary service in Iraq and Afghanistan.

Iraq and Afghanistan have, however, raised questions about the future. A professional military must compete for members with other employers. As a result, it is expensive, and it is thus smaller than a conscript force. When military commitments are small, as they were in the 1990s, these smaller resources are not strained by overuse. Iraq and Afghanistan have strained these resources to their near breaking point and have raised questions about whether the concept is sustainable in the face of larger-scale demands.

Professionalization also brings the citizen–soldier concept into question. The modern American military member is still a citizen, but have contemporary soldiers become "more" soldier and less civilian than the country's past citizens would have countenanced? Americans who do not wish to serve are no longer troubled by the prospect of forced service. But has there been a price for that convenience that has yet to be paid?

CONCLUSION: THE CONTEMPORARY PERIOD, 1989 TO PRESENT

The end of the Cold War represented a major change in the environment and thus in the ways Americans think about matters of national security. This change was not immediately recognized, nor was there a great initial effort to test the nature and implications of the collapse of the Soviet empire. The response to September 11, 2001, further stimulated changed thinking.

With nearly two decades of the new environment and the second fault line of terrorism revealed as context, how will the American tradition adapt to and be shaped by the contemporary situation? Key elements in the past two situations have included the role of the United States in the international system and the level of threat the environment provided, as noted earlier. The American past experience reveals a contrast on these two variables, as shown in Table 4.1. As the table reveals, the two historical periods show the United States has exemplified both the "pure" combinations: high threat and a large international role during the Cold War and low threat and a small role during most of the formative period.

The contemporary period represents a hybrid. Clearly, the American role in the world is large, and with the collapse of the Cold War, it arguably became larger than it had ever been before. The question was and is, Which part of the American tradition will dominate the contemporary view of the world? A declining number of Americans would reduce the United States' assertive presence and role, representing

Table 4.1: American Roles and Threats

	Threat	
Role	High	Low
Large	Cold War	?
Small	?	Formative

the legacy of the formative period's preference basically to be left alone. The cutback in active-duty troop strength and the disappearance of conscription as part of the potential political agenda suggested that all the elements from the formative period have not disappeared and may reassert themselves as the United States returns from the "abnormality" of the Cold War to a more comfortable past.

The role of the United States, however, has not receded to where it was in the formative period but has remained at least as prominent as it was during the Cold War. Does this mean that the internationalism that dominated the Cold War approach of the United States toward the world has become such a permanent part of the landscape as to be inescapable? The Bush administration entered office in 2001 with the stated intention of trimming back the United States' commitments in areas

Challenge!

How Much Has Changed?

Did the terrorist attacks on New York and Washington and the subsequent worldwide campaign against international terrorism fundamentally change the threat and role of the United States in a security sense? Prior to the attacks, the United States was in a new situation of having a large role in an international milieu that posed few meaningful threats—a kind of hybrid of the formative and Cold War experiences. But how much did the situation change?

The question requires an assessment of how fundamental the threat posed by international terrorism really is. In the immediate wake of the 2001 incidents, the initial response of both the administration and the public was to portray the problem as global, pervasive, and extremely threatening. The Bush administration's pronouncements and actions seemed to reinforce, even to inflame, this perception. Troops were sent to Afghanistan in 2001 and the Philippines in early 2002 to fight the "war" on terrorism, and deployments were contemplated in numerous other places. Bush's labeling of Iran, Iraq, and North Korea as the "axis of evil" extended the problem beyond a contest with nonstate actors to an interstate basis. Domestically, the Office of Homeland Security was created and began periodically issuing terrorist alerts, while an alternative government went underground to ensure governmental continuity in the event of a massive, crippling terrorist attack. The creation of the Cabinet-level Department of Homeland Security (see Chapter 5) capped this effort.

Was all this activity warranted by the actual scale of the threat? Al Qaeda certainly does not have the capabilities to wreak havoc that a nuclear-armed Soviet Union could, but it also has shown the ability to launch an operation that killed three thousand Americans. Where does that place the current environment in the matrix presented in Table 4.1? Is it in a high-threat environment, a low-threat environment, or somewhere in between? What reassessment should the Obama administration undertake? How should it answer the question, How much has changed?

such as peacekeeping, but it was mere months before the terrorist attack caused it to quietly jettison that rhetoric and adopt an aggressive military posture favored by the neoconservatives toward the international environment. In 2001, it committed U.S. forces to Afghanistan, and in 2003, it invaded and occupied Iraq. The continuing struggles in Afghanistan and Iraq provide the challenge that faced the Obama administration when it entered office in 2009.

The past is never, of course, a perfect road map for the present or future, but the past is the context within which the future comes to be. As suggested in the preceding pages, there have been two distinct historical influences on how the American military tradition has evolved and shaped the way Americans view the role of force in the world. Whether one of those influences will dominate the future or whether that future orientation will be a polyglot of those influences is an interesting question to ponder and to observe. As the *Challenge!* box asks, "How much has changed?"

STUDY/DISCUSSION QUESTIONS

1.   What are the three conditioning factors affecting the American view of national security? Discuss each, including how each has changed.
2.   What is the formative period of the American national security experience? What principles did it produce? Which have been the most enduring, and which have changed the most? Why?
3.   How did the Cold War represent a major change in how the United States views national security? Discuss.
4.   What are the major influences on national security that came out of the Cold War? Discuss each, including how each influence has evolved.
5.   The ways in which the American experience has influenced how the United States has viewed Iraq and how Iraq has affected how the United States may view national security in the future have been major themes throughout the chapter. Discuss these influences in both directions.

SELECTED BIBLIOGRAPHY

Ackerman, Bruce. *Before the Next Attack: Preserving Civil Liberties in an Age of Terrorism*. New Haven, CT: Yale University Press, 2006.

Applebaum, Anne. "In Search of Pro-Americanism." *Foreign Policy*, July/August 2005, 32–41.

Boehlert, Eric. *Lapdogs: How the Press Rolled Over for Bush*. New York: Free Press, 2006.

Brodie, Bernard. *War and Politics*. New York: Macmillan, 1973.

Chandrasekaran, Rajiv. *Imperial Life in the Emerald City: Inside Iraq's Green Zone*. New York: Alfred A. Knopf, 2007.

Clausewitz, Carl von. *On War*. Rev. ed. Translated and edited by Michael Howard and Peter Paret. Princeton, NJ: Princeton University Press, 1984.

Cole, David, and James X. Dempsey. *Terrorism and the Constitution: Sacrificing Civil Liberties in the Name of National Security*. New York: New Press, 2002.

Dupuy, D. Ernest, and Trevor N. Dupuy. *The Encyclopedia of Military History*. New York: Harper and Row, 1972.

Gaddis, John Lewis. *Strategies of Containment: A Critical Appraisal of Postwar American National Security Policy*. Oxford, England: Oxford University Press, 1982.

Hassler, Warren W., Jr. *With Shield and Sword: American Military Affairs, Colonial Times to the Present*. Ames: Iowa State University Press, 1984.

Heymann, Philip B., and Juliette Kayyem. *Protecting Liberty in an Age of Terror*. Cambridge, MA: MIT Press, 2005.

Isikoff, Michael, and David Corn. *Hubris: The Inside Story of Spin*. New York: Crown Publishers, 2005.

Leckie, Robert. *The Wars of America*. Rev. and updated ed. New York: Harper and Row, 1981.

McMaster, H. R. *Dereliction of Duty*. New York: Harper Perennial, 1997.

Millett, Allan R., and Peter Maslowski. *For the Common Defense: A Military History of the United States of America*. New York: Free Press, 1984.

Snow, Donald M., and Dennis M. Drew. *From Lexington to Baghdad and Beyond: War and Politics in the American Experience*. 3rd ed. Armonk, NY: M. E. Sharpe, 2009.

———. *When America Fights: The Uses of U.S. Military Force*. Washington, DC: CQ Press, 2000.

Tucker, Robert W., and Donald C. Hendrickson. "The Sources of American Legitimacy." *Foreign Affairs* 83, no. 6 (November/December 2004): 18–32.

Weigley, Russell F. *The American Way of War*. New York: Macmillan, 1973.

Williams, T. Harry. *A History of American Wars: From Colonial Times to World War II*. New York: Alfred A. Knopf, 1981.

Yingling, Paul (Lt. Col.). "A Failure in Generalship." *Armed Forces Journal* [online], May 2009.

Zakaria, Fareed. "Beyond Bush." *Newsweek*, June 11, 2007, 22–29.

CHAPTER 5

The Domestic Environment

PREVIEW

How environmental changes affect policy and approaches and responses to national security challenges is more than just an abstract matter. This chapter examines how the influences of the domestic political environment have an impact on political processes and outcomes. Because there is some difference in generalized views of how the environment operates in the area of national security, the chapter begins by looking at the domestic context. It then turns to the question of how internal political processes affect and are affected by national security changes. In particular, it examines the chief institutional response to international terrorism, the Department of Homeland Security, and its enigmatic evolution, as well as related policy areas.

The final contextual element in viewing national security concerns is the influence of domestic politics. Just as the threat environment is largely defined by international political forces that oppose American interest and even reflect harmful desires toward the United States, so, too, is the domestic political system an important factor in defining the national security environment. Domestic politics interacts with the world in both directions. In one direction, forces in the international environment define the threats with which the country must cope, and domestic actions can make those threats more or less dangerous and poignant. International religious terrorism, for instance, emanates from the international environment, but actions taken by the United States (for instance, successfully pursuing and disabling terrorists, increasing or lowering their appeal as the result of U.S. policies in the Middle East) can make the environment more or less troubling and hostile.

National security policy is largely about how the country responds to threats, suggesting the other direction. To some large degree, what threatens the United States and the extent to which those threats require different levels of response are subjective determinations arising from the psychological dimension of security. As already pointed out, at this level, people can and do disagree, particularly when decisions require the expenditure of scarce resources (which they inevitably do) that reduce or eliminate risk in one area, while potentially neglecting other priorities. The politics involved in such situations can often be quite intense, sometimes in ways not always directly connected to national security. The debate over border security (highlighted later in this chapter and in Chapter 14) is an example where there is disagreement over the nature and seriousness of the problem and what to do about it, with both strictly domestic and national security implications. Whether to continue building the 700-mile fence along the United States–Mexico border authorized in 2006 by Congress is a dramatic example of this kind of conflict.

Disagreement, sometimes fundamental, about national security is reflected in domestic politics. Partly, the debate is a philosophical discussion about the extent of American activism in the world that reflects an assessment of what the world out there is really like and the degree to which the United States has some role, obligation, or ability to affect the environment. The pendulum of opinion swings on the issue. The Clinton years, for instance, were marked by a high degree of international activism expressed in joint actions with other countries in an atmosphere of low threat and high cooperation. The terror-driven atmosphere impacting the Bush years was typified by a much more confrontational, unilateralist view of the American role in a hostile environment. The Obama predilection is to move back toward a more internationalist, cooperative stance.

National security problems and their resolution can be fully analyzed and understood only in their political setting. Defending the country is one of the most important functions for which government exists, even arguably the ultimate purpose of the state and its government. No one questions the importance of security among state purposes, and for this reason, there is a tendency to elevate the processes by which national security policy is made above the normal political dialog as too vital to be subjected to the rough-and-tumble of "politics as usual." At its best, this instinct can provide a sense of purpose in times of crisis that is unmistakable to enemies as a sign of national resolve. At its most controversial, this same exercise can result in a rancorous debate about policies, such as the disagreement about the treatment of detainees that marked the transition from the Bush to the Obama administration and is discussed in Amplification 5.1.

Politicians seize upon this importance to try to create the belief that their particular solutions to problems are the only "reasonable" means to achieve national security ends and that alternative analyses are not only incorrect but also even insidious or seditious. National security, in other words, is not above politics, whether it should be or not.

The problem that arises from following this line of reasoning is that it denies that national security is part of the normal process by which scarce resources are allocated to deal with national problems and priorities, which always exceed those resources. Within the realm of national security, there are always multiple threats that are candidates for attention, and there are also inevitably disagreements on which situations do and do not constitute threats to security, the relative importance of threats, and what solutions in what order of priority should be undertaken. In some rare cases—September 11 stands out—the situation is crystalline, as is what must be

Amplification 5.1

EXTREMISM IN THE DEFENSE OF LIBERTY?

During his unsuccessful 1964 campaign for the presidency, Republic candidate Barry Goldwater of Arizona made the assertion that "extremism in the defense of liberty is no vice." Although Goldwater was primarily defending acts of overt patriotism such as expressions of love of country, the term *extremism* was a liberal lightning rod, suggesting the legitimacy of political extremism. Similar concerns, not using the Goldwater language, have come to surround some actions by the Bush administration in its conduct of the "war" on terror.

One of the first acts of the Obama administration was to honor a campaign promise to close the facilities at Guantanamo Naval Base in Cuba that have housed suspected terrorists captured by Americans in Afghanistan and Iraq. The action raised questions about what would happen to those still detained, at least some of whom were dangerous individuals everyone agreed should not be released into society.

The ensuing domestic political debate had two largely partisan political bases. One concern was where to put those detainees who would continue to be incarcerated. Predictably, politicians on both sides of the aisle, reflecting their constituents' views, wanted these individuals locked away anyplace but where they lived.

The second political dustup was more personal and partisan. The closing of Guantanamo also included repudiating Bush administration policies regarding treatment of prisoners, notably interrogation procedures that arguably included torture. Rescinding authorization for the use of these techniques, when combined with the closing of Guantanamo, led former Vice President Richard Cheney to assert in public appearances since leaving office that President Barack Obama's actions had weakened national security and placed Americans at greater personal risk than they had been under Bush. The Obama administration quickly rebuked Cheney, in effect arguing that extremism is unacceptable, even in the defense of liberty.

done about it. Most of the time, however, politicians must reconcile threats with available resources in a situation of scarcity of resources.

If national security policy is part of the broader political process, it occupies a distinct place in that process, for two reasons. The first is the unique subject matter of national security. At the bottom line, national security policy is about national survival, a distinction not shared by other policy areas. The second is the amount of national resources devoted to national security. Although the country spends more on entitlement programs than on national security, the defense budget is the largest discretionary part of the budget (a distinction discussed later in the chapter).

Too much can be—and often is—made about the life-and-death nature of national security policy. Decisions made in the health and medical areas—whether to fund stem-cell research, for instance—also affect who lives and dies and the quality of life and conditions surrounding death, but the connection is neither as immediate nor as causally consequential as it would be if a national security decision emboldens a national enemy to launch a massive attack against the United States that would not have occurred in the absence of that decision. This worst-case possibility always lurks in the background of national security decisions as a rejoinder against precipitous change—and especially reductions in defense efforts. The logic behind being "better safe than sorry" is particularly powerful when the potential outcome is catastrophic. The result is a process that is weighted toward maximum risk reduction, where the response to additional threats is to expand the resources available to reduce risk (i.e., to spend more), and where efforts directed at risk management are perpetuated even if their causal relationship to risk abatement is not demonstrable or is questionable (since change could lead to the worst case). These dynamics guarantee a very expensive, highly conservative national security process.

How these influences come together provides the domestic context for national security concerns. To understand how this process operates, the discussion begins by looking at the historical context, including the attitudes of the founding fathers and the framework created for the Cold War through the National Security Act of 1947. This context leads to the institutional framework for the national security process within and between the executive and legislative branches of government. The chapter then moves to applications of the process in action, institutionally through the homeland security reaction to September 11 and more politically through the controversy over border security.

THE HISTORICAL DOMESTIC CONTEXT

The national security mechanisms and attitudes that influence the way Americans act in contemporary situations are partly the product of the same American experiences that created aspects of the security culture discussed in Chapter 4. When the founding fathers were designing the American political system, matters that are now considered national security concerns were not major concerns for them. The American Revolution had expelled foreign forces from American soil, and the major priorities of the country concentrated on devising and developing a new polity in a largely virgin, undeveloped land. Most of the "security" problems facing Americans were peripheral and marginally threatening (e.g., subduing and replacing American Indians on the frontier) or aberrational (the self-infliction of the Civil War). Because the founding fathers neither envisioned nor sought extensive international interactions that could become conflictual, they were particularly spare in creating a constitutional framework in this area. The framework they did create is summarized in Amplifications 5.2 and 5.3 and is discussed in the next section.

A skeletal political and legal framework served the country adequately before World War II, but in the wake of the world's bloodiest conflict and the Cold War, it was clear that the traditional, more informal system would be inadequate for the "national security state" that would manage the Cold War. The major initial political response was the National Security Act of 1947. A related theme was the attempt to reform the military to make it more functional for the threat environment. Both elements continue to influence the contemporary environment.

The National Security Act of 1947 created the institutional framework that has defined the national security policy process to this day. A remarkably comprehensive and foresighted document that was signed into law on July 26, 1947, the act transformed a highly fragmented and inefficient governmental structure that had been greatly strained during World War II into a highly durable structure that managed the Cold War successfully and that has remained the basic framework to this day. Efforts to reform the national security apparatus start from the structure created in 1947.

The National Security Act created five institutions, each of which remains a vital part of the domestic national security effort. The first was the *Department of Defense (DOD)*. Prior to 1947, each of the independent military services (the Army and the Navy) was an independent Cabinet-level agency, a condition that had proven an impediment to the most efficient conduct of World War II, and there was great pressure to create a unified military department to supersede the old prewar structure. The basic idea was to force greater cooperation and coordination among the military services in the areas of planning, war fighting, and budgets, as well as to establish more firmly the principle of civilian control of the military. The new structure was originally called the National Military Establishment and was changed to the current DOD by the amending National Security Act of 1949. At the time, this merger of military assets into one department was generally favored by the Army and what would become the Air Force (which was then the Army Air Corps, a part of the Army) and opposed by the Navy (which felt it could lobby for its budget more effectively as an independent Department of the Navy). As partial compensation for the Navy, Admiral James Forrestal was named the first secretary of defense.

This structure remains essentially intact and has been durable. Among the areas of some continuing controversy is the relationship between civilian and military elements within the department. The original intent was to subordinate military influence on policy making through the establishment of an Office of the Secretary of Defense (OSD) at the top of the organizational pyramid of the department. After the Vietnam War and surrounding decision making for Iraq, questions were raised about whether the result is a military leadership that is *too* subservient to its civilian leaders, failing to advise the civilian leadership of the operational impossibility of implementing some of the policies civilians may favor. McMaster wrote the definitive statement of this position on Vietnam; Yingling recently produced a similar statement about Iraq.

As part of the DOD structure, the act created a second institution, the *Joint Chiefs of Staff (JCS)*. The purpose of the JCS was to create a staff of senior officers from the various services who would work together to coordinate and cooperate on military problems facing the country and provide military advice directly to the president. Opposition to this idea arose from individuals fearful that the new JCS might become a super-elite group like the Prussian General Staff in Germany. Under provisions of the act, the chief of staff of each service serves as a member, with the chairmanship of the body (the chairman of the JCS, or CJCS) chosen from the services basically on a rotating basis. By statute, the CJCS is the chief *military* advisor to the president, as opposed to the secretary of defense (SECDEF), who is the chief *defense* advisor to the president. Because the retrospective on the Vietnam War suggested that this structure had not produced a maximally integrated effort to fight that conflict (air missions against North Vietnam by the Air Force and Navy, for instance, were often uncoordinated), the Congress passed the *Goldwater–Nichols Act of 1986* mandating much greater and more meaningful cooperation and coordination (known as *jointness*), a policy that resulted in much more interservice cooperation in both the Persian Gulf and the Iraq wars.

The third institution created by the act was the *Central Intelligence Agency (CIA)*. Prior to World War II, the United States had possessed no peacetime civilian intelligence-gathering and -analyzing organization. To remedy that situation, President Franklin D. Roosevelt had created the Office of Strategic Services (OSS) under the leadership of Colonel (retired) William Donovan to provide intelligence to the government during the war, but the OSS mandate ended with the conclusion of hostilities. Recognizing the emerging threat posed by an increasingly hostile Communist bloc led by the Soviet Union, this condition was deemed intolerable and resulted in the creation of the CIA as the country's first permanent peacetime intelligence agency.

Even at the time of its inception, the new CIA was plagued with two problems that continue to be part of the contemporary debate about the agency. The first was its place within the community of intelligence assets of the country. In addition to the CIA, there are major intelligence capabilities in several other areas of government. The most notable of these are within the DOD—the National Security Agency, the Defense Intelligence Agency, and the intelligence assets of the various services (which cumulatively comprise about four-fifths of the country's intelligence assets). The CIA was designated as the lead agency for intelligence (with the responsibility of providing intelligence information and advice to the president). Its head, the director of central intelligence (DCI), was also designated as the chair of the intelligence community. This arrangement put the DCI in the awkward position of being both the head of one intelligence agency (CIA) and the official designated to oversee and coordinate the activities of all agencies, including his own. The result was a conflict of interest that was part of the reason for creating the position of Director of National Intelligence (DNI), one of the actions recommended by the 9/11 Commission, discussed later in the chapter.

At the same time, there has always been some controversy about what the CIA does or should do. The gathering, compilation, and reporting of information (intelligence) is its basic and least assailable mission, but there has always been debate about what the CIA should be able to do in addition to intelligence collection. The controversy has centered on the area known as "operations," which refers to active efforts the CIA may clandestinely undertake to influence international events (known as covert actions). Within the original legislation creating the CIA is a provision for the agency to carry out "other functions and duties related to intelligence." This somewhat vague formulation has led to a variety of actions that have been deemed offensive by some within the political realm, such as extreme renditions (the practice of sending prisoners to countries that practice torture as a means to extract information from them) and the Guantanamo detention facilities.

The fourth institution created by the act was an independent *U.S. Air Force*. During World War II, the air assets of the United States were divided among the Navy (including the Marines) and the Army (the Army Air Corps). The proponents of airpower had long lobbied for an independent air force to consolidate the various roles and missions assigned to airpower. They were successful to the extent of extricating themselves from the Army and being established as an independent U.S. Air Force (USAF). They were not successful in that the Navy and Marines maintained control of their own air forces, and the Army managed to get back into the air business through the application of helicopters for military purposes. Rationalizing the military uses of the atmosphere (and beyond) has been a recurring theme in attempts at military reform, also discussed below.

The fifth, and in many ways the most important, accomplishment of the National Security Act was the creation of the *National Security Council (NSC)*. The NSC was of enormous symbolic importance in depicting the American role in the postwar world. At its most basic level, it recognized the new and growing importance of the United States and the consequent need for some formal mechanism to assist in how the United States would react in the world. It also implied and boosted the centrality of defense matters within the hierarchy of foreign policy concerns. The statutory members of the NSC were the president, the vice president, the secretary of state, and the new secretary of defense (the president can add other members as he chooses, and subsequent legislation and practice have increased the normal membership to include the DCI, CJCS, and others). The symbolism of the composition was the placement of the secretary of defense as the lineal equivalent of the secretary of state, indicating that the line between foreign policy (with diplomacy as its heart) and national security policy (with the military at its core) would be less clear than in the past and that much of foreign policy would indeed be virtually indistinguishable from national security policy. The fact that the Cold War emerged as a political competition largely framed in military terms reinforced this placement of the SECDEF within the structure. The NSC has proven an exceptionally durable institution and has been further elaborated through a system of executive branch mechanisms known collectively as the interagency process (discussed in the next section).

A recurring subtheme was also part of the crucible of concerns that surrounded the National Security Act. That theme is military reform, and it is as lively today as it was in 1947. It is worth raising in passing here because the call to reform how the services define what they do (internally and in relationship to one another) and how they carry out those missions remains a point of contention.

Interservice rivalry had been evident in World War II. The American role in the war even enhanced that rivalry, as the war was, at the operational level, two separate wars in which the two major services had contrasting roles. The war in Europe was essentially a ground war and, as such, was dominated by the U.S. Army, which had primary responsibility for its successful conduct, with a subordinate role for the Navy (essentially ferrying personnel and supplies to the theater of operation). In the Pacific, the Navy was the dominant service, as the Navy first eliminated the Japanese Navy and then employed the Marines (an institutional part of the Navy) in the campaign of island hopping closer and closer to Japan. The Army was assigned the basic task of consolidating (or "mopping up" resistance) control of the islands the Navy/Marines captured. This structure discouraged cooperation between the services, which would be dysfunctional against a comprehensive Communist opponent after the war.

Admiral Forrestal foresaw this difficulty and commissioned the first roles and missions conference among the services at Key West, Florida, in 1948. Without going into details, the services basically agreed to concentrate on what they had done previously and to split the new defense budget in rough terms into thirds, with one-third for each service: the Army, the Navy (including the Marines), and the new Air Force. The division left some anomalies that have continued across time. The most famous of these is duplication of effort. It is said, for instance, that the United States possesses four air forces (the USAF, the Navy's land- and sea-based air forces, the Marines' air forces for close air support, and the Army's helicopter-based forces) and three armies (the U.S. Army, the Navy's army—the Marines—and the Air Force's smaller army to guard air bases). The same is true in the area of special forces, as each service has its own special operations forces, although they are coordinated through the U.S. Special Operation Command (USSOCOM). Periodic efforts are made to rationalize this structure, with varying success.

THE STRUCTURE OF DOMESTIC POLITICS

National security policy is among the most contentious political areas within the American federal system. As already noted, the content of national security policy is potentially very important, ultimately including decisions that can affect the very physical survival of the country and, less dramatically, decisions about when Americans may be compelled to put themselves in harm's way to defend American interests.

National security policy is also highly political because it involves the expenditure of very large amounts of money. Defense spending is generally the second-largest category in the federal budget, behind spending on entitlements (social security, Medicare, and the like) and just ahead of service (paying interest) on the national debt. During the Cold War, it involved roughly a quarter of the federal budget and 5 to 6 percent of gross national product (GNP). In the mid-1950s, before many of the entitlement programs were enacted, it accounted for nearly half of federal spending.

Defense spending is highly political for other reasons as well. One of the important characteristics of the defense budget is that it is the largest discretionary element within the federal budget. One way to distinguish items in the federal budget is to divide them into discretionary or controllable and nondiscretionary or uncontrollable elements. A discretionary element is one that must be appropriated annually; thus, the Congress exercises its discretion over whether that element will be funded. A nondiscretionary element is one that is automatically appropriated unless there is specific legislation altering or rescinding the appropriation (social security is the best example). Nearly two-thirds of the discretionary money in the federal budget goes toward defense, meaning that attempts to increase, decrease, or alter the pattern of federal spending often begin with the defense budget.

The political nature also reflects the impact of national security spending on Americans. Not only is a lot of money spent on defense, but also those expenditures are made in a large number of physical locales, wherever concentrations of military installations and defense industries are found. The competition for defense contracts and for the locations of bases or posts is a highly charged process wherein the financial health and prosperity of communities can be vitally affected by the effectiveness of congressional delegations in winning federal contracts for their states and districts.

National security spending is also contentious because much of the money is spent on highly durable procurements. The decision, for instance, to build an aircraft carrier not only involves appropriating several billion dollars for its construction (money that is fed into the local community wherever the ship is built, of course), but also involves investment in a weapons "platform" that is expected to be in the arsenal for thirty years or longer. Procurement decisions affect not only the arsenal characteristics of whatever administration authorizes them, but also the military capability available to a commander in chief a quarter-century or more in the future. The same is true of procuring new fighter or bomber aircraft, a new model of main battle tank, and the like.

There is an old saw that "policy is what gets funded," and that truism is particularly applicable to national security. Two things are coming together to create a sharp poignancy for the political, and especially budgetary, elements of the national security decision process. One is the nature of the current military arsenal. The military characteristics of the current force include the fact that it was largely shaped to confront a Soviet military threat that no longer exists and is not being replicated by any emerging potential adversary. Moreover, the force is getting old, and much of it needs replacement. A major question is how to modernize the force. During the Bush administration, Secretary of Defense Donald Rumsfeld led a movement for an aggressive revolution in military affairs (RMA), applying the fruits of technological innovation to create a smaller but more lethal and expensive U.S. force. Faced with budgetary restraints associated with the economic downturn of 2008, the Obama administration deferred this reform and asked the military to explore less expensive means of dealing with problems.

The politics of national security is played out at various levels that come together in the budget process. One level is within the executive branch of government, where the representatives of various government agencies and functions compete for priority within federal policy, including the budget. This competition extends to the legislative branch, where the same kind of competition occurs within the various layers of the committee system in hammering out what budget the executive will ultimately have to spend. Ultimately, decisions involve the interaction of the two principal legislating branches of the government (a process in which the judiciary is rarely involved).

The Executive Branch

National security policy within the executive branch of the government operates on two separate tracks that are, in some ways, paralleled conceptually within the Congress. The day-to-day conduct of national security (as part of overall foreign policy) occurs within the federal agencies with authority in the field—such as the Department of State, Department of Defense, and the CIA—at the direction of the president. Policy decisions are coordinated and implemented through the *interagency process*, the chief vehicle of which has been the NSC and its subordinate bodies. New institutional actors, such as the Department of Homeland Security (DHS) and the director of national intelligence (DNI), are being integrated into this system. This process of policy development and implementation is conceptually similar to the role of the authorizing committees of the Congress. The other track is the competition for funding, which is the heart of the budgetary process, and it pits parts of the national security community against one another and against competing functions of the government. The framework for this interaction, of course, is the constitutionally mandated roles for the various branches of government laid out by the founding fathers, as discussed in Amplification 5.2.

Amplification 5.2

THE PRESIDENT, THE CONSTITUTION, AND NATIONAL SECURITY

Because the founding fathers did not anticipate a level of involvement in international affairs that even mildly resembles the extent to which the country interacts with the rest of the world today, the U.S. Constitution does not lay out an elaborate list of powers for the president in the area of national security or foreign policy, as noted. Such specific powers as are provided are found in Article II of the Constitution, and essentially all are counterbalanced by contrary powers given to the Congress as part of the "checks and balances" system that characterizes the entire document. The result is an "invitation to struggle" (see Crabb and Holt) intended to make the two branches coequal in this area.

The Constitution lists six powers for the president that directly apply to national security and defense policy. They are the positions of chief executive, chief of state, commander in chief of the armed forces, treaty negotiator, nominator of key personnel, and recognizer of foreign government.

Chief Executive. In this capacity, the president is designated as the major presider over the executive agencies of the government, all of which report directly to the president. In the area of foreign and national security policy, these agencies include the Departments of State and Defense, the Central Intelligence Agency, and the various economic agencies, including the Departments of the Treasury and Commerce and the U.S. Trade Representative. These agencies collectively are the chief repositories of the expertise of the federal government on foreign matters, and the president's access to them provides an important advantage in dealing with foreign and national security matters.

Chief of State. In this largely symbolic role, the president is designated as the chief representative of the U.S. government to all foreign governments. This means, for instance, that officials of foreign governments (ambassadors, for example) are accredited to the president, and when the heads of other states interact with the U.S. government, it is with the president or a representative of the president.

Commander in Chief. The president is designated as the commander in chief of the armed forces of the United States. This means, among other things, that he or she is the highest military official of the government to whom all members of the armed forces are subsidiary and that it is the president's authority to employ the armed forces in support of various public policies, including the commitment of force in combat (although this power is circumscribed by congressional limitation).

Treaty Negotiator. Only the president of the United States or his or her specified representative (known as plenipotentiary) is authorized to enter into negotiations with foreign governments leading to formal relationships and obligations on behalf of the U.S. government. Although only a small percentage of agreements between the United States and foreign governments come in the form of formal treaties, this nonetheless sets the precedent for presidential leadership in all arrangements with foreign governments.

Nominator of Key Personnel. The president alone has the power to name key officials of his or her administration. The most important appointments are the Cabinet members (the various secretaries of executive agencies), the members of the NSC, and the deputy and assistant secretaries, such as those who serve on the various committees of the NSC system.

Recognizer of Foreign Governments. Only the president has the authority to extend or remove formal recognition of foreign governments by the U.S. government. This is one of the few powers of the president that does not require some form of formal supporting action by the Congress.

The Interagency Process. The interagency process has evolved since the Eisenhower administration in the 1950s as the mechanism for implementing the National Security Act of 1947. The act was not specific about how the NSC would function at the operational level, and both its structure and its operations have changed over time. Dwight Eisenhower used it extensively as a kind of military advisory board, and John F. Kennedy used it much less often. Lyndon Johnson expanded its use during the Vietnam War, and it began to take on its present form during the Nixon and Ford years. How it works at any time is largely a matter of presidential preference rather than legislative mandate. There is, for instance, no provision for a national security advisor (NSA) in the legislation, and that position has expanded from being a coordinator and office manager to being a major presidential advisor on foreign affairs. Similarly, there is no provision for a system of committees and subcommittees within the NSC structure, but that is what has evolved.

The NSC system began to congeal during the Eisenhower administration of the 1950s. In its present form as the interagency process, it came into being during the 1980s, and it is a fairly elaborate system. By statute, the NSC itself consists of the four permanent members and whomever else the president may designate to attend and participate for any particular purpose. The White House chief of staff is normally always included, and on military matters, so are the CJCS and the NSA. The purpose of the NSC is purely advisory. The members offer advice to the president that he is free to accept or reject. No votes are ever taken, ensuring that the president will not feel obligated by what the majority may favor.

Directly below the NSC is the *Principals Committee (PC)*. This group is composed of the same membership as the NSC itself, except the president does not attend. There are two basic occasions when the NSC meets as the Principals Committee. If there are matters that do not require direct presidential involvement, the others may meet without him. At the same time, the president will occasionally absent himself when he wants to facilitate a more frank exchange of views than might occur when he is present and when he feels the other members might be unwilling to champion views they think he might oppose. This latter reason was used by John F. Kennedy during portions of the Cuban Missile Crisis when the Principals Committee was known as the ExComm (Executive Committee).

The next layer in the system is the *Deputies Committee (DC)*. As the name suggests, this group is composed of the principal deputies of the members of the NSC. The meetings are traditionally chaired by the president's principal deputy for national security, the NSA, although in the early days of the Bush administration there was an unsuccessful attempt by Vice President Richard Cheney to usurp that role from then NSA Condoleezza Rice. The Deputies Committee is more of a working-level body, and its roles include formulating policy proposals for action by the NSC or Principals Committee and figuring out how to implement decisions made in those bodies. Other members of the Deputies Committee include the undersecretary of state for political affairs, the undersecretary of defense for policy, the deputy director of national intelligence, and the vice chairman of the JCS.

At the bottom of the process are the *Policy Coordinating Committees (PCCs)*. This is a series of committees formed along both functional and geographic lines. Each functional committee is chaired by the assistant secretary (or equivalent) from the Cabinet department with the most direct and obvious responsibility. There are, for instance, functional PCCs for defense, intelligence, arms control, and international economics. Each geographic PCC is chaired by the assistant secretary of state for that particular region. It is the role of the PCCs to monitor their areas of responsibility (the PCC for the Near East and East Asia keeps tabs on the activities of Iraq, for instance), to provide options to the Deputies Committee and above on assigned problems, and to carry out the detailed policies adopted elsewhere in the process.

Reflecting his own interests and perceptions about change in the international environment, President Bill Clinton created a parallel body, the *National Economic Council (NEC)*, by executive order in January 1993. It differed from the NSC in that it was not created by legislation and thus could be dismantled without congressional action. Clinton gave it four charges that parallel the duties of the older body: (1) to coordinate the economic policy-making process with respect to domestic and international economic issues; (2) to coordinate economic policy advice to the president; (3) to ensure that economic policy decisions and programs are consistent with the president's goals; and (4) to monitor implementation of the president's economic agenda.

The NEC was a prominent and important part of national security policy during the Clinton years and reflected the paramount importance of economic policy during the 1990s. The NEC was chaired personally by Clinton, and in addition, it had its own Deputies Committee and staff capability through the Trade Policy Review Group and the Trade Policy Staff Committee. The first task assigned to the first director of the NEC, Robert Rubin (later secretary of the treasury), was Clinton's comprehensive budget reduction plan, which succeeded in balancing the budget in 1998, and the NEC was prominent in trade policy and multilateral negotiations on trade promotion. When he came to office in 2001, President George W. Bush threatened to do away with the NEC as an unnecessary relic from his predecessor but has retained it at a much lower level of visibility and with much less personal involvement.

The NEC became prominent again under President Obama as one of the two principal advisory groups to the president (along with the NSC). The spearhead of the NEC is Dr. Lawrence Summers, a prominent economic advisor from the Clinton years and former president of Harvard University, who was named director of the White House–based council and who consults on a daily basis with Obama on his economic recovery program. This return of the NEC to a Clinton-like status reflects the administration's elevation of economic policy as both a domestic and an international priority.

The interagency process works largely the way the president wants it to operate. The NSC is assisted by the NSC staff, all of whom are members of the president's personal staff and thus not subject to congressional confirmation, review, or scrutiny. Because they serve at the president's pleasure, they are highly loyal to the chief executive and generally closely reflect the president's views. The degree to which the president utilizes this asset depends on presidential prerogative. Richard Nixon, for instance, had a long and deep-seated distrust of the State Department. State Department officials have civil service protection and cannot be fired (except in extreme circumstances), and most generally opposed Nixon's policies. As a result, he enlarged the NSC staff and used it in effect as an alternate State Department to ensure his policy preferences would be implemented. Presidents who are highly activist in foreign affairs, such as George H. W. Bush and Bill Clinton in his second term, rely heavily upon the NSC to carry out their desires, whereas those with less interest (such as Gerald Ford and George W. Bush) use the NSC less and rely more on the executive agencies to conduct policy on their own. The Obama administration's early concentration of effort on the economy left uncertain the president's personal level of involvement. The signals were mixed. On one hand, he filled key posts with very prominent people (such as Secretary of State Hillary Clinton) who could relieve him of the national security spotlight. On the other hand, he is both highly knowledgeable of and interested in foreign affairs (he was an undergraduate major in international affairs) and may well assert his personal leadership.

Funding Security. The other dimension of policy making within the executive branch focuses on the competition for resources to fund various government functions and programs. The principal manifestation of this political battle is the formulation of the presidential budget request to the Congress and how that is translated into the working budget of the federal government of the United States. The budget process is one of the most complicated, arcane, yet fundamental political activities of the government. If one accepts the notion that policy is what gets funded, it is also the heart of the political process.

The complexity of the process of allocating public monies for the various things government does goes well beyond the purposes of this volume to unravel in detail. Instead, two aspects of the politics of national security budget making—the competition among the services for resources and the competition between defense and other government functions in the formulation of the executive branch's request to the Congress (some consideration of the politics of the congressional response to the president's budget request is found in the next section)—will be examined.

Budgeting is an ongoing, continuous process within the U.S. government. At any point in time, the DOD, for instance, is working on at least three different budgets: the budget for the current fiscal year, which has been appropriated and is being expended; the budget proposal for the next fiscal year, which has been proposed to Congress and to which the Congress is responding; and the budget proposal for the year after that, which is being formulated for presentation to the Congress in the following fiscal year. In addition, some long-range programs are funded over several years, meaning funds appropriated in earlier budget cycles are also being spent at any given time (known as "out years").

The competition between the services and between defense and nondefense spending is closely related to this process. Under the provisions of the planning, programming, budgeting, and spending (PPBS) system first introduced by the McNamara Pentagon in the early 1960s, initial planning for a budget begins approximately two and a half years before the first money is spent (assuming the Congress and the executive branch agree on a budget before the beginning of the fiscal year in which spending is to occur). Thus, planning for spending in fiscal year 2010 (which began on October 1, 2009) began in January 2008, when initial planning requests were sent to operational units within the DOD and elsewhere in the government. In spring 2008, the requests from defense units such as the military services were compared with other equivalent requests and reconciled with one another and then processed through the programming and budgeting phases during the late summer and fall of 2008. In turn, the DOD's proposal was compared with requests from other executive agencies and reconciled into a budget request that accompanied the president's State of the Union address to the Congress in January 2009. Legislative enactment would occur between January and September 2009, and if all went well, there would be a budget agreed to by both branches of the government that would go into effect on October 1, 2009, or a budget resolution that continued spending after October 1 until a final budget was approved (which is what happened). While legislative action was going on in 2009 on the fiscal year 2010 budget, the planning process for the fiscal year 2011 budget was set in motion, and the DOD was spending resources from the fiscal year 2009 budget.

Much of the politics within the executive branch occurs during the initial phases, when the president's budget request is being formulated. At the beginning, the military services are asked to formulate their individual requests. All units know that the aggregated requests (what are sometimes known as the "wish list") of the services will exceed by some large order of magnitude the resources that will actually be available to the services. Nonetheless, each makes the request for everything it wants, regardless of funding expectations, for two reasons. First, doing so creates a record of what, say, the Army feels it really should have to carry out its mission most effectively. Second, since all the services know their requests will be cut—and, based on experience, approximately by what percentage they are likely to be cut—submitting a request that combines what the services think they will actually receive plus what they assume will be cut reasonably ensures that after cuts are made, the services will get roughly what they expected. Submitting a more modest and realistic request and having it cut probably means getting less than expected and needed.

The politics of interservice competition are particularly important regarding military procurement of new equipment, and especially major weapons systems. During the process of proposal and negotiations, it is fair to say the services provide a valuable public service to the budgeting process by offering detailed critiques of the requests of the *other* services in order to find weaknesses in the other services' requests that might be turned to their own advantage. The motivation combines self-interest and civic-mindedness, and it serves the useful purpose of providing a kind of informal check and balance within the process through expert monitoring of rival service requests.

Once the defense request has been formulated, the national security budget comes into direct competition with other spending priorities within the federal budget. As in the internal defense process, the requests from agencies representing the range of government activity invariably exceed the total amount of money the Congress is likely to be willing to appropriate in any given year, meaning budget compromises must be negotiated to get the total budget request within realistic parameters.

The defense budget is especially vulnerable during this phase of the process. The first and most obvious source of vulnerability has already been mentioned: the defense budget contains the largest discretionary elements within the total federal budget and is thus a tempting target for budget cutters with other priorities. Increases in social security benefits are mandated and automatically appropriated in the absence of specific legislation changing those benefits; the funding for new fighter aircraft for the Air Force must be expressly appropriated each year. At the same time, despite colorful political campaign rhetoric to the contrary, there is relatively little "fat" in other budgets that can easily be used to compensate for other priorities.

The vulnerability of the defense budget became obvious in the first Obama budget for FY 2010, announced shortly after the new president took office. Normally, a new administration makes only incremental changes in the budgetary documents it inherits at inauguration because those priorities have been developed for well over a year and because action is necessary in the first few months of the new term.

With the economic crisis as its rationale, the Obama team proposed a major overhaul and expansion of budget priorities, and the defense budget was not spared, especially since many of its discretionary elements provided tempting targets for revision. One area where potential cuts were apparent was in the area of military procurement of new and often expensive weapons systems, the need for which was open to debate. As a result, Obama ordered a thorough review of the whole procurement process aimed at reducing wasteful and unnecessary spending and a review of new procurement spending.

The budgeteer's axe did not stop there. Obama noted that much of the funding for the Iraq and Afghanistan wars had been "off the books" of the budget through use of the supplemental appropriations process (discussed in the next section). He vowed to include the real war costs in new budget submissions and pointed out that winding down the wars would be a source of considerable savings that would be available for other spending priorities or deficit reductions.

One of the areas where new spending needs were identified was in veterans' services, and especially medical (including psychological) treatment for returning veterans, an area conspicuously underfunded by the Bush administration. Additional funding for problems such as post-traumatic stress disorder (PTSD) and brain injuries added to the budget stresses facing the Obama team.

The Congress

The Constitution establishes the executive, legislative, and judicial branches as coequals in governing the country. As a matter of practice, the judicial branch does not insert itself into the national security policy process except in limited areas such as the parameters of executive authority during times of war. In the area of national security, the "invitation to struggle" is largely between the president and the Congress. The basic principle involved in modulating this competition is checks and balances: for every executive power, there is a countervailing congressional power. The formal provisions are summarized in Amplification 5.3.

Amplification 5.3

THE CONGRESS, THE CONSTITUTION, AND NATIONAL SECURITY

The U.S. Constitution is similarly as compact in its enumeration of congressional responsibility over foreign and national security affairs as it is with the executive branch. The powers of the Congress are enumerated in Article I of the Constitution. Some of these are direct responses to and limitations upon presidential powers, and others derive from the application of more general congressional authority to the national security arena. These powers include lawmaking power, the power of the purse, war-making power, confirmation, ratification, and general oversight of the executive branch.

Lawmaking Power. Nearly all of the actions taken by the government are the result of the passage of legislation by the Congress or the application of previous legislation. As noted in the text, all legislation must begin in one house of the Congress or the other and must have the concurrence of both houses. The president may, of course, veto any legislation he or she deems unacceptable.

Power of the Purse. The Constitution specifies that all authorization of the expenditure of public funds must be initiated in the House of Representatives and have the specific concurrence of both houses of the Congress. Particularly in the area of national security, this is a significant power because large amounts of money are spent on national security and because most of those funds are controllable and must therefore be appropriated each year.

War-Making Power. Although the president is the commander in chief of the armed forces, the Congress has important countervailing powers. The Congress sets the size and composition of the armed forces (promotions for officers, for instance, must formally be approved by Congress before they can take effect). The president can have no larger armed forces than the Congress authorizes. Moreover, the Congress is the only agency of government that can declare war. While this provision has been used only five times in the country's history, it remains a strong limitation on the president's practical ability to place American armed forces into harm's way.

Confirmation of Officials. Presidential appointees to high offices in the administration (with the exception of the National Security Council staff, who are considered part of the president's personal staff and thus are exempt) are subject to confirmation by the U.S. Senate. The purpose of this provision is to ensure that the president does not appoint personnel who are personally obnoxious or politically objectionable in a policy sense.

Ratification of Treaties. Although the president is the only official who can negotiate agreements with foreign governments, none of these can take force until they have the positive advice and consent of two-thirds of the U.S. Senate. This limitation is necessary because a ratified treaty is coequal to laws passed by the Congress. Because of the sheer volume of the relations between the United States and other governments, only a small portion of the dealings with other governments takes the form of treaties (executive agreements, which do not require senatorial ratification, are most common), but most of the more important relationships are in the form of treaties.

Oversight. Although it is not specifically enumerated in the Constitution, the power to review how laws are implemented by the executive branch and to examine how well executive agencies operate has long been an accepted form of congressional limitation on executive actions. The chief mechanism for this oversight is the various congressional authorizing committees that mirror major executive branch functions (the Armed Services Committees and the Department of Defense, for instance).

The nature and tenor of this competition change depending on circumstances. In the first six years of the George W. Bush administration, for instance, the clash between the branches was not as obvious as it often has been and as it became in 2007. There were two basic reasons for this aberration between 2001 and 2007. On one hand, the reaction to September 11 created a "rally round the flag" effect of support for the global war on terrorism (GWOT), which centered (as it normally does during national emergencies) around the presidency and was reflected in support for Bush. Normal partisan and interbranch disagreements were muted because critics were afraid of being depicted as unpatriotic and wanted to lend support for a united response to the tragedy. Also, between January 2001 and January 2007, both the presidency and the Congress were controlled by the Republican Party, and the congressional leaders were less critical of a president of their own party than they might have been had the president been a Democrat.

In 2007, both conditions changed. After four increasingly unpopular years of fighting, the public turned by a two-thirds majority against the administration's major symbol of the GWOT, the war in Iraq. Partly because of this change of heart about Iraq, the Democratic Party was returned to a majority status in both houses of Congress with a broad mandate to end the war. These Democrats confronted a president in the last two years of his tenure (and thus a so-called lame duck) in increasingly partisan ways. Among other things, the change gave the Democrats control of the committee chairs in both houses, a powerful tool. In the early Obama term, the situation resembled the early Bush relationship because both the presidency and the Congress were controlled by Democrats.

The formal political process within the U.S. Congress is theoretically simpler and more compact than that within the executive branch. The structure for considering the budget request of the administration is more direct, for instance, consisting of three prescribed steps rather than the multiple steps in the formulation process within the executive branch. Compactness is facilitated because the Congress does not have to develop a budget on its own. It only has to respond to a presidential request, which it can accept, reject, or modify.

Other factors also influence this process. For instance, the two houses of Congress are in fact two large and often unruly committees, consisting of 100 highly independent senators and 435 equally independent members of the House of Representatives. Unlike the politically appointed officials of the executive branch, they are divided politically by party and by political philosophy. Moreover, the disposition of the defense budget is particularly important to individual members because defense dollars are spent in individual congressional districts and states. Members of Congress thus have an acute built-in self-interest in the outcomes. The result is quintessential politics.

The heart of congressional action in the area of national security occurs largely through two mechanisms: the committee system and the budget process. The budget process is important because it produces the resources that fund efforts to ensure the national security and thus provides much of the shape and nature of the national security effort. The budget process is also of particular importance to the Congress because it is this power, imbedded in the American

Constitution, that gives it the most leverage over the executive branch in matters pertaining to national security.

The Committee System. Because of its size and consequent unwieldiness, the Congress does relatively little of its most important business acting as overall houses of Congress. The real, detailed business of the Congress is performed by the committee system, wherein smaller groups of senators and representatives, all of whom have volunteered for the committees on which they serve (although by no means do all members get membership on all the committees they desire), hammer out congressional positions, draft and vote on legislation, oversee the activities of the executive agencies they parallel, and respond to presidential budgetary and policy initiatives. When the Congress is working properly (which it does not always do), the agreements that are reached in committee are ratified by the overall bodies.

One might reasonably ask why committees are so important and powerful within the Congress. For one thing, the various committees (including their staffs) are the major repositories of congressional expertise on the area of their focus. Congressional members typically volunteer for committee assignments in which they or their constituents are interested or in which they have particular expertise. Thus, a congressional district with a large concentration of military facilities or defense contractors will produce congressional members who will develop an interest in and knowledge of defense matters because the outcomes of defense issues may affect their constituents. The longer members of Congress stay in the Senate or House and remain on the Armed Services Committees, for instance, the more expertise and seniority they acquire and the more influence they develop. The most prominent and knowledgeable members attain the status of congressional leaders in their area of expertise.

These experts—especially the chairs and the ranking members of the minority party (who become chairs if their party attains a majority)—become chief congressional spokespeople in their area of expertise. Members with less expertise than the experts tend to defer to the judgments of these leaders (especially members of the same party) and generally vote the way the chairs or ranking members recommend. The same is true of the major subcommittees of the major committees, where the chairs develop great expertise in their narrower subject area (military manpower, for instance). The rise in partisanship and especially ideological division within both houses of Congress during the 1990s has made members more independent of their leadership and thus has decreased some of the deference paid to the chairs, but the impact of the chairs on legislation remains formidable. It has also hardened divisions along party lines on important matters.

Another reason the committee system is so powerful is because of the smaller and more manageable size of committees compared to the full houses of Congress. It has often been said of the houses of Congress themselves that their size and organization make them great debating forums for the discussion of public policy, but that they are so large and unwieldy as to be terrible places to enact and especially to frame legislation. The major committees of Congress, normally with memberships of twenty or fewer members, are more compact and can give more thorough and knowledgeable consideration to matters of legislative review, including such things as calling for and considering the views of expert witnesses. The recommendations of the appropriate committees thus have a considerable impact on how the Congress as a whole acts on matters that come before it. If one wants to get a sense of what the Congress thinks about a particular matter, the persons to listen to are the appropriate committee's chair and its ranking member of the minority party (who generally becomes the chair if the minority gains a majority in either house).

Being the majority or minority party in Congress has particular importance in establishing control of the Congress. At the beginning of each congressional session, members of each house are assigned to committees in numbers reflecting their majority or minority status. In turn, the committees elect their chairs, almost invariably from the majority party or its allies. Barack Obama, the first sitting member of Congress to be elected president since John F. Kennedy in 1960, showed early deference to this system in his initial attempts to create bipartisanship for his ambitious reform package. Whenever he met with congressional leaders, the chair and ranking member of the appropriate committee in each house were invariably prominent members of the discussion, a de facto acknowledgment of the continuing centrality of the committee system.

The Budget. The budgetary process represents the essence of the congressional committee system in operation. It consists of three steps. The first comes reasonably early in the legislative session that convenes in January and consists of actions leading to a *budget resolution*. When the president's proposed budget is submitted to the Congress, the budget committees of the two houses receive and analyze the request, both overall and by budget category (one of which is national defense). The review establishes likely budgetary ceilings for the overall budget and for each category. When the committees of the two houses reach agreement on these general goals and their acceptability is acknowledged by the executive, the result is the joint budget resolution.

This resolution is a nonbinding agreement about the general shape of the budget that is supposed to guide other congressional committees in legislating the details of the budget package. Sometimes the final budget conforms fairly closely to the guidelines, but often it does not. The resolution provides the basic parameters about what can and cannot be spent within the budget.

After the budget resolution is in place, the serious work of budgeting begins in the Congress. This process, depicted in Table 5.1, is, in a sense, both simpler and more complicated than it may seem. The second and third steps in the congressional budgeting process for national defense occur through the actions of the authorizing committee of each house, the Senate and House Armed Services Committees (SASC and HASC, respectively), and the appropriations subcommittee on defense of each house. The role of the authorizing committees in budgetary action is programmatic: they review the programs requested in the budget and decide which of these to authorize and at what level of support. They do not, however, make specific recommendations about how much should be spent on individual programs and the overall budget, although there are clearly budgetary implications in areas such as procurement—approving a program for a given quantity of a particular weapons system has predictable budgetary consequences.

Table 5.1: The Budget Process

House		Senate
	President's Budget Request	
Budget Resolution		Budget Resolution
	Joint Budget Resolution	
Authorizing Committee		Authorizing Committee
(HASC)		(SASC)
Appropriations		Appropriations
Subcommittee		Subcommittee
	Conference Committee	
House		Senate
	President	

Actual recommendations on the size of the budget and on what can be spent are made by the appropriations committee of each house and, in the case of defense, by the appropriations subcommittee for defense of each house. The role of the overall appropriations committee is to develop the total congressional version of the federal budget, and that of the subcommittees, one of which parallels each functional authorizing committee (including defense), is to make recommendations for their functions that are aggregated in the overall budget.

The process becomes political and controversial when there is disagreement among the various initiating and reviewing bodies, as there normally is. These disagreements can come about in three basic ways. First, the authorizing and appropriating committees in either or both of the houses can disagree on both programmatic priorities and budgetary size. The result is a mismatch between approved programs and resources to fund them. Second, the committees in the two houses, when each reaches accord on its vision of the budget, can disagree. The results can be different programs or appropriations between houses. Third, the president can disagree with parts of the congressional version of the budget or with the overall outcome. The more these possible points of disagreement come into conflict, the more contentious the overall process becomes and the more problematic the outcome is. These disagreements are particularly vivid when the executive and legislative branches (or the two houses of Congress) are controlled by different political parties. The extreme difficulty in crafting health reform legislation in 2009 demonstrates each of these difficulties: the two houses debating substantively different bills, appropriations subcommittees and authorizing committees in each house disagreeing over priorities, and the president disagreeing with various implications of different permutations of the Congressional deliberations.

The authorizing and appropriations functions theoretically should be sequential. In a totally rational world, the authorizing committee would review the budget request programmatically and decide which programs are meritorious and worthy of funding and which are not. The committee would then pass its recommendations along to the appropriations subcommittees, which would allocate appropriate funding. Alternatively, the appropriations subcommittees could first decide how much money is available, and then the authorizing committee could pick the programs that could be funded with the available resources. Neither of these models is followed in practice. In fact, the two forms of committee actions occur more-or-less simultaneously and independently within each house and with little formal coordination either within or between the houses. The result is often four more-or-less conflicting recommendations (two in each house) that require reconciliation before a budget bill can be passed along to either house for enactment.

If this seems a disorganized approach to enacting a budget, the reasons derive from the consequences of the outcomes. Members of appropriations subcommittees, like their counterparts on authorizing committees, commonly represent constituencies with interests in the outcomes and hence want to be certain their interests are thoroughly represented. This not only is true regarding the defense budget, but also has parallels in every other area of budgetary and policy concern—the agricultural committees and subcommittees in both houses, for instance, overwhelmingly have members from farm states who want to protect the interests of their constituents.

When differences exist between the authorizing committees and appropriations subcommittees within each house, they are resolved by joint meetings whose purpose is to produce accommodations and compromises acceptable to all. Normally, there is informal contact with the parallel committee leadership in the other house. In some cases, the president may well invite the committees' leadership to the White House to "jawbone" them into reaching agreements as close as possible to his position. President Obama early established the practice of traveling to the Capitol and meeting with congressional leaders on their own "turf" as his method of conducting these discussions.

The ultimate outcome unfolds from this interaction. Each house passes a defense budget allocation based on the interaction of the authorization committee and appropriations subcommittees. If these are identical (which they rarely are), they go directly to the president. If they are different, they are sent to a conference committee composed of members of the appropriate committees of the two houses to reach agreement on identical bills, which are then sent back to the individual houses to be voted upon. When each house has approved the bill, it is then sent to the president for his signature. The president may accede and sign the budget, veto it, or ask for revisions.

The budgetary process has been further complicated by the increasing reliance on *supplemental appropriations* as a means to finance important governmental operations, particularly in the area of national defense and security. What are these supplemental appropriations? A study by OMB Watch, a watchdog group that studies and critiques government spending, offers a useful definition. According to that study, supplemental appropriations involve "spending legislation, generally but not exclusively requested by the President, intended to address a need not known or foreseen when the annual budget for a given fiscal year was drawn up." The use of this form of funding dates back to the first Congress in 1790 and has been used, to a greater or lesser degree, ever since. The key notion historically has been tying such appropriations to the need to deal with emergency situations; particularly during the Bush administration, they were extended to a variety of other purposes.

The use, and some would argue abuse, of this process was a prominent part of the budgeting process during the Bush administration for funding the war in Iraq and other priorities to the point that over 6 percent of government-proposed spending for fiscal year 2007 was proposed through supplemental requests. As the OMB Watch study asserts, "The use of supplemental appropriations has mushroomed during the Bush administration, and the emergency requirement has faded. The Iraq and Afghanistan wars have been almost entirely financed by emergency supplementals." The arguably pernicious effect of funding non-emergency needs through supplemental appropriations is to distort what the government spends on planned activities. Spending on the war effort in Iraq in 2007, for instance, could hardly be described as unforeseen, and funding it through supplemental appropriations effectively takes it "off the books" of the regular budget. In the case of Iraq, a perusal of expenses based on regular budget appropriation reveals a much smaller financial commitment than the country actually made.

The amount of funds involved is not inconsequential. For fiscal year 2006, a supplemental appropriation of $91 billion was passed by Congress on March 8, 2006. Approximately $68 billion of that amount were earmarked for Iraq, Afghanistan, and the GWOT; about $19.5 billion were allocated to Hurricane Katrina relief (an expenditure more in line with original intent), and slightly over $4 billion were allocated for international activities such as relief for Darfur and for Pakistan following the catastrophic 2005 earthquake. The request for fiscal year 2007 was $99.7 billion.

Why has this device been such a popular way to fund government activities? Clearly, some of the reasons are legitimate and unimpeachable. Supplemental appropriations to deal with the original intent of spending on truly unanticipated events such as Katrina relief are certainly a case in point. One can make a case for using this process for dealing with one-time expenses so that they do not get built into the permanent budgets of agencies and result in the difficult task of rescinding a budget element. Aid for Darfur probably qualifies. Also, the process allows the administration to adjust funds to pressing needs when emergencies apply.

Historically, supplemental appropriations have been rendered less controversial through the inclusion of "offsets" in supplemental requests. These offsets represented reductions in budgeted spending or increased revenues to compensate for— or offset—emergency appropriations. During the Bush years, supplemental appropriations were typically proposed without offsets, meaning they were net increases in government spending not accounted for in the formal federal budget. The Obama administration promised to end the funding of the wars through supplemental appropriations when it came to office.

APPLICATIONS: THE HOMELAND SECURITY RESPONSE TO THE ENVIRONMENT

The interaction between the changing international environment and the vagaries of domestic politics can best be demonstrated by looking at actual policy arenas where the two intersect. In the post–September 11 context, the major change in emphasis has been in dealing with terrorism. The GWOT (renamed Overseas Contingency

Operations by the Obama administration in March 2009) has been concentrated on military efforts to track down and suppress foreign terrorists. The greatest domestic change has been in the creation of the DHS as the institutional response to organizing and coordinating efforts aimed at reducing the risks posed by terrorists.

The Department of Homeland Security

One of the most important questions raised after September 11, 2001, concerned the institutional adequacy of the U.S. government to confront terrorism. In the days and months following the attacks, information became available that there had been intimations of the impending attacks circulating at lower levels of the government in the months before the actual attacks and even a planning document and monitoring held over from the Clinton administration specifically aimed at Al Qaeda. Despite this activity, the attacks appeared to come as an awful surprise. Why? In order to answer the question and to make some sense of the process, three aspects of homeland security are examined: the historical evolution of concern with homeland security, its institutionalization as DHS through the Homeland Security Act of 2002, and problems of the homeland security effort.

Background and Evolution

Although the term *homeland security* appeared abruptly after September 11 and thus seemed to be a very new kind of phenomenon, it is not. If homeland security is defined as that part of the national security effort focusing primarily on the protection of the physical territory and citizens of the United States, then homeland security has been a major cornerstone of American national security policy since the formation of the republic. The name may have been new; the function it describes is not.

As suggested in Chapter 4, however, what is now called homeland security has not been a major operational problem for the United States throughout American national history. The reason, of course, has been the accident of geography that provided the United States with nonthreatening neighbors and broad oceans that protected it from harm. The vulnerability of the American homeland to attack was not a problem until the latter 1950s, when Soviet nuclear-tipped missiles became capable of attacking and destroying the American homeland. That danger, of course, remained theoretical and abstract throughout the Cold War; the terrorist attacks of September 11 made the problem concrete and immediate. The impact of the attacks was to wed homeland security to a concrete threat, that of terrorism.

The modern evolution of homeland security has proceeded along two policy thrusts. The first of these is emergency management. Largely associated at the federal level with the actions of agencies such as the Federal Emergency Management Agency (FEMA) and at the state and local levels with first responders like police and fire agencies, this effort had two major emphases: protection against and reaction to natural disasters (hurricanes, tornados, earthquakes, etc.) and man-made disasters. Problems with the former were vividly illustrated by continuing responses to Hurricanes Katrina and Rita; the latter was associated primarily with civil defense efforts in the event of a nuclear attack against the American homeland.

The suppression of terrorism was added to the homeland security portfolio during the 1980s, although at a much more muted level of publicity than the current effort. During the 1980s, a number of actions were taken within the federal government to create federal capabilities in the areas of antiterrorism and counterterrorism and to elevate and attempt to coordinate the efforts of the principal federal agencies with responsibility for terrorism: the CIA, FBI, and Immigration and Naturalization Service (INS). INS functions are now assigned to DHS, and specifically to Immigration and Customs Enforcement (ICE). Operational responsibility for dealing with on-site efforts when terrorists might strike has remained at the state and local levels.

The two efforts have remained parallel, although with some tensions that were apparent from the beginning but that lacked enough urgency before September 11 compelled rationalization. Terrorism suppression is primarily a federal function, for instance, whereas emergency management is mostly state and local in execution. Operationally, the federal government is more interested in preventing disasters like terrorist attacks and is secondarily concerned with dealing with the consequences of disasters; the order of emphasis is reversed for the emergency managers. These differences are manifested in historical allegations of poor communications between the federal and the state and local levels and in the competition for funding for homeland security. FEMA, with responsibilities in both areas, has become something of a whipping boy for problems of coordination, particularly in light of its poor coordination of efforts in New Orleans, which was one of the most visible deficiencies in the federal response to Katrina.

The process of trying to organize the government to deal with these matters dates back to the Reagan administration. In 1986, President Reagan issued National Security Directive (NSD) 207, which did three things. First, it created the Interagency Working Group (IWG) under the National Security Council. Second, it designated the IWG as the mechanism to coordinate responses to terrorism. Third, it established the lead agency designation (the federal agency with primary responsibility) of the State Department in regard to international terrorism and the FBI over domestic terrorism.

The Clinton administration was also active during the 1990s. In 1995, Clinton issued Presidential Decision Directive (PDD) 39, with three emphases: preventing terrorist acts, responding to terrorist acts and provocations, and managing the consequences of terrorist attacks. The FBI was given broader responsibility domestically, including the formation of domestic emergency support teams (DESTs) to act in the event of significant problems. Clinton also authorized the suspension of *posse comitatus* (an 1869 law that prevents the use of the military for domestic police functions) during emergencies and designated FEMA to lead "consequence management" efforts. Clinton issued two other relevant documents in 1998. PDD 62 created the Office of the Coordinator for Security, Infrastructure Protection, and Counterterrorism, and PDD 63 added the problem of cyberterrorism specifically to the agenda under the designation of "information infrastructure." (Much of this evolution is detailed in Richard Clarke's *Against All Enemies*.)

The point of this discussion is that there was governmental activity in the area that has become homeland security for at least a decade and a half before September 11, 2001. The potential for terrorism was known within specialized parts of the federal government, but the efforts were low-key and generally low priority, as terrorism remained, for the most part, a peripheral concern for most Americans despite overseas instances of terrorist attacks against Americans and American facilities (the African embassy bombings of 1998, the attack on the USS *Cole* in Yemen in 2000) and despite even the 1993 attack on the World Trade Center towers (later linked to Al Qaeda) in New York. During this time period, the dual emphases on terrorism suppression and emergency management were established, and homeland security was largely equated with terrorism as a military and law enforcement problem. These efforts, however, remained at the peripheries of the public agenda until a compelling event caused them to be thrust on center stage.

The Homeland Security Response to September 11

The Al Qaeda attacks against New York and Washington instantly elevated the concept of homeland security to the heart of the national political process. The initial institutional reactions included the creation of a Homeland Security Council parallel in structure to the National Security Council, the establishment of an Office of Homeland Security, and the appointment of a director for the effort. Militarily, the DOD established a Northern Command (from the old Force Command) to coordinate military responses to threats against the American homeland. This process ultimately resulted in the passage of the Homeland Security Act of 2002, which President Bush lauded as the single most important and sweeping reorganization of government in fifty years (a comparison with the National Security Act of 1947). The DHS came into existence in 2003 as a result of that legislation. Its role and structure are still evolving.

The initial response to the September 11 problem was the creation of the Office of Homeland Security within the White House and the appointment of former Pennsylvania Governor Tom Ridge as its director. Ridge was given a position conceptually conceived of as similar to that of the national security advisor and was charged with rationalizing and coordinating improved government capabilities for dealing with terrorism. Critics at the time maintained that Ridge's position left him as little more than a figurehead who could not compel agencies to do anything, especially to cooperate with one another in activities in which they had not previously done so.

In June 2002, the administration proposed a stronger way to institutionalize the effort—the creation of the DHS. The new department, with full Cabinet status, was legislated into being in November 2002 and mandated to perform four functions: border and transportation security; emergency preparedness and response; chemical, biological, radiological, and nuclear countermeasures; and information analysis and infrastructure protection. To accomplish its tasks, the president proposed pulling resources from a number of existing agencies and putting them under the control of the new department.

Virtually no one opposed either the general proposition of this effort or its implementation in principle. As is often the case, however, the devil proved to be in the details of implementation. The kinds of reorganization authorized by the act moved over 170,000 employees from twenty-two major federal agencies under the umbrella of DHS. Such a transfer in and of itself is daunting, as many agencies, individuals, and organizations with contrasting work cultures and methods of operation and little or no tradition of interaction and coordination were suddenly thrust in positions in which they were expected to work as a team acting in a common effort. At the same time, there were significant "turf wars" over which agencies (and their budgets) found their way into DHS and which remained within their traditional homes. These political problems have spilled significantly over into the oversight relationship between DHS and the Congress.

The first and most difficult problem was which agencies would be drawn into the new department and which would not. As already suggested, three federal agencies have primary responsibility operationally in the terrorism field, forming a kind of golden triangle of federal efforts. Ideally, the CIA (which, until legislation establishing the DNI passed in 2004, was an independent agency) had primary responsibility for discovering and monitoring the existence and activities of overseas terrorists; the INS (originally part of the Department of Justice; now Immigration and Customs Enforcement, or ICE, in DHS) had responsibility for monitoring and intercepting aliens entering the country; and the FBI (also part of Justice) monitored and arrested terrorists committing acts within the country. Within this relationship, the CIA should tell the INS who is attempting to enter the country, and when suspicious aliens do come into the United States, the INS should then inform the FBI so it can begin its role of monitoring. In order to maximize the likelihood that this relationship is seamless and effective against terrorism, it follows that all three agencies should have been included in DHS.

They are not. The INS and the Customs Service were made part of DHS (mostly because INS had so many political problems that Justice was glad to get rid of it) with the INS redesignated as ICE. The CIA and the FBI remain independent of DHS, directed only to coordinate with DHS. Why? Both the CIA and the FBI effectively argued that terrorism is only one part of their responsibilities. Virtually all the agencies that have been included in the new department could make the same argument, but the FBI and the CIA were sufficiently powerful that their arguments succeeded, while others failed. In the process, of course, the traditional budgets of the FBI and the CIA were protected as well. FEMA, also an independent agency created in 1979, was included in DHS, mostly because it lacked enough powerful supporters to block its inclusion.

The amalgamation of agencies into DHS has been analogized to a similar process that created the Department of Energy (DOE) in 1977. Both agencies share three major commonalities. First, they were both created as responses to national emergencies: the oil shocks of the 1970s led to demands for a DOE, just as the terrorist attacks of 2001 created the momentum for a DHS. Second, both departments represent attempts to reorganize the federal government by rearranging the federal organization chart, pulling agencies and responsibilities out of existing structures and putting them under the umbrella of the new agency. In the case of DHS, this has been a daunting task internally. The analogy with DOE, however, provides another invidious political comparison that has plagued both agencies—the problem of congressional oversight. Third, both were done "on the cheap." The Bush administration initially argued that the DHS would require no added funding because resources would be made available by agencies contributing people and other resources to the DHS (which proved largely false). Underfunding remains a problem: the DHS budget for 2004, for instance, was under $30 billion. In fiscal year 2007, it was around $50 billion.

The oversight problem has proven especially arcane. Each function of the executive branch of government is overseen for programmatic and budgetary purposes by committees and subcommittees of the two houses of Congress. The oversight function is a significant part of the power base of the members of Congress because it provides real clout in determining who receives and does not receive funding under whatever function they may control. As a result, members of Congress are quite jealous of their prerogatives with regard to oversight and are particularly resistant to the idea that a function over which they have some control might move from the department their particular committee oversees to a committee created to oversee a new department like DOE or DHS, on whose committee they do not serve. Reform at the executive level, in other words, threatens the power of members of Congress. The result was resistance to change of the effective structure that can make the work of the new agencies all the more difficult.

DOE is a miniature version of the congressional problem faced by DHS. The DOE solution in Congress was largely to leave budget and programmatic aspects of agencies included in DOE under their previous committee purviews. The result is that the DOE secretary must report to seventeen committees and subcommittees of the Congress, a daunting and time-consuming way to get policy advice and funds. Moreover, since most of these bodies do not have energy per se as their sole or even primary focus, the advice and funding recommendations are likely to be at odds with one another. No one recommends the DOE precedent as the right way to organize a new department.

The DOE's problem with Congress is child's play compared to that faced by DHS. In aggregating the various agencies into the DHS organization chart, the responsibilities of no fewer than eighty-eight committees and subcommittees in the two houses were affected by the transfers. When the DHS came into being in 2003, a survey showed that *all one hundred* senators and all but twenty members of the House were on committees whose jurisdictions were potentially affected by the reorganization. While everyone could agree in abstract principle that the new DHS would face the smoothest possible sailing in admittedly troubled waters if there was a single authorizing committee and a single appropriating committee in each house (which is the case for traditional departments), the potential consequence of moving toward that ideal end was to erode the power of virtually every member of the Congress by removing some power from a committee or subcommittee on which he or she sits. This potential erosion of power has caused sufficient opposition to reforming the congressional part of the relationship that there is no permanent Homeland Security Committee in the Senate and a Committee on Homeland Security with largely symbolic value in the House of Representatives.

Two other important problems attended the creation of DHS. One concerned funding. The Homeland Security Act was passed at the same time that President

George W. Bush was pushing for additional tax cuts beyond those he had achieved during his first year in office, and one consequence of this emphasis was that he did not want to appear to be increasing funding in other areas of the federal budget at a time when he was arguably reducing revenues. As a result, the decision was made that the new effort would require no additional funding because funding would simply follow transferred departments into the new agency and provide the budgetary base for DHS. This assertion was, of course, a fiction: agencies fought tooth and nail to maintain their budgets, and the new mandates given DHS clearly required new funds. The precedent, however, was set, and DHS attempts to gain additional resources have suffered from the albatross created by the original fiction.

There has been the additional problem of mandate. At one level, protecting the American homeland from foreign enemies—notably terrorists—would seem to be a fairly straightforward task, but in operation, it has proven to be complicated. Securing American territory encompasses a wide range of duties, from monitoring who comes into the country through customs to providing border security to protecting specific potential terrorist targets to ensuring port security. Each of these duties requires different skills and puts demands on the system for additional resources, not all of which have been available, particularly if one aggregates all of these sources of threat and tries to eliminate them. Funding and other resource deficiencies associated with the DHS response to Katrina (largely through FEMA) illustrate the consequences of assuming this risk.

Nowhere have these anomalies been more evident than in the current controversy over illegal immigrants coming across the United States–Mexico border. The flow is not strictly a national security problem because the immigrants are overwhelmingly peaceful, law-abiding job seekers fleeing poverty and pose no military or other security risk (that they may pose other political problems is a separate matter). Their status has politically been raised to threat status by advocates of stricter control of access to the United States across the border. The DHS is caught in the middle of this conflict because the Border Patrol and ICE, both parts of DHS, have roles in regulating entrance into the country, including the possible penetration of the borders by terrorists. More recently, drug cartel violence in Mexico spilling over into the United States, a problem that does have potential homeland security implications, has been added to the complex problem of border security. The illegal immigrant part of the problem is not a duty DHS needs or wants, but it is one it cannot avoid altogether. This problem is discussed more fully in Chapter 14.

Ongoing Problems and Controversies

Some of the difficulties associated with the evolution of the new DHS can be attributed to growing pains. Whether one accepts the claim of the monumental stature of the Homeland Security Act as accurate or as political hype, it has created the basis for a very large governmental overhaul in a large, high-priority area of concern. As suggested, the effort was institutionally politicized from the beginning, and this has made accomplishment of the ambitious goals set forward for the new agency even more difficult. In turn, of course, the agency has been at the center of several political controversies, including the effort against terror, the disastrous handling of Hurricane Katrina relief, and most recently, drug trafficking and violence across the Mexican border. The result has been a tumultuous early history of DHS.

Several ongoing questions and controversies thus surround the DHS and its mission. For present purposes, three of them can be mentioned and briefly examined: the emphasis of the agency between the federal and the state and local levels, with special attention to budgetary and political concerns exemplified by the border question; the division of responsibilities between DHS and other agencies, of which Katrina relief is an example; and the extent to which the DHS effort collides with the rights of citizens, an extension of the terrorism problem.

Mission and Political Emphases. Although it was the stated intention of the homeland security legislation to elevate this important governmental function above the political fray, that effort has not been altogether successful. The reason, simply enough, is that setting priorities and emphases has budgetary implications, and that means politics inevitably intrudes.

Beyond the question of moving funding among federal agencies, this question of emphasis has come to center on the debate over relative emphasis on combating and preventing attacks against the United States (the federal emphasis) and on emergency management by first responders (the state and local emphasis). Originally, the pattern was for the federal government to mandate actions by the states and localities, for which they were to find funds (unfunded mandates). As concern with avoiding new spending ebbed, however, funding became available for the first responders, mostly in the form of equipment grants and funding for emergency plans and the like. The availability of these kinds of funds, in turn, provided opportunities for members of Congress to endear themselves to their constituencies by gaining funding for new ambulances, fire trucks with hazardous materials (hazmat) capabilities, police communications capabilities, and the like. To some observers, provisions like this are evidence of a commitment to first response; to others, they are pure "pork," a form of earmarking. Benjamin Friedman, writing in *Foreign Policy*, cites 2003 allocations of $725,000 for port security in Tulsa, Oklahoma, and $1.5 million in federal funds to Fargo, North Dakota, to purchase trailers equipped to respond to nuclear attacks and "more biochemical suits than it has police officers." The issue of border security with Mexico offers a contemporary example. While the issue of border security is complex and multifaceted (and is discussed in detail in Chapter 14), it flared up politically in early 2009 over the danger that Mexican drug cartel violence would spill over into the United States. Obama DHS Secretary Janet Napolitano announced that additional funds would be allocated to securing the border, but since these funds are limited, debate quickly emerged over how to spend the money (fences or more border guards, for instance), where (in which border states), and at what level (federal, state, and/or local).

Conflicting DHS Mandates. The diversity of agencies included in DHS is manifested in a large number of sometimes conflicting mandates for the agency. Since it was created to respond to terrorism, that mandate was overarching, even

Challenge!

THE "ANGRY LIBRARIANS" AND CIVIL LIBERTIES

While a number of provisions of the USA PATRIOT Act have been the subject of opposition and even derision, one provision, Section 215, has come to symbolize what critics believe is most egregious about it. Because it deals partly with governmental access to library records of individuals, it has been given the nickname "the attack of the angry librarians."

The section contains three provisions its detractors find obnoxious. First, it permits government investigators access to a wide range of information about suspects, including what library books they have checked out (which critics view as invasion of privacy). Second, secret subpoenas that cannot be contested in court (should someone find out about them) can be issued to gain access to patron activity at the library (thus denying the right to contest the subpoenas). Third, there is no requirement that the government disclose its investigations to those under scrutiny (thereby denying rights of due process). All the provisions are justified as necessary national security actions in the "war" on terrorism.

Are such actions justified by the homeland security threat? In the absence of the assertion of a national security basis for them, they would unambiguously be declared unconstitutional as violations of fundamental rights guaranteed to all Americans. The government's counterargument is that in the state of war between the United States and terrorism, they are necessary and appropriate actions. Courts have ruled the provisions unconstitutional, but these rulings have been appealed and were unresolved as of September 2009. Do you agree? How much individual freedom can and should be sacrificed in the name of security? What do you think?

consuming, during the Bush years, and the occasional result was to give short shrift to other priorities. Katrina relief was the most extreme result.

Responding to natural disasters at the federal level has been the chief responsibility of FEMA since its creation in 1979 (it was created in response to inadequate responses that year to hurricanes). When it was folded into DHS, that first responder role was redefined as response to terrorist attacks such as coordinating efforts for catastrophes like biological or chemical attacks. In the process, emergency relief for natural disasters was deemphasized, leaving the agency deficient in supplies and personnel to deal with an event like Hurricane Katrina, which had a huge impact on the Gulf Coast. The result was avoidable human suffering and extremely bad publicity for FEMA and DHS.

Homeland Security and Civil Rights. A fairly muted but significant level of concern has been raised about the impact of homeland security efforts on the civil rights of American and other citizens. The problem of potential infringements on people's rights has not been specific to DHS but has tinged the entire problem.

Much of the concern centers domestically on provisions of the USA PATRIOT (Uniting and Strengthening America by Providing Appropriate Tools Required to Intercept and Obstruct Terrorists) Act of 2001, most of which were renewed in 2005. Critics argue the act's provisions represent an unreasonable infringement on civil liberties, and supporters contend the provisions are necessary for the successful pursuit of terrorists (see the *Challenge!* box). Internationally, the open-ended detention of suspected terrorists and their sympathizers at Guantanamo Bay, Cuba, has added to the global concern about the problem.

Responding to these criticisms created some controversy for the Obama administration as it sought to recraft both homeland security and foreign policy more generally. At least partially because he is a lawyer and former constitutional law professor, President Obama was particularly sensitive to allegations of U.S. violations of American civil rights and of international law in areas such as detention of suspected terrorists and even torture of those prisoners. His efforts to end these practices created a brief firestorm of protest, most notably that by Cheney (noted above), which did not persuade the new administration to back down from its strong advocacy of individual rights.

CONCLUSION: THE ENVIRONMENT SINCE SEPTEMBER 11, 2001

Through constitutional provisions and evolved practice, the American political system has developed ways of dealing with national security problems that are part of the context within which the country views these concerns. The institutions and views have evolved and changed as the national condition has changed as well, but the bedrock institutions of the American political system remain as conceptual pillars within which the adaptation to a changing environment occurs.

Thinking about and dealing with the national security environment was set on its head by the events of September 11, 2001. Suddenly, a mostly benign and tranquil environment was revealed to have a very dark and hostile side that had heretofore been an abstract concern but that was suddenly very real. Before the attacks on major symbols of American military and financial power, the only instances of foreign-inspired and foreign-committed acts had been small and relatively primitive—the most notable example was the 1993 attack on the World Trade Center towers by a single truck laden with explosives that killed six people. The scale of the 2001 attacks and the enormous loss of life revealed a level and quality of vulnerability that few Americans had imagined in their worst nightmares. The body politic was thrown into convulsion about how it could have happened, how it could be avoided in the future, and how to punish those behind the atrocity.

The shock of the attacks and the ambiguity about appropriate responses confused the debate, raising doubts but few obvious solutions. The conventional debate was particularly muddied. National security planning had concentrated on dealing with the concrete, conventional military threats posed by other sovereign states or groups within states. Suddenly, the area of homeland security moved to the center of our attention; as the preceding discussion has suggested, fashioning an organizational and policy response is still a work in progress.

The massive attacks by nonstate actors engaging in the most unimaginable forms of "warfare" did not fit within standard categories. Shadowy, private terrorist organizations that do not represent states and that have small, elusive units (or cells) do not lend themselves to conventional military responses. The idea of using commercial aircraft heavily laden with jet fuel essentially as cruise missiles to attack urban, civilian targets had no precedent within military doctrine or practice and could be found only in escapist fiction (Tom Clancy's *Badge of Honor* revolves around using an airliner to attack the national capitol). How does the country define such a threat? Moreover, how can forces and capabilities be developed that can counter and negate this kind of problem? The answers were and are not clear, but it was evident that one had to move beyond conventional thinking to formulate responses. How that thinking has evolved over time is the subject of the chapters of Part II.

STUDY/DISCUSSION QUESTIONS

1. What is the National Security Act of 1947? Why was it necessary? What are its principal provisions? Why are they important today?
2. What are the constitutional powers provided to the executive branch in the area of national security? What are the congressional powers? Compare and contrast them.
3. What is the interagency process? Discuss its structure and its role in the national security decision process.
4. Discuss the budget process within the executive branch. Compare it to the process in Congress. How do they fit together? Why is the defense budget so important and so controversial?
5. Why has the relationship between Congress and the executive changed since the 2006 election? Do you think divided government (different parties controlling the legislative and executive branches) or unified government (one party controlling both branches) better serves the national security of the country? Why?
6. What are supplemental appropriations? Why do they exist? Why are they important in understanding contemporary defense spending, especially on the Iraq War?
7. The major political response to September 11 domestically has been the creation of the Department of Homeland Security (DHS). Discuss the process leading to forming the DHS, its structures (including those agencies included and excluded), and the difficulties associated with the new agency.
8. What are the major ongoing controversies surrounding homeland security? Discuss each.

SELECTED BIBLIOGRAPHY

9/11 Commission. *The 9/11 Commission Report: Final Report of the National Commission on Terrorist Attacks upon the United States.* Authorized ed. New York: W. W. Norton, 2004.

9/11 Public Discourse Project. *Report on 9/11 Commission Recommendations.* Washington, DC: Public Discourse Project, December 5, 2005.

Ackerman, Bruce. *Before the Next Attack: Preserving Civil Liberties in an Age of Terrorism.* New Haven, CT: Yale University Press, 2006.

Ball, Howard. *The USA PATRIOT Act: Balancing Civil Liberties and National Security: A Reference Book.* Santa Barbara, CA: ABC–CLIO, 2004.

Berkowitz, Peter, ed. *The Future of American Intelligence*. Palo Alto, CA: Stanford University Press, 2006.

Clarke, Richard. *Against All Enemies: Inside America's War on Terror*. New York: Free Press, 2004.

Crabb, Cecil V., Jr., and Pat Holt. *Invitation to Struggle: Congress, the President, and Foreign Policy*, 2nd. ed. Washington, DC: CQ Press, 1984.

Flynn, Stephen. "The Neglected Home Front." *Foreign Affairs* 83, no. 5 (September/October 2004): 20–33.

———. *America the Vulnerable: How Our Government Is Failing to Protect Us from Terrorism*. New York: Harper Perennial, 2005.

Friedman, Benjamin. "Think Again: Homeland Security." *Foreign Policy*, July/August 2005, 22–29.

Fullilove, Michael. "All the President's Men." *Foreign Affairs* 94, no. 2 (March/April 2005): 13–18.

Goodman, Amy, and David Goodman. "America's Most Dangerous Librarians." *Mother Jones* 33, no. 5 (September/October 2008): 42–43.

Harty, Maura. "U.S. Visa Policy: Securing Borders and Opening Doors." *Washington Quarterly* 28, no. 2 (Spring 2005): 23–34.

Heymann, Philip B., and Juliette Kayyem. *Protecting Liberty in an Age of Terror*. Cambridge, MA: MIT Press, 2005.

Hillyard, Michael J. "Organizing for Homeland Security." *Parameters* 32, no. 1 (Spring 2002): 75–85.

Hilsman, Roger. *The Politics of Policy Making in Defense and Foreign Affairs: Conceptual Models and Bureaucratic Politics*, 3rd ed. Englewood Cliffs, NJ: Prentice-Hall, 1993.

Irwin, Paul M., and Larry Nowels. *FY 2006 Supplemental Appropriations: Iraq and Other International Activities, Additional Katrina Hurricane Relief*. Washington, DC: Congressional Research Service, March 10, 2006.

Johnson, Loch. *Bombs, Bugs, Drugs, and Thugs: Intelligence and America's Quest for Security*. New York: New York University Press, 2000.

Kettl, Donald L. *System Under Stress: Homeland Security and American Politics*. Washington, DC: CQ Press, 2004.

Lehrer, Eli. "The Homeland Security Bureaucracy." *Public Interest* 256 (Summer 2004): 71–85.

Maxwell, Bruce, ed. *Homeland Security: A Documentary History*. Washington, DC: CQ Press, 2004.

McMaster, H. R. *Dereliction of Duty: Lyndon Johnson, Robert McNamara, the Joint Chiefs of Staff, and the Lies That Led to Vietnam*. New York: Harper Perennial, 1997.

Nakayama, Andrea C., ed. *Homeland Security*. Detroit, MI: Greenhaven Press, 2005.

OMB Watch. *Background Brief: Supplemental Appropriations*. Washington, DC: OMB Watch, March 2007. (http://www.ombwatch.org/budget/supplementalbackgrounder.pdf)

Rothkopf, David J. "Inside the Committee That Rules the World." *Foreign Policy*, March/April 2005, 30–41.

Snow, Donald M. *United States Foreign Policy: Politics Beyond the Water's Edge*, 3rd ed. Belmont, CA: Wadsworth, 2005.

Yingling, Paul (Lt. Col.). "A Failure in Generalship." *Armed Forces Journal* [online], May 2007.

PART
II

HISTORICAL CONTEXT

The ways in which the United States confronts and is confronted by national security problems have changed over time with evolving circumstances. Inevitably, past experiences affect the way the country and its leaders view existing and future problems, and because of this, Part II examines the American national security experience over the past quarter-century.

Much of contemporary national security has been affected by two monumental historical events : the end of the Cold War and the terrorist attacks of September 11, 2001.Both have had a particularly strong impact on the United States, and it is with these events and their ramifications that the section begins. Calling these events "Fault Lines," Chapter 6 introduces the notion of critical events as exemplified by the two major crises and how they have shaped the way the United States views the contemporary world. Chapter 7, "The Nature and End of the Cold War," examines specifically how the end of the Cold War conditions both the way many Americans view national security and how the events of the period from 1989 to 1991 changed those perceptions. One of the major consequences of the end of the Cold War was a relatively tranquil decade in terms of national security concerns in the 1990s. New influences, notably economic globalization, became a major international factor, and Chapter 8, "Globalization and Beyond," explores those new influences.

Whatever tranquility existed in the 1990s was, of course, shattered by the terrorist attacks against New York and Washington on September 11, 2001. Chapter 9, "Legacies of 9/11," looks specifically at that impact and, among other things, how it has led to contemporary problems such as the wars in Afghanistan and Iraq. Chapter 10, "Ongoing Military Problems," lays out continuing national security concerns as they have emerged from the recent past and considers how they have been altered by but continue to influence current and new challenges to national security.

CHAPTER 6

Fault Lines

PREVIEW

This chapter elaborates on themes introduced in Chapter 1 to organize thinking about the evolution of national security policy. First, it examines the impact of two traumatic events, or fault lines, and how these events have accentuated and defined deep divisions among Americans about adaptation to the evolving order. The text looks at factors that contribute to that debate, including the relative roles of geopolitics and globalization in the evolving nature of the world environment, the central role of the United States in the evolving international system, and the environmental response to the post-9/11 world. The chapter concludes with some initial speculation about the continuing role of force, leavened by Iraq, in the national security system of the second decade of the twenty-first century.

The United States has been on an intellectual roller coaster over matters of national security, and more specifically the role of force, in the last quarter-century. The Cold War was both a political and a military competition, but it was heavily defined in military terms and thus elevated the role of force to levels unprecedented in the American experience, as chronicled in Chapter 4. The 1990s provided a respite of sorts from the militarily dominated competition, and new influences like economic globalization arose in a system where the United States was the sole remaining superpower. The second fault line spawned the global war on terrorism (GWOT) and thus returned the centrality of military power as the lingua franca of international relations. The first post-9/11 administration, that of President Barack Obama, wrestles with how to adapt to an environment where international terrorism remains a salient force but may have lost some of its sense of immediacy.

This chapter examines the debate from two angles. The first is the impact of the fundamental change events (the fault lines) on the operation of world politics. The second is the contrasting views of how the United States should deal with these changes based on differing perceptions about the nature and degree of change.

As noted, interest in and concentration on matters of national security have varied across time, driven largely by the ebb and flow of events in the world and American reactions to them. In relatively tranquil times, when the United States has felt unthreatened by forces that might do it harm, the level of interest and concern has tended to be low. Most of American history between the end of the American Revolution and World War II was of this nature; only the self-infliction of the Civil War seriously interrupted national tranquility and made a concern about and commitment to the most obvious form of national security, military force, seem particularly important. Americans languidly reestablished the "normalcy" of nonconcern between the world wars and will almost certainly look back on the period between the end of the Cold War and the terrorist attacks of 2001 as a time of similar tranquility.

Times have not always been so tranquil, of course, and when they have not been, the level of concern with national security matters—with geopolitics—has been heightened. The Japanese surprise attack on Pearl Harbor—delivered an hour before the Japanese ambassador to Washington presented the American government with an ultimatum tantamount to a declaration of war (which was part of the plan)—rocked the American psyche, ended the appeal of isolationism, and propelled the country into a patriotic war to crush fascism. In the words of Japanese Admiral Isoroku Yamamoto after learning of the failure to deliver the ultimatum before the attack began, "We have awakened a sleeping giant and filled him with a terrible resolve." That resolve carried over to the Cold War that followed World War II. The terrorist attacks of September 11, 2001, were similar in form and effect to Pearl Harbor; once again, attention is focused on matters of geopolitics and national security.

Prior to World War II, the traumatic events in U.S. history were infrequent enough and sufficiently separated in time that they did not have much accumulated effect. The "shots heard round the world" at Lexington and Concord in April 1775 signaled the beginning of the "first" major event in American military history—the American Revolution—and the firing on Fort Sumter, South Carolina, initiated the country's most painful self-induced trauma, the Civil War. The country experienced other significant challenges between these events and the Japanese attack on December 7, 1941, but none as traumatic or precedent-setting as the onset of World War II. That war, in turn, thrust the United States onto the center stage of world politics and began a process whereby traumatic events would become more frequent.

There have been two such events in the past two decades. The distinguished Harvard political scientist Graham T. Allison, Jr., analogized the first event, the end of the Cold War, to an earthquake, a "tectonic shift" in the structure of international relations and the American place in them; the effect of September 11 was similar. Put another way, 1989 and 2001 revealed major fault lines in the evolution of the international environment. Before the fault lines were revealed, the world looked one way; afterward, it looked very different. Before the end of the Cold War, geopolitics was the large concern in a hostile world environment, and that emphasis and perception returned after New York and Washington were victims of commercial airliners turned into lethal missiles. The period between the two major events witnessed a major ascendancy of the emphasis on economic globalization and interdependence. Arguably, the second trauma has been absorbed enough for a new paradigm to emerge.

These alternate emphases are not mutually exclusive, of course. The seeds of the globalization of the 1990s were sown in the last decades of the Cold War, and the contemporary system is struggling with how globalization is affected by and must adapt to an environment in which dealing with the geopolitical reality of international terrorism occupies center stage. Similarly, concern with geopolitics did not disappear in the geopolitical tranquility of the 1990s; it was just not as pronounced a concern as before and after the globalization decade.

The first fault line was revealed between 1989 and 1991 when the Cold War ended. Whether the beginning of that change is attributed to the rise of Gorbachev, to Poland's defiant election of a non-Communist president in 1989, to the breaching of the Berlin Wall on November 9, 1989, or to the official demise of the Soviet Union at the last tick of the clock in 1991 in Moscow's Red Square, the Cold War structure that dominated international politics for forty-plus years after the end of World War II crumbled. The process of adjustment to those changes was still under way when the airplanes slammed into the World Trade Center and the Pentagon.

The end of the Cold War traumatized policy makers mostly because it was so unanticipated. Certainly, a few observers saw it coming: George F. Kennan prophesied in 1948 that vigilant containment could cause Communism's implosion, and New York Senator Daniel Patrick Moynihan consistently suggested its demise—but they were lonely beacons whose message was largely ignored. The Soviet Union crumbled as Soviet republics declared their withdrawal from the union throughout 1991, but the policy of the American administration of George H. W. Bush tried to keep that mortal enemy of forty years intact nearly to the end, fearful and suspicious of the alternatives to a known enemy.

Had the United States anticipated what was going to happen, it might have been better prepared for it. World War II had hardly begun, for instance, when planning for the postwar world after the Axis defeat was instituted. As a result, the institution of a new structure for the international system could be implemented quickly after the guns were stilled. Unfortunately, so few believed in the end of the Cold War—and those who did were ridiculed for their "naïveté"—that no real planning was done to accommodate the possibility. The world was caught completely off guard.

The result was to leave the large contours of foreign policy adrift, and there is no place where that drift was more apparent than in thinking about and planning for national security. In some ways, the trauma is natural because of the nature and impact of change. The Cold War was, after all, a quintessentially geopolitical competition, and the centerpiece of that confrontation was the military might that both sides possessed and projected against one another. Two great land masses were locked into a deadly dance, and keeping the competition below the level of mutual incineration was a time-consuming and energy-draining enterprise. With the stakes so great and the possibilities so grim, it is not surprising that those committed to the process would find the peaceful alternatives to the Cold War to be the stuff of mere dreams.

But the Cold War ended, and observers and policy makers struggled for a decade conceptually and practically to describe and understand how the world was different. During the 1990s, the forces of economic globalization slowly overshadowed the forces of geopolitics within the American administration and raised questions about something like a paradigm shift from geopolitics to globalization. When George W. Bush entered the White House in 2001, he brought with him a foreign and national security team of Cold Warriors (people who had gained much of their knowledge and expertise in global affairs during the Cold War). Like the Clinton administration that preceded them, they struggled during their early months in office for a basis upon which to reorient national security policy, until responding to the terrorist attacks provided that focus for them. The Obama administration is a step further away in both personnel (among national security advisors, only Secretary of Defense Robert Gates and Vice President Joe Biden have significant Cold War ties on their credentials) and attitude.

The United States is still struggling to describe the new international system and appropriate policies and strategies with which to cope with it. This book examines the ensuing debate and its impact on national security policy. The two perspectives through which to view the question, as already suggested, are those of traditional geopolitics and more contemporary influences like globalization. The first lens through which to conduct that examination is focused on the fault lines and their impacts.

THE FIRST FAULT LINE: THE WORLD AFTER THE COLD WAR

The new century began with a very different atmosphere and with very different perspectives and expectations than did the 1990s. In 1990 and 1991, breathtaking political change was virtually the norm; the central feature of that change, of course, was the death of Communism, as country after country peacefully (except in isolated cases like Romania) eschewed Marxism–Leninism, and the Soviet Union, the leader and enforcer of Communist orthodoxy worldwide, stood idly by. As noted, in 1991 constituent parts of the Soviet Union itself began the process of secession; ultimately, the Soviet empire (and it was, in many important respects, the last European empire, since much of the territory had been acquired by force by Russia) broke into fifteen independent states, all of which officially disavowed Communism. By the end of the decade, when the dust had settled on the Marxist experiment, only four states in the world remained nominally Communist. Two of those states, Cuba and North Korea, entered the twenty-first century professing a continued dedication to the principles of Communism, although most observers expect that façade to disappear when Fidel Castro leaves power in Cuba and North Korea reaches an accommodation with the South—both of which are events that could occur in the relatively near future. The other Communist states, China and Vietnam, retain the dictatorship of the Communist Party politically but openly reject Marxist economics and are enthusiastic participants in the globalizing economy. As a competitive political ideology, the belief system articulated by Karl Marx and Friedrich Engels has essentially been consigned to the intellectual dust pile of history.

The implosion of Communism was the most obvious, dramatic, and important change of the last decade of the twentieth century and was arguably the most important international event since World War II. It was a unique series of events in the sense that a major global power source simply vacated the playing field without a shot being fired. The same Soviet Union that had, for the most part, brutally imposed Communist systems on most of what was known as the Second (or Socialist) World simply watched those systems being toppled with scarcely a shrug of its national shoulders. The virtually peaceful implosion of the Soviet Union itself was an act of nonviolence without precedent; large states and empires had, of course, disappeared before, but virtually all the other dismemberments were the direct result of major hot wars. The Cold War ended with a whimper, not a bang, to borrow an old phrase.

The end of "operational Communism" (Communism as the official political organizing system for a country) has had major systemic impacts to which the world is still adjusting. The Cold War international system was what political scientists call a *bipolar system*, which means a system dominated by two opposing states (the United States and the Soviet Union) around which other states congregated in differing degrees of association. The nature of bipolarity had evolved during the Cold War period. In the first decade or so of the Cold War, the system was described as one of *tight* bipolarity, which meant the two dominant parties could influence or control the actions of their "client" states to a large degree. For a variety of reasons, this control was gradually relaxed, and the system evolved into one of *loose* bipolarity. The ultimate manifestation of loosening of control, of course, was the inability of the Soviet Union to keep the members of its bloc adherent to the political principle of Communism that was the source of their sameness.

The result has been a power vacuum. With one pole non-existent, the system can no longer be described as bipolar. There is only one pole left because Russia, the successor to the Soviet Union, has lacked the stature and resources to be a "superpower" in the Cold War sense beyond its continued possession of a large but, thanks to arms control agreements, shrinking arsenal of nuclear weapons (which was the major criterion for superpower status during the Cold War).

In recent years, there have, however, been some potential signs of a Russian revival, possibly as an adversary. This possibility, which some observers have suggested may have the potential to create a new Cold War–like environment, is introduced in Amplification 6.1.

No one was willing to designate the resulting system *unipolar* because that would imply a level of American control that does not exist and that most other states would (and do) oppose. The United States remains the central power, but defining what that centrality means has been a critical and evolving part of defining the new system. It is probably of some symbolic importance that a consensus never formed on what to call the new system and that the most common name describes what it is not—the post–Cold War world.

As it evolved over time, the Cold War had the major physical and intellectual advantage of developing a very orderly set of rules of interaction. The competition for global power and influence between the Communist and non-Communist worlds was well defined, as were the rules by which that competition was carried out. It was conceptually a *zero-sum game* in which the gains of one side were assumed to be the losses of the other and the possibility of *positive-sum* outcomes to

Amplification 6.1

RUSSIAN RESURGENCE?

Are events in contemporary Russia creating the prospect of a renewed competition between the United States and the major successor state of the Soviet Union? During the 1990s, Russia emerged from the rubble of the Communist state as an apparently democratizing but desperately poor country. Both these conditions have changed. Is the result a rejuvenated Russian superpower capable of and intent on reviving something like the Cold War?

Russia is indeed changing. The most visible aspect has been the erosion of political democracy (at least by American standards) by President Vladimir Putin, the successor of the late Boris Yeltsin, a trend arguably continuing under Putin's successor, Dmitry Medvedev. The most visible manifestation of the erosion has been the gradual accumulation of power by the president at the expense of the legislative branch. At the same time, Russia has emerged as the world's second largest exporter of petroleum, providing considerable wealth that allows the country to be, among other things, much more assertive in foreign affairs. Where is Russia and U.S.-Russian relations headed? When Presidents Obama and Medvedev met for the first time at the G–20 summit in April 2009, they vowed a new era of relations between the countries, and Obama met with Medvedev in Moscow in July 2009 to continue the dialog. Where will it end?

situations (in which both sides gained) were infrequent and considered unlikely in any particular situation. The lingua franca of this competition ultimately was the enormous military machine each side maintained, capped by the possession of enormous arsenals of thermonuclear weapons that, if ever employed against one another, would probably have ended civilization as the world knows it.

Yet the system produced an orderliness around which the Cold Warriors could think about world problems and dynamics based in the competition and its management short of war. The end of the Cold War shattered that order. As Georgi Arbatov, director of the Soviet USA and Canada Institute and a member of the Central Committee of the Communist Party of the Soviet Union, put it to the Americans in mid-1991, "We have done a terrible thing. We have deprived you of an enemy." Conceptually, it was indeed a terrible thing in the sense that national security thinking, clearly grounded in the Soviet threat and deflecting and managing that threat, suddenly lost most, if not all, of its relevance. The result was both physical and intellectual disorder in how to think about the world. While the process was going on in 1990, University of Chicago political scientist John Mearsheimer even lamented in the title of an *Atlantic Monthly* article, "Why We Shall Soon Miss the Cold War." What Americans would miss, he contended, was the order and predictability of events and the ability to act appropriately within the bounds of that order.

The debate over what should replace the bipolar international political system raged inconclusively until the debate was suspended by the events of 2001. The changes have produced clear benefits that hardly anyone could or would try to deny. At the same time, there are evolving systemic dynamics about which there is a considerable amount of disagreement within the academic and policy communities that continue to enliven debates within both of those communities.

Undeniable Benefits

The most obvious and most dangerous manifestation of the Cold War was the military confrontation between the competing blocs led by the United States and the Soviet Union. Managing that confrontation was a serious consequence of the nature of international politics and one that, given the possible consequences of a misstep, had to be taken very seriously. The prospect of general war employing nuclear weapons even produced a political culture that was fatalistic about the future, resulting in the expenditure of large amounts of resources in its possibility. Keeping the Cold War cold was the preeminent international responsibility beside which other priorities paled by comparison.

The post–Cold War world produced no equivalent of the East–West, Communist–anti-Communist military confrontation, and this fact had two obvious and overwhelming benefits for the citizenry of the 1990s. Both benefits condition how to think about the problem of national security in the contemporary world, even after the second fault line was revealed.

The first positive change, and the one most relieving for those who participated in the Cold War period, is the absence of any real concern about the possibility of a general systemic war that could threaten national and international survival. Within the context of the Cold War, the possibility—thought by some to be a probability—of a global World War III in which nuclear weapons would be used massively was ever-present, a problem that never went away. The two sides were certainly politically opposed enough to find adequate cause for war between them, and managing the competition in such a way to reduce the likelihood that such a war would begin was a major task.

Since then, the situation is both radically different and the same. Physically, Russia and the United States have reduced the size of their nuclear arsenals and conventional forces significantly, but they retain large enough nuclear forces to be able to do great damage to one another on a scale only slightly smaller than during the Cold War. The demise of Soviet Communism, however, has removed the political differences that could provide the rationale for war. Only a radical change in relations could change that situation. The world is still deadly but less dangerous.

This changed dynamic enormously relaxed the security environment because it removed the "worst case" planning problem from the heart of concern to a lower order of likelihood and thus concern. All of the realistic military contingencies for the present and foreseeable future are more limited in conduct and potential for expansion to general war. It is virtually impossible to conjure a realistic scenario that would lead the world to a general war that would cause the nuclear bombs to start being hurled in a general, systemic way. Terrorism reminds mankind that the world could still be a dangerous place; the unlikelihood of nuclear escalation makes the prospects less deadly.

The result was to take some of the urgency and fervor out of the national security debate. To borrow a distinction from one of the author's other books (*When America Fights*), the United States faced very few potential situations in which it would *have* to fight and especially to use its total military might (employments of necessity); rather, Americans debated in which kinds of places the United States *might* use its forces, knowing the decision would not likely compromise American interests greatly one way or the other (employments of choice).

The second change flows from the first. During the Cold War confrontation, both potential adversaries and their major allies maintained large and expensive military machines that could be quickly inserted into the fray should war somehow break out. Given the destructiveness such a war could rapidly produce, it was assumed that it would be fought and completed with the forces on hand when it began—the "force in being"—and both sides maintained large forces for that possibility.

It was a very expensive proposition. During the 1950s, the United States dedicated as much as half the federal budget to defense. After a spate of entitlement legislation was passed during the 1960s, the proportion fell to about 25 percent of the budget and into second place among categories of federal expenditures. Although reliable budget figures for the Soviet Union were always elusive, the estimates were that they spent between 15 and 25 percent of gross national product (GNP) on the military (with a much larger economic base, the spending equivalent for the United States never exceeded 6 percent of GNP).

The end of the Cold War was accompanied by a sizable demilitarization among the major players, and especially the leaders of the Cold War coalitions. Troop strength for the United States went from 2.15 million active-duty troops in 1988 to 1.4 million in 1998. The Russians have cut their forces down even more, although the ten-year comparison is distorted in that 1988 figures reflect the entire Soviet Union, whereas 1998 figures (which showed an active force of 1.16 million) reflect only Russia. In any case, force sizes and expenditure levels went down substantially for all the major powers, a trend that has, by and large, continued since.

Debatable Changes

While the danger of global war and the need to prepare for it undeniably were receding, the effects of other changes in the environment caused some level of disagreement. While making no pretense of inclusiveness or exhaustiveness, three interrelated changes with some impact on the security equation and the relevance of geopolitics and globalization are worth mentioning in this context.

One change, from which the others to an extent follow, was a greater emphasis on the developing world. In one sense, this emphasis did not represent much of a change at all in national security terms. While national security during the Cold War focused on the major power competition, virtually all the actual fighting involving American forces occurred in the developing world. The United States, for instance, *deployed* forces worldwide, including in the developed world (Europe, Japan); it *employed* force exclusively in the developing world (Korea, Vietnam, Grenada, for example). The reasons for this are complex, of course, but the fact that most of the violence and instability was in the developing world had something to do with this pattern of employment. More importantly, in most instances violent confrontations between clients of the two sides could be waged without a real danger of escalation to direct superpower confrontation. Since many of these conflicts had Communists battling anti-Communists, the use of force could be argued to have been necessary to avoid shifting the geopolitical balance between the East and the West.

The post–Cold War situation both echoed and diverged from the pattern. Virtually all violent conflicts still take place in the developing states, and most are still internal in nature (the Balkans, Haiti, Afghanistan, for instance). This phenomenon has continued since 2001 because the developing world is also the seedbed for most international terrorism, the combating of which became the fulcrum of national security concern after 9/11. Thus, most of the opportunities to employ force are where they always were.

The result of tranquility among the major powers is that much more attention can be directed at the developing world than it could before. In a direct national security sense, this fact is reflected in debate over the nature and appropriate uses of force in the developing world that will be energized even more by the post-Iraq and post-Afghanistan debates.

The point of contrast and continuity cannot be overstated. Using military forces to influence internal wars and instabilities in the developing world is nothing unique to the post–Cold War world at all. What was different is the rationale for putting American or other troops potentially in harm's way and the ways in which they are employed.

During the Cold War, the uses of American armed forces in the developing world were conventional in terms of purpose and methods of employment: the reason to use American military might was to thwart Communist takeovers that might occur in the absence of American assistance, a direct extension of the central geopolitical competition. Whether that force was warranted or wise in particular places such as Vietnam was a matter of disagreement, but the central purpose was not. In those circumstances, the way forces were used—strategically, if not always tactically—was conventional: the idea was military victory over a well-defined enemy. That enemy might fight unconventionally (asymmetrically) and thus create the need for tactical adjustment to bring about enemy defeat, as was the case in Vietnam, but the goal was traditional—fighting to support traditional governments.

Opportunities to employ force in the period between the fault lines were different on both counts. The disappearance of Communism meant that such involvement could no longer be justified in terms of the kinds of geopolitics that underlay Cold War actions. More typically, justifications became "softer," framed in terms of arresting and reversing humanitarian disasters in situations where clearly military conflict between defined military forces was not present. The purpose was more often framed in terms of reinstituting peace and protecting civilian populations from the return of atrocity. As a result, military victory in a traditional sense gave way to an open-ended commitment to imposing, enforcing, and keeping a fragile peace.

That reorientation ran counter to traditional military ways of thinking about the use of force in the American experience.

When the new Bush administration entered office in 2001, it clearly demonstrated the ambivalence created by this debate over how and when to use force. During the 2000 campaign, Bush had come out strongly in opposition to future uses of American force for peacekeeping when American interests were not clearly engaged. Dr. Condoleezza Rice, who became national security advisor in the first Bush term and secretary of state in the second, was the point spokesperson for this position, arguing that the United States should not act as the "world's 911," that it was an improper role for elite American troops like the 82nd Airborne to be used to escort children to kindergarten in places like Kosovo, and that endless deployments were eroding troop morale. The Bush team even suggested the desirability of terminating American involvement in Kosovo and Bosnia.

These positions did not long survive the oath of office. The United States' European allies quickly informed the Bush administration of the necessity of maintaining the missions in the Balkans and of the vital nature of the American presence in those missions. The rhetoric of non-involvement was quietly cooled, and Secretary of Defense Donald Rumsfeld quickly announced a comprehensive review of American military strategy and missions. The Bush administration did, however, continue to harbor a disdain toward one of the obvious experiences of the 1990s—state building—which would be disastrously demonstrated in Iraq.

Globalization is the other 1990s trend with a significant developing-world element, and disagreement exists about what it does and how or whether it should be promoted. Bursting upon the scene and coinciding with or stimulating (there is disagreement about which) the worldwide economic expansion and prosperity of the global economy in the most developed states, globalization spread to selected parts of the developing world during the 1990s. During the first half of the decade and beyond, the results appeared overwhelmingly positive and formed the core of the Clinton administration foreign policy of engagement and enlargement (engaging those countries most capable of joining the global economy and thereby enlarging what he called the circle of market democracies). In its purest form, the expansion of the globalizing economy would be accompanied by political democratization and contribute to a spreading *democratic peace* around the globe. In this scenario, as democracies increasingly came into power, peace would follow, since it is asserted that political democracies do not fight one another. Moreover, as the global economy reached out and encompassed more and more countries, the motivation to fight would give way to economic interdependence.

In this happy scenario, a geopolitical perspective that seeks to minimize violence and instability in the world appeared to coincide with and reinforce globalization, since they are both aimed at the same ends. Unfortunately, the rosy outlook of the 1990s began to fade as the twentieth century wound to an end. As the international system faced the new century, the desirability and contribution of globalization became more debatable.

At least three things contributed to the ambivalence about globalization. First, its proponents were too optimistic in their advocacies, and events proved their most expansive projections to be at least partially wrong. During the height of the "go-go" 1990s economy, some analysts predicted that globalization had fundamentally altered the nature of traditional economics; modern technology could make adjustments heretofore impossible in areas like product mix and inventory control, meaning the business cycle of boom and bust could effectively be surmounted, even eliminated.

These predictions proved overly optimistic, even wrong in some cases. Knowing they were producing too many automobiles did not keep the world's automakers from producing 80 million cars a year for a market that could absorb only 60 million in the late 1990s, and the result was large excess inventories as the century changed that resulted in layoffs, unprofitable discounting, and other phenomena familiar in the old economy. In 1997, a currency crisis broke out first in Thailand, spread rapidly to other East Asian states that were considered pillars of globalization, and even adversely affected the U.S. economy for a time. When the signs of economic weakness became evident even in Japan, the "economic miracle" that accompanied globalization seemed suspect.

The geopolitical consequences of globalization provided a second source of controversy. The approach of using economic globalization as a way to entangle and drag countries into the web of market democracies was no more vigorously pursued anywhere than it was in China. The prevailing idea was that by tying the Chinese to the global economy through mechanisms like most favored nation (MFN) status and membership in the World Trade Organization (WTO), pressure could be brought to bear that would force the Chinese to improve their human rights record and to allow for increased political democracy in the country. The Communist regime's obdurate resistance to loosening its political monopoly or to allowing greater political (as opposed to individual) freedoms has made that strategy suspect and has kindled a renewed debate on how to treat China, which has continued as China proceeds through the transition to the fourth generation of Communist leaders.

The failure of globalization to produce all of its most optimistic (and probably unrealistic) outcomes has created a third problem, which is a backlash against the phenomenon of globalization—and especially its most prominent institutional manifestations. The first overt demonstration of strident, organized opposition to globalization came in late November 1999 at the Seattle annual meeting of the WTO, where an estimated twenty thousand demonstrators voiced their objections to the consequences of globalization (and engaged in considerable destructive vandalism in the "Emerald City"). Prominent participants included labor unions fearful of the movement of jobs to cheap labor markets and environmentalists fearful that multinational corporations and other private firms would ignore environmental protection. Other groups with parallel concerns, such as those fearful of U.S. global domination and groups seeing globalization as an assault on sovereignty, added their voices to the dissent.

This backlash became a regular and continuing part of the institutionalization of globalization in its various aspects and of the dialog on globalization. Attempts to disrupt organizations meeting to promote global values like free trade have become an apparently inevitable part of such meetings. The 2000 meeting of the International Bank for Reconstruction and Development (IBRD) in Washington, D.C., was interrupted by roughly the same coalition of rejectionists that had appeared in Seattle. In April 2001, this phenomenon was internationalized amid great worldwide television coverage as demonstrators at the third Summit of the Americas in Quebec City, Canada, battled tear gas–wielding police to oppose progress toward forming a Free Trade Area of the Americas (FTAA) among the thirty-four democratically elected governments of the Western Hemisphere (all countries except Cuba) by 2005. This opposition was repeated during demonstrations at the 2005 meeting in Argentina. The groups that have attracted demonstrators are diverse. The WTO has been in existence for over a decade with the purpose of promoting and monitoring the removal of trade barriers among its members (currently about 140 states); the World Bank is one of the original Bretton Woods institutions that came out of World War II to reorder the world economy, principally by making loans to creditworthy countries; and the FTAA is an unratified proposal unlikely ever to come to fruition. The common thread among all three, however, is that they are a general part of the process of globalization.

The Second Fault Line: The World After September 11

Although September 11 was a traumatic event of the same order of magnitude as the end of the Cold War, describing the distinctive characteristics of the resulting world has been more difficult. Like the post–Cold War world (1991–2001) it superseded, it did not have a universally accepted name: the closest anyone has come in the immediate wake of the traumatic events is to proclaim it as the GWOT, but it is not clear that label is adequate. For one thing, the response to the terrorist acts was not a war in any traditional, recognizable way (a point argued at length in Chapter 13); for another, it is not yet certain that the GWOT represents or accompanies a profound and *lasting* change in the way the system works. It is possible that international terrorism will be reduced to the status it had before the attacks (a peripheral place in the scheme of things) or eliminated, in which case history may view this period as an interlude in the post–Cold War world. Alternately, terrorism may be an enduring problem with which to contend concertedly for some indefinite time.

An accurate perspective is further clouded by subjective factors. Because the traumatic events are so recent, there is less perspective on the events and their long-term impacts than for the forty-year Cold War. Powerful symbols of the United States were attacked, which makes the events of September 11 more personal and emotional than they might otherwise have been. The obvious equation of the attacks with the Japanese attack at Pearl Harbor creates a sense of "infamy" around the events, seeming to dictate a swift and decisive retribution that continues to remain elusive and adds to frustrations. The amorphous nature of a terrorist opponent that operates in the shadows makes it difficult to fashion images to depict how to eradicate the "evil" that terrorism represents.

If it is difficult to agree on all aspects of the new environment in any detail, it is possible to discern differences on the post–September 11 side of the second fault line. Among other things, the balance between traditional geopolitical and globalization concerns has clearly shifted from the latter to the former. Geopolitics, and thus the relevance of force, has had a rebirth that is clear and undeniable as the search continues for adequate ways to describe and cope with the new geopolitical reality. One of the new forces that clearly entered the public international calculus is the emergence of so-called nonstate actors in the form of international terrorists whose base and loyalties do not coincide with any country. Most of the members of Al Qaeda are not Pakistani, nor are they Afghans, but they have found safe haven among the Pashtun tribesmen living on both sides of and traversing the border between those countries. One result is an enemy hard to classify in national terms and hard to attack without alienating the government and people of the countries in which the terrorists reside.

The revealed vulnerability of American soil to attack quickly revived an interest in the tool of geopolitics—military forces—in the American debate after a decade or more when they received much less attention. One of the most obvious beneficiaries has been military spending. In the patriotic outpouring following the terrorist attacks, this shift to an almost obsessive emphasis on national security went virtually unchallenged. In the area of defense spending, for instance, the expected tough debate over modernization—which new systems to buy—turned into a frenzy of trying to procure everything on the menu despite the tenuousness of the arguments of how different capabilities would contribute to the central thrust of combating terrorism. In 2009, calls by Secretary of Defense (SECDEF) Gates to rein in defense spending met great resistance, at least part of the basis for which was grounded in the GWOT.

The ascendancy of geopolitics has been accompanied by the assertion that the United States is locked in a new and different kind of war, a theme raised shortly after September 11 by the Bush administration and dutifully adopted by the media. While it was never quite clear what was new about combating terrorism, it was widely advertised that the new and amorphous enemy engaged in *asymmetrical warfare*. Calling such approaches "new" strained credulity to the breaking point. The adoption of methods to negate the advantages of a larger and superior force is as old as the first time a weaker foe outdid a superior enemy, and the United States confronted—unsuccessfully—this kind of enemy in Vietnam a third of a century ago. There is certainly nothing new about the use of terrorism—only the instruments have changed. What *is* new in the contemporary context is the relative emphasis now being placed on combating unconventional opponents. During the Cold War, for instance, most emphasis was on strategic nuclear and large-scale conventional war with the Soviet Union in Europe—a sort of grand-scale reprise of World War II. Some emphasis on asymmetrical warfare—in forms such as antiterrorism and guerrilla warfare—was part of planning, but it was relegated to a lower order of priority. Special Operations Forces (SOFs) were largely responsible for this concern, and because those missions were considered less important than the central conflict, the result was to help trivialize the importance of the SOFs and their missions. In a contemporary environment where there are few dangers of large-scale conventional warfare, priorities have been essentially inverted—witness the reorientation of the priorities of American forces announced by SECDEF Gates in 2009 as part of constraining military spending (see Chapter 10).

A more prominent characteristic of the new geopolitical order is its increased emphasis on nonstate actors, organizations that have neither a permanent territorial base nor loyalty to any particular country but that engage in activities that cross state borders. In a generic sense, such actors are also nothing new; the most prominent examples of nonstate actors are nongovernmental organizations (NGOs)—nonstate-based international organizations that perform a variety of useful functions within the system from providing humanitarian assistance (CARE, Doctors Without Borders) to monitoring human rights violations (Amnesty International, Human Rights Watch), for example.

The terrorist attacks riveted attention on a subcategory of nonstate actors who are violent in their actions. Once again, violent transnational groups are not a novel feature of the post–Cold War world and beyond. In contemporary terms, the international drug cartels have been a prototype of sorts, and international terrorist organizations have operated for years. What is different is that organizations such as Al Qaeda have attained a central position in national security attention.

Dealing with nonstate actors in the form of international religious terrorist organizations poses some unique problems for national security policy makers beyond the fact that they were not given high priority in the past. The United States' historical experience has been combating the agents of state-based governments who represented a conventional (or symmetrical) threat in conventional warfare. Armed forces, doctrines for warfare, and the whole legal and ethical framework for warfare are geared to fighting such foes. International terrorism stands these concepts and rules on their head in several ways.

One problem is how to depict efforts to combat international religious terrorists. The analogy of "war" has its roots and designations in conventional interstate war and classic internal war over control of governments but does not clearly fit an opponent that has no territorial base or loyalty and is apparently uninterested in gaining and exercising authority over territory. Whom does one attack in this war? Historically, acts of war are committed against states and their agencies. In the case of international terrorists, such distinctions are at best indirect—for example, the designation of the Taliban regime in Afghanistan in 2001 as an opponent because of its shielding of Al Qaeda. It is relatively easy to assign blame when actions can clearly be identified with a particular state (and especially when that state acts overtly); it is more difficult when dealing with a nonstate-based opponent.

/ This difficulty became particularly clear in the case of Taliban and Al Qaeda prisoners sent to Guantanamo Bay (nicknamed "Gitmo") in Cuba in 2002 and afterward after the campaign to overthrow the Taliban in Afghanistan succeeded. Were these individuals to be considered prisoners of war (POWs), in which case they were clearly subject to treatment as such under the Geneva codes of war (see Amplification 6.2)? Or were they detainees, as the administration maintained? Had there been a literal, legal state of war, there would have been no question about POW status. Since there was not, their status was debatable and controversial. The compromise solution of treating Taliban prisoners as POWs because they were soldiers of the Taliban regime and treating Al Qaeda prisoners as something else was not legally or politically pleasing, particularly when allegations of mistreatment, even torture, arose, since such acts are prohibited under the rules of war and international conventions regardless of the status of those against whom such acts are administered.

THE RULES OF WAR: WHO IS A POW?

One of the fallouts of American participation in the campaign to overthrow the Taliban government of Afghanistan was the question of the status of hostile prisoners captured by American and Afghan forces. It was a complicated problem in two ways. The first complication revolved around whether a state of war existed, since war was never declared formally by the Afghan government, the coalition of forces seeking to overthrow that government, or the intervening United States. The other complication was that the prisoners included both soldiers supporting the Taliban regime and Al Qaeda terrorist members fighting alongside the Taliban.

The question of prisoner status was first raised when a number of captured Afghans were transported to the U.S. naval base at Guantanamo Bay, Cuba. The explanation for the transfer was that the "detainees," as the Bush administration labeled them, were dangerous individuals who, if left in Afghanistan, might escape and cause havoc there. In addition, the United States wanted to isolate and interrogate suspected Al Qaeda members to aid in the campaign against terrorism.

The question became critical at this point. The Bush administration maintained that the detainees did not qualify for POW status under the Geneva Conventions of War (more specifically, Convention III: Relative to the Treatment of Prisoners of War, Geneva, August 1949), to which the United States is a signatory. After some discussion, it was conceded that the Taliban detainees, as representatives of the government of Afghanistan, qualified under Article 4 of the convention but that the Al Qaeda detainees did not. The administration, anxious to get as much information as possible from the detainees, initially resisted differentiating between members of the two groups. Article 5 of the convention, however, is quite clear on this matter: "Should any doubt arise as to whether persons, having committed a belligerent act and having fallen into the hands of the enemy, belong to any of the categories enumerated in Article 4, such persons *shall enjoy the protection of the present convention until such time as their status has been determined by a competent tribunal*" (emphasis added). Over seven years after their arrival, no tribunals had been convened for that purpose.

Why was the Bush administration so reluctant to afford POW status to the Afghans? The answer was straightforward: if the detainees were legal POWs, there were sharp limits on the American right to extract information from them. Part III, Section 1, Article 17, defines the problem: "Every prisoner of war, when questioned on the subject, is bound to give his surname, first names and rank, date of birth, and army, regimental, personal or serial number, or failing this, equivalent information." Since that is *all* the information a POW is required to provide, granting that status would clearly have hamstrung the antiterrorist effort. The question is whether the additional information was worth the price of the United States apparently violating a basic treaty obligation. The questions remain unresolved and contentious.

Source: Convention III: Relative to the Treatment of Prisoners of War. Geneva, Switzerland, August 1949. (Text available from the Society of Professional Journalists at http://www.spj.com/genevaconventions/convention3.html)

Nonstate actors such as international terrorists are difficult to combat in conventional military terms, as the U.S. military has learned. These groups do indeed engage in asymmetrical forms of combat, in the process not honoring traditional rules of engagement or conventional laws of states. Terrorist acts invariably break laws and are considered criminal by the targets, just as these same acts are considered acts of war by the terrorists.

A further characteristic of the changed environment is how the American role in the world is viewed. In particular, the question that has been raised quite frequently is whether dealing with terrorism has predisposed the United States to act in concert with its allies and the international community (a position known as multilateralism) or on its own with little regard for others in what it believes to be its individual self-interest (unilateralism).

In the immediate aftermath of September 11, 2001, there was great agreement on the perfidy of the attacks and on the need to combat them through concerted, broadly international action, and the Bush administration responded by calling for such action. The rationale was that since international terrorism represented a threat that did not honor borders, the response to it must be international as well in areas such as intelligence gathering and sharing and detention of suspected terrorists. The internationalist instinct seemed to prevail.

By the beginning of 2002, however, that consensus had begun to erode as the campaign to capture and destroy Usama bin Laden and his associates proved more difficult than originally imagined. In the atmosphere of the time, the U.S. government began proposing more militarily oriented actions that met with cool receptions almost everywhere else. The first lightning rod for international concern was the detainees at Guantanamo and the stern refusal of the United States to listen to international entreaties about their treatment. When President Bush announced the "axis of evil" designation of Iraq, Iran, and North Korea in his 2002 State of the Union address and threatened vaguely about the likelihood of military action to deal with their alleged transgressions without consulting American allies in advance, many in the international community saw a return to the unilateralism they had suspected before the attacks.

Finally, September 11 dampened discussions and emphases on globalization and other nonmilitary aspects of security. Some of the optimism about spreading globalization had already been dampened by economic events of the end of the 1990s. The shock of the terrorist events further removed the luster that had surrounded globalization, as the system reoriented its focus toward the problem of international terrorism. The more profound effects of the changed environment on globalization are examined in more depth in Chapter 8. For present purposes, it is sufficient simply to suggest the contours of short- and long-term prospects.

In the immediate wake of the attacks, negative impacts on the system that had evolved in the 1990s tended to be emphasized. For example, one of the reasons the Al Qaeda terrorists were able to enter the United States was the relative ease that people and products have in entering and leaving the country. That penetrability is a distinct asset for increasing international economic activity such as trade, but it also makes monitoring and intercepting terrorists (as well as illegal immigrants and drug traffickers, as noted in Chapter 13) more difficult than would be the case with greater restrictions on movement. As discussions turned to the prospects of terrorists moving weapons of mass destruction into the country, there were quite understandable calls for increased security at U.S. borders, a concern that has continued and is discussed in Chapter 14. One question was how this could be accomplished without unduly strangling trade, effectively undoing globalization, and threatening freedoms integral to the American way of life.

In the longer term, it is possible to think of the emphases on geopolitics and globalization as being potentially reinforcing, part of a comprehensive policy toward the world. A reasonable consensus has emerged that a basic reason for terrorism is abysmal living conditions in parts of the world that are breeding grounds for the hopelessness that makes terrorism an attractive option. Economic development—draining the "swamps" in which terrorism thrives—thus becomes part of a longer term strategy aimed at eliminating the terrorist threat. Since a major component of alleviating human misery is improving living conditions through economic prosperity, the spread of the globalizing economy to places that have hitherto been those swamps can become part of overall geopolitical strategy.

There are two "aftershocks" of the September 11 fault line that continue to affect U.S. national security policy. One, of course, is the continuing vitality of international religious terrorism. Despite some hard-fought efforts that have brought individual terrorists to justice and have disrupted or disabled their efforts, no one is arguing that "victory" in the struggle is on the horizon. The other aftershock has been the Iraq War and the domestic and international reaction to it. The war is clearly tied to September 11: the clearest reasons for concern about Iraq (at least in public advocacies) were the formal and potential ties of the Saddam Hussein regime to terrorism (the alleged tie to Al Qaeda, the fear weapons of mass destruction would be shared with terrorists). Without the ability to allege these connections, the invasion would likely have remained the idle delusion of neoconservatives within the Bush administration. Internationally, very few countries accepted the alleged connections, and thus, the world community overwhelmingly rejected the American actions that flowed from them.

In the years since 9/11, the effort against international religious terrorism has lost some of its immediacy and intensity, if not its seriousness and importance. That emotions have cooled somewhat is not surprising. Emotional heat has a tendency to dissipate with time and the fading of memories. The absence of subsequent attacks on U.S. soil has dampened the sense of immediacy, even if it has sparked an ongoing debate about what has kept the country attack-free since 2001. Al Qaeda, however, remains a viable threat as it continues to commit acts of terror elsewhere in the world and threatens to extend these back to American territory. The question is how best to deal with that threat.

TOWARD THE NEW INTERNATIONAL SYSTEM?

The emergence of the fault lines has had major impacts on both the nature of the international system and how we think about our place in that system. This section introduces and briefly explores three aspects of these changes and how they may have an impact on contemporary actions in the post-9/11 world. First, it looks at the system's dynamics in terms of the relative ascendancy of the geopolitics- or the globalization-based paradigm in the period between the end of the Cold War and the second fault line, a theme elaborated in Chapter 8. Second, one of the obvious changes in the international system is the enhanced primacy of the United States in the international order, and that requires examining the nature and some of the implications of the U.S. position as the sole remaining superpower and how that position may have eroded in the past decade or so. Third, the aspects of change currently coalesce on the post-9/11 incumbency of Barack Obama, so this chapter introduces some of the themes suggested in Chapter 1 about the post-9/11 environment.

Paradigm Choices

As the discussion of the fault lines clearly suggests, the relationship between geopolitics and globalization and related emphases is an intertwined, intimate, and evolving proposition, not an either/or matter. During the Cold War, geopolitical concerns were clearly and appropriately dominant, given the nature of the international situation. Yet, while the geopolitics of the East–West confrontation dominated the international agenda, the forces that would propel globalization were being set in place, ready to enter the calculus.

During the 1990s, two quite opposite forces were at play that changed the relative importance of globalization and geopolitics and ended up creating an exaggerated view of the post–Cold War world. One of these was the apparently receding importance of the most visible manifestation of geopolitics: military forces. The demise of the superpower military confrontation clearly devalued traditional military force within the major power conglomerate of important countries, and this devaluation led many states sharply to reduce their forces. Following the apparent last hurrah of twentieth-century-style warfare in the Persian Gulf War, military concerns shrank to considering smaller tasks, such as peacekeeping.

At the same time, the impact of globalization was making enormous headway as the leading edge of the great and spreading prosperity of the 1990s. During the first seven or so years of the decade, economic growth and prosperity seemed inexorable at the very same time that major systemic instability and the prevalence of violence faded from the world stage. The result was a euphoria that would prove with time to be partially false. But to enthusiasts of the time like *New York Times* correspondent Thomas L. Friedman, the world was entering the "age of globalization," a systematic transition from the old to the new.

At one level, the rise of globalization and other concerns in the 1990s was nothing more than the latest conceptual and physical reaction to the realism represented by the geopolitically dominated Cold War period. As noted in Chapter 2, realism and geopolitics represent the conflictual side of international relations, the dark side or yin in politics. Globalization and other cooperative dynamics, on the other hand, emphasize the cooperative side of the international equation, the idealist assault on the worst outcomes of a realist-dominated world—war. This assault has known many names, from interwar idealism and its attachment to international organization to the functionalism of the early post–World War II emphasis on the United Nations system as a means to make war functionally impossible. The more direct lineage attaches to the idea of complex interdependence popularized by Robert Keohane and Joseph S. Nye, Jr., in the 1970s. Globalization emerged as the yang to the geopolitical yin.

The result has been a fast-moving and changing international dynamic. The seemingly inexorable ascent of globalization was delivered a sobering blow by the East Asian crisis that swept through the global economy in 1997 and 1998 and reminded the world that the growing prosperity was neither automatic nor nonreversible. In turn, the ensuing turmoil brought geopolitical elements back to the fore in diverse places. In Indonesia, for example, the crash laid bare the last vestiges of corruption in the Suharto dictatorship, hastening his resignation from a presidency to which he had had himself appointed for life and setting in motion centrifugal forces in the archipelago that continue into the new century. In order to straighten out the economic mess revealed by the crisis, the old-fashioned economic instrument of power (although not called that) was invoked in the form of International Monetary Fund sanctions in offending countries. At the same time, the carrot and stick of WTO membership and MFN status were dangled in front of the Chinese in order to secure their adherence to other quite different standards such as human rights. The dark side of geopolitics was reasserted decisively as the commercial airliners slammed into the icons of geopolitics (the Pentagon) and globalization (the World Trade Center).

What this reveals is that globalization and geopolitics have become intertwined in complicated ways that continue to evolve in the post-9/11 world. In some ways, the economic aspects of globalization replaced—at least part of the time and in some instances—the military aspects of geopolitics during the 1990s. Certainly, this was true in relations within the developing world. At the same time, globalization may be the servant of geopolitics, as in the complex motivations and debates about the use of economic incentives toward China to entangle that country in a spiderlike web that will draw it toward the economic and political values of the First World–dominated system. As the world's countries emerge from the economic recession that began in 2008, the relationship will take yet another turn.

Geopolitics and globalization may thus be the yin and yang of modern international relations, sometimes competing with one another and other times complementing one another. Before beginning the journey to try to decide the direction, nature, and velocity of that relationship, it is necessary to introduce one other major characteristic of the contemporary environment: the central role of the United States.

The American Role in the New World System

One of the ways the new international order is clearly different from the Cold War era is in the distribution of power and influence among states. The language of bipolarity and multipolarity is clearly no longer descriptively accurate, and the use of the term *unipolarity* has connotations of a level of control, even hegemony, that the United States does not possess and to which most Americans do not aspire.

While it became fashionable in the 1990s to describe the United States as the remaining superpower, a new term entered the lexicon to describe how much more influential the United States is than other states in the system. That term is *hyperpower*, and it connotes the great qualitative advantage of the United States in addition to quantitative advantages such as having the world's largest economy and most lethal military. It is a term sometimes used out of awe and respect, but it is also attached to what the late Arkansas Senator J. William Fulbright called in a book title in 1966 "the arrogance of power."

What have the bases of American preeminence in the world been? It is possible to use the traditional measures of national power—the political, economic, and military instruments of power—to compose that advantage. During the Cold War, the United States had the advantage in each of these measures of power, but these advantages were challenged in each category. Marxism–Leninism posed a challenge (that turned out to be overestimated) to the political appeal of western democracy, the economies of Japan and the European Common Market (now the European Union) posed an economic challenge, and Soviet nuclear and massive conventional forces challenged American dominance on the military dimension as well.

During the 1990s, the United States clearly established its preeminence on all three measures of power. Part of the reason was that the United States outperformed its rivals, especially in the economic realm. At the same time, the demise of the Soviet Union meant the source of both the political and the military dimensions of opposition quit the field, leaving the United States alone as the sole possessor of significant amounts of all the instruments of power.

Politically, the United States emerged as "the indispensable nation," to use former Secretary of State Madeleine Albright's phrase. The basis of American political advantage was at least twofold. The power and appeal of the American system and its political ideals (Nye's "soft power") made the United States the model that many states and peoples worldwide sought to emulate. At the same time, the United States was the only country with truly global interests. This means that whenever situations arise almost anywhere, the United States is affected and has an interest in influencing the outcome, a situation highlighted when the United States became the direct victim of international terrorism. Because of American power in the other dimensions, American preferences are consequential and sought out regardless of the location.

The economic dimension has been similar. After nearly two decades of economic doldrums during the 1970s and 1980s, when it became popular in this country and abroad to talk about American decline, the American economy revived and led the expansion of the globalizing economy during the 1990s and into the 2000s. The United States had remained the world's largest economy even during the down years, but as expansion occurred and the globalization system became ultimately a trading system, the United States also blossomed as the world's great market, which everyone sought to enter. At the same time, the United States' primary economic rivals relatively declined. The German economic "miracle" was slowed by the greater-than-anticipated burden of absorbing the former German Democratic Republic (East Germany) into the Federal Republic in the early 1990s. By the end of the 1990s, the Japanese economy was faced with a serious downturn; joining the

American-inspired and American-led "circle of market democracies" added to the luster of its soft power.

American military advantage increased the most. The most obvious reason for this was the decline of the United States' military rivals. Russian forces are far inferior in size and quality to the old Soviet military machine, and the burdensome retention of a nuclear arsenal comparable to that of the United States, which the Russians cannot afford to maintain adequately, is about the only way in which the United States' past rival poses any threat. This Russian decline may not be permanent, a prospect explored in Chapter 7. Similarly, the People's Republic of China retains the world's largest army but has no way to project it far from its borders and spends much less proportionately on defense than the United States does despite a major commitment to defense in recent years. As the adversaries have melted away, the U.S. allies have also cut back their forces at a more rapid rate than has the United States, contributing to the substantial gap in military capability between the United States and everybody else.

The gap is qualitative as well as quantitative. As was first demonstrated convincingly in the Persian Gulf War, the results of the *revolution in military affairs* (RMA) in adapting technologies like electronics to the battlefield have given the United States (and its close allies) an enormous qualitative advantage militarily. The only other states that have undergone aspects of the RMA are First World allies like France and Great Britain. Third World states (like Iraq in 1991) simply stand no realistic chance when confronted by a military machine such as that which can be fielded by the United States and its North Atlantic Treaty Organization (NATO) allies—at least in traditional warfare.

The result of these military advantages is that the United States has the military reach to match its global interests, and it is the only country that can project military power globally. At the operational level, the United States is the only remaining power with a true global blue water (major oceangoing) Navy, and it is the only country that has global air power projection capabilities. This means not only that the United States has great advantage in projecting its own forces into faraway places, but also that others must rely on American capabilities to get their own forces to distant battlefields or to deployments in the name of peacekeeping or emergency humanitarian relief, for instance.

This position of preeminence is not always or universally appreciated, and it has become commonplace to hear objections to American global leadership on grounds such as American "arrogance" or some similar charge. At the same time, one of history's lessons would seem to be that nature abhors vacuums in all guises, including balances of power. Some argue that American singularity of power will create rivals to fill the vacuum left by the Soviets, and occasionally, there is some mention of the possible formation of rival coalitions (such as Russia and China). These never seem to come to fruition, and American preeminence has remained unchallenged for well over a decade. In fact, following the initiation of the Afghan campaign and American threats to bring down the government of Saddam Hussein unilaterally in the face of international opposition, there was speculation that American military prowess may have gotten too great—to the point the United States no longer needs its allies to accomplish military goals and thus can ignore their advice. Such concerns have been lessened to a degree in light of the quagmire of Iraq, where the American military "juggernaut" has been effectively tied down by a low-level insurgency in that country, and by the apparent lack of progress in Afghanistan. Acceptance of American leadership, in other words, remains controversial, and many other countries hope that the American reaction to Iraq will be to chasten American action in the future.

As the 2000s have moved toward a close, these trends may have begun to become less evident. The American military impasse in Afghanistan and Iraq and increasing charges of arrogant unilateralism hurled against the Bush administration had arguably eroded the American position of political and military preeminence, and many blamed the United States for causing the economic downturn that began in late 2008. Against that backdrop, the Obama administration came to office in January 2009 with a distinctly different view of American security than its predecessor.

The Post-9/11 Era?

As suggested in Chapter 1, there have always been two basic views of American foreign and national security policy that have competed over time. The dominant view since World War II has been liberal internationalism, featuring a high level of commitment to international cooperation, multilateralism, and the reservation of force to situations of last resort. This had been the orientation of most American administrations during the Cold War and represented the worldview of the first post–Cold War presidents, George H. W. Bush and Bill Clinton. The other view has been conservative nationalism, featuring a lesser commitment to international cooperation, a penchant for unilateralism, and a more inclusive view of the utility of force. This was the view of George W. Bush and his neoconservative advisors. Clearly, this paradigm shift was influenced by the fault line of September 11.

Obama represents an intellectual return to the liberal internationalist tradition. Although he has pronounced a dedication to the eradication of terrorism as strong as that of his predecessor, his preferences for achieving those results more clearly mirror those of traditional liberal internationalists than the more radical, unilateralist solutions of the Bush neoconservatives.

Obama rapidly established himself as a foreign and national security activist less encumbered by the traumas of the fault line than was his immediate predecessor. In his initial international foray to Europe in April 2009, he made a point of demonstrating his intention to listen and adapt American policy in light of the advice of friends and allies, a display of internationalism in stark contrast to the unilateralist determination of the Bush administration. Although Obama failed to gain the accession of NATO allies on additional troop commitments to Afghanistan, his response that a dialog on the subject should continue was received as a welcome change from what many NATO allies saw as the somewhat churlish Bush "my way or the highway" response to disagreement and rebuff. Opening negotiations with Cold War adversaries like Cuba was a further sign of change.

Some of the change is less tangible but no less real. Obama's immense international popularity alters significantly the context within which the United States deals with other countries. In the years after 9/11, dislike of the United States grew as the international opinion of President Bush became more negative, and as a result, it became politically difficult for leaders to support American positions regardless of their merits. Popular support of "rock star" Obama, on the other hand, makes support of American policies less of a liability and opposition to Obama-initiated positions the more politically perilous course.

The Obama responses to a changed post-9/11 world reflect some of the changed perceptions of the environment. In the first months of the new administration, change was reflected both in the policy guiding the inherited wars in Afghanistan and Iraq and in the American posture toward future uses of American force. Although both these redirections are discussed in more detail in subsequent chapters, they can be introduced here to illustrate adaptation to the post-9/11 environment.

The change in war policy was more incremental than dramatic. Candidate Obama had promised an end to American military involvement in Iraq, and he sought, sometimes more hesitantly than antiwar activists preferred, to honor that pledge. In addition to announcing the removal of all U.S. combat troops by late 2010, he reiterated in his surprise April 2009 visit to Baghdad the need for the Iraqis more quickly to shoulder the burden of their own security as well as his determination to end the U.S. role. In Afghanistan, he increased the American troop and economic commitment but simultaneously opened regional talks on resolving the conflict, made cooperation with Pakistan a more prominent aspect of policy, defined more clearly the defeat of Al Qaeda as the real U.S. goal, and emphasized that resolution of the Afghan crisis was ultimately a political rather than a military task amidst considerable pressure to change that policy either toward greater or lesser levels of involvement in October 2009.

SECDEF Gates became the point man in efforts to reshape the post-9/11 military. The vehicle, announced initially in April 2009, was fundamental reform of the military procurement process, which the administration asserted was geared to the purchase of large, expensive weapons systems more appropriate to a Cold War environment in which large-scale war with the Soviet Union was the central planning problem than to the smaller-scale asymmetrical wars of the twenty-first century. To this end, the administration created a political firestorm by cancelling a number of "big ticket" military projects that created concerted opposition among defense contractors and communities in which those projects would be built.

CONCLUSION: THE CONTINUING ROLE OF FORCE

There are two broad interpretations of the extent to which the recourse to force has changed in the post–Cold War world. If one begins from an emphasis on the potential applications of force, then change has been dramatic, since the most notable potential use was the ultimate employment of necessity, a military confrontation with the Soviet Union. That contingency has obviously disappeared, and much of the potential use of force in conventional interstate warfare has faded in the general tranquility among those countries with conventional forces, notably the most developed countries. It is still possible to conjure interstate wars on the peripheries (the identification of the "axis of evil" states of Iraq, Iran, and North Korea as possible targets for American military wrath by the Bush administration, for instance), but none of these has the immediacy and importance of the Cold War confrontation. Combating terrorism has replaced large-scale warfare at the pinnacle of national security priorities. This assessment, of course, has major implications for the kinds of forces the United States develops and the missions for which they are prepared.

The other way to look at the problem is how and where force was actually employed in the past and how it is employed in the present or will be in the future. From this vantage point, change is not very dramatic at all. As noted, the United States employed force exclusively in the old Third World during the Cold War, and the current pattern emphasizes deployments in the less developed countries of the world. In both periods, the conflicts were generally internal affairs, civil wars of one kind or another. The difference is in the motivation underlying involvement: during the Cold War, the United States was primarily motivated by ideological, Cold War reasons, whereas now the temptations to intervene are either to relieve human-induced chaos and suffering, in effect to save countries from themselves, or to root out sources of international terrorism.

This distinction regarding motivation for using force is not insignificant for at least three reasons. One is the relative importance attached to potential involvement. In the Cold War context, one could make the argument—admittedly sometimes a stretch—that the United States was impelled to act in the developing world because of the geopolitical implications of the outcome. Should our side lose, it would be yet one more instance of the "victory" of Communism in the global struggle. Thus, intervention could be arguably a matter of necessity. Such geopolitical motivations are generally missing in many contemporary situations, where the goal often is to restore order after some humanitarian disaster, promote democracy, eradicate terrorism, or some combination of those reasons. In any geopolitical sense, these are clearly employments of choice (efforts to combat terrorism are at least a partial exception). The employments of necessity deal with terrorism; the elusive, secretive nature of the terrorist opponents, however, makes specification of where and how engagement might occur difficult.

The nature of involvement in internal wars has changed as well. During the Cold War, conflicts were usually clearly drawn competitions between a government and an insurgent group, each of which fielded an organized armed force and sought militarily to defeat the other. In these circumstances, the purpose of inserting American armed forces was to assist "our" side in defeating the enemy. American forces were sent "to fight and win," in familiar military terms. In the contemporary environment, this is not the case. Often, the situation is one of more-or-less great chaos, where the contending parties are shadowy organizations with inarticulate political goals and are supported by armed bands that are barely military in composition. The purpose for using force in these situations is to suspend the fighting and in effect to impose peace on the area. This is best done by simply intimidating the warring parties with a show of force and then keeping them physically apart. Ideally, the soldiers do no fighting at all because their simple presence accomplishes the goal. Force used in this manner is more difficult to understand than more traditional employment. The first phase of the

Afghan campaign, where American force was used to help topple a regime, represents a return to a more traditional reason for fighting, but it has been superseded by involvement in a murky civil war, where outcomes are uncertain and American stakes arguable. The ongoing battle with terrorism is complicated by the fact that none of these descriptions clearly holds for dealing with terrorists.

This overview suggests that an understanding of the current American national security situation requires looking at the factors that underlay the two fault lines and that form the context within which the current reorientation of policy by the Obama administration is occurring. While the memories of the Cold War are rapidly fading and many, if not most, of the policy makers whose orientation toward national security was formed during the "long peace" are leaving power, it still remains the historical base for much of world politics today. One cannot, for instance, fully understand the dynamics underlying U.S.-Russian relations without knowledge of their Cold War relationship, and the ongoing security threat posed by North Korea makes sense only as an extension of the Cold War.

The post–Cold War era of the 1990s also unleashed forces that remain important contributions to the current political map. The 1990s were, for many purposes, a tranquil interlude between the traumas of the fault line events, and they produced dynamics like globalization, drawing the world together and engendering a spirit of cooperation that produced substantial international agreements—on war crimes and global warming, for instance—that are still part of the national security environment. In addition, the dynamics of the 1990s may provide the model for how the post-9/11 United States comes to orient itself toward the world and are interesting for that reason.

The fault line of 9/11 is currently the most vivid "marker" affecting American attitudes toward the world, with the GWOT as the conceptual banner of U.S. policy after the terrorist trauma. The events of 9/11 are now almost a decade in the past, and the degree to which those events have been absorbed and adapted to is now a prominent part of the current legacy. Each of these influences on the current state of affairs is discussed in the three chapters that follow (Chapters 7–9), and their impact on current military problems is the subject of Chapter 10.

STUDY/DISCUSSION QUESTIONS

1. Describe the first fault line (the end of the Cold War) and the impact it had on the structure of the international system and the problems affecting American security policy. What were the major benefits and debatable impacts of that change?
2. Describe the second fault line (September 11) and the impact it had on the structure of the international system and the problems affecting American security policy. What does it mean to describe Iraq as an "aftershock" of this fault line?
3. Geopolitics and globalization have been described in the text as the yin and yang of the contemporary international system. What does that mean? Discuss.
4. What is the United States' role in the contemporary international system? What does it mean that the United States is the only remaining superpower?
5. Is the international system moving toward a post-9/11 phase, where the fight against terrorism is a less central, compelling characteristic? If so, how? If not, why not?

Selected Bibliography

Allison, Graham T., and Robert Blackwill. "America's Stake in the Soviet Future." *Foreign Affairs* 70, no. 3 (Summer 1991): 77–97.

Campbell, Kenneth J. *A Tale of Two Quagmires: Iraq, Vietnam, and the Hard Lessons of War.* New York: Paradigm, 2007.

Campbell, Kurt M., and Derek Chollet. "The New Tribalism: Cliques and the Making of U.S. Foreign Policy." *Washington Quarterly* 30, no. 1 (Winter 2006–2007): 193–203.

Ferguson, Niall. "The Axis of Upheaval." *Foreign Policy*, March/April 2009, 56–60.

Friedman, Thomas L. *The Lexus and the Olive Tree: Understanding Globalization.* New York: Farrar, Straus, Giroux, 1999.

Fukuyama, Francis. *The End of History and the Last Man.* New York: Free Press, 1992.

Fulbright, J. William. *The Arrogance of Power.* New York: Random House, 1966.

Gaddis, John Lewis. "Setting Right in a Dangerous World." *Chronicle of Higher Education: The Chronicle Review* 48, no. 18 (January 11, 2002): B7–B10.

Gates, Robert M. "A Balanced Strategy." *Foreign Affairs* 88, no. 1 (January/February 2009): 28–40.

Haass, Richard N. "The Age of Nonpolarity." *Foreign Affairs* 87, no. 3 (May/June 2008): 44–56.

Kagan, Robert. "The September 12 Paradigm." *Foreign Affairs* 87, no. 5 (September/October 2008): 25–38.

Keohane, Robert O., and Joseph S. Nye, Jr. *Power and Interdependence,* 2nd ed. Glenview, IL: Scott Foresman/Little Brown, 1989.

Mearsheimer, John J. "Why We Shall Soon Miss the Cold War." *Atlantic Monthly* 266, no. 2 (August 1990): 35–50.

Nye, Joseph S., Jr. *Bound to Lead: The Changing Nature of American Power.* New York: Basic Books, 1990.

———. *The Paradox of American Power: Why the World's Superpower Can't Go It Alone.* New York: Oxford University Press, 2003.

Peters, Ralph. *New Glory: Expanding America's Global Supremacy.* New York: Sentinel, 2005.

Shevtsova, Lilia. "Russia's Ersatz Democracy." *Current History* 105, no. 693 (October 2006): 307–314.

Singer, Max, and the Estate of the Late Aaron Wildavsky. *The Real World Order: Zones of Peace, Zones of Turmoil.* Rev. ed. Chatham, NJ: Chatham House, 1996.

Slaughter, Anne-Marie. "America's Edge." *Foreign Affairs* 88, no. 1 (January/February 2009): 94–118.

Snow, Donald M. *When America Fights: The Uses of U.S. Military Force.* Washington, DC: CQ Press, 2000.

Snow, Donald M., and Eugene Brown. *International Relations: The Changing Contours of Power.* New York: Longman, 2000.

Zakaria, Fareed. "The Future of American Power." *Foreign Affairs* 87, no. 3 (May/June 2008): 18–42.

CHAPTER 7

The Nature and End of the Cold War

PREVIEW

Although the Cold War has been over for nearly two decades, the international and domestic structures and attitudes it produced continue to have an impact on the contemporary world. A distinctly American form of geopolitics was one product of the forty-year confrontation, many of the national security leaders who have shaped policy had their intellectual grounding during the Cold War, and the American military structure still reflects preparation to fight World War III against a Soviet-style opponent. The Cold War is still a dominating influence on the American experience as the country faces a changed environment. Understanding how the Cold War occurred and evolved—especially in a military but also in a political sense—and what residues remain is therefore crucial to understanding how the United States is predisposed to respond to the future.

The contemporary international environment can fully be understood only in the context of the Cold War international system from which it evolved and which helped form the contemporary world. These impacts of the Cold War on the present and future include the enormous influence the Cold War had on reforming the American attitude toward the world and the United States' role in it; the influence the Cold War had on the worldview of the generations who presided over it, including many in the present leadership; and the traumatic effect of the Cold War collapse on the international system and American attitudes toward it.

The Cold War was a national baptism for the United States into the world arena. In the country's formative period, the United States had not been a consistent major player in international relations for reasons already discussed: the accident of geography, disdain for a corrupt international system, and a general preference to be left alone to realize American manifest destiny. These factors combined to keep the United States on the periphery of a European-centered international system for most of its first century and a half. That system, in turn, had little need most of the time for American involvement in its affairs except during systemic traumas like the world wars.

The end of World War II left a return to isolation from the world impossible and thrust a reluctant, inexperienced United States onto the center stage of world events. When the last guns of the war were stilled, only two states, the United States and the Soviet Union, retained enough power to influence international events and to reorganize an international system laid prostrate by the war. The implications of this bipolar balance of power—and especially its adversarial content—were not clear immediately but took shape in the five-year period climaxed by the Korean conflict. As a result, the United States was propelled into the *realpolitik* of international relations for the first time.

The changed nature of the international system was especially dramatic. Through most of American history, the system's configuration was *multipolar*, a condition in which there were several countries of importance in the system that competed for positions of power but in which no single state predominated (although Germany arguably came close twice in the twentieth century). In this system, the United States gradually rose from being a weak, peripheral power to a more central role.

The post–World War II world was different. Except for the United States and the Soviet Union, all the traditional powers were so weakened by the war effort that they were unable or unwilling to remain major powers. In this situation, the system became *bipolar*, with the United States and the Soviet Union as the major powers (or poles) around which other states more or less willingly congregated, and eventually these resulting blocs of states became competitive. With the end of the Cold War, the Soviet pole disappeared, and the system has been undergoing a process of reconfiguration ever since.

Understanding and managing the Cold War became the central task for the next generations of American policy makers, strategists, and scholars who had to manage and explain change as the world slid toward the Cold War between 1945 and 1950 and then had to adapt to the Cold War system for another forty years. Lurking constantly over their shoulders was the shadow cast by the possibility the Cold War could go very hot in a totally ruinous nuclear war.

The major organizing construct they built and managed was, of course, the realist paradigm discussed in Chapter 2. It was a harsh, confrontational relationship for most of its existence, and it became a very *conservative* construct in the pure sense of that term: it sought to conserve the system below the level of general war, which both sides quite rightly feared. In the end, that construct and the fear it produced helped contribute to the end of the Cold War. But while the Cold War lasted, it provided a virtually uncontested worldview, and those who challenged it were dismissed as dreamers and visionaries whose suggestions were too risky or foolhardy to be considered seriously.

It is important to emphasize the pervasive nature of the Cold War because it affects the way many people continue to look at the world. The military people who have flag rank (generals or admirals) in the services today were by and large educated in the late 1970s and early 1980s and had their first personal experiences in the world in the 1970s and 1980s, and the same is true of the many civilians in the foreign and national security community. Many have, with varying degrees of success, sought to shed some of the inapplicable aspects of the Cold War mentality, but they remain at least partly Cold Warriors nonetheless. The equation of the U.S. response to terrorism with a war between good and evil, for instance, has antecedents in the Cold War against "godless Communism." President Bush's "axis of evil" and President Reagan's "evil empire" come from the same intellectual cloth. While many observers consider Barack Obama the first post–Cold War president, he was 27 years old when the Berlin Wall fell and thus had most of his formal education within the Cold War framework.

The way the Cold War ended influences the present as well. It was neither a planned nor an anticipated event. With the considerable benefit of hindsight, there was a whole series of signs of the impending doom of the Soviet Union that were nowhere nearly as obvious at the time as they are in retrospect.

The Cold War and its demise are history, but it is important history that is relevant to understanding the present. As a result, this chapter is devoted to the Cold War. It begins by looking briefly at the essence of the Cold War relationship as a distinct international system. The text then turns to the military competition that was at the center of U.S.-Soviet conflict. That military confrontation, in the end, helped contribute to the end of the Cold War. Finally, some residues of the Cold War remain part of the current reality. For instance, as the United States aligns itself with former Soviet states in the name of fighting terrorism, some of these holdovers influence the content of policy and its effects on the future, and Russia strains to reassert its preeminence in the global community.

THE COLD WAR SYSTEM

At the end of World War II, the international system was confronted with two fundamental questions, the consequences of which would evolve and dominate international relations for most of the rest of the twentieth century. One question centered on nuclear weapons. The use of atomic bombs against Hiroshima and Nagasaki, Japan, by the United States helped to break Japan's will to continue the war and meant these novel and enormously deadly weapons would be part of the calculation of future military affairs. Hence, a fundamental question facing planners was what difference these weapons would make in the future.

The other question was about the wartime collaboration between the United States and the Soviet Union. Would friendship continue in the postwar world, or would the deep ideological differences between them result in a future of conflict and confrontation? In retrospect, the answer seems stunningly obvious, and most observers at the time suspected that the collaboration could not be sustained. But if continued cooperation could be maintained, the result could be a much more tranquil international environment, and at the time, this hopeful possibility could not be dismissed out of hand.

Planning for dealing with these postwar contingencies had gone on throughout the war in the United States and especially in collaboration between the Americans and the British. Unlike the end of the Cold War, which caught everyone off guard, there was ample time to think about and plan for the postwar world. Uncertainty about what kind of relationship would exist among what became the superpowers of the Cold War system dominated the policy process. In the face of this uncertainty, the planners devised a structure to accommodate either outcome—collaboration or confrontation.

The principal instrument for organizing the postwar world was the United Nations Charter. The primary purpose of the organization was to create a viable mechanism to organize the peace that would avoid a repetition of the slide to World War II. Critical to crafting a viable, working system was whether the major powers, the United States and the Soviet Union, could agree upon a form of the peace they were willing to enforce.

Since the two powers had very opposing worldviews, the task of finding a mutually acceptable peace to defend was not going to be easy. Clearly, the United States preferred a world of western-style political democracies and capitalist-based economies like its own, and the Soviets equally fervently wanted to promote the expansion of Communism in the world. Both sides were evangelical, and the secular "religions" they promoted were incompatible. Thus, the prospects of peace and cooperation were prejudiced from the beginning.

What the U.N. Charter drafters sought to do was create a mechanism that would allow enforcement of the peace if the major powers could cooperate on a common vision but that would be disengaged if they could not. Cooperation would be accomplished institutionally through the U.N. Security Council, which the Charter empowers (through Chapters VI and VII) to take effective actions to squelch threats to or breaches of the peace. Each of the permanent members of the Council (the major victorious allies in the war—the United States, the Soviet Union, Great Britain, France, and China) was given a veto over any action, thereby providing the disabling mechanism when the major powers disagreed in any given situation. In the event that disagreement became pervasive, the Charter, through Article 51, allowed the members the right to engage in "individual and collective self-defense," providing the basis for the opposing military alliances that eventually came to institutionalize the Cold War confrontation.

Collaboration was not sustainable, of course, because the two sides could not agree on the world they preferred. Thus, the mechanisms for organizing the peace through cooperation remained disabled and disengaged for the duration of the Cold War. The United Nations was able to act on Korea in 1950 because the Soviets were boycotting the organization in protest of the American-led refusal to seat the new Communist government of China rather than the Nationalist government of Chiang kai-Shek in Taiwan and thus did not veto the action. After Korea, the mechanisms for enforcing the peace in essence went into a veto-induced hibernation for forty years. After the Cold War, a Russia that was no longer Communist had no ideological grounds to veto U.N. potential actions, and the world body returned to life as promoter of the peace.

By 1950, both wartime questions had been answered. The North Korean invasion of that year removed any lingering doubt that confrontation rather than collaboration would be the central feature of the Soviet-American relationship. After the Soviets exploded their first atomic bomb in 1949, the question of the role of nuclear weapons was added to the calculus of what became the Cold War international system. This system had at least three prominent characteristics that are worth considering. It also had within it the sources of future change.

Characteristics

First, the Cold War *political and military competition dominated international politics*. While only the United States and the Soviet Union emerged from World War II with enough residual power to organize and influence international events, their power bases differed. The bases of American power were economic and military. The American industrial system was strengthened by the war and towered above those of everyone else (for a period in the 1940s, the American economy accounted for nearly 40 percent of world productivity, as opposed to less than half that today). Military power was guaranteed through the sole possession of nuclear weapons. The much weaker Soviet economy had been virtually destroyed by the war, but the Soviets kept a force of close to 12 million under arms (the United States was demobilizing to around 1 million in 1946).

This distribution of power defined the international system as *bipolar* in nature: the United States and the Soviet Union stood as the two remaining powers (or poles) around which other states congregated and could be controlled or influenced. The American lever of power was economic; everyone in the West needed American money and goods for recovery. The Red Army occupation in Eastern Europe was able to impose friendly regimes in the occupied countries that became reluctant parts of the Soviet orbit, but the Soviet Union could not then and was truly never able to compete economically.

The Cold War's pervasive nature took root first in a Europe divided by what British statesman Winston Churchill first called the Iron Curtain in a speech in Fulton, Missouri, in 1947. The relationship became formally militarized through the formation of the North Atlantic Treaty Organization (NATO) in 1949 and later its Communist counterpart, the Warsaw Treaty Organization (WTO or the Warsaw Pact), in 1955. The ideological struggle spread to the developing world as countries emerged from colonial rule, principally in Asia and Africa, during the 1950s and 1960s.

Nothing symbolized the fervor of the Cold War more dramatically than the superpower nuclear competition. At one level, the competition was incongruous, as both sides built arsenals for potential use against one another so large and excessive that a war between them would almost certainly destroy both. It became popular to depict the relationship as two scorpions in a bottle: each scorpion was ready to kill the other and itself in a conflict both feared the other might be tempted to initiate if they showed weakness or vulnerability. Each came gradually to dread the prospect of that conflict enough that nuclear weapons contributed to defusing the Cold War. The ultimate lunacy of the relationship, however, did not prevent either side from spending lavishly to ensure that the other did not gain what was sometimes described as an "exploitable advantage" in some measure of the weaponry.

Second, the conflict was viewed as *protracted*, a long-term competition for which only great patience would suffice and the management of which required great vigilance. The Cold War was a battle between two diametrically opposed systems of political belief that was enduring and that had an uncertain outcome. There was very little consideration of a peaceful end of the relationship. It was broadly assumed that the only means by which closure could come was through a massive military clash, World War III, that would likely become nuclear and could destroy both sides.

The protracted nature of the competition became both a prediction of the future and a prime value, given its extremely destructive alternative. There was always something curious in this assessment, however. It was a matter of firm belief in the West that the Communist philosophy was inherently inferior to its capitalist economic and democratic political ideals. Somehow this belief was hardly ever translated into the idea that Communism might collapse on its own as those flaws became manifest (which, of course, is exactly what happened). Instead, the operating assumption was that the Cold War was both immutable and fatalistically preferable to its believed alternative, hot war. One particularly fatalistic expression is captured in Amplification 7.1.

The perceived basis of Communist strength was the totalitarian nature of Soviet rule. Soviet Communism, the argument went, could not fail because its coercive strength was so great that any opposition would be crushed mercilessly. Thus, even if the regime lacked broad popular support, as it did, its power could not be challenged effectively.

Amplification 7.1

BETTER DEAD THAN RED?
BETTER RED THAN DEAD?

The 1950s was the decade when the Cold War was at its most intense and assessment of the future was most pessimistic. The Korean War, which had become intensely unpopular after it stalemated in 1951 but dragged on until 1953, was a recent memory of apparent failure. The liberation of North Korea had not been accomplished, and the Communist Viet Minh of Ho Chi Minh had prevailed in French Indochina, another victory for expanding Communism. When the Soviet Union beat the United States into space by launching *Sputnik* into the heavens first and Americans peered into the nighttime sky and saw it blink by overhead, there seemed reason to be suspicious of who was prevailing in the competition. Nuclear war drills in schools and public buildings only added to the growing hysteria. The flaws of operational Communism had not become obvious to anyone.

In this atmosphere, a kind of despair emerged about how the Cold War might end. One possibility was that the Soviet Union might actually prevail, in which case the debate was whether it would be preferable to accept Soviet domination or to go down fighting in a cataclysmic nuclear war: better Red than dead? The second possibility was that war between the two systems was inevitable. It was not a question of whether there would be war but *when*. The debate was turned around to ask if perishing in such a conflict was preferable to Communist overlordship: better dead than Red? In that atmosphere, hardly anyone could imagine the outcome that eventually prevailed: *neither dead nor Red*.

In retrospect, this was also a curious proposition. In the western tradition, democratic theory argues that the basis of political stability is popular support for the government, or legitimacy. Legitimacy is the source of strength in democracies. Arguments about the endurance of Communism implicitly maintained that legitimacy simply did not apply if a regime had enough guns and other forms of coercion to control the population. Coercion effectively trumped legitimacy. What this line of reasoning failed to consider was that the reason Communist governments needed to be totalitarian was because they were illegitimate. The monopoly on power was really an indirect indication of the weakness, not the strength, of regimes. When populations throughout the Communist world shucked the system with no remorse or regret starting in 1989, it demonstrated that coercion only artificially and temporarily substitutes for legitimacy.

These intellectual blinders meant that there was much less consideration about ending the Cold War than if participants had begun with the proposition that the competition was intellectually tilted in favor of the democracies. Over the years, a few observers had seen this, but their prophecies were largely ignored. George F. Kennan, the American diplomat who was the intellectual father of the American foreign policy of containment, argued that a policy of diligence could contain Communism within the boundaries it had achieved. If containment was applied consistently, the inherent inferiority of the Communist system would eventually cause it to implode. He was, of course, proven correct.

A third characteristic of the Cold War system was that it became *global*. Originally, it was geographically limited to the boundary between Western and Eastern Europe and, after 1949, the area surrounding China. As independence movements produced new states in Asia and Africa during the 1950s, 1960s, and early 1970s (decolonization was effectively over in 1975 when Portugal granted independence to the last members of its empire), both sides scrambled to gain favor, even allegiance, from newly installed governments in new states.

Because the new countries gained their independence from European states and most adopted nominally democratic systems based upon the colonialist form of government, the West initially was thought to have the advantage in this competition. Most of these new states, however, were desperately poor and in need of developmental assistance that was generally not available in adequate supply. Their new governments often proved to be inept or corrupt (or both), leading to a spiral of instability and violence. Those circumstances presented the Soviets with an opportunity to attempt to spread their influence by arguing they advocated a superior alternative to the West.

This global spread of the competition universalized the Cold War, meaning Cold War concerns permeated even the most remote parts of the globe. The American policy of containment was extended all along the Sino-Soviet periphery (over the objections of Kennan) and was manifested in a whole series of bilateral and multilateral collective defense arrangements (alliances) that globalized U.S. commitments and both justified and demanded robust forces capable of global projection. While the competition generally remained below the level of direct military confrontation, American- and Soviet-supported forces did fight in areas where American interests consisted mainly of denying Soviet interests, and vice versa.

The nature and tenor of the Cold War competition changed over time. The presumption of an intractable, encompassing, negative relationship in the 1950s softened with experience to the point that, at the time the Cold War ended, Soviet political leader Gorbachev was one of the most popular politicians in the West and adorned the cover of *Time* magazine as its Man of the Year.

Sources of Change

The Cold War dynamics changed in two ways. The first was the result of events in the 1950s but was not widely recognized at the time—the two superpowers began to lose some control over their individual blocs. The early postwar system had been known as one of *tight* bipolarity, meaning the major powers could control events within their blocs fairly closely. The system evolved, however, to one of *loose* bipolarity, wherein the ability to order events slipped for both.

Two events in 1956 started the change from tight to loose bipolarity. First, Great Britain joined France and Israel in an attack on Egypt, the purpose of which was to occupy the Suez Canal Zone (which Egyptian President Gamal Abdul Nasser had nationalized the previous year). The action was taken without prior consultation with the U.S. government (which almost certainly would have opposed it). When the United States subsequently joined the Soviet Union in sponsoring a Security Council resolution condemning the invasion, the French concluded the United States could no longer be trusted and began the process of moving away from the United States to a more independent position in international affairs. The American ability to control its bloc suffered a major setback.

The second change event was the brutal suppression of the Hungarian Rebellion by Soviet forces later in that same year. Initially seen as proof of Soviet ruthless control over its bloc, there was a longer-term and quite opposite lesson and effect. The United States took the lead in an anti-Soviet publicity campaign that included widely disseminating pictures throughout the developing world of Soviet tanks rumbling through Budapest. The Soviets suffered an enormous propaganda black eye because they had portrayed themselves as the peace-loving champions of freedom and self-determination, and they were clearly lying. The result was that the Soviets—and their client states—realized they needed to avoid another similar embarrassment. East European countries learned that as long as they did not threaten Soviet security, they could act more independently than before, a sign of decay in the Soviet control of its bloc.

The second great change was in the nature of the competition, and the symbolic event was the Cuban Missile Crisis of 1962. In that confrontation over the Soviet attempt to deploy nuclear-tipped missiles aimed at the United States on Cuba, there was a military standoff that almost all observers believed was the closest the two sides had come to nuclear war. That realization convinced both powers that their prior assessment—that they had nothing in common—was at least partly wrong. At a minimum, both sides realized a joint interest in avoiding destroying one another and possibly the world.

The Cuban crisis was the watershed in the confrontational nature of the Cold War. Prior to the crisis, the relationship was regularly marked by direct confrontations with at least some potential to spiral out of control—the Berlin blockade, Korea, and the Berlin Wall incident, to mention three. These crises shared a potential to escalate to direct confrontation. After the Cuban missile crisis, that dynamic changed, and direct Cold War confrontations with obvious escalatory potential essentially disappeared.

The Cuban watershed changed the nature of the relationship in two ways, both of which reduced the likelihood the superpowers would once again meet at the precipice of nuclear war. First, they began a process of nuclear arms control, whereby the two sides signed a whole series of treaties aimed first at limiting where nuclear testing could occur and later at limiting the size and characteristics of the arsenals they aimed at one another (a process that has continued to the present). This process became a prominent forum for Soviet-American dialog for the rest of the Cold War. Second, the shared realization of an interest in avoiding mutual incineration provided the compelling rationale for the beginning of a gradually broadening discussion that eroded the confrontational basis of the relationship. After the missile crisis, direct confrontations with escalatory possibilities simply vanished from the international scene, although some argue that the Yom Kippur crisis of 1973 is an exception to that dynamic.

From a twenty-first-century perspective, much of this flavor of the Cold War may seem odd, even anachronistic and unreal. It was, however, very serious business to those who made and implemented policy, many of whom, to repeat, are still active in national security policy today. Nowhere is the furtiveness of the competition more evident than in the way the two sides prepared themselves for potential armed conflict.

FORMS OF MILITARY COMPETITION

The Cold War was both a military and a political competition, with primary emphasis centering on one aspect or another across time and in different places. Originally, it was both. The communization of the occupied Eastern European countries was accomplished almost exclusively by the Red Army rather than the political interplay of Communist and non-Communist elements. At the same time, Communist parties competed politically in several Western European countries and even enjoyed some electoral success in France and Italy. By the end of the 1940s, however, the totalitarian nature of Communist regimes had been clearly demonstrated in countries like Czechoslovakia (where a democratically elected government was overthrown by the Soviets and their Czech surrogates). From 1950 until 1991, the Cold War in Europe was almost exclusively a military competition between NATO and the Warsaw Pact (after the latter became operational in 1956).

The political dimension of the Cold War was limited to the peripheries—Africa, Asia, and to a lesser extent, Latin America. The process of decolonization and the subsequent emergence of inexperienced postindependence governments created considerable political ferment into which both sides plunged, hoping either to gain influence or, more modestly, to deny influence to the other side. One of the means of currying favor was providing military aid to various governments (or factions within countries). Occasionally, involvement would devolve into military intervention, as it did for the United States in 1965 in the Dominican Republic and Vietnam and for the Soviets in Afghanistan a decade and a half later. Nonetheless, the competition in the developing world had both a political and a military dimension.

The heart of the Cold War, however, was played out in Europe along the Central Front in Germany, the presumed focus of a Soviet invasion of Western Europe. That possibility formed the worst-case scenario against which NATO planners prepared. The rarely questioned presumption within NATO was that the Soviet Union had serious designs on controlling Western Europe and might unleash the vast Red Army into NATO territory unless NATO demonstrated sufficient military strength and resolve to convince them of the futility of such an attack.

How serious a threat the Soviets indeed posed to Western Europe is not the point here. Certainly, the Soviets maintained military forces far in excess of those needed for a purely defensive stance in Europe (as did NATO), and there was ample ideological antagonism between the two sides to place the worst possible interpretations on the intentions of the adversaries. Thus, it was not at all difficult for NATO members to project a real and lively threat against which vigilant defensive preparation was the only prudent recourse. The underlying point is thus that planners *believed* in the existence of the military threat and acted militarily on those beliefs.

The perceived nature of the military threat was colored by the time and place in which it occurred. The fact that the competition emerged in Europe on the heels of history's largest conventional war affected the shape and purposes of military forces to this day, when the military situation is quite different. Militarily, the Cold War began as an extension of the global conflict featuring conventional armed forces preparing to fight symmetrically. The military dimension of the Cold War mirrored this inherited reality in terms of both how it would be fought and with what kinds of forces. Even though the weapons became more sophisticated and deadly across time and would have produced a much bloodier result, a war in Europe where the United States and the Soviet Union were the principal adversaries would have been very much like World War II. Since the military and political leaders on both sides were mostly veterans of World War II, this was not an unsurprising projection and basis for preparation for them. Hidden within the assumptions about preparing for World War III was the notion that the forces and doctrines would also be effective against smaller, unconventional (asymmetrical) foes. That assumption has proven dubious.

The wild card, of course, was nuclear weapons. The Cold War provided the first occasion when a war could be fought by two opponents both armed with these remarkably destructive weapons. Whether a war in Europe could be fought without releasing the nuclear genie was a hotly debated issue in military, political, and academic circles around which no real consensus ever emerged. A second lively question was whether their employment could be restricted to the immediate theater of operations (a possibility about which the Europeans who would experience a nuclear defense understandably had little enthusiasm) or whether their use would somehow inexorably spread beyond the battlefield to society at large. Whether conventional war in Europe would escalate into a general nuclear exchange engulfing the homelands of the superpowers was the ultimate concern for American, and presumably Soviet, planners.

These concerns have not entirely disappeared. The nuclear balance remains intact, if at reduced levels, even if Russia and the United States lack the realistic motivation to attack one another. American conventional armed forces are still largely structured basically the same way they were during the Cold War. Despite the efforts of a host of reformers, of whom Secretary of Defense (SECDEF) Robert Gates is the most recent example, to try to reshape that force, such efforts continue to be resisted by military and civilian leaderships at least implicitly clinging to Cold War perceptions of military reality. Understanding those forces and why they are constructed the way they are is a necessary preface to dealing with contemporary forces for contemporary problems.

Conventional Forces

The heart of the Cold War was a confrontation between conventional (nonnuclear) forces facing one another across the no-man's-land that comprised the Iron Curtain, and most especially the so-called inter-German border that divided East and West Germany and was widely expected to be the initial battleground in a NATO–Warsaw Pact war. For NATO planning purposes, a heavily armored Soviet breakout at the Fulda Gap in Germany seemed the most likely way that war would begin.

World War II and the military predilections of the leaders of the two coalitions heavily colored the way they conceptualized the problem. Everyone envisioned that the battlefield would be somewhere on the northern European plain, relatively flat terrain that gave the advantage to mobile yet heavily armed forces, such as the tank armies that leaders like General George S. Patton had popularized in World War II.

Both the Americans and the Soviets embraced this style of warfare in which huge forces slugged it out in an orgy of incredible violence until one side collapsed. For the Americans, this had historically meant committing the superior American productive system to building so much sophisticated equipment that the enemy eventually was beaten down by the sheer weight of arms. The Soviet experience on the Eastern Front had taught them that overwhelming numbers of troops could eventually carry the day, if at terrible human costs. The prospect of these two behemoths colliding on the battlefield created a nightmare scenario of unprecedented carnage and destruction that, among other things, would leave the European landscape on which it was fought largely devastated.

The way the war would likely be fought affected the politics of war preparation. The focus of NATO preparation was to provide a sufficiently daunting prospect to the Soviets that they would be deterred from starting a war. But politics got in the way. Since the Soviets always had a quantitatively much larger force than NATO and would have the advantage of choosing when and where to attack, how was NATO to provide such an inhibiting presence? The domestic politics of the NATO democracies made it politically suicidal to suggest conscripting a force that could match the Soviets soldier for soldier. Moreover, the longer that war was avoided, the less support there was for the need for the sacrifice of military service.

The major concern was with what NATO fought, and this concern was colored by perceptions of the conventional military balance that heavily favored the Communists. In 1985, for instance, the Red Army was nearly two-and-a-half times the size of its American counterpart and had four times the number of tanks and armored vehicles and half again the number of combat aircraft. The United States had the advantage in helicopters and naval vessels, but their direct applicability to the central front in Germany was questionable. Numbers favored the Soviets.

Regardless of how the relative quality of the two forces was rated, these comparisons left the very real prospect that a Soviet-led assault in Germany might succeed *if the war remained strictly conventional*. What the NATO allies needed was so-called force multipliers, ways in which to enhance the comparative capability of those NATO forces (multiply their effectiveness). The most obvious candidates for this enhancement were battlefield and theater nuclear weapons, and analysts wondered out loud whether it would be better to accept conventional defeat on the battlefield or to escalate to nuclear exchange, with all the uncertainties that such a change would create for possible escalation to a general homeland exchange between the two superpowers, raising grim prospects such as those raised in Amplification 7.1.

How did the United States respond to these challenges? The question is germane because the blueprint for defending Europe is still largely in place as the rationale for current forces (despite efforts at change) and was the basis for the plan that defeated Saddam Hussein in 1991.

These strategies were never implemented in Europe, of course, but they did produce a distinctive force structure and a mindset for fighting that continue to this day. To many military planners, the plans were vindicated in the Persian Gulf War, where the basic blueprint for engaging and defeating the Iraqis was the highly mobile air-land battle concept designed for Europe, made easier to implement because there were no natural or man-made obstacles to rapid mobility in the Kuwaiti desert. That very success reinforced the continuing adherence in the Army to a heavily armored concept and in the Navy to forces based on aircraft carriers (which carried out a large part of the air mission in Desert Storm), despite arguments that both tanks and carriers are vulnerable and obsolete in an era dominated by missiles. Overwhelming force, a core element of the strategy, appeared to work in 2003 in Iraq, but unaccompanied by conventional mass (large members of forces), it proved inadequate for the ensuing occupation.

Nuclear Forces

Nuclear weapons were the second legacy of World War II. A number of countries were studying nuclear physics on the eve of the war, and Albert Einstein convinced President Franklin D. Roosevelt of the need to engage in research on the weapons potential of nuclear power to hedge against the success of the German research program (which never reached fruition in large part because a number of the critical German scientists were Jewish and fled the country). The American Manhattan Project succeeded in producing a bomb in early 1945, and the United States emerged from the war as the only nuclear power.

The U.S. nuclear monopoly did not last long. The Soviet Union exploded its first atomic (fission) device in 1949, and both countries successfully developed far deadlier nuclear explosives in the early 1950s. These thermonuclear (fission–fusion) devices replicate the energy production methods of the sun and produce explosions measurable in the equivalents of *millions of tons (megatons) of TNT*; by contrast, the atomic bombs of the 1940s produced explosions the equivalent of thousands of tons, or kilotons, of TNT. For some real-world comparison, the explosion of Mount St. Helens in Oregon in the 1980s was estimated at 40 megatons.

Parallel research was going on in the area of delivering nuclear and other weapons to their targets. Advances in rocketry produced the first successful Soviet intercontinental ballistic missile (ICBM) in 1957, a feat rapidly duplicated by the United States. Combined with similar work on shorter range missiles, both sides had missile-borne nuclear bombs aimed at one another by the time of the Cuban crisis, and the weapons could be delivered against their targets with no reasonable expectation they could be intercepted or neutralized. During the 1960s and 1970s, the arsenals grew enormously on both sides, with strategic inventories (those aimed at one another's homelands) numbering over ten thousand apiece and shorter range missiles dedicated to the support of military forces in the European or other theaters numbering in the tens of thousands. Nuclear weapons thus served two distinct functions. The more dramatic and better publicized function was that assigned to the strategic nuclear forces (SNF), developed for potential use against the adversary's territory. The other was to support conventional operations.

As the arsenal sizes grew and became impossible to defend against, the thrust in nuclear weapons thinking and planning shifted to *deterrence*, the development and maintenance of weaponry to convince the opponent not to use its weapons against you. Since neither side could defend itself against an attack that was launched against it by nuclear-tipped missiles, the threat had to be based in retaliation and punishment of a nuclear transgressor. The idea was that a potential aggressor would realize that the victim of the attack would retain such a large surviving force as to be able to launch a devastating retaliatory strike, making the initial attack in effect suicidal. One concept used to describe this dynamic and the strategy to implement it in the 1960s was *assured destruction*, to which a detractor added the prefix *mutual*, thereby creating an acronym reflecting his assessment of the idea: MAD.

It required the mindset of the Cold War for this nuclear balance to make sense, especially as the arsenals grew to the point that an all-out attack by either side (or especially both sides) could effectively immolate the enemy several times over—"make the rubble bounce," in Winston Churchill's phrase. Both sides continued aggressively to research and deploy yet more deadly weapons out of the fear that failing to do so would create some advantage the other might feel it could exploit in a nuclear attack. Lamenting this aspect of the nuclear arms race, President Jimmy Carter's SECDEF Harold Brown summarized it: "We build, they build; we stop, they build." That the result was a policy and effective strategy of genocide and countergenocide (the effect if the arsenals were used) mostly bothered the nuclear disarmers.

The other role for nuclear weapons was in support of conventional operations, primarily in Europe. The purpose of these "battlefield" or "theater" nuclear weapons (TNWs) was as a force multiplier. In American planning, for instance, a major mission for TNWs was to help blunt the massive Soviet tank offensive that was presumed to be the opening foray of World War III. When masses of Soviet tanks approached the border, they would be attacked with nuclear warheads, thereby breaking up the assault. A special form of nuclear explosive, the enhanced radiation warhead, or neutron bomb, was to be applied specifically to this purpose (see Amplification 7.2).

Amplification 7.2

THE CAPITALIST BOMB

A major objection to the contemplated use of nuclear weapons in Europe was the enormous devastation their use would create for the very territory they were designed to defend. Europe—and especially Germany, where the bulk of the initial fighting would take place—would be a scarred and cratered radioactive moonscape unlikely to sustain life for many years to come. On the other hand, nuclear weapons seemed militarily an effective way to destroy the concentrated armored tank assault that would spearhead the Soviet attack and against which there were inadequate alternatives.

These two diametrically opposed priorities were partially reconciled by a new form of nuclear explosive first tested in the early 1970s and proposed for deployment by the Carter administration during the latter 1970s. The new technology was something called the enhanced radiation warhead (ERW), which quickly earned the popular name the neutron bomb. Its innovation was to rearrange the relative effects of nuclear explosives. Any nuclear explosive produces four effects: a fireball of heat, extremely high winds known as blast overpressure, initial or prompt (beta and gamma ray) radiation, and residual radiation, also known as fallout. The chief culprits in a conventional nuclear explosion were blast overpressure, which knocks down structures and craters the landscape; the fireball, which causes fires; and fallout, which lingers in the physical environment for years to come. The fourth effect, prompt radiation, sends out deadly rays during the explosion itself, but once the explosion ends, it becomes comparatively benign.

The neutron bomb rearranged nuclear effects so that 75 to 80 percent of the nuclear explosion involved the release of prompt radiation. This had two advantages, given the problem it sought to overcome. First, the other effects of the weapon were reduced greatly, thereby doing less environmental damage—the concern of the local citizenry. Second, it seemed ideal against the Soviet tank threat. If the weapons were detonated over advancing Soviet tank columns, the deadly gamma and beta rays would penetrate Soviet armor and incapacitate and eventually kill the crews without destroying the tanks. The attacks would thus be halted, and one grisly plan was to have NATO troops remove the bodies and turn the tanks on the aggressors with NATO crews.

The Soviets howled at the proposal. They labeled it "the capitalist bomb," a weapon that killed people in a grotesquely cruel manner but did not destroy the productive system it sought to protect. They threatened to produce their own neutron bombs, and the Europeans could never quite bring themselves to support any nuclear defense of Europe. Deployment was delayed, and eventually the plan to deploy the capitalist bomb in Europe was scrapped with the signing of the Intermediate Nuclear Forces (INF) Treaty in 1988, which removed most nuclear weapons from Europe.

Theater nuclear weapons were always more controversial than their strategic counterparts, especially among the European allies who would be "defended" by them. There was deep suspicion in Europe that their use could not be controlled—that once the first nuclear weapons were used on the battlefield, the result would be escalation to broader use. Whether expansion would be limited to the theater or would expand to homeland exchanges between the superpowers could not be demonstrated. Since nuclear weapons had never been used in anger when both sides possessed them, there was absolutely no evidence to support or refute claims about whether or how escalation might occur.

Regardless of escalatory potential, most Europeans agreed that anyplace nuclear weapons were used would be a loser, an irradiated wasteland that would be uninhabitable until the radiation dissipated. Some Europeans even suspected that after decimating parts of Europe, the superpowers would pause, conclude that any further escalation placed their own territory at risk, and stop, arguing that they had done their duty to defend their allies.

DEADLOCK OF THE COMPETITION

Even when the Cold War competition was proceeding in its most vigorous manner, the seeds of its demise were being sown. By the 1970s, two trends, unrecognized at the time, were beginning to congeal that would militate toward the end of the Cold War. One trend was the weakening of the Soviet economy both absolutely and in comparison to that of the United States. The other was a growing recognition of a deadlock in the military competition between the superpower blocs. By the 1980s, these trends coalesced to create the conditions that led to the end of the Cold War.

The Economic Dimension

The economic implosion that eventually engulfed the Soviet state had its roots in the 1970s or even before. By the 1970s, economic growth began to slow, and by the end of the decade, the Soviet economy had stopped growing altogether, what Soviet economists would later call the "era of stagnation." By the early 1980s, the only economic growth in the Soviet Union was apparently in the production of vodka, and if vodka production was removed from measures of productivity, the Soviet economy was in absolute decline. Indeed, when Gorbachev mandated limits in vodka production in the mid-1980s, the economy was adversely affected.

This problem was known to some Soviet academic economists, but they lacked access to the leadership cadre associated with Soviet leader Leonid Brezhnev (known as the *nomenklatura*), who benefited from the system and were uninterested in seeing change that might adversely affect their privilege. Instead, the academic economists allied themselves with a rising star within the Communist Party, Mikhail S. Gorbachev, whose wife, Raisa, was their colleague at Moscow State University. When Gorbachev achieved power in 1985, this cadre was ready to roll out the mechanisms of reform. Unfortunately for them, their efforts were too little and too late.

A good bit of the Soviet decline was due to lagging behind in science and technology. The Soviets were largely excluded from the high-technology revolution in the West that underlay the economic expansion of the 1980s and 1990s and the process of globalization of the world economy. Part of this exclusion was purposive—to shield a shaky economy from outside competition. Two additional dynamics exacerbated this technological gap. First, the problem was progressive. The motor of technological growth was the development of more-sophisticated generations of computers. This is a progressive process because the major tool for designing the next generation of computers is the current generation. Thus, the computer industry's future health depends on its current competitiveness. Moreover, the developmental time between generations has grown shorter because of the greater power of newer machines. Translated, that means the farther a country is behind (the more generations it is removed from the cutting edge), the farther it gets behind in the future. By the early 1980s, the Soviet Union was approximately three generations behind the United States, and the gap was widening.

The Soviets could not close the gap. In the 1960s, the decision had been made to concentrate on military development at the expense of the computer research section of the Soviet Academy of Scientists, and its personnel were assigned to military research. As a result, the best scientific minds in the Soviet Union were devoted to unproductive (in economic terms) military activity rather than basic research or on consumer applications. The Soviets became so desperate that they even stole computers, tore them down, and put them back together again so they could replicate the system (a process known as reverse engineering). It did not help. The systems they stole represented current technology becoming obsolete, and reverse engineering took longer than the development of new generations.

The second dynamic was that the Soviets were forbidden from collaborating with the West in technology. Almost all the technologies in which the Soviets were behind were *dual use*, meaning they had both civilian and military applications. For instance, a computer designed for research in theoretical physics could be converted to applying physics principles to weapons design. As long as the Soviet Union was the avowed enemy, the United States and the rest of the West were not going to provide the Soviets with capabilities that might produce weapons with which to menace them. The resulting isolation simply exacerbated the existing economic gulf.

Most of these dynamics went largely unnoticed in the West at the time. Soviet economists were rarely allowed to communicate with their western counterparts, the Soviet government doctored economic statistics that were notoriously inaccurate anyway (and thus disbelieved), and the military production system, on which attention was concentrated, seemed to be working well. In fact, when the Central Intelligence Agency produced an analysis of the Soviet economy in the middle 1970s suggesting the possibility of its decline, the report was condemned, and an alternate panel was assembled to reassess the material. That group produced a more ominous analysis, which was largely wrong. Since its conclusions reinforced what officials believed to be the case, it was widely accepted. The façade was cracking, and hardly anyone noticed.

The Military Dimension

By the end of the 1970s, the military competition was also undergoing change to the ultimate disadvantage of the Soviet Union. The competition had essentially deadlocked into a very deadly but ritual confrontation in which neither side seemed to be able to obtain meaningful advantage. This competition was enormously burdensome to a Soviet economy that was much smaller than that of the United States and that needed to divert resources devoted to the military for economic purposes if the Soviets hoped to compete economically. The military competition, in a word, became a millstone around the neck of the Soviet future. The weight became unbearable in the late 1980s, when their ill-fated, expensive, and unpopular intervention in Afghanistan contributed to the demise of the Soviet state.

The seeds of military deadlock can be traced back to the Cuban crisis, when both sides confronted the potential reality of nuclear war and did not like what they saw. Despite the recognition of a mutual interest in avoiding nuclear war that was the major outgrowth of that crisis, the military competition, if anything, expanded and intensified in the following years. Many in the American national security community remained deeply suspicious of anything the Soviets did (and vice versa) and continued to build up stocks of arms, especially in the area of strategic nuclear forces, as if the Cuban experience had not changed anything.

While the potential deadliness of the nuclear balance expanded, the danger of nuclear war was actually declining, even if this decline was mostly unrealized. The prospect of nuclear war with the levels of arms available in 1962 was sobering, but the prospect of such a war fought with the arsenals of the 1980s was positively catastrophic. Leaders on both sides going back as far as President Dwight D. Eisenhower in the 1950s and Soviet Premier Nikita Khrushchev in the early 1960s had publicly proclaimed the unacceptability of nuclear war as a means to resolve East–West differences. These original pronouncements were made when arsenal sizes numbered in the hundreds; when both sides recognized what could happen if the ten thousand or more weapons both possessed were unleashed, avoiding such a war became imperative.

The necessary step to reduce the danger—or likelihood—of war between the two sides was to add the unacceptability of conventional war to the relationship. The key element in accomplishing this was the uncertainty of the escalatory process. A conventional war would become a nuclear war if escalation occurred, and there was no empirical basis on which to predict confidently whether that escalation would occur. In that circumstance, the only certain way to avoid nuclear war between the superpowers was to avoid *any* war between them.

This "necessary peace," as I described it in a 1987 book with that title, reduced the Cold War military competition to ritual status. Both sides developed and deployed weapons and conducted war games with them for the precise reason of avoiding their use in war. The old military axiom of "preparing for and fighting the country's wars" became twisted to "preparing to avoid fighting the country's wars."

The recognition of military deadlock came at a time when the burden of the arms race was clearly contributing to the crisis of the Soviet economy. The Soviets were plowing upward of one-quarter of their gross national product into defense spending from an economy probably only about one-third the size of the American economy. When support for foreign adventures in places like Cuba and Mozambique and the direct expense of the war in Afghanistan were added to the Cold War "bill" for the Soviets, the burden was becoming overwhelming. In 1981, the administration of Ronald W. Reagan announced the largest arms buildup in peacetime American history, and one of the explicit purposes of the increase in arms was to force the Soviets into an economically ruinous arms race by trying to keep up with the American expansion.

Convergence

These two dimensions had converged as Gorbachev succeeded Konstantin Chernenko as the Soviet leader in 1985. Gorbachev seemed a new kind of Soviet opponent. He was the first chief executive of the Soviet Union with a college degree, was a lawyer by training, and was clearly more urbane and sophisticated than his predecessors, preferring well-tailored Italian silk suits to the baggy gray gabardine associated with older Soviet Communists. His professor wife, Raisa, was also a handsome, urbane, and very public figure—in contrast to the dowager images of Gorbachev's predecessors' wives (some of whom were never seen in public). When Gorbachev went to London as one of his first acts and clearly charmed British Prime Minister Margaret Thatcher, it was clear that he was a different character than those he succeeded.

Gorbachev faced a daunting set of problems. He knew about the economic problems from the Soviet professors, and he sought to reform the economic system. As a believing Marxist, his initial approach was to fine-tune the existing system, but that system itself was beyond repair, and he was slow in recognizing that it and the assumptions on which it rested were the problem.

He also realized that much of the economic problem was the result of the isolation of the Soviet economy. Gorbachev ultimately recognized that the only chance for economic redemption was to open the country to the West. Western technology was absolutely critical to any attempts at economic modernization and hence competitiveness, and an influx of Western capital was clearly necessary to fund improved economic performance. But how could the Soviets convince a suspicious West to engage itself with the Soviet economic system? How could they convince an even more suspicious American national security establishment that shared technology would not be turned into hostile tools of war?

The military problem was much the same. When Gorbachev entered office, the Soviets were engaged in their fifth year of a frustrating, unsuccessful war in Afghanistan that was draining the treasury and corroding the society in ways not dissimilar to the effects of the Vietnam War on the United States. Eventually, Soviet forces would have to withdraw from Afghanistan in disgrace, which became a factor in the ultimate demise of the Soviet Union. The effects of trying to match the Reagan buildup were adding to the strains, and pitiful client states like Cuba looked increasingly like unaffordable luxuries.

What was Gorbachev to do? The choices were not attractive. The status quo could not be sustained, and trying to tinker with the system through the economic and political reforms known as *perestroika* was not working. The Soviet Union was sinking fast as a state and as a power. A radical solution was needed.

The answer was to end the Cold War. The logic of the Soviet situation dictated the decision. Economic stagnation was eroding the standing of the Soviet Union in the world and was progressively reducing the standard of living of Soviet citizens. The Soviet Union was becoming, as many critics described it, "a third-world country with nuclear weapons." To change that situation, they needed access to western technology and capital, and their only hope was to cease being the enemy and to join the community of states as a normal rather than a rogue member. The same logic held for the military dimension. Competing with the Reagan buildup, continuing the frustrating burden of the Afghanistan war, and supporting losers like Castro were becoming unbearable and unsustainable. Cancelling the losing game the Cold War had become was an increasingly attractive option.

The world stood by in stunned silence as the Soviet leader began to unravel the forty-year-long confrontation. Gorbachev published a blueprint of the changes he proposed in a 1987 book, *Perestroika: New Thinking for Our Country and the World*. In it, he proposed a detailed internal reform plan. In the international realm, he detailed the transformation of the Soviet Union into a "normal" state by policy changes such as non-interference in the affairs of other states and renunciation of the so-called Brezhnev Doctrine, which had justified Soviet intervention in the socialist states and had been used as the rationale for Soviet invasions of Hungary, Czechoslovakia, and Afghanistan.

Perestroika was initially greeted skeptically in the West. Many analysts presumed that the book was nothing more than an elaborate web of lies to lower the West's guard. But then Gorbachev began to act in accordance with the book's proposals. In 1989, the Soviet Union completed its military withdrawal from Afghanistan, despite having accomplished none of its goals. That same year it stood idly by when the Polish parliament seated a non-Communist government, an act that opened the floodgates for the rapid decommunization of Eastern Europe and, in 1991, the formal dissolution of the Warsaw Pact. These inactions seemed to constitute renunciation of the Brezhnev Doctrine and implementation of the principle of non-interference in the affairs of other states.

Domestic reform was not dramatic or attractive enough to avoid the breakup of the Soviet Union itself. Led by the Baltic states (Lithuania, Latvia, and Estonia), the constituent republics of the Soviet Union announced their intention to withdraw from the union and establish themselves as independent states. On the last tick of the clock of 1991, the red Soviet flag came down from the Kremlin for the last time, replaced the next day by the Russian tricolor of red, white, and blue.

The peaceful implosion of the Soviet state was—and is—an unprecedented political act in world history. States, including major powers, have from time to time ceased to exist through Carthaginian peaces or partition at the ends of wars, but for one of the world's two most powerful countries simply to vote itself out of existence was absolutely and entirely unanticipated both within and outside Russia. Ultimately, the outcome hardly anyone considered adequately, a peaceful end of the Cold War, had happened.

So why did Gorbachev do what he did? The short answer is that he had no choice. The old system was broken, if not exactly in the way he and his advisors thought at the time. Knowing the system could not be revived without considerable outside assistance, Gorbachev understood that the *sine qua non* for assistance was to end the Cold War and to remove its most obviously annoying symbols: the Iron Curtain, the Berlin Wall, and most important, the structure of military confrontation. He and those around him did not foresee that the cost would be the destruction of the edifice they had sought to strengthen.

Fascinating questions remain. Could the Cold War have been ended without the destruction of the Soviet Union? If so, what would world politics look like today? If Gorbachev had anticipated the real price of ending the Cold War, would he have gone through with it? In another vein, was the outcome foreordained regardless of who was in the Kremlin in the middle 1980s, or was it the unique contribution of Gorbachev to stimulate the destruction of the internal barriers to change and the Soviet state itself? What problems did the end of the Cold War leave behind? More recently, the question "Could it return?" has been added to the mix.

COLD WAR RESIDUES

The end of the Cold War left a geopolitical void in the international system. The most gaping hole was in Europe and centered around two axes. The first, and potentially most traumatic, was what succeeded a former Soviet Union now divided into fifteen independent states, of which the Russian Federation is the pivot, and the second was the collapse of the Communist order in Eastern Europe. There still remains some process of adjustment among the states of the former Soviet Union itself, and most of the East European transitions from Communism to western forms have occurred or are well under way. More recently, however, the possible resurgence of Russia as a world power (introduced earlier) has become a cause for concern.

Russia and the Successor States

When the Soviet Union dissolved, Russia was the largest single state that emerged from the breakup, containing roughly half the population and three-quarters of the land mass of the old Soviet Union. Russia also has maintained most of the military power of the old Soviet Union, notably the thermonuclear arsenal. Although beset by enormous and debilitating political and economic problems that unquestionably diminished its place in the world in the 1990s, Russia's growing oil wealth has reversed that fate, and Russia and its future remain an important international concern.

The Russian situation can be divided into political, economic, and military questions. The political and economic aspects focus on the transformation of the Russian system away from its totalitarian, socialist past to some more western democratic and capitalist future. Its progress in these areas has been mixed. Militarily, Russia has been in a process of decline that began before the fall of Communism, but it remains a nuclear superpower.

The political and economic transformation of Russia has moved forward in interrelated fits and starts. The political system is still developing democratic support in a situation where economic chaos and even free fall became virtually institutional features in the 1990s. Economically, an attempt to institute market practices was grafted onto an inherited institutional framework woefully inappropriate and inadequate for the market to take hold and prosper. When the Soviet Union became Russia, for instance, the country had essentially no banking or other financial laws or institutions, making it virtually impossible to regulate financial dealings. It lacked mechanisms to collect taxes to run the government. The breakdown of the Communist levers of state coercion left the country with inadequate policing capacity, which resulted in the ascendancy of the *Mafioso* and other forms of lawlessness. Pensioners who believed the Communist state would support them in their old age found themselves holding the bag, as the "social net" promised by the Communist state was withdrawn from them.

Politically, the record has also been mixed. Russia has held five relatively free elections for president, and in the third one in 2000, power was peacefully passed from Boris Yeltsin to Vladimir Putin, a momentous occasion in Russian history. When Putin was reelected in 2004, some international concern was raised (especially by the United States) about the Russian president's commitment to western democracy as a result of actions that have greatly centralized power in his hands. In 2008, the Russian electorate voted Putin's hand-picked successor, Dmitry Medvedev, to office, and Putin became prime minister. Medvedev has asserted his independence of Putin in important ways, but Putin's underlying power remains a concern.

Russia also has serious military and security problems. One of the major themes of Russian history has been a concern with—some argue paranoia about—military security that has been reinforced by invaders as diverse as the Mongol hordes, Napoleon Bonaparte, and Adolf Hitler. A major reason for constructing the Communist empire in Eastern Europe after World War II, after all, was to provide a *cordon sanitaire* (buffer zone) between Russia and future invaders. That buffer zone is gone.

The relative assurance of Russian physical security was a victim of both the end of the Cold War and the breakup of the Soviet Union. The demise of the Cold War meant Russia lost its Warsaw Pact allies; the breakup of the Soviet Union meant Ukrainians, Moldavians, and others were no longer part of the Russian security scheme and might even become part of the new security problem.

Russia has other military problems. Partly because of budgetary problems, the military itself has deteriorated markedly. Because Russian soldiers are unable to subsist on wages that often are not paid, it has not been unusual to see them in uniform working second jobs or panhandling on the streets of Moscow. The backbone of the Russian army remains first-term conscripts, many of whom desert at the first possible opportunity with the implicit approval of the society. When it has been called upon to perform in former Soviet areas, the military's record has been mixed. In the 1990s, its performance was less than exemplary in putting down secessionist violence in the strategically vital region of Chechnya (see Amplification 7.3), and lingering Chechen terrorism remains a problem, although apparently minor enough that the Russians announced an end to the military occupation of Chechnya in April 2009.

Amplification 7.3

CHECHNYA AND THE PIPELINE

One place where Russian security concerns and adaptation to a post–Cold War world have coalesced is over Chechnya, a renegade republic in the Caucasus region of Russia that declared its independence from the Russian Federation in 1994 and has been fighting the Russians ever since to become an independent Muslim state. Like many other areas of the southern part of Russia, the citizens are not ethnic Russians and live in areas forcefully annexed to Russia.

Chechnya represents the Russian dilemma of dealing with the post–Cold War period in at least three ways. One is clearly the precedent that would be set if Chechnya were allowed to secede from a Russia already diminished by the dissolution of the Soviet Union. Second, the ferocity—even barbarism—of the fighting created a public relations nightmare for the Russian government. The once proud Russian army was largely ineffective in putting down the rebellion and was reduced to leveling Chechen cities like Grozny, with pictorial documentation widely available worldwide. In the process, widespread accusations by human rights groups of atrocities committed by the Russians have caused embarrassment to the Russians and slowed the flow of developmental assistance to Russia. Since September 11, 2001, the Russians have sought to portray the Chechens as part of the web of international religious terrorism. Some of the Chechen "freedom fighters" have been shown to have common roots with Al Qaeda and other terrorist groups, and this depiction by the Russians has stilled much of the criticism of their brutality toward Chechnya.

The real heart of the Russian problem in Chechnya, however, revolves around getting Caspian Sea oil from Azerbaijan to markets in the West. Because the pipelines that will carry the oil can be taxed, there is great potential wealth that can be accrued to whatever country wins the competition to have the pipeline built across its territory. The possible routes are across Iran (not much of an alternative, since much of the reason for exploiting Caspian oil is to reduce dependence on the Persian Gulf), Turkey, and Russia. The Russians argue the revenue is absolutely vital to Russian economic development because it would greatly augment the central government's tax revenues. The problem, however, is that by far the most direct and economically viable way to build a pipeline across Russia is to build it through Chechnya. As long as there is an embarrassing armed rebellion in that republic, Russia's chances are visibly diminished.

In 2008, the military was more successful in assisting ethnic Russians and Ossetians and Abkhazians in their separatist cause against the government of Georgia.

The solution to the Russian security problem may center on its evolving relationship with NATO. Originally, of course, NATO was formed largely to deter Soviet aggression; today, security is served by courting and embracing Russia. The question is, How? Full NATO membership for Russia is one possibility, but it faces opposition that has to this point proven insurmountable. The chief obstacle is the status of Russia if it is a member—would it be a regular member like France or Germany or a "special" member like the United States? Currently, the solution is Russian participation through the NATO-Russian Council, a consultative relationship and arrangement that allow Russian access to NATO short of being a member. The courtship between Russia and NATO continues to be an off-and-on proposition, as both sides attempt to resolve their historic animosity and distrust with contemporary reality.

From a western viewpoint, the ideal outcome to the Russian situation is the gradual emergence of Russia as a fully westernized political democracy with a growing and prosperous market-based economy that is a full participant in the international system. The alternative is the possible resurgence of an authoritarian and possibly antagonistic Russia.

Russian Resurgence

Russia is a very old and proud country that has strived for centuries to be seen and treated as one of the world's major powers. Located as it is on the eastern edge of Europe, the Russian Empire was a member of the European-dominated Balance of Power from the seventeenth into the twentieth centuries, but it was widely regarded as the most backward, even marginal, member of that system. It ascended to superpower status as the Soviet Union after World War II, assuming the kind of lofty status Russian nationalists had always dreamed for it to hold. When the Soviet Union disintegrated, that status declined, leaving many Russians discontented with their returned diminished status and yearning to reassert Russian greatness.

The 1990s, after the Soviet Union dissolved, were problematical for Russia. The Soviet superpower that Russia had dominated shrunk physically and geopolitically. A mixture of often antagonistic regimes arose in the successor states, which the Russians referred to as the "near abroad" (indicating a special relationship with the Russians generally not felt in those countries but reflecting the sizable remaining Russian minorities that had been planted there as part of Soviet policy), and these regimes viewed Russia with defiant distrust. Despite Russia's maintenance of Soviet nuclear weapons, its conventional power receded to the point that many who had feared the Soviets ceased fearing Russia. As the 1990s progressed, the Russian economy continued to decline into a state of chaos that left many wondering if the non-authoritarian regime could maintain power. Russian political democracy hung in the balance. As the change of millennia took place, the prognosis for the Russian state was clearly in question.

By the middle of the 2000s, that prognosis had changed radically. The cause of that change has been a resurgent Russian economy, and the engine of that resurgence has been Russia's emergence as the second-leading exporter of petroleum in the world, as noted earlier. The economic results have been striking. As Ukrainian political leader Yuliya Tymoshenko pointed out in a 2007 *Foreign Affairs* article, Russia is now sustaining a 6.5 percent annual economic growth rate and is in the process of paying off most of the external debt accumulated during the 1990s. Economic prosperity has come—albeit selectively—to Russia and Russians.

The political dynamics associated with this resurgence have been more potentially troublesome both domestically and internationally. Domestically, there has been a gradual accumulation of power to the presidency at the expense of the Russian parliament (the Duma) under Putin, and that trend was particularly pronounced during the second Putin term, which coincided with Russia's emergence as a major petroleum exporter. The concentration of power in the presidency has caused concern among observers (Tymoshenko and Azar Gat, for instance), and many observers are anxiously viewing the evolution of the Medvedev regime to see if it will continue this trend. This problem, however, seems to trouble outsiders more than it does Russians themselves. Why?

There are two basic answers, one largely domestic and the other international and at the heart of international concerns. Thomas L. Friedman describes the domestic side in terms of Russia's emergence as a *petrolist* state. In states that have great petroleum wealth but that lack firm democratic traditions, governments can sometimes strike a kind of Faustian bargain with their populations wherein petroleum wealth is distributed to the citizenry to improve their material conditions, and in return the citizens cede some political rights to the government. The dynamic is what Friedman calls the first law of petropolitics: "the price of oil and the pace of freedom always move in opposite directions in oil-rich petrolist states." Putin and Venezuela's Hugo Chavez have been specifically cited as practitioners of petrolist politics.

This movement toward authoritarian politics has impeded Russia's full entrance into the circle of democratic states, but it also has potentially troubling international repercussions. During the 1990s, Russia was a non-assertive, compliant member of the international order, at least in part because its increasingly desperate economic condition left it in no position to pursue the assertive, expansionist foreign policy of its predecessor. This change was humiliating to many Russians seeking a return to Russian status as a major world power. The decline of Russian military power was especially vexing in its response to Chechen resistance and has only partially been restored in "near abroad" states like Georgia.

Russian oil wealth at least partly mitigates this condition. The possession of a scarce resource provides Russia with a new source of leverage unavailable to its Soviet predecessor, and European dependence on Russian oil and natural gas provides the Russians with significance in Europe. Oil wealth also provides the possibility of significantly rebuilding Russia's shattered armed forces, should it choose to do so.

Hardly anyone is confidently projecting the international impact of Russian resurgence. The worst-case scenario is that Russia will be transformed into a new authoritarian—if capitalist—state that could become as antagonistic as the fascist states of the 1930s and reinstate something like a new Cold War. Most observers find this extreme outcome unlikely or at least premature to project at this time. Nonetheless, the retreat of Russia from the democratizing trajectory of the 1990s and very early 2000s represents a troubling phenomenon. One of the challenges facing the Obama administration is how to deal with Russia and to try to help shape its future. As suggested in the *Challenge!* box, much of this effort initially surrounded the disposition of a proposed U.S. missile defense system in Eastern Europe, a problem at least temporarily defused by the September 2009 American decision to abandon the system based in Eastern European and to rely on a ship-based alternative.

Challenge!

WHAT KIND OF RUSSIA?

It is clear that the United States would like to see Russia evolve into a nonthreatening, democratic country that participates in international relations as a helpful partner rather than as an antagonist. For that kind of Russia to emerge, the country will have to evolve and strengthen its democratic institutions, but doing so must occur within the specific context of a Russian mentality where resurgent Russian nationalism competes for support with democracy. After Russia's humiliation during the 1990s, it is not entirely clear what Russians would do if they had to choose between being a democracy and being a great power.

How can the United States help redefine and influence that choice? One way is to treat the Russians with the respect and deference to which they feel they are entitled. One place this can clearly be attempted is in discussions of deploying a missile defense system in Poland and the Czech Republic.

The Russians have fundamentally opposed the plan since it was first proposed by the Bush administration and have seen it as evidence of disrespect for their status as a major power. The Russians dismissed American arguments that the system was not aimed at them but at a potential rogue power like Iran, arguing instead that it was a hostile act of military encirclement and a brazen move that the United States would consider only if it did not respect the views of a fellow great power. To Russians, it was evidence that the United States regards Russia as a marginal power, an assessment they find intolerable.

What the United States should do in this situation was a matter of considerable disagreement before the Obama administration scrapped the plan. One possibility was that it should insist on the security benefits of the system for the United States, even if it threatens U.S.-Russian relations and the evolution of the Russian state as a democratic partner? This possibility was discussed when President Obama visited Moscow in July 2009, but it was not been positively resolved. Deciding on a ship-based alternative using current weaponry has been a compromise solution: it placates some opponents of the system because it is cheaper than the Bush plan and overcomes Russian objection about the Czech-Polish deployment. Champions of the Bush plan counter that the decision amounts to giving in to the Russians and will provide less protection against a hypothetical Iranian threat. Did the United States make the right decision in abandoning the Bush plan? What do you think?

CONCLUSION: THE END OF THE COLD WAR IN PERSPECTIVE

Viewed strictly from the vantage point of the twenty-first century, the Cold War years must seem an anomalous period, one that probably should be consigned mainly to the history books. Although many of the problems and tensions associated with the second half of the twentieth century have proven to be less enduring than those who witnessed them thought they would be, such a view would be shortsighted and would miss the point of how the Cold War continues to influence the present and possibly the future.

The Cold War remains the backdrop from which the contemporary system is emerging. Among the overarching concerns of the new millennium is the integration of the formerly Marxist-Leninist states into the globalization system, a problem that clearly could not have existed had there not been a furtive competition between ideologically defined contenders in the first place. This process of integration is being stimulated by the enlistment of former enemies as allies in waging the campaign against terrorism and in shaping a new world order. For better or worse, many of the contemporary difficulties with which the world grapples have their origins in the Cold War and can be fully understood only in that light.

The Communist world of the Cold War encompassed much of the Eurasian landmass, with China and the Soviet Union as its anchors. China remains nominally Communist but has become the United States' second largest trading partner and a major international actor relations with which remain controversial (see the discussion in the next chapter). Russia, on the other hand, has emerged from the rubble of the Communist experience as much the same enigma that Sir Winston Churchill ascribed to the Soviet Union well over a half-century ago. Where is Russia headed in the community of states?

Russia's evolution is not yet complete. Russia may be neither Communist nor the Soviet Union, but it is still the largest country in the world physically, it is the largest unexploited source of many mineral and energy resources, it still has nuclear weapons, and petroleum and natural gas are fueling its resurgence among the world's powers. The decline of Russia so dramatically witnessed in the 1990s is giving way to a new, possibly more traditional power role in the 2000s, the contours and dimensions of which are not entirely clear.

STUDY/DISCUSSION QUESTIONS

1. How and why did the dissolution of the Soviet Union and the end of the Cold War represent a traumatic event for the international system? Discuss.
2. Discuss the Cold War system. What were its major characteristics, and how did they help define how the system operated? What were the sources of change that occurred over time?
3. The heart of the Cold War system was the military competition between the United States and the Soviet Union. Discuss the dimensions of that competition.
4. How did the East–West competition deadlock? Discuss the economic and military dimensions of that deadlock and how they led Soviet leader Mikhail S. Gorbachev to conclude the competition had to be ended.
5. What are the two major residues of the end of the Cold War? In particular, analyze the problem of Russian resurgence as part of that residue.
6. Based on your reading, what kind of Russia do you think is likely to evolve in the future? Why?

SELECTED BIBLIOGRAPHY

Aslund, Anders. "The Hunt for Russia's Riches." *Foreign Policy*, January/February 2006, 42–49.

Bialer, Seweryn, and Michael Mandelbaum, eds. *Gorbachev's Russia and American Foreign Policy.* Boulder, CO: Westview Press, 1988.

Brzezinski, Zbigniew. "The Cold War and Its Aftermath." *Foreign Affairs* 71, no. 4 (Fall 1992): 31–49.

Clark, Ronald W. *The Greatest Power on Earth: The International Race for Nuclear Supremacy, Earliest Theory to Three Mile Island.* New York: Harper and Row, 1980.

Claude, Inis L. *The Changing United Nations.* New York: Random House, 1967.

Friedman, Thomas L. "The First Law of Petropolitics." *Foreign Policy,* May/June 2006, 28–36.

Fukuyama, Francis. *The End of History and the Last Man.* New York: Free Press, 1992.

Gaddis, John Lewis. *The United States and the End of the Cold War: Implications, Reconsiderations, Provocations.* New York: Oxford University Press, 1992.

Gat, Azar. "The Return of Authoritarian Great Powers." *Foreign Affairs* 86, no. 4 (July/August 2007): 59–69.

Goldman, Marshall. "Moscow's New Economic Impact." *Current History* 107, no. 711 (October 2008): 322–330.

Gorbachev, Mikhail S. *Perestroika: New Thinking for Our Country and the World.* New York: Harper and Row, 1987.

Lieven, Anatol. "The Essential Vladimir Putin." *Foreign Policy,* January/February 2005, 72–74.

Mearsheimer, John J. "Why We Shall Soon Miss the Cold War." *Atlantic Monthly* 262, no. 2 (August 1990): 35–50.

Mendelson, Sarah, and Theodore P. Gerber. "Failing the Stalin Test." *Foreign Affairs* 85, no. 1 (January/February 2006): 2–8.

———. "Soviet Nostalgia: An Impediment to Russian Democratization." *Washington Quarterly* 29, no. 1 (Winter 2005–2006): 81–96.

Rose, Richard, William Mishler, and Neil Munro. *Russia Transformed: Developing Popular Support for a New Regime.* New York: Cambridge University Press, 2006.

Sestanovich, Stephen. "What Has Moscow Done?" *Foreign Affairs* 87, no. 6 (November/December 2008): 12–28.

Shevtsova, Lilia. "Russia's Ersatz Democracy." *Current History* 105, no. 693 (October 2006): 307–314.

Simes, Dmitri. "The Return of Russian History." *Foreign Affairs* 73, no. 1 (January/February 1992): 67–82.

Snow, Donald M. *The Necessary Peace: Nuclear Weapons and Superpower Relations.* Lexington, MA: Lexington Books, 1987.

———. *The Shape of the Future: The Post–Cold War World,* 3rd ed. Armonk, NY: M. E. Sharpe, 1999.

———. *Cases in International Relations: Portraits of the Future,* 3rd ed. New York: Pearson Longman 2008.

Stephenova, Ekaterina. "War and Peace Building." *Washington Quarterly* 27, no. 4 (Autumn 2004): 127–136.

Stoner-Weiss, Kathryn. "It Is Still Putin's Russia." *Current History* 107, no. 711 (October 2008): 315–322.

Tymoshenko, Yuliya. "Containing Russia." *Foreign Affairs* 86, no. 3 (May/June 2007): 69–82.

CHAPTER 8

Globalization and Beyond

PREVIEW

The geopolitical perspective that casts national security largely in terms of military power is not the only way to think about security. Other ways of thinking about what makes the United States safe have historically competed with the military conceptualization; in the 1990s, economic considerations in the guise of globalization arguably challenged geopolitics as the dominant security paradigm. Globalization and other security concerns will continue to be important influences on national security in a post-9/11 world. This chapter looks at the post–World War II emergence and evolution of the economic factors culminating in globalization in the 1990s. It then examines the lower-profile influence of globalization in the 2000s, including domestic and international reactions to globalization and the emergence of alternate sources of security concern—notably, energy, the environment, and the U.S. border. The chapter concludes by speculating on possible effects globalization and these other concerns may have on the developing conceptualizations of security.

Americans have historically not been entirely comfortable thinking of the world and their place in it entirely in geopolitical terms, in which war and the use of military force play a prominent part in the national existence. In the 150-plus years of the formative period, military affairs—and especially the use of military force—were considered aberrations, unwelcome interruptions to the normalcy of peace. As the United States emerged on the world stage after the American Civil War, it was American economic prowess, not military power, that distinguished the country as a world power. The economic instrument of power, of which globalization is the most recent manifestation, has long held a place in American life.

Since the end of World War II, geopolitics has been boosted to the forefront first by the Cold War and more recently by September 11 and its aftermath—notably in Afghanistan and Iraq. The end of the Cold War provided a reprise during the 1990s in which globalization served as the instrument of economic challenge to geopolitics.

Will the reaction to the outcomes of wars in Iraq and Afghanistan, along with other concerns, create a similar reaction? How will globalization be reshaped by the global economic downturn of 2008? In order to assess these possibilities, it is first necessary to examine the nature and evolution of globalization and other challenges such as energy, the environment, and more recently, the U.S. border.

Globalization and the impact of the globalizing economy were the centerpiece of the 1990s, just as terrorism was the lightning rod of the early 2000s. During the 1990s, the international system moved away from its Cold War emphasis on geopolitically based national security concerns. After the global economic recession of 1991 faded in 1992 and 1993, a period of growing economic prosperity and expansion blossomed as a trade-driven global phenomenon, and the economies of participating countries expanded in nearly a decade of unprecedented economic growth. This phenomenon was felt in most of the developed and parts of the developing world, but nowhere was it more evident than in the U.S. economy and for individual Americans. The U.S. economy emerged from a decade or more of relative economic listlessness to reclaim its position as the dominant economic force in the world. Whether there will be a similar reaction to the far deeper economic crisis that began in 2008 remains to be seen.

The 1990s era of economic expansion induced an overreaction about the degree and depth of transformation that had occurred. Until the system endured a major shake-up in the form of the East Asian crisis of 1997, there was a near-euphoria about the benefits and endurance of globalization's seemingly inexorable benefits. Analysts suggested that this new phenomenon of globalization was fundamentally altering the world system. To its most vocal adherents, realism-based geopolitics was giving way to globalization as the dominant force in international relations.

The relative roles of geopolitics and globalization fit into the broader debate about the United States' place in the post-9/11 world developed throughout the book. The internationalist strain in the U.S. worldview has always been strongly represented in the economic debate, and the United States has been a leader in the promotion of increased world trade since it emerged as an industrial power after the American Civil War. Even when the country withdrew *politically* from international affairs into "splendid isolationism" between the world wars, it remained a very active member of the international economic system. The same internationalism that manifests itself in a politically activist role and an expansive view of the country's military obligations is also a part of the economic debate, the current focus of which is globalization.

The purpose of this chapter is to create a foundation for thinking about the role of economic and other concerns and their impact on foreign and national security policy. It proceeds historically from the end of World War II, dividing the American international economic experience into three distinct periods. The discussion begins with the American-dominated economic system that emerged from World War II, the Bretton Woods system. It then moves to the transitional period between the American denunciation of the gold standard in 1971 and the emergence of globalism somewhere around the end of the 1980s. It concludes with the contemporary period of globalization and where it may be leading, particularly in light of the resurgence of terrorism-led geopolitics in 2001. This contemporary period has also witnessed the addition of other national security agenda items.

THE BRETTON WOODS SYSTEM, 1945–1971

What became known as the Bretton Woods system had its roots in World War II. It reflected perceptions about how the interwar international economic system had helped precipitate the war and about what the nature of the postwar international economic situation would be. The result was a series of international negotiations dominated by the Americans and the British that produced an institutional framework that organized the revised and rejuvenated economic order.

The Setting

Two overarching economic facts dominated the international scene in 1945 and were the major concerns of postwar planners seeking to recreate an international system that would not slide back to instability and yet another devastating war. How could the international economic system contribute to the geopolitical goal of war avoidance in a changed environment? The United States had emerged from the war with the overwhelmingly largest and most robust economy in the world, and it was thus the only country capable of leading a postwar reconstruction of the global economy. Most economic observers believed that economic policies pursued between the world wars had contributed significantly to the slide toward war and thus needed to be revised to avoid a recurrence.

The U.S. economy had been hard hit by the Great Depression (as had Germany's, and that impact was partially blamed for the rise of Hitler and thus the war). When the United States entered the war, its unused industrial capacity was activated to transform the country's industrial base into the "arsenal of democracy," producing the war materiel that would bring down the Axis powers. The unemployment that had been the most visible symbol of the depression evaporated in the economic and military mobilization. The American economy was thus rescued and strengthened absolutely and relatively by the war.

American economic preeminence meant the United States was the only candidate to lead any global economic recovery. Because the United States possessed an enormous amount of leverage to structure that system, it was very difficult for the other World War II participants to resist American preferences. The question was whether the United States would lead the world economy to a stable new prosperity or whether it might revert to prewar isolationism.

Answers about the direction of the global economy were worked out as part of the wartime allied collaboration that also produced the United Nations. The security problem during the interwar years had been a League of Nations that was not strong enough to enforce policies that would maintain the peace. The economic realm was even worse: an international institutional void in the area of economics allowed states to pursue policies that created an economic crisis in the 1930s that many believed led to the war.

A major culprit in interwar economics had been the punitive nature of the Versailles peace treaty, which ended World War I. In 1919, Germany was forced to accept total responsibility for starting the war through the War Guilt Clause, Article 231. This provision justified sizable reparations from Germany to pay for the destruction in France (where most of the physical fighting on the western front occurred) and also to pay Great Britain. The reparations payments virtually ensured that Germany could not recover from the war economically. The effect was that the Great Depression hit Germany harder than any other country on the continent.

The Great Depression also set off a wave of economic nationalism that worsened matters worldwide. As the effects of the depression spread throughout Europe and threatened the integrity of industries and businesses, governments responded with protective barriers in the form of very high tariffs and other devices designed to protect indigenous industries from foreign competition by making outside goods and services artificially more expensive than domestic counterparts. These barriers reduced trade to a trickle of its predepression levels and added to the general animosity between countries that was greasing the slide to world war.

These perceptions helped predispose those who would take the lead in fashioning the postwar economic system. The isolationism that had been a firm part of the economic nationalism—some called it economic warfare—of the 1930s was firmly rejected. So was the notion of a punitive peace that had crippled the defeated Central Powers of World War I, ensured they could not fully embrace the peace settlement, and ultimately encouraged another global war.

The Bretton Woods Institutions

Formal planning for the revised economic order was a wartime enterprise dominated by the Americans and the British. Each had somewhat different perspectives on what should be done after the war ended, and each produced different blueprints for the future.

The initial international conference to craft a new set of structures was held in July 1944 in the New Hampshire resort town of Bretton Woods at the picturesque Hotel Washington, nestled at the foot of Mount Washington in the White Mountains. Representing forty-four countries, the planners at Bretton Woods began by agreeing that the economic protectionism of the interwar years had contributed to the war and that protectionism had to be attacked if economic stability was to be reinstated. Specifically, they were concerned about international financial and economic practices: large fluctuations in the exchange rates of currencies, chronic balance-of-payments problems experienced by some countries, and the high tariffs that had dominated the 1930s. All of these problems restricted the flow of international commerce, and there was a clear underlying preference for moving toward a system of considerably freer trade than had existed before the war.

The conferees produced agreements that created two institutions forming the core of the Bretton Woods system. At the same time, they deferred consideration of the more politically divisive issue of institutionalizing free trade until after the war was over. The institutions created were the *International Monetary Fund (IMF)* and the *International Bank for Reconstruction and Development (IBRD or World Bank)*. Both had the initial purpose of dealing with the specific economic problems identified during the war. The IMF would deal with currency stabilization and balance-of-payments problems by authorizing what amounted to lines of credit to countries suffering difficulties in these areas. The World Bank was authorized to grant loans, as its formal name implied, to assist in reconstructing war-torn economies and later in developing less developed countries. Both organizations were funded by subscriptions from the members, with weighted voting privileges depending on the amount of the initial subscription. Because the United States had the most money to subscribe, it received the largest bloc of votes (about one-third at the time) in both organizations.

The attempt to institutionalize international free trade did not go so smoothly. It began when the war ended but faced a perilous political course, especially in the United States. Within the American administration of Harry S. Truman, there was great support for an institutional commitment through an organization parallel to the IMF and IBRD, thus completing the Bretton Woods troika of international economic organizations. This idea, however, had both domestic and international opponents who effectively blocked the movement.

The Truman administration's strategy for lowering trade barriers consisted of two parts, both of which have their parallels in the contemporary debate over trade. One of these was to pursue bilateral and multilateral reductions in tariffs and quotas under the provisions of the Reciprocal Trade Agreements Act (RTAA) of 1934. The RTAA, passed in reaction to the extreme protectionism of the Smoot–Hawley Tariff Act of 1930, authorized the administration to reduce tariffs on specific items by up to 50 percent with other countries—but only if the reductions were reciprocal. It did not authorize the elimination of any trade barriers and thus was only a modest first step toward the administration's goal of freeing trade. It was the precursor to the so-called fast-track (or what the Bush administration called trade promotion) authority.

The heart of the free trade initiative was to be an international organization, the *International Trade Organization (ITO)*. The purposes of this organization were to promote free trade among its members and to create an enforcement mechanism to investigate and punish those who violated trade agreements into which they had entered. In order to draft a statute for the ITO similar to those of the Bretton Woods institutions, a preliminary meeting was held in 1947 in Geneva, Switzerland, to lay out trading principles under the name of the *General Agreement on Tariffs and Trade (GATT)*. The GATT was intended as a temporary umbrella, an expedient device wherein general principles could be drafted to govern the permanent ITO.

The meeting at which the ITO was formally proposed was held in Havana in November 1947. By the time it was convened, domestic and foreign opponents to the principle of universal free trade had organized themselves well enough to dilute the outcome. These early "rejectionists" argued against the domestic and international impacts of loosening trading restrictions and for the protection of special arrangements, such as the British Imperial Preference System (which created a special tariff status between Great Britain and members of the empire and Commonwealth). In addition, other national delegations refused to grant the United States the deference accorded it through weighted voting in the IMF and IBRD. Instead, they insisted that the United States be given a single vote like any other country.

Geopolitics and globalization clashed, and the ITO never came into being. President Truman refused to submit the ITO treaty to the Senate in 1948. He feared that in an election year, free trade, with considerable opposition in Congress and from the public (see Amplification 8.1), might become a campaign issue. In 1949, the administration's effort to gain ratification of the North Atlantic Treaty (the first peacetime military alliance in American history) pushed the ITO off the agenda. By the time the president submitted the treaty to the Senate in April 1950, enthusiasm for international organizational solutions to problems had cooled, and the outbreak of the Korean War in June 1950 reinforced that sentiment. In November 1950, Truman withdrew the ITO proposal from Senate consideration, and it was a dead horse until revived in 1993 as the World Trade Organization (WTO).

The GATT, however, survived. Although protectionists did not like it much more than the ITO, it was less threatening to their cause. The GATT was not an organization at all but a series of periodically convened negotiating sessions between sovereign states. This lack of structure meant that it would have no permanent investigating or enforcing staff that could enforce objectionable rules on countries and thereby infringe on their sovereignty. Also, because it was a series of negotiations (that became known as "rounds"), the individual states retained maximum control over what they were willing or unwilling to accept by signing or not signing individual proposals.

Amplification 8.1

THE ITO AND THE ANTI–FREE TRADERS

The noteworthy failure of the Bretton Woods process was the inability to bring the International Trade Organization (ITO) into existence. The result stymied the maximum promotion of free trade, which was one of the major objectives of the architects of the Bretton Woods system. Reflecting the long-standing American ambivalence about the proper role for the United States in the international economic order, the United States both proposed the ITO to the international community and brought about its defeat by failing to ratify the ITO treaty.

As a domestic political event, the scenario was familiar. The principal backers of the ITO were in the executive branch: the original impetus for the body came from State Department planners during World War II, and when Harry S. Truman succeeded the late Franklin D. Roosevelt as president, his administration took the lead in proposing a United Nations Conference on Trade and Development in 1946 to draft the statute for the ITO.

Major opposition congealed in the Congress. The major elements in the protectionist coalition were Republicans who were influenced by major business and commercial interest groups that believed in protecting American products from foreign competition. Both manufacturing and farm elements were represented in this effort. At the other extreme, a number of liberal Democrats believed the ITO statute was too timid a document in promoting free trade and joined the opposition, as did conservatives who opposed the ITO on the grounds that it represented a dangerous assault on American sovereignty. The opposition successfully blocked Senate advice and consent on the matter and provided a precedent for the kind of odd-bedfellows coalition that continues to this day.

The GATT became the banner around which the free traders congregated until the time was right for them to assert their case for a permanent international organization. In the process, the GATT developed a set of four principles that defined its operation and remain important points of reference to this day (summarized in Rothgeb, p. 75). These include *nondiscrimination* (the promotion of most-favored-nation—MFN—status for all subscribing countries), *transparency* (the unacceptability of secret trade restrictions and barriers), *consultation and dispute settlement* (resolution of disputes through direct negotiations), and *reciprocity* (the idea all members should incur balanced obligations).

The free trade issues raised in the 1940s are instructive because they parallel and even anticipate the same kinds of debates and problems that enliven the 2000s. The debate over the extent to which free trade should be an active part of American international economic policy stands at the vortex of the issue. Generally speaking, there has been a domestic political debate with strong interbranch implications: the White House in the 1940s was the epicenter of free trade advocacy under Roosevelt and Truman and has been for the last decade under Clinton, Bush, and now Obama. On the other side of the coin, organized political opposition has largely come from elements in Congress with constituencies harmed by and thus opposed to free trade. What is different is that in the 1940s, most of the organized congressional opposition was Republican, whereas much of the contemporary opposition is Democratic.

Much of the disagreement was over the international institutionalization of free trade. Congressional opposition effectively killed the ITO when Truman determined he did not have the votes in the Senate for ratification, and the issue remained dormant for over four decades. The call for an international organization, the WTO, emerged from the 1993 Uruguay Round of the GATT, and in a changed economic atmosphere where cutting-edge American industries in areas such as telecommunications and financial services would clearly benefit from institutionalization, the Senate passed the treaty forming the WTO (which took effect on January 1, 1995). The ITO was thus reborn as the WTO.

The Breakdown of Bretton Woods

The Bretton Woods system dominated in international economics for over two decades. During this time, the United States held sway over the international economic system basically because the U.S. economy was the dominant economic force in the world. Because countries needed U.S. economic resources and goods, the dollar became the only "hard" currency in the world (the only currency universally accepted in international trade). Regulating the supply and availability of dollars in the international system provided a considerable source of leverage for the United States in international financial circles.

The attractiveness of the dollar was enhanced because it was tied to the gold standard. Every dollar in circulation was backed by gold, with one ounce of gold determined to be worth $35. The gold standard meant that, at least theoretically, anyone with $35 in cash could trade it in for one ounce of gold. The gold standard was always a fiction (the United States never possessed enough gold to redeem all the dollars in circulation), but the promise of the gold standard created an aura of confidence around the value of the dollar that stabilized the entire financial system.

The strength of the Bretton Woods system was predicated on the preeminence of the American economic system and currency, and the system was bound to founder as the relative position of the United States in the world economic order shrunk in the 1960s. Some of these changes were the direct consequence of American actions in the world; others were the result of domestically based political decisions.

Part of the change was the postwar recovery in Europe and Japan. In the late 1940s, the American economy was producing about 40 percent of all the goods and services produced worldwide. This remarkable testimony to American productivity also reflected the absence of productivity in the other traditional industrial countries, all of which were struggling to recover and rebuild from the ravages of the war.

Faced with the geopolitical Soviet menace, it had been explicit U.S. policy starting in the 1940s to assist in the recovery of the European and Japanese economies through programs such as the Marshall Plan. The motivation for this was largely geopolitical—to increase the status of these countries as anti-Communist bastions and to ensure that Communism did not appeal to their citizens. Pumped up by American dollars, the European and Japanese economies did recover—as intended—and became economic competitors to the United States. In the process, the American relative share of global gross national product (GNP) began to shrink, moving downward to the low 20 percents in the 1970s, where it has essentially remained since. The United States did not cease to be the preeminent economic power in the world, but it no longer enjoyed the same overwhelming level of superiority it once occupied—a possible precedent for the current world economic situation.

Since purchases of goods and services in international trade are by and large made in the currency of the country from which those purchases are made, there suddenly was a demand for currencies other than the dollar to pay for goods and services from other countries. In addition, political and economic events during the 1960s were making continuing adherence to the gold standard an increasingly impossible fiction.

Several domestic events and trends in the 1960s contributed to this problem. In the mid-1960s, President Lyndon B. Johnson made the fateful decision to simultaneously finance the Vietnam War and the complex of entitlement programs known collectively as the Great Society without raising taxes. The result was the first sizable budget deficits and consequent accumulation of national debt in the United States since World War II. One outcome was a decline in confidence in the American economy, which, coupled with rising inflation and competition from foreign goods and services, created a new atmosphere in which American economic predominance was actually called into question for the first time since the end of the war.

The ultimate event occurred in 1971, when adherence to the gold standard became such a millstone on the American economy that it could no longer be sustained. The inflationary spiral of the 1960s had resulted in such a flood of dollars into circulation that the fiction of redemption of dollars for gold was increasingly obviously hollow. Moreover, pegging the value of the dollar to gold resulted in overvaluation of the dollar against other currencies, which made it difficult for American producers to compete with their overseas counterparts (it took too many units of a foreign currency to buy enough American dollars to purchase American goods compared to goods from other countries).

These factors combined to force the U.S. government to renounce the gold standard in 1971. Dollars would no longer be redeemable in gold. More important, the value of the dollar would no longer be determined against a set quantity of the precious metal. Instead, the dollar would be allowed to "float" against other currencies, with its value set at whatever price others were willing to pay for it in other currencies. The dollar thus essentially became a commodity like other commodities and would have to compete with other currencies in the marketplace. Almost instantly, other currencies (especially those from places such as Germany and Japan, which produced goods and services desired in world markets) became hard currencies. American preeminence was no longer to be taken for granted.

THE TRANSITIONAL PERIOD, 1971–1990

American renunciation of the gold standard ushered in a period of change in the structure of the international economic system. The broad theme was apparent American decline in military and political power arising from the Vietnam experience, but especially economic decline during the 1970s, followed by resurgence by the end of the 1980s.

The 1970s were a difficult transition period in the United States. Economic turbulence was assured by the oil shocks of 1973 and 1977. Led by its Middle East members, the Organization of Petroleum Exporting Countries (OPEC) took a series of joint actions that greatly raised the price of oil to all consuming countries. In 1973, these actions were accompanied by a boycott of countries that did not denounce Israel after the Yom Kippur War. Since most developed economies were heavily dependent upon oil as an energy source, the result was a markedly higher level of economic competition to gain funds to pay for oil, principally from the Middle East. This competition, in turn, contributed to, even accelerated, eroding American economic competitiveness and the appearance of decline.

American Decline

Economic bad news accompanied the United States' political and military mishaps. One of the apparent legacies of deficits created by financing the war in Vietnam was a high rate of inflation. By the end of the 1970s, it had become "double digit" (over 10 percent annually). Inflation eroded consumer buying power and created a sense of economic malaise. Worse yet, there was growing evidence that American industry was losing its competitive edge against other countries, especially Germany and Japan. The question in the minds of many Americans was not whether the United States was in decline but how pervasive and how permanent the phenomenon was.

The evidence of economic decline seemed to cut across the board. American industries appeared to have become soft, no longer innovating as were competitors in Europe and Japan. American industries were losing market share in a wide variety of products from consumer electronics to heavy machinery, from hospital equipment to automobiles. Some dark predictions hinted this condition might even worsen to the point that the United States would fade into second-class status. Yale historian Paul Kennedy went so far as to prophesy that the United States would fade as a world power due to imperial overreach.

Driven by advances in high technology and changing policies and attitudes within the business and policy communities, things began to change in the 1980s. It was a quiet, virtually subterranean revolution. Much of the perception of malaise from the 1970s continued to dominate the public debate, and until the latter part of the decade, the Cold War continued to be the focal point of international concerns. One was much more likely to hear about the lack of competitiveness of American electronics or the seemingly endless military competition with the Soviets than about the crumbling of the Soviet empire or the resurgence of the American economy.

American Revival

Beginning in the 1970s and accelerating in the 1980s, policy and science coalesced to promote positive change. The policy arena of the 1980s was heavily influenced by the efforts of the Republican administration of Ronald W. Reagan in the United States and Conservative British Prime Minister Margaret Thatcher, both of whom preached for and advocated a reduced role for government in the economic sector and a much more pure form of capitalism. Reagan's domestic economic program is remembered most distinctively for the huge tax reduction he pushed through Congress in 1981 that resulted in runaway government deficits and a skyrocketing debt, the reduction of which became the centerpiece of Clinton fiscal policy in the 1990s. The recurring theme of the Reagan policy was "getting government off the people's backs."

Reagan and those around him also believed that the less government interference in and control over the economy, the better. Reagan's general belief, supported by Thatcher, was that in economic matters, the private sector almost always made better decisions than did government officials and thus should be as unfettered from government intrusion as possible.

The result was two policy thrusts. *Privatization* involved getting government out of operating businesses and turning formerly government-operated functions over to private entrepreneurs and corporations. The idea was that privatization would result in increased efficiency and thus greater value for consumers. In the United States, the breakup of government-controlled monopolies such as long-distance telephone service illustrated this philosophy.

Deregulation was the other shibboleth. The Reaganites believed a major cause of the supposed economic decline was too much regulation of the private sector by the government, thereby stultifying the ability of the private sector to be flexible and to compete both domestically and internationally. By removing strictures on how business could be done, the result was to be greater efficiency in operation and hence competitiveness. Airline deregulation is a primary example of this philosophy in action.

Other forces reinforced this set of policy predilections. A major source of change was the area of high technology, where the fruits of advances in computing and telecommunications (and the merger of these two industries to create the information age) were together changing the content and nature of what composed the cutting edge of economic and scientific activity. If the early post–World War II period had been dominated by the manufacture of goods, services and the monopoly on the most desired information came to represent the "commodity" of greatest value in the evolving economy. Figuratively speaking, software replaced steel-belted tires as the symbol of productivity. American preeminence in these areas became the basis for the American resurgence.

The attractiveness of the American political and social system contributed to this growing American strength, which became the basis for American resurgence in the 1990s. Fired by technological developments in computing, the birth of the Internet, and the like, the centers of American attraction emerged in the 1980s as magnets for the best young minds and the most ambitious entrepreneurs in the world. They tended to congregate in places where there were clusters of great universities and pleasant living conditions and lifestyles. The Silicon Valley in California, nestled between and nurtured by great universities like Stanford and California–Berkeley, became the model for the further development of emerging technology, followed by places such as the Route 128 corridor outside Boston (in the shadow of Harvard and the Massachusetts Institute of Technology, among other schools), the Research Triangle in North Carolina, and others. These enclaves became the collective seedbed of the United States' return to preeminence.

Governmental restructuring and the early glimmers of what became the telecommunications revolution emerged as the pillars of the so-called Reagan revolution that American conservatives continue to view as a model for economic activity. The two influences did fuel a revitalized U.S. place in the global economy and formed the foundation of the "Washington consensus," which provided the intellectual basis for the 1990s growth of globalization, and for those reasons, it is worth considering in some detail.

The globalizing economy of the 1990s formed the base for American and world prosperity and for a more relaxed, less militarized basis of security for that decade. The operation of the globalization-dominated system was, of course, derailed by international religious terrorism, but some of its own dynamics carried to extremes contributed as well. Deregulation carried to extremes that Reagan himself likely would have opposed contributed to the Wall Street meltdown of 2008, and as the United States grasps for a security paradigm for the 2010s, the experiences of both the 1990s and the 2000s offer lessons and cautions.

THE GLOBALIZING ECONOMY, 1990–PRESENT

The system of globalization resulted from a series of individually unspectacular but cumulatively significant trends that came together in the 1990s, unlike a traumatic economic event like American renunciation of the gold standard in 1971. The collapse of Communism provides a political benchmark of that emergence with some economic ramifications for the rise of globalism. The fall of Communism concluded the economic competition between socialism and capitalism. The economic disparities created by globalization might have been the economic force that toppled the Communist world in the 1990s, although many analysts argue that the inability of the Soviets to compete militarily was an equally or even more important factor in the collapse. Imagine the pressure on the socialist societies of Eastern Europe to join the general prosperity if they had remained on the wrong side of a still-existing Iron Curtain but could see how the West lived. Even more dramatically, imagine the trauma for China of being a geopolitical enemy of the United States, while simultaneously trying actively to participate in trade with this country.

Globalization began with a distinctive set of values forged during the transition period during the 1970s and 1980s, and the value of trade was the 1990s' most important contribution to its evolution. Acceptance of the rules and values of globalization has been the sine qua non for membership in the global economy and thus, for most purposes, participation in the prosperity that was a part of the globalizing economy in the 1990s. Those countries that rejected participation had to suffer the economic consequences in terms of prosperity.

The emergence of the globalizing economy coincided with and helped contribute to the general global prosperity of most of the 1990s. At its height, the pressures toward globalization seemed ineluctable, and criticisms were weak and overwhelmed by advocates—even cheerleaders—such as the *New York Times'* Thomas L. Friedman. The euphoria has proven to be at least partially overly inflated. As chinks appeared in the armor of globalization enthusiasm, the domestic and international critics came forward in increasingly public ways.

The basic arguments for and against globalization go back to fundamental arguments in the American political debate about the American place in the world (internationalism versus isolationism) and participation in the global economy (free trade versus protectionism), to say nothing of the parallel debate about national security (realism versus idealism). The result is a debate about the attractiveness of globalization as an alternative paradigm to geopolitics that requires looking at its characteristics and objections to it.

Characteristics and Values

The building blocks of the evolving "system of globalization" (to borrow Friedman's phrase) are central economic phenomena from the 1980s and the 1990s. The major contribution of the 1980s was the reassertion of the capitalist ethic of market-based economics. This philosophical underpinning proposed to free national economies from the government meddling and interference that, it was argued, had been a barrier to entrepreneurial growth and innovation. Privatization and deregulation were major tools in this policy change.

The major contributions of the 1990s represented not only a continuation, but also a reversal of some policies with their roots in the 1980s. The continuity came in the form of the election of free trader Bill Clinton to succeed free trader George H. W. Bush as president. As a result, free trade advocacy dominated in the executive branch of the U.S. government during most of the 1990s and beyond.

The reversal in policy came through Clinton's successful commitment to wiping out budget deficits and reducing government debt as a way to improve the atmosphere in which economic entities did business in the 1990s, an emphasis largely abandoned after September 11.

A caveat to the legacy of the 1980s with relevance for the 2010s—market capitalism *within* national economies—must be added. The market capitalists rejected governmental management of economic activity, but they did *not* reject all governmental participation in providing a nurturing business environment. The specific area of policy in which government participation was welcome is governmental regulation, especially in overseeing the activities of financial institutions and in adopting macroeconomic policies that facilitate how business operates.

The willingness to accept some regulation of fiscal activity—especially the actions of banks and other financial institutions—has its American roots in the so-called S&L (savings and loan) scandal of the 1980s. The scandal is important because almost the same problems and solutions have been encountered as part of the economic crisis beginning in 2008. Prior to the S&L crisis, the country had deregulated this banking sector, in much the same way as the expansion of financial institutions into new areas was left unregulated in the 2000s.

The result in the 1980s was the collapse of the savings and loan industry. The "thrifts," as they were known, were limited-purpose financial institutions specializing in activities such as home mortgages and business lending. Their attractiveness to investors was that they generally paid higher interest rates than regular banks and were thus desirable depositories for the savings of small investors. They were not, however, subject to the same standards of reporting of activities as were regular banks, a matter that was not of great concern because savings accounts were insured by the government and no S&Ls had ever failed.

The scandal emerged when a number of S&Ls went bankrupt and threatened to dishonor investor accounts. The most famous bankruptcies were associated with the S&L empire of Arizona entrepreneur Charles Keating, Jr. The investigation of a number of his institutions revealed a pattern of investor fund misuse through bad loans that could not be repaid (called nonperforming loans) and even bribes to public officials. As the modest savings of many Americans were threatened, the U.S. Congress passed legislation aimed at guaranteeing investor confidence by ensuring honesty and "transparency" (having records of transactions, the financial conditions of financial institutions, and the like publicly available for inspection) within these institutions. The reforms enacted in response to the S&L crisis restored public confidence and willingness to invest in institutions that loan funds to entrepreneurs. Over the objections of a Clinton administration that wanted them strengthened, these rules regarding accounting standards were relaxed after 1994. The results included corporate scandals (Enron, for instance) in the early 2000s and more fundamental difficulties since in the financial industry culminating in the economic crisis of 2008.

The same rationale—bolstering public trust—applies to other forms of macroeconomic policy. Proponents of the Reagan-based model believed the government has a limited useful role in the economy beyond making sure that bankers and others are honest. More specifically, the government can provide a useful service in creating a favorable fiscal climate for business and in providing services that are otherwise burdensome for the private sector.

The major beneficial macroeconomic policy of the 1990s was deficit reduction and elimination, a direct reversal of the practices of the Reagan years championed by Clinton and his closest economic advisors. A major impact of the Reagan deficits was to force large-scale government borrowing to cover obligations for which there were inadequate tax receipts. Much of this borrowing came from the American private sector, to which the government had primary access before private enterprises. Some of the money borrowed came from foreign sources (a controversial matter in its own right), but a sizable amount came from American sources. With the government in effect skimming funds available for borrowing before private firms got a chance, the result was a smaller pool of financial resources available for private firm innovation and investment. This problem recurred and contributed to slower economic growth rates in the mid-2000s; it has become an even more fundamental problem as the United States seeks to rebound from the current crisis.

Under this model of limited government participation in the capitalist system, the government encourages entrepreneurial activity by providing the social net in the form of social programs such as the social security benefits originally instituted in the 1930s and expanded across time to include Medicare and Medicaid and related benefits for the general population. One of the purposes of universal health care reform will likely be health care portability, thereby removing some of the responsibility for health care from businesses. Doing so frees private concerns from having to develop such systems themselves, thus becoming the social net for their employees, and provides considerable flexibility for firms in their operations. In theory, employees are no longer tied closely to individual companies upon which they rely for things like health care and social security upon retirement. Instead, devices such as portable health insurance and government-provided pensions theoretically free companies to tailor and downsize their workforce without undue regard for the social consequences of laying off workers whose functions have been bypassed by change.

The other policy triumph of the 1990s was the victory of free trade, a primary emphasis and legacy of Clinton. In concept, free trade represents the extension of David Ricardo's theory of comparative advantage to international economics. Politically, it represented the triumph, at least for the balance of the 1990s, of the free traders over the protectionists.

The ascendancy of free trade represented more of a practical than an ideological victory. When Clinton came to office, one of his first priorities was the successful passage through the Congress of the North American Free Trade Agreement (NAFTA), negotiated by George H. W. Bush. The traditional coalitions had lined up in support and opposition based upon general preferences about American participation in international economics and the like. The authorizing legislation for NAFTA passed by a narrow margin in both houses of Congress (as an economic agreement rather than a treaty, it required House as well as Senate approval). NAFTA was followed by a flood of other activity supported by the free traders that, by the end of the decade, had locked the United States into a web of free trade associations in addition to NAFTA, such as the Asia–Pacific Economic Cooperation (APEC) at the regional level and the WTO at the global level.

Advocacy of globalization has become more subdued in the contemporary environment for both economic and geopolitical reasons. Why? Economically, the broad answer is that economic circumstances have changed. When Clinton came to office, the recession of 1991 that had helped defeat the incumbent Bush in the 1992 election was lifting, replaced by an eight-year period of sustained growth in the local and global economies. One can debate the degree to which Clinton was responsible for or simply the beneficiary of this expansion, but it was a period of unprecedented growth from which the vast majority benefited economically. The trade that Clinton promoted was clearly a major element in the prosperity, as cheaper foreign goods poured into the country to benefit consumers. While some American industries such as textiles suffered, in most cases there was enough prosperity to absorb most of those displaced. The argument that freeing trade was at least partially responsible for the prosperity was difficult to refute in that atmosphere, a situation that free trader Clinton nurtured and exploited.

In geopolitical terms, of course, the emphasis moved away from globalization to a virtually total interest in the aftermath of September 11—notably, the global war on terrorism (GWOT) and extensions of it, such as the Afghanistan and Iraq Wars. Globalization did not disappear from the scene—trade levels continued to grow, and efforts to expand free trade continued. What changed is the relative emphasis given to globalization. Large, spectacular efforts such as the Free Trade Area of the Americas (a proposal to make a free trade area of all the Western Hemisphere other than Cuba) have been deemphasized or quietly shelved in favor of bilateral or more limited international agreements that require less energy to consummate. The lowering of the profile of globalization has also coincided with growing domestic and international criticism of globalization and the continuing intrusion of other concerns on the national security agenda.

Objections to Globalization

The glow that surrounded globalization in the 1990s was probably too bright to sustain under the best of circumstances. In the early and mid-1990s, the globalization-driven expansion in the world economy seemed to be a "rising tide that lifts all boats," promising a growing prosperity to all that joined it and a seemingly brighter alternative to the dreary, bellicose ambience of the Cold War. Globalization seemed to provide a brighter future to everyone.

That bright future, as it turns out, was overblown. As the millennium changed, the global economy cooled, and many national economies suffered setbacks that led to modifications of the rising tide analogy. It became apparent that the tide of globalization lifted some boats much higher than others and that it even swamped some of the smaller, less seaworthy boats. Domestically, the Ricardian consequence of comparative advantage was being felt as uncompetitive industries were being undercut, costing Americans and non-Americans jobs. This, in turn, helped fan the flames tended by those who had objected to globalization all along. The economic crisis starting in 2008 only adds to these problems.

International Objections. Globalization became controversial in ways that would have seemed inconceivable except among its most diehard opponents in the 1990s. The January/February 2007 issues of *Foreign Policy* and *Foreign Affairs* featured articles titled "How Globalization Went Bad" and "Has Globalization Reached Its Peak?" Both assertions would have generally been considered heretical a decade earlier, but they captured the tone of global criticisms, which can be grouped around four objections.

The first objection centers on the western, and especially American, domination that accompanies subscription to globalization and participation in the global economy. In order to become an active, participating partner in the globalization system, countries have been required to accept the rules of conduct of the so-called Washington consensus, mentioned earlier. These rules are based heavily on the American conceptualization of capitalism and require governments to do a series of things to become "eligible" to participate in the system (which effectively means gaining the kind of international rating that encourages investment and trade with other members). These requirements include things like balancing governmental budgets, instituting strict banking and other procedures that make the financial sector more "transparent" (open to outside inspection), and removing subsidies for noncompetitive industrial and other sectors of the economy—only some of which are actually practiced in Washington.

The imposition of the Washington consensus may distort the economies of target countries, especially during the transition from whatever form the economy of a given country possessed to the "golden straitjacket" (Friedman's term) of conformance with the Washington consensus. Almost all countries undergoing globalization are required to undergo economic belt-tightening, which has negative economic and political effects on these regimes and their populations. During the good times of the 1990s, when all boats were being lifted enough that differentials could be ignored, these strictures seemed acceptable, if painful. In the less economically expansive 2000s, the sacrifices have seemed more painful and less acceptable, triggering negative reactions that have resulted in the election of antiglobalization governments in a number of countries that sought to enter the globalization system in the 1990s. One reaction has been the election of populist, antiglobalization administrations in countries like Argentina, Bolivia, and Venezuela, to cite three examples.

Another objection involves the difference between the broad systemic (or macro) and the individual or group (or micro) effects of globalization—a factor with both international and domestic impacts. Generally speaking, most of the arguments favoring globalization are made at the macro level: globalization—and its handmaiden, free trade—expands the global economy and the economies of various countries that are part of the globalization system. That is true, and in some countries, it has resulted in a broad enthusiasm and embrace of globalization (India is a notable example). While the macroeconomic argument is generally not assailed, its impacts at the microeconomic level are. The micro level reflects the impact of globalization on individuals and groups within societies, and the impacts can be quite negative.

Two examples of the microeconomic malaise that fuels opposition to globalization stand out. The first, which is basically domestic in the countries where it occurs, results because forcing uncompetitive industries out of business does not always lead to retraining displaced workforces for productive careers. Instead, those displaced simply become unemployed (or underemployed in lower-paying, less skilled jobs), where they become a source of political dissent. The second is the process of so-called outsourcing: maintaining competitive advantage by moving production away from its current base to somewhere else where the function can be performed at lower costs. Those industries employing electronic media have been particularly notable in this regard; shipping telemarketing jobs from the United States to India, is one example. In any case, the result is unhappy former workers who now find foreigners doing the jobs they had performed. The result may be a stronger economy at the macro level but opposition at the micro level.

Despite these objections, is globalization inevitable under any circumstances? Resistance to the inexorable nature of globalization comes from two basic sources. For some countries (mostly the poorest), there is essentially nothing that they produce at comparative advantage, meaning they do not benefit from participation. In fact, adopting free trade means undercutting their domestic production, which is, by definition, uncompetitive. It is notable that the largest group of countries that are not members of the World Trade Organization are extremely poor countries. The other countries that respond negatively to the notion of inevitability are those that have politically consequential groups that are adversely affected by globalization. One of the consequences of making the transition to the globalization system is accepting economic austerity measures, and these measures tend to create privation that is absorbed primarily by the lower classes in developing countries. Where there is a tradition of populism (as is the case in many countries in South America), these disaffected groups can wield (or be mobilized to wield) significant opposition to globalization. The rise of populists like Venezuela's Hugo Chavez is at least partly the result of this phenomenon.

These objections did not seem of great consequence during the 1990s, when it appeared that globalization was not only inevitable but also universally beneficial. When it began to become evident that those benefits were neither as automatic nor as munificent as first argued, then opposition began to surface. That opposition, in turn, has weakened the power of globalization as an instrument around which to organize the system because it means the lever that grants or denies participation is not so universal. It would, for instance, be helpful to the U.S. government to be able to threaten Chavez with the prospect of nonparticipation in globalization if he does not moderate his anti-American policies; however, since Venezuela has basically opted out of the globalization system and rejected its values, such a threat lacks force. On a smaller scale, the same is true elsewhere.

Domestic Objections. Some of the foreign objections to globalization are also present in the United States. During the heyday of globalization during the 1990s, opposition was mostly limited to traditional anti–free trade groups that were the successors of opponents of the ITO during the 1940s. Their composition is described in Amplification 8.2.

Amplification 8.2

THE REJECTIONISTS

As noted earlier, resistance to free trade has a long-standing history in the United States. In the 1940s, one coalition of opponents managed to help jettison approval of the ITO. With the rise of globalization in the 1990s, rejection of free trade and its institutionalization through the WTO returned, if with somewhat different actors leading the movement.

Who are the rejectionists? They are a single-issue coalition bound together in their opposition to various aspects or implications of globalization that have very few, if any, other common interests. The interests they represent, however, have been present for a long time. First, there are the protectionists, who feel personally threatened by lowering trade barriers. In the 1940s, the protectionists were mostly conservative Republicans representing big business and commerce; today, they are predominantly Democrats representing the interests of trade unionists in industries that cannot compete successfully without trade protection. Second are those who feel that efforts to institutionalize globalization are too timid. Environmentalists, for instance, believe that institutions like the WTO will not adequately regulate environmental degradation by international corporations and governments (they believe that globalization is dominated by private interests with little environmental sensitivity). At the same time, others believe that the interests of developing world countries left out of the globalization policy are underrepresented. Finally, there are objections from groups that feel globalization undercuts national sovereignty.

The domestic opposition tends to focus on the micro level of adverse economic impacts of globalization on different groups within American society. One strong strain of this opposition comes from the perceived bias of globalization toward big business. William Greider, writing in *The Nation*, for instance, complains of "corporate-led globalization" and its alleged pernicious effects. These include "all the benefits of being American—government services and subsidies, the protection of the US military—while discarding reciprocal obligations to the country: jobs, economic investment and paying a fair share of the tax burden."

The second, and loudest, complaint is the impact on jobs. Even Ben Bernanke, chairman of the Federal Reserve Board, admitted this problem in August 2006 (quoted in Abdedal and Segal). "Changes in the pattern of production are likely to threaten the livelihoods of some workers and the profits of some firms, even when these changes lead to greater productivity and output overall," he said. "The natural reaction of those affected is to resist change, for example, by seeking the passage of protectionist measures." This statement encapsulates the micro-macro level of disagreement; while Bernanke is attempting to make the macro point, he is also acknowledging the micro perspective.

The United States in a Multipolar Economic Environment

Contemporary conditions may resemble those that surrounded the breakdown of the Bretton Woods system in the 1970s. After a long run of American preeminence after World War II, the United States was increasingly challenged in the 1970s; the same kinds of factors may be present in the global economy facing the 2010s.

The shape and standing of globalization will almost certainly be altered by the global response to the global economic recession/depression (there continues to be disagreement about which it has been) that began in fall 2008 and lingers to the present. As noted, a milder recession in 1991–1992 served as a springboard for an American-led (some would argue American-dominated) surge of globalization during the balance of the 1990s. That may recur, but there are factors this time that limit the likelihood of a reprise.

One negative influence is the global perception that practices in the United States—notably on Wall Street—were basically responsible for the crisis and its depth. Most observers ascribe much of the blame to underregulated financial markets in the United States that permitted and arguably even encouraged risky, irresponsible behavior by Wall Street manipulators whose actions spread to infect other countries' financial sectors as well. While the United States has begun a process to lessen the likelihood of a recurrence, the experience has raised questions about the infallibility of American economic leadership in the future. When the global economy rebounds, it is unlikely to be on the basis of unquestioned American leadership.

The productive underpinnings of American leadership are also not so clearly apparent in the contemporary environment. Fueled largely by U.S. predominance in the telecommunications revolution, the American economy was clearly the beacon to which other countries were drawn in the 1990s. That is no longer so clearly the case. In terms of the production of goods, the United States slipped behind China in 2008 (before the crisis began), and American technological superiority is no longer so obvious. Countries like India now compete with the United States in areas such as applying technology to consumer outcomes. The United States is no longer so clearly king of the hill in global economics.

The result is a much more multipolar economic environment, in which multiple states are important, competing factors in influencing global economic agendas and the outcomes of disputes over agenda items. The United States retains the advantage of being overwhelmingly the world's largest market, but it is also increasingly the world's largest debtor—a dubious and controversial distinction. The result is that it is not entirely clear that the United States will be able to dictate the contours and face of globalization for the 2010s the way it did in the 1990s.

New Additions to the National Security Agenda

The more relaxed geopolitical environment of the 1990s and the more charged atmosphere of the 2000s also saw the addition of several other concerns to the list of items that affect national security. These new items represent an expansion of the basic concept of what constitutes security beyond its roots in protecting American soil from hostile military threats. Security has become more than military and economic security.

No list of these new agenda items will be complete enough to satisfy everyone, so no claim of inclusiveness is made here. Rather, several new factors that represent the additional kinds of concerns that have been added to the national security agenda are presented. For this purpose, there are three candidates for national security concern: energy security, environmental security, and border security. All three have some relationship to globalization: energy consumption is the motor of economic productivity, the environment is clearly one of the concerns surrounding globalization, and border security has become an issue because globalization has had more beneficial impacts in some places than in others. Each topic is examined by raising three questions: How important is the issue (does it represent a threat to vital interests, the traditional criterion for military-based national security concerns)? Does its outcome affect the country's basic security, and if so, how? And what means, military or nonmilitary, are most appropriate for dealing with it?

Energy Security. As suggested in Chapter 4, the problem of having secure access to energy supplies is relatively new for the United States. Historically, the United States had within its boundaries adequate supplies of necessary sources of energy (coal, petroleum, later uranium) to meet the country's needs as it developed as a major power. That situation changed during the period after World War II and has evolved to a situation where the United States is now dependent on energy—principally petroleum—from foreign sources. The reasons for this change are numerous but include the exhaustion of cheap domestic sources of petroleum (oil that could be extracted at low enough prices to be profitable because of depletion of cheaply recoverable supplies) and increases in demand for petroleum-based energy.

This transition has created vulnerability for the United States that is shared by most of the world that does not possess large, easily accessible petroleum resources. The United States, for instance, consumes nearly 22 million barrels of oil a day (out of a global supply of 85 million barrels a day). Half of that petroleum is imported from the volatile Persian Gulf region, and other parts of its come from places like Venezuela and Nigeria, neither of which is the most reliable supplier to the United States (Nigeria because of unstable politics, Venezuela because of its political difficulties with the United States). Worldwide demand for petroleum is increasing: the decisions by China and India to mass-produce automobiles for their populations will add a major source of demand for petroleum beyond current available supplies (worldwide demand is about 83 million barrels a day). If demand continues at current levels, the results will include a much more furtive competition among oil consumers to curry friendship and favor with current and projected producers and a resultant increase in the political leverage of those producers.

The energy problem will not solve itself. It is linked vitally to two contradictory international imperatives. One is the prosperity attached to the globalization system: energy consumption is the single strongest correlate of economic productivity. To join the economic prosperity or to keep (or increase) one's place in the globalizing economy, secure access to energy, which means petroleum-based energy for the foreseeable future, is absolutely necessary. The contradictory influence is the effect of fossil-fuel burning on the atmosphere (greenhouse gas emission) and hence global warming (see below). Environmentalism seems to militate for reduced (or alternate) energy use, whereas prosperity—and an alternative to a geopolitical basis of security—calls for greater consumption and thus greater geopolitical competition.

The continued addiction of the United States (currently the world's leading importer of foreign petroleum) to foreign energy creates distinctive national security dilemmas that would, at a minimum, be different in the absence of that need. The most obvious is in the Middle East. Two-thirds of the world's established reserves of petroleum are in the Persian Gulf littoral area, and secure access to it has been deemed so important to the United States that President Carter declared that access to be a vital interest to the United States in his 1980 State of the Union address (the so-called Carter Doctrine). That declaration has formed the basis for American policy in the region ever since Carter declared it. The consequences are, of course, debatable but include American leadership in the Persian Gulf War of 1990–1991, continued military interaction with Iraq throughout the 1990s (Operations Northern and Southern Watch), and the Iraq War. Whether these involvements would have occurred or would have been the same without the United States' requirement for petroleum from the area is debatable. That need has, however, created the perceived dictate for a continuous American military presence in the region since 1990, which Usama bin Laden has repeatedly stated is one of the major bases of his animus toward the United States (see Chapter 13).

Another consequence, raised in Chapter 7, surrounds the emerging role of Russia, given its newfound prominence as a petroleum and natural gas exporter. As noted, Russia is now the world's second-largest exporter of petroleum and controls very large reserves of petroleum and natural gas in the Caspian Sea area and in Siberia. The United States' closest political allies in Europe are highly dependent on Russian energy, and the potential to interrupt that supply gives the Russians enormous potential leverage in Europe (a point of some relevance, for instance, regarding the cancelled American-proposed and Russian-opposed missile defense scheme in Eastern Europe, discussed in Chapter 9). While the United States is not itself dependent on Russian energy, that energy is underpinning the Russian revival as a world power.

Energy accessibility will remain a major, direct American security issue as long as the United States depends critically on foreign supplies for its vitality. Lessening that dependency has become recognized as a major priority for American security, although exactly how to achieve it is controversial because all the solutions entail painful political decisions. The chief proposed alternatives are making the transition to alternate energy sources and conservation (independently or in combination), but both have drawbacks. Alternate sources are either questionably adequate (wind and solar energy, for instance), questionably responsive to other problems (coal and the environment, as an example), or opposed on other grounds (nuclear energy waste storage and disposal, for instance). The other alternative is conservation, but implementing meaningful conservation measures (those that would reduce imports noticeably) either requires lifestyle changes Americans are reluctant to undergo (e.g., driving less in lighter, smaller, and more fuel-efficient vehicles) or is potentially disastrous (the effects of energy reductions on economic productivity). The failure to come to grips with the current energy problem, of course, means that measures—including military deployment and employment—to keep access to necessary foreign energy sources will remain high on the national security agenda.

The entire energy issue, including its security aspects, is a major priority of the Obama administration. General James Jones, the retired Marine Commandant who serves as national security advisor (NSA) to Obama, is known to be a particularly strong advocate of conceptualizing energy as a security concern, and the president is a strong supporter of developing alternative, especially domestic, sources of energy. The administration has both environmental and national security motivations. Although essentially no one believes the United States can, in the foreseeable future, achieve the absolute security of total sovereign control over all the energy it consumes, the combination of reduced consumption and alternate sources can reduce dependency and attendant security concerns. The problem of protecting oil tankers from Somali pirates is an example of a security threat that would not exist if the United States was independent of Middle Eastern oil. Environmental impact has also been added to the mix of influences affecting national security.

Environmental Security. The ties between efforts to sustain the environment and national security are less direct than with energy. The idea that the maintenance, protection, and promotion of a healthy, sustainable environment should be a security concern is of reasonably recent vintage, and equating the two concerns tends to galvanize two politically opposing forces, environmentalists and those with a primarily traditional national security orientation grounded in military affairs. Thus, the process of identifying whether and how the two concepts are conjoined has not been an entirely easy one.

The major environmental issue with national security implications is global warming. Part of that conjunction has already been suggested: the fact that much of the carbon dioxide problem at the root of the global warming phenomenon is the result of producing energy from the very fossil fuels discussed directly above. Reductions in petroleum consumption would clearly assist the efforts to reduce or reverse greenhouse gas emission and would thus aid the global environmental condition (unless it is replaced with other polluting sources). Efforts to do so, however, have geopolitical implications, since reductions by some countries but not others could hurt the productivity of the compliers, while promoting the productivity of the abusers, and thus affect the global power formula. It is this fear, for instance, that fueled at least part of the Bush administration's insistence on including China in the formula for carbon dioxide reductions mandated by the Kyoto Protocol (China and India, potentially two of the largest polluters, are excluded from Kyoto provisions as developing countries).

A major difficulty of treating environmental issues within a national security framework is the problem of immediacy. Most national security analyses focus on immediate, here-and-now threats to the country, of which military and even economic examples are plentiful. Environmental threats, however, lack such urgency. No one, for instance, argues that the worst possible outcomes of global warming (or even some of the less drastic consequences) would not affect the security of many Americans (and citizens elsewhere). A modest rise in sea levels, for instance, would have very strong impacts on the millions of Americans living in the coastal southeastern United States (the Carolinas, Georgia, and most of Florida), where homes and businesses are only a few feet above current sea levels. Should these be endangered immediately (as was the case in New Orleans because of Hurricane Katrina), it would be considered a national security emergency. Because these projections are both conjectural (not everyone agrees when or if they will to occur) and generally distant (over the next fifty to one hundred years), they do not evince the same immediacy of concern as, for instance, the dangers of an international religious terrorist attack.

There are two generally underemphasized national security concerns that are environmentally based. One regards environmental pollution by the military. Many military bases (Ft. Ord in California is a prime example) were so polluted by military activities (firing artillery shells, burying waste, etc.) that their future use has been endangered pending expensive cleanup that the military has been reluctant to undertake as an unnecessary diversion of scarce resources. The other concern is that the United States was at the forefront of opposition to environmental activities during most of the 2000s, and this soured its relations with various countries in other areas. While there is, for instance, no direct link between what foreign governments feel about American opposition to participation in the Kyoto process (which most deride) and support or opposition to other American security concerns (Iraq, for instance), at a minimum the United States standing at odds with much of the world community on environmental issues did not enhance support for the United States on other issues. The announced agreement of the United States to participate in follow-on talks beyond Kyoto that began in Copenhagen in late 2009 is an indication of a changed perspective on the importance of environmental issues.

Border Security. The problem of lack of immediacy does not extend to the current national security issue of border security for the United States, especially its long border with Mexico. Making the borders safe from unwanted incursion is one of the major responsibilities of any government; without that ability, there is little operational meaning to sovereign control of territory. Thus, the frontiers between countries and between countries and the bodies of water that may form their boundaries are a natural and basic national security concern for all countries.

As in other matters, border security has not occupied a high priority historically for the United States. Especially through the long formative period of the republic, ocean boundaries provided a buffer for the United States from potential hostile others who would have to sail either the Atlantic or the Pacific Ocean to exact harm against the country. The land borders with Canada and Mexico were likewise innocuous from a security vantage point, since neither country posed any particular threat to the United States. The result was that both boundaries, and especially the long United States–Canada border, were essentially unfortified and unguarded.

That pristine condition has, of course, disappeared, and the sanctity of U.S. borders has become a major political issue. The catalyst for this concern was originally the issue of illegal immigration by Mexicans and Central Americans across the southern border into the United States, but that is not the only reason the U.S. government worries about the status of the border. In addition, the flow of illegal drugs across the Mexican-U.S. border (where estimates are that up to 90 percent of illicit drugs entering the country transit) and onto the American shoreline became an issue as part of the "war on drugs" during the administration of George H. W. Bush between 1989 and 1993, and increasing drug cartel violence in Mexico with the potential to spill over the border into the United States has recently intensified that concern. The GWOT has added the prospect of terrorist penetration of the United States to the mix. Illegal immigration (by other than terrorists) and drugs are not a particular problem regarding the Canadian border, and most of the emphasis on securing the coastline has centered on the smuggling of drugs into the country by sea and by air. The three aspects of the border problem—immigration, drugs, and terrorism—come together on the currently volatile issue of the U.S.–Mexican border.

Each of these aspects is a separate problem. Illegal immigration has become a major problem since the middle 1990s, when the number of Mexicans and other illegal residents of the United States began to soar from about 1.5 million to current estimates of 12 million or more. This focus has become the epicenter of political concern, although it is not a national security problem in any conventional manner (the immigrants pose no military threat to the United States, for instance). Their numbers do, however, contribute to other domestic problems, affecting such areas as health care, education, and jobs. As a national security concern, immigration is most clearly relevant to conditions that make life commodious and is secondarily a concern as an indication of the ability to make territory inviolable.

The drug problem has a more conventional national security aspect, since the trafficking in drugs contributes to criminality, including violence, against American citizens and has a major corrupting and destabilizing effect politically in countries through which the drugs pass on their way to the United States, notably Mexico. The drug interception problem contains domestic as well as international concerns. At one level, the problem is primarily domestic: the reason there is a problem of drugs crossing the border is, after all, the huge market for illicit drugs in the United States. If the domestic drug problem were to disappear, so would the border problem, including the reverse flow of narcotics profits and weapons out of the United States, flows that add to the international aspect of border security that deals with drug cartel violence transiting the border from Mexico to the United States. The upshot is that this aspect of the border problem is much more than simply a border concern.

The problem of terrorists sneaking across the border, of course, has direct national security impact, since people entering in this manner successfully clearly evade identification and detection by appropriate authority, making it more difficult to interfere with any terrorist act in which they may seek to engage. It is difficult to determine how great this part of the problem is. Unlike efforts that result in the capture of illegal immigrants or the interception of drugs, the interception of potential terrorists coming across the border is never publicized for fear that doing so would compromise future efforts. Clearly, preventing the violation of the border by terrorists is the most important and potentially consequential of the three aspects of border security, but assessing the extent of the problem or the effectiveness of border security efforts in this area is the most problematical.

The current focus of the border problem has been how to seal the border from the unwanted intrusion of all three of these problems—with the emphasis on illegal aliens and more recently on drugs and drug violence. Currently, the major proposal for doing so has centered on a fence that would put a physical barrier along about 700 of the 1,933 miles of the United States–Mexico border. Building such a fence was authorized by legislation passed by Congress and signed by President Bush in 2006 (the Border Protection, Antiterrorism, and Illegal Immigration Control Act), but construction has been slow because of controversies surrounding the proposal. These include whether a fence that leaves almost two-thirds of the border not barricaded will work (most of Texas, for instance, will not have a fence), whether any fence can stop the immigration (some argue that building a fence will simply make it more expensive for immigrants to get across the border by hiring criminal guides), and how to build the fence. According to the Department of Homeland Security, which would have jurisdiction over the project, a "state of the art" fence would cost between $4 and $8 billion (for the 700 miles), whereas a ten-foot prison-style fence (chain link topped with concertina wire) would cost about $850 million (plus an extra $360 million to electrify it) and a twelve-foot high, two-foot thick concrete wall would cost about $2 billion. Past experience (notably the fence built along the border adjacent to San Diego) suggests the probability of significant cost overruns. Moreover, it is not entirely clear how this fence would protect against people simply walking across the border at unprotected locations (often at considerable personal danger) or burrowing under the fence (a favorite method among drug dealers).

The other question raised by a multipurpose fence is that of jurisdiction. Different agencies, after all, have jurisdiction over the various objects with which the fence is supposed to deal, and it is apparently not unusual to find representatives of the Drug Enforcement Agency (drugs), Immigration and Customs Enforcement (terrorists), and the Border Patrol (immigrants) at odds in particular cases. The most notorious case to date has involved the arrest and conviction of two Border Patrol agents for shooting and killing a drug trafficker with connections to the Drug Enforcement Agency who was crossing the border, a conviction overturned in 2009.

CONCLUSION: GLOBALIZATION AND OTHER FACTORS IN AMERICAN SECURITY

Globalization in some evolving form will simply be a continuing factor of international life in the 2010s, and the only way it or other concerns raised in this chapter could be reversed altogether would likely be as the result of some catastrophic international event such as a global war. That outcome may seem unlikely in the current context, and the shock of the global recession has not shaken the basic global belief in either the inevitability or the basic desirability of globalization.

Does globalization add to or detract from the American place in the world and thus American security? And what can be done to improve problematical aspects to make the process better serve those interests, including enhancing security? In the prosperous 1990s, when globalization was given credit—rightly or wrongly—for helping to create and sustain prosperity, the answer was likely to be automatically positive. In the more cautious economic condition of a postmillennial era more focused on terrorist and other assaults on physical security, the assessment is likely to be more guarded and critical.

One aspect of the question, which also provides an intellectual bridge to the next chapter, may illustrate the difficulty of reaching expansive conclusions. It is the connection between globalization and sovereignty. As noted in Chapter 2, the retention of state sovereignty is a core realist value that has always been particularly important to the United States. Guarding American sovereignty has sometimes forced the United States out of step with the rest of the world.

By definition, the retention of effective state sovereignty is a major element of the country's national security, making the relationship between sovereignty and globalization an important matter. At the same time, if globalization contributes to the greater economic well-being of Americans, is any dilution of sovereignty that results from globalization a good bargain? Moreover, a virtue of globalization has been to impose American economic values on others, bringing them into conformance with American ideals. Should the question therefore be, Whose sovereignty is compromised?

An example may clarify thinking about this. One part of the statute creating the WTO gives it the power to investigate allegations of trade violations by member states and, where it finds violations, to prosecute and impose mandatory sanctions against violating governments. In the ratification debate over the WTO, this provision was widely condemned by defenders of American sovereignty, as had been the case over a similar provision in the proposed ITO in the 1940s. The counterargument was that most of the rules of the WTO would enforce were American values, making vulnerability minimal and assuring that others would be forced to conform as well. Conformance to the WTO charter thus cuts both ways: it dilutes the sovereign control of both the United States and those other countries it seeks to influence.

The statute has indeed had both effects. A major argument for sponsoring Chinese membership in the WTO was that it would force China to reform its economic practices in ways that would lessen the ability of the Chinese government to maintain authoritarian control over the economy and ultimately, it was hoped, over the political system. While this was a difficult step for a Chinese government that is also a prime defender of state sovereignty, it is the price China had to pay for full membership in the global economy.

As an example of how the statute cuts both ways, shortly after the WTO came into force in 1995, the Clinton administration sought to improve the United States' balance of payments situation with Japan by forcing the Japanese to buy more American automotive components to put into Japanese cars. To this end, Clinton announced his intention to place a high excise tax on Japanese luxury cars entering the United States, which would have made them uncompetitive with domestic models. The hope was that the Japanese would cave in and agree to import more American car batteries and tires to avoid these penalties. Instead, the Japanese cried unfair trade practices and threatened to drag the United States before the WTO, where the United States would certainly have lost any judgment rendered. Faced with that likelihood, the Clinton administration withdrew the threat to exercise its state sovereignty through the excise tax.

Challenge!

OTHER NATIONAL SECURITY CHALLENGES?

If the 1990s ushered in a broadening of the kinds of issues and concerns that are described in national security terms, will the 2010s witness a similar expansion? One example may be the need to respond to state failure resulting from terrorist intervention, of which the case of Pakistan, discussed in the next chapter, may be an example. The availability of adequate supplies of potable water in the world may be another.

But are there additional candidates? Are there new and more-or-less foreseeable man-made or natural disasters or trends that will rise to national security status? Is, for instance, the depletion of ocean fisheries such a problem? In 1990, hardly anyone would have conceived of a large military involvement by the United States in Iraq, but that clearly happened—twice. What may be next? Think about it!

The 1990s also witnessed other concerns muscling their way onto the national security agenda, and three that were discussed in this chapter have survived the national fixation with 9/11 that dominated most of the first decade of the new millennium. Doubtless there will be new concerns that will arise in the future, and the *Challenge!* box invites the reader to think about these new influences.

The national security environment will continue to evolve, conditioned by experience and new challenges. Nearly a decade after its occurrence, it may be possible to begin to sort out the national security legacies of the second fault line of 9/11 as part of the clarification process of looking forward to a new era. Chapter 9 begins that process by examining some of the legacies of the terrorist experience.

STUDY/DISCUSSION QUESTIONS

1. Compare and contrast the concepts of globalization and geopolitics. Are they compatible and mutually reinforcing, or antithetical, or both? Discuss.
2. What was the Bretton Woods system? What institutions did it create for what purposes? How has it evolved? How do the concepts of globalization and free trade fit into its evolution? Discuss in terms of the ITO–WTO process. How and why did the Bretton Woods system break down?
3. What distinguished the transitional period between 1971 and 1990? How did its evolution form the base for the globalization system?
4. What is the globalization system? What are its major characteristics and values?
5. What have been the major international and domestic objections to globalization? How are they related to one another?
6. Discuss energy as a national security problem. How would the use of military power by the United States have been different over the past twenty-five years without U.S. dependence on Middle Eastern oil?
7. How and why can environmentalism be thought of as a national security problem? Discuss.

8. Discuss the various aspects and locations of the U.S. border problem. Regarding the current emphasis on the Mexican-U.S. border, what are the most important aspects of the problem? How are they national security problems (or are they)? Will building a fence along roughly one-third of the border solve the problem?

SELECTED BIBLIOGRAPHY

Abdedal, Rawi, and Adam Segal. "Has Globalization Reached Its Peak?" *Foreign Affairs* 86, no. 1 (January/February 2007): 103–114.

Altman, Robert. "The Great Crash." *Foreign Affairs* 88, no. 1 (January/February 2009): 2–14.

Blinder, Alan S. "Offshoring: The Next Industrial Revolution." *Foreign Affairs* 85, no. 2 (March/April 2006): 113–128.

Diehl, Paul R., and Niles Peter Gleditsch, eds. *Environmental Conflict*. Boulder, CO: Westview Press, 2001.

Dregner, Daniel W. *U.S. Free Trade Policy: Free Versus Fair*. New York: Council on Foreign Relations Press, 2006.

Dunn, Robert. "Has the United States Really Been Globalized?" *Washington Quarterly* 24, no. 1 (Winter 2001): 53–64.

Feldstein, Martin. "A Self-Help Guide to Emerging Markets." *Foreign Affairs* 78, no. 2 (March/April 1999): 93–109.

Friedman, Thomas L. *The Lexus and the Olive Tree: Understanding Globalization*. New York: Farrar, Straus, and Giroux, 1999.

———. *The World Is Flat: A Brief History of the Twenty-First Century*. New York: Farrar, Straus, and Giroux, 2005.

Fukuyama, Francis. *The End of History and the Last Man*. New York: Free Press, 1992.

Greider, William. "Comment: A Globalization Offensive." *The Nation* 284, no. 4 (January 27, 2007): 5–6.

Kennedy, Paul. *The Rise and Fall of the Great Powers: Economic Change and Military Change from 1500 to 2000*. New York: Random House, 1987.

Keohane, Robert O., and Joseph S. Nye, Jr. *Power and Interdependence*. 2nd ed. Glenview, IL: Scott Foresman/Little Brown, 1989.

Levey, David H., and Stuart S. Brown. "The Overstretch Myth." *Foreign Affairs* 84, no. 2 (March/April 2005): 2–7.

Luttwak, Edward. "From Geopolitics to Geo-economics: Logic of Conflict, Grammar of Commerce." *National Interest* 20 (Summer 1990): 17–24.

Lynn-Jones, Sean, and Stephen Miller, eds. *Global Dangers: Changing Dimensions of International Security*. Cambridge, MA: MIT Press, 1995.

Mattoo, Aaditya, and Arvind Subramanian. "From Doha to the Next Bretton Woods." *Foreign Affairs* 88, no. 1 (January/February 2009): 15–26.

McBride, Stephen, and John Wiseman, eds. *Globalization and Its Discontents*. New York: St. Martin's Press, 2000.

Nye, Joseph S., Jr. *Bound to Lead: The Changing Nature of American Power*. New York: Basic Books, 1990.

Payan, Terry. *Three U.S.-Mexican Border Wars: Drugs, Immigration, and Homeland Security*. Westport, CT: Greenwood, 2006.

Pirages, Dennis C., and Theresa Manley Degeest. *Ecological Security: An Evolutionary Perspective on Globalization*. New York: Rowman and Littlefield, 2004.

Podesta, John, and Peter Ogden. "The Security Implications of Climate Change." *Washington Quarterly* 31, no. 1 (Winter 2007–2008): 115–138.

Rockenbach, Leslie J. *The Mexican-American Border: NAFTA and Global Linkages*. Oxford, England: Routledge, 2001.

Rothgeb, John M. J. *U.S. Trade Policy: Balancing Economic Dreams and Political Realities*. Washington, DC: CQ Press, 2001.

Sachs, Jeffrey. "International Economics: Unlocking the Mysteries of Globalization." *Foreign Policy* 10 (Spring 1998): 97–111.

Snow, Donald M. *Cases in International Relations: Portraits of the Future*. 3rd ed. New York: Pearson Longman, 2008.

Victor, David G., M. Granger Morgan, Jay Apt, John Steinbruner, and Katherine Ricke. "The Geopolitical Option." *Foreign Affairs* 88, no. 2 (March/April 2009): 64–76.

Weber, Steven, Naazneen Barma, Matthew Kroenig, and Ely Ratner. "How Globalization Went Bad." *Foreign Policy* (January/February 2007): 48–54.(FP doesn't have volume nos.)

Yergin, Daniel. "Ensuring Energy Security." *Foreign Affairs* 85, no. 2 (March/April 2006): 69–82.

CHAPTER 9

Legacies of 9/11

PREVIEW

The fault line of 9/11 brought the problem of terrorism to the forefront of international concerns affecting American national security, and it remains the most obvious and powerful national security legacy of the 2000s. Terrorism became a ubiquitous factor in national security concerns for that decade and a vital part of the backdrop for ongoing concerns in the 2010s. Because of that importance, this chapter investigates the nature of the terrorist problem, how it is changing, and what can be done about it. It begins by examining the dynamics of terrorism: what it is, what terrorists seek to do, who they are, and what causes people to become terrorists. It then moves to how terrorism has evolved as a problem since September 11. Finally, the discussion considers how the terrorism past affects the present—its legacies—by looking at two important issues that likely would not have been as important otherwise: torture and the fate of Pakistan.

The two fault lines were very different in content and effect on the United States. Both, of course, were traumatic, but in different ways. The first fault line represented the end of a forty-year confrontation; failure to manage the Cold War could have threatened civilization, and its cessation, while surprising and initially disconcerting, opened the way for a true relaxation of tensions (détente) among the major players. In retrospect, it was clearly a positive event that made possible the relative tranquility of the 1990s described in the last chapter.

The second fault line was, in important ways, just the opposite. It created a period of tension and conflict that has remained the single most important national security challenge for the last decade. Moreover, international religious terrorism is the underlying force that has propelled American national security policy and efforts since 2001, and it remains a potent part of the environment for the 2010s.

Because the role of terrorism remains pervasive, it must be given full attention here. The discussion of terrorism will be divided into two separate expositions befitting its impact on American and world thinking about national security. In this chapter, attention will be directed at the phenomenon of terrorism and how the dynamics of terrorism have become such a ubiquitous part of the overall national security effort. The purpose of this discussion will be to show terrorism as a primary legacy of the 2000s for the national security problem for the 2010s. In Chapter 13, the discussion will move to how terrorism can be suppressed and, if not extinguished, at least brought under some reasonable degree of control—at best, an outcome parallel to ending the Cold War.

The extent of the legacy of 9/11 remains to be written, of course, since terrorism remains a lively force and its perpetrators beyond American control. Terrorism came as a shock to Americans and remains an amorphous, shadowy phenomenon, so the discussion will begin by describing terrorism in some detail, with an emphasis on international religious terrorism centered in the Middle East and providing the primary threat to Americans. Following that exposition, the chapter will turn to two special legacies, one primarily domestic and one mostly international, that illustrate the legacies of terrorism. The primarily domestic instance is the problem of purported torture authorized and carried out by officials of the U.S. government in the prosecution of the war on terror, actions that, if indeed undertaken, represent violations of American and international law. As a legacy, they raise questions about what is appropriate in the pursuit of national security. The international example concerns Pakistan, one of the world's most fragile countries, which has been pushed to the brink of national chaos because of terrorists. Whether American efforts have made Pakistan's situation better or worse is part of the legacy that this case will have for the future. (see note on p. 1)

Terrorism and the well-publicized global war on terrorism (GWOT) have dominated the national security agenda in the United States since the September 11 attacks by Al Qaeda against New York and Washington, D.C., targets. The problem of terrorism was not unknown within the government and expert communities before September 11, and it has been revealed after the fact that there had been premonitions and even fairly specific warnings that Al Qaeda would attempt something like what it did. Because terrorism had heretofore been an apparently minor problem that had not captured the central attention of the public or top political leaders, the warnings went unheeded, and American vulnerability was revealed in shocking, bloody relief.

The problem of terrorism is unique and enigmatic. It is an ancient practice that most historians date back at least to biblical times, and it has recurred episodically and persistently ever since, to the point that it is not unfair to characterize the phenomenon of terrorism as a permanent feature of the international environment. Individual terrorists and their causes come and go, but terrorism remains. Finding a way to deal effectively with terrorism has thus been a central factor in modern, post–September 11 defense policy, and it remains so.

The effort to contain terrorism and to hunt down and suppress its perpetrators is now almost a decade old. It has had some successes, notably in capturing or otherwise suppressing elements of the old Al Qaeda network, but the problem of terrorism and Al Qaeda has not abated. The apparently monolithic threat posed by Al Qaeda itself is arguably smaller than it was in 2001, but the problem of terrorism itself is not: new permutations have arisen that are, if anything, more provocative and dangerous. Al Qaeda in Iraq (Mesopotamia) is an example. Most share radical Islam as a foundation, but from Chechnya to Indonesia, new and different organizations have emerged as new challenges: international terrorism has become a hydra-headed beast.

Before turning to an examination of the phenomenon, three related observations are necessary to provide context for the comments that follow. First, although people speak of a global war on terrorism, the use of the term *war* is unfortunate, deceiving, and distorting. As the term is normally used, *war* refers to armed combat between combatants organized as states or between states and organized oppositions within these states. War, in other words, is an action that pits people against other people, and the groups attack one another to impose their will on those other people. Terrorism, on the other hand, is a more intangible idea, a method by which people seek to accomplish goals. One cannot attack and subdue an idea as if it were an enemy army. What one can do is to oppose and subdue people who act from ideas—to make war on terrorist organizations like Al Qaeda (although their lack of a territorial base makes subduing them difficult); the best one can do with an idea is to discredit it.

The second observation flows from the first: the war analogy is further flawed because it implies that the opposition can be defeated—that the purpose of the war is to suppress and eliminate the opposition. Terrorism is indeed an ancient practice that transcends efforts to suppress and defeat individual manifestations—defeating Al Qaeda or any other terrorist organization will not eliminate the phenomenon, just particular practitioners. There will always be terrorists somewhere, and the realistic purpose of those opposed to terrorism is to *contain* the problem, not eliminate it.

Third, because terrorism cannot ever be eliminated altogether, efforts in opposition to it are exercises in *risk reduction*, not risk elimination. Risk, as already noted in Chapter 3, is the difference between threats to interests and capabilities (or resources) to counter, contain, or eliminate those threats. Although the level of terrorist threat ebbs and flows across time, it is essentially always potentially greater than the resources available to effectively thwart all manifestations of the threat. Terrorism, to paraphrase former German Chancellor Helmut Schmidt, is a problem to be worked, not solved once and for all. Any strategy or policy that is aimed at "smashing" or "defeating" terrorism is bound to come up short.

The discussion will proceed through three steps, all aimed at putting terrorism into perspective. It will begin by defining terrorism, centering the discussion on what is unique about terrorism as a phenomenon. Because there is disagreement about why people have become terrorists (and thus why others may reach that decision in the future), the discussion will move to alternative explanations. Finally, it will move to the first part of the legacy, the evolution of international religious terrorism since 9/11.

DEFINING TERRORISM

What exactly constitutes terrorism is confusing to many people. Thus, the first step in coming to grips with terrorism is defining the term. Many phenomena in the contemporary international arena are labeled terrorist. For some, terrorism became the sobriquet for anything or anybody to be opposed after 9/11. This makes a definition particularly important as a means to measure whether a particular movement or act is terrorist or not. Without a set of criteria to define what does and does not constitute terrorism, one is left disabled in trying to make a determination.

Having an agreed-upon definition of terrorism helps answer questions about potential terrorist activities, but unfortunately, such an agreement does not exist. Rather, there are virtually as many different definitions as there are people and organizations making the distinctions. There are also some commonalities that recur across definers, making it possible to adopt a definition for present purposes. A few arguably representative examples aid in drawing distinctions.

The U.S. Department of State offers the official governmental definition, which is applied in its annual survey of international terrorism. Its definition of terrorism is "premeditated, politically motivated violence perpetrated against noncombatant targets by subnational groups or clandestine agents, usually intended to influence an audience." In *Attacking Terrorism*, coeditor Audrey Kurth Cronin says terrorism is distinguished by its political nature, its nonstate base, its targeting of innocent noncombatants, and the illegality of its acts. Jessica Stern, in *Terrorism in the Name of God*, defines terrorism as "an act or threat of violence against noncombatants with the objective of exacting revenge, intimidating, or otherwise influencing an audience." Alan Dershowitz (in *Why Terrorism Works*) offers no definition himself but notes that definitions typically include reference to terrorist targets, perpetrators, and acts.

These definitions and similar ones from others in the field differ at the margins but have common cores. All of them share three common points of reference: terrorist acts (illegal, normally violent), terrorist targets (usually innocent noncombatants), and terrorist purposes (political persuasion or influence). The only difference among them is whether they specify the nature of terrorists and their political base: the State Department, Cronin, and Dershowitz all identify terrorist organizations as nonstate-based actors. Cronin, in particular, emphasizes that "although states can terrorize, by definition they cannot be terrorists."

The definition used here incorporates the three components of terrorist acts, targets, and purposes but not the criterion of terrorist organizations as nonstate actors. Historically, states have been leading terrorists either by condoning the actions of government organizations like the secret police or by creating, commissioning, or controlling the activities of terrorists. In the contemporary setting, almost all terrorist organizations are nonstate-based, and this fact is at the heart of the difficulty in dealing with them. Defining terrorism as a nonstate-based activity, however, removes an important category of past (and conceivably future) activity from the definitional reach of terrorism. The nonstate basis is a characteristic of modern terrorism, not a defining element.

For present purposes, terrorism is defined as the commission of violent acts against a target group, normally to gain compliance with some demands the terrorists insist upon. Terrorism thus consists of three related phenomena, each of which must be present in some manner for something to be considered an act of terrorism. If all three elements are present, so is terrorism. If one or more elements are missing, the phenomenon is not terrorism but something else. Discussing each helps contribute to an understanding of what constitutes terrorism.

Terrorist Acts

The first part of the definition refers to *terrorist acts*, which are the visible manifestation of terrorism and the part of the terrorism dynamic with which most people identify. Several comments can be made about terrorist acts.

Terrorist acts are distinguished from other political expressions in that they are uniformly illegal. Terrorist acts are intended to upset the normalcy of life through destructive actions aimed at either injuring or killing people or destroying things. Although terrorists normally couch their motives in lofty political terms, the actions they commit—and especially their focus on noncombatants whose only "guilt" is being part of the targeted group—break laws and are subject to criminal prosecution. By raising the rhetoric of terrorist actions to acts of war (currently holy war, or *jihad*), terrorists may seek to elevate what they do to a higher plane ("one man's terrorist is another man's freedom fighter"), but the simple fact remains that terrorist acts are criminal in a legal sense.

The general purpose of terrorist acts is to frighten the target audience: indeed, the word *terrorism* is derived from the Latin root *terrere*, which means "to frighten." The method of inducing fright is the commission of normally random, unpredictable acts of violence that seek to cause such fear that those who witness or learn of the acts will conclude that compliance with terrorist demands is preferable to living with the fear of being future victims themselves. Acts of terrorism are not necessarily aimed at the actual victims themselves (who are often randomly selected and whose individual fates do not "matter" to the terrorist) but at the audience who views the actions. As Brian Jenkins once put it, " *Terrorists want a lot of people watching and a lot of people listening, and not a lot of people dead"* (emphasis in original). The dynamic of inducing this fright is the disruption of the predictability and safety of life within society, one of whose principal functions is to make existence predictable and safe. Ultimately, a major purpose of terrorism may be to undermine this vital fiber of society.

Beyond frightening the target audience, individual terrorist acts are committed for a variety of reasons, not limited to the normally expressed political goals of particular terrorist organizations. Al Qaeda, for instance, says that its most fundamental goal is the expulsion of the West (especially the United States) from the holy lands of Islam and that its acts (especially those serving bin Laden's *fatwa*, calling for killing Americans everywhere) are intended to further that goal. But that is not the only motivation for particular actions.

Terrorists sometimes act for other reasons. Jenkins provides a list of six other, generally less lofty, purposes for terrorist actions. First, terrorist actions may be aimed at exacting special concessions, such as ransom, the release of prisoners (generally members of the terrorist group), or the publicizing of a message. A case in point is the capture and threatened (or actual) beheading of foreigners by Iraqi resistance groups in the early stages of the Iraq War to force countries to withdraw their nationals from Iraq. In that case, the capture of foreign nationals was at the base of demands to release prisoners and efforts to force foreign countries to withdraw from the international relief effort in that country. Jemaah Islamiyah carried out its 2004 attack on the Australian embassy in Jakarta, Indonesia, and promptly announced that it would perpetrate similar attacks if its leader, Abu Bakar Bashir, was not released from prison.

Second, terrorists may act to gain publicity for their causes. Before Palestinian terrorists kidnapped a series of airliners and then launched an attack on the Israeli compound at the Munich Olympics in 1972, hardly anyone outside the region had ever heard of the Palestinian cause; the terrorist actions resulted in global awareness of that cause. The publicity may be intended to remind a world that has shifted its attention away from a particular group and its activities that it is still active and pursuing its goals. One of the apparent reasons for the spate of Chechen violence in 2004, for which Chechen leader Shamil Basayev claimed credit, was to remind the world that the Chechen movement to gain independence from Russia were still alive.

A third, and more fundamental, purpose of terrorist acts is to cause widespread disorder that demoralizes society and breaks down the social order in a country. This, of course, is a very ambitious purpose and one that presumably can be undertaken only through a widespread campaign that includes a large number of terrorist acts, and it is the kind of objective most likely to be carried out by governments or semigovernmental actors. The suicide terror campaign by Hamas against Israeli civilians (and arguably Israeli counterattacks against Palestinians) provides an example of terrorism for this purpose.

A fourth, more tactical use of terrorism is to provoke overreaction by a government in the form of repressive action, reprisals, and overly brutal counterterrorism that may lead to the overthrow of the reactive government. This was a favorite tactic of the Viet Cong in the Vietnam War and evoked the ironic analogy among Americans of building schools during the day (as a way to pacify the population) and then bombing those schools at night (because those schools were occupied by and used as staging grounds by the Viet Cong after nightfall).

A fifth purpose of terror may be to enforce obedience and cooperation within a target population. Campaigns of terror directed by the governments of states against their own citizens often have this purpose and are often assigned to a secret police or similar paramilitary organization. The actions of the KGB in the Soviet Union, the Gestapo and other similar organizations in Nazi Germany, and the infamous death squads in Argentina during the 1960s and 1970s provide examples of the government use of terror to intimidate and frighten its own population into submission. At a less formal governmental level, many of the actions of the Ku Klux Klan during the late nineteenth and early twentieth centuries against Black Americans qualify as well.

Jenkins's sixth purpose of terrorist action is punishment. Terrorists often argue that an action they take is aimed at a particular person or place that is somehow guilty of a particular transgression and is thus being meted out appropriate punishment for what the terrorists consider a crime. Although the Israeli government would disagree that its counterterrorist campaign to bulldoze the homes of the families of suicide terrorists or to bomb the homes of dissident leaders on the West Bank were acts of terror, the Palestinians clearly viewed them this way. The Israelis suspended the policy in 2008.

Stern adds a seventh motivation that is internal to the terrorist organization: morale. Like any other organization, and especially terrorist groups in which the "operatives" are generally young and not terribly mature, it may be necessary from time to time to carry out a terrorist attack simply to demonstrate to the membership the continuing potency of the group as a way to keep the members focused and their morale high. As Stern puts it, "Attacks sometimes have more to do with rousing the troops than terrorizing the victims." Improving or maintaining morale may also have useful spin-off effects, such as helping in recruiting new members to the group or in raising funds to support the organization's activities.

A final comment about terrorist acts concerns whether, or to what degree, they are successful. The answer is rather clearly mixed and is related to the scale of the actions and their intended results. In some cases, terrorism has been highly successful—but usually in relatively small ways where the terrorists' purposes were bounded and compliance with their demands was not overly odious. To cite one example, terrorist demands for release of jailed members of their groups have, on occasion, been complied with, although some countries are more prone to comply than others.

It is when terrorists make large demands and follow them up with sizable actions that they tend to be less successful. When terrorists come to pose a basic perceived threat to the target country because of the audacity of what they have done or the perceived obnoxiousness of what they propose, the reaction by the target may be, and usually is, increased resolve rather than compliance. The September 11, 2001, attacks, after all, did not result in a groundswell of sentiment for the United States to quit the Middle East (especially Saudi Arabia), as bin Laden and Al Qaeda demanded; rather, they stiffened the will of the country to resist. This poses something of a quandary to the terrorist: the more ambitious a group becomes, the more likely it is to increase opposition to achievement of its goals. On the other hand, sizing terrorist acts downward to levels that will not increase resolve may result in less positive and less satisfying outcomes.

What this discussion of terrorist acts seeks to demonstrate is that, like virtually everything else about the subject, terrorists act for a variety of reasons. Some of these are more purposive and "noble" than others, but it is not clear what may motivate a particular action. Moreover, different reasons may motivate different groups at different times and under different circumstances. Knowing that a terrorist attack has occurred, in other words, does not necessarily tell one why it has been committed.

Terrorist Targets

The targets that terrorists attack can be divided into two related categories. The first is people, and the objective is to kill, maim, or otherwise cause some members of the target population to suffer, usually as an example for the rest of the population; in some cases, terrorists target and kill specific people whom they oppose in order to eliminate them, of course. The second category is physical targets, attacks against which are designed to disrupt and destroy societal capabilities and to demonstrate the vulnerability of the target society. The two categories are obviously related in that most physical targets are located where people will be killed or injured in the process. As well, attacking either category demonstrates the inability of the target population to provide protection for its members and valued edifices, thus questioning the efficacy of resisting terrorist demands.

There are subtle differences and problems associated with concentrating on one category of target or the other. Clearly, attacks directly intended to kill or injure people are the most personal and evoke the greatest emotion in the target population, including the will to resist and to seek vengeance. From the vantage point of the terrorist, the reason to attack people (beyond some simple blood lust) is to attack the target population's will to resist the demands that terrorists make. Snow and Drew refer to this as *cost-tolerance*, the level of suffering one is willing to endure in the face of some undesirable situation. Terrorists seek to exceed the target's cost-tolerance by making the target conclude that it is less painful (physically or mentally) to accede to the terrorists' demands than it is to continue to resist those demands—that is, by maximizing the level of fear and anxiety that the target experiences because of the often hideous effects of attacks on other members of the target group. If cost-tolerance is exceeded, the terrorists win; if the target remains resolute, the terrorists do not succeed (which may not be the same thing as saying the terrorists lose).

Recognizing that producing fright is the objective reinforces Jenkins's observation about the intent of those committing terrorist acts against targets. It is, after all, impossible to frighten dead people, nor can the victims of murder capitulate and accede to demands. Only survivors who view the carnage and wonder if they will be next can be so manipulated, and terrorists have a vested interest in keeping enough around to buckle to their demands.

Overcoming target cost-tolerance is not an easy task, and it usually fails. For one thing, terrorist organizations are generally small with limited resources, meaning that they usually lack the wherewithal to attack and kill a large enough portion of the target population to make members of that population become individually fearful enough to cause them to give in to terrorists. Blowing up people on airplanes may be a partial exception. One of the great fears associated with terrorist groups obtaining and using weapons of mass destruction is that such a turn of events would change that calculus. However, attacking and killing innocent members of a target group (at least innocent from the vantage point of the group) may (and often does) infuriate its members and increase rather than decrease the will to resist. If this is the case, then the result is counterproductive from the terrorists' viewpoint.

When the targets are physical things rather than people per se, the problems and calculations change. When the target of terrorists is physically a whole society, the range of potential targets is virtually boundless. In attacking places, the terrorist seeks to deprive the target population of whatever pleasure or life-sustaining or life-enhancing value the particular target may provide. The list of what used to be called *countervalue* targets when speaking of nuclear targeting (things people value, such as their lives and what makes those lives commodious) covers a very broad range of objects, from hydroelectric plants to athletic stadiums, from nuclear power generators to military facilities, from highways to research facilities, and so on. Compiling a list for any large community is a very sobering experience. The problem is further complicated because acting to protect one class of targets may simply cause terrorists to move on to another class (a process known as target substitution).

It is unreasonable to assume that the physical potential target list for any country can be made uniformly invulnerable. There are simply too many possible targets, and the means of protecting them are sufficiently discrete that there is little overlap in function (protecting a football stadium from bombers may not have much carry-over in terms of protecting nuclear power plants from seizure). As a result, there will always be a gap between the potential threats and the ability to negate all those threats, and the consequence is a certain level of risk remaining: realistically, protecting targets is an exercise in risk reduction, not elimination.

Terrorist Objectives

The final element in the definition of terrorism is the objectives, or reasons, for which terrorists do what they do. These objectives, of course, are directed against the target population and involve the commission of terrorist acts, so the discussion of objectives cannot be entirely divorced from the other two elements of what constitutes terrorism.

For present purposes, the discussion of terrorist objectives refers to the broader outcomes that terrorists seek (or say they seek) to accomplish. Objectives are the long-range reasons that terrorists wage campaigns of terrorism. In the short run, terrorists may engage in particular actions for a variety of reasons, as already noted (group morale or recruitment, for instance). What they seek ultimately to accomplish is the province of terrorist objectives.

It is useful to distinguish among types of goals terrorists pursue. The major objectives of terrorists, their ultimate or strategic goals, refer to the long-term political objectives to which they aspire. For Al Qaeda, for instance, the removal of Americans from the Arabian Peninsula is a strategic goal; for Chechen separatists, independence from Russia is the ultimate objective. At the same time, terrorists also pursue interim, or tactical, goals, which generally involve the successful commission of terrorist acts against the target population. The purpose, in the case of tactical objectives, is to demonstrate continuing viability and potency, to remind the target of their presence and menace, and to erode resistance to their strategic goals.

Because most terrorist groups are ultimately political in their purposes, terrorist objectives are political as well. To paraphrase the Clausewitzian dictum that war is politics by other means, so, too, is terrorism politics by other, extreme means. The objectives that terrorists pursue may be extreme to the target population but not to the terrorists themselves. Sometimes terrorist objectives are widely known and clearly articulated, and at other times, they are not. Ultimately, however, campaigns of terror gain their meaning in the pursuit of some goal or goals, and their success or failure is measured by the extent that those goals are achieved.

As a form of asymmetrical warfare, terrorism is, of course, the method of the militarily weak whose ideas are generally unacceptable to the target population, a subject examined in detail in Chapter 11. The extremely asymmetrical nature of terrorist actions arises from the fact that terrorists cannot compete with their targets by the accepted methods of the target society. Terrorists lack the military resources to engage either in open, conventional warfare, at which they would be easily defeated, or in the forum of public discourse and decision, because their objectives are unacceptable, distasteful, or even bizarre to the target population. Thus, terrorists can neither impose their purposes on the target nor persuade the target to adopt whatever objectives they want. These facts narrow the terrorists' options.

The fact that terrorist objectives are politically objectionable to the target sets up the confrontation between the terrorists and the target. Normally, terrorist goals are stated in terms of changing policies (Palestinian statehood or the right to repatriation within Israel, for example) or laws (releasing classes of unjustly detained people) in ways that the majority in the target state find unacceptable. Since the terrorists are in a minority, they cannot bring about the changes they demand by normal electoral or legislative means, and they are likely to be viewed as so basically lunatic and unrealistic by the target audience that it will not accord seriousness to the demands or those who make them. To the terrorists, of course, the demands make perfect sense, and they are frustrated and angered by the treatment their demands are given. The stage is thus set for confrontation.

Terrorists achieve their objectives by overcoming the will of the target population to resist, or by exceeding cost-tolerance. The campaign of terrorist threats and acts is intended to convince the target population that acceding to the terrorist demands is preferable to the continuing anxiety and fear of future terrorism. If the target population concludes that giving in to the terrorist demands is better than continuing to resist, cost-tolerance has been exceeded, and the terrorists win. If continuing resistance (even increased defiance) is the outcome, then cost-tolerance is not exceeded, and the terrorists do not succeed.

The failure to achieve strategic objectives is not the same thing as total failure, however. The successful terrorizing of a large society by a small group of terrorists is a tall order, one for which the terrorists (almost by definition) do not have the resources to achieve. At its zenith, after all, Al Qaeda consisted of probably fewer than ten thousand active members, who could hardly bring the United States to its knees. Terrorism is, after all, the "tactic of the weak," and there are real limitations on the extent of the danger such groups can physically pose. The degree to which a target society inflates—even overinflates—the extent of the threat is, arguably, an indicator of terrorist success.

Determining whether terrorists achieve their goals or fail is complicated by the contrast between the tactical and strategic levels of objectives, making the compilation of a "score card" difficult. Modern terrorists have rarely been successful at the strategic level of attaining long-range objectives. Al Qaeda has not forced the United States from the Arabian Peninsula (although American presence has declined), Russia has not granted Chechnya independence, and Jemaah Islamiyah has yet to achieve a sectarian Islamic state in Indonesia. At the same time, the terrorist record of achieving tactical objectives (carrying out terrorist attacks) is, if not perfect, not a total failure either. As long as terrorists continue to exist and to achieve some of their goals, they remain a force against the targets of their activities. Thus, the competition between terrorists and their targets over the accomplishment of terrorist objectives continues to

Amplification 9.1

THE UNITED STATES–AL QAEDA STANDOFF?

The concerted campaign by Al Qaeda against the United States and the countercampaign by the United States against Usama bin Laden's terrorist organization have now been ongoing for nearly a decade since 9/11, and neither side is measurably close to overcoming the cost-tolerance of the other and bringing the competition to a conclusion. The United States has been unable to "disrupt, dismantle, and destroy" Al Qaeda, in President Obama's terms, and Al Qaeda has been incapable of launching a successful tactical attack, much less a strategic attack, against American soil.

Is the situation effectively a standoff? For the confrontation to end successfully for the United States, it must obliterate Al Qaeda, a task that the United States has not been able to accomplish. Given the geopolitical situation along the Afghanistan–Pakistan border, it may continue to prove impossible without actions that could have worse repercussions, particularly in Pakistan (see the discussion of Pakistan later in the chapter). Al Qaeda, on the other hand, remains an irritant for the United States as long as it cannot be destroyed, and continuing in that status may be the most it can expect and thus be satisfactory to its members.

If this assessment is at all accurate, the standoff could last for a long time. As long as the standoff does not include successful attacks on American soil, is that outcome acceptable? In other words, is it possible to eradicate terrorism, or must accommodation to the reality of some continuing terrorist threat form the basis of policy? The answers depend to some degree on how people look at and what causes terrorism.

exist within a kind of netherworld where neither wins or loses decisively and thus both can claim some success: "We do not give in to terrorism," defined as resisting terrorist strategic objectives, versus "We succeed by killing the infidels," defined as the successful commission of acts of terrorism. This may mean that, in some cases, terrorism may become a permanent fixture of the environment, where particular terrorists can neither succeed nor be eliminated, a prospect raised in Amplification 9.1.

PERSPECTIVES ON AND CAUSES OF TERRORISM

For most people, terrorism is such an alien phenomenon that they have difficulty conceptualizing exactly what it is and why people would engage in acts of terrorism, up to and including committing terrorist acts that involve their own planned deaths (suicide terrorism). And yet the historical and contemporary public records are strewn with enough instances of terrorism to make confronting the conceptual "beast" necessary for understanding and coping with reality and devising strategies and policies that will combat it.

Terrorism may be too complex a phenomenon to capture entirely in a few pages of text, but it is possible to gain some insights into it by viewing it through two lenses. The first is by examining three perspectives that try to capture terrorism and its place in international politics. The second is by looking at three of the explanations commonly put forward to answer the question, Why is there terrorism?

Three Perspectives

Where does terrorism fit into domestic and international politics? Is terrorism ever a legitimate enterprise, or is it always something outside the realm of legitimacy? Answers to these questions depend on one's perspective, as captured in a typecasting of terrorism as legitimate or illegitimate behavior. Two polar opposite perspectives are generally the basis for such a discussion: terrorism as crime and terrorism as war. To these two distinctions, a third, developed throughout the discussions, is terrorism as a specific kind of warfare, asymmetrical war.

The basic distinction serves two purposes. It speaks to the legitimacy of terrorism: a depiction of terrorism as crime clearly stamps it as illegal and thus illegitimate, whereas depicting it as war (of one sort or another) raises its status among actions of states and groups. The distinction also suggests the appropriate approach to dealing with terrorism either as a legal problem or as a military problem, which is also a contentious matter.

The *terrorism as crime* perspective focuses on terrorist acts and their acceptability, with an emphasis on their illegality. It is primarily the perspective of the victims of terrorism. All terrorist acts against people and things violate legal norms in all organized societies: it is against the law to murder people or to blow up things, after all, regardless of why one does so. If acts of terrorism are, at their core, criminal acts, then terrorists are little more than common criminals and should be treated as such. Terrorism thus is at heart a criminal problem, and terrorists are part of the criminal justice system, subject to arrest, incarceration, trial, and, where appropriate, imprisonment or execution. This is the perspective that most European countries have toward terrorism.

Terrorists simultaneously reject and embrace this depiction. They reject the notion that what they do is criminal because their acts—while technically illegal—are committed for what they believe are higher political purposes. Terrorists kill people, but they do not murder them. Terrorists are not criminals; rather, they are warriors (in contemporary times, "holy" warriors). Thinking in this manner elevates the status of the terrorist from criminal to soldier, a far more exalted and acceptable position. At the same time, terrorists prefer for target societies to think of them as criminals in those situations in which they are captured and brought to justice (assuming the capturing society adheres to its own criminal procedures, which is not always the case). The reason is simple: at least in the West, criminal procedures are considerably more stringent in procedural and evidentiary senses than military law, affording terrorists greater protections under the law and making their successful prosecution more difficult. Attempts in the United States to relax criminal safeguards regarding terrorists seek to change that status but have created controversy in civil rights and liberties terms.

Terrorists prefer the second perspective, *terrorism as war*. This viewpoint emphasizes the political nature of terrorism and terrorist acts, in essence adopting the Clausewitzian paraphrase that "terrorism is politics by other means." If one accepts the basic premise of this perspective, then terrorist acts are not crimes but acts of war and, as such, are judged by the standards of war, which apply different rules regarding the killing of people. The interactions between terrorist organizations and their targets are thus warlike, military affairs. Killing outside situations of war is always illegal, but within war, it is permissible, at least within certain bounds regarding who is killed and in what conditions that killing occurs.

The current global war on terrorism implicitly accepts this perspective, if not its implications. Within the GWOT, the term *war* is used rather loosely and almost allegorically rather than literally, and almost all apostles of the designation do not view terrorists as warriors but rather as wanton criminals to be brought to justice or their demise. Within the antiterrorism campaign in Afghanistan, for instance, members (or alleged members) of Al Qaeda were not treated as prisoners of war, which would have afforded them certain legal rights under the Geneva Conventions on War, but instead under the legally vague and controversial designation of "detainees," who the Bush administration apparently believed do not possess Geneva Convention protections.

The problem of treating terrorism as crime or as war is that, in most cases, it is both. Terrorists do engage in criminal acts, but they do so for reasons more normally associated with war. This suggests that there should be a third way of depicting terrorism, which can be called *terrorism as asymmetrical war*. Asymmetrical warfare is different from the conventional forms of warfare that are covered by the traditional laws of war; indeed, a major characteristic of asymmetrical warfare is the rejection of traditional norms and rules as part of the attempt to level the playing field of conflict. As noted in Chapter 11, for instance, the asymmetrical warrior does not distinguish between combatants and noncombatants, just as the terrorist considers all members of the target group equally culpable and thus eligible for attack.

Terrorism as asymmetrical war is a hybrid of the other two perspectives. The terrorists' rejection of accepted rules means they can treat their actions as acts of war, while the target society rejects this contention and can continue to consider their actions crimes against mankind. The status of asymmetrical warriors as warriors may be ambiguous within the rules of war, but leaving their actions within criminal jurisdiction satisfies the target society's depiction, while affording captured terrorists the legal protections they seek. This perspective also allows terrorism to be depicted as both a criminal *and* a military problem, which it is, and thus allows both law enforcement and military responses to terrorists. The only difficulty is in determining the appropriate mix of criminal justice and military responses generally and in specific situations.

Three Causes

The motivation to become a terrorist and to engage in the often gruesome and dangerous acts that typify terrorism is also the source of considerable speculation and disagreement among experts and lay observers. Much of the difficulty in making such assessments derives from the absolute inability most people have in imagining why anyone would become a terrorist and kill people who, from the victims' perspective, are innocent. Whatever leads people to become terrorists is so alien that people cannot draw analogies from their own experiences or those arising in society as they know it.

Three vantage points on what causes people and groups to adopt terrorism are often put forward, reflecting in some ways the disciplinary vantage points that various students of the phenomenon represent. Most of these explanations surfaced during the 1960s and 1970s, during the third or "New Left" wave of modern terrorism, according to David C. Rapoport (the first two were anarchism and anticolonialism; the fourth and present wave is religious). This is worth noting because the 1960s and 1970s tended to be more tolerant of, and even sympathetic to, politically aberrant movements than is true today. At any rate, terrorism is typified as primarily a societal, a psychological, or a political problem. The three explanations are neither mutually exclusive nor agreed upon.

The *societal* argument is that social conditions provide the breeding grounds for terrorism. Societies that consistently underachieve, that fail to provide adequate material or spiritual advances or hope for their people, and that leave their citizens living in an unending and hopeless condition of deprivation provide a kind of intellectual and physical "swamp" in which terrorism "breeds" a ready supply of potential terrorism followers who are willing recruits for causes that promise to bring meaning and direction to their lives. These "failed societies" may even oppress specific groups that are even more prone to the appeals of terrorism recruiters and may prevent other groups from achieving the goals to which they aspire (what Gurr calls "aspirational deprivation"). A variant of this argument suggests that some societies' values may be better suited than others for producing terrorists. In the contemporary setting, for instance, some observers note that Islam has a more prominent, positive role for religious martyrdom than do other religions, making the terrorist path, and especially suicide terrorism, more acceptable than it would be in other places.

If this argument is substantially correct, it leads to a potential solution to the terrorism problem: if the wretched (or frustrating) conditions are removed and the society ceases to be a failed one, then the conditions that breed the terrorists may also be removed. These failed societies are not necessarily the poorest societies (which tend to produce criminals but not terrorists) but those where opportunities are limited or missing. This is the heart of the argument for "draining the swamp" as a way to combat terrorism. The tool for doing so is the infusion of (probably massive) amounts of developmental assistance to create the physical basis for greater prosperity and a sense of meaningful futures: people do not volunteer for potential self-immolation (such as suicide terrorist missions) if they have hope for a more positive, promising future. In the current debate, feeding resources into the Pakistani education system to create a peaceful alternative to the religious *madrassa* schools, which teach anti-Americanism, is a prime example of the application of the societal argument, and indeed, the Obama thrust for developmental assistance in places like Afghanistan and Pakistan is at least implicitly based on the implications of the societal argument.

Critics point to a hole in this explanation of what creates terrorism. They argue that many modern terrorists are the product not of objective societal deprivation but of aspirational deprivation. Sixteen of the nineteen September 11 terrorists, after all, were Saudi citizens who could hardly be accused of coming from abjectly deprived backgrounds. Such an observation is obviously true, but it does not completely negate the argument that inferior societal conditions produce terrorists. Rather, the observation conditions the argument by saying that *not all* terrorists come from physically deprived backgrounds. Most terrorist leaders, it appears, and some of their followers come from middle-, even upper-class backgrounds (bin Laden, for instance), but a lot of their followers indeed emerge from the "swamp."

The second explanation moves from the group to the individual. Rather than focusing on failed societies, the *psychological* argument shifts the emphasis from the failed society to failed persons. The psychological argument is not entirely divorced from the societal argument in that it basically contends that certain traits in people, certain psychological states, make them more susceptible to the terrorist appeal and thus more willing to commit terrorist acts than is true of other individuals. Since not everyone who possesses these traits becomes a terrorist (lots of people are frustrated but do not react by blowing themselves up, for instance), there must be triggering societal conditions that activate these tendencies.

Terrorist profiling is a clear example of the psychological explanation of terrorism. In many contemporary arguments, for instance, it has been observed that many of the individuals who perpetrate religious-based terrorism from Middle Eastern settings share several characteristics. Most of the terrorist followers (as opposed to the leaders who recruit, train, and direct them) tend to be teenaged boys with high school educations who do not have jobs at all, or if they do, their jobs pay them sufficiently poorly that they have few prospects. They tend to be unmarried with few prospects of finding a wife (often because they cannot support one). They also tend to have low self-esteem intermixed with a high sense of helplessness and hopelessness about their futures. These perceptions lead to a high sense of humiliation, embarrassment, and impotence with respect to the future. Individuals with this kind of profile are believed to be especially vulnerable to recruitment by terrorist leaders who promise to restore meaning and purpose and thus a sense of self-esteem. A particularly troubling recent trend has been the emergence of females with similar profiles in terrorist roles. The profile of a particularly troublesome type, the suicide terrorist, is discussed in Amplification 9.2.

The implications of this profile are particularly disturbing because the Middle East has a population "bulge," which includes a large number of young males who exhibit the basic enabling characteristics described in Amplification 9.2. Moreover, the societal conditions in most Middle Eastern states offer few prospects for reducing these conditions—notably for providing employment, which could turn the situation around. As long as life does not contain meaningful prospects that can prevent the triggering of psychological processes leading to terrorism, there will be fertile breeding grounds for new generations of terrorists. It might be added that far fewer studies suggest similar profiles for terrorist leaders, except that they come from higher socioeconomic situations.

The third explanation is *political*, that failed governments produce the societal and psychological conditions in which terrorism emerges or produce conditions in

Amplification 9.2

Profiling Suicide Terrorists

The problem posed by terrorists willing to kill themselves to commit their terrorist acts burst on the scene during the clash between Israel and the Palestinians that erupted in 2000 (*Intifada* II) and has been given further publicity by the suicidal actions of many terrorists since, including increasing instances in places like Afghanistan and Pakistan. Suicide/martyr terrorism is neither truly new nor unique to the present: Americans, for instance, encountered suicide bombers during the conquest of Okinawa in World War II, which was one reason they sought to avoid an invasion of the Japanese home islands. The whole idea of self-immolation, especially by the young people associated with Palestinian suicide terrorism, is, however, totally alien to most Americans.

The Israelis (as reported in Stern) have developed a profile of these terrorists. They tend to be young, often teenagers, and they are generally mentally immature. In nearly all cases, they are under pressure to get a job but, due to a lack of connections, are unsuccessful in doing so. As a result, they have no money or reasonable prospects for improving their situations. Among other things, they cannot afford girlfriends or fiancées, and marriage is not an option for them. They thus feel a profound sense of helplessness and hopelessness. For many, God and the Mosque are their only refuge.

Becoming a suicide terrorist remedies some of these problems. Being a member of a terrorist organization can restore a sense of purpose and self-esteem: the recruit (*shaheed*) is now an important person, and his willingness to make the ultimate sacrifice only adds to his social prestige and acceptance. Martyrdom reestablishes his worth.

What is frightening is that the population bulge in the Middle East means there are a large number of young men (and increasingly young women) who fit the profile. Unless steps—whatever they may be—can be taken to reverse the conditions that give rise to suicide terrorists, more suicide terrorists can be expected in the future.

which terrorists emerge or are nurtured. Although it hardly exhausts the possibilities, state action can lead to terrorism in two ways. First, state oppression (indeed, including the use of terrorism *by* the government) may lead to political opposition that must be clandestine and must resort to terrorism as the only means of survival (terrorism as the tool of the asymmetrical warrior). The Chechen resistance would certainly view itself in this manner. In other cases, the government may be so inept or ineffective that it provides a haven for terrorists to exist without being able to do anything about it. The ineffectiveness of the Pakistani government in suppressing remnants of Al Qaeda and other sympathetic groups in the mountainous areas bordering Afghanistan is an example discussed later in the chapter. In yet other cases, sympathetic governments may even provide refuge and sanctuary for terrorist organizations. The relationship between Afghanistan's Taliban regime and Al Qaeda is a frequently cited example.

As with the other explanations, the political model also suggests remedies. If it is bad governments that create, put up with, or consort with terrorists, then there are two ways to deal with the problem. One is to convince the government to abandon the terrorists, quit creating them, or apprehend them, using either positive inducements (military or economic assistance) or threats of some form of sanctions to induce compliance. This has been the basic American strategy with Pakistan. If those efforts fail, a second option may be to replace those governments with more compliant regimes. That is at least part of the rationale for the American invasion of Iraq. The effectiveness of these solutions is, of course, open to question.

As noted, these explanations are not mutually exclusive. Failed governments have failed societal conditions as one of their causes and consequences, and it is failure at these levels that may create the triggering conditions for psychological forces that activate terrorists. It may be, as well, that these explanations are not comprehensive but may be characteristic of the variants of terrorism from the 1960s and 1970s, which were, among other things, noticeably secular rather than religious. Those who develop strategies for dealing with the terrorism problem must sort out the influences of the various explanations and determine how well they apply to the current and evolving forms of terrorism.

TERRORISM SINCE SEPTEMBER 11

The events of September 11 understandably focused national attention on a specific terrorist threat posed by Al Qaeda. The focus was natural, given the audacity and shock value of the actual attacks, the novelty of an organization such as Al Qaeda, and the underlying hatred of Americans that they revealed. To the extent that Americans had much of an understanding of terrorism, it was associated with more "classical" forms such as highly politicized anticolonialist movements like the Irish Republican Army (IRA), with state terrorism in the form of suppression by totalitarian regimes like Hitler's Germany or Stalin's Soviet Union, or with isolated anarchist assassinations or individual acts like the bombing of the Murrah Federal Building in Oklahoma City.

Understanding the nature of the threat has been difficult for at least two reasons. First, the contemporary form of terrorism appears very different from anything encountered before. It is nonstate-based terrorism that does not arise from specific political communities or jurisdictions but instead flows across national boundaries like oil slipping under doors. It is therefore conceptually difficult to make terrorism concrete and to counter it. It is also religious, showing signs of fanaticism that are present in all religious communities. Slaughter in the name of God goes beyond most people's intellectual frameworks. It has been fanatically anti-American and thus in sharp contrast to the general pro-Americanism that at least seemed to dominate the end of the twentieth century. It also employs methods such as suicide terrorism that, if not historically unique, are deviant enough to go beyond most people's abilities to conjure.

Second, understanding is made more difficult by the extremely changing nature of contemporary terrorist opponents. The Al Qaeda of 2001 was hard enough for us to understand, but it has evolved greatly since then. Partly this is because international efforts since 2001 were quite effective in dismantling the old Al Qaeda structure by capturing and killing many of its members. This success, however, has caused the threat to disperse and transform itself into newer and arguably more deadly forms. Currently, the geographic focus is in the mountainous regions of Pakistan, effectively beyond the reach of the Pakistani government and difficult for the U.S. military to assail because doing so could further destabilize Pakistan in potentially fundamental ways, an outcome arguably worse for the United States than dealing with Al Qaeda.

This changing nature is manifested in two ways. One is organizational. The success of western efforts in penetrating and disrupting conventionally organized (what Stern calls command-cadre) terrorist groups, has turned them into much more loosely organized networks (Stern calls them "protean" organizations). The reason for this loosening of control is that penetration of these organizations has largely been the result of monitoring and tracking internal electronic communications, and the protean response has been to reduce communications among terrorist network organizations greatly. The outcome has been that terrorist organizations are more difficult to penetrate but also less effective in planning and carrying out complex activities that require coordination.

The other change has been even more to imbed terrorist organizations into physical sanctuary environments beyond the reach of those who seek to destroy them. Al Qaeda is the prime example. Since the overthrow of the Taliban in Afghanistan in 2001, no national government will provide official sanctuary for terrorist organizations, but Al Qaeda has managed to find a safe, hospitable location in the mountainous tribal regions of Pakistan that has proven to be beyond the political and military reach of the United States, a legacy problem discussed in the next section.

This background forms the basis to describe the current structure of the global terrorist problem that remains the principal legacy of 9/11. The authoritative source of terrorist organizational activity is the U.S. Department of State's list of designated foreign terrorist organizations, an annual publication. *Infoplease*, an on-line publication of Pearson Education, takes this list and annotates it with additional information about the nature, goals and targets, membership, year of formation, and alleged activities of each organization. This information can be used to describe the current pattern of terrorist activity in the world. The most recent list available at the time of writing was from 2006. Although the list changes marginally from year to year, it is representative of current activity.

Forty-two organizations made the list. They come from four of the Earth's continents (Asia, Europe, Africa, and South America), and a slight majority (23 of 42) are Islamic in membership and purposes, but a sizable minority are not. They are summarized by origin and membership in Table 9.1.

It is a diverse lot of organizations. The largest concentration is Muslim Middle Eastern organizations, with almost one-third (13 of 42) of the total, including prominently Al Qaeda and Al Qaeda in Iraq as separate organizations. The formation of an Islamic state is a strategic goal of most Muslim organizations—including

Table 9.1: Demography of Terrorist Organizations

Location	Muslim	Non-Muslim	Total
Middle East (excluding Turkey and Pakistan)	13	4	17
Other Asia	6	6	12
Africa	4	—	4
South America	—	4	4
Europe	—	5	5
Total	23	19	42

groups in Iraq, Kashmir, Egypt, Algeria, Lebanon, the Philippines (which also has a Marxist group seeking to overthrow the government), Uzbekistan, Indonesia, Pakistan, Libya, and Morocco. Not all of these movements are anti-American, depending on whether the United States opposes or ignores their goals. Non-Muslim groups vary from an Israeli extremist group (Kahane Chai) to separatist groups in Europe (the Irish Republican Army splinter groups and the Basque Fatherland and Liberty, or ETA) to Marxist groups supporting the narcotics trade in South America. The point is that the worldwide roster of terrorist organizations is far wider and more diverse than the current GWOT emphasis on international religious terrorists (principally Al Qaeda) would suggest and that the United States is not the particular target of many of these groups. It also suggests that a "successful" GWOT against Al Qaeda and its affiliates might eliminate that source of terrorism in the world and come close to eliminating the American concern with terrorism but that it would not eliminate the practice of terrorism worldwide.

OTHER LEGACIES

The 9/11 terrorist attacks spawned and spun off a number of other national security concerns that either would not have existed at all or would have been quite different in the absence of the elevation of international religious terrorism to the center stage of national concern. Some of these spin-offs have been in the form of two ongoing major military involvements for the United States in Iraq and Afghanistan. Since both of those engagements have and continue to represent major commitments by the United States, their discussion is reserved for Chapter 12.

It is probably impossible to list in any comprehensive manner all the legacies that 9/11 has left and continues to leave in its wake. As a result, the discussion here will instead be concentrated on two obvious and important outcomes that have been and continue to be influences on the American pursuit of its national security.

One example, as noted earlier, is the allegation that the U.S. government engaged in the use of torture to obtain information regarding actual and potential terrorist activities from prisoners in its control from 2002 probably at least until 2007. This alleged activity has become both domestically and internationally controversial because, if it is true, it means officials of the American government committed or suborned actions that are illegal under international and domestic laws and that specifically violate provisions of international treaty agreements of which the United States is a signatory. The problem is at once domestic and international in both a legal and a political sense. The domestic argument tends to blend the legal and political arguments regarding both the permissibility of the actions, given national security concerns, and the political propriety of the Obama administration's attempt to prosecute members of the administration it succeeded. The international aspect affects considerations of the role of the United States as a leader and the quality of its leadership in upholding or resisting international norms. Both aspects have important elements of precedent for the future.

The other example is the problem of Pakistan, a country that has been caught up—largely against its will—in the pursuit of Al Qaeda by virtue of its border with Afghanistan. In a nutshell, Pakistan has become the unwilling, even unwitting, sanctuary for international religious terrorism, a situation the notoriously unstable but nuclear-armed Pakistani government is almost perfectly incapable of confronting successfully. The result has become a potential firestorm of unintended consequences for both Pakistan and the United States, whereby the American interest in dislodging and destroying Al Qaeda leads it to actions that could further destabilize, possibly to the point of dismembering, the Pakistani state. Without the influence of Al Qaeda and religious terrorism, Pakistan would be a tenuous place, as it always has been. The influence of religious terrorists and their pursuers runs the risk of pushing this fragile society of 173 million people over the brink.

The Problem of Torture

Accusations that the Bush administration authorized the use of interrogation methods widely suspected of constituting torture have become one of the most emotional and controversial legacies of the post-9/11 period. The decisions that authorized the "enhanced interrogation techniques" date back to internal Bush administration documents from 2002 that formed the rationale for the use of such techniques against Middle Eastern nationals under U.S. control (so-called "detainees") until at least 2007. The rationale was that it was necessary to use harsh methods against those who might have information about planned future terrorist attacks against the American homeland or American forces. Although these methods were suspected previously, they were first given widespread publicity following the disclosure of questionable practices at the Abu Ghraib prison in Iraq in 2004. The controversy reached crisis proportions with the inauguration of Barack Obama, who had campaigned vigorously about his opposition to the practice of torture by Americans under any circumstances. Since accusations of authorizing and conducting torture could be made against members of the administration Obama succeeded, a political and legal firestorm has followed, the outcome of which will likely influence how the American government does its national security business in the future.

What exactly is torture? The practice of what is generally considered torture is certainly nothing new; it was practiced by the Roman Republic and Empire to gain information from its enemies, and it has been used subsequently for a variety of purposes, including gaining intelligence during war and even in the name of religious conversion, notably in the Spanish Inquisition. Torture has also been used as a means of execution (crucifixion is often cited as an example), and torturers have devised methods that have been hideous and often excruciating—and unacceptable in civilized society. Given dire, threatening conditions, however, specific acts of torture have received at least tacit support among many members of society across time. The current debate in the United States is only the latest instance of this disagreement.

The contemporary effort to eradicate the practice of torture is a post–World War II phenomenon that arose from the same general movement that outlawed war crimes, a reasonable connection, since torture is considered a war crime when committed during war. The United Nations Universal Declaration of Human Rights of 1948, for instance, specifically states in Article 5, "No one shall be subject to torture or to cruel, inhuman, and degrading treatment or punishment." The Fourth Geneva Convention on War specifies that torture is a war crime (a crime against humanity), and jurisdiction over the prosecution of accused torturers is claimed by the International Criminal Court (ICC or War Crimes Court) in Articles 7 (crimes against humanity) and 8 (war crimes).

The major international document covering torture is the United Nations Convention Against Torture and Other Cruel, Inhuman, or Degrading Treatment or Punishment (UNCAT). The convention was passed through the U.N. in 1987, and the United States acceded to its provisions in 1994, when it received the advice and consent of the U.S. Senate. As required by the UNCAT, the United States has passed legislation (notably a federal antitorture act in 1994 and the War Crimes Act of 1996) implementing the provisions into American law and has reported as follows to the U.N. Committee Against Torture: "Every act of torture within the meaning of the Convention is illegal under existing federal and state law, and any individual who commits such an act is subject to penal sanctions as specified in the criminal statutes. . . . Torture cannot be justified on the basis of an order from a superior officer." The Eighth Amendment to the U.S. Constitution, which prohibits "cruel and unusual punishment," is often cited as a basis for the American position, as is the Fifth Amendment's protection against self-incrimination.

Under the UNCAT and supporting law, the definition of torture is explicit (Article 1): "any act by which severe pain or suffering, whether physical or mental, is intentionally inflicted on a person for such purposes as obtaining from him or a third person information or a confession, punishing him for an act he or a third person has committed or is suspected of having committed, or intimidating or coercing him or a third person, or for any reason based on discrimination of any kind, when such pain or suffering is inflicted by or at the instigation of or with the consent or acquiescence of a public official or other person acting in an official capacity." Some defenders of the Bush administration have attempted to argue that these definitions are vague, but if there is any point of ambiguity or debate, it is limited to what constitutes "severe" pain, and much of the legal argumentation produced by the Bush administration sought to establish the boundary of actions severe enough to constitute torture. The prime example is *waterboarding* (subjecting a person to a procedure that simulates drowning): almost all outside experts agree it is torture, while Bush officials, including former Vice President Richard Cheney, maintain it is not. The convention further denies the acceptability of torture within states that are at war and against combatants or noncombatants (Article 2). The definition of torture itself, parallel to the reasoning on war crimes developed at the Nuremburg and Tokyo war crimes trials after World War II, suggests that legal vulnerability extends throughout the entity that authorizes acts of torture. This latter point has been used to suggest that culpability could extend all the way into the Oval Office if prosecuted vigorously.

The debate about the use of torture extends to political argumentation regarding its utility as a device to obtain information. Within the American debate, no one, of course, openly supports the practice of torture as a general principle, at least partly because to do so would be to advocate criminal behavior. Thus, the critics of the practice have been more vocal than the supporters.

Critics of the use of torture cite four reasons not to carry out torture. The first is that such practices are immoral, based on the commission of acts of evil that are morally and ethically reprehensible and in fundamental opposition to the Golden Rule's entreaty to treat one as you would wish to be treated. The counterargument is that if one's opponent commits such acts, one is unnecessarily restrained if torture is prohibited: barbarous acts by terrorists, for instance, may justify retaliation in kind in some circumstances. The retort is that two rights do not make a wrong. The entire argument is reminiscent of debates during the Cold War about permissible intelligence activities—notably "wet" operations such as assassinations—when the opponent engages in such actions. In that debate, there was disagreement over whether the United States was unduly handicapped by self-restraint or whether the commission of such acts left the United States in effect no better than (not morally superior to) an immoral opponent. Much the same logic applies to the torture debate.

The second argument is that torture is illegal under both international and domestic law. Once again, that assertion cannot be seriously questioned, as documented above. Those who support at least the occasional recourse to dubious acts are forced to contend that what is done does not rise to the definition of torture, that reasons of state based in national security can justify otherwise illegal acts, or that the highest political authority can interpret law in a broad manner. The last defense raises comparisons to Richard Nixon's defense of Watergate activities that actions are not illegal if the president does them and even to Fawn Hall's famous testimony before the Iran–Contra Committee in 1987 that "sometimes you have to go beyond the written law" (Hall was the secretary to Iran–Contra notable Oliver North). Critics of torture simply reply that in a society of laws, those laws must be supreme.

The third and fourth arguments are less theoretical. The third argument is that torture is an ineffective way to gain desired information: torture does not work. Revelations that some terrorist suspects were waterboarded literally hundreds of times before yielding any information are cited in support of this notion, and many experts maintain that the information obtained by torturing subjects is notoriously unreliable. Torture victims, it is asserted, will tell their inquisitors whatever they think will end their suffering, whether it is the truth or not. The fourth argument is that committing torture invites retaliation. Much of the law of war is based on the principle that certain acts will not be carried out as a matter of reciprocity, and this extends to the use of torture. In effect, the principle is that if I do not torture your members, you will not torture mine. If, on the other hand, the United States engages in acts of torture against people it captures, what can Americans expect in return when they are captured?

Supporters of the alleged Bush practices do not disagree fundamentally with these arguments but make counterarguments at the peripheries. Cheney, for instance, denies that the use of enhanced techniques is ineffective, maintaining that the full disclosure of documents will reveal that such techniques were critical in preventing a variety of terrorist actions against the United States. Moreover, defenders maintain that self-abnegation creates a critical disadvantage that, if allowed to exist, would place American officials in the morally unconscionable position of failing to take actions that could protect American lives and security. The argument, simply, is that morality exists at different levels and that what may be immoral in some (even most) circumstances may be the only morally defensible position in situations where the failure to act in ways deemed immoral in some circumstances would result in even more immoral consequences. In some ways, it goes back to a long-standing constitutional and legal debate over the extent to which national security imperatives provide an acceptable exception to other constitutional principles, an ongoing matter of disagreement.

Much of the formal debate on this issue became obscured in the partisan political debate that emerged in 2009 surrounding the torture issue. In April, a number of Justice Department memoranda were released that reflected the internal Bush administration debate on authorizing the practices, and these were followed by a flood of actions by various entities like the military and the intelligence communities trying to distance themselves from legal culpability for the practices. Meanwhile people in the process like former National Security Advisor and Secretary of State Condoleezza Rice attempted to "clarify" their roles. Among those most closely associated with the program, former Vice President Cheney was among the few who refused to recant any of his involvement.

The debate has threatened to obfuscate the underlying issue of the acceptability of torture. The Obama administration was quickly accused of conducting a political "witch hunt" against its predecessors by investigating whether those officials indeed engaged in the authorization of illegal torture. The allegations and their denials tended to break along partisan lines, suggesting that the pursuit of these questions was more about political retribution than about legal wrongdoing. The Obama administration sought to separate the two strands of debate by assigning the investigation of potential lawbreaking to the Justice Department and effectively exempting high-level Bush officials from prosecution, saying it had no interest in such prosecutions. The assignment of the legal matter to the Justice Department was procedurally correct but nonetheless controversial, since the Justice Department under Bush had produced the dubious legal opinions on which the alleged torture was justified. Thus, its objectivity was questioned, and Republicans accused the Obama administration of abandoning the bipartisan approach that Obama had very publicly proclaimed. The result was to muddy the waters of the underlying questions, which were whether the United States had engaged in illegal acts of torture, what it would do about those accusations, and where the boundary lies between national security and the rule of law.

The exact legacy of the controversy over torture has not yet been written. Certainly, a short-term effect will be to lessen the likelihood that the U.S. government will suborn or participate in those kinds of actions for the foreseeable future; American public and world opinion would simply be too outraged for a reprise. At some point, however, the controversy will find its place in the more general, unresolved debate about what can be done in the pursuance of national security. The debate has tended to be enlivened by instances where the U.S. government arguably overstepped legal, even constitutional grounds in its zeal to protect the country from its enemies: Abraham Lincoln's suspension of habeas corpus legal protections during the Civil War and the forced internment of Japanese-Americans during World War II come to mind. In both cases, Americans knew or had strong reason to believe their government was acting in ways that violated the basic premises of their society, but in both cases, they acquiesced in those practices out of fear for their own safety. The World War II experience has become notorious and the source of considerable national shame. Whether the question of torture rises to that level of notoriety remains to be seen.

Pakistan and the Law of Unintended Consequences

The second example surrounds the overflow into Pakistan of American efforts to reduce and destroy the terrorist threat that has emanated from Afghanistan. The situation is ironic in several ways. One is that the underlying purpose of American efforts is to attempt to bring stability to the region between Russia and India, but the initial effect is to cause greater instability instead, an irony made more poignant by the fact that Pakistan has a nuclear arsenal generally believed to number 60–100 warheads, the security of which (especially from terrorists) is arguably the United States' most important interest in the region. Another is that the chief manifestation of the danger created by the American escalation of the antiterrorist campaign into Pakistan is that it has energized the Taliban in Pakistan, an organization that the Pakistan government had a large role in creating in the first place, to rise against the government in Islamabad. The law of unintended consequences thus comes full circle, as an American attempt to solve its terrorism problem has the effect of turning a Pakistani-created scorpion on its master and creator.

The extension of the antiterrorist campaign into Pakistan has had the effect of worsening conditions in a Pakistani state that is already on the brink of being or becoming a failed state, a designation its rulers deny. Pakistan is a classic artificial state that has no historical basis. It was carved from the British Raj in south Asia that created the Hindu state of India and a Muslim state from the rest. The result was initially a Pakistan of two distinct geographical areas, West Pakistan and East Pakistan (which became Bangladesh in 1970), separated by 1,000 miles of Indian territory. Islam was supposed to provide a nationalist glue for the diverse areas, but it could not. Instead, the preexisting tribalism has survived the creation of Pakistan. Before Bangladesh successfully seceded (with Indian help), the chief rivalry was between the dominant Punjabis of the west and the Bengalis of the east. Since the establishment of Bangladesh, the rivalry in what is left has been between the Punjabis and other remaining tribal concentrations.

The tribal balance is relevant to the current crisis, as is geography. Punjabis, who are concentrated in the eastern, generally less mountainous parts of Pakistan adjoining India, make up about 45 percent of the Pakistani population of 173 million, and they dominate both the government and the military. The second-largest group within the country is the Pashtun, about 15 percent of the population, who live in the mountainous regions adjoining Afghanistan. The Pashtun are the largest ethnic group in Afghanistan, and their population is bisected by the Afghanistan–Pakistan border (the so-called Durand line discussed in Chapter 12). The Pashtun neither honor this border nor accept Pakistani rule in the tribal regions where they are dominant. This area is extremely mountainous and difficult to assault militarily, and the result has been that the Federally Administered Tribal Areas (FATA) there have historically been largely autonomous from control by the central government, an arrangement that has dampened activism for creation of a state of Pashtunistan. In addition, the Baluch areas along the Iranian border harbor separatist tendencies, and numerous other tribal groupings are also present.

Pakistan is a poor country under the best of circumstances, and maintaining some semblance of intertribal peace has meant that the Pakistani military has always occupied a very central role in the country. Its central mission has always been the defense of the country from India, a particular concern of the Punjabis who live beside India. This level of concern (some would argue obsession) is particularly relevant to the current impasse. For one thing, the military has been particularly interested in governance because of the overarching threat. This has manifested itself in numerous military governments in the country (the recently deposed government of Pervez Musharaff is an example) and in a high level of tension between the military and democratic advocates in the country. At the same time, the result has been an army built to confront a highly conventional, heavily equipped Indian armed force on the generally gentle geography between them. This structure of the armed forces is appropriate for conducting the World War II–style conflicts the Indians and Pakistanis have fought in the past, but it is almost totally inappropriate for fighting a guerrilla-style, asymmetrical war in the mountainous, undeveloped FATA. The classic Pakistani response has been to neutralize the mountainous areas by granting them effective autonomy and even sponsoring movements to destabilize their neighbors (the major motivation for Pakistani complicity in helping create the Taliban to weaken Afghanistan). When these strategies fail and the Pakistanis must confront their enemies in the tribal regions—as the United States demands as the Pakistani contribution to eradicating Al Qaeda—they do not fare well.

This situation further creates a quandary for the United States in helping to bolster Pakistani military efforts because it is not clear that only a basic reorientation of those forces toward counterinsurgency warfare will improve their performance against the Taliban, whereas the easiest way to help them is to provide more ineffective conventional materials. In addition, the Pakistani military fears that a reorientation of their forces toward the counterinsurgency role will weaken their ability to deter or fight the Indians, which they continue to view as the more fundamental threat.

The result has been a very delicate balancing act for the Pakistanis. Some of their current difficulties are, of course, of their own making. In their efforts to weaken neighboring Afghanistan, they were, after all, partly responsible for creating the Taliban in the 1990s, a strategy intended to help assure the government in Kabul could pose no threat to them. It is a strategy that has also been used in Kashmir, and in both cases, the effect was to neutralize opposition to the central government and to advance Pakistani security interests, which they believe requires concentrating their efforts on India.

The determination by the United States to destroy Al Qaeda, and by extension the Taliban, has thrown a wrench into these mechanics. The American effort has been concentrated in Afghanistan (see Chapter 12), but its effects have spilled over into Pakistan. The reason, of course, is that the escape of Al Qaeda in 2001 and the eviction of the Taliban from Afghanistan landed them on the Pakistani side of the frontier dividing Pashtunistan, where both organizations have found safe haven and have regrouped and strengthened. From its Pakistani bases, Al Qaeda continues to organize and carry out terrorist activities, and the Taliban have launched an increasingly effective insurgency in Afghanistan. Both of these phenomena frustrate U.S. policy on Afghanistan and have led to the conclusion that Afghanistan cannot be stabilized and Al Qaeda defeated as long as that safe haven continues to exist. The result has been increased American air attacks across the Durand line that fuel anti-Americanism in Pakistan and American pressure for the Pakistanis to bring military pressure to bear against the Taliban in Pakistan. Anti-Americanism is inflamed both because the attacks violate sovereign Pakistani soil and because they inevitably result in civilian casualties (collateral damage). The demands for greater Pakistani participation put the Pakistanis in an untenable situation as well. Their military is ill-suited for the task, compliance aligns the government with the United States (a not particularly popular position), and the whole task requires unraveling Pakistani strategy in the region.

It is against this background that the ongoing situation continues to evolve. The situation is, as hinted at already, ironic. Had one asked Americans before 9/11 which parts of the region between India and Russia were important and which were not, the answer would almost certainly have been that Pakistan—especially after it exploded its first nuclear device in 1998—was very important and that Afghanistan was not. That recognition was accompanied by an acknowledgment of the delicacy of the Pakistani state and a consequent belief that the United States should treat the internal situation in Pakistan very carefully.

Part of the legacy of 9/11 has been to stand those perceptions and their policy consequences on their head. The situation in Afghanistan has caused the United States to insist that the Pakistani government reverse its historic posture toward its mountainous tribal regions in ways that threaten the stability of Pakistan, which is hardly the consequence the United States intends in Pakistan and the region. How fundamental the threat to Pakistan's stability will eventually be remains to be seen. There was great alarm when the Taliban made major inroads within sixty miles of Islamabad in spring 2009, but the resulting concern was overblown. The Taliban, after all, represent at most 15 percent of the population (assuming all Pashtun support them, a questionable proposition), and their military capability would largely evaporate if they came out of the mountains and confronted the Pakistani armed forces in conventional warfare on the relatively flat plains at which the latter are skilled at fighting.

The military equation is made all the more emotional because of the fear that a destabilized Pakistan could lose control of its nuclear arsenal, with the absolute worst case being that those nuclear warheads could somehow come under the control of the Taliban and their Al Qaeda allies. That outcome, of course, would represent what has been the worst nightmare of American antiterror planners since 2001 and would bring the issue of unintended consequences to its most stark realization. As the United States attempts somehow to create an atmosphere of cooperation among the governments of Pakistan, Afghanistan, and itself in defeating the Taliban, an enemy that has a much different significance to the United States than it does to the others, it must also figure out a way to reach a conclusion that adds to the stability of these countries. That, in turn, requires a fairly fundamental reorientation of Pakistani relations with the contested areas, a concern the United States has been reluctant to fully embrace.

The legacy of 9/11 in Pakistan may thus reside in the recognition that policies devised and applied in one place and for one purpose may have quite different consequences, some of them unanticipated and unintended, when those policies are extended to other places. The United States did not intend to destabilize Pakistan when it decided that Pakistani sanctuaries for the Taliban and Al Qaeda were intolerable, and the end result may be that Pakistan will emerge from the experience a better place. That outcome is not, however, guaranteed, and if it is not realized, the unintended consequence could be a bigger problem in a far more consequential place than Afghanistan.

CONCLUSION: TERRORISM, TORTURE, AND UNINTENDED CONSEQUENCES

The attacks of 9/11 represented such a great national trauma that it is not surprising that they have had multiple long-term effects. As a response to these events and their aftermath has been devised and implemented, the results have become part of the national experience that shapes perceptions about how to deal with the present and the future.

Exploring a sample of these legacies has been the subject of this chapter. Terrorism itself, exploding into the public awareness and being catapulted to the top of the national security agenda by the 9/11 events, is the clearest and most overwhelming legacy of the 2000s and has thus received the greatest attention in this chapter. Spin-off phenomena such as the problem of torture and the intensification of conflict in and over Pakistan have served as further legacy events. Each continues to create difficulties as the 2010s begin.

The dilemma presented by confronting terrorism is twofold. First, it is a very complex problem of the kind with which political institutions are loathe to deal. Declaring a GWOT was a great deal simpler than dealing with the incredible complexities only broadly suggested in these pages. Second, the suppression of terrorism is not a conflict that can easily be won, if it can be "won" at all. Terrorism as an idea has been around for a long time, and it will likely continue to persist for a long time. The goal of terrorism strategy is to contain terrorism, to reduce the risks arising from it, but not to exorcise it from national and international existence. That is not as high-flown a goal as obliterating terrorism, but it is more realistic.

The first and obvious step in dealing with terrorism is deciding what the goal of such an effort should be. It is clearly not enough to say the goal is to "win" the struggle; one must specify what winning means. During the latter stages of the 2004 presidential campaign, the principal candidates effectively—if inadvertently—framed this question. Democratic nominee John Kerry, in the second presidential debate argued the only realistic goal was to contain the problem, to reduce it to the status of a nuisance rather than a central, encompassing fixation; he drew an analogy with containing prostitution and gambling. George W. Bush replied fierily that Kerry was wrong and that the goal of the GWOT had to be to hunt down and destroy terrorism everywhere it existed; winning means eradicating terrorism.

Which of these goals should be adopted as the bedrock of policy? Eradication of terrorism is clearly more emotionally attractive, but is it a realistic or attainable goal? As noted, terrorism has been around as a more-or-less permanent force for at least two thousand years (many scholars date it back to the first century A.D. to groups like the Sicarii and the Zealots), and although it has ebbed and flowed in its prominence across time, it has never disappeared altogether. Similarly, terrorist movements, such as the current religiously based terrorist groups, come and go, but they seem always to be replaced by something else. In that case, is a strategy based in destroying terrorism (more properly, terrorists) bound to fail and frustrate those who pursue it? Is it more realistic (if less emotionally satisfying) to aim to minimize terrorism?

There is the further question of what is to be done. At least two concerns can be raised in this regard. Clearly, one way to eliminate or lessen the problem of terrorism is to discourage or lessen its appeal to potential terrorists: fewer terrorists, by definition, would pose a smaller terrorism problem. Antiterrorism and counterterrorism efforts discussed in Chapter 13 may influence the actions of current terrorists, but they apparently do little to discourage, and may actually encourage, the recruitment of future terrorists. Israeli destruction of the family homes of Palestinian suicide terrorists has rather clearly not discouraged others from signing up for that grisly mission, and it has been argued that the American military effort in Iraq—regardless of the merit of its stated aims—has had the ancillary effect of increasing regional anti-Americanism and thus intensifying efforts to recruit terrorists to oppose Americans.

How can terrorism be made less attractive to potential recruits? One approach is to relieve the human conditions in which terrorism seems to prosper—to "drain the swamp" of terrorism-producing societal, psychological, and political conditions and thus make terrorism a less attractive alternative. Intuitively, such efforts appear to make sense, but they face objections. One is expense: uplifting societies to the point that terrorism is unappealing to their citizens would require extensive monetary and other resources. For instance, what would it cost to fund a Pakistani education system that would make the terrorist-producing *madrassa* system obsolete? Are Americans willing to pay for such an effort? In addition, the results are uncertain: as many analysts point out, the September 11 terrorists came from Saudi Arabia, not some wretched backwater "swamp," and all the developmental assistance in the world presumably would not have had a positive impact on these people and what they did.

A second possible thrust to discourage terrorism might be to make terrorist targets less appealing as targets. Current Middle Eastern religious terrorism is fueled by a virulent anti-Americanism that Americans find intellectually ludicrous and incorrect. Should the United States be mounting a much more comprehensive campaign to convince people in the region that the western model is superior to the worldview that fanatical religious spokespersons are propounding? Is the neoconservative plan of imposing democracy—as has been attempted in Iraq—the way to do this? Or is there some other, better way?

There is also the question of exposure. One reason for the underlying anti-Americanism in parts of the Middle East is the level of supposedly corrupting American physical presence in the region (this has been a particular obsession of

Challenge!

TERRORISM AND YOU

Terrorism is both a frightening and a confusing phenomenon. The attacks of September 11 established that all of us are potentially targets of terrorist actions, removing some part of our senses of safety and tranquility. Some of the resulting anxiety has abated as time has passed and renewed attacks have not occurred, but simultaneously, people are warned of an ever-present, if virtually invisible, threat. The confusion is the result of trying to come to grips with this elusive, shadowy phenomenon. It makes reaching personal judgments all the more difficult.

What does the terrorism problem mean to *you*? Is it a "war," as it is advertised, or is it something else, something more or less frightening? Does it belong at the absolute top of the list of national security concerns, or is it somehow a lesser problem than that? Has the problem, in other words, been "hyped"?

And what about our efforts to deal with the problem? We are spending a large number of tax dollars on the problem, but are we getting our money's worth? Do we have a coherent approach to dealing with the problem? If you had the ability to change the policy, how would you do so? What do you think about terrorism and yourself?

bin Laden for some time). The obvious reason for that presence is Middle East oil, and without that need, the reason for American presence is reduced greatly or disappears altogether. If that is the case, should national energy policy not be an important element in reducing the problem of terrorism? Some of the most vocal proponents of the GWOT in the United States simultaneously oppose higher fuel-efficiency standards for vehicles (the so-called corporate average fuel efficiency—CAFE—standards), standards updated and made more stringent in 2009. Since oil revenue has clearly been linked to private support for terrorists in Saudi Arabia and elsewhere, is it not inconsistent to support strong terrorism suppression, while driving a large, gas-guzzling sport utility vehicle? All these questions suggest difficult personal choices, as the accompanying *Challenge!* box and the discussion in Chapter 14 suggest.

The spin-off legacies reflect these difficulties and frustrations. While there have undoubtedly been isolated situations in American history—mostly when the country was at war—when torture has been used against national enemies, the sanctioned application of such techniques as a systematic adjunct of policy is a product of the reaction to 9/11. As the shock of the attacks fades, so, too, may the willingness to justify the attacks justified in terrorism's name fade. The analogy with later revulsion over the treatment of Japanese-Americans during World War II may be a guide. No one would, based on the 1940s internment experience, put forward a similar proposal should apparently parallel conditions exist because of what happened then. The reaction to torture may produce a similar legacy of shame.

The Pakistani precedent is still too uncertain to assess as a legacy; it is not at all clear what the outcome will be and thus what lesson is to be learned. Part of that potential lesson may fall under the umbrella of state building, the subject of Chapter 13. Aspects of the experience may provide positive or negative precedents for future actions in the developing world, prospects explored in Chapter 14.

STUDY/DISCUSSION QUESTIONS

1. How is terrorism defined? Why is it important to have an agreed-upon definition of terrorism? What elements can go into a definition?

2. What are terrorist acts? Why do terrorists commit them? When are they successful or unsuccessful?

3. What are the two kinds of terrorist targets? Distinguish one kind from the other. What different problems are associated with each?

4. Define terrorist objectives at both the tactical and the strategic levels. At which levels are terrorists most and least successful?

5. What are the three perspectives on terrorism? Compare and contrast them. Which do you find most persuasive?

6. What three causes are sometimes attributed to terrorism? Compare and contrast them. Which do you find most convincing?

7. Discuss post–September 11 terrorism in terms of the types of terrorist organizations and the current pattern of targets and actions of those organizations, with an emphasis on Al Qaeda.

8. Define *torture*. Is there ambiguity about what constitutes torture or about its legality? Separate out the political and legal aspects of the debate about torture. What arguments do you find compelling? Why?
9. What are the potential unintended consequences of U.S. actions in Pakistan? Are these possible consequences worth the risk? Why or why not?

SELECTED BIBLIOGRAPHY

Allison, Graham. *Nuclear Terrorism: The Ultimate Preventable Catastrophe*. New York: Times Books (Henry Holt & Company), 2004.

Atwan, Abdul Beri. *The Secret History of Al Qaeda*. Berkeley: University of California Press, 2006.

Bergen, Peter. *Holy War Inc.: Inside the Secret World of Al Qaeda*. New York: Simon and Schuster, 2001.

Betts, Richard K. "How to Think About Terrorism." *Wilson Quarterly* 30 (Winter 2006): 44–49.

Bloom, Mia. *Dying to Kill: The Allure of Suicide Terror*. New York: Columbia University Press, 2005.

Burke, Jason. "Think Again: Al Qaeda." *Foreign Policy*, May/June 2004, 18–26.

Cobban, Helena. "Think Again: International Courts." *Foreign Policy*, March/April 2006, 22–28.

Convention Against Torture and Other Cruel, Inhuman, or Degrading Treatment or Punishment. New York: United Nations, December 10, 1984.

Cronin, Audrey Kurth. "Sources of Contemporary Terrorism." In *Attacking Terrorism: Elements of a Grand Strategy*, edited by Audrey Kurth Cronin and James M. Ludes, 74–93. Washington, DC: Georgetown University Press, 2004.

Dershowitz, Alan M. *Why Terrorism Works: Understanding the Threat, Responding to the Challenge*. New Haven, CT: Yale University Press, 2002.

DeYoung, Karen. "U.S. Options in Pakistan Limited." *Washington Post* (online). May 4, 2009.

Enders, Walter, and Todd Sandler. *The Political Economy of Terrorism*. New York: Cambridge University Press, 2006.

Greenberg, Karen Joy. *The Torture Debate in America*. Cambridge, MA: MIT Press, 2005.

Gunaratna, Rohan. "The Post-Madrid Face of Al Qaeda." *Washington Quarterly* 27, no. 3 (Summer 2004): 91–100.

Gurr, Ted Robert. *Why Men Rebel*. Princeton, NJ: Princeton University Press, 1973.

Habeck, Mary. *Knowing the Enemy: Jihadist Ideology and the War on Terror*. New Haven, CT: Yale University Press, 2005.

Hoffman, Bruce. *Inside Terrorism*. 2nd ed. New York: Columbia University Press, 2006.

Hoge, James F., Jr., and Gideon Rose, eds. *Understanding the War on Terrorism*. New York: Council on Foreign Relations (*Foreign Affairs* Books), 2005.

Jenkins, Brian. "International Terrorism." In *The Use of Force: Military Power and International Relations*, edited by Robert J. Art and Kenneth N. Waltz. 6th ed., 77–84. New York: Rowman and Littlefield Publishers, 2004.

Juergensmeyer, Mark. *Terror in the Mind of God: The Global Rise of Religious Violence*. Berkeley: University of California Press, 2003.

Mueller, John. "Is There Still a Terrorist Threat?" *Foreign Affairs* 85, no. 5 (September/October 2006): 2–8.

Nacos, Brigette L. *Terrorism and Counterterrorism: Understanding Threats and Responses in the Post-9/11 World*. New York: Penguin Academics, 2006.

Pape, Robert. *Dying to Win: The Strategic Logic of Suicide Terrorism*. New York: Random House, 2005.

Pillar, Paul R. "Counterterrorism After Al Qaeda." *Washington Quarterly* 27, no. 3 (Summer 2004): 101–113.

Rapoport, David C. "The Four Waves of Terrorism." In *Attacking Terrorism: Elements of a Grand Strategy*, edited by Audrey Kurth Cronin and James M. Ludes, 46–73. Washington, DC: Georgetown University Press, 2004.

Reidel, Bruce. "Al Qaeda Strikes Back." *Foreign Affairs* 86, no. 3 (May/June 2007): 24–40.

Rubin, Barnett R., and Ahmed Rashid. "From Great Game to Grand Bargain." *Foreign Affairs* 87, no. 6 (November/December 2008): 30–44.

Schmid, Alex P., and Ronald D. Crelinsten. *The Politics of Pain: Torturers and Their Masters*. Boulder, CO: Westview Press, 1994.

Simon, Jeffrey. *The Terrorist Trap: America's Experience with Terrorism*. Bloomington: Indian University Press, 2001.

Simon, Steve, and Jeff Martin. "Terrorism: Denying Al Qaeda Its Popular Support." *Washington Quarterly* 28, no. 1 (Winter 2004–2005): 131–146.

Sloan, Stephen. *Beating International Terrorism: An Action Strategy for Preemption and Punishment*. Montgomery, AL: Air University Press, 2000.

Snow, Donald M. *September 11, 2001: The New Face of War?* New York: Longman, 2002.

———, and Dennis M. Drew. *From Lexington to Baghdad and Beyond: War and Politics in the American Experience*. 3rd ed. Armonk, NY: M. E. Sharpe, 2009.

Stern, Jessica. *Terrorism in the Name of God: Why Religious Militants Kill*. New York: ECCO, 2003.

———. "The Protean Enemy." *Foreign Affairs* 82, no. 4 (July/August 2003): 27–40.

The 9/11 Report: The National Commission on Terrorist Attacks upon the United States, Thomas H. Kean, Chair, and Lee H. Hamilton, Vice Chair. New York, St. Martin's Paperbacks, 2004.

U.S. Department of State. *Patterns of Global Terrorism*. Washington, DC: U.S. Department of State (annual publication).

"U.S. Designated Terrorist Organizations." *Infoplease*. New York: Pearson Education, 2007. (http://www.infoplease.com/ipa/A0908746.html)

Whittaker, David J. *Terrorists and Terrorism in the Contemporary World*. New York: Routledge, 2004.

CHAPTER 10

Ongoing Military Problems

PREVIEW

Thinking about and planning for large-scale war between armed forces as they were developed for and fought in World War II—conventional forces for symmetrical warfare and strategic nuclear war—predate and postdate September 11, 2001. The traditional purposes for which these forces were developed largely disappeared with the end of the Cold War, and only the United States retains a robust traditional capability that it proposes to augment through force modernization. At the same time, critics say these large, European-style forces are anachronisms in a world of shadowy asymmetrical threats. Before assessing these criticisms, it is necessary to describe traditional forces and missions, first nuclear forces and then conventional forces and the residual problems associated with each that have a continuing impact—notably weapons of mass destruction (WMD) and the problems their spread to other states and nonstate entities (proliferation) creates. The chapter concludes with some assessment of the relevance of these forces in the future.

The past, it is sometimes said, is the prologue of the future, and nowhere is that observation more applicable than in the area of military forces. War is an ancient institution, and it has evolved and changed over time, but it retains significant continuities in how and why it is fought. Doctrine—beliefs about the best ways to accomplish military ends—has a long past, and much of the doctrine employed today is rooted in the cumulative worldview that existed before September 11. The past is thus relevant to the future.

In the current environment, past experience has been called into question as the United States seeks to grapple with the legacies of 9/11, especially in the Middle East, where the military problems tend to be unconventional and traditional ways and means of thinking about the use of military force are questionable. The result has been a drive, spearheaded by Secretary of Defense Robert Gates, to rethink and reorient the American military toward contemporary realities. This reorientation, of course, begins with traditional thinking and forces as its base.

What does it mean to refer to traditional problems, forces, and solutions? Basically, such allusions describe the structure of the American armed forces in the European style that evolved through the formative period of the American military experience and congealed in World War II. The structures of armies, navies, and air forces armed with nuclear and nonnuclear (conventional) weapons are designed to confront and defeat similarly armed and organized opponents in symmetrical warfare. These forces remain the backbone of American capabilities. A major question against which they must be measured is their relevance in a world of asymmetrical threats. This chapter describes those forces; Chapters 11 and 12 assess their relevance in a world of asymmetrical threats.

Why is this description important? There are four reasons. First, traditional, nonnuclear forces and uses have been important in the past. Second, they are still major components of the package of forces with which the United States confronts the world—the components military planners best understand and are most comfortable with. The ways in which forces have been designated and employed in Iraq and, until recently, in Afghanistan are testimony to this endurance. Third, modernizing and enhancing the capabilities they represent make up one possible aspect of added defense expenditures after the current wars are concluded and thus will be a major concern in the post-Iraq debate. Finally, it may be necessary to use these forces again in the future against some currently unforeseen or foreseen foe. Their continuing relevance and applicability to the evolving structure of threat are a relevant concern. Any of these reasons is sufficient to warrant a review and analysis of the traditional security components of national security; collectively, these reasons are compelling.

This chapter examines the inheritance of two major functions of armed forces during the Cold War competition: (1) thermonuclear forces and the strategies governing their potential use and (2) so-called traditional armed forces. Both capabilities were developed explicitly for a Cold War confrontation and environment that no longer exist, but the capabilities and plans for their use remain essentially intact today and influence the current national security debate. Moreover, these forces frame what the United States can and cannot do militarily in the world and especially in the most militarily stressful situations it may face. Their continued relevance in a world where hardly anyone else has a counterpart force is a major question.

This chapter approaches the traditional problems of national security sequentially. It begins with nuclear forces and deterrence, the historically unique military problem of the Cold War. The possibilities of nuclear Armageddon, however remote, were of such enormous potential consequence as to receive the highest priority in defense planning and thinking. While a nuclear World War III has faded as a major concern, the possible spread of nuclear weapons to potential opponents, so-called nuclear proliferation, remains a central concern.

The other side of the traditional balance is the continuing utility of traditional (or nonnuclear) forces. The Cold War's military competition featured very robust nonnuclear forces—large, heavily equipped armies; highly capable surface, subsurface, and aerial navies; and sophisticated bomber- and fighter-based air forces—developed to deter and, if necessary, fight the "central battle" in Europe. The preparations undertaken came from a vision of an even larger and bloodier reprise of World War II. Of the two massive forces that conducted that competition, only American forces remain as large and configured with the kinds of capabilities the Cold War dictated.

Large-scale nuclear war and massive World War II–type war are no longer major operational probabilities, although they remain worst-case possibilities, however remote. There are, however, residual issues arising for each type. For nuclear forces, these include the problems of nuclear proliferation and missile defenses. For conventional forces, military manpower and military force reform are important residues.

NUCLEAR FORCES AND DETERRENCE

The nuclear age was formally born in the predawn hours of July 16, 1945, when the first atomic explosion lighted the skies around ground zero at the Trinity Site at White Sands, New Mexico. The light from the explosion could be seen as far as Albuquerque, New Mexico, a hundred miles or so away. Robert Oppenheimer, the physicist considered the "father" of the atomic bomb, was so overwhelmed by the event that he said later, "There floated through my mind a line from Bhagavad-Gita, 'I am become death, the shatterer of worlds.'" General Lesley Grove, the military commander of the Manhattan Project that produced the bomb, intoned, "This is the end of traditional warfare," as he viewed the explosion. His view was, of course, overstated, and traditional warfare continued despite this monumental change in destructive capability. The clear difference, however, is that wars are now conducted with nuclear escalation as a possibility, especially when nuclear-capable states are involved.

The thought surrounding nuclear weapons has its rich, distinct history, much of which has faded from public view and policy concern. The "shadow of the mushroom-shaped cloud" is, however, a remaining artifact of the second half of the twentieth century, and thus, it is worthwhile to briefly sketch its dynamics, highlighting those with continuing relevance.

Seminal Events of the Nuclear Age

The nuclear age did not burst upon us suddenly at White Sands. Scientific research into nuclear physics went back nearly a century through more-or-less independent investigations in Europe and North America. (Clark's *The Greatest Power on Earth* is a particularly good history of this evolution.) The impending clouds of World War II and intelligence reports that Nazi Germany was attempting to harness and weaponize nuclear physics alarmed Albert Einstein to the extent that he wrote a letter at the behest of more politically active colleagues like Enrico Fermi to President Franklin D. Roosevelt, warning of the potential problem such weapons could pose in the hands of the Nazis. Roosevelt's response was to commission the Manhattan Project, which began the crash program that produced nuclear bombs shortly before the end of the war.

The first operational atomic bombs were, of course, used against Hiroshima and Nagasaki, Japan, on August 6 and 9, 1945, to shorten the war in the Pacific by forcing Japanese capitulation short of an anticipated bloody invasion of the Japanese home islands. (This vision was made especially vivid by the spirited Japanese defense of Okinawa, which, interestingly, included Japanese soldiers wrapping themselves with explosives and committing suicide by blowing themselves up.) When the second bomb exploded, the American arsenal was temporarily exhausted; for the last time, the world had no nuclear weapons. In the next quarter-century, the nuclear world evolved from those primitive days through the cumulative impact of a series of nuclear events.

The Atomic (Fission) Bomb. The successful conclusion of the Manhattan Project was, of course, *the* seminal event of the nuclear age, since none of the other sophistications would have been possible without having taken this first step. The original atomic bomb was what is known as a fission device—the basic physical reaction that makes the bomb explode and produce its deadly effects occurs through the breaking apart (or fission) of atoms of unstable isotopes of uranium. The atomic bomb represented a quantitative change in the deadliness of war. The delivery of an atomic bomb over a target could produce deadly effects that otherwise could have been produced only by literally hundreds or thousands of attacks by conventional bombardment. The campaigns against Dresden, Germany, and Tokyo with incendiary bombs (both of which were cumulatively more destructive than the atomic attacks) had required attacks by many hundreds of aircraft to wreak the deadly havoc of a single nuclear bomb. Atomic bombs thus made bombardment incredibly more "efficient" than it was in the prenuclear age.

The Hydrogen (Fission–Fusion) Bomb. The second major event was the successful development of a qualitatively larger form of nuclear explosive, the fission–fusion or hydrogen bomb. Known as the "Super" at the time because of the order of magnitude by which its deadly effect had increased, a prototype of the hydrogen bomb was successfully tested by the United States in 1952. The Soviet Union followed suit a year later. As the name implies, the physical reaction behind this new form of nuclear explosion involves two steps—the explosion of a small fission "trigger" to induce the second step, which is fusion. This reaction involves the fusing together of atoms of heavy hydrogen (deuterium or tritium), which releases an enormous amount of energy far in excess of that possible with a fission reaction.

The effects of a thermonuclear explosion are awesome. Fission bombs produced yields that were the equivalent of thousands of tons (*kilotons*) of TNT; fission–fusion devices produced explosions with destructive effects measured in *megatons* (*MT*), or the equivalents of *millions* of tons of TNT. During the Cold War, the Soviet Union was reported to have tested a fission–fusion device that produced an eight-five MT blast.

The entry of thermonuclear bombs into the arsenals of the two sides altered the calculus of nuclear weapons and their use in two ways. First, it altered the calculation of survivability in a nuclear war. A society might endure grievous damage as the result of an attack with atomic bombs, but it could reasonably anticipate surviving such an attack. The same attack with thermonuclear bombs—a quantum leap in destructive capability—made survivability questionable and meant the new weapons represented a *qualitative*, rather than a quantitative, increase in the deadliness of war. Second, during the early 1950s, scientists achieved considerable success in designing bombs that were more compact and much lighter than the Hiroshima and Nagasaki prototypes. This made possible the delivery of these deadly weapons by missiles, a further qualitative change.

The Intercontinental Ballistic Missile (ICBM). The effort to weaponize rocketry began in the period between the world wars, when the first rockets were developed and tested in Germany and the United States, among other places. In World War II, the first prototypes, the V-1 "buzz bombs" and the V-Rockets, were used against Great Britain in a desperate act by the Germans to break British will. These early designs were so grossly inaccurate as to have little impact on the war, and rockets were considered little more than terrorist weapons. By the 1950s, advances in rocketry allowed nuclear weapons to be transported over intercontinental ranges and land close enough to their targets to destroy them.

These advances fundamentally altered the impact of nuclear weapons on war more than any of the other seminal events. The reasons were (and are) profound and cumulative. The thermonuclear bomb had removed the ability to calculate surviving a nuclear war if a large number of these devices were used. The ICBM produced the perfect delivery device for such weapons, since there was (and arguably still is) *no known defense capable of defending against a nuclear rocket attack*. The result is total societal vulnerability to nuclear devastation, and when both sides have this offensive capability, the condition is known as *mutual societal vulnerability*. In this situation, the only way to avoid being killed in a nuclear war was to avoid having such a war at all. Nuclear war avoidance (or nuclear deterrence) became and remains the prime value and concern.

The Multiple Independently Targetable Reentry Vehicle (MIRV). The fourth development was a major increase in the deadliness and extensiveness of nuclear arsenals—the perfection of a means to dispense more than one nuclear bomb (or warhead) from the tip of a single rocket. This military capability was achieved by the United States in 1970, when it began to add MIRV capability to its arsenal; the same feat was achieved by the Soviet Union in 1975.

The MIRV had two major effects on the nuclear equation. The first was to multiply the size of nuclear arsenals without increasing the number of nuclear missiles within those arsenals, a phenomenon known as *fractionation*. This meant that a single rocket's capacity could be increased by the number of additional warheads that the MIRV permitted to be added (or fractionated). The MIRVing of superpower arsenals had a second, anomalous effect. During the 1970s, arms control negotiations with the purpose of reducing the likelihood of nuclear war between the superpowers were particularly active, and one of their purposes was to place limits on the size and capabilities of the two offensive arsenals. MIRVs, however, had been excluded from those discussions by the Soviets (who lagged in the technology and did not want to negotiate away their chance to catch up), and the process of converting arsenals to MIRV status meant that the number of warheads actually increased greatly during the decade. The MIRV was the reason.

Ballistic Missile Defense (BMD). The fifth seminal event—defenses against missile attacks—has not yet definitively occurred but is instead a residue of the Cold War. It was a high priority of the George W. Bush administration and could, in certain circumstances, alter the nuclear calculus as much as the others. The current round of debate about missile defenses is nothing new. In fact, investigation of how to try to destroy incoming ballistic missiles proceeded parallel to the development of offensive applications of rocketry, and all the theoretical problems of missile defense had been solved before the first ICBM was launched in 1957. The problem has not been the concept; the difficulty has been, and continues to be, execution of the proposed mission, as discussed later in the chapter.

Why would the development of effective defenses represent a seminal event in the nuclear age? The answer is that a truly effective system should be capable of intercepting and destroying all of an incoming nuclear missile attack. A truly effective, reliable defense would thus remove dependence on deterrence as the only basis on which to prevent the ravages of a missile-launched nuclear war. Rather than relying on the threat of robust retaliation after absorbing an attack (the basic threat under theories of deterrence as they have been practiced), a defensive system that worked could render such an attack ineffective and futile and make nuclear weapons "impotent and obsolete," in Ronald Reagan's depiction of the purpose of his Strategic Defense Initiative. A truly effective defense would rank with the ICBM in importance in nuclear evolution and change the way we thought and think about nuclear weapons.

Theories of Deterrence

As the nuclear balance evolved, two broad conceptualizations of deterrence emerged to dominate defense theorizing and planning in the United States, including the development and deployment of nuclear arsenals. Both positions were first articulated in two works published in 1946, one very famous (Bernard Brodie's *The Absolute Weapon*) and one not so well known (William Liscum Borden's *There Will Be No Time*).

These formulations sound strange, even macabre or bizarre, when taken out of the context of the times. Brodie's formulation evolved to the strategy of assured destruction, which a detractor modified by putting the word *mutual* in front of it to produce the acronym MAD. Borden's position evolved by the 1980s to a strategy known as limited nuclear options or countervailance; a detractor gave its adherents the title nuclear utilization theorists, or NUTS. The intellectual debate about what best deterred a nuclear attack thus became a dialog between those who were MAD and those who were NUTS.

Assured Destruction. The title of Brodie's book gave its thesis away. According to Brodie and his associates at Yale University who collaborated on *The Absolute Weapon*, nuclear weapons fundamentally changed the nature and calculation of war. The destructiveness of those weapons was so great that, in Brodie's opinion, conventional war—which could escalate to nuclear war—was now obsolete. Thus, the only reason states could have for maintaining military forces (including nuclear weapons) was to avoid their use against them—in other words, deterrence. Borden disagreed, arguing that nuclear weapons were weapons, after all, and that weapons are eventually used.

Much of the debate lay fallow for over a decade. The event that enlivened the question of deterrence, of course, was the successful testing and deployment of ICBMs in the latter 1950s. Since the only way to guarantee not being killed in a nuclear war when ICBMs were present was to make certain that a nuclear war did not occur, the question became, What kind of nuclear strategy best assured the avoidance of nuclear hostilities?

The Brodie position was the first answer to dominate the debate and was articulated in the early 1960s as assured destruction. The first premise of the strategy, which came directly from Brodie himself, was that all sides would lose in any nuclear war, meaning that only war avoidance was acceptable. The question was how best to assure that no one could ever miscalculate the possibility of succeeding in a nuclear war and thus decide to start one. The answer was the assured destruction threat.

The basic dynamic of assured destruction was that any Soviet nuclear attack would be met by a fierce and destructive American retaliation that would destroy the Soviet Union and rob it of any possible calculation that it had "won" anything. ICBMs guaranteed the condition of mutual societal vulnerability under which such retaliation would occur against an initial attacker; the upshot was that launching a nuclear strike became the equivalent of committing national suicide.

The implementation and implications of assured destruction are ghoulish and created a lively opposition. In order to reinforce to Soviets the suicidal nature of an attack, the strategy features *countervalue targeting* by American retaliatory forces against Soviet targets. This antiseptic term means aiming weapons at the things people value most, notably their lives and the conditions that make life commodious. The prototypical countervalue target is an urban complex—the larger, the better—since the purpose is to convince the adversary's leadership and population that they will die if they attack the United States.

Limited Nuclear Options. The murderous implications of assured destruction did not go unnoticed or uncriticized. Arguing that such a threat was both gruesome beyond belief and incredible because of the ghoulish consequences, a second strand of thought emerged within nuclear strategy circles, suggesting a different role for nuclear forces. In the curious world of nuclear weapons and deterrence, the argument began with the belief that the assured destruction threat was unbelievable because of the moral abyss that implementation of the strategy promised and then posed a supposedly more humane alternative. Thus, nuclear planning must contain ways to use nuclear weapons that do not necessarily entail Armageddon.

This basic idea, extrapolating from Borden, became known as limited options in the 1970s and 1980s and posited proportionality as the basis of deterrence. The defenders began by arguing that the assured destruction threat was believable only in the event of an all-out Soviet first-strike attack against the United States. Since the Soviets knew the consequences of such an attack, it was the least likely form of attack for them to undertake. Thus, any nuclear attack they might actually contemplate would be less than all-out, leaving the president with only the option of doing nothing or launching the entire arsenal. As a result, the assured destruction threat emerged from this analysis as a credible threat against the least likely form of nuclear aggression and an ineffective threat against other and, by definition, more likely forms of provocation.

The limited nuclear options strategy remedies this deficiency by creating within the Single Integrated Operational Plan (SIOP, the actual plan for implementing nuclear attacks) a series of options short of all-out response (hence the name *limited options*). The idea is to provide the president with a whole array of possible responses proportional to the original attack by the Soviet Union. Thus, for instance, if the Soviets were to launch twenty to thirty missiles against U.S. ICBM fields in North Dakota, the United States should have the capability and plan to respond by taking out a similar target in the Soviet Union. Presumably, the threat and ability to do so would have two salutary effects. First, a proportional response would be more believable than an all-out counterattack. Second, knowing the United States could effectively play tit-for-tat in the event of any provocation, the Soviets would realize that any action they might initiate would be countered effectively; their attack would be trumped and provide no advantage.

Nuclear Residues

Nuclear weapons have lost the prominent role they played during the Cold War, when the central competition involved two nuclear-armed superpowers, but that does not mean nuclear considerations have disappeared from national security concerns. There are at least two related concerns about nuclear weapons that remain important items on the national security agenda: problems of nuclear proliferation and the alleged need for BMD. Neither is a new concern. The spread of nuclear weapons to states that do not currently have them was one of the earliest worries of nuclear thinkers in the 1960s, and the prospects of and debates about missile defenses predate the actual deployment of the missiles that the defenses seek to stymie.

Nuclear Proliferation. The problems associated with the prospect or reality that states that had previously lacked nuclear weapons would attain that capability were born, as a practical matter, when the United States reached nuclear capacity at

White Sands and began to worry about the prospect that a potentially antagonistic Soviet Union would follow suit. They are problems that have created agony among politicians and analysts as the nuclear "club" (the states with nuclear weapons) has increased across time. The current concern over Iran "going nuclear" is just the latest instance of a venerable problem.

The traditional nuclear proliferation concern centered on the additional problems produced if additional sovereign states gained nuclear weapons. In the contemporary context, that concern remains but with a twist that did not concern nuclear planners during the Cold War but does today. In the contemporary context, additional states that might gain nuclear weapons capability like Iran and North Korea remain problematical, but there are two other matters of concern. The first is that the proliferation concern has broadened beyond nuclear weapons, which are difficult to acquire, to other forms of WMD such as biological and chemical weapons that are less deadly but more accessible. The second concern is that the WMD, but especially nuclear weapons, might fall into the hands of nonstate actors and, more specifically, terrorist organizations. These two additional concerns are conjoined because of the fear raised most dramatically (if falsely) about the possibility that a WMD-armed Iraq might have shared these weapons with terrorist organizations like Al Qaeda.

Nuclear proliferation can take on two guises. The first is *horizontal proliferation*, which refers to the spread of nuclear weapons to states that do not currently possess them. This is the proliferation problem that most commonly forms the basis of contemporary concerns. The second form, however, is *vertical proliferation*, which refers to growth in the arsenals of current nuclear weapons states. As particularly the superpower nuclear arsenals mushroomed after the advent of MIRV, this phenomenon became entangled with horizontal proliferation, as potential new nuclear club members (notably India) argued that their continuing abstention from joining that club was tied (as specified in the Non-Proliferation Treaty or NPT) to a reduction in the arsenals of the superpowers. The failure of the United States and the Soviet Union to engage in arsenal cutbacks was used to justify the Indian decision to join the nuclear club in 1998.

The dynamics of horizontal proliferation are captured in a construct called the $N + 1$ *problem*. This artifact of the Cold War is as valid today as it was forty years ago when it was articulated. In this formulation, N stands for the number of states that currently possess nuclear weapons, and $+1$ refers to the additional problems created if additional states gain these weapons. The problems are conventionally described in terms of how new members destabilize the system by adding additional "fingers to the nuclear button" (increasing the number of states that, by virtue of having the weapons, can start a nuclear war). Implicit in this formulation is the assumption that new members are *more likely* to start a war than current members; if they were not, the concern would be less well grounded.

The heart of the $N + 1$ problem is the different perceptions of the two groups. The N states implicitly (sometimes explicitly) argue that the possession of the weapons by states that already have them is acceptable, and their evidence is that the current possessors have avoided nuclear war. Additional states, however, pose unpredictable new dangers and dynamics that it is safer to avoid, thus forming the basis for opposition. At least implicit in this assessment is the premise that new possessing states would act more irresponsibly with the weapons than current possessors do. Since the same charges were made against current members before they joined N (China in particular), it is difficult publicly to defend this position without being openly condescending to the potential proliferators.

Potential new members (the +1 states) discount that *their* possession would make things more unstable and argue that, if anything, their membership in the club would increase their own security. This seems to be a prime argument made by Iran and North Korea, who state that they need nuclear weapons to deter the *United States* from attacking them. Once +1 states get the weapons, however, they tend to accept the argument that N (of which they are now a part) produces an acceptable balance but that additional accretions to the club would be unacceptable.

The divide between states that do and do not possess nuclear weapons over *whether* an N + 1 problem exists cannot be overstated because it reflects basic cleavages about how states view one another. Put bluntly, the supposition that it is all right for currently possessing states to perpetuate their nuclear arsenals and destabilizing for other states to join them is discriminatory at a minimum and condescendingly racist at worst. The loudest detractors of nuclear weapons spread have been the United States, Russia, Great Britain, and France, all of which are European by tradition. Obviously, some possessors (China, India, and Pakistan, for instance) are not European, but they are also the most worrisome members of N. Somewhat interestingly, the possession of these weapons by Israel rarely evokes this concern in the West.

The +1 states, on the other hand, come mostly from the developing world. Moreover, claiming that some countries are more responsible than others in possessing these weapons in effect accuses the pretenders of being more reckless and irresponsible, which, at a minimum, is condescending. Why, for instance, does the United States so vociferously oppose the spread of nuclear weapons to Iran and the Democratic People's Republic of Korea (DPRK or North Korea)? The answer is that such spread would be destabilizing, which effectively means that those countries would likely be less responsible possessors. Operationally, this means they would be more likely to use nuclear weapons against their enemies (including the United States) or might provide access to them to terrorists. Why? Because the Kim Jong Il regime of the DPRK and the Mahmoud Ahmadinejad regime of Iran (how much power he actually would wield over these weapons is questionable) are less responsible than the current possessors. That logic may make sense to Americans; it cannot possibly be viewed by North Koreans or Iranians as anything other than insulting.

This logical dilemma infects the major international effort to discourage nuclear weapons acquisition, the Non-Proliferation Treaty that was negotiated in 1968 and entered into force in 1970. The treaty in essence creates a caste system. On the one hand are the states that already possess nuclear weapons, who are required not to encourage or help nonpossessors to gain these weapons and who are committed to reducing their own possession to zero (reverse vertical proliferation). These states have been much better at meeting the former requirement than the latter. Nonpossessing states are required to renounce their intention ever to build these weapons. Those states unwilling to make that pledge (Israel and India are the most prominent examples) simply refuse to become members of the treaty (North Korea and Iran *are* members, although the DPRK at one point dropped out of the treaty).

The concern over horizontal proliferation extends beyond nuclear weapons. The other forms of WMD include biological weapons (using agents of biological origin) and chemical weapons. Both forms are prohibited by international treaties of which most counties are members. Biological and chemical weapons are of a lesser order of concern mostly because their effects are more limited. An attack with a chemical or biological aerosol may kill or debilitate those on whom it falls, but generally, the radius of destruction is limited. Moreover, the use of either is problematical, particularly because airborne agents are subject to vagaries such as the shifting direction and velocity of wind. Most of these weapons lack the potential for massive devastation of a target population that nuclear weapons possess. On the other hand, they are easier to construct using materials that are much more readily available internationally than the fissile materials necessary to build nuclear weapons, and their development and stockpiling are relatively easier to accomplish clandestinely than are nuclear programs. The fear that Iraq had manufactured and was secretly stockpiling such weapons was, after all, a primary justification for invading that country.

How does one deter horizontal proliferation? There are two basic approaches. One is *acquisition deterrence*, which consists of attempts to dissuade countries from acquiring the weapons. The techniques for accomplishing this form of deterrence include positive incentives not to engage in provocative actions, such as providing safeguarded nuclear fuels (fuel sources that cannot be transformed into weapons-grade materials) and monetary incentives for demurring from weapons development, and negative actions, such as sanctions. Both techniques are currently being used against the DPRK (sanctions when the North Koreans engage in nuclear developments and assistance such as nonnuclear fuels and foodstuffs when they comply) and Iran. If countries like India, for instance, cannot be dissuaded from developing these weapons, then one must revert to *employment deterrence*, which consists of efforts to avoid the use of nuclear weapons by states who gain them. The techniques for doing so tend to be those associated with traditional bilateral U.S.–USSR deterrence during the Cold War.

Two more points should be made about nuclear proliferation. First, the key to avoiding new states getting such weapons is avoiding the transfer of weapons-grade materials (particular isotopes of uranium and plutonium) to acquiring states. The physics of making nuclear bombs is generally well known, and most potential proliferators can assemble the scientific and engineering teams to create nuclear weapons (it is not, it should be added, clear that most terrorist groups can meet this criterion). The secret is the control of weapons-grade materials, and that has been the heart of most attempts to limit the spread of nuclear weapons.

The second point concerns the addition of nonstate actors (most prominently terrorist groups) to the list of nuclear pretenders. Arguments about the irresponsibility of this category of potential nuclear club members are much more convincing than the same arguments made against states. Notably, the allegation is made that a terrorist group such as Al Qaeda would be more likely to use such weapons if it had them because its members lack the fear of the consequences—retaliation—that impedes state possessors. There are two reasons for this. On the one hand, the principle of martyrdom is built into the ethos of many of these groups, who would thus not fear retaliation the way most states would. On the other hand, nonstate actors lack identified, claimed territorial bases against which to retaliate. Should Al Qaeda launch a nuclear attack somewhere (blow up a bomb in an American city, for instance), what would the United States annihilate in retaliation? If the attacker is Russia, the answer is obvious. But if it is Al Qaeda, does that mean leveling parts of Waziristan, which is a province of an American ally, Pakistan?

There are currently seven admitted members of the nuclear club (in order of "admission," the United States, the Soviet Union/Russia, Great Britain, France, China, India, and Pakistan), one state that neither confirms nor denies its possession but is universally considered a member (Israel), one state that developed these weapons but subsequently dismantled them and renounced their possession (South Africa), and one state that periodically admits or denies its possession (the DPRK). Predictions made several decades ago suggested that twenty to thirty states might by now have gained the capability, but they have not. Moreover, proliferation has not been accompanied by its most dire possible consequence, nuclear war. The potential that other states and, more ominously, nonstate actors might join the club keeps the concern over the proliferation problem lively because the potential consequences of a rogue +1 entity gaining possession of the capability are so dire.

The proliferation question remains controversial. No one—with the exception of countries attempting to obtain the weapons—thinks that proliferation is a good idea or that the world would be a better place with more nuclear weapons–possessing states. At the same time, there is disagreement about *how much* of a problem it is, as already suggested. In recent years, there has been an additional and dynamic concern among potential proliferators that they may need the weapons to protect themselves from current possessors like the United States.

The irony about proliferation in the current context is that countries seek nuclear weapons in order to guard against being attacked by their enemies—a deterrence argument. Nuclear weapons possession, it is argued, provides status and respect from potential predators: no state in possession of nuclear weapons has ever been attacked by another state. The irony is that this argument is currently voiced most prominently as a reason for gaining nuclear weapons in Iran and North Korea, and the country they seek to deter with those weapons is the United States. To support this concern, some argue that Saddam Hussein's greatest mistake was *not* pursuing nuclear weapons because, if he had possessed them, the United States might not have attacked him for fear of a nuclear retaliation by Iraq. Thus, nonproliferation may be more dangerous to some states than proliferation.

This argument has particular resonance in Iran. Many Iranians fear being attacked by two nuclear states, the United States and Israel. Both states have identified a nuclear-armed Iran as unacceptable, and especially the Israelis have

Amplification 10.1

IRANIAN PROLIFERATION AND ISRAEL

Privately, most American officials admit there is little the United States can do to prevent Iran from building nuclear weapons if that country is determined to do so. This conclusion is based on ruling out military action against Iran's program as problematically effective and possibly leading to a major war with Iran they believe would be unwise. Thus, American efforts center on deterrence—to convince Iran not to build nuclear weapons (acquisition deterrence) or, if that fails, not to use them (employment deterrence).

The Israelis view the situation more desperately, fearing a nuclear-armed Iran might attack them or provide the weapons to terrorists who would use them. Thus, Israeli threats to attack and destroy Iranian weapons are quite sincere and create a real quandary for the United States. Such an attack would likely have to be quite massive to have any real chance of destroying the widely dispersed, hardened, and clandestine Iranian program and would almost surely produce widespread calls for *jihad* against the Israelis throughout the region. How would—or should—the United States react in these circumstances? The best answer is to prevent the scenario and thus avoid the question. But what if that fails?

threatened military actions to prevent the Iranians from obtaining nuclear weapons. Such threats were made and carried out by Israel against Iraq and Syria, adding credence to them. One way for Iran to negate that threat would be to obtain the weapons and their deterrent properties. This prospect creates the additional concerns suggested in Amplification 10.1.

Missile Defenses. The long-standing Bush administration proposal to build a missile defense inherited by the Obama administration is not a new idea. In fact, the idea is the third generation of advocacy for developing and deploying a defense against ballistic missile attack. The first proposal was put forward in the latter 1960s and early 1970s as the Sentinel and later as the Safeguard system to guard against a Chinese nuclear capability that was projected for the future, and as such, it was similar to the Bush plan in intent (see Amplification 10.2).

In 1983, President Ronald Reagan proposed a much more ambitious system, the *Strategic Defense Initiative (SDI)*. The Reagan SDI had the grand purpose of providing a comprehensive, totally effective shield against a massive launch of nuclear weapons (essentially an assured destruction attack) by the Soviet Union. The impenetrability of the SDI screen would render nuclear weapons "impotent and obsolete," in Reagan's own words. Reagan's longer view was that such a shield would make nuclear weapons themselves irrelevant and thus lead to nuclear disarmament, his real goal. The SDI program lost focus during the first Bush administration and was formally scuttled by

Amplification 10.2

THE CHINESE NUCLEAR THREAT

Recent proposals to deploy a missile defense in Europe bear an eerie resemblance to similar arguments made nearly forty years ago, when the People's Republic of China's fledgling nuclear capability was the major objective of the United States' proposed Sentinel and later Safeguard antimissile systems. What critics argued is particularly instructive about the comparison is that the "threat" posed by China was, at the time, potential rather than actual. In the 1960s, China had nuclear warheads but no ballistic missiles capable of delivering them against the United States. The projected problem was the assertion that China would soon acquire such a capability and that missile defenses were needed to deter a Chinese launch against the United States when they indeed acquired the capability.

In retrospect, the arguments appear nearly hysterical, although the state of United States–China animosity in the late 1960s made them appear more plausible than they do today. In 1967, after all, the United States had no formal relations with the Chinese (and had not since the Communists assumed power in 1949) and had fought Chinese "volunteers" in the Korean War (Chinese forces sent to Korea were officially designated as volunteers to avoid a direct legal and political confrontation between the two countries). Moreover, after China joined the nuclear weapons club, Chinese leader Mao Zedung had publicly proclaimed that China's huge population meant it was the only country that could physically survive a nuclear war.

The irony of the rationale was not only that the projections of Chinese acquisition of delivery capacity against U.S. targets were premature, but also that the capability has never been meaningfully achieved. The Chinese arsenal, although undergoing modernization, remains very small even today, consisting of a handful of unreliable, liquid-fuel, land-based and sea-based missiles that cannot be kept at a high state of readiness because their means of propulsion cannot be stored in the rockets and they would have to be "gassed up" before a launch. These missiles arguably pose a potential threat to neighboring Taiwan but not the United States. The question is whether potential acquisition of delivery capability by "axis of evil" states such as Iran and North Korea may be as fanciful as the Chinese "threat" against which the first missile shield was proposed.

President Clinton. What remained after the demise of SDI was research on a more limited form of defense. The Bush proposal came from this program.

The Clinton White House never showed great enthusiasm for missile defense, and the program was kept alive largely because of congressional interest. President George W. Bush took up the cause of missile defense in his 2000 campaign and continued that advocacy once elected. The events of September 11, 2001, temporarily sidetracked what had been active attempts both to gain support for the program and to overcome foreign (notably Russian, but also Chinese) objections to deploying such a system, objections that continue to the present and are reflected in Russia's opposition to a missile shield in Eastern Europe (which, as noted earlier, has been mollified by the Obama administration decision to abandon the deployment of the system). This proposed system was a major source of friction in U.S.-Russian relations under Bush and has been a bargaining chip in Obama's effort to improve relations between the two countries.

The idea of missile defense has inherent appeal arising from the realization that deterrence can in fact fail (i.e., a nuclear terrorist attack can be launched). In that event, the absence of some form of defense leaves the population absolutely vulnerable to being killed, a decidedly unappealing prospect and one against which it is attractive to try to hedge. It is even suggested by advocates that it is immoral not to try to mount a defense against a missile attack.

There are several objections to developing and deploying missile defenses. The first and most fundamental objection is *workability*. Although the theoretical principles for missile defenses had been surmounted before the first ICBM was fired successfully, developing a system that actually could shoot down missiles with any proven reliability has been and remains illusive. This problem was ultimately the undoing of the SDI, a system that would have been so complicated that no one could ever convincingly argue it would work.

A second critique deals with the *need* for a defense. As Amplification 10.2 points out, the original Sentinel/Safeguard system was designed to thwart a projected Chinese nuclear threat to the United States that has yet to emerge more than forty years later. While no one questioned that the Soviets posed a threat for which an effective SDI might have provided a remedy, the Bush proposal was more similar to Sentinel/Safeguard than to SDI. It is designed not as a counter to an existing threat but rather as a hedge against the emergence of a threat by rogue states or, in the wake of the September 11 terrorist attacks, by nonstate actors. Critics argue that, as in the 1960s, this threat may never emerge, and if it does, it is far enough in the future to wait until a truly effective system can be designed.

The third objection is *cost*. A major characteristic of all three missile defense proposals has been widely diverging speculation about how much a system designed to fulfill its mission would cost. The numbers are always high. The most extreme case was the comprehensive SDI, the most ambitious of the proposals. The cost of deploying the SDI was estimated at anywhere between $500 billion and $2 trillion over a ten-year deployment period. Estimates for the national missile defense (NMD) have run upward of $60 billion.

While the Obama administration did inherit the Bush-designed program for a thin shield in Eastern Europe consisting of radars and interceptors in Poland and the Czech Republic to protect against a small nuclear missile launch from a Middle East location, that program has been shelved. The Obama White House first put implementation of the accord signed with the Czechs and Poles on hold, with Obama stating that no action would be undertaken until the system's workability was clearly demonstrated. At least partially to assuage Russian misgivings about the Bush system, the Obama administration announced in September 2009 that it would instead field a ship-based system using existing anti-missile systems to protect against a potential Iranian launch while continuing research on other possibilities. Such a system, it is hoped, will be both cheaper than the Bush system and will be viewed as less provocative by the Russians.

Worries about the U.S. proposal have caused the Russians to revive their historical objections to American intentions to build a missile defense in Eastern Europe. Russia, which has opposed missile defenses for decades, opposes the deployment on three grounds. First, it argues that the threat is bogus and that Iran neither does nor will pose such a threat in the foreseeable future (similar to the Chinese nuclear threat). Second, Russia opposes operational missile defenses close to its borders as provocative and aimed implicitly at Russia. Third, it has never accepted that defensive systems can work (at least *Russia* has never been able to build one) but fears that an American deployment might provide the kind of operational experience that could lead to perfection of such a system, thereby leaving Russia at a disadvantage. Pique over the controversy became so great that in July 2007, despite Bush's assurances to Putin at a mini-summit earlier that month at the president's father's retreat in Maine, the Russians announced they were suspending their participation in the Treaty on Conventional Armed Forces in Europe signed in 1990 and the basis of constrained conventional force levels in Europe since. The July 13, 2007, announcement in Moscow suggested the Russian move was necessitated by "extraordinary circumstances . . . which affect the security of the Russian federation and require immediate measures" (quoted in Kramer). The fate of the proposed system will likely be an ongoing item in future U.S.-Russian relations.

TRADITIONAL FORCES AND THE FUTURE

Both of the fault lines highlight the question of the future of traditional forces. As already noted in the introduction to this chapter and in Chapter 7, the bulk of American military forces and the expenses associated with them were devoted to maintaining and modernizing a force that was largely designed and configured to fight World War III in Europe. The end of the Cold War made this kind of a conflict extremely unlikely; no realistic potential adversary has emerged to confront the United States in traditional symmetrical warfare (both sides fighting a stand-up, western-style war), nor is one likely to emerge in the near future. Saddam Hussein challenged the United States on its own military terms in the Persian Gulf War in 1990–1991, and he failed miserably. His experience was instructive for all who might challenge the West, and especially the United States, on its own terms in the future. The end of the Cold War started the process by which the United States' traditional power has become so great that it has made itself virtually obsolete, a kind of self-fulfilling prophecy in which American prowess has eliminated the problem for which it was devised.

The campaign against terrorism has simply accentuated this situation. Following the fairly conventional first phase (overthrowing the Taliban), the campaign in Afghanistan has witnessed a very different way of waging hostilities and raises some further questions about the continuing relevancy of traditional military forces to deal with these kinds of problems. Where do traditional forces fit in this environment? The remaining pages of this chapter will look at the traditional roles such forces have played and the fate of attempts to reform those forces, the question of force modernization in light of environmental changes and revised missions for the military caused by dynamics associated with fault lines, and the impact of recent events on the equation.

American military predominance in these traditional forces has helped fuel a debate on their continuing relevance. The last time the traditional force structure and model were applied in toto was in the Persian Gulf War of 1990–1991, although, in modified form, it was also the model for the invasion and conquest of Iraq in 2003. As one looks at future possible scenarios where the United States might contemplate involvement, traditional, World War II–style wars are hard to imagine. Indeed, the strongest argument for retaining and modernizing these forces is that an unforeseen contingency might arise where they would be needed.

The Vietnam War introduced another model of warfare, unconventional or asymmetrical war, a form of armed conflict where the structure and mission of forces do not conform to the traditional model. This unconventional model has been encountered in the postinvasion (occupation) phase of the Iraq War and in Afghanistan and is the kind of conflict in which Pakistan has become enmeshed. The Obama administration has concluded that this kind of war represents the future for American arms, a position embraced and articulated by Secretary Gates.

These opposing views, and the roles, missions, and forces that implement them, form the basis for debate as the United States enters the 2010s. One model, the extension of traditional uses of force, can be called conventional and the forces it emphasizes "heavy." The other model is unconventional and the forces it emphasizes "light." In practice, the two models are to a great extent incompatible.

The Heavy Forces (Conventional) Model

World War II was the major formative period for American military forces as they now exist and are configured today. The purpose of that conflict was the defeat of Nazi aggression by large, heavily armed, mechanized forces fighting European style, and the United States and its allies responded with symmetrical forces. Although the structure of active-duty forces was largely dismantled in the years immediately after World War II, that war still served as the model for the Korean conflict, with some peripheral modifications to reflect technological innovations (such as jet aircraft and helicopters). Since this force remained in being after Korea, rather than following the American tradition of mobilization for war and then rapid demobilization at war's conclusion, the conventional force for the Cold War was one with which veterans of World War II were comfortable and familiar. Only the adversary changed, and since the Soviets were similarly organized and were likely to fight symmetrically, the model seemed vindicated. This force structure has largely survived reductions in size since the end of the Cold War but is under more intense scrutiny in a new century.

The bulk of the American nonnuclear armed forces can be reasonably accurately described using two adjectives, *heavy* and *conventional*, which define what the military likes to refer to as *legacy forces*. The term *heavy* refers to the way the force is configured and how it is equipped to perform its mission. More specifically, it describes a force designed to fight in large-unit, concentrated-firepower combat, using mobile mechanized units, against a similarly configured opponent in brutal, positional land, air, and naval warfare. The symbols of heavy warfare are tanks and mobile artillery on land, bombers with large payloads in the air, and large capital ships (battleships, aircraft carriers) on the sea. By contrast, *light* forces feature more lightly armed and mobile forces capable of engaging in a variety of forms of warfare and generally not preferring the kinds of direct confrontations between armies, navies, and air forces typical of heavy forces.

Heavy forces are designed to fight *conventional*, traditional warfare, which is the style that was perfected during World War II and that has been called European. Sometimes referred to as the "Western way of war," its military purpose is to overcome adversary "hostile ability" (the capacity to resist the other side's armed forces physically) through the direct confrontation of armed forces. The military purpose is to destroy "in detail" or to break the cohesion of enemy armies, sink enemy navies, and shoot down enemy air assets. Collectively, the objective is to gain military superiority over an adversary in order to impose political objectives on that enemy by overcoming its physical ability to resist that imposition. Warfare employing heavy forces is most closely attached to wars of total political purpose (in which the objective is the overthrow of the enemy government) such as World War II, although in some circumstances these forces are effective in lesser contingencies. Heavy forces are designed and best suited for confronting similar forces possessed by the opponent. They are the tools of symmetrical warfare.

A heavy force was appropriate for the Cold War confrontation with the Soviet Union and its allies. The U.S. and Soviet armed forces were virtual mirror images of one another physically, and both shared similar plans in the event of war. The doctrines of both sides emphasized mass (having more force at the point of engagement). A war between them, it was assumed, would resemble World War II, except that it would be much bloodier and more violent, and one side or the other would exhaust its weaponry and its ability to continue first. Moreover, such a war would likely be total in purpose, with one side or the other having its government overthrown (unless, of course, the war escalated to system-destroying nuclear war, in which case both sides would lose). The heavy model proved durable for fighting and winning World War II and confronting the Soviet Union short of war during the Cold War.

The heavy force model has dominated American military thinking at least since the American Civil War, and some argue that Ulysses S. Grant was the conceptual "father" of the American heavy tradition. As the United States plans and equips itself for a post-9/11 world, the question of the continuing propriety of this emphasis has been raised. Are future American wars likely to be traditional affairs, dominated by heavy forces?

The Obama administration thinks not. In April 2009, Secretary Gates cancelled major weapons projects for all three of the major independent services branches (the army, navy, and air force), each of which was designed to project traditional military superiority into the future. The rationale was not only that those commitments would be terribly expensive, but also that the capability they would create was not relevant to likely future military needs. A prime example was the F–22 fighter–bomber, an air superiority jet whose relevance was questioned in a world where the skies were already ruled by the United States and its allies and where the emergence of a new adversary seemed fanciful.

A further symbolic example occurred in May 2009, when Gates relieved General David McKiernan, an army general with a "heavy" background and orientation in armor, with Lt. General Stephen McChrystal, a former Joint Special Operations Command (JSOC) commander, as leader of U.S. forces in Afghanistan. Special Forces (the core of JSOC) is a major "light" force, and McChrystal's elevation was a commentary on both the nature of the Afghan campaign and the general direction of U.S. armed forces.

The Light Forces (Unconventional) Model

The alternative approach to building heavy military forces is the light forces model. Light forces is a term that generally refers to military structures that deemphasize large military equipment and that, at the extreme, are largely limited to equipment that can be carried physically by soldiers on foot or transported by helicopter or similar conveyance (e.g., rifles, small-caliber mortars). The emphasis of light forces is on speed, maneuverability, and surprise. They are not designed to confront and "slug it out" with heavy forces, against which they stand little chance in symmetrical warfare. Rather, they are best adapted to rapid movement, to special assignments for which speed and deception are critical, and to missions that heavy forces cannot accomplish because of their relative lack of speed and flexibility—capturing fugitives or rescuing hostages, for instance.

In the developing world, light forces have been associated with guerrilla warfare, particularly in the jungles of the mountainous "green belt" surrounding the Equator and similar inhospitable physical environments, where it is easier for such forces to maneuver, and especially to engage in hit-and-run tactics in the face of more firepower-intensive heavy forces. The Viet Cong were classic practitioners of this style of warfare during the Vietnam War, and it consistently frustrated the efforts of much more heavily armed American regular forces until they adopted similar approaches.

The light forces model has always been a part of the western tradition, although its relative importance has varied. Some might suggest that the cavalry tradition is the prototype for light forces in the American system, comparing the cavalry on horseback with helicopter-borne "air cavalry." Special Forces and Rangers are also examples of the light forces model.

A major criticism of light forces is their inability to match up with heavy forces in direct combat; a soldier with a rifle stands little chance against a tank. This criticism is valid and carries considerable weight when the opponent is heavy, in which case heavy forces are the necessary counterweight. A light force facing a heavy force can deal with it successfully only by avoiding the kind of direct confrontations in which the superior firepower of the heavy force can be brought to bear to "frame" and destroy the lighter force. This was the lesson painfully learned by Taliban light forces that remained massed in the face of American air forces in 2001. Heavy forces, however, have not always prevailed over light forces in unconventional asymmetrical warfare, as Vietnam provides ample evidence. If the future is likely to hold more asymmetrical than symmetrical foes, then the primacy of heavy forces is not to be taken for granted.

Light forces have always been "orphans" within a U.S. military establishment more committed to traditional warfare methods and specialties. The Obama conclusion that their relevance will be greater in the future helps explain the reorientation toward these kinds of forces. Advocate Gates explained in a 2009 *Foreign Affairs* article, "I just want to make sure that the capabilities needed for the complex conflicts the United States is actually in and most likely to face in the foreseeable future also have a strong and sustained institutional support over the long term."

Light or Heavy Futures?

If the heavy forces model served the United States well in the twentieth century, is it equally durable and serviceable for confronting the environment of the twenty-first century? Clearly, the environment within which the use of armed forces is contemplated has changed. The prospect of fighting a symmetrical war against heavy forces using conventional means has all but disappeared. In the words of the original 1997 version of the Quadrennial Defense Review (QDR) (a review of American strategy and forces mandated by Congress once every four years), the United States lacks a "peer competitor" or even a foreseeable adversary that poses the kind of military threat for which those forces have been historically appropriate. The question becomes whether this type of force and this style of warfare are appropriate for the challenges ahead. The experience of the United States in Afghanistan, where both heavy and light forces were employed in both symmetrical and asymmetrical settings and ways, does little to clarify this debate, as Amplification 10.3 explains. However, there is nothing really new in the debate, nor is it likely to be resolved definitively anytime soon.

TRADITIONAL RESIDUES

The proper types of traditional military forces and their applications in today's environment remain in question, and the experience of the United States in Iraq and Afghanistan further clouds the outcome. In fact, this evolving experience has called into strong relief two related residual questions about these forces that must be answered for the future application of traditional forces. One question centers on military manpower: how many forces will be needed for what purposes, and how will the United States acquire them? The other question involves military reform and centers on what kind of forces the United States will need or be able to develop to confront the environment in the future.

Amplification 10.3

LIGHT AND HEAVY FORCES?

For a country with considerable resources available to it, the debate over heavy or light forces is not an either/or proposition. Very poor countries may have no affordable alternative to lightly armed forces. The United States, on the other hand, can afford both kinds of forces, and although there will always be a debate over which kind to emphasize at different times and in differing situations, one form or the other is extremely unlikely to disappear.

There are several good reasons why the debate is over emphasis, not the exclusive existence of one kind of force or the other. First, keeping both kinds of forces is politically the easiest solution, especially in the relations between civil authorities and the military itself. An emphasis on light forces has considerably more support within the civilian community than it does within the career military, most of whose leaders have emerged from backgrounds in "heavy" military specialties. Considerable political capital is preserved by arguing the need for both kinds of forces.

Second, it is difficult to argue for the elimination of either emphasis in an uncertain environment. As military apologists are quick to point out, for instance, no one foresaw as little as a few months before the fact that Iraq would invade and conquer Kuwait in 1990. In order to oust the Iraqis, heavy forces were clearly necessary to confront and defeat a heavy Iraqi opponent. Had the choice been made in advance to drastically draw down American heavy assets, the effort would have been considerably more difficult and expensive. A wide variety of forces, in other words, is a hedge against unforeseen contingencies.

Third, eliminating or drastically cutting back heavy armed forces would eliminate the principal military advantage the United States possesses in the world. Confronting the United States frontally in symmetrical combat may be unthinkable under current circumstances, but if the United States self-abnegated its advantage, then such warfare might once again emerge as a real and lively problem.

Military Manpower

The United States has faced a mounting manpower problem that threatens to become more acute, to the point of jeopardizing the American military ability to meet current and future military obligations. The major symptom of this crisis was the inability of the armed forces to meet recruiting goals (numbers of recruits necessary to replace retiring members) for several years, necessitating increasingly long, involuntary, and unpopular deployments of existing forces. The economic downturn of 2008 provided a temporary respite, as unemployment rates drove more young Americans into the services, and 2009 was a banner years in which all armed forces met their recruitment quotas. Whether that trend will survive economic recovery remains to be seen.

The manpower crisis has been, in its most general sense, the result of the reversal of two trends from the 1990s. The first is greater utilization of the force, increased operational tempo (or op tempo in military jargon), than in the 1990s. Some increase in force deployment and employment is a natural outgrowth of the attacks of September 11 and the increased need for military force in places like Afghanistan. The principal cause of increased deployment, of course, has been the war in Iraq, which is also the cause of much of the manpower crisis.

The Iraq commitment has greatly stressed American manpower resources in ways that reveal both the nature and the limits of the All-Volunteer Force (AVF) concept that has predominated in the military since the Vietnam War. Because all AVF members are volunteers who want to be in the military, the result has been a highly motivated, competent, professional force. It is, however, a relatively expensive force because professionals must be paid well, and it is relatively small, since only a limited number of Americans volunteer. This size has limited military operations in Iraq, which has required relatively large occupation forces. To deal with these limitations, the armed forces have resorted to multiple tours of duty in Iraq for active-duty members and extensive use of the Reserves, each of which has created its own problems.

The result, of course, is the manpower crisis that has emerged. It has three major components and one major implication for the United States. One component is recruiting shortfalls—all of the services have, at one time or another, failed to meet their recruitment goals, and in some cases, the deficits have been substantial. The problem is most acute for ground forces—the so-called combat arms—as is normally the case. The most commonly cited reason that eligible young Americans are not enlisting was their reluctance to serve in Iraq. The combat arms problem is especially acute in the Guard and Reserves. The second component is lower-than-normal reenlistment rates for current military members. Once again, the greatest part of the problem is in the Guard and Reserves, where non-reenlistment rates have approached 50 percent in some cases and might be higher except for "stop loss" orders, which have kept soldiers involuntarily in uniform and deployed beyond the periods of their enlistment. The scheduled withdrawal of American combat forces from Iraq in 2010 will alleviate this problem somewhat but will not address the third problem, which is combat-stress disorders suffered by American forces, and especially those subject to multiple deployments. The result has been highly elevated rates of mental illness and suicide among Iraq War veterans.

What can the United States do about this problem? The answer is parallel to the discussion of risk. One way to reduce risk is to increase capability to deflect risk; the parallel for the military is to increase the size of the armed forces. The question is, How? One way is to increase recruitment, either by creating greater incentives to join (e.g., more money for college tuition, signing bonuses) or offering better terms of service (e.g., shorter enlistment periods, fewer overseas deployments). The problem in the current context is the opposition of parents to their children's enlistments— opposition that incentives are unlikely to change. The other way to increase the force, of course, is through involuntary service—conscription or the draft—a prospect that is politically suicidal.

Challenge!

MILITARY SERVICE AFTER IRAQ

No American who was not at least eighteen years old on January 1, 1972, has ever been subjected to the possibility of involuntary conscription into the U.S. armed forces. One of the consequences of that condition—the result of negative reactions to the Vietnam War—is that few young Americans have had to give serious thought to the prospect of military service. Since exemption from involuntary service now spans two generations, this means that relatively few Americans in what used to be the "draft eligible" age pool of eighteen- to twenty-six-year-olds even have fathers who served voluntarily or involuntarily.

The attacks on the World Trade Center and the Pentagon produced a spike in interest in enlistment in the armed forces from young men and women across the board, including college students, who were heretofore among the least likely to enlist. This proved to be a temporary reaction—enlistments by college students did not rise appreciably after September 11. The problem of enlistment is more acute regarding Iraq.

What will the future situation be like? Has military service seriously occurred to you? If it has, what did you conclude about joining one of the services? Has your attitude changed because of the Iraq War? More specifically, has your view changed enough that you give more consideration or less to the services than before?

Another way to reduce risk is to reduce the threat. In military manpower terms, the parallel is to decrease op tempo for the force. With fewer overseas deployments, for instance, major objections to enlistment would be eased, and more current members would likely reenlist (especially Guard and Reserve elements). Clearly, the way to decrease op tempo most dramatically would be to make a major reduction in the force in Iraq, a move that would have enormous policy implications. The accompanying *Challenge!* box explores this future.

Military Reform

Changes in how and what the military does—military reform—come in several forms, not all of which are relevant for present purposes. Reform may, for instance, refer to changing rules about who can join the military (females, gays) and for what purposes (women in combat roles). It can refer to proper military conduct, the relationship between civilian and military authorities, or any of a broad variety of other areas of military concern.

For present purposes, consideration will be limited to the questions of military missions and the appropriate and most efficiently configured forces to carry out those missions, which is related to the debate over heavy or light forces. The questions, generally speaking, are logical and sequential. The first concern is what kinds of situations the military will be forced to confront and what outcomes are likely. The second is whether current forces are appropriate for achieving current and future assigned missions, and if they are not, what changes should be made to better align missions and forces. The debate over forecasting and preparing for an unknown and somewhat unknowable future is a venerable military concern.

Military reform in this context is a dynamic and ongoing process, since situations are always changing, as is the ability to deal with the changes that occur. Military reform, however, is an especially wrenching task for military professionals to undertake. The nature of the problem for which military forces are developed is profoundly serious—ultimately the protection of the population from harm, even their survival. That mission tends to make the military conservative in approach—that is, more prone to "tried and true" methods than to untested innovations that might fail at critical points. Institutionally, most military professionals get into positions where they may be charged with assessing reform proposals only after they have served long careers in specific warfare specialties to which they have great allegiance and loyalty and which they believe are necessary to the successful prosecution of war. Moreover, the "American way of war" emphasizes the western tradition in warfare and has been relatively successful in prosecuting warfare fought by forces with similar values, rules, and conventions of war. Military traditions and values are simply resistant, if not impervious, to reform efforts unless truly traumatic experiences force change upon the military establishment of the day. This observation is not intended to be demeaning or insulting to those charged with reform but only to reflect sources of and reasons for resistance.

The history of military reform efforts since the end of World War II reflects this resistance. The first systematic effort was convened by new Secretary of Defense James Forrestal in 1948 at Key West, Florida, to rationalize military roles and missions. In the early 1990s, President Clinton's first defense secretary, Les Aspin (a former chair of the House Armed Services Committee) commissioned the "Bottom Up Review" (BUR) to conduct an exhaustive review of how the military should operate with the collapse of the Soviet threat. When that effort failed to produce meaningful reform, a frustrated Congress pushed through legislation requiring the QDR. The initial report was produced in 1997. When the George W. Bush administration entered office in January 2001, one of the first assignments facing Secretary of Defense Donald Rumsfeld was to complete the 2001 QDR by September 30 of that year. Overwhelmed by the terrorist attacks of September 11, the new QDR was issued without fanfare on October 1, 2001. A subsequent QDR was produced in 2006, but many of its calls for change were sidetracked when Rumsfeld resigned as secretary shortly after the 2006 election. That requirement remains in place for the Obama administration.

The situation created by 9/11 complicated the reform process in illustrative ways. When Rumsfeld became secretary of defense, he was dedicated to reforms seeking to apply technology in ways that would produce a smaller but leaner, more lethal (and hopefully cheaper) force, ideas resisted by the military establishment. His proposals were derailed by the responses to 9/11, first in Afghanistan and then in Iraq, which dominated the remainder of the Bush presidency.

The spirit of reform may have been sublimated by 9/11, but it did not disappear altogether. The point person toward the end of the Bush incumbency was Robert

Gates, and one of the major reasons he apparently agreed to stay on in the job of secretary of defense under Obama was the promise that he could go forward with re-form in a post-9/11 environment.

One of the major characteristics of the post-Iraq situation will be, in conven-tional terms, the lack of a concrete opponent. There is thus no measurable threat against which to develop capabilities. Instead, in the 2001 QDR's words, "the United States is likely to be challenged by adversaries who possess a wide range of capabilities, including asymmetric approaches to warfare, particularly weapons of mass destruc-tion." With uncertainty as the backdrop, force planning may thus be based on capabil-ities rather than threats in the face of a potentially diverse set of requirements.

A capability-based approach to force development works in two ways. First, it attempts to identify the range of likely problems the country may confront and to develop forces to nullify that range of threats. An example is the projected prob-lem of possession of weapons of mass destruction by rogue states or nonstate actors like Usama bin Laden. The Bush missile defense system was advertised by its champions as an example of a capability-based response to this potential threat. At the same time, the approach is designed to exploit American technological su-periority in weapons development through the revolution in military affairs. The environment, the 2001 report argues, "requires the transformation of U.S. forces, capabilities, and institutions to extend America's asymmetric advantages well into the future."

One of the more interesting questions regards military manpower. The numbers of Americans either on active duty or in the Reserves and National Guard have shrunk by about one-third from Cold War numbers. Partly in response to these re-duced overall numbers, the armed forces have turned to the Reserves for a variety of tasks formerly assigned to active forces. Reserves were prominent in the Persian Gulf War (the first major Reserve activation since Korea), and they have played an increasingly major and controversial role in Iraq, as noted.

CONCLUSION: THE CONTINUING RELEVANCE OF TRADITIONAL FORCES

By and large, the traditional military problems discussed in this chapter are artifacts of the Cold War and thinking about that period, conditioned by the experience of the first half of the twentieth century (notably the world wars). The end of the Cold War provided a reprieve from the worst possible consequences of the Cold War going "hot" and produced a decade of relative relaxation of military concerns, effectively reversed by September 11. The decade of the 2000s has been dominated by 9/11-generated defense efforts, but it is drawing to a close. What is next?

What seems clear is that the military requirements of the post–September 11 de-fense environment are considerably different than those of the Cold War. The large end of the scale of threat, with huge arsenals of nuclear weapons and massive conven-tional forces facing one another in what could have been mankind's most destructive, and possibly last, war, has largely disappeared from operations consideration. Russia, the successor to the menacing Soviet Union, is no longer a significant opponent and is often a friend, even if there remain some sources of strain such as those over the European-based missile defense system cancelled by Obama. The titanic clash that once seemed inevitable now seems a more fanciful possibility. The military artifacts of that confrontation like massive nuclear arsenals seem oddly archaic as well.

The small end of the scale with no "peer competitor" is now the most likely source of scenarios. The threats to American security come from more remote places where American interests are less engaged and where the scale and nature of American involvement are less well defined but generally more limited. The terrorism of bin Laden against the American homeland was the apparent exception to that rule, but it is not yet entirely clear whether this, or some other, form of terrorism will fill the center stage of concern or prove to have been a historical aberration.

How relevant are the military concerns and forces of the Cold War for the present and the future? Certainly, the conventional forces and structures inherited from that era proved to be highly useful during the Persian Gulf War of 1990–1991, which helps explain why a more thorough critique of future roles was delayed as long as it was. The defenders of tradition received a reprieve in the Kuwaiti desert. That critique was further delayed by the more immediate need to react to 9/11 and its spin-offs in Afghanistan and Iraq. American combat operations in Iraq are winding down amid mixed assessments of their effectiveness, and the apparent inadequacy of the effort in Afghanistan has caused restructuring of the effort there. The Gates reorientation of forces is one important institutional response to traditional approaches to contemporary problems.

The huge nuclear arsenals and the elaborate constructs for their deterrent roles seem particularly anachronistic, which has led to initiatives to reduce them. Nuclear weapons are not completely irrelevant, of course, because several states possess them and others, including terrorists, may attempt to get them. Both the United States and Russia will clearly maintain arsenals adequately large to promise that an aggressor contemplating attacking either one with WMD will have to consider the suicidal consequences of such actions. In the meantime, the emphasis will be on arsenal reductions, the security of remaining forces from undesirable hands, and whether the threat from those undesirable others is sufficient to undertake highly expensive defenses against ballistic missile delivery of WMD.

The structure of conventional forces is also questionable. As noted, the heavy composition of American (and most other western) forces was designed for a massive, western-style World War III clash with like forces from the Soviet world. Now, the only countries that possess those kinds of forces are American allies or friends, and it is not clear how adaptable those forces are for other contingencies, especially the kinds of asymmetrical wars that may seem to be the future.

Conventional forces are buffeted from both ends of the spectrum. On one hand, their relevance in the face of unconventional forces bent on devising ways to negate their advantages has not been proven. If technological proficiency and mass always prevail, the United States must have won in Vietnam. Newer and more sophisticated means of conducting traditional warfare have been developed and proposed for deployment, but their fate seems dubious. The Gates reforms have slammed the door on conventional force modernization for now, based on the dual grounds that the kinds of wars for which they are designed are so unlikely as not to justify their expense and that no conceivable opponent challenges American conventional military superiority. The current round of discussions about possible non-nuclear futures has largely been won by the unconventional warriors.

The debate about roles, missions, and forces is never conclusive because times and circumstances change. The contemporary judgment is that the traditional concerns that this chapter has described are no longer as important as they were a generation ago and that alternative directions are more relevant and should be pursued with greater vigor. That judgment is, however, not consensual and certainly not eternal. The pendulum may have swung away from traditional warfare, but it easily could—and probably will—swing back at some time in the future. For now, the future seems asymmetrical and unconventional, problems examined in the final part of the text.

STUDY/DISCUSSION QUESTIONS

1. How are current American conceptions of traditional military problems tied to the Cold War? Discuss.
2. Discuss the evolution of strategic nuclear forces and plans for their use in terms of the seminal events of the nuclear age, the concept of deterrence, and U.S. nuclear strategies of deterrence.
3. What is nuclear proliferation? Discuss its aspects and evolution, its dynamics (the $N + 1$ problem), and the current state of the concern, including the problems associated with attempts to limit proliferation.
4. What is missile defense? What are the arguments for and against it? What is the current controversy over American plans to deploy such defenses in light of the cancellation of the Bush plan?
5. Discuss the traditional role of conventional forces, including the debate over heavy and light forces.
6. What is the contemporary debate over military manpower? How has this debate been made more lively by the Iraq War?
7. Why is the debate over military reform so contentious? What is the current state of this debate?

SELECTED BIBLIOGRAPHY

Borden, William Liscum. *There Will Be No Time: The Revolution in Strategy.* New York: Macmillan, 1946.

Brodie, Bernard. *The Absolute Weapon: Atomic Power and World Order.* New York: Harcourt Brace, 1946.

———. *Strategy in the Missile Age.* Princeton, NJ: Princeton University Press, 1959.

Carter, Ashton B. "How to Counter WMD." *Foreign Affairs* 83, no. 5 (September/October 2004): 72–85.

Clark, Ronald W. *The Greatest Power on Earth: The International Race for Nuclear Supremacy from Earliest Theory to Three-Mile Island.* New York: Harper and Row, 1980.

Clausewitz, Carl von. *On War.* Princeton, NJ: Princeton University Press, 1976.

Collins, John M. *Grand Strategy: Principles and Practices*. Annapolis, MD: Naval Institute Press, 1973.

Deutch, John. "A Nuclear Posture for Today." *Foreign Affairs* 84, no. 1 (January/February 2005): 49–60.

Drew, Dennis M., and Donald M. Snow. *Making Strategy for the Twenty-First Century: An Introduction to National Security Processes and Problems*. Montgomery, AL: Air University Press, 2006.

Gabel, Josiane. "The Role of Nuclear Weapons After September 11." *Washington Quarterly* 28, no. 1 (Winter 2004–2005): 181–195.

Gates, Robert M. "A Balanced Strategy." *Foreign Affairs* 88, no. 1 (January/February 2009): 28–40.

Gormley, Dennis M. "Missile Defence Myopia: Lessons from the Iraq War." *Survival* 45 (Winter 2003–2004): 61–86.

Guertner, Gary L., and Donald M. Snow. *The Last Frontier: An Analysis of the Strategic Defense Initiative*. Lexington, MA: Lexington Books, 1986.

Harrison, Selig. "Did North Korea Cheat?" *Foreign Affairs* 84, no. 1 (January/February 2005): 99–110.

Ivanov, Igor. "The Missile Defense Mistake: Undermining Strategic Stability and the ABM Treaty." *Foreign Affairs* 79, no. 5 (September/October 2000): 15–20.

Kramer, Andrew E. "Russia Steps Back from Key Arms Treaty." *New York Times* (online), July 14, 2007.

Lieber, Kier A., and Daryl G. Press. "The Rise of U.S. Nuclear Superiority." *Foreign Affairs* 85, no. 2 (March/April 2006): 42–54.

McCaffrey, Barry R. "Looking Beyond Iraqi Freedom: Future Enemies Won't Roll Over So Easily." *Armed Forces Journal* 140 (July 2003): 8–9.

McNamara, Robert S. "Apocalypse Soon." *Foreign Policy*, May/June 2005, 28–35.

Nuechterlein, Donald E. *A Cold War Odyssey*. Lexington: University of Kentucky Press, 1997.

Payne, Keith B. "The Nuclear Posture Review: Setting the Record Straight." *Washington Quarterly* 28, no. 3 (Summer 2005): 135–152.

Perkowich, George. "How to Be a Nuclear Watchdog." *Foreign Policy*, January/February 2005: 28–35.

Pilat, Joseph F. "Reassessing Assurances in a Unipolar World." *Washington Quarterly* 28, no. 2 (Spring 2005): 59–70.

Quadrennial Defense Review. Washington, DC: U.S. Department of Defense, 1997, 2001, and 2006.

Rhodes, Richard. *The Making of the Atomic Bomb*. New York: Touchstone Books, 1998.

Snow, Donald M. *Nuclear Strategy in a Dynamic World: Policy for the 1980s*. Tuscaloosa: University of Alabama Press, 1981.

———. *The Necessary Peace: Nuclear Weapons and Superpower Relations*. Lexington, MA: Lexington Books, 1987.

Specter, Arlen, with Christopher Walsh. "Dialogue with Adversaries." *Washington Quarterly* 30, no. 1 (Winter 2006–2007): 9–26.

Winner, Andrew C. "The Proliferation Security Initiative: The New Face of Interdiction." *Washington Quarterly* 28, no. 2 (Spring 2005): 129–143.

PART

III

NEW CHALLENGES

The dominant theme of American national security policy during the first decade of the twenty-first century has been reaction to the terrorist attacks on September 11, 2001, and this theme has been most evident in American military action in the Middle East aimed at controlling or eliminating the terrorist threat. The two most obvious manifestations of this theme have been the wars in Afghanistan and Iraq, both of which have been, or have displayed characteristics of, asymmetrical wars. Moreover, the short- to mid-term likelihood is that the United States will continue to find interests in these kinds of conflicts and appropriate responses to them.

Part III reflects these concerns. It begins with Chapter 11, "Asymmetrical Warfare," which attempts to describe and examine the characteristics and problems of unconventional warfare and why it is the kind of warfare the United States will likely continue to confront in the future. Chapter 12 looks specifically at the two major violent conflicts of the 2000s in which the United States has been embroiled, "The Unresolved Dilemmas in Iraq and Afghanistan." Since the seedbed of much American concern lies with terrorism and its eradication, Chapter 13 examines two aspects of that problem under the title "Terrorism and State Building," on the premise that attempts to suppress terrorism can be successful only if the societies in which terrorism occurs are transformed into stable, prosperous states wherein terrorism has less appeal. Chapter 14, "Extending Security Under Obama," returns to themes introduced in Chapter 8 by examining four nontraditional elements of the future national security agenda: border security, energy security, environmental security, and health security.

CHAPTER 11

Asymmetrical Warfare: The "New Kind of War"

PREVIEW

The events of September 11, 2001, reintroduced the United States to a form of warfare that it had experienced in the past—in Vietnam nearly forty years ago—and that it would see shortly thereafter—in Afghanistan and Iraq. Because the United States prefers to engage in traditional, conventional (symmetrical) warfare and has had an undistinguished history against unconventional foes, this trend has been difficult to adapt to and embrace. Had the United States indeed discovered a new kind of war that represents the future? Or had the emergence of the United States as the world's premier symmetrical warrior forced others to adopt asymmetrical warfare as the only way to confront American might? To answer these questions, this chapter first defines and describes asymmetrical and symmetrical warfare, with an emphasis on the more unfamiliar former. Because the Obama administration has largely embraced this kind of war as representing the likely future, it looks at asymmetrical futures in the forms of fourth-generation warfare, the new internal wars (NIWs), and Iraq, with the current instability in Pakistan as an indicator of how difficult this problem can be. The chapter concludes by looking at how "new" this kind of war really is.

The horrendous events of September 11, 2001, and the Afghanistan and Iraq Wars have revived the public debate over the uses of American military force for the future. In the relative tranquility of the decade following the end of the Cold War, important American interests were largely unchallenged militarily, and as a result, the debate over how and when to use force was largely muted. The principal international dynamic in a national security sense was the interest–threat mismatch in which American vital interests were hardly threatened anywhere and the threats that did exist were so peripheral as to be hardly interesting. No country on Earth appeared to pose a meaningful threat to basic American security. The only remaining superpower reigned supreme, and the only apparent needs for American armed forces were in "deployments of choice" (situations in which the United States elected but was not compelled to employ armed forces) in remote and obscure locales such as Haiti, Bosnia, and Kosovo to quell humanitarian disasters.

This seeming tranquility did not mean that questions were not being asked about the future of American military activity. Within the professional defense intellectual community, the future was a lively concern that centered on two related questions. The first question concerned the kind of circumstance in which Americans might have to employ arms, and the answers tended to suggest that the most likely scenarios were nontraditional conflicts occurring in the developing world. A few writers were even predicting the kinds of concerns that have been raised since September 11, 2001, although their exhortations were clearly not prevalent during the 1990s. The other question was how the United States should prepare for future contingencies, and answers focused on issues of force modernization and possible restructuring, introduced in Chapter 10.

The future came home with a literal crash with the terrorist attacks against New York and Washington, D.C. The events themselves were galvanizing and shocking enough to raise basic concerns about national security. As the reaction to the airplane attacks settled in the collective consciousnesses of Americans, an immediate victim of the exposure of the second fault line was American complacency about a supposedly tranquil and nonthreatening environment. At the bottom line, the attacks revealed that the United States was indeed vulnerable to attack. Even if the country lacked a major foe that could imperil its survival, its previously assumed invulnerability to harm was shown to be false and could not be easily or quickly restored by traditional military means.

In the immediate, shocked response, the analogy that dominated descriptions of the new situation was that of "war." President Bush rapidly described the attacks as acts of war equivalent in their infamy to the Japanese attack on Pearl Harbor sixty years earlier. The media, and especially the electronic news networks, promptly seized on the analogy, with the Cable News Network (CNN), for instance, proclaiming the "new kind of war" as the masthead of its news coverage for months after the fact.

Shock masked an important dynamic of the new environment. In the decade or so since the Cold War, the United States had developed the most powerful conventional (symmetrical) armed forces in the world, forces that were compared to the Roman legions in their presumed dominance. These forces were so potent at symmetrical warfare, as demonstrated against Iraq in 1991, that no other country could face the Americans on their own terms and hope to succeed. The United States had become a military juggernaut that could not be defied.

The result was that the United States failed to grasp fully the inevitable reaction to its prowess. Realizing that a symmetrical response to the Americans was suicidal, opponents did what groups have always done: they adopted approaches to fighting—what is now called asymmetrical warfare—that negate the American advantage. The unrecognized consequence of American strength was to negate its application: the United States became so good at symmetrical warfare that, in a classic self-fulfilling prophecy, it made such warfare obsolete. No one will (or should) play the game the way Americans want to play it.

The law of unintended consequences was at work in these dynamics. The United States developed its prowess to advance its interests in the world, but the world responded by changing the nature of the competition to give itself a chance against the American behemoth. The unintended consequence of American power is that the country is now confronted by a new problem, asymmetrical warfare, which it has not dealt with successfully in the past.

It is not a problem likely to disappear anytime soon. The simple fact is that asymmetrical warfare does succeed in leveling the playing field and gives what appears to be a hopelessly outmanned force a chance to compete, even to succeed. The Iraqi and Afghan insurgencies are only the most recent instances of this dynamic.

The extension of the antiterrorist campaign to Afghanistan and the effort to remove the Taliban government shielding Al Qaeda from capture added to the conceptual confusion in 2001. In Afghanistan itself, forces loyal to the Taliban had been waging a very traditional civil war against a series of opponents led by the Northern Alliance. It was traditional, or *symmetrical*, warfare in the sense that both sides were fighting in similar manners and for the traditional goal of maintaining or gaining control of the government. When the United States entered that situation, it was indeed involved in what quite properly could be described as a war, where American airpower and special forces were employed in absolutely traditional ways to help overthrow the Taliban government. When the Taliban were overthrown and the objective returned to rooting out Al Qaeda from its hideouts in the caves of the Tora Bora Mountains along the Afghanistan–Pakistan border, the enterprise moved away from traditional warfare. The Afghan campaign thus mixed symmetrical and asymmetrical elements from the beginning and helped obscure the emergence of the distinctive asymmetrical problem.

Thinking about and acting on this change have evolved in the 2000s. Terrorism is one extreme form of asymmetrical warfare, and while dealing with it is not an entirely military task, reorienting American thought toward waging a "war on terror" required challenging some long-held precepts within the U.S. military. The resistance to the American military occupation of Iraq and the Taliban campaign to regain control of Afghanistan have largely employed asymmetrical means, and the challenge posed by the Taliban in Pakistan is a classic case of the dynamics of symmetrical and asymmetrical force interaction.

These Middle Eastern events have dominated American activity in the 2000s and are reflected in thinking about the 2010s. The future face of war has, for instance, very strong implications for the future evolution of American forces and missions, as argued in Chapter 10. As the war in Afghanistan began to take shape, American Special Operations Forces (SOFs) were very prominent in the early going, serving as advisors to the anti-Taliban forces and as spotters directing American air strikes to their targets. Later they helped organize and conduct operations against remnants of the Taliban and Al Qaeda hiding in caves in the Afghan mountains. The result, of course, was that the Pashtun-based Taliban slipped across the border into Pashtun tribal areas in Pakistan, where Al Qaeda outsiders were treated as protected guests (see Chapter 12). In that setting, they reconstituted into a formidable force that threatens the American-backed governments in Afghanistan and Pakistan. In both cases, their methods are unconventional, requiring nontraditional responses by the Afghans, Pakistanis, and Americans.

The aftermath of September 11 thus has provided a new emphasis for the debate about war in the future. What is clear is that the menu of violence has changed in at least two ways. First, the likelihood of American involvement in classic conventional war has been reduced dramatically (there is no one else who will fight this way if the Americans are involved), meaning future involvements will likely be asymmetrical. Second, the asymmetrical pattern will—by definition—change. Asymmetrical warfare is an approach to war, not a set of instructions for making war. The asymmetrical warrior fights in whatever way works at any place and point in time, and that is an evolving process of experience and adaptation.

SYMMETRICAL AND ASYMMETRICAL WARFARE

A basic consideration in thinking about the nature of warfare is the conceptualizations of war that the different participants have. For most of the American experience, wars have been fought by traditional, conventional military forces, where both sides were organized in very much the same way, had largely the same (if opposing) purposes, served as representatives of sovereign states (or of groups seeking to gain or maintain control of states), and accepted the same general conventions (or laws) surrounding proper and improper ways to conduct war. The term used to describe warfare among similar opponents is *symmetrical warfare*, meaning that the contending sides resemble or mirror one another along the axes of organization, purpose, affiliation, and intent. The world wars represent the epitome of symmetrical wars.

Symmetrical warfare suggests the existence of its opposite. One of the newer terms to enter the public debate is *asymmetrical warfare*, and it has been used throughout the text. In its broadest connotations, asymmetrical warfare represents the opposite of symmetrical warfare. In this form of combat, one side fights traditionally, while the other side organizes itself differently, may or may not share the same objectives as its opponent, may or may not represent a government or a movement aspiring to become a government, and rejects the conventions or laws of warfare propounded by the conventional side.

In the current context, symmetrical warfare is associated with the western military tradition practiced in modern Europe and, more recently, North America and other parts of the world that have adopted its norms. The salient characteristics of countries operating in this tradition include the fielding of mass armies, navies, and air forces that are similarly organized and configured (e.g., wearing regular uniforms, organized in traditional rank orderings), follow Clausewitzian principles regarding the subordination of war to its political purposes, fight as representatives of state governments seeking to realize the interests of states, and accept common rules about what is permissible and impermissible in war (e.g., treatment of prisoners, acceptability of purposely targeting civilians, prohibitions on torture). While not all wars fought in this tradition completely mirror all of these characterizations, it is the general and expected means of war. Those who hold these values view adherence to them as honorable and deviation from them as somehow less than honorable.

In the current debate, asymmetrical approaches are more closely related to what is described as the Asiatic (including Middle Eastern) approach to war. This tradition goes back to the beginning of recorded theories of war and is currently manifested in military conduct in which at least one of the opponents is organized in a manner different from a standard armed force (guerrilla fighters, for instance), may or may not have gaining or maintaining government control as its central purpose, may not represent governments or insurgents, and does not accept or practice warfare (especially limits on permissible actions) in accord with western conventions.

There is nothing new about asymmetrical warfare other than the name. Its underlying motivations are clear and have deep roots. As already argued, asymmetrical approaches to warfare are attractive to those who cannot compete successfully using conventional methods and whose only chance for success requires changing the playing field so that they do have a chance. As Vincent Goulding, Jr., put it, it is the approach by which "weaker opponents have sought to neutralize their enemy's technological or numerical superiority by fighting in ways or on battlefields that nullify it." If one cannot win fighting one way, it makes sense to find another way at which one can at least hope to succeed. The principle is as old as the first armed group that faced a superior enemy it could not possibly defeat if it fought according to the accepted rules of the day.

Put a slightly different way, asymmetrical warfare is unconventional warfare. Symmetrical warfare is the preference of those entities that are advantaged under accepted forms of war, whereas asymmetrical approaches are appealing to those who cannot compete successfully within the constraints of those rules. In the current environment, the world's most vociferous champion of symmetrical warfare is quite understandably the United States, whereas its opponents are inexorably drawn to asymmetrical approaches.

Evolution of Asymmetrical Warfare

As already stated, the term *asymmetrical warfare* is much newer than the general phenomenon it describes. Methods of warfare displaying some or all of this style of warfare have a long history, have been described with a variety of names, and have long been at least a small part of the American military tradition.

The idea of trying to negate the advantages of opponents fighting the conventional warfare of the day is as old as organized warfare. Although styles and tactics have changed, conventional warfare has almost always been conducted by massed, uniformed armies divided into ranks who used their weight and firepower to confront and overwhelm opponents. It is how the Roman legions generally fought, and it is how the various combatants in World Wars I and II conducted war. Normally, this style of warfare is conducted in conformance with some broad set of rules of engagement that specify acceptable and unacceptable conduct in battle. Through history, there have been, of course, notable exceptions to this depiction—the Mongol Hordes substituted maneuver for mass and ignored conventions on the treatment of prisoners, for instance. The tradition of this style of warfare, now called symmetrical warfare, is highly western in content and values. More to the point, it is key to the "American way of war."

Normally, an opposing force that lacks the mass of a conventional armed force in either quantitative or qualitative terms cannot successfully confront a conventional force on its own terms and prevail. In that circumstance, the options available to the inferior force are to quit the contest and surrender, to stand before and be destroyed by the superior force, or to adopt a style of warfare that seeks to negate the advantages of the superior force and thus provides an opportunity for success. In other words, the only possible avenue for victory is to fight asymmetrically.

The asymmetrical tradition is most associated with Asian styles of fighting. The original Chinese military manual, Sun Tzu's *The Art of War*, is a virtual primer on how to shift the advantage from a superior to an inferior force (see Amplification 11.1). Many of the principles originally laid out by Sun Tzu were adapted and operationalized by Mao Zedung in his campaigns against the Guomintang led by Chiang kai-Shek in

Amplification 11.1

SUN TZU ON ASYMMETRICAL WARFARE

Little is known about Sun Tzu, a Chinese military thinker who advised several warlords in China approximately three thousand years ago. Some argue that he did not exist at all and that the work attributed to him was the collection of experiences of others. His classic military manual *The Art of War* (similar in intent to Machiavelli's political manual *The Prince* for Italian leaders in the sixteenth century) was little studied in the West until it became known that it was one of the sources of inspiration for Mao Zedung in his campaign to seize control of China over a twenty-year period ending in 1949.

The heart of Sun Tzu's military advice, which would be familiar to practitioners of what is now called asymmetrical warfare, was knowing when and how to fight. His philosophy of indirection and asymmetry is best stated in his advice to military leaders of his time: "When the enemy advances, we retreat; when the enemy halts, we harass; when the enemy seeks to avoid battle, we attack; when the enemy retreats, we pursue." In addition, he adds that the victor on the battlefield has a superior understanding of his opponent that allows him to deceive and thus alter favorably the battle: "All warfare is based on deception. . . . To subdue the enemy without fighting is the acme of skill." Thus, what is of supreme importance is to attack the enemy's strategy." Echoing that sentiment three thousand years later, Goulding adds, "War might usually favor the side with the heaviest battalions, but it *always* favors the smartest." Does war really change?

the twenty-plus years of the Chinese Civil War and were, in turn, adapted by the Vietnamese historian-turned-general Vo Nguyen Giap in his campaigns first against the French and later against the Americans between 1945 and 1975. Hundreds of years earlier, during the thirteenth century, the Vietnamese had successfully evicted Kublai Khan and the Mongols from Vietnam using similar techniques.

The style of warfare represented by the asymmetrical tradition has known different names across time. A parallel term is *guerrilla warfare*, used to describe a particular style of warfare involving highly unconventional tactics employed for the traditional end of gaining control of government. Unconventional warfare is to conventional warfare what asymmetrical is to symmetrical. Terms like *partisan* or *people's war* have also been used as synonyms. The purpose of saying this is not to confuse the reader but to point out that asymmetrical warfare has known many names and that the names change more than the underlying principles on which they are based.

It is also part of the American military tradition, beginning in the earliest days of White settlement of North America. Most of the Indians whom the settlers encountered fought unconventionally at the tactical level, engaging in ambushes, hiding behind trees and rocks, and otherwise behaving in ways that did not conform to the tactics of linear warfare practiced in Europe. When the American Revolution began, it quite quickly became apparent that the fledgling Continental Army could not successfully contest the British Army in linear battles, and some of its tactics moved from the symmetrical to the asymmetrical. The colonies' first great victory in the Revolutionary War, at Saratoga in 1777, was a classic linear clash, but its success was largely the result of attrition of the British expeditionary force coming down from Lake Champlain by American militiamen fighting Indian style. By the time General Burgoyne's army finally reached Saratoga, attrition had reduced it to about half the size of its American counterpart. Francis ("the Swamp Fox") Marion in South Carolina and George Rogers Clark in the Northwest Territories were notable practitioners of this form of warfare during the Revolution. The United States faced asymmetrical opponents in the Seminole Wars in the 1820s in Florida, in its campaigns against the Western Indians after the Civil War, in the Filipino Insurgency at the turn of the twentieth century, and in its actions against Pancho Villa in New Mexico and Arizona in the 1910s.

The United States' most extensive and traumatic encounter with an opponent practicing a form of asymmetrical warfare was, of course, in Vietnam. The basic situation conforms neatly to the distinctions already made and has some parallels in the ongoing campaigns against the Taliban in Afghanistan and Pakistan and against insurgents in Iraq.

Consider the basic structure of the military situation in Vietnam. The Vietnamese insurgents (the North Vietnamese and Viet Cong) faced an American-organized and hence thoroughly conventional South Vietnamese opponent. Following the basic outlines of the Maoist mobile-guerrilla warfare strategy (see Snow, *Distant Thunder*, Chapter 3, for a description), the North Vietnamese Army (NVA) and the Viet Cong (VC) had worn down the Army of the Republic of Vietnam (ARVN) through a guerrilla war of attrition and, by 1964, had gained such a military advantage that it converted to conventional warfare, confronting the ARVN in a symmetrical fashion for the purpose of destroying the ARVN and seizing political power.

The United States entered the fray with combat forces in 1965. The South Vietnamese were in desperate straits when intervention occurred, but American conventional military power quickly reversed the military situation. This change was first demonstrated in the two-day Battle of the Ia Drang Valley in November 1965, an encounter vividly captured in Moore and Galloway's *We Were Soldiers Once . . . and Young* (which was the basis of the motion picture *We Were Soldiers*). On the first day of the battle, an NVA conventional force encountered and engaged an American force in a conventional battle. The overwhelming American advantage in firepower (mass) turned the confrontation into a deadly shooting gallery in which the NVA was severely bloodied. On the second day, however, the Americans began a march to the staging area from which they were to be evacuated that stretched the troops single file over three miles, and the NVA responded by reverting to guerrilla tactics of ambush and hit-and-run attacks by small units that could avoid American concentrated firepower. The result was a defeat for the Americans.

Although largely unrecognized at the time, the Ia Drang experience was a parable of sorts for understanding the dynamics both of Vietnam and of symmetrical and asymmetrical warfare. Prior to the American intervention, the NVA and VC were fighting symmetrical (conventional) war against the ARVN, and they were succeeding (the ARVN continued to fight that way because, although it was losing, this was the only way they knew how to fight). When the United States entered the contest, however, the much more modestly equipped NVA and VC realized they could not compete with American firepower in symmetrical combat, leaving them the choice to surrender, lose, or change the rules to provide them with a chance of success.

The asymmetrical style they selected was the guerrilla phase of mobile-guerrilla warfare. Instead of standing toe-to-toe with the Americans, they reverted to guerrilla tactics such as ambush and avoidance of concentrations of American forces. Capturing and holding territory ceased to be a central concern; instead, they sought to wear down the American forces, to drag out the war until the Americans wearied of the contest and public opinion demanded they leave. It was the classic Vietnamese approach that they had used seven hundred years earlier to rid themselves of the Mongols, and it ultimately worked equally well against the Americans. And, of course, when the Americans left in 1973, the NVA abandoned asymmetrical methods and returned to conventional, symmetrical warfare to finish off the job the Americans had interrupted during their stay.

The Contemporary Setting

The American military experience in Vietnam was a harbinger of later encounters with asymmetrical warfare that are a leading fixture of the post–September 11 environment. The 1990s witnessed the emergence of the United States as the military hyperpower: although U.S. troop strength declined during this period, the forces of other countries declined even more. A major reason for this gap was the application of electronic technology to warfare, the revolution in military affairs (RMA), that resulted in the overwhelming and growing conventional military disparity between the most advanced countries—and especially the United States—and the rest, including the developing countries in which violence most often occurs.

Conventional Dominance and the RMA. The growing gap in qualitative military capabilities was largely the result of the RMA. Without going into diverting detail, the RMA (there have been several of them historically) is the impact of a particular technology or series of technologies on the battlefield when those scientific discoveries are applied to warfare. The classic study of how new weaponry changes the nature and outcome of war was the Brodies' *From Crossbow to H-Bomb*. A good twentieth-century example of the effects of applying new technology to warfare was the impact of the internal combustion engine, which allowed the development of weapons such as the tank and the armored personnel carrier and made possible the *blitzkrieg* tactics introduced by the Germans in World War II and widely employed by all combatants in that war.

The contemporary RMA features the application of advances in computing and telecommunications to modern warfare. The "computer revolution" was first applied by the United States in the Vietnam conflict in ways such as using electronic sensing to track VC and NVA troop movements. At the time, the applications were fairly primitive (for example, the VC stymied some sensors by hanging sacks of human waste above the sensors, which emitted heat and chemical signatures that caused the sensors constantly to record troops going by when none were), and there was an inadequate appreciation of the strategic implications of the application of technology to the war. The early attempts in Vietnam, however, were no more than the tip of the iceberg of contemporary applications.

The weaponization of high technology began to mature in the years following Vietnam. Although technology has had a pervasive influence, it has been most dramatic in two related areas that have most widened capability disparities: reconnaissance and weapons accuracy. Reconnaissance has been enhanced dramatically by satellite imagery, which, when wedded with the most modern telecommunications equipment, reveals the location of both friendly and adversary forces over a wide area and in considerable detail. To aid in visualization of the battlefield, for instance, high-definition television (HDTV) was subsidized by the U.S. Department of Defense to produce the most vivid, detailed pictures of combat areas possible. Particularly when this kind of information is available to one side but not the other, the result is a considerable advantage for the possessor and an almost insurmountable disadvantage for the side lacking the capacity. In its most extreme manifestation, the possessor knows where his opponent is and can target him all of the time, whereas the nonpossessor never knows where his opponent is or when and how that opponent is likely to strike.

The second advance has been in guidance capabilities that allow the precision delivery of munitions—usually airborne from cruise missiles or aircraft—over long distances with astonishing accuracy. This capability makes it possible for the possessor, once his opponent is found, to attack promptly and with a very high degree of success. Because the munitions normally can be fired from distances outside visual range and at speeds such that they cannot be seen, the victim is helpless to protect himself. The most vivid example currently in use is the Predator, an unmanned aircraft (or drone), used to bomb targets in Afghanistan and Pakistan.

Reconnaissance and precision delivery are just two of the more important aspects of the current RMA. All these applications have the effect of being *force multipliers*, or enhancers of the effectiveness (lethality) of the force that possesses them. In addition, they all dramatically reduce the vulnerability of the warriors who possess them, thereby also dramatically reducing casualty rates for the possessing state, while increasing those rates for the victims.

The results have been mixed. Applications of the RMA have, for instance, made American forces considerably more lethal against a vulnerable opponent and, in the process, have greatly reduced American casualties. For the kinds of missions for which RMA capabilities are relevant, these capabilities also reduce the manpower requirements for American forces. Enigmatically, this lethality often raises casualties among target civilian populations, may create the illusion that smaller forces work for all purposes, and may cause the opponent to adopt offsetting strategies. The result is a mixed impact.

The technology gap thus becomes a problem that the asymmetrical warrior must negate. Electronic surveillance works only when the target can be found, and thus, the asymmetrical warrior will likely take countermeasures (like hiding) to avoid detection. It does not matter how accurate a weapon is if it cannot find its target, so denying "target acquisition" is a major asymmetrical objective. The feckless campaign to locate and capture or kill Usama bin Laden demonstrates that the asymmetrical warrior can sometimes succeed in foiling the fruits of the RMA.

The Persian Gulf War Example. The first overwhelmingly successful application of this growing disparity occurred in the Persian Gulf War of 1990–1991. After the Iraqi invasion, conquest, and threatened annexation of tiny Kuwait in August 1990, a military coalition was created to reverse that outcome. The United States took the lead in organizing the effort under United Nations auspices and eventually brought together a coalition of twenty-five states, including some Islamic countries from the region, to oppose Saddam Hussein.

At the time, there was great concern about how difficult the military task of dislodging the Iraqis from Kuwait would be. Iraq possessed the fourth-largest army in the world, it was pointed out, and it was a battle-tested force, having fought for eight years in the Iran–Iraq war that ended in 1988. In those circumstances, many predicted a stout defense by the Iraqis, and speculation abounded about, among other things, the level of casualties the United States would incur.

Those who predicted large numbers of casualties, of course, were proven wrong, as the war turned out to be a walkover in military terms. The applications of the RMA to the forces of the major western powers had created such a technological disparity between the two opponents that the traditionally organized and equipped Iraqis stood no practical chance against the coalition troops. Saddam Hussein also misperceived American will (he believed the United States was still so traumatized by Vietnam that it would not react decisively) and the relative strength of his forces arrayed against the Americans and their allies. As a result, he engaged his Soviet-trained and Soviet-styled armed forces in conventional, symmetrical warfare, thus fighting on the terms of the coalition, against which he could not prevail.

The major difference was the effect of the RMA. When the air war commenced, the Americans attacked and destroyed the Iraqi radar and communications infrastructure on the first day. For the rest of the campaign, the United States had uncontested control of the skies, while the Iraqis were limited in their ability to monitor activities of the coalition literally to what they could see standing on the ground. Meanwhile, satellites provided detailed images of Iraqi locations and movements that Iraq absolutely lacked. As an example, the now familiar global positioning system—or GPS—meant Americans always knew where they were in the featureless Arabian Desert, whereas the Iraqis were never certain of their own location, much less the enemy's. At the same time, the Americans, positioned well out of range of Iraqi retaliatory capabilities, were able to locate Iraqi targets and to direct precision munitions to them. Although subsequent assessments have indicated that some of the more dramatic claims of superiority were inflated, nevertheless, the result was an overwhelming coalition victory with very few coalition—and specifically American—war deaths (less than 150, not all of which were the result of hostile action). The implication for developing countries of taking on the United States symmetrically using American rules was clear to all concerned.

The Iraq War. The impact of the RMA, combined with *blitzkrieg*-style maneuver techniques, was also felt dramatically in Iraq in 2003. The Americans and the British were able to sweep through the country virtually unopposed except in a few cities like Basra. In addition to the "shock and awe" effects of massive precision bombing, the heart of the success was the extreme speed with which the coalition forces moved, demoralizing and dispiriting their Iraqi foes.

The Iraqis, who had suffered the consequences of trying to match the United States militarily in kind a decade earlier, did not repeat their mistake. After a brief show of stout resistance by the regular Iraqi armed forces, they simply dissolved back into the population, either putting down their weapons or hiding them for later use in unconventional warfare. The United States apparently did not anticipate this reaction, in which Iraqi forces simply absorbed the inevitability and prepared to resist the ensuing occupation they were powerless to prevent. American mesmerism with its own RMA-induced superiority inadvertently added validation to this concept.

The RMA had at least one perverse impact on military planning. To Secretary Rumsfeld and his supporters, the technological prowess of RMA-equipped forces meant the effectiveness of individual soldiers was magnified (the force multiplier effect), and the implication was that numerically smaller forces could accomplish the same—or even broader—objectives that historically larger forces carried out. This principle underlay the numbers and tactics employed in Operation Iraqi Freedom, and their "shock and awe" effects were apparently quite effective in the invasion and conquest phases of the war, but they proved to be inadequate for Phase IV operations (the occupation of Iraq). The implications are discussed in Chapter 12.

Afghanistan and Pakistan. The dynamics that applied to Iraq in 2003 have largely been mirrored in the American effort in Afghanistan and, in a somewhat different manner, in the Pakistani efforts against the Taliban. Both cases illustrate the difficulties faced by the symmetrical warrior confronting an asymmetrical opponent in hostile physical circumstances.

The American problem in Afghanistan is discussed intensively in Chapter 12, but its underlying asymmetrical base can be raised here. The United States became involved in Afghanistan in October 2001 in its attempt to capture and destroy Al Qaeda, which was headquartered in Afghan sanctuaries protected by the Taliban regime. The United States aided in overthrowing the Taliban, who fled to Pakistan and regrouped. The United States remained in Afghanistan as part of its global war on terror (GWOT) campaign, and when the Taliban began to return in 2003 to resume their campaign to control the country, the United States joined in the fight.

The Taliban campaign has largely been an asymmetrical effort employing unconventional tactics in the mountainous region along the Afghanistan–Pakistan border and basing its support in Pashtun areas on both sides of the frontier. The Taliban are mostly Pashtuns, and much of the secret to overcoming them requires weaning those Pashtuns who do not support the Taliban away from the insurgents. As discussed in the next section, this, in turn, requires a level of penetration and control of those Pashtun areas that has yet to be achieved.

The Taliban problem has also infected Pakistan. The Pashtun tribal areas are on both sides of the Afghanistan–Pakistan border, including the Federally Administered Tribal Areas (FATA) of Pakistan. Historically, the FATA has been essentially autonomous, with the Pakistani government permitting self-rule in return for Pashtun neutrality in Pakistani politics. Since the Taliban arrived in force in 2001, however, they have become an increasingly assertive force, along with their Al Qaeda allies. The American attempt to destroy Al Qaeda has required that the Pakistanis break this standoff and aid in the campaign against the terrorists. The result has been to transform the FATA into a war zone.

The upshot has been the confrontation between the Pakistani armed forces and the Taliban that broke out in May 2009 and that illustrates the relationship between traditional and asymmetrical forces. The Pakistani armed forces are designed for conventional war with India in the relatively flat terrain along their mutual border. They are classic "heavy" forces and, as such, are ill-suited and ill-equipped for fighting in the rugged, primitive mountains of the FATA. They thus have resisted deployment in these areas historically and have been generally ineffective against the mountain tribesmen. The Taliban, on the other hand, are classic "light" guerrilla fighters who are equally unprepared to fight effectively outside the mountains in the centers of Pakistani power.

In May 2009, the Taliban were only 60 miles from Islamabad in the Swat Valley, but in order to menace the capital, they would have had to come out of the mountains and confront the Pakistanis in such a way that they would have been severely disadvantaged and probably would have been decisively defeated. Similarly, when the Pakistanis counterattacked into the mountains, they were playing into the Taliban's strength and had limited success. The result has indeed been a standoff that shows symmetrical and asymmetrical approaches are not so much superior or inferior to one another as they are appropriate or inappropriate in different situations.

The Strategic Effects. The dual lessons of the Persian Gulf War and the Afghanistan campaign, along with the Pakistan situation, should be clear, as should their implications for likely uses of American force in the future. The assessment is not without irony, as already noted. At the bottom line, the United States and its closest allies have become so proficient at conventional warfare that they are likely to be able to engage in such methods only against extremely foolish or masochistic opponents. At the same time, the maintenance of such force will continue to be necessary to remind potential future opponents of the folly of challenging the United States symmetrically and to perform the kinds of tasks at which such forces are adept, such as military occupation.

The two experiences clearly reinforce the gap in conventional capabilities that has been widened to a chasm between RMA-proficient forces and conventional forces that do not share those capabilities. In Kuwait, Afghanistan, and Iraq, when the opponents of the United States both stood and to some extent fought symmetrically in circumstances where they realistically had no chance of prevailing, their conventional forces were thoroughly and efficiently routed. This gap in capability between the military "haves" and "have nots" will only widen further in the future, meaning the consequences will remain in the future as well.

Much has been said since Vietnam about the failure of American will, especially the American aversion to accepting casualties. Two factors from the Kuwait and Iraq experiences should mitigate this perception and thus temper future assessments of how or if the United States will respond when provoked. One of the consequences of American conventional dominance that was first demonstrated in Kuwait and reinforced in Afghanistan has been the ability to greatly reduce American casualties through the application of technology. The mass of American firepower and the distance from which it can be employed not only devastate opponents if they try to confront this firepower directly, but also save American lives. The perception that an opponent can force an American withdrawal by killing a few American soldiers (based on American actions in Lebanon, Vietnam, and Somalia in the twentieth century) does not seem to hold up when opponents are fighting symmetrically with the Americans. The current testing ground of American willingness to incur losses is the ongoing Afghanistan war.

The Afghanistan experience provides another rejoinder about American willingness to accept battle losses. The reaction to the terrorist attacks reminded the United States that Americans have always been willing to put lives at risk *if the cause was sufficient*. The question of the unacceptability of casualties has arisen when people thought the cause was insufficient to justify the sacrifice, as in places such as Somalia. In that sense, the analogy between the terrorist attacks on September 11, 2001, and Pearl Harbor is apt: the United States may be reluctant to respond when the situation does not clearly dictate a response, but it will when the reasons are obvious and compelling. When American support for the cause wavers, as it has in Iraq, then the aversion to casualties returns.

The lessons of these combined experiences for future potential American (or more broadly western) opponents should be fairly obvious. The most obvious lesson, of course, is that it is fool's work to challenge the western powers at their own game; symmetrical warfare with the West is suicidal. It has been suggested that one way for weaker states to level the playing field would be to introduce weapons of mass destruction (WMD) such as chemical or biological weapons on the battlefield. Such a suggestion misses the essential point and actually reinforces the disparity. Should Saddam Hussein have introduced chemical or biological agents into the Gulf War (as it has been suggested he contemplated doing), the overwhelming western advantage in WMD would have simply made his defeat all the more decisive, with the United States, for instance, responding to a chemical attack against its forces with a more-or-less controlled nuclear response. Fortunately for most potential opponents of the West, they lack the military resources for a symmetrical challenge anyway.

The other obvious lesson is how to fight the West if a clash becomes inevitable. The overwhelming weight of American and other western might means a challenger cannot confront that power directly and has some chance of success only by changing the rules. Vietnam again provides a model of sorts. The North Vietnamese government understood shortly after the American intervention that it could not defeat the United States symmetrically, so its forces reverted to an asymmetrical style (guerrilla warfare) that negated the American advantages in technology and firepower. They attacked the American will to continue the contest by inflicting a large enough number of casualties on the Americans (although the numbers were trifles compared to the casualties they incurred themselves) to convince the American public and its leaders that persevering was not worthwhile. What ultimately undermined the American campaign was not, as Saddam Hussein and Usama bin Laden apparently concluded, American unwillingness to incur losses; it was the unwillingness to do so in what many concluded was a *less than worthy cause*. The fate of the Iraq campaign will likely ultimately be decided in those terms: Americans have concluded that Iraq was not worth the amount of sacrifice that it entailed, and the result has been a demand to terminate the involvement.

This assessment leaves some ironic implications for American preparation for the future. On one hand, the only countries that could possibly confront the United States in conventional, symmetrical warfare are its closest allies (members of the North Atlantic Treaty Organization [NATO]) and other countries with which we have developed such close relations that war is unthinkable (Russia, China). On the other hand, those groups and countries that might confront the United States do not have the forces to do so symmetrically and will only challenge the United States asymmetrically. Thus, the very kind of application of force at which Americans most excel is the least likely kind of force the United States will have occasion to use in the near future. The clear lesson of the Iraq occupation, however, is that mass and numbers, the data of symmetrical warfare, still matter in these situations.

Thus, conventional force cannot be abandoned, dismantled, or substantially diminished. While one can argue about whether current American forces deter *all* kinds of attacks on the United States (future terrorist assaults, for instance), they certainly do deter conventional attacks that might be contemplated in their absence.

Pakistan illustrates the point: its conventional forces may not ensure victory over the Taliban, but they likely preclude defeat.

What this analysis suggests is that, in the future, most of the situations in which the United States will have the opportunity to use force will be against an opponent adopting asymmetrical methods to try to obviate the American dominance in conventional warfare. This would suggest an emphasis on light forces (see Chapter 10) and on special purpose forces, such as SOFs, as well as precision airpower. At the same time, it is equally clear that asymmetrical opponents will continue to make adaptations to the means they employ against us, thus requiring flexibility in countering new methods they devise. On the other hand, if the United States wants to engage in conventional missions, like military occupations, it will need the mass of symmetrical forces to be successful.

ASYMMETRICAL FUTURES?

The asymmetrical approach to warfare—changing the rules to negate disadvantages—is ancient, even if some of the tactical means of applying asymmetrical warfare principles are new and evolving. In order to get a better idea of what the dynamics of asymmetrical warfare are and how they may affect the future, it is helpful to look at two models. One of them is a more-or-less theoretical construct predicting what some analysts during the 1990s thought about the likely future of warfare and providing a generic description of that future—what has been called *fourth-generation warfare*. The other, about which I have written in *Uncivil Wars* and other works, is a description of the empirical nature of a series of chaotic civil wars of the 1990s and beyond that I have called the *new internal wars* (NIWs). NIWs essentially serve as concrete examples of how the fourth generation of warfare may look in parts of the world. The two types suggest some of the dynamics of successful ways to resist this kind of warfare currently being contemplated and implemented by the United States.

Fourth-Generation Warfare

A body of thought among military historians and other analysts has for some time argued that conventional, western-style warfare, especially warfare conducted along Clausewitzian lines, represents an aberration rather than a universal phenomenon. In particular, these analysts maintain the kind of warfare described here as symmetrical is a temporal oddity. Among the champions of this position has been the British historian John Keegan, who argues there has been a kind of Clausewitzian interlude beginning with the Napoleonic era and ending with World War II when Clausewitz's trinitarian relationship among the people, government, and armed forces was dominant and western norms of warfare prevailed. Keegan argues that era has passed and the dominant pattern of warfare in the future, as it was in the past before the Napoleonic period, will be what has been identified here as asymmetrical warfare. A persistent band of contemporary analysts agrees; for some of them, the dominant analogy is fourth-generation warfare.

Fourth-generation warfare represents a conceptual and physical departure from the dominance of western-style warfare. One of the earlier depictions of this change was described by a group headed by William Lind, a former aide to Senator Gary Hart. This group examined the evolution of warfare from the Napoleonic period forward in an article published in the October 1989 *Marine Corps Gazette*. The authors maintain that the first generation of warfare was dominated by linear formations of armies clashing in open fields where the dominant weaponry was the smooth-bore musket. This form of fighting favored the offensive actions of the conventional armies in combat. The second generation was the result of the introduction of much more accurate rifles and muskets that made the charges of tightly configured formations suicidal. The trench warfare of World War I is the epitome of this kind of defensively dominated war. With the weaponization of technologies like the truck and tank and the storage battery (for propelling submarines), the pendulum swung back to the offensive advantage, as maneuver was reintroduced onto the battlefield. The epitome of this type of warfare was the *blitzkrieg* style of fighting mastered by Germany in World War II.

What is notable about these three generations is how geopolitically and militarily traditional they are. In all three cases, they describe warfare fought by western national armies organized conventionally and with clear and identifiable political purposes for their actions. The changes from generation to generation are not radical but largely the result of changes in weapons technologies and adaptation of strategies and tactics that reflect those changes. At the same time, this western-style warfare features the clash of armies directly when the major purpose of conflict is for one side or the other to defeat the enemy on the field of battle as a necessary preface to imposing its political will on the vanquished. It is fundamentally a Clausewitzian vision of war.

Those who suggest a new kind of war, whether or not they use the fourth-generation analogy, maintain that the world is entering a period of radical change in warfare. One of the apostles of this change is the Israeli analyst Martin van Creveld, who described the magnitude of the change he foresaw in 1991 in his *The Transformation of War*. His basic argument is that the western paradigm of war is being broken. The Clausewitzian base, for instance, is shattered because, "should present trends continue, the kind of war that is based on the division between government, army, and people seems to be on its way out." The result will be the crumbling of conventional nationally based military forces. As he puts it, "Much present-day military power is simply irrelevant as an instrument for extending or defending political interests over much of the globe."

What replaces conventional, trinitarian warfare in the van Creveld scheme? He argues the change is fundamental in terms of the units that wage war, the methods of combat they use, and the purposes for which they fight. In his words, "In the future, wars will not be waged by armies but by groups whom we today call terrorists, guerrillas, bandits and robbers. Their organizations are likely to be constructed on charismatic lines rather than institutional ones, and to be motivated less by 'professionalism' than by fanatical, ideologically based loyalties." The new kind of war, in other words, turns the traditional warfare of the first three generations on its head both organizationally and in terms of its underlying purposes. It also describes Al Qaeda and the Iraqi resistance well before they existed.

The arguments surrounding this alleged transformation are, of course, controversial. While they have been made for two decades or more, until recently most of the discussions have been confined to places like the war colleges, where they have been extensively debated and dissected. The events of September 11, 2001, have brought these arguments out of the shadows and onto center stage. The actions by bin Laden and his cohorts clearly coincide with aspects of the future war described by van Creveld, and the popularization of the term *new kind of war* has sent many scrambling to find out what this newness is. There is no consensus at this point.

All the controversy cannot be settled here. What can be done is to describe what the champions of the new form of war claim about it. Because the terrorist attacks and the subsequent campaigns against the Taliban, Al Qaeda, and the Iraqi resistance proved the stimulus for consideration of the fourth generation, one can also ask how an assessment of that experience reinforces or undercuts the claims of those arguing fundamental change.

The 2007 "surge" in Iraq (where additional American forces were inserted in a counterinsurgency role) brought this approach to war and dealing with it to the forefront. The apostle was General David Petraeus, an army general who commanded U.S. forces in Iraq at the time and has since been promoted to commander of Central Command (CENTCOM), with total overall responsibility for U.S. Middle East military matters, including Iraq and Afghanistan. Petraeus oversaw the most recent U.S. doctrinal statement on asymmetrical warfare, *Field Manual (FM) 3-24*, which was the basis for the surge, the underlying rationale of the Gates reforms, and the organizing concept for the Obama reorientation of U.S. strategy in Afghanistan. It is not unfair to say that these efforts have brought concern with asymmetrical warfare into the mainstream of American military consideration.

Characteristics of Fourth-Generation Warfare. Although there are other depictions available that differ in detail, the framework of Lind and his colleagues remains useful for describing what people mean when they talk about fourth-generation warfare. What is interesting about their analysis is that it not only argues the change that marks the fourth generation, but also points out how important elements of the new environment have their roots in the past and evolving kinds of war.

Lind and his colleagues argue that there is a series of characteristics of fourth-generation warfare that can be traced to the past. In terms of the conduct of hostilities, for instance, they maintain that in the future there will be no distinctions between civilians and military forces in terms of targeting: society is the battlefield in the new environment. There will be an absence of definable battlefields or fronts, and the places where fighting occurs will be dispersed and undefined: everywhere and nowhere are the front lines. The result is a much more fluid military situation in which traditional concerns like battlefield encounters and measures such as land gained or lost will largely lose meaning as measures of military success.

The purposes of fighting will also change, at least for those who adopt the methodologies of the fourth generation. The goal will not be traditional military defeat but instead the internal political collapse of the opponent and its will to continue. The manipulation of the media will be a skill that is highly valued by practitioners of the fourth generation, and the target of much of this activity will be popular support for the government or whatever force against which the campaign is waged.

To this point, the description of fourth-generation warfare is still not terribly innovative. While one can see elements of it in more recent terrorist attacks (not distinguishing between military and civilian targets, for instance), almost all of these characteristics could easily be ascribed to the NVA and VC asymmetrical campaign against the United States a third of a century ago. In fact, this part of the description is largely attributable to the postmortem of the American experience in Vietnam.

Lind and his colleagues extend these characteristics in trying to describe the basic nature of the fourth generation. First, they argue explicitly the nonwestern, Asiatic (including Middle Eastern) basis of this form of warfare. In October 2001, Keegan embellished this connection: "The Oriental tradition, however, has not been eliminated. It reappeared . . . particularly in the tactics of evasion and retreat practiced by the Vietcong against the United States in the Vietnam war. On September 11, 2001, it returned in an absolutely traditional form. Arabs, appearing suddenly out of empty space like their desert raider ancestors, assaulted the heartlands of Western power in a terrifying surprise raid and did appalling damage."

Second, they argue that terrorism is a standard tactic of practitioners of the fourth generation. Because they are militarily weaker in the traditional (symmetrical) sense, their terrorist tactics provide an asymmetrical way to bypass the conventional strength of western militaries and to strike at the homeland. They are aided in accomplishing these acts by the very openness of free societies that makes them more easily penetrable. Third, a major objective of fourth-generation practitioners is the disruption of target societies, what Lind and his colleagues call the "culture of order," which is the direct objective of the attacks. Finally, they argue that movements adopting fourth-generation warfare will often not be nationally based governments but will have a transnational and, on some occasions, even a religious base.

These descriptions, published twelve years before the September 11 attacks, have an eerily prescient ring in terms of what happened in New York and Washington. Van Creveld adds (once again, in 1991) other evidence of similarity: "There will be a tendency to treat leaders as criminals who richly deserve the worst fate that can be inflicted on them. Hence, many leaders will probably decide to remain unattached and lead a semi-nomadic life."

The Fourth Generation and September 11, 2001. The descriptions of the nature and implications of fourth-generation warfare seemed virtually to predict the terrible events of September 11, 2001, a decade before they occurred, which is, in large measure, why they are reproduced and quoted in some detail. Imbedded in these discussions, however, is the further assertion that nonstate-based warfare fought using asymmetrical methods and for nonconventional purposes will become the dominant form of warfare in the future. Implied in that prediction is the further assertion that traditional, western national military forces will become obsolete relics because of the new form of warfare.

Does the experience of the terrorist attacks and responses to them bear out these implications? In some ways, they clearly do. The attacks against the Pentagon and the World Trade Center towers clearly fit the descriptions and motivations of the purveyors of this new "model" of warfare. Not all the attributes were new, of course—terrorism is a decidedly old tactic, and terrorist acts committed by nonstate actors are hardly novel in the American or international experience. What sets the attacks apart in the contemporary context is their audacity and scale. Terrorist attacks by individuals and groups with no formal state affiliation that kill a relatively small number of people are, if not common, not entirely uncommon. When thousands of innocent people are killed in such attacks, then the problem achieves another order of magnitude.

Did the attacks and the subsequent campaign to overthrow the Taliban, destroy Al Qaeda, and capture bin Laden vindicate the apostles of the fourth generation of warfare? In other words, were the attributes of how the United States' asymmetrical foes fought sufficiently frustrating to the United States that one feels the need to reformulate how the military goes about its business in the face of future repetitions that may become the norm for future violence?

The short-term answer is mixed. Asymmetrical warfare is successful when the conditions for its success hold. Thus, the Taliban, who were roundly defeated when they stood and fought the Americans and the Northern Coalition after October 2001, slipped across the border into Pakistan, where they reorganized and reconstituted themselves as an asymmetrical force that has enjoyed considerable success in Afghanistan and is a major thorn in the side of Pakistan. They have proven incapable of establishing total control in Afghanistan or of evicting the Pakistani government completely from the FATA, but neither the Afghans and their American and NATO allies nor the Pakistanis have been able to defeat them. Indeed, both situations remain draws, wars of attrition where the contest of wills ultimately will decide the outcome. Much the same is true of Al Qaeda.

Al Qaeda ended up in the Tora Bora Mountains and across the border into Pakistan in 2001, where they were pounded by the combined conventional might of the Americans and the various Afghan factions. They were not, however, entirely broken. All of the adherence to apparently novel forms of warfare did not keep them from being forced to go deep underground, and bin Laden and his closest cohorts evaded the dragnet out to snare them. Conventional force and counterterrorist actions have been able to reduce Al Qaeda to a shadow of its prewar status but have not been able to destroy it completely. The resilience that Al Qaeda has demonstrated will, in all likelihood, be part of the model for future asymmetrical warriors, as well as a characteristic of Al Qaeda's own continuing existence.

The dramatic capture and subsequent rescue of the *Maersk Alabama* in May 2009 brought to the public attention an ancient practice with distinctly asymmetrical warfare characteristics, piracy. The practice of piracy—defined as armed robbery at sea if committed within the territorial waters of a country and as "illegal acts of violence committed for private ends—outside of a state's territorial waters" (Kraska and Wilson)—is an ancient phenomenon. In recent years, its widespread practice has moved from the Straits of Malacca and South Asia to an area off the coast of Somalia where those who attacked the *Maersk Alabama* resided.

Piracy shares some characteristics with asymmetrical warfare on land. It is clearly unconventional activity based on the same kind of tactical surprise ascribed earlier to the 9/11 attackers. The vast expanses of the world's oceans make it difficult to locate and attack pirates, and effective "counterpiracy" would be prohibitively expensive and manpower intensive. On the other hand, piracy is clearly criminal behavior with no redeeming political rationale, making its justification problematical. One can, however, think of piracy as asymmetrical warfare at sea.

New Internal Wars

Before the events of September 11, 2001, caught the world's attention, another form of warfare had been raging over the last decade or more in parts of the developing world in the form of often grotesque and hideous conflicts that I have identified as the new internal wars (NIWs).

These kinds of wars broke onto the public scene during the 1990s, although there were a few internal conflicts during the Cold War that met all or most of the criteria for classification as NIWs. What sets these conflicts apart is their disorderliness and the extreme violence and apparent senselessness of the suffering being exacted mainly against civilian populations by their countrymen. Moreover, although NIWs have occurred most often in places far from the geopolitical spotlight, the conditions that gave rise to them continue in many parts of the world and form part of the rationale for engaging in state building (Chapter 13) and thinking about future contingencies (Chapter 14).

The end of the Cold War contributed to the emergence of the NIWs as a major phenomenon in the pattern of world violence. Internal conflicts were, of course, the dominant form of war during the Cold War, and in that sense, the NIWs represent a continuation of the pattern that occurred during the period of superpower competition. At the same time, civil conflict during the Cold War generally had the character of traditional insurgency, where the structure of the violence featured a government that sought to maintain itself in power and was supported by one of the superpowers (usually the United States) and an insurgency employing some form of mobile-guerrilla war model that sought power and was supported by the other superpower (usually the Soviet Union). Superpower presence provided an often irrelevant Communist–anti-Communist aspect to contests more properly understood in other terms (ethnic or tribal dominance, for instance), but it also brought restraint to the fighting, since neither superpower wanted its client (and by extension, itself) charged with atrocities.

The war in Cambodia in the 1970s between the Khmer Rouge and its opponents was the major exception to this rule (the contending sides were sponsored by the Soviet Union and China), and in many ways, it was the prototype for the NIWs. The brutal, genocidal campaign by the Khmer Rouge government to transform Cambodia into a pastoral, docile society produced a litany of horrors that war crimes investigators are still unraveling. It also provided a frightening portent of the future of internal war that was largely ignored at the time.

The list of the most prominent instances of these new internal wars is familiar. The post–Cold War prototype occurred (and in limited form is still going on, partly as the source of piracy) in Somalia, where a combination of a long drought and the use of international food supplies as weapons in the clan-based conflict for power threatened to result in massive starvation until an international peacekeeping force intervened to interrupt the suffering. "Ethnic cleansing" was added to the language of international politics as Serbs, Croats, and Bosnian Muslims struggled to partition the Bosnian successor state to Yugoslavia, and that phenomenon was reprised a half decade later in Kosovo. Between those Balkan conflicts, the United States intervened in Haiti, and the Rwandan nightmare was added to the list in 1994.

Characteristics of New Internal Wars. The characteristics of NIWs can be divided into political and military categories. At the political level, the most striking feature of these wars is their nearly total reversal of the kinds of goals found in traditional insurgencies. Unlike traditional civil wars, the control of government is often not the clear objective of both sides. In a number of cases of NIWs, the "rebel" force articulates no political objectives or statements of ideological principles about how it would organize itself to rule. The Revolutionary United Front (RUF) of Sierra Leone, for instance, never issued a manifesto of any kind, and this is not unusual. The apparent reason for this was that the RUF movement had neither the intention nor the desire to gain control of and govern the country. Rather, in a number of cases, the highly nontraditional political purpose is anarchical, in the sense of seeking to destabilize the country, preventing governmental control by anyone. Creating anarchy is, of course, a political goal but not one that is accorded legitimacy in a state-centered, Westphalian world. In these cases—most notably the narco-insurgencies of South America and some parts of Asia and the criminal insurgencies of parts of Africa—the real goal is to create a sense of total lawlessness that maximizes the group's ability to enrich itself either through thievery and worse or by controlling or protecting narcotics trafficking. Such groups often adopt splendid political ("revolutionary front") or otherwise high-sounding (the "Lord's Army" of Uganda) names to mask the basic criminality that forms their purpose.

There is another political characteristic that also helps differentiate NIWs from traditional internal wars and explain the savagery that often dominates these conflicts. Traditional civil wars are fought for control of the government of a country, and a central factor in which side prevails is the loyalty of the country's population—the "hearts and minds" of the people. This "center of gravity" is a point of competition for both sides, and neither wants to drive the people into the other side's arms by committing hideous and unacceptable acts of violence against the population. The need to appeal to the people thus moderates the violence, especially against noncombatant civilians.

Since the goal in NIWs is not to govern but to intimidate or kill those members of the population who might be in opposition, there is no such motivation toward moderation. In Bosnia during the first half of the 1990s, Bosnian Serbs did not seek to appeal to Bosnian Muslims or vice versa; rather, their aim was to drive people from their homes, move in, and claim the land by virtue of possession. Similarly, the Rwandan Hutus were clearly not appealing politically for the support of the Tutsi as the rampage proceeded; they simply wanted to kill as many people as possible. The racial purification of the Darfur region of the Sudan by murdering African Muslims is similar. This absence of a shared center of gravity that needs to be nurtured makes NIWs effectively like wars between states (interstate wars) rather than internal wars (intrastate wars) politically. Like interstate wars, the purpose is to subdue, not to win over, the opponent. Unlike traditional intrastate wars, there is no battle for the hearts and minds of the people to moderate the slaughter. The internal fighting in Iraq certainly exhibits this characteristic as well.

The military characteristics of NIWs follow from these nontraditional political characteristics and provide a close parallel with the military characteristics of fourth-generation warfare. Since there are often no clear political objectives for these affairs, they do not translate into strategic guidance to form conventional military objectives and operations. The military units that conduct these forms of hostilities are typically highly irregular, not uniformed or organized into coherent rank orderings of officers and enlisted soldiers. They are poorly trained, if they have received any military training at all, and are unaware or contemptuous of normal conventions of war. Similarly, they normally lack a sense of military order or discipline. In a number of instances, these fighters have been little more than children, with members of the ranks reportedly no more than ten- to twelve-year-olds, often kidnapped and forced into service by the fear of personal or family consequences if they refuse (the Lord's Army of Uganda, for instance, kidnaps children from orphanages and threatens to kill them if they resist becoming "soldiers").

Given these characteristics, the savagery and atrocity associated with these wars should come as little surprise. Echoing the fourth-generation lack of distinction between civilians and military targets, they are marked by frequent incidences of attacks by fighters against unarmed civilians, notably women and children, the elderly, and other similarly helpless beings (atrocities in the Sudan are a particularly gruesome example). In most NIWs, there are rarely any encounters between the organized armed forces of the two (or more) contending sides. The main reason for this pattern is that the sides are not organized into military forces that can contend against other organized forces; attacking, mutilating, or killing helpless, innocent civilians is their form of asymmetrical warfare.

Countering Asymmetrical Warfare. Finding effective ways to negate asymmetrical enemies is arguably the largest military challenge facing the United States. It is a difficult, bedeviling problem because asymmetrical wars are idiosyncratic and the methods used to combat one asymmetrical foe may be quite inapplicable to another. Part of the difficulty is that asymmetrical warfare is an approach to war, not a set of principles and doctrines that can be countered with opposing tactics and doctrines. Moreover, asymmetrical warfare is a continually changing, chameleon-like phenomenon, with practitioners selecting from the past those things that have worked or failed for others and adapting them to their particular circumstances. The old conundrum that the military prepares to "fight the last war" is particularly inapplicable when the next opponent is an asymmetrical warrior.

Still, there are general guidelines, mostly incorporated into *FM 3-24*, that can guide, if not direct in detail, counter-asymmetrical warfare. Three will be raised here: the paramount importance of security in contested areas, the battle for the hearts and minds of the target population as the key to the center of gravity (objective) of both sides, and the inherent limitation of outsider effectiveness in these conflicts, be they fourth generation wars, NIWs, or hybrids like those currently being fought in Afghanistan and Pakistan.

Since today's (and likely tomorrow's) asymmetrical opponents are broadly insurgents (people who are native to the country in which they operate and seeking political goals from an established government), then principles of counterinsurgency, preached and laid out by General Petraeus in *FM 3-24* and others (an extensive discussion by the author can be found in *Distant Thunder*), are applicable to counteracting asymmetrical foes. The essence of successful counterinsurgency is the successful competition for the loyalty of the target population. That competition begins with providing security to the population one is seeking to influence.

Providing physical safety for those people whose allegiance is sought or is to be maintained is critical because one of the first priorities of an insurgent group is to demonstrate that the government cannot provide them that security and thus does not deserve their allegiance. Among the methods the insurgents use is suppressing (including killing) government supporters and officials, and one intended effect is to terrorize potential supporters into nonsupport. This technique is ubiquitous in these kinds of wars, from the American Revolution (see Snow and Drew, *From Lexington to Baghdad and Beyond*) to the operation of the Taliban in Afghanistan and Pakistan.

If one cannot protect potential converts from physical danger, little else is possible, but doing so is difficult and both time and manpower intensive. The provision of security must be constant and comprehensive; if counterinsurgent forces are not always on duty to protect the population, the insurgents will exploit their absence to terrorize the population. Their goal of creating insecurity does not require their constant presence, only the possibility of their return when the government leaves (thus saving their resources). Outside forces can augment efforts to provide security, as the United States did in the Iraqi surge and is doing in Afghanistan—but the bulk of the effort must be indigenous, for two reasons. First, there will never be enough outsiders to do the job (Afghanistan is, after all, the size of Texas). Second, outsiders will always kindle some opposition in the target population because they are foreigners whose motives are suspect.

The purpose of security is to create a shield behind which the real business of counterinsurgency can proceed—what Lyndon Johnson called the battle for the hearts and minds of men. At heart, internal wars are more about political loyalties than anything else: whichever side has that loyalty is likely to prevail. Insurgents will attempt to influence this contest positively, by demonstrating superior claims to loyalty through promises of better governance or appeals to ethnic or other kindred connections, but they may also use coercion to gain compliance in areas they control. The counterinsurgents, on the other hand, seek to establish loyalty to the regime, but they are normally in a situation where their leadership has been called into question by the insurgents, and if the insurgency is lively, there is some basis for their appeal. This is often a very difficult dynamic, as Amplification 11.2 seeks to suggest about Afghanistan.

Amplification 11.2

HEARTS AND MINDS IN AFGHANISTAN

The problem of loyalty in Afghanistan is extremely difficult for the United States and its ally, the Afghan government of Hamid Karzai. The difficulty has three bases. The first reflects the political and economic condition of the country. Afghanistan is an extremely poor country, and it is also one of the most corrupt countries in the world, ranking near the bottom of international indices on the subject. The result is that the government is alienated from much of the population, which considers it incompetent, venal, or both and is thus open to appeals that promise a less corrupt, more responsive alternative.

Second, the battle is largely couched in ethnic terms. Afghanistan is dominated by a group of ethnic tribes who hold the loyalty of many Afghans. The largest ethnic group is that of the Pashtuns, which has traditionally dominated Afghanistan and is the second-largest ethnic group in Pakistan. Although there is no indication that a majority of Pashtuns support the Taliban, the Taliban is almost exclusively Pashtun, and its operating base is in the Pashtun regions of the two countries. Successful defeat of the Taliban in both countries requires somehow creating enough anti-Taliban sentiment among Pashtuns to convince them to turn into active opposition to the Taliban. Since neither the Afghan nor the Pakistani government controls those regions, neither can provide security within which to nurture a transfer of loyalty to the government. The Taliban, of course, maintain control by ruthlessly rooting out any signs of opposition to them. In this circumstance, it is not clear how or if the transfer of loyalty to the government of either country can occur.

The third element is the inherent limitation of outside intervention in the internal affairs of other countries, notably in asymmetrical wars. Outside intervenors will always elicit some opposition and suspicion because they are outsiders whose motives will be suspected. This is particularly true in a country like Afghanistan, which has a long history of successful resistance to outside invaders and which tends to view any foreigners as the next invaders. At the same time, the need for outsiders to help in the prosecution of an asymmetrical war is itself evidence of the impotence of the government to do the job itself and is a source of derision, which, in the worst case, will stain the government as the "puppet" of the outsiders (providing the insurgents with a rallying call for their cause in the process). Finally, the cause being contested is almost always more important to the internal factions, and especially the insurgents, than it is to the intervening power. One of the true lessons of the Vietnam War, for instance, was that ultimately who won was more important to the North Vietnamese than it was to the United States. As a result, those who oppose American intervention efforts are likely to adopt a strategy of attrition against the symmetrically superior Americans, dragging out the war effort and inflicting just enough pain on the Americans that they conclude continuation of the war is not worth the costs incurred. That strategy of outlasting the interveners worked in Vietnam, may still prove to have worked in Iraq, and will almost certainly be part of the dynamic in Afghanistan.

CONCLUSION: NEW FORM OR NEW FACE OF WAR?

The chapter concludes by going back and asking the question raised at the beginning of the chapter: Is the kind of warfare that the United States faces literally something new? Or is asymmetrical warfare a "back to the future" proposition, borrowing from the title of Goulding's article in the U.S. Army's journal, *Parameters*? As the analysis has sought to demonstrate, in a purely military sense, what is now called asymmetrical warfare does not represent a great change in war but is instead the approach that has been taken throughout history by weaker protagonists when facing superior forces. The American reintroduction to this kind of warfare in Vietnam did not, however, prepare it for an opponent who would change the rules of engagement so radically as to attack and destroy the kinds of civilian targets that were attacked on September 11, 2001. The innovation was not the dynamics of war; it was the physical object of attack. It is not the last major innovation the United States will likely encounter.

The United States had better anticipate that it will face more asymmetrical foes in the future. One of the other clear characteristics of the contemporary environment is the huge and growing chasm of conventional military capabilities between the countries of the West and the rest of the world. The RMA means, to repeat, that no developing world country or movement has any military chance against the United States or its friends and allies if it fights on western terms (symmetrically). The Iraqis did not understand that in 1991 and paid a price they were unwilling to pay again in 2003. The Taliban either did not understand it or could not adapt quickly enough when confronted with western airpower in 2001; they also learned their lesson.

That leads to the conclusion that, at a minimum, future opponents are likely to confront the United States with highly unorthodox, unconventional, and unanticipated problems. If the lesson learned from September 11, 2001, is how to combat terrorism (see Chapter 13) and no more, the United States will have missed the real novelty of the "new kind of war," which is the need to change and adapt and to be ready for the unexpected. The alternatives are unattractive. As Goulding puts it, "Military forces like those of the United States and its allies who constitute the bulk of 'well organized and well paid regular forces' and generally play by the rules may, in their next battles, wish fervently that it was against soldiers of their own ilk they were fighting."

If the concepts underlying asymmetrical war are hardly new, the ways in which it is conducted are constantly evolving and adapting to changed physical and political circumstances. The tactics that worked in the Vietnamese mountains and jungles are not directly applicable to arid Iraq, so the Iraqi resistance to the American occupation fought differently in order to rid themselves of the Americans than did

Challenge!

IS THERE A NEW KIND OF WAR?

The initial, highly emotional reaction to the terrorist attacks of September 11, 2001, in the United States suggested that these were somehow an unprecedented phenomenon, and the rage and smoldering desire for revenge could most easily be translated into the analogy of militarily crushing those who had committed these atrocious acts. The idea that Americans were faced with a new kind of war was born of this conjunction of the apparent uniqueness of the act and the desire for a military reaction.

Is the analogy accurate? The thrust of much of the analysis in this chapter has been that it is not. The central point has been that terrorism has long been a central manner in which weak groups attempt to assert their will over stronger groups. A major focus of these efforts involves changing the rules of engagement between contending forces to remove some of the advantage the stronger party has and in effect to level the playing field or tilt it in the weaker party's favor. Since part of that leveling entails rejecting the rules and conventions under which the dominant player operates, the result is likely to be outrage when the weaker party attacks. This dynamic of fourth-generation or asymmetrical warfare dates back to antiquity. The uniqueness of the current application lies in its scale and the fact it has been visited directly against the American population. Would Americans have the same sense of rage and the same depth of reaction if airliners had attacked the 1,381-foot Jin Mao building of Shanghai in China? Or the world's tallest buildings, the 1,483-foot Petronas towers in Kuala Lumpur, Malaysia?

The question asked in the title of this *Challenge!* is really two related questions. Is the form of activity in which the United States is engaged properly described as a form of war? And is that activity something new? The answer to the second question is fairly clearly no, but the answer to the first question is not so clear. Is it more useful to think about this kind of campaign in warlike terms, or is some other framework more useful? What do you think? If you believe war is not the best way to think about countering terrorism, what do you think is a better way?

the Vietnamese. Future asymmetrical opponents will also seek to present the United States with novel problems for which the Americans are unprepared. The secret to confounding asymmetrical warriors is anticipating and preparing for what they will do before they can do it. But, as the *Challenge!* box asks, is there *really* a new kind of war?

STUDY/DISCUSSION QUESTIONS

1. What are symmetrical and asymmetrical forms of warfare? Describe each. Under what circumstances does a country or group prefer one approach to the other?
2. Is asymmetrical warfare a new idea? Describe its history and evolution, with some emphasis on Vietnam.

3. Describe the contemporary military setting facing the United States. What is the RMA? How has it affected the American approach to force and the international environment? Apply this impact to the Persian Gulf War, Afghanistan, and Iraq.
4. What is fourth-generation warfare? Where does the term come from? What are the characteristics of fourth-generation warfare? Cite examples, including September 11.
5. What are the new internal wars? Discuss how and when they emerge, what their political and military characteristics are, and what makes them different than other kinds of wars.
6. Why is it so difficult to counter insurgencies? What are the major elements of a counterinsurgency strategy? What makes it difficult for an outsider to be decisive in this kind of war?
7. Is asymmetrical warfare the military challenge of the future? Is it something new to the United States? What should the United States do about it?

SELECTED BIBLIOGRAPHY

Barnett, Thomas P. M. *The Pentagon's New Map: War and Peace in the Twenty-First Century.* New York: Berkley Books, 2004.

Boot, Max. "The Struggle to Transform the Military." *Foreign Affairs* 84, no. 2 (March/April 2005): 103–118.

Brodie, Bernard, and Fawn M. Brodie. *From Crossbow to H-Bomb: The Evolution of Weapons and Tactics of Warfare.* Bloomington: Indiana University Press, 1973.

Cothran, Helen, ed. *National Security: Opposing Viewpoints.* San Diego, CA: Greenhaven Press, 2004.

Dobbins, James. "Iraq: Winning the Unwinnable War." *Foreign Affairs* 84, no. 1 (January/February 2005): 6–25.

Duncan, Stephen M. *A War of a Different Kind: Military Forces and America's Search for Homeland Security.* Annapolis, MD: Naval Institute Press, 2004.

Field Manual 3-24: Counterinsurgency. Washington, DC: United States Army and United States Marine Corps, 2007.

Gallagher, James J. *Low-Intensity Conflict: A Guide for Tactics, Techniques, and Procedures.* Mechanicsburg, PA: Stackpole Books, 1992.

Gerstein, Daniel M. *Securing America's Future: National Security in the Information Age.* Westport, CT: Praeger Security International, 2005.

Goulding, Vincent J., Jr. "Back to the Future with Asymmetrical Warfare." *Parameters* 30, no. 4 (Winter 2000–2001): 21–30.

Haass, Richard N. "Regime Change and Its Limits." *Foreign Affairs* 84, no. 1 (January/February 2005): 66–78.

Hentz, James J., ed. *The Obligation of Empire: United States' Grand Strategy for a New Century.* Lexington: University Press of Kentucky, 2004.

Keegan, John. *A History of Warfare.* London: Hutchison, 1991.

Kraska, James, and Brian Wilson. "Somali Piracy: A Nasty Problem, a Web of Responses." *Current History* 108, no. 718 (May 2009): 227–231.

Lacquement, Richard A. *Shaping American Military Capabilities After the Cold War.* Westport, CT: Praeger, 2003.

Lewis, Bernard. "Freedom and Justice in the Modern Middle East." *Foreign Affairs* 84, no. 3 (May/June 2005): 36–51.

Lind, William S., Keith Nightengale, John F. Schmitt, Joseph W. Sutton, and Gary J. Wilson. "The Changing Face of War: Into the Fourth Generation." *Marine Corps Gazette*, October 1989, 21–26.

Luttwak, Edward N. "Iraq: The Logic of Disengagement." *Foreign Affairs* 84, no. 1 (January/February 2005): 26–36.

Mao tse-Tung. *Mao tse-Tung on Guerrilla Warfare*. Translated by Samuel B. Griffith. New York: Praeger, 1961.

Moore, Lt. General Harold G., and James L. Galloway. *We Were Soldiers Once...and Young: Ia Drang: The Battle That Changed the War in Vietnam*. New York: Harper and Row, 1993.

O'Hanlon, Michael E. *Defense Strategy for the Post-Saddam Era*. Washington, DC: Brookings Institution Press, 2005.

Peters, Ralph. *Fighting for the Future: Will America Triumph?* Mechanicsburg, PA: Stackpole Books, 2001.

Snow, Donald M. *Uncivil Wars: International Security and the New Internal Conflicts*. Boulder, CO: Lynne Rienner Publishers, 1996.

———. *Distant Thunder: Patterns of Conflict in the Developing World*. 2nd ed. Armonk, NY: M. E. Sharpe, 1997.

———. *When America Fights: The Uses of U.S. Military Force*. Washington, DC: CQ Press, 2000.

———, and Dennis M. Drew. *From Lexington to Baghdad and Beyond*. 3rd ed. Armonk, NY: M. E. Sharpe, 2009.

Sun Tzu. *The Art of War*. Translated by Samuel B. Griffith. Oxford, England: Oxford University Press, 1963.

van Creveld, Martin. *The Transformation of War*. New York: Free Press, 1991.

CHAPTER 12

The Unresolved Dilemmas in Afghanistan and Iraq

PREVIEW

The major legacies of the post-9/11 period are the ongoing American involvements in wars in Afghanistan and Iraq. Because Al Qaeda had its headquarters in Afghanistan and was sheltered from pursuit by the United States and others by its Taliban regime, this was a logical place for the United States to send forces in 2001. These forces have been augmented and their mission enlarged, and the Afghanistan War proceeds with no direct end in sight. In 2003, the United States invaded, conquered, and occupied Iraq on grounds justified by 9/11. That involvement is winding down. This chapter examines both conflicts and what they mean for the United States.

In his May 25, 2009, Memorial Day message, President Barack Obama asked the American people to observe a minute of silence. He asked that they remember those Americans who have died in war and pray for a time when war no longer scourges the world. Despite this latter hope, the United States has been, and remains, enmeshed in two wars in the Middle East. The precipitating events for ongoing American involvements in Afghanistan and Iraq can be traced, directly or indirectly, to 9/11 and the reaction to it. In the case of Afghanistan, that lineage is direct: American forces were dispatched to that country in October 2001 specifically to pursue and attempt to capture or kill the leadership of Al Qaeda, which was responsible for the 9/11 attacks. That mission brought the United States into direct conflict with the Islamist Taliban regime of Afghanistan that was providing physical sanctuary for the terrorists. In the process, the United States became embroiled in the anti-Taliban side of a civil war in Afghanistan. Over time, the anti–Al Qaeda and anti-Taliban distinction has blurred to the point that President Obama, in his

June 5, 2009, speech in Cairo identified the mission by saying, "We would gladly bring every single one of our troops home if we could be confident that there were not violent extremists in Afghanistan and Pakistan determined to kill as many Americans as they possibly can. But that is not yet the case." Presumably the term "violent extremists" encompasses both Al Qaeda and the Taliban.

The connection between 9/11 and the Iraq War seemed intimate when the United States invaded in 2003 because the Bush administration argued Iraq was a theater of the global war on terrorism (GWOT). As the war has dragged on and more information and analysis have become available, that connection has become more tenuous and questionable. The Iraq involvement, however, is an intimate part of the post-9/11 environment, and although American combat forces are scheduled to be withdrawn completely in 2010, an American presence in Iraq will remain for the foreseeable future. The U.S. commitments in Afghanistan and Iraq are not over, and it is unlikely either will end completely in the near future. Since legacies are lessons from past, presumably completed events, the ability to extrapolate beyond these conflicts is thus limited.

That having been said, certain predictions seem sufficiently rooted in actual experience to appear reasonably safe (recognizing that hypothesized predictions can prove right or wrong). One reasonably safe projection is that American participation in the Iraq War will start to wind down in the not-so-distant future, even if there is some continuing American presence after U.S. combat participation formally ends. The end will not likely be because of some dramatic turn of events that supporters and critics can agree constitutes "victory" for the United States or for the Iraqis (or at least certainly not all Iraqis). Rather, the ultimate resolution of the Iraq situation will be determined by Iraqis (probably influenced by their regional neighbors) after the Americans leave. Although a resolution is clearly further away in Afghanistan, it will also likely not be decisive in any definitive way (one side surrendering, for instance). This ambiguity of resolution may simply be a characteristic of contemporary asymmetrical warfare.

Supporters of both wars in the United States will likely contest the desirability of these outcomes. A bloody form of conflict resolution in Iraq will likely occur regardless of when the United States decides to end its involvement, and the violence that ensues after that departure will increase American angst over the outcome because of the unavoidable knowledge that most of it probably would not have occurred (if any of it would have) had the United States not intruded itself into Iraq in the first place. While the same criticism of American initial involvement in Afghanistan is unlikely, a similar angst over the protracted nature of involvement is emerging.

A second safe assumption is that Americans will be divided about the outcomes of both wars. If one rules out the likelihood in either case of a clear-cut American "victory" (depending on how that is defined) around which almost all Americans could unite, the American people will likely be divided into three groups regarding the outcomes. Some Americans will support the outcomes because they feel these outcomes either were inevitable or produce what they view as the greater good of removing Americans from harm's way. Some Americans, most of whom have been generally supportive of the wars, will decry the outcomes because they do not achieve the American political objectives for going and because the result will entail additional suffering for those whose suffering was one of the reasons for supporting the involvements in the first place. Yet others, who may have been supporters or opponents or even neutral for some time, will simply be relieved the wars are over and will not care a great deal about what happens afterward, a sentiment widely felt in the United States after the fall of Saigon in 1975.

A third reasonably safe prediction is that the postwar assessments of the wars—the "lessons learned," in military parlance—will be contentious, and in some cases acrimonious and vindictive. Because the Iraq War became intensely unpopular and divisive in a way and to an extent not seen in the United States since the Vietnam War, there will be a "blame game" of recriminations about how and why the United States stumbled into what a growing consensus agrees was a mistaken adventure. The postmortem about Afghanistan is more likely to focus on whether the U.S. effort was a noble but doomed attempt that morphed from a crusade against terrorism into partisan involvement in an ethnic civil war in which the United States had no real stake.

A fourth safe prediction is that the Afghanistan and Iraq Wars will produce a revived debate about the circumstances and means of using American forces in the future. In some ways, this debate will be a revival of discussions begun in the 1990s and suspended by September 11 and the subsequent GWOT—of which, after all, both wars have been described as applications or "theaters." This debate will likely be reminiscent in tone and thoroughness to a similar retrospective after the American disengagement from Vietnam. Whether the analogy will hold regarding conclusions is, to some extent, unknowable, but both wars have the significant potential to have as profound an impact on American national security as did Vietnam.

With these likely commonalities in mind, the two ongoing conflicts can be viewed individually. Because the initial involvement militarily in Afghanistan in October 2001 precedes the invasion of Iraq in March 2003 by nearly a year and a half, it will be reviewed first, followed by an examination of Iraq. The two analyses will be roughly parallel in structure. Each will begin by examining the process by which the United States initially became involved ("The Road to War"), including the feasibility of the mission. The discussion will then move to errors as the missions unfolded ("What Went Wrong and Why") and will include some speculation on how each war will end. The concluding section of the chapter will examine some likely political and military legacies of the two wars.

Although the wars share similarities, they are also distinctly different. In retrospect, the Iraq War was rather clearly a "war of choice," the result of decisions reached before 9/11 that it was desirable to overthrow Saddam Hussein. The result was a choice to go to war, which Obama acknowledged in his Cairo speech, since the Iraqi regime, even if it was an annoyance, represented no real threat to the United States, arguments to the contrary made at the time notwithstanding. Al Qaeda's physical presence in Afghanistan after 9/11 was different. As Obama put it in Cairo, "We did not go by choice, we went because of necessity."

The United States made strategically consequential mistakes in both wars, but they were distinctly different errors. In Iraq, the crucial mistake was virtually nonexistent planning for the postinvasion occupation period (Phase IV), which resulted in actions that made the situation even worse than it needed to be, prolonged the occupation, and made the war's eventual outcome even more problematical than it would have been had the early stages been handled competently. In Afghanistan, the principal error was—and to some extent still is—the failure to distinguish between the two distinct aspects of the conflict—the campaign against Al Qaeda and the civil war for the control of Afghanistan. A focused effort on the objective that truly activated American interests (Al Qaeda) was allowed to be diffused by increased attention to an aspect of the conflict that does not clearly represent American interests (the Taliban versus the government).

The two conflicts will also likely end differently for the United States. Neither is likely to conclude the way the United States would prefer—a democratic Iraq that is a beacon of moderation and stability and a stable, unified Afghanistan that provides no succor to regionally based violent extremists. The questions are how far each situation will end up diverging from these ideal outcomes, what the regional consequences of this divergence will be, and how Americans will react to and learn from those outcomes.

THE AFGHANISTAN WAR

What has become the American war effort in Afghanistan was the first direct American military response to 9/11. The connection between the two events was clear and unambiguous. The 9/11 attacks were devised and executed by the terrorist group Al Qaeda, whose headquarters and sanctuary were in Afghanistan under the protection of the Taliban-controlled government of that country. When the Taliban refused to relinquish the Al Qaeda leadership to the United States, the Bush administration began military action in October 2001, the month after 9/11.

At the beginning, the U.S. effort was highly focused and easily justifiable: the destruction of Al Qaeda by either killing or capturing those who were responsible for 9/11 and who might be planning additional attacks against the United States. Thus, American actions could be justified as defensive and necessary, in addition to providing retribution for the nearly 3,000 killed in New York, Washington, and the Pennsylvania countryside.

The problem would have been simply and painlessly resolved had the Afghan government arrested and turned the terrorists over to the United States as requested, but it did not. The Taliban (the root of which, *talib*, translates roughly as "student") and Al Qaeda had a long history dating back to the Afghan resistance to the Soviet occupation of the 1980s: many of the Pashtun tribesmen who formed the core of the Taliban had fought alongside foreign fighters (including Usama bin Laden) who formed the core of Al Qaeda. When bin Laden was evicted from Sudan in 1996, he moved to Afghanistan at the invitation of the then new Taliban regime.

The Taliban and Al Qaeda formed a bond that has endured and forms the basis of the most conspicuous contemporary difficulties the United States and its allies have in trying to extract Al Qaeda from the mountainous regions on both sides of the Afghanistan–Pakistan border. Although Al Qaeda is not universally revered in these regions, Pashtun tribesmen still protect them from—or at least do not expose them to—American attacks for three reasons. First, there is a sense of kindredness between many Pashtuns and Al Qaeda dating back to the 1980s resistance to the Soviets. Second, one of the pillars of the Pashtun code of behavior (known as *Pashtunwali*) is the honoring and protection of guests from outsiders. Third, the Taliban treat harshly any dissident Pashtuns who might violate the sanctuary relationship.

The unwillingness of the Taliban to relinquish Al Qaeda to U.S. control created a problem for the American government, which was under pressure, some of it self-inflicted, to bring the terrorists to justice. That problem was access to the terrorists. In the absence of Afghan cooperation, the only way the United States could pursue Al Qaeda was on its own with armed force. In turn, the determination to do so brought the United States into direct confrontation with the Taliban and into the middle of a civil war between the regime and its opponents, symbolized by an alliance of largely non-Pashtun tribesmen known as the Northern Alliance.

The clear and compelling American objective of dismantling the Al Qaeda terrorist threat thus became entangled with the most recent Afghan civil war (some form of civil unrest being endemic to the country), a conflict in which the United States had shown no interest prior to 9/11 other than expressing disdain for some of the more byzantine behavior of the Taliban regime toward its own citizens. Pursuing Al Qaeda, however, required overcoming Taliban opposition, and removing the Taliban from power was one way to achieve that goal.

This background is necessary to frame the evolution of American engagement in Afghanistan. Prior to 9/11, American interest in that country was indirect, very limited, and restrained by a lack of obvious U.S. interests in the country. During the 1980s, for instance, the United States supported the mujahidin resistance to the Soviet occupation (a resistance that was the spawning ground of both the Taliban and Al Qaeda). That support had virtually nothing to do with inherent American interests in the country but rather was motivated almost entirely by a desire to deny influence to the Soviet Union as part of the Cold War competition.

The presence of Al Qaeda created a U.S. interest in Afghanistan that had not previously existed and justified American military action in a war of necessity in a country wherein such necessity was otherwise unthinkable. That justifiable action, which was and continues to be unsuccessful in its original intent, enmeshed the United States in a civil war in which it had no previous interests. The slender tendril that held the two quite distinct bases for involvement together was opposition to the Taliban, not because the United States has any real interest in who rules Afghanistan but because one faction (the Taliban) makes pursuit of the real objective (Al Qaeda) harder. The actual fighting and killing, however, has gradually come to be directed at the Taliban, and thus the outcome of the civil war, rather than against the primary objective, Al Qaeda. President Obama as much as admitted this merger in his Cairo speech, referring to the enemy in Afghanistan as people who want to kill Americans, a term that can be extended to both groups.

The Road to War: Was the United States Justified?

Although the Taliban–Al Qaeda link complicates matters, an assessment of American involvement in Afghanistan must separate it into its two parts: the destruction of Al Qaeda and the outcome of the struggle for control of Afghanistan. The two aspects are of different importance: destroying Al Qaeda is a direct response to a vital, even survival, interest of the United States, while who rules Afghanistan is of relatively little importance to the United States beyond the question of whether the regime shields Al Qaeda from American attack. Put another way, the United States can live—and has lived—with any Afghan regime that does not protect Al Qaeda; any regime in Kabul that would vow not to protect the terrorists is probably acceptable to the United States. On the other hand, the Taliban provide a much more concrete and identifiable, if asymmetrical, opponent than does Al Qaeda.

The road to war in Afghanistan is entirely straightforward as a response to 9/11. Certainly, the United States had some interests in the country prior to the 9/11 attacks because it was the known Al Qaeda sanctuary and American anti-Taliban covert operations had undoubtedly been carried out in Afghanistan. The American foot was thus at least partly in the Afghan door before 9/11; the terrorist attacks caused that door to be kicked down.

Some confrontation between the two countries had been brewing ever since the Al Qaeda terrorists arrived in Afghanistan and took up residence in training camps originally developed (with some CIA assistance) to train mujahidin to resist the Soviets. These facilities were used to train and dispatch terrorists to carry out a series of missions against American targets (the American embassies in Dar es Salaam, Tanzania, and Nairobi, Kenya, in 1998 and the USS Cole in a Yemeni port in 2000, for instance) and had even resulted in a cruise missile attack against a site thought to be inhabited by bin Laden in 1998. Thus, Afghanistan and Al Qaeda were well on the American radar at the time of 9/11. Doing something decisive about them became the prime national priority after the attacks on the American homeland.

The problem would have been conceptually and physically simple had the Taliban acquiesced in American demands to relinquish the terrorists. In that case, the real objective of American policy would have been realized, the terrorist threat associated with Al Qaeda would have been eliminated, and the United States could have rested secure in knowing that effective retribution had been exacted. Although some might disagree on this point, in all likelihood the United States would also have been willing to leave the Taliban in power as part of any agreement by which the Al Qaeda leadership was turned over to the Americans. That, of course, did not happen for reasons already discussed. At the same time, had the operations undertaken to capture bin Laden and his associates in the Tora Bora mountains along the Afghanistan–Pakistan border to which they fled when the United States initially intervened been successful, the U.S. objective would have been accomplished without the need to remain.

Since neither of those conditions occurred, the United States was left with the question of what to do. To answer the question raised in the section heading, there is little question whether the United States was fully justified in its original purpose of going after Al Qaeda, and an impressive international coalition lined up in support of American action. For a time, world opinion stood solidly behind the United States and whatever it sought to do in response to the 9/11 attacks. The problem was that once the members of Al Qaeda had eluded the American dragnet and snuck across the border into Pakistan (although their exact location was unknown at the time), there was little direct way to attack the primary opponent, and the war shifted its center of gravity to the competition between the Taliban and the Northern Alliance. American interest in the outcome of that conflict, as noted, was indirect. The United States opposed the Taliban regime because of its failure to honor American requests about Al Qaeda, but beyond that, it is not at all clear the United States had any particular interest in aiding the overthrow of the regime and its replacement with an alternative.

That is, however, exactly what happened. American direct military involvement in pushing the Northern Alliance over the top in its military efforts against the Taliban was limited to supplying the insurgents, trying to smooth over differences among the factions, and providing air attacks against Taliban forces (using U.S. and British special forces as spotters to help direct the attacks). At the time, there was no public pronouncement that the primary emphasis on the ground against Al Qaeda had shifted to the Taliban, but that is what occurred. In November 2001, the Taliban was defeated, and in December 2001, a Northern Alliance government headed by Hamid Karzai (who was himself a Pashtun warlord, but one who had opposed the Taliban) came to power. In January 2002, the first contingents of international peacekeepers entered the country, and in May 2002, the United Nations extended the mission of the International Security Assistance Force (ISAF) to December 2002. Among the major purposes of the ISAF, which remains the official sponsor of ongoing efforts (although largely with NATO forces assisting the United States), was to keep the Taliban from returning to power. At the time, it was generally believed that the actions of late 2001 had destroyed the Taliban. In fact, the remnants of the Taliban retreated to remote Pashtun regions of Afghanistan and the Federally Administered Tribal Areas (FATA) of Pakistan, which are largely controlled by the Pashtuns. This sanctuary allowed the Taliban to regenerate, and they began to return to Afghanistan to renew the competition for control in 2003.

Was the United States justified in its efforts in Afghanistan? The question really has two distinct parts. One is whether the United States was justified in employing armed forces to destroy Al Qaeda. Given the recalcitrance of the Taliban regime in acceding to the U.S. demand to relinquish the perpetrators of 9/11, the answer is overwhelmingly positive and is reflected by the international support the United States received for its efforts. Support for destroying Al Qaeda has been consistent and strong throughout U.S. military involvement in Afghanistan, and the basis of most American support for the ongoing effort is the belief that this remains the principal goal. Opposition that has arisen largely since 2008 has tended to have as its origin a belief either that the mission is unattainable or that the real focus has moved away from the original objective.

The other part of the question is whether the United States is justified in its efforts to maintain an anti-Taliban government in control in Kabul. This question is much more controversial. The positive answer is derived mainly from the conjunction of Al Qaeda and the Taliban and tends to treat the two entities as the same. Thus, the Taliban must be defeated in order to strip away the shield behind which Al Qaeda hides. The negative answer is that the United States has little other interest in who wins a tribally based civil war in a country with no tradition of strong central governance in which the United States effectively finds itself opposing the country's majority tribal faction (the Pashtun) and which has spread over into and destabilized Pakistan, a country in which the United States does have distinct, strong national interests. Moreover, the ability to accomplish the goal of positively affecting the outcome of the civil war in Afghanistan is open to direct question. The question of justifiability is thus not a simple one to answer.

Was the Mission Feasible?

Unless one believes in the virtue of quixotic quests, it is necessary to ask whether the missions that the United States has set out for itself are attainable. The fact that the United States has been enmeshed in Afghanistan for over eight years with no obviously positive outcome in sight suggests, at a minimum, that the mission is not easily achievable. Unraveling the question of feasibility, however, requires looking both at the two parts of the objective already identified and at the mission from both political and military perspectives.

The Political Objective. Although the U.S. government does not distinguish clearly between political goals for what are in fact its two distinct missions, they must be separated and viewed individually, both because they project different outcomes of the effort and because they are of considerably varying feasibility.

There is a critical link between the two objectives, and that is the Pashtuns. The Pashtuns are, as noted, the largest ethnic group in Afghanistan (at one point they were a majority, but migration has left them with a plurality of about 40 percent of the population) and the second largest group in Pakistan. In some quarters, the term *Pashtun* (or its variations) is considered synonymous with Afghans. Moreover, their tribal lands lap over the Afghanistan–Pakistan border (the so-called Durand line after the nineteenth-century British diplomat who drew it), which the Pashtuns do not honor. "Pashtunistan," as it is sometimes known, encompasses the rugged, forbidding landscape that protects both the Taliban and their Al Qaeda guests and is territory that has historically been only nominally controlled by governments in Kabul and Islamabad. Moreover, the Taliban are almost exclusively Pashtun, although the majority of Pashtuns do not support them, and it is the Pashtun code of honor behind which Al Qaeda hides. For all these reasons, the Pashtuns hold the key to the accomplishment of either goal—destroying Al Qaeda or preventing a Taliban government in Kabul—that the United States seeks to accomplish.

For the United States to succeed, it must have the support, or at least the lack of opposition, of the Pashtuns, a realization that is occasionally made implicitly. This recognition comes in the form of initiatives to try to split so-called moderate supporters of the Taliban (if such exist) away from the radical Islamist movement. While it is unlikely that actual Taliban can be redirected in any meaningful way, what this may mean is that an attempt can be made to influence non-Taliban Pashtuns into opposition to the Taliban cause. The purpose of such conversion would be to deny the Taliban and Al Qaeda untrammeled domain over the tribal regions, thereby facilitating efforts to pursue either Al Qaeda or the Taliban.

Is such a strategy feasible? Once again, it probably depends on which political objective is being pursued. There has been some survey evidence, for instance, that many Pashtun tribesmen are disaffected with Al Qaeda, both because they are foreigners (the Afghans have always been highly suspicious of outsiders) and because they disapprove of Al Qaeda terrorism. The question then becomes how the United States or the government of Afghanistan makes an appeal to those apparently dissident Pashtuns so that they will cooperate in apprehending Al Qaeda.

The most obvious way to attempt such a conversion would seem to be for the government in Kabul to wrest loyalty from the Taliban to itself. There are, however, at least three difficulties in doing so. One is that the government is associated with Kabul, and there has always been a deep rift between the political elite in Kabul and the countryside (since the majority of Afghans are not urban dwellers, the result has historically been a weak central government), in which most Pashtuns live. Moreover, they view those who, like Karzai, have become urbanized citizens as tainted. Second, the current regime may be headed by a Pashtun (Karzai), but its support base and its military leadership are largely non-Pashtun, including heavy participation by ethnic Tajiks, who are the principal rivals of the Pashtuns. This non-Pashtun character of the current regime adds to the appeal of the Taliban. Alleged Tajik domination of the military is a particular point of contention among Pashtuns. Third, the Afghan government is among the most corrupt in the world, and its world-class venality has alienated it from large parts of the population, a problem Karzai refuses fully to acknowledge or confront. General Stanley McChrystal, American military commander in Afghanistan, acknowledged the need for "good government," which means legitimate, honest governance, as a condition for U.S. success in his Commander's Assessment of the war on August 30, 2009 calling for additional U.S. troops.

All of this suggests that a process of converting the Pashtuns (and other Afghans who currently do not support the Karzai regime) is going to be difficult, and it is not at all clear what the United States can do to bring it about. Once again, the problem is formidable if directed at either objective, but it is especially difficult when dealing with the civil war. If the goal is to create a political situation wherein whoever rules Afghanistan does not provide aid and succor to Al Qaeda, however, the barriers are somewhat less formidable than if the goal is assuring a government in the country that is both anti-Taliban and anti–Al Qaeda.

Pursuit of the original goal of eradicating Al Qaeda requires negotiating with whichever faction prevails in the civil war to agree not to provide sanctuary to

Al Qaeda, and this is, at least in principle, a goal that can be discussed with either a Taliban- or a non-Taliban-dominated regime. Clearly, it would be easier to deal with the current regime or with one that succeeds it but that is also anti-Taliban, but such a government likely would supply the willingness but not the ability to aid in eradicating Al Qaeda unless conditions change radically. A Taliban-run or -influenced government, on the other hand, would likely be more difficult to negotiate with because of the war that has been waged against it by the United States and others and because of its relationship with Al Qaeda. Since the sanctuary Al Qaeda enjoys requires the cooperation of Pashtuns, however, a Taliban government would probably be better able to isolate Al Qaeda by withdrawing support for it. There is no present indication the United States has devised an effective way to drive a wedge between the Taliban and Al Qaeda, but the prospect is at least hypothetically possible.

The goal of "winning" the civil war by defeating the Taliban is clearly more desirable but less obtainable. It is more desirable because an Afghanistan in which Taliban influence is removed would almost certainly be more cooperative in the pursuit of Al Qaeda than would any Taliban regime (especially if such a regime could cooperate with the Pakistanis in the effort to destroy Al Qaeda). That result is, however, arguably much less feasible, partly for reasons already discussed. The real key, of course, is finding some way to incorporate the Pashtuns into a much larger role in governing Afghanistan. This, in turn, requires a process of political conversion that the military situation makes very difficult.

The Military Objective. The accomplishment of either political objective, but especially the triumph of the government in the civil war, requires a level of control of the Afghan countryside that the government sorely lacks. Even with considerable ISAF military activity, the government securely controls very little territory outside the Kabul region, and such control is crucial to any effective form of counterinsurgency in the area. Put very simply, it would be foolhardy for Afghans to change allegiance to the government in areas that the government does not control and in which their security from hostile retaliation from the Taliban cannot be assured. The Afghan National Army (ANA) is incapable of providing that security, and although it is a primary goal of the augmented U.S. plan for Afghanistan to increase their capability, no one expects it to achieve that capacity in the near future.

That leaves the United States and its ISAF allies (whose numbers are dwindling as states remove themselves from the conflict) in the possibly impossible position of providing the security shield behind which a policy of political conversion by the Afghan government can proceed. The weakness of the government makes such an effort problematical in the best of circumstances, but it is further compromised by two other dynamics. First, there are simply not enough foreign troops available to secure any large part of a country the size of Afghanistan. The quality of security necessary for citizens to develop enough of a sense of safety to convert requires the virtual constant presence of forces to prevent Taliban disruptive efforts, and the size of forces available is simply inadequate for that task. General Shinseki's estimate of the 300,000 necessary for the occupation of Iraq may be a benchmark for Afghanistan. Second, it is not clear, as suggested in the last chapter, that this kind of process of security and conversion can be provided by outsiders, who will always be viewed with some suspicion by some natives of the country. Particularly if the political end result is the defeat of the Taliban in the civil war, it is probably necessary that the instrument of that defeat be Afghan forces.

The American military's answer to this part of the problem is the rapid expansion of the Afghan National Security Forces (ANSF, composed of the army and police) to take over the role of securing and holding territory currently being contested by foreign troops. The reasons are twofold. One is that the ultimate reconciliation of the Afghan people and their government can only by accomplished by the Afghans themselves, not by foreign surrogates. The second is the realization that American and other public opinion will not tolerate an indefinite occupation of Afghanistan, meaning the buildup of the ANSF is necessary to allow the Americans and their allies to leave. The linchpin of the viability of this solution is whether a viable ANSF is possible, which remained an open question.

What Went Wrong and Why?

How did the United States get itself into the difficult position in which it finds itself in a conflict with such an apparently righteous beginning? While the war effort has been ongoing for nine years, the answers to that question really go back to the earliest stages of the conflict in terms of what the United States both did and did not do to accomplish its changing objectives in Afghanistan.

The Afghan effort has been most prominently criticized, as in statements made forcibly by candidate Obama during the 2008 presidential campaign, for our "taking our eye off the ball" in Afghanistan by diverting American attention and resources to the mounting effort in Iraq. Although it is not entirely clear that focusing attention on Afghanistan would have yielded a significantly different result than the one that faces the United States, the criticism nonetheless has merit.

The charge of diverted attention has three major bases. The first is that the initial military effort to capture and destroy Al Qaeda suffered from a lack of adequate military resources because military assets that might have been used against the terrorists before they escaped Afghanistan into Pakistan were withheld as part of the buildup for Iraq. The gist of this argument is that, had more American military force been brought to bear in places like the cave networks in the Tora Bora mountains where the terrorists were hiding after October 2001, they might not have slipped through the tightening grasp of symbolically named Operation Anaconda. Since more force was not used and the escape occurred, this criticism can be made and supported; since that extra force was not applied, however, it is counterfactual to argue it would have been decisive. This is a point on which disagreement will always exist.

The second argument is that the United States complicated matters by shifting its objective from capturing Al Qaeda to propping up the Karzai government after the unsuccessful attempt to eradicate Al Qaeda and that the result has been a different, less important, and ultimately less attainable set of objectives for the United States in the country. The evidence used to support the added difficulty and consequences comes at least partially from the third alleged basis of mistakes.

The third allegation is that the United States made matters worse in Afghanistan by essentially reneging on promises to the Karzai government to provide significant economic and other assistance after Karzai came to power that would have allowed him to stabilize the country. In fact, the U.S. government did initially promise a multi-billion-dollar aid package, most of which was never appropriated, meaning that assistance in recovering from the damage created by the effort to overthrow the Taliban in 2001 never entered the Afghan economy. The result was that support for the new regime that might have been created by a growing prosperity, and thus a stake in support for the regime, never materialized. One can, of course, argue that the extremely corrupt nature of Afghan politics is such that even the most generous aid package would have been frittered away or stolen by venal politicians, but the fact remains that the United States did not live up to the rhetorical commitments it made to Afghanistan in late 2001 and 2002. It has also been argued in some quarters that the lack of American aid contributed to the regime's instability and corruption, since the regime was so poor that it had to turn to nefarious methods simply to survive (there are, for instance, reports of Afghan cabinet ministers who moonlighted driving taxis in Kabul because they did not receive their salaries from the government). The diversion of funding for the war in Iraq is normally blamed for this initial failure, and the growing costs of prosecuting the war in Iraq meant that requests for money to aid the Karzai government have been extremely scarce ever since.

These criticisms of the Afghanistan effort adhere primarily to the goal of influencing the outcome of the ongoing civil war in Afghanistan. One can argue that the United States has *acted* as if it has no real stake in the outcome of that contest by its treatment of the Karzai government, but the rhetoric and rationale for American presence have operated from the assumption that avoiding a Taliban takeover and suppressing Al Qaeda are necessary partners as objectives. Once again, the validity of that association is premised on the assertion that the United States cannot work out a bargain with a new Taliban regime that would include its cooperation in the campaign against Al Qaeda. The previous experience in 2001 offers evidence for this presumption, but the proposed strategy of trying to convert "moderate" Taliban suggests it is not universally accepted.

The result, of course, is a deepening confusion that becomes more important as American attention and resources move from the winding down of the effort in Iraq into Afghanistan. The United States has already been in Afghanistan longer than it has been in Iraq, although the scope and costs have until now been much more modest. As the focus shifts, questions about what the United States hopes to accomplish in Afghanistan will undoubtedly increase. Is Afghanistan worth it?

Afghanistan as a War of Necessity

Public opinion has not until recently turned decisively against the Afghanistan War in the way that it has against the Iraq War. Part of the explanation has to be that the Afghan campaign has been much more muted, in terms of both the amount of American suffering and the level of publicity that the war has attracted. Both of these factors have changed as Afghanistan has become more of a focal point of U.S. foreign and military policy and the American commitment there have become relatively more prominent. At the same time, however, there is a sense of necessity about the United States being in Afghanistan that evaporated in Iraq with revelations that the original rationales for that war were false.

The linchpin of the basis for American participation in Afghanistan is, of course, the pursuit of terrorists (or, in Obama administration language, violent extremists) represented by Al Qaeda. Bin Laden and his associates have demonstrated that they can pose a very real threat against the United States in a very direct sense, and they could and almost certainly may pose a future threat unless they are effectively countered. Criticisms of the American action have centered on the execution of this mission, not on whether it is necessary for American national security. As such, the continuing future menace of Al Qaeda makes the war in Afghanistan a war of necessity for the United States.

When one separates the war effort into its two constituent parts, however, that claim of necessity is diluted and the situation is once again muddied. The objective of eradicating Al Qaeda is necessary, but it is not crystalline that pursuit of that objective is what American service members are fighting over. Rather, it has been the bulk of the argument here that the real impact of the American effort has been directed against the Taliban in their quest to regain control of Afghanistan, an outcome that in itself may not be necessary to the United States. The connection that can elevate saving the Afghan government to the status of necessity has to be that the absence of doing so will make the necessary goal of defeating Al Qaeda more difficult or impossible. If that is true (and its truth or falsity are debatable), then the mission the United States is actually engaged in can be argued as a deployment of necessity. If, on the other hand, the net effect of that action is simply to try to prop up the current Afghan regime and doing so does not measurably contribute to defeating Al Qaeda, then the actual mission quite possibly qualifies as a war of choice, not necessity.

The evidence for what kind of war is being waged in fact is not clear. The direct combat in which the United States is engaged is in Afghanistan, where the Taliban are actively fighting to overthrow the government but where Al Qaeda presence is rarely asserted (indeed, the American government estimated in late 2009 that as few as 100 Al Qaeda operatives may be active in Afghanistgan). The only action directed against Al Qaeda has been in the form of controversial air raids against suspected terrorist hideouts in Pakistan. Because these attacks have been fiercely opposed by Pakistan (on the grounds of intrusion into sovereign territory) and have created enough "collateral damage" in attacked areas (alleged civilian deaths), the Obama administration has been under considerable pressure to suspend them. If these direct attacks are indeed ceased, then the only direct connection between American military action and the goal that creates its necessity is the extrapolation of the defeat of the Taliban to the campaign against Al Qaeda. Whether this connection will continue to be adequate in the public mind will depend, to some degree, on the outcome of the war in Afghanistan.

How Will the Afghanistan War End?

This question cannot, of course, be answered with any certainty as long as fighting continues and the situation remains fluid. During the period between 2003, when the Taliban returned to the country, and 2008, when a change in American leadership signaled a shift in priorities away from Iraq and to Afghanistan, the situation had not been going well from an American vantage point, an argument Obama made repeatedly to bolster his reorientation of policy. The Taliban had gradually been increasing their control over larger parts of Afghanistan—even menacing the approaches to Kabul—and the United States was making little visible progress toward defeating Al Qaeda. Since his election, Obama has both increased American troop strength in Afghanistan and raised it as a priority. In the process, the prospect that the war will spread into Pakistan has also been increased.

Will the new American gambit succeed in producing a favorable outcome in Afghanistan? The new administration has admitted that the campaign will be, in Rumsfeldian terms, a "long slog" that will not end soon, and the outcome is uncertain. Obama, in turn, has faced criticism that is almost certain to continue that the effort is futile and should be terminated, an outcome many of his supporters expected him to implement based on the 2008 campaign.

There are, of course, three possible outcomes, two of which seem unlikely in this particular instance of modern asymmetrical warfare. The two unlikely outcomes are the extremes: a clear and unambiguous military victory or defeat for the United States or its adversaries. A clear-cut defeat of American forces is beyond the capacity of the insurgent forces the United States faces. Insurgent forces lack the wherewithal to administer the kind of decisive defeat that can force the Americans from the field. The best they can hope for is to persevere longer than the Americans—to exceed their cost-tolerance—in which case the United States will simply withdraw, as it did in Vietnam and may be doing in Iraq (see below). At the same time, it is probably equally unlikely that the United States will be able to decisively destroy either the Taliban or Al Qaeda as long as those adversaries adhere to an asymmetrical approach to the war.

The elimination of those possibilities leaves the third option, which is an outcome in between the extremes of defeat or victory for either side. The dynamics of such an outcome can vary considerably, from a virtual defeat of one side or the other in the civil war to the continuation of the contest more or less indefinitely. The history of Afghanistan suggests that the retention of power by the Karzai government or the return to power of the Taliban could be transitory, since the country lacks any real tradition of stable, enduring central rule. If the United States realizes this, then its strategy (implicit in what it is currently doing) may be simply to try to bolster the government to the extent it can through greater preparation of the ANA and then declare it has done what it can and begin withdrawal. This in essence is what the United States did in Vietnam and is doing in Iraq; "Afghanization" may be the only course there as well.

The situation is somewhat more complicated if the United States focuses on its primary objective, the defeat of Al Qaeda. Given the physical nature of the problem,

Amplification 12.1

AFGHANISTAN, PAKISTAN, AND AL QAEDA

The longer the war in Afghanistan continues, the more apparent it becomes that the major objective of the war effort, destroying Al Qaeda, cannot occur there because Al Qaeda is located in Pakistan. As a result, the contribution of the actual fighting in Afghanistan to the campaign against Al Qaeda is effectively limited to keeping Al Qaeda in Pakistan, where they are outside the reach of the American military effort.

The only way to direct military pressure onto Al Qaeda is thus to attack them in Pakistan or cause the Pakistanis to do so themselves. The current Pakistan government has taken some measures in this direction, but it is not well prepared to fight in the mountainous retreats where Al Qaeda resides and faces considerable opposition from its own people in doing so. Moreover, Pakistani actions have caused Al Qaeda and the Taliban to widen their efforts into Pakistan, further threatening to destabilize the already fragile situation in Pakistan. This prospect is all the more disturbing because it raises the possibility that Pakistani nuclear weapons might fall into the hands of the Taliban and Al Qaeda, which has always been the worst nightmare the United States faces with the terrorists. It is not at all clear how to navigate and resolve this dilemma.

a resolution of this necessary objective requires the cooperation of *both* the Afghan and the Pakistan governments and their forces with the United States, since attacking Al Qaeda in one country simply sends them scurrying into the other if there is not joint action. As noted in the last chapter, the Pakistani armed forces are not well configured or predisposed to such cooperation and such a mission, and, as Amplification 12.1 suggests, the expansion may produce worse outcomes than the continued existence of Al Qaeda in the country. In turn, the United States must ask itself which is worse, a continued Al Qaeda threat or a potentially destabilized nuclear Pakistan.

THE IRAQ WAR

Prior to 1990, most Americans had barely heard of the Middle Eastern country of Iraq, let alone know who its leader was or what relationship the United States had with that country. Then, in August 1990, Iraq invaded neighboring Kuwait, thereby imperiling the access of the United States and others to the region's primary commodity, petroleum. Suddenly, the United States took the global leadership in evicting Iraqi dictator Saddam Hussein from Kuwait under the banner of Operation Desert Shield/Storm, leading to the brief and highly successful Persian Gulf War of 1990–1991. Equally suddenly, all Americans knew about Iraq and Saddam Hussein.

The Persian Gulf War did not end to the satisfaction of all observers. The coalition formed to reverse Saddam Hussein's aggression fulfilled its United Nations mandate to restore the status quo ante, which meant evicting Iraq from Kuwait and restoring Kuwaiti sovereignty. The Hussein government, however, remained intact and unrepentant, and this fact troubled some observers, including a group who became known as the *neoconservatives* (or neocons, for short) who had advocated his overthrow for years before his action in Kuwait. In the eyes of some (but not all) observers, the Iraq War of 2003 was born of the decision not to overthrow Hussein in 1991.

The Iraqi situation remained contentious but less than critical between 1991 and the terrorist attacks of 2001. The neoconservatives (e.g., Richard Perle, Paul Wolfowitz, and Douglas Feith), who had argued volubly for going ahead and marching into Baghdad in 1991 and toppling the Iraqi regime, left power with the election of Democrat William J. Clinton in 1992. Iraq never left the public agenda altogether, as the United States, Great Britain, and (for a time) France maintained a "no-fly zone" over much of northern and southern Iraq to keep the Hussein regime from wreaking revenge on Kurdish and Shiite groups that had engaged in a 1991 plot (encouraged informally by the United States) to overthrow the regime. Operation Provide Comfort (renamed Northern Watch) and Southern Watch put the United States at odds with the Iraqi regime, resulting in numerous incidents of the Iraqis attempting to shoot down allied reconnaissance aircraft. In addition, President Clinton authorized a limited bombing campaign against Iraq in 1998 (Operation Desert Fox). Policy toward Iraq was part of the broader regional policy of *dual containment*, aimed at containing the ambitions of both Iraq and Iran. When George W. Bush was elected the forty-third president of the United States in 2000, Iraq policy was once again on the table, leading to the Iraq War.

The Road to War: Was the United States Justified?

The election of George W. Bush was critical to the road to war in three ways. First, Bush himself had become convinced that Saddam Hussein needed to be overthrown. In December 1997, he had given an interview to a San Antonio newspaper in which he argued that his father had been correct in not taking the Iraqi regime down because the result would have been a "civil war." By 1999, he had changed his mind, hinting broadly in a December speech at the Ronald Reagan library that he favored "regime change" (the early euphemism for overthrowing Saddam Hussein). As Bush prepared for the 2000 election campaign, Wolfowitz, who would later be christened the "father" of the Iraq War, was one of his closest foreign policy advisors. Even before September 11, war against Iraq was not far from the center of the foreign policy agenda. Haass, for instance, reports that then National Security Advisor Condoleezza Rice told him the decision had been made as early as April 2001.

Second, the election of Bush brought the neoconservatives into key policy positions. Supported by figures like Vice President Richard Cheney and Secretary of Defense Donald Rumsfeld, a number of advisors like Wolfowitz found their way back into government in more powerful and influential positions than they had previously held under Bush's father. Among their major agenda items were overthrowing Saddam Hussein and replacing his regime with a "model" democracy in Iraq and guaranteeing the security of Israel. The two policies were linked by the belief that the flowering of democracy in Iraq would result in demands in other Middle Eastern countries for democratization, which, in turn, would produce more peaceful regional regimes that would be less hostile to Israel.

The third event, of course, was the terrorist attacks of September 11. Their direct ties to activating plans for attacking Iraq are disputed, and many observers such as Clarke and Woodward maintain that one of the first post–September 11 queries by President Bush was for evidence of Iraqi complicity. The Bush administration denies this assertion, but as Chandrasekaran (among others) maintains, Bush "gave the order to begin planning for the invasion of Iraq just a few months after the September 11, 2001, attacks." This claim is widely accepted by others (see Gordon and Trainor, Packer, Record, Ricks, and Woodward, for instance) and is obliquely admitted by the commander of the operation, General Tommy Franks, in his autobiography. At a minimum, the September 11 tragedy brought to the fore the possible ties of Iraq to terrorists, although the relationship was likely instrumental (9/11 as an excuse to invade Iraq).

The rising justification for an invasion of Iraq was thus the result of a pastiche of motivations that were gradually tied together. Bush himself had virtually no experience in foreign affairs and no known expertise on the Middle East, but he disliked Saddam Hussein because the latter allegedly authorized an assassination attempt in 1993 against Bush's father (on a visit to Kuwait) and because Bush had apparently been influenced by advisors who favored the overthrow. As a result, Iraq was included in the "axis of evil" designation (along with the Democratic People's Republic of Korea and Iran) in Bush's January 2002 State of the Union address. The resulting demonization of the regime was completed by allegations of ties between the Iraqis and Al Qaeda (although not Al Qaeda in Iraq, which did not come into existence until 2004). This confluence provided the fuel needed by the neoconservatives to press the case successfully for what they had wanted to do all along—overthrow Saddam Hussein.

Were the invasion, conquest, and occupation of Iraq justified? In other words, should the United States have done what it did? In the debate that has surrounded the prosecution of the war, this question has largely been submerged on the basis that the *real* problem is what to do now. The imputation is that whether the effort was justifiable in the first place is academic, since the United States is engaged and must figure out how to make the best of the situation.

Whether the United States should have gone into Iraq in the first place is, however, critical in determining what can be learned from the experience. Comparisons with Vietnam are tempting. In retrospect, most observers would agree that American participation in the Vietnam War was unwarranted and that the country would have been better off had it abstained. The basic retrospective argument is that American vital interests were never engaged in Vietnam, and the evidence is that the worst-case outcome, the North Vietnamese uniting of the country, occurred and the United States was not especially affected fundamentally by that outcome.

If anything, all the involvement did was to prolong the war and cause enormous suffering for the Vietnamese and for the Americans, simply delaying an outcome that would have occurred much more rapidly and with much less bloodshed had the United States not intervened. Moreover, the erosive effects on the United States that participation in the eight-year-long war caused would have been avoided. It is hard to argue that the United States would not have been better off if the country had never intervened in Vietnam.

The situation in Iraq, of course, was not the same as that in Vietnam. In Vietnam, there was an ongoing conflict (whether it was an internal civil war or a war between sovereign countries—North and South Vietnam—was disputed) that the United States sought to influence. In Iraq, there was undoubtedly great privation and injustice, but there was no war until the United States started it by invading. That said, the question remains whether the United States should have taken the action it did. Like Vietnam, that is a two-part question that is a matter of perspective. The parts include whether the case for invasion was adequate at the time and whether it appears to have been justifiable in retrospect. People can reasonably disagree, depending on the perspectives from which they come and based on the determination of facts not as clear at the time as they became later.

Vietnam was justified largely in terms of the spread of Communism and specifically the so-called domino effect, which argued that if Vietnam fell to Communism, other neighbors would follow like rows of dominos being toppled. This assessment proved correct but largely irrelevant, since the companion assumption that U.S. interests would be vitally affected by the dominos falling proved false—something not entirely knowable at the time initial decisions were made. The decision to invade Iraq was based officially on arguments already mentioned: Saddam Hussein's purported possession of weapons of mass destruction (WMD) and his intransigence in the face of international inspectors of the country; his alleged ties to terrorism, thus tying the Iraqi regime to the GWOT; and, more nebulously, the desirability of instituting a model democracy in Iraq that would serve as a regional beacon.

Two questions must be raised about these justifications for invading Iraq. First, were they accurate (and should those who made the allegations have known if they were not)? In the acrimony over Iraq, it has been generally established that the Iraqis did not have WMD (none has ever been found) and that there were no ties to Al Qaeda (in fact, the secular Hussein regime opposed the religious terrorism associated with Al Qaeda). One can debate the desirability of democratizing Iraq, although the question of whether this was ever feasible remains contentious. The question of whether those who made the decision did or should have known the truth of their justifications also remains contentious; there were, however, numerous critics in and out of government who denied both the principal reasons were true. Whether there were other, hidden reasons also remains a matter of disagreement, discussed in Amplification 12.2.

The second question is whether these justifications, even if true, constituted sufficient grounds to undertake the actions that were carried out. This question largely pits the traditional realists against the neoconservatives and centers on the question of vital interests. Would the worst possible outcome of the situation in Iraq (possession of

Amplification 12.2

HIDDEN AGENDAS IN IRAQ?

The war in Iraq has fueled speculation about whether the stated objectives of the United States were the *actual* reasons for the war or whether there were other, more subterranean motivations. Such speculation was stimulated by judgments that the stated objectives did not justify the options chosen, so that there *must* have been deeper, but not publicly stated, reasons. In Iraq, two alternate objectives have been put forward (and denied by those in decision-making positions): petroleum and Israeli security.

The argument about petroleum is straightforward and is believed by many Iraqis. Proponents of this argument maintain the real underlying motivation of the United States is control of the considerable Iraqi oil reserves through the overthrow of the Saddam Hussein regime and its replacement with a compliant Iraqi regime that would guarantee the United States secure access to Persian Gulf petroleum at a reasonable price—and thus help to free the United States of its dependence on a fickle ally, Saudi Arabia. As Record puts it, "The creation of an American client state in Iraq would, it was believed, provide a substitute for a U.S.-Saudi security relationship compromised by Saudi promotion of Islamic extremism," a reference to Saudi Arabia's reluctance to suppress known anti-American, pro–Al Qaeda supporters. Indeed, a rumor circulated in the Pentagon before Operation Iraqi Freedom (OIF, the code name for the invasion) began that planners had initially favored calling the mission Operation Iraqi Liberation before someone pointed out the potentially embarrassing acronym (OIL) the name would create.

The other argument is that the real underlying reason for the invasion was to ensure Israeli security in the region. This argument is consistent with the general neoconservative belief that American and Israeli interests and security in the region are closely intertwined—if not synonymous—and that the requisite for Israeli security is a reduction of animosity toward Israel among the Islamic states of the region. Extrapolating from this premise and adding the *democratic peace hypothesis* (that democratic states do not attack one another), it then follows that the installation of a model democratic regime in Iraq (which would be envied and emulated by its neighbors) is a necessary and important first step toward securing Israeli security and thus a more tranquil Middle East (which, incidentally, would be more amenable to guaranteeing American access to the region's petroleum). In addition, Record argues, "a benign Iraq...would redound to the immense strategic benefit of Israel, America's chief client state in the Middle East and a major focus of neoconservative security strategy."

WMD, ties to terrorists, possible collaboration with terrorists on WMD) create a situation so intolerable that force was necessary to bring about a tolerable outcome? The answer varied, depending on the perspective from which the analyst comes.

From the neoconservative position, the question was irrelevant: the goal of creating a new Middle East reality was so compelling that traditional concerns based in vital interests did not apply. Indeed, one administration aide, in response to a question on the subject of the relevance of realism to the situation, allegedly replied, "We make our own realities." From the other side of the ledger, traditional realists answered the vital interest question negatively, arguing that the policy of dual containment had effectively managed relations with Iraq and that the prospect that Iraq would supply terrorists with WMD that might ultimately be used against the United States was theoretically possible but too remote to justify the strong measures taken. The subsequent revelations that both the WMD and the terrorism arguments were based on false assertions only added to this criticism.

Was the Mission Feasible?

The other major prewar question was whether the objectives the United States laid out for itself in Iraq were attainable. If the Iraq mission was in fact impossible to achieve, was that assessment known or knowable when the decision was made? Answering it requires examination from both a political and a military standpoint, with implicit comparisons to the parallel process in Vietnam.

The Political Objective. Whether the political objective in Iraq was feasible depends on what that objective was. If the purpose was the overthrow and removal from power of Saddam Hussein—which was certainly at least an instrumental goal necessary before others could be attained—or the removal of non-existent Iraqi WMD, then it was clearly attainable, if arguably bogus. But what else did the United States hope to achieve?

The other public explanation for American action was the neoconservative goal of democracy promotion. If one accepts that the real political objective in Iraq was to transform that country into a model democratic, free-enterprise country, then the question of feasibility arises. As virtually anyone who has ever studied Iraq knows, it is an almost totally artificial state—a country with no historical, linguistic, religious, or other reason for being in its present configuration—with enormously deep rifts within the population that virtually guarantee its instability. The familiar divisions within the population (Arabs versus Kurds, Sunnis versus Shiites, for instance) were widely known in an expert community that almost universally regarded Iraq as one of the worst places on Earth in which to try to create a political democracy. Moreover, most of the economy was state-owned, and transforming it into a kind of American-model free-enterprise status (also part of the neoconservative dream) was a daunting physical and legal proposition.

Was this perspective known and available to the Bush administration when it reached the decision to invade Iraq (regardless of exactly when that determination was made)? The answer is yes. More specifically, *all of the problems associated with Iraq that later became obvious after the occupation began were known in advance of the invasion, and they were ignored.* That is a harsh indictment, but it is one supported overwhelmingly by the evidence. On the eve of the war, Deputy Secretary of Defense Paul D. Wolfowitz was so bold as to tell a congressional committee that invading Iraq would be much easier than dealing with Afghanistan because there were *no ethnic divisions* in

Iraq. As plans for the occupation were being made and implemented, so-called Arabists (people with knowledge and experience in the area) were consciously excluded from the process because their experience allegedly prejudiced them against the goal of democratization (this allegation is confirmed by virtually all the sources listed in the "Selected Bibliography"). To cite an example of this ignorance, Chandrasekaran raises the case of one U.S. official sent to Baghdad as part of the occupation, Thomas Foley, an investment banker and classmate of President Bush at Harvard Business School. Foley's mission was to privatize the Iraqi economy, which meant expropriating state-owned enterprises and selling them to private investors. Under the Geneva Conventions of War (1899), such expropriations by an occupying power are illegal under international law. When informed of this fact, Foley allegedly replied, "I don't give a s--- about international law. I made a commitment to the president that I'd privatize Iraq's businesses."

There was thus considerable sentiment within the academic and policy-examining communities that an attempt to democratize Iraq faced, at a minimum, an uphill fight. Larry Diamond, who was a pro-democracy scholar and former colleague of Condoleezza Rice at Stanford University and who became a part of the administration's attempt to institute democracy, provides a particularly detailed account of the problems encountered. Moreover, the president himself had, as noted, correctly predicted that overthrowing Hussein would result in a civil war, an assessment also made by the State Department and concurred in by the Central Intelligence Agency (CIA), both of which produced detailed assessments of the problems that would be encountered in an occupation (among other things, that the occupation would not long be viewed as a liberation). Indeed, a prewar study in early 2003 by Crane and Terrill of the U.S. Army's Strategic Studies Institute (an arm of the Army War College) conclusively made the argument in some prescient detail about the problems war on Iraq would create. Yet there was relatively little vocal objection in advance, and there is hardly any evidence that negative assessments were considered within the administration. Why not?

The answer is important. If the stated mission in Iraq was indeed quixotic, then one can argue that it should not have been undertaken in the first place. As the prospects of a democratic outcome faded, the fallback position became that the United States did remove a hated and ruthless dictator and gave the Iraqi people the ability to engage in self-determination. Three questions, however, remain, that must be part of the post-Iraq assessment.

The first and most obvious is whether the stated goal of the mission—democratization of Iraq—was a reasonable goal or a neoconservative pipe dream. Was it possible to attain the objective? If not (and those involved did or should have known it was not), should it have been attempted? Second, was attaining the goal worthy of the use of the military instrument of power? Were American vital interests involved in instituting democracy in Iraq? How is the international environment more or less tolerable for the United States with a democratic or nondemocratic Iraq? Third, was the current result (Iraq in the midst of a tortured transition to self-rule with uncertain results) predictable in advance? Did, in other words, the invasion do more harm than good? And was that outcome knowable in advance? There can be no definitive answers to these questions until the war is over. Even under the best of circumstances and outcomes, there will be substantial disagreement about whether the political outcomes justified the military effort.

The Military Objective. Militarily, Iraq is a tale of two wars, one highly successful and one arguably less so. The successful phase was the *invasion and conquest* of Iraq. With a few minor problems that are predictable in war (see Franks and Gordon and Trainor), this phase of the war went smoothly. Whether the ease of attaining the necessary (but clearly not sufficient) goal of toppling the regime was the result of exquisite planning and execution (the official view) or the lack of an organized resistance by the Iraqis is a question that eventually will have to be answered, but the military has, by and large, been highly self-congratulatory about the operation with little dissent.

The other part of the war, the *occupation*, is another matter. This aspect, known as Phase IV by war planners, has been the subject of withering criticism, on two basic grounds. First, critics (including the preponderance of military professionals) have argued that the size and composition of the occupation force was and continues to be grossly inadequate for the task of occupying, pacifying, and rebuilding the country. The OIF force that invaded the country was around 150,000 strong, despite admonitions from, among others, Army Chief of Staff Eric Shinseki (named Secretary of Veterans Affairs by Obama) that a force of 250,000–300,000 was needed to conquer *and* pacify the country. When the invasion's initial phase was successful with lower numbers, Shinseki (and others like him) were dismissed as alarmists by overly optimistic supporters of Secretary Rumsfeld, who had demanded the smaller-sized force that carried out the mission. Rumsfeld (and Cheney) believed before the war that the Americans would be treated as liberators and that only a small residual American force would remain in Iraq after summer 2003. The need to augment the 130,000 Americans remaining in Iraq in 2007 with a "surge" of additional combat troops to put down the insurgency (and help create the conditions for Iraqification) provides further evidence that, over four years after the invade-and-conquer phase, the numbers were still not adequate for Phase IV occupation and rebuilding. These forces were designated to perform a primarily counterinsurgency role, and while their presence did apparently lead to a lowering of violence, it is not clear their numbers were adequate to perform the kind of counterinsurgency mission described in Chapter 11.

The second criticism of Phase IV has been about the inadequacy of planning and execution for what followed the conquest. The available literature suggests that planning was flawed in at least two ways. One is that it was not considered very important by wartime planners, who simply assumed that things would work out on their own. Rumsfeld's famous "freedom's untidy" response to reports of looting in Baghdad is exemplary of this lack of concern. Such planning as occurred went on in Douglas Feith's Office of Special Plans within the Pentagon, a midlevel part of the Department of Defense bureaucracy, and was heavily influenced by Iraqi exiles like neoconservative favorite Ahmed Chalabi. The expert community was studiously ignored: the State Department because of its negativity toward the prospects of success in Iraq and United Nations experts in postconflict reconstruction and state building because they were deemed to be "too liberal." In retrospect, those ignored experts very accurately predicted the problems that would be encountered and that were predictable.

Possibly the most egregious error made in the planning, and a particular chestnut of Vice President Cheney, was the expectation that the Iraqis would treat the Americans as liberators and that they would continue to hold the Americans in that regard even as the occupation continued This assumption might not have been entirely specious if, as the planners apparently assumed, the occupation was very short. Indeed, there was apparently an initial positive reaction among many Iraqis at being liberated from the Hussein regime; that perception faded as the Americans continued to stay and did not improve living conditions in the country. This point was made by Sir Robert Thompson in describing the 1948 Malay insurgency in his book *Make for the Hills*: "There is no hope for democracy if nothing works. Reliance on a military solution will always fail, particularly when sought by foreign troops." There is considerable evidence that the seemingly open-ended American occupation was responsible for creating the conditions that allowed for the formation of and support for Al Qaeda in Iraq (see Chandrasekaran, among others). The present author discussed this dynamic in *Distant Thunder*: "The level of involvement (by outsiders) and the ability to influence the outcome are often inversely related. The more public the intervention and the more obvious the degree to which the regime depends on the assistance, the more resentment is likely to be created in the population. The insurgents' propaganda will be fueled by that dependence." If true, this observation is devastating for arguments made in defense of the occupation that the longer the United States stays, the more likely success is.

The other flaw was the execution of the plans—Phase IV was a poor plan poorly executed. This criticism has run through the critical literature on Iraq and has centered not only on the conceptual paucity and lack of preparedness of American officials to oversee Phase IV, but also on the incredible ineptitude and, in some cases, arrogance of those given the jobs of carrying out the occupation and rebuilding of the country.

This criticism has two distinct aspects. One is the sheer paucity of preinvasion planning, which meant occupation administrators (carefully not designated as such) arrived in Iraq with no programs to administer, since details of what happened after the fall of Hussein were simply supposed to work themselves out. Diamond, for instance, went to the country with a missionary zeal about democratizing the country, but was disillusioned by the actual situation. He records starkly the reality he found: "from the moment the war ended, Iraq fell into a deepening quagmire of chaos, criminality, insurgency, and terrorism. . . . Iraq became a black hole of instability." This "black hole" covered the range of public services from basic security and public services to the reform of the economy and the rebuilding of Iraq's schools and other parts of the infrastructure. While many of the things that needed doing (for instance, many aspects of the infrastructure) had suffered under Saddam Hussein, Iraqis presumed the Americans would fix them and improve their conditions of life; when this did not occur (or did so with remarkable slowness), the Iraqis became increasingly disillusioned with the Americans, who came to look increasingly like occupiers rather than liberators. This change of perspective, in turn, helped spark and fuel the armed resistance to the Americans by various factions.

The role of the military itself must inevitably be part of any assessment. The professional military had been chastened greatly by the Vietnam experience, in which it had been remarkably compliant in accepting the mistaken political leadership that had impelled the military into a war that many of its leaders knew at the time could not be won, an arguable parallel to Iraq. Dissent was not rewarded in Vietnam. One of the Kennedy and Johnson administrations' top experts on guerrilla warfare, Roger Hilsman (who had served as an organizer of guerrilla opponents to the Japanese in World War II), served as assistant secretary of state for Far Eastern affairs as the decision to intervene in Vietnam was being made. As he put it at the time, "those of us against escalating the struggle in Vietnam reached exactly the opposite conclusion: that the mistake would not be letting Vietnam go down the drain but for the United States to intervene." His views did not prevail, and he left the government on March 15, 1964, removing an obstacle to implementing what proved to be a disastrous military and political decision.

The military itself was not blameless in Vietnam (see McMaster's scathing indictment of the military's acquiescent role in that conflict). It was even less blameless in Iraq because most of the senior leaders who agreed to the decision to invade Iraq were products of the professional military education system that had dissected the Vietnam experience and concluded such a mistake should not be made again. At the middle ranks of the officer corps (majors through colonels), there was opposition based on the application of those lessons to Iraq. At the top of the ranks, however, there was, by and large, silence. Some of that undoubtedly was the result of the experience of General Shinseki, who was publicly ridiculed and quietly forced into retirement after his opposition to the war plans. In Vietnam, the generals said "can do" to a mission they could not successfully complete, and they did not, at a minimum, say "can't do" in Iraq. Lieutenant Colonel Paul Yingling, a serving U.S. Army officer, summarizes the "failure of generalship" in Iraq most vividly: "America's generals have repeated the mistakes of Vietnam in Iraq. First, throughout the 1990s our generals failed to envision the conditions of future conflict and prepare their forces accordingly. Second, America's generals failed to estimate correctly both the means and the ways necessary to achieve the aims of policy prior to beginning the war in Iraq. Finally, the generals did not provide Congress and the public with an accurate assessment of the conflict in Iraq."

The decision to invade Iraq was made not only on the basis of questionable premises about whether it was necessary and desirable, but also on the basis of questionable views of the objective (a free and democratic Iraq) and how easily that objective could be attained. If, for instance, the administration had told the American public on the eve of the invasion that the result would be a long (over seven years and counting) and expensive (in treasure and blood) quagmire, would the American people have accepted the idea of the invasion? They did not offer a negative judgment because the basis for one was not forcefully presented to them by figures whose judgment they would have recognized and respected. As in Vietnam, there were dissenters, but they were too few and isolated, and they were pilloried by war supporters for their dissent. Did that process serve the American interest well? If not, what lessons can be taken to assure that the same mistakes are not made again? There would not, after all, have been an inept administration of the occupation of Iraq had there been no war.

What Went Wrong and Why?

Hardly anyone, even those in an administration that continued to assert that progress was somehow possible and occurring, would argue that the Iraq effort represents any kind of exemplary experience that should be repeated. The Bush administration's early assertions of a quick, bloodless, and highly successful experience that would cost the American taxpayers essentially nothing (Iraqi oil revenues were supposed to cover most of the costs) seem almost comical in retrospect, but they are not. The projections that led the United States into Iraq were almost systematically wrong, as were the projections of what would happen afterward. Why? One answer is that the United States failed to understand at critical junctures the nature of the conflict, and the other is that the United States failed to understand Iraq as a very different war of choice.

Iraq as a War of Choice

Part of the reason the Iraq War is both confusing and controversial is the disagreement about whether the United States should have or needed to become involved in that country's affairs with military force. Unlike the American initial entrance into Afghanistan, it is not entirely clear that American vital interests were jeopardized once the WMD and terrorist arguments were discarded.

A democratic Iraq is arguably better than an authoritarian state would be there, but is its promotion necessary for American well-being? Many Americans have concluded that the outcome was not sufficiently important to justify expending American forces, especially to the extent it has been used. Iraq was, in other words, a war of choice, not of necessity.

Wars of choice are always more problematically justifiable than wars of necessity, and this is especially in a democratic society where decision makers are accountable to the electorate and must justify their actions to them. The reason is obvious: war involves the expenditure of lives and treasure, precious commodities not to be expended frivolously. A war that cannot be avoided and must be fought is far easier to rationalize than one where the need is not so pressing.

Members of the Bush administration were aware of this dynamic, although they apparently underestimated its potentially erosive effects. Their underestimation stems from their implicit characterization of the action as a war of necessity through the WMD and terrorism assertions. Had the war been over quickly and painlessly as planners like Rumsfeld presumed, it might have been concluded before the choice/necessity dichotomy was raised. The underestimation was failing to recognize that Iraq would become, once again in Rumsfeld's term, a "long slog" where the necessity of the war would be questioned.

American public opinion turned against the Iraq war when the majority of the U.S. population concluded it was a war of choice that did not justify the sacrifice being made in its name. A major conundrum of the contemporary period illustrated by both Afghanistan and Iraq is that the American population will support actions of dubious importance/necessity under two circumstances: if they are either too short or too painless to create controversy. The American rescue of medical students in Grenada in 1983 demonstrates the first acceptable set of circumstances, the longer but less painful U.S. involvements in the Balkans in the 1990s (Bosnia and Kosovo) represent the latter.

Iraq directly violates both criteria: it has been long, indecisive, and painful. In these circumstances, it is not at all surprising that it would become unpopular and difficult to sustain. The conundrum is that Iraq-like situations—potential military involvements where vital interests are not unambiguously engaged and where military involvement is likely to be protracted, painful, and indecisive—are considerably more likely than simple and easily resolvable wars of choice or situations where the United States clearly must use armed force.

How Will the Iraq War End?

The answer to this question has two distinct, if interrelated, parts about what Iraq will be like after the war. One part is the causation and timing of American withdrawal from Iraq, and the other is the physical situation on the ground in Iraq when that withdrawal occurs.

The possible outcomes form a continuum, the extremities of which can be safely eliminated as highly improbable. One extreme is a total and unambiguous U.S. "victory," which means the creation of a stable, model democracy in Iraq that can defeat an insurgency that lacks popular support (which has been transferred to the government) and that unites Iraqis into a pro-American postwar polity. This outcome would be easily as much a victory for the United States as it would be for the Iraqis, since it is unclear what conditions would be acceptable to the Iraqis as a whole to allow this outcome. It is highly improbable because of the deep divisions within Iraq—arguably exacerbated by the Americans—that were present before the war, but suppressed by the Hussein regime, and that form the heart of critical judgments about intervening in the first place. There is also almost certainly not sufficient support for the American-favored outcome in Iraq either.

The second extreme is an abject American loss in Iraq. Proponents of the war argue this is the outcome most likely if the United States withdraws "prematurely" (it is never quite clear when the situation is "mature" enough for withdrawal). Such a scenario would mean the American withdrawal would result in a new dictatorship (the apotheosis of a democracy) that would turn Iraq into a full-blown terrorist-supporting state. This outcome is also unlikely. The imposition of a new autocracy (almost certainly Shiite if it occurs) would be widely opposed regionally and would further ignite Kurdish separatism. A multicommunal authoritarian state that can gradually democratize over time may be the more realistic possibility.

This leaves an outcome somewhere in between, some form of Iraqification, as the remaining candidate. Some form of this strategy is clearly being implemented along lines parallel to the Vietnamization policy. Vietnamization had as its major purpose preparing the South Vietnamese to defend themselves against attempts to reunify all of Vietnam by force. The operational tools for attempting to accomplish this goal included maximum training and equipping of the South Vietnamese, the provision of military assistance to their operations (the use of U.S. close air support when the North Vietnamese attempted to invade in 1972—the Easter Offensive), and the insulation of South Vietnam from outside intervention by sealing infiltration routes through Cambodia and Laos (efforts that ultimately failed).

The same dynamics have been applied in Iraq since about 2005. They have centered on building Iraqi armed forces and police to defend the country against the various forms of the insurgency, a direct parallel to similar efforts in Vietnam. As in Vietnam, the effort has been partially hamstrung by the inability to recruit and train a force sufficient for the job, if for different reasons (the need to conscript the South Vietnamese force, coercion and violence and ethnic loyalties in Iraq). The result, at some point, will be the same: the declaration that the Iraqis are as prepared as the Americans can make them and that it will be up to them to defend the country, at which point the Americans will withdraw. At the same time, the United States will try to make Iraq as impervious to outside influence as possible. In the Iraqi case, this will be attempted by using diplomacy to try to ensure the absence of outside intervention and by posting American forces "over the horizon" in places from which they could conceivably redeploy into Iraq, such as Kuwait and Kurdish Iraq.

The remaining debate over the terms of American withdrawal from Iraq falls within this middle range of possibilities. If unambiguous victory is unattainable (and always was) and equally unambiguous defeat is too politically unacceptable in the United States to be allowed, then some form of ambiguous withdrawal that leaves the final outcome to the Iraqis themselves and allows Americans to rationalize that "we have done all we could" is the best that can be expected. It is essentially a face-saving device, which is what Vietnamization was. The reluctance to call it Iraqification arises both from the reluctance of Iraq War supporters to admit the parallels with Vietnam and from the recognition that Vietnamization ultimately failed. Iraqification by whatever name may also fail, in which case Americans will be left to bicker about whether it would have succeeded if some other disengagement point (e.g., level of preparedness of the Iraqis) had been chosen. As the United States moves to and especially beyond the 2010 deadline for withdrawing American combat forces, the answers will begin to emerge. As pressure mounts within Iraq for a total withdrawal of U.S. forces, it will become even clearer.

THE LEGACIES OF AFGHANISTAN AND IRAQ

Afghanistan and Iraq have been two distinctive experiences forged from the same crucible. Their common heritage is 9/11, but their connections to that event are very different, as have been the political and military legacies of each. The individual and collective impacts of these two wars will, however, influence the way the United States military does its business in the years to come.

For better or worse, Afghanistan and Iraq are thus the foundations on which the military and political leaderships must prepare for the future. Iraq in 1990, and to an extent in 2003, is the last of the traditional wars, in which the United States is likely to encounter a traditional military opponent. In Zinni's colorful terms (quoted in Clancy and Zinni), "we managed to go up against the only jerk on the planet who was stupid enough to challenge us to refight World War Two." Future situations will be much more like what Afghanistan always was and Iraq became (the insurgency). Using the Vietnam War as a base, the present author published a book, *When America Fights*, in 2000 that discussed these same matters; in essence, the lessons and legacies of Afghanistan and Iraq are not that much different. They simply provide another example of what happens when one ignores the legacies of the past. In the Afghanistan and Iraq cases, these lessons are political, military, and related to the structure and uses of future U.S. forces.

The Political Legacy: Be Careful Where You Intervene

At the turn of the millennium, the United States was afflicted with the belief that it had unprecedented and ineluctable power in the world, and one heard frequent analogies between the United States and the Roman Empire at its apex. The terrorist attacks of September 11 sent the country reeling temporarily, but it rebounded with a fierce determination to right that wrong. The might of the United States could be applied to "make reality," in the neoconservative sense. After an early apparent success (tempered by time) in Afghanistan, Iraq became the next great political battleground. In Iraq, the United States would take its first step toward transforming the Middle East and the world. Afghanistan was largely forgotten, but it did not go away.

American power was, of course, exaggerated in these descriptions, and the failure to bring democracy to Iraq or to stabilize Afghanistan should cause the United States to reassess what it can and cannot do, especially unilaterally or with limited international support, in the world. The decision to go into Iraq reflected the triumph of the idealistic neoconservatives and the temporary defeat of the traditional realists. The neoconservatives were voted out of office in 2008, and in their places, a new generation of people with views closer to those of the traditional realists has arisen, one that will ask different questions about involving the United States in different situations. The outcome in Afghanistan will further temper their concerns.

Although the questions can be arranged in various ways, one possible ordering suggests three basic questions. The first surrounds the feasibility of adopting any particular political objective: Is success possible? Is it likely or unlikely? How can you assess likelihood in advance? The second surrounds the desirability or necessity of involvement: Is a proposed involvement one of necessity (where the failure to act will result in intolerable disadvantage—affect vital interests) or one of choice (where vital outcomes are not engaged)? If vital interests are not involved, should force be considered, or should alternative means be explored and the use of force eliminated or at least shelved? The third, and related, question has to do with the endurance of support for an action if taken: Will the United States remain diligent even if achieving the objective is long and costly?

These three questions are, of course, related to one another. Following an unattainable objective is quixotic, and a negative answer to the question of attainability should counsel a negative reaction unless the objective is so overwhelmingly important that it must be pursued as a matter of unavoidable principle. An easily achievable goal will not test the vitality or endurance question, since such goals can be achieved with minimum effort and expense. Likewise, the American people are more likely to provide enduring support for an effort that is clearly vital to the country's interests than one that is not.

These kinds of questions will be asked in the future about American military involvement in unstable situations in the world. Most of the situations will be ambiguous and the answers difficult to determine easily. The Afghanistan and Iraq experiences should, however, create skepticism about optimistic assessments that sound anything like the ramp-up to the invasion in 2003. Because these situations will be in places that are foreign and alien to many Americans, expert opinion should have a greater impact on the debate than it did in the past. The more of the basic questions that are answered negatively—or that cannot be convincingly argued positively—the less the likelihood that a positive decision for involvement will be sustainable.

The Military Legacy: What Kind of Foe to Prepare For

It was a virtual mantra before the Iraq War that asymmetrical warfare was the wave of the future, and that warfare fought by unconventional means represented the kind of military exigency with which the United States would most likely have to deal. Although the American military leaders accepted this vision publicly, it was not a style of warfare that they liked or one with which they could identify. The Persian Gulf War, fought under the leadership of Zinni's last "jerk" to take on the United States conventionally, provided a respite from the new reality, and by and large, the invasion and conquest phase of the Iraq War of 2003 was fought in a modified version of World War II–style maneuver warfare, seemingly providing evidence for not abandoning the "old" ways of war. Operation Iraqi Freedom was used to vindicate two continuing illusions about the application of military force. Military traditionalists saw it as proof of the applicability of the conventional application of force, even if many of them chafed at the size of the force, especially for the postmilitary phase (Phase IV) of the action. Supporters of Donald Rumsfeld's concept of a smaller, more technologically oriented force that could move more quickly and lethally than the old force believed the rapid movement of forces through Iraq vindicated his vision of the future as well. The campaign to overthrow the Taliban in 2001 showed the vitality of both special operations and traditional aerial bombardment.

The various forms of the Iraq insurgency and the long slog in Afghanistan have brought that illusion to an end. Even as American forces moved through Iraq, they encountered—much to their surprise—isolated pockets of resistance, such as individual fighters or groups engaged in ambushes and harassing actions against them. The disbanding of the Iraqi Army and police provided a virtual trove of potential recruits for the various insurgent groups—armed, angry, unemployed men who could blame their conditions on the occupiers. That all major sides—the Kurds and their *pesh merga* ("those who face death") and the Sunni and Shiite militias, augmented by Al Qaeda in Iraq foreigners after 2004—emerged to form a multisided resistance that the Bush administration refused to designate a civil war should not have come as a surprise. Similarly, no antidote has been found to Taliban and Al Qaeda activity in the tribal regions of Afghanistan and Pakistan. Despite thirty years of studying the dynamics of insurgency and counterinsurgency (culminating in the publication of *Field Manual 3-24* on counterinsurgency in 2007, among whose lead authors was General David Petraeus), the United States has not found a successful way to quell the violence after over five years of trying.

Both wars either began as or became asymmetrical. Two points of note should be mentioned about that dynamic. The first is that asymmetrical warfare against the American effort in each case has been sufficiently successful that it will almost certainly be adopted by future opponents of the United States. The insurgencies have not defeated the Americans on the battlefield, but they have held at bay the American military goliath. Depending on the final nature of American withdrawal from each country, some of its proponents will almost certainly claim they have prevailed over the Americans. At any rate, the lesson will almost certainly be that asymmetrical warfare is the way to combat the United States, and as a result, that is the kind of opponent the United States should anticipate and attempt to overcome in the future.

The other point is how the insurgents in both countries have learned to adapt their method to maximize its effectiveness. Iraq offers the clearest example. Earlier forms of asymmetrical warfare, such as Vietnam, were fought in rural settings, generally in the tropical green belt that surrounds the Earth's Equator. In Iraq, most of the fighting has been in the setting of urban guerrilla warfare, and the asymmetrical opponents have adapted classical insurgent techniques like ambush to the new setting. In Iraq, two innovations have stood out. The most prominent, of course, has been the use of improvised explosive devices (IEDs), essentially booby traps to destroy Americans riding in what have turned out to be inadequately armored vehicles, and this tactic has been enhanced by lying in wait with antiaircraft missiles to shoot down helicopters trying to reach the scene of IED attacks to ferry out survivors. The other has been the use of suicide bombers against urban targets, a method adopted by the Taliban, especially in Pakistan. Neither technique is entirely novel, but both have confounded the American occupiers. Their legacy is twofold: these kinds of tactics will almost certainly be used the next time the United States faces an asymmetrical opponent, and just as these were novel tactics in the Iraq War, the next opponent will almost certainly have equally ingenious adaptations to present as problems for the Americans.

Afghanistan, Iraq and the American Military: What Kind of Force

A consequence of the reaction to Afghanistan and Iraq is that the U.S. military will have to regroup before it faces a future foe. Depending on the outcomes, one political impact is likely to be some reluctance to employ force in the future. While this reluctance to see Americans put in harm's way will provide a breathing space for this regrouping, it is not clear what happens if, during the period of skepticism about military employments, a real crisis—a war of necessity—is thrust upon the country. Some analysts are concerned about such a possibility in Pakistan, but the Obama administration seems committed to lowering the military content and raising the diplomatic content of policy there. Events will influence which emphasis succeeds.

At least two elements will play into the equation as the military looks forward. The first has to do with how it physically regenerates itself in the face of the almost certain hemorrhage of many from its ranks and a likely lack of enthusiasm among potential new recruits. The other is conceptual and has to do with how (or whether) the military can make the transition from an almost exclusively heavy, symmetrical structure with some asymmetrical add-ons to a force that balances more enthusiastically and physically a future where asymmetrical threats at least equal symmetrical ones, as Secretary Gates proposes.

Manpower. The manpower problem is the more immediate and pressing concern. First, in Iraq and now in Afghanistan, the government has essentially "robbed Peter to pay Paul" in the sense of overextending, overusing, and even arguably abusing the force it has to the breaking point. The litany is familiar: for example, multiple deployments of active-duty and reserve units, arguably without adequate breaks; "stop loss" measures to prevent those whose terms of enlistment have expired from leaving the service; and mistreatment of wounded and other veterans when they return to the United States. These conditions have already made many potential recruits wary of joining, despite Obama's promises to relieve the conditions. Moreover, when the American withdrawal finally occurs and there is inadequate reason to keep military members involuntarily in service, there will almost certainly be a large number of resignations and failures to reenlist. The recruitment "boom" of 2008-2009 (where all services met their quotas) seems temporarily to reverse that trend. Whether enhanced enlistment rates will survive the recovery of the economy is another matter. Historically, military recruitment and prosperity have been inversely related.

The military faced this same problem after Vietnam, and the short-term results are not encouraging for current military planners. The problem was probably worse in Vietnam because the military itself was largely blamed (rightly or wrongly) for the outcome, a verdict that it resented but could not deflect altogether. In Afghanistan and Iraq, the military bears part of the blame but has not been discredited institutionally by the effort in either country. Nonetheless, the experience that American soldiers and sailors have had in these wars will make the task of military recruiters more difficult than it was before the wars.

The size and nature of the future military and its future missions are intimately related. If the United States projects more involvements of the size and nature of Iraq, then it will require a substantially larger force than would be the case if it envisages smaller deployments and missions. Conversely, the size of the military makes possible and impossible different kinds of missions. A clear lesson of Iraq, for instance, is that the current U.S. armed forces are not large enough comfortably to accommodate the military occupation of a middle-sized or larger opponent. One of the lessons discussed in Chapter 10 is that the All-Volunteer Force concept produces a very good but not necessarily a very large force.

The military, of course, does not determine its own size, which is a prerogative of the Congress. What size forces the United States needs after Afghanistan and Iraq will be the decision of the political system, which will pass judgments both on the desired size and missions of the military and on the physical and political difficulties of attaining different sizes and qualities of force. In looking at the question, there are five possible ways for the armed forces of the post-Iraq era to "man" themselves.

The first is the *status quo*: the continuation of the ongoing all-volunteer force recruited in the current manner. This will almost certainly be the approach attempted initially after the current involvements end. The rationale for continuing the present system will be that it worked before in producing the kind of force the country desired and it represents a structure and approach with which the military is familiar and comfortable. Moreover, removing the shadow of Iraq should reduce the reluctance of new recruits to come forward and existing troops to reenlist. The negative side of this argument is that the shadow of Iraq will linger and that potential new members (as well as reenlisting present members) will be reluctant to commit until they see tangible evidence that there will not be another Iraq in their futures.

If the status quo is inadequate, as it arguably will be, the second option is *enhanced recruitment*. This can take on several guises. It can mean increased incentives for enlistment/reenlistment, such as larger bonuses, college tuition vouchers, and the like. It can also mean reaching out to new constituencies, such as recruiting more females or members from minority groups into the service. Shorter terms of enlistment and guaranteed leave time can also be part of the package, as can amenities like better living conditions for military members (greater access to the Internet and e-mail for deployed troops, for instance). These approaches seek to widen the recruitment/retention base of the armed forces and to keep members satisfied, while not diluting their quality. The problems include the expense of bonuses and incentives and the danger of turning the force into one of more disproportionate minority composition than it already is.

A variant of enhanced recruitment offers a third possibility—*lowering standards for recruits*. To some extent, this has already been incorporated into attempts to maintain force levels in Iraq, and it can consist of two actions, both of which enlarge the potential pool of military accessions. The first is to lower educational/intellectual standards. By statute, the military can recruit only a very small percentage of troops who lack high school diplomas (the standard measuring stick), and increasing the percentage of nongraduates increases the pool. The problem is that high school dropouts, as a group, are probably less capable and more unreliable than those who graduate, resulting in a less capable force with greater discipline problems. The other method, which is more controversial, is to allow recruitment of people convicted of some categories of crime who are now precluded from service.

If the first three methods are inadequate or unacceptable, a fourth is a return to *conscription (the draft)*. Although it has not been activated or used since the end of 1972, the United States still retains a selective service system that registers eighteen-year-olds and that could be reactivated without specific legislation. The draft system, by which the military obtained most of the force that fought in Vietnam, was a victim of the backlash against that conflict. Since Vietnam, even raising the possibility of a return to involuntary military service creates a political firestorm of opposition that no political actor will seriously advocate (Representative Charles Rangel

(D–NY) regularly presents an advocacy of the draft but for the symbolic purpose of pointing to inequities and flaws in the current system). Much of the opposition to the draft arises from the inequities of the old system, but many of these have been overcome. Nonetheless, the idea of a draft continues to be problematical, as investigated in the *Challenge!* box.

Challenge!

THE DRAFT OPTION

A major reason for opposition to the old selective service system was that it was riddled with inequities that allowed those with money, privilege, or power to evade service but ensnared those lacking such advantages. To some extent, the issue of equity will always plague any conscription system, although those inequities can be minimized.

Inequity has two sources. The first is at the front end of the process and involves who is "eligible" to be drafted. Under the Vietnam-era system, there was an extensive set of exemptions from service, including educational participation (attending college), family concerns (marital status), and even employment in occupations deemed to be vital to national security. Moreover, all women were exempt. This created an economic and educational gap between those who might be chosen to serve and those who would not. This form of inequity can be lessened by removing all sources of exemption (except strictly defined physical or mental disability), thereby also increasing the eligibility pool beyond what used to exist. The problem is that this would mean the children of those with power and wealth would be part of the eligible pool rather than being exempt, making implementation even more difficult to achieve.

The other source of inequity, which cannot be erased, is inequity in terms of who serves. A *selective* service system is premised on the idea that the military (or any alternative forms of service) does not need or want all of the members of the eligible pool and thus selects some and bypasses others. The result is inequity: some endure the sacrifice of service, and others do not. A major approach to reducing this inequity is to provide rewards (e.g., college expenses) for those who serve but not for those who do not. Because selection and induction into the armed forces potentially involve being placed in harm's way, the gap cannot be removed altogether.

The military also opposes a conscript force because it entails unwilling, discontented members who create disciplinary and morale problems that dilute force quality. The dilemma, as already pointed out, is that an entirely volunteer force will always be smaller than a conscript force can be, because less people will volunteer than can be compelled to serve. The result is to impose limits on force size and thus uses.

Imagine the situation wherein the AVF concept cannot yield a large enough force to meet the country's need in some future crisis. Would you favor a draft to produce more service members? More to the point, would you be willing to be drafted? Would you favor removing all sources of inequity—including some from which you might benefit—from the system?

The fifth alternative is largely an artifact of Iraq: the *privatization of parts of the force*. In Iraq, for instance, Avant reports that Rumsfeld estimated there were 20,000 "private security personnel" in Iraq in 2004, making them "the second largest member of the 'coalition of the willing.'" The use of these forces, provided by so-called private security contractors (PSCs), has certain advantages, as catalogued by Avant: they can be mobilized quickly to provide flexibility and surge capacity; they often possess special skills, since they are recruited from the open market; they can be recruited internationally; and they are politically less costly than regular soldiers. The disadvantages include cost, especially when they are used in high-risk situations; reliability, since they do not report through normal military chains of command; integration into regular forces; and legal ambiguity (status under the laws of war).

In one sense, privatization of the military is simply an extension of the principle of privatizing government functions generally and has been extended to a number of other military tasks already—food service is an example. On the other hand, the use of these kinds of forces strikes many as a resort to mercenary forces (defenders argue that they are not mercenaries because they only sign up to fight for the United States and are not generally available to the highest bidder, as mercenaries are); moreover, they raise the same kinds of problems of control and responsibility as does an organization like the French Foreign Legion, to which private forces like Blackwater have been analogized. Moreover, scandals surrounded Blackwater Worldwide private security forces (renamed Xe Services LLC in February 2009)in 2007 (see Snow, *What After Iraq?*). One intriguing question is whether one is more willing to risk these kinds of forces in situations where one would not place citizen–soldiers whose "expenditure" would have greater political consequences.

Manpower and Missions. The impact of Afghanistan and Iraq on military manpower will be to make it more difficult, at least after the effects of the recession recede, to recruit a force that replaces the current force, and especially to create a larger force more adequate for Iraq-sized or larger future missions. For some, this limitation will be viewed as a virtue because it means the United States cannot contemplate another episode like Iraq (this was clearly the case after Vietnam).

The relationship between military mission and manpower requirements will be one of the most important elements of the post-Iraq debate. Barring unforeseen changes of fortune, the exit from Afghanistan and Iraq will tend to reinforce rather than negate the tendency of Americans to eschew military solutions to problems for a time, during which the military services (and especially the Army and Marines) will physically and psychologically attempt to assess the experience and try to recuperate from the harm the war has done to their ranks and their images in the world. If there are no calls for large-scale deployments over the next half decade or so, the combat arms will not complain.

There are likely to be two major lightning rods in the postmortem in the wake of Afghanistan and Iraq. One is how to reassess, and probably scale back, the military's activism, while still keeping a strong commitment to security. The Obama administration in 2009 inherited the problem of international religious terrorism, but Al Qaeda itself will likely remain solidly, if unofficially, domiciled in the mountainous outreaches of the Pakistan–Afghanistan border region (Waziristan) unless things change. In the short run, the response may well be restricted to aerial raids. The advantage is that such raids do not directly tax the overused Army and Marines, and their violation of Afghan and Pak sovereignty is not as great as if ground troops were used. The disadvantage is that such forms of attack are rarely conclusive and have not successfully targeted bin Laden and his cohorts in the past. The Obama administration is trying to partially demilitarize the effort against terrorism, but it cannot ignore it or the contention by many that the military is an, or the, appropriate instrument for this war.

The manpower problem will be ubiquitous. Will the United States rebuild the Army and Marines back to their pre–Iraq War levels? Or will they be made larger or smaller? The Iraq War so tied down American ground forces that it has been virtually impossible (and fortunately not necessary) to conduct a major deployment elsewhere simultaneously. Is that what Americans want? Conversely, a smaller force—even if technologically augmented to create force multipliers—can presumably be used less than a larger force, which some see as an advantage. A larger force, on the other hand, can be used for purposes that may allow it to guarantee a greater level of security or to get into more mischief, depending on one's perspective.

CONCLUSION: SECURITY AFTER AFGHANISTAN AND IRAQ

The Afghanistan and Iraq Wars make planning for and executing policy aimed at furthering national security more difficult than before the wars. Although the military itself is likely to avoid the tarnish of blame for the lack of success in both cases more than was the case for the post-Vietnam military, there will indeed be a postwar hangover that will, at a minimum, make the necessary reconstitution of the armed forces more difficult than it otherwise would be. At the same time, the notion that military force is a multifunctional instrument that can solve a wide range of problems has also been brought into question by the wars. The prime promoters of this multifaceted dimension of military force, the neoconservatives, have largely been discredited by the effort, and their influence has clearly declined.

The Obama administration appears to view the use of force more cautiously than did the Bush administration. Military activism will lie fallow for a time while the military rebuilds itself, both physically and in terms of what it does and how it does it. The increased commitment to Afghanistan is an exception to this tendency. One can only hope it takes advantage of its enforced introspection to provide an outlook more forward looking than the post-Vietnam assessment did.

Although one hates to do so, it is necessary to end the chapter on a somber note. The lesson of Vietnam was "no more Vietnams," which roughly meant no more involvement in quixotic causes where the realistic prospects of success were minimal. Iraq, unfortunately, met the definition of what was to be avoided, and the United States immersed itself in yet another Vietnam-like lost cause. Afghanistan has arguably evolved in the same direction. One of the lessons of Iraq will likely be "no more Iraqs." Will the same be true in Afghanistan? And will the United States actually learn the lesson this time? Or will there just be another interval before it forgets and repeats the same errors again?

STUDY/DISCUSSION QUESTIONS

1. The text predicts certain characteristics about the post-Iraq environment. What are they? Will they prove true or false? How do any discrepancies between the predictions and the reality affect the text's assessment of that environment and its predictions about the post-Iraq world?
2. How did the United States become involved in Afghanistan? Was war necessary or a matter of choice? Explain.
3. What does it mean to say there are two wars in Afghanistan? What are they? How does their existence complicate thinking about and acting in that country?
4. What went wrong in Afghanistan? How is the war likely to end?
5. Discuss the road to the Iraq War, starting with the legacy of the Persian Gulf War and moving forward to 2003. Include a discussion of the role of the neoconservatives in your answer.
6. Was the U.S. action in Iraq politically or militarily feasible? Assess the feasibility on both measures.
7. How will the Iraq War end? Assess the possible outcomes and the effects of those outcomes on both Iraq and the United States.
8. What are the broad lessons of the Iraq War? Discuss and assess each lesson.
9. How should the United States decide to man the post-Iraq military? At what levels and for what purposes should it be sized? How should the requisite numbers be obtained?

SELECTED BIBLIOGRAPHY

Avant, Deborah D. *The Market for Force: The Consequences of Privatizing Security.* New York: Cambridge University Press, 2005.

———. "Contracting for Services in U.S. Military Operations." *PS: Political Science and Politics* 40, no. 3 (July 2007): 457–460.

Bacevich, Andrew J. "Who's Bearing the Burden? Iraq and the Demise of the All-Volunteer Army." *Commonweal* 132 (July 15, 2005): 13–15.

Baker, James A., III, and Lee H. Hamilton, co-chairs. *The Iraq Study Group Report: The Way Forward—A New Approach.* Authorized ed. New York: Vintage Books, 2006.

Chandrasekaran, Rajiv. *Imperial Life in the Emerald City: Inside Iraq's Green Zone.* New York: Alfred A. Knopf, 2007.

Clancy, Tom, with General Tony Zinni and Tony Koltz. *Battle Ready.* New York: G. P. Putnam's Sons, 2004.

Clarke, Richard. *Against All Enemies: Inside America's War on Terror.* New York: Free Press, 2004.

Coll, Steve. *Ghost Wars: The Secret History of the CIA, Afghanistan, and bin Laden from the Soviet Invasion to September 10, 2001.* New York: Penguin Books, 2004.

Crane, Conrad C., and W. Andrew Terrill. *Reconstructing Iraq: Insights, Challenges, and Missions for Military Forces in a Post-conflict Scenario.* Carlisle Barracks, PA: Strategic Studies Institute, February 2003.

Crews, Robert D., and Amin Tarzi, eds. *The Taliban and the Crisis of Afghanistan.* Cambridge, MA: Harvard University Press, 2008.

Diamond, Larry. *Squandering Victory: The American Occupation and the Bungled Effort to Bring Democracy to Iraq.* New York: Times Books (Henry Holt and Company), 2005.

Ewans, Martin. *Afghanistan: A Short History of Its People and Politics.* New York: HarperCollins Perennial, 2002.

Franks, General Tommy, with Malcolm McConnell. *American Soldier*. New York: Regan Books, 2004.

Frum, David, and Richard Perle. *An End to Evil: How to Win the War on Terror*. New York: Random House, 2003.

Glantz, Aaron. *How America Lost Iraq*. New York: Jeremy P. Tarcher/Penguin, 2005.

Gordon, Michael R., and General Bernard E. Trainor. *Cobra II: The Inside Story of the Invasion and Occupation of Iraq*. New York: Pantheon, 2006.

Haass, Richard N. *War of Necessity, War of Choice: A Memoir of Two Iraq Wars*. New York: Simon and Schuster, 2009.

Hersh, Seymour M. *Chain of Command: The Road from September 11 to Abu Ghraib*. New York: HarperCollins, 2004.

Hilsman, Roger. *American Guerrilla: My War Behind Japanese Lines*. Washington, DC: Brassey's (U.S.), 1990.

Kagan, Robert, and William Kristol, eds. *Present Dangers: Crisis and Opportunity in American Foreign and Defense Policy*. San Francisco: Encounter Books, 2000.

Kattenburg, Paul M. *The Vietnam Trauma in American Foreign Policy, 1945–1973*. New Brunswick, NJ: Transaction Books, 1980.

Mann, James. *Rise of the Vulcans: The History of Bush's War Cabinet*. New York: Viking, 2004.

McChrystal, Stanley J. *Commander's Initial Assessment*. Kabul, Afghanistan: NATO International Security Assistance Forces, Afghanistan U.S. Forces, August 30, 2009.

McMaster. H. R. *Dereliction of Duty: Lyndon Johnson, Robert McNamara, the Joint Chiefs of Staff, and the Lies That Led to Vietnam*. New York: HarperPerennial, 1997.

Moore, Lt. General Harold G., and Joseph L. Galloway. *We Were Soldiers Once . . . and Young: Ia Drang: The Battle That Changed the War in Vietnam*. New York: HarperPerennial, 1992.

Neville, Leigh. *Special Operations Forces in Afghanistan*. New York: Osprey Publishing, 2008.

Packer, George. *The Assassin's Gate: America in Iraq*. New York: Farrar, Straus, Giroux, 2005.

Peters, Ralph. *Beyond Baghdad: Postmodern War and Peace*. Mechanicsburg, PA: Stackpole Books, 2003.

Pollack, Kenneth M. *The Threatening Storm: The Case for Invading Iraq*. A Council on Foreign Relations Book. New York: Random House, 2002.

Record, Jeffrey. *Dark Victory: America's Second War Against Iraq*. Annapolis, MD: Naval Institute Press, 2004.

Ricks, Thomas E. *Fiasco: The American Military Adventure in Iraq*. New York: Penguin Press, 2006.

Snow, Donald M. *Distant Thunder: Patterns of Conflict in the Developing World*. 2nd ed. Armonk, NY: M. E. Sharpe, 1997.

———. *When America Fights: The Uses of U.S. Military Force*. Washington, DC: CQ Press, 2000.

———. *What After Iraq?* New York: Pearson Longman, 2009.

———, and Dennis M. Drew. *From Lexington to Baghdad and Beyond: War and Politics in the American Experience*. 3rd ed. Armonk, NY: M. E. Sharpe, 2009.

Thompson, Sir Robert. *Make for the Hills: Memories of Far Eastern Wars*. London: Lee Cooper, 1989.

Woodward, Bob. *State of Denial: Bush at War, Part III*. New York: Simon and Schuster, 2006.

Yingling, Paul (Lt. Col.). "A Failure of Generalship." *Armed Forces Journal* (online). May 2007.

CHAPTER 13

Terrorism, Peacekeeping, and State Building

PREVIEW

In modern warfare, the cessation of active fighting does not necessarily signal the end of hostilities or the onset of peace. Rather, domestic reconciliation and the building or rebuilding of societies torn apart by either internal war or international military action must be parts of efforts to stabilize the military situation (peacekeeping) and to create conditions in these countries where stability and peace will be self-sustaining. In the 1990s, American involvement in situations where these problems were present was largely justified on humanitarian grounds; today, the rationale is suppressing terrorism. To address this issue, the chapter begins by looking at the problems associated with suppressing terrorism. Since the roots of terrorism (and other problems) lie in destabilizing conditions in some societies, it then looks at why, how, and where to intervene in the future. The possibilities for improving the situations, peacekeeping and state building, are then examined, and the chapter concludes with likely effects of these actions for the future.

The ongoing wars in Afghanistan and Iraq are symptomatic in at least two ways of the kinds of national security problems that face the United States and the rest of the world for the foreseeable future. One is that both occurred in unstable countries—sometimes referred to as failed or failing states—where political, economic, cultural, and other problems make stability difficult, if not impossible, to achieve. This instability often cannot be contained entirely within the boundaries of the state in which it occurs, and consequently, it spills over into its neighbors or into the international system more generally. The form that this spillover often takes is manifested as terrorism directed either internally or at real or imagined outside enemies, including the United States. For the most part, the United States believes its interests are best served by international stability and tranquility. Thus, self-sustaining countries where conditions do not breed violence and instability, particularly societies that do not provide the "swamp" in which terrorism breeds, as argued in Chapter 9, are preferable. The problem is how to create those conditions and the motivation to do so.

Since 9/11, the motivation underlying U.S. efforts has been in the area of terrorist suppression, and the chapter begins by examining how the United States has and continues to try to contain or eradicate terrorism directed against it. The heart of these efforts, however, is aimed at stopping actual manifestations of terrorism rather than at changing the underlying conditions that lead to terrorist-producing instabilities. The discussion thus moves to the more fundamental underlying questions of how to address and cause the cessation of violent instability in developing world countries (peacekeeping) and how to build alternative structures and conditions in which a return to violent instability will be eliminated or minimized (state building). Iraq, Afghanistan, and potentially Pakistan offer particularly poignant crucibles within which such efforts are occurring. The abeyance of terrorist activity would be one of the clearest and most desirable effects of the success of such efforts.

THE CONTEMPORARY SCENE

One of the most lasting, indelible legacies of the Iraq War has been the failure of the Phase IV operation, chronicled in detail by a number of critics of the war effort (Chandrasekaran, Diamond, Glantz, Record, and Ricks, for instance). These failures have included efforts to establish security and end violence and to build or rebuild the country to the point that it can be (or return to being) a self-sufficient, peaceful society, and the same dynamics apply to Afghanistan. The task of fully securing the peace in any unstable, war-torn society is the necessary precondition to rebuilding the country and is known as *peacekeeping*. The second task, building a country's infrastructure or rebuilding it (especially if one is responsible for destroying it in the first place), is known as *state building*. No contemporary military problem, prominently including those associated with terrorism, can be said to be ended completely successfully until both these tasks are accomplished.

The historical and contemporary records in regard to these tasks are mixed. The United States (and the rest of the world) encountered these problems in the 1990s and gained some understanding of them in places like the Balkans (Bosnia and Kosovo). The Bush administration came to power openly disdainful of these kinds of operations (notably peacekeeping operations) and professed no obvious interest in state building. As a result, there was virtually no consideration of the dynamics and complexities of peacekeeping and state building in what passed for Phase IV operations planning in Iraq, and the results have arguably contributed to the unrest and instability in that country.

Iraq and Afghanistan offer the primary rationale for why the United States must come to grips with the peacekeeping/state-building "dilemma." It is a dilemma for two reasons. On the one hand, almost all the opportunities and temptations to use military force that the United States will encounter in the upcoming years will be in countries where, like Iraq, the conflict will not be resolved until peacekeeping operations and state building are complete and successful. On the other hand, there is no proven international, and certainly no American, blueprint for state-building success. Indeed, John Hulsman of the Heritage Foundation, drawing upon the experience of T. E. Lawrence, argues that each potential situation is sufficiently unique that one must "avoid a cookie-cutter approach to state-building."

Contemporary, normally asymmetrical wars share three characteristics that endow them with their unique nature and that define the problems the United States and others must confront if they become involved in them. First, they share an important, sometimes exclusive, internal or civil component: elements within the state are fighting one another, meaning that part of the military and political problem of ending the war and restoring the peace is reconciling formerly warring factions. The Pashtun-based Taliban and the Afghan government are an example. Second, these wars occur essentially exclusively in the developing world, so when outsiders like the United States involve themselves, there is inevitably some resentment about that involvement, at least partially the result of a less-than-perfect understanding of the local situation by the intervening party.

The third characteristic is the most consequential, most difficult, and least well understood: these wars almost always have three distinct phases, all of which must be surmounted before success can occur. The first is the actual fighting phase, and the normal response is to bring that fighting to an end on some terms (what will be called *peace imposition*). The period after the fighting has ended is one of adjustment and unstable peace, and the problem is maintaining the peace and beginning to improve conditions in the target country (what will be called *peace enforcement*). Finally, the situation must be improved physically and politically (*state building*) so that outsiders can prepare for their exit (what will be called *peacekeeping*). In Iraq, peace imposition refers to the conquest of Iraq; peace enforcement and state building refer to the occupation. Afghanistan is in the peace imposition stage.

The question of American involvement with force in the developing world was skewed by the events of September 11, 2001. Prior to the terrorist attacks, there was a lively, partisan political debate about the degree of American activism in the developing world. During the 2000 election campaign, then candidate George W. Bush and close advisors such as Condoleezza Rice actively derided American intervention and continuing involvement in locales like Kosovo and Bosnia, maintained that the United States should cut back its involvement by scaling back or withdrawing American troops where they were present, and publicly promised that the United States would no longer be "the world's 911." More to the point, the commitment of American forces to missions such as peacekeeping and American resources to state building was derided as a misapplication and overextension of scarce and valuable American assets.

This whole question appeared to change fundamentally when the United States set its sights on Afghanistan in the fall of 2001 and Iraq in 2003. The United States had tolerated the repressive, virulently anti-American stance of the Taliban regime in Afghanistan since it came to power in 1996 on the grounds that no American interests were affected by its objectionable attitudes and actions. The regime's sanctioning of terrorism was, of course, regrettable, but until its refusal to hand over the terrorists dictated its removal from power, the Taliban regime was not very high on the American agenda.

The apparent need to change terrorist-prone societies altered the calculus of involvement in poor, unstable developing-world countries for the Bush administration. In the period between the fault lines, the motivation to become involved was primarily humanitarian, trying to alleviate great human suffering because it was, in President Clinton's justification for intervention in Bosnia, "the right thing to do." Terrorist-proofing similar societies became Bush's reason for involvement, a rationale applied first to Afghanistan and then to Iraq. How the Obama administration will view situations beyond the current Iraq and Afghanistan involvements remains to be seen.

Assessing the likely future of American activism requires making two judgments, both of which are controversial and both of which apply equally to terrorist-suppressing and humanitarian motivations. The first is what the United States and its *developed* world allies seek to accomplish in the developing world. The Bush administration suggested the aggressive role of promoting democracy as its distinctive answer. The Obama administration has quietly backed away from this goal as a primary rhetorical device but has not articulated a clear alternative.

The other judgment is about how much *can* be accomplished. The experience of transforming developing states into modern or postmodern states is limited and spotty. The United States succeeded in South Korea but failed in Iran. Moreover, most of our experience has been in countries that were not among the most destitute; most of the candidates in the future will be in those difficult places. Afghanistan is almost a textbook case of the difficulties that will likely be faced more generally. Iraq magnifies the difficulties.

All these concerns apply equally well to potential terrorist-suppressing and humanitarian situations because the West believes the same underlying set of circumstances breeds asymmetrical warriors in the form of terrorists and practitioners of other forms of violence. Those conditions are poverty, despair, and oppression, which we believe constitute the swamp that, once drained, will cease to be the breeding ground for future instability and violence.

The post-9/11 emphasis on terrorism means the discussion must begin with efforts directed at its suppression. It is probably not unfair to assert that, if terrorism could be eliminated without addressing the underlying conditions that give rise to it, many Americans would embrace that solution. The question is whether terrorism can be controlled without "draining the swamp." Because solving the problem may also include attention to conditions in which terrorism breeds, the discussion then moves to peacekeeping and state building.

DEALING WITH TERRORISM

The attacks of 9/11 elevated terrorism and responding to it to the top of the national security agenda. The Bush administration described the effort as a "global war on terrorism" (GWOT) and raised terrorism to the pivot of American national security concerns. After eight years of soaring rhetoric, the Obama administration ratcheted down the tone of the debate, dropping the term *war* and replacing it with a descriptor borrowed from the Bush years as a campaign against *violent extremists*. The troop buildup in Afghanistan, however, belied any substantial reduction in intensity of the effort.

But what does all this rhetoric mean? Exactly what (or who) has been the opponent in this competition by whatever name? There are three possibilities. One is that the opponent is terrorism, but terrorism is a method, a way to do things, not a concrete entity. How does one defeat and subdue a method—and specifically a method that has endured for over two thousand years? A second possibility is that the opponent is terrorist purposes, but these are ideas that can be "defeated" only by being discredited, an intellectual process. The third possibility is that the contest is against terrorists, those who actually commit terrorist acts. Terrorists are at least a concrete opponent, but can eliminating particular terrorists extinguish terrorism as long as the method works at least some of the time and there are adherents to terrorist ideas?

These are all valid questions for which definitive, agreed-upon answers do not exist, but which must be dealt with if a coherent strategy for dealing with the problem is to be found. Examine each possibility. It is frequently argued that it makes no sense to talk about a campaign against an abstraction and the idea of terrorism is an application of a method, a means to accomplish goals. Can you "kill" an idea in some concrete or abstract form? If so, how do you know you have accomplished the task?

The war analogy suffers even if one switches emphasis and says the effort is directed against global terrorists. Switching the emphasis at least has the virtue of making it a war against people, a conceptual improvement, but it still retains two problems in the current context.

First, warfare against terrorists is warfare against asymmetrical warriors. That means that the countries seeking to defeat terrorism are militarily superior in conventional terms and that terrorism is the asymmetrical method by which terrorists seek to create a situation in which they have a chance of succeeding. The problem lies in the criteria for success for those seeking to snuff out terrorists and for the terrorists themselves. For any country seeking to engage in terrorist suppression, the criterion is very exacting: the effort cannot be won until all terrorists specified as the object of the action have been defeated. Those seeking to suppress terrorists must crush their opponents; in a phrase, they can only "win by winning."

The situation is different for the terrorists. Knowing they cannot succeed in the traditional sense of crushing their opponents themselves, they also know that their enemies cannot claim victory as long as the terrorists continue to operate. Thus, terrorists come to realize that their criterion for success is to avoid extinction and that the longer they do that, the more likely they are to be a sufficient irritant that their opponents conclude it is easier to accede to their demands than to continue the effort. The terrorists, in other words, can "win by not losing" or, at a minimum, prevent their enemy from declaring victory by avoiding defeat.

The problem of defeating terrorists is made more difficult by a second problem associated with modern asymmetrical warfare: contemporary terrorist organizations are nonstate actors. The majority of contemporary terrorist organizations are Muslim and have connections to parts of the Islamic Middle East. All Muslims in the area do not support terrorists (although enough do to provide safe havens and recruitment bases), and no state government has claimed association with a major terrorist organization since the Taliban were overthrown in 2001. To make matters worse, these nonstate actors generally imbed themselves within physical areas and among people sympathetic to them. They move around, sometimes crossing national borders, such as the Waziristan area of the FATA along the Afghanistan–Pakistan border, and they rarely establish physical symbols that can be associated with them.

The problem this creates for a "war" on terrorism is finding targets that can be attacked and defeated. When Al Qaeda was openly running training camps in Afghanistan in the 1990s, this was not so much of a problem, and occasionally, a military attack would be launched against these facilities, such as the cruise missile attacks in 1998 in retaliation for Al Qaeda bombings of American embassies in Kenya and Tanzania. Since the fall of the Taliban and their dispersal into non-state anonymity, targeting actions against Al Qaeda has been much more difficult and less successful. The result, according to Audrey Kurth Cronin, is "that it is virtually impossible to target the most vulnerable point in the organization." Until (or unless) the problem of identifying targets that can be attacked without significant civilian casualties is solved, military efforts are likely to remain frustrated.

The current dilemma regarding Al Qaeda illustrates the problem. It is widely known that Al Qaeda's leadership and infrastructure are located in the Pakistani "badlands," where the Pakistani government has historically exercised only token control, ceding effective governance to tribal leaders in return for their allegiance to the regime. The tribal leaders, in turn, have had working relations with Al Qaeda that leave the terrorist group secure and allow it to transit back and forth across the Afghan border. Until recently, the Pakistani government has not dared to conduct large-scale operations against Al Qaeda because it lacks detailed information about where Al Qaeda is located and it would meet local resistance.

In this case, how can the antiterrorist campaign be brought to bear against Al Qaeda? Politically, American ally Pakistan can neither conduct effective ground operations in much of the FATA nor permit the United States to conduct air attacks because of concerns with sovereignty. Additionally, American intelligence capabilities are too limited to pinpoint Al Qaeda targets (such as bin Laden) for aerial attacks. The result is a very frustrating situation that is a major point of contention between the United States and Pakistan.

Suppressing terrorist activities involves a variety of activities, not all of which can be described in detail here. All are aimed at either eliminating terrorist activities or containing them at some "acceptable" level (normally undefined). For present purposes, these efforts can be organized around three distinctions: the forms of terrorist suppression (antiterrorism and counterterrorism), the focus of these efforts (international and national), and the objectives of these efforts.

Antiterrorism and Counterterrorism

In conventional terrorism-suppression circles, two methods for dealing with the terrorism problem are most often invoked: antiterrorism and counterterrorism. The terms are often used interchangeably, although each refers to a distinct form of action with distinct purposes. Any program of terrorist suppression will necessarily contain elements of each form, but failing to specify which is which only confuses the issue.

Antiterrorism refers to defensive efforts to reduce the vulnerability of targets to terrorist attacks and to reduce the effects of such attacks that do occur. Antiterrorism efforts thus begin from the premise that terrorist attacks will in fact occur (or at least be attempted) and that two forms of effort are necessary to counter those efforts. First, antiterrorists seek to make it more difficult to mount terrorist attacks. Airport security to prevent potential terrorists from boarding airliners and the interception and detention of potential terrorists by border guards are examples, as is placing barriers around public buildings so that terrorists cannot drive bomb-laden vehicles close enough to destroy the buildings. Second, antiterrorists seek to mitigate the effects of terrorist attacks that do occur. This form of activity is also known as civil defense and is largely the province of first responders such as police and firemen.

At least four related difficulties hamper an effective antiterrorist campaign. One is that antiterrorism is necessarily reactive: terrorists choose where attacks will occur and against what kinds of targets, and antiterrorists must respond to the terrorist initiative. A second problem is the sheer volume and variety of targets to be protected. The potential list of terrorist targets is almost infinite, and one of the purposes of attacks is often randomness so that potential victims are always on guard but uncertain of where the terrorist may strike. The third problem is target substitution: if antiterrorist efforts are sufficiently successful in protecting one target or category of targets to make success problematical, the terrorists will simply look for and choose a less-well-defended target. The fourth problem is the political economy of the enterprise: suppressing terrorism is much more expensive than terror is, a dynamic explored in Amplification 13.1.

The other form of terrorist suppression is *counterterrorism*, offensive and military measures against terrorists or sponsoring agencies to prevent, deter, or respond to terrorist attacks. As the definition suggests, counterterrorism consists of both preventive and retaliatory actions against terrorists. Preventive acts can include such things as penetration of terrorist cells and taking action—including apprehension and physical violence against terrorists—before they carry out their acts. Retaliation is more often military and paramilitary and includes attacks on terrorist camps or other facilities in response to terrorist attacks. The purposes of retaliation include both reducing terrorist capacity for future acts and hopefully deterring future acts by instilling fear of the consequences. In addition, Special Operations Forces are sometimes used to penetrate terrorist staging areas for reconnaissance and intelligence purposes.

Amplification 13.1

THE COST-EFFECTIVENESS OF
SUPPRESSING TERRORISM

The economics of terrorism and its suppression favors the terrorist. Generally speaking, it is cheaper to mount a terrorist attacks against a target than it is to protect that target. The reason is simple: the terrorists know what particular target in a target set they plan to attack and need only expend resources on preparing to attack that object. Antiterrorists, on the other hand, do not know far in advance (if they know at all) which part of the set is being targeted, and thus, they must plan to protect all objects in the set. The larger the target set, the more advantage goes to the terrorists.

Protecting the whole target set is clearly more expensive than protecting individual targets, and since most members of the set are not actually under threat, the additional costs of protecting them are costs not incurred by the terrorists. Since the terrorists can always change targets from more- to less-well-protected targets, the result is that the terrorists can always further disadvantage the antiterrorists by simply expanding the list of target categories that must be protected at economic disadvantage for the defenders.

Counterterrorism is inherently and intuitively attractive. Preventive actions are proactive, taking the battle to the terrorists and punishing them in advance of creating harm. If effective, they prevent terrorist operations from being carried out and weaken the terrorist organization by capturing or killing its members. In its purest form, preventive counterterrorist actions reverse the tables in the relationship, effectively "terrorizing the terrorists." Pounding a terrorist facility as punishment from enduring a terrorist attack at least offers the satisfaction of knowing the enemy has suffered for the suffering it has caused the victim.

The problem with counterterrorism, like antiterrorism, is that it is insufficient on its own as a way to quell terrorism. Preventing terrorist actions requires a level of intelligence about the structure of terrorist organization that is quite difficult to obtain, and it has been a central purpose of terrorist reorganization into protean forms, discussed in Chapter 9, to increase that difficulty. If one does not know the terrorist organization in detail, it is, for instance, difficult to penetrate, learn of its nefarious intentions, and interrupt those actions. The absence of a state base that can be attacked means it is more difficult to identify terrorist targets whose retaliatory destruction will cripple the organization, punish its members, or frighten it into ceasing future operations.

Ideally, antiterrorism and counterterrorism efforts act in tandem. Counterterrorists reduce the number and quality of possible attacks through preventive actions, resulting in less frequent and thus more manageable antiterrorist efforts to ameliorate the effects of attacks that do succeed. Counterterrorists' retaliation, then, can hopefully reduce the terrorists' capacity for future mayhem. In practice, however, these efforts sometimes come into operational conflict. The antiterrorist emphasis on lessening the effects of attacks may lead to publicizing the possibility of particular attacks as a way to alert citizens (the color-coded warning system, for instance), whereas counterterrorists prefer to keep operations as secret as possible to facilitate clandestine penetration and interruption.

International and National Efforts

There has been considerable discussion since 9/11 about the appropriate level at which to conduct operations aimed at suppressing this current wave of international terrorist activity. In the immediate aftermath of the attacks, there was an enormous international outpouring of sympathy for the United States and willingness to join a vigorous international effort to deal with terrorists around the globe. That resolve resulted in a good amount of international cooperation among law enforcement and intelligence agencies in various countries, much of which continues quietly to this day. The more visible manifestations of that internationalization faded as the United States "militarized" the terrorism-suppression effort (the GWOT as primarily "war") and moved in directions opposed by major allies through unilateral actions in places like Iraq. The Obama administration's general preference for international cooperation will likely result in a resurgence of international cooperative behavior.

Does the evolving nature of the threat suggest a greater inward or outward turning of efforts? Former Central Intelligence Agency (CIA) expert Paul Pillar suggests that the evolving nature of the threat reinforces the need for greater internationalization. As he describes it, "In a more decentralized network, individuals will go unnoticed not because data on analysts' screens are misinterpreted but because they will never appear on those screens in the first place." Much of the added data on the successors to Al Qaeda can be collected only in the countries where they operate, but Pillar sees two barriers to sustained international cooperation. On the one hand, "an underlying limitation on foreign willingness to cooperate with the United States is the skepticism among foreign publics and even elites that the most powerful nation on the planet needs to be occupied by a small band of radicals." This leads to the second misgiving, which is the perceived "ability to sustain the country's own determination to fight" the terrorist threat.

The internationalization or nationalization of focus has become somewhat sublimated in the militarization of efforts to destroy Al Qaeda in Afghanistan and Pakistan. As noted in Chapter 2, the effort is rhetorically aimed at Al Qaeda, but the actual opponents on the ground are Taliban contesting control of the government of Afghanistan; increasingly, North Atlantic Treaty Organization (NATO) members of the International Security Assistance Force (ISAF) who signed on for the terrorist goal have become less enthusiastic about effective involvement in the civil war. Pakistani national resistance to outside (mainly U.S.) incursion on its sovereign soil to destroy Al Qaeda sanctuaries has progressively isolated the United States from the international community as well.

Objectives of the Effort

A final problem of the conceptual nature of terrorism suppression is capturing the entirety of the problem that it has been asked to solve. The GWOT, as suggested, was really an effort aimed at suppressing terrorists, as are the forms of dealing with terrorists discussed in the previous section. Somehow capturing or killing all the existing terrorists does not, however, destroy *terrorism*, which is the underlying purpose of the entire enterprise. As long as individuals and groups choose terrorism as a means to realize their ideas, terrorism cannot be wholly eradicated; only its current manifestations can be contained.

This other part of any effort to suppress terrorism is intellectual, a war of ideas that has two parts. The first is the intellectual competition between terrorists and their enemies—the underlying reasons terrorists emerge and the appeal they have among populations that hide, nurture, sustain, and form the recruitment base for movements that employ terrorism as a method. In the current wave of religious terrorism, virulent anti-Americanism is the activator; the United States and the American way of life are portrayed as the major threat to Islam and the way of life it promotes. As long as the United States (and the West generally) does not compete with this idea and assert and convince those in the Middle East that our ideas produce a superior existence *for them*, there will be an endless stream of recruits to the banner that no terrorism-suppression effort can even hope to overcome. The best chance for "defeating" these ideas may be that their millenarian goals will eventually be abandoned as unattainable—as has happened in the past.

The second part of the intellectual battle is over the use of terrorism as the method of those ideas Americans oppose. This requires competing in the forum of ideas that can lead to terrorism and also dealing with what causes people to become terrorists. Regardless of the level of causation at which one begins (societal, political, or psychological), one must persuade people that volunteering to be terrorists is not a rational act that will allow them to achieve their own personal or societal goals. Delegitimizing terrorism, in other words, is a key element in "draining the swamp" in which terrorists breed and is a clearly necessary part of any successful future strategy.

PEACEKEEPING AND STATE BUILDING

Although the assertion is not without critics, the general policy community consensus is that the source of international instability manifested most dramatically by international religious terrorism cannot be defeated or contained as long as there are unstable societies that produce the kinds of frustration in which violent extremism is nurtured. The result has been an emphasis on efforts to pacify such vulnerable societies (peacekeeping) by stabilizing the underlying conditions in which violence occurs.

The Afghanistan effort by the United States and the ISAF peacekeepers attracted more attention than previous peacekeeping missions because of the association of the mission with international terrorism. The missions in which the United

States was involved in the 1990s—Somalia, Haiti, Bosnia, and Kosovo—generated some initial publicity when the United States embarked on them and, in the case of Somalia, when the United States withdrew under less-than-ideal circumstances and with a less-than-favorable outcome. Interest, however, was never enormous, because these missions neither involved significant U.S. interests nor entailed significant costs in blood or treasure. In Afghanistan, until recently interest was high and the costs moderate. Although Iraq has never been characterized as a peacekeeping operation, the problems of dealing with an occupied Iraq are basically the same as those encountered in peacekeeping operations.

The 1990s missions had peacekeeping and, at least implicitly, state building as objectives. In Haiti, the mission involved restoring Jean-Bertrand Aristide to the elected presidency from which he had been removed by a military coup and creating the conditions for future stability. The first objective was achieved during the four years the United States remained in the country as the lead member of the Operation Uphold Democracy coalition. The second objective is hard to label a success because Haiti still lacks the basis of a stable, prosperous state.

In Bosnia and Kosovo, the United States was part of a U.N.-sanctioned peacekeeping mission with the purpose of restoring order and preparing the countries for postmission stability; in the case of Kosovo, the mission explicitly included state building. The Stabilization Force (originally Implementation Force) entered Bosnia in 1995, and the Kosovo Force was formed in 1999.

Although the terms were developed for 1990s operations, peacekeeping and state building are used to describe Afghanistan and Iraq, even though these situations are sufficiently different as virtually to defy comparison. The efforts arise out of very different situations. In Kosovo and Haiti, repressive governments were suppressing the population, and the first goal was to end the suppression. In Bosnia, the problem was to separate warring parties as the first step in implementing the Dayton Accords, which called for a separation of factions. In Afghanistan, there was a conventional civil war going on between the Taliban government and its opponents, which the United States joined on the side of the insurgents (although prior to the stimulus of the terrorist attacks, the United States had essentially ignored the war). In Iraq, of course, the United States overthrew the oppressive Hussein regime.

The structure and purposes of interventions are also different. The United Nations initially authorized the ISAF to restore and enforce order in Kabul, but its mission beyond that was not clear. The Afghans themselves expressed interest in a long deployment providing security for more of the country while the situation stabilized. The United States, meanwhile, established its own longer-term presence both by establishing and maintaining control of airfields and the like in Afghanistan itself and by establishing bases in adjacent former republics of the Soviet Union (e.g., Uzbekistan), while initially opposing the extension of the ISAF mission and declining to participate in it. Establishing bases outside Afghanistan was rather clearly a hedge against outliving the American welcome in Afghanistan itself. Meanwhile, international leaders were pledging support for rebuilding an Afghanistan ravaged by over two decades of war (in other words, state building), without being very specific about what that entailed.

Iraq is a unique situation not often described in peacekeeping/state-building terms, but it arguably should be. After the United States successfully overthrew the Iraqi government, its first mission was to establish, maintain, and strengthen internal order and peace within the country (essentially peacekeeping). It also adopted a state-building role by declaring its intent to assist in the establishment of political democracy and the rebuilding of Iraq's society and economy during Phase IV operations. What principally differs is that the United States *created* the need for such actions by starting the war rather than by reacting to preexisting conditions.

Basic Distinctions

Outside interference in the affairs of other states is always problematic. While the motives underlying interference may be noble and pristine (they may also not be), they are never going to be viewed by those in whose countries interference occurs in the same way they are by the intervening parties. The initial motivation during the 1990s among intervenors (usually under the flag of the United Nations) was publicly humanitarian, and helping the suppressed and suffering is always among the motives that impel such actions. This is as true in American-dominated missions like Iraq as it is in U.N. operations. Such efforts will always likely meet some initial opposition, which will increase the longer the operation lasts and the intervening parties stay. This is true because intervention always has the effect—if not the intention—of providing advantage to some internal factions at the cost to others, and the losers will eventually not appreciate the effort or view it as benign. At the same time, lengthy interventions, especially in the formerly colonized world, will almost certainly begin to look like recolonization and create rumblings of imperialism. No country's citizens long embrace being occupied by a foreign army.

This uncertainty of reception helps create the frame within which outside interference is contemplated. What outsiders propose to do really consists of two determinations. The first is what it will try to accomplish—its concept. To this end, the basic alternatives are conflict suppression and state building. The other question is how it will accomplish the task—its form. This examination requires looking at a continuum of actions with peace imposition and peacekeeping as its poles.

The first distinction is between conflict suppression and state building. One of the frequent, recurring criticisms of American involvements in developing-world conflicts in the past has been the open-endedness of these missions. Part of this criticism is focused on the failure to establish a clear initial objective to be accomplished. This criticism, in turn, leads to the more frequently alleged shortcoming, which is the lack of a clear point at which the mission is accomplished, sometimes called an end or exit strategy that tells Americans when to go home. When, for instance, will the United States have sufficiently influenced conditions in Afghanistan to allow withdrawal from that country? The longer the stay and the more seemingly ubiquitous the presence of the outsider, the greater the resentment of that presence will be among some groups, especially those that do not benefit from that presence. This dynamic will occur regardless of how noble the outsider's personal intentions are.

When entering the chaos of a war-torn developing-world country that has been unable to terminate the violence itself (the normal reason in the first place), a state can have one of two missions. The first is conflict suppression—either stopping the ongoing fighting (peace imposition) or maintaining a recently established but volatile ceasefire (peace enforcement). These actions do no more than cause the fighting and killing to stop; they do not in and of themselves assure postwar domestic tranquility. The simplest measure of success is whether the fighting is discontinued.

Conflict suppression itself does not address or solve the problems that led to fighting. A more ambitious definition of successful conflict suppression is that it results in continued peace after the force has been withdrawn. This is necessary because, unless the underlying causes of fighting are addressed, fighting is likely to be rekindled after the intervening parties leave. Conflict suppression deals, in other words, with the symptoms of violence, not the underlying disease. It is a bandage to staunch the wound, not a cure.

Since intervention usually occurs in failed or noncompetitive states, leaving behind a stable, nonviolent environment in which the return to violence will seem unappealing to the formerly warring parties is the clear requisite to success. The societies that tend to collapse into violence generally require both political reform (institution building, political reconciliation, etc.) and economic development to create a sense of present or future tranquility and prosperity that is clearly preferable to war and that thus commands the loyalty of the population (in other words, results in the conferral of legitimacy to the regime). The collective actions taken to accomplish this goal constitute state building.

Conflict suppression and state building are sequential. A conflict must be terminated before any state building can begin. Although a country can engage in conflict suppression without engaging in state building, the outcome is likely to be incomplete: a reversion to war after the conflict-suppressing force withdraws. Conversely, state building cannot normally be undertaken unless successful conflict suppression has occurred; it would not be safe to try to do so, and state-building efforts would themselves be the object of future violence.

This leads to distinctions about what the intervening state attempts to do—the forms of intervention. In common terms, interventions are known collectively as peacekeeping, although the term is misleading in its generally accepted form and describes only a part of what is undertaken when intervention occurs.

Intervention can encompass three distinct activities that form a continuum paralleling the three phases of contemporary asymmetrical war. At one end of the spectrum is peace imposition, which refers to actions taken to stop the violence in a war zone. In most but not all cases, peace imposition is undertaken for neutral purposes to stop the fighting and killing, what may be called neutrality of intent. The effect of stopping the fighting will never, however, be neutral in effect, if for no other reason than stopping the fighting halts the military success of whoever was winning and increases the likely failure of whoever was losing. The result is that some will congratulate and embrace the intervenors (the winners, like the Iraqi Shi'a) and some will not (the losers, like the Iraqi Sunni). In Afghanistan, the Pashtuns suffer most from American peace imposition efforts.

At the other end of the continuum is peacekeeping. In its classic sense, peacekeeping consists of monitoring and observing an established ceasefire between warring parties when the peacekeepers' intent and effect are to oversee a temporary condition of peace conducive to discussions intended to produce a lasting, stable peace. In the terms introduced above, a peacekeeping setting is one where statebuilding activities can be undertaken with the relative assurance that the peacekeepers will not be the victims of violence while they build or rebuild the economic and political infrastructure of the target country.

Lying between these two extreme forms of activity is peace enforcement. It is an activity undertaken when the physical fighting has been concluded but wherein it is uncertain that peace would be sustained in the absence of the outside force. Whereas peace imposition and peacekeeping represent responses to concrete, finite situations (states of war, peace desired by all parties), peace enforcement constitutes a range of situations, from a near state of war in which few of the participants prefer war to its alternative, to a situation in which almost all the parties prefer peace. Most real situations into which outside forces are committed rightfully fall in the category of peace enforcement.

These concepts can be applied tentatively to Iraq. The ultimate goal in Iraq, which may or may not be realized, is state building to produce a democratic, prosperous Iraq that will be a regional model. Within this neoconservative construct, the primary instrument for change has been U.S. military force. The conquest and the overthrow of the Hussein government can be thought of as peace imposition—although with the added step of destroying and then restoring peace. The occupation has largely been an exercise in peace enforcement, since the "peace" has clearly been fragile and might well break down if peace enforcers (the occupation troops) are withdrawn. The situation has not evolved to the point that the occupation is an exercise in peacekeeping, since that requires that all (or nearly all) groups prefer the peaceful status quo to continued violence. Since state building occurs best in a peacekeeping environment (where there is little violence to disrupt it), the absence of such an environment helps explain the relative lack of state-building progress. Afghanistan, by contrast, clearly remains a peace imposition problem.

Peacekeeping

The term *peacekeeping* has its contemporary origins in a specific set of U.N. operations conducted during the Cold War that constituted one of the few notable successes of the world organization in the security area during that period. Those activities basically conform to the definition of peacekeeping described earlier and emphasize the observation and monitoring of ceasefires between formerly warring parties. In most cases, these peacekeeping forces were put in place between sovereign countries and had the passive purpose of making sure the terms of ceasefires were honored. Their success occurred when the parties truly preferred peace to war and thus preferred maintenance of the status quo to a return to violence. In those circumstances, peacekeepers could be neutral both in intent and in effect, thereby adding positively to the situation for all concerned. Peacekeeping works, in other words, when the parties want peace roughly in conformance with the conditions the peacekeepers are assigned to enforce.

That set of circumstances rarely holds in internal wars, as the United Nations learned in its two major Cold War intrusions into domestic fracases in the former Belgian Congo (later Zaire, now the Democratic Republic of Congo) and Cyprus. In the Congo in 1960, U.N. peacekeepers opposed the attempted secession of Katanga (now Shaba) province and found themselves in the position of partisans rather than neutrals, to the organization's discomfort and the mission's ineffectiveness. In Cyprus in 1967, the United Nations was so successful in imposing peace and a ceasefire line that the Greeks and Turks concluded there was no real need to settle their differences as long as UNFICYP (U.N. Forces in Cyprus) remained in place. The U.N. mission is still there, with no real prospect of being concluded and withdrawn.

When the Cold War ended, these distinctions and limitations were largely lost in the euphoria of the U.N.-sponsored Desert Storm coalition. The security role of the world body was greatly enhanced, and it appeared likely the U.N. role would become central to international security. In 1991, the Security Council instructed Secretary-General Boutros Boutros-Ghali of Egypt to draw up a blueprint for U.N. participation in the promotion of international peace in the post–Cold War world. In 1992, he produced *An Agenda for Peace*, which labeled almost any international intervention, regardless of whether it was in wars between states (which have been virtually nonexistent since the Persian Gulf War) or internal wars (which virtually all wars have been), as peacekeeping. The confusion over roles and missions has been ongoing ever since.

The problem, of course, is that the wake of internal wars or other interventions rarely resembles the tranquil situation for which traditional peacekeeping is designed. In most cases, missions are not contemplated until violence has been going on for some time and when the trigger for international action is the public revelation of hideous, often grotesque atrocity (such as in Sudan). In those circumstances, the impulse for reconciliation will likely be overwhelmed by the desire for retribution, which peacekeepers can only interrupt (Albanian Kosovar reprisals against their Serbian former persecutors provide an example). The situation is normally tentatively one of peace enforcement—at best—wherein intervening forces must actively work to sustain the absence of violence rather than simply observing and monitoring an established peace.

This situation has operational consequences as well. Classic, traditional peacekeepers are lightly armed forces (generally with only handheld weapons to be used exclusively in personal self-defense) that require a minimum of physical or military support, since it is not anticipated they will be placed in harm's way. This also makes them relatively inexpensive, an attribute that makes them appealing to the United Nations, which must rely on the often fickle collection of member-state contributions to support its activities. Since it is cheaper than fighting a war, the characterization of situations as peacekeeping appeals to a perpetually financially strapped organization like the United Nations.

The problem is that few contemporary situations are peacekeeping in nature. The so-called U.N.-sponsored peacekeeping operation in Darfur, for instance, is

Table 13.1: Situations, Missions, and Force Requirements

Situation:	War	Unstable Peace	Peace
Mission:	Peace Imposition	Peace Enforcement	Peacekeeping
Force Required:	War Fighters	War Fighters/Police	Police

there to *impose* and *enforce* a peace that not everyone (including the *janjaweed* "rebels" and the Sudanese government) wholeheartedly embraces. The classic passive peacekeeping model does not clearly apply, nor is it clearly appropriate to the situations in Afghanistan or Iraq.

The tasks and complexities surrounding generic peacekeeping take on added meaning if two other dimensions are added to the peace imposition–peace enforcement–peacekeeping continuum, as shown in Table 13.1.

In the figure, the situation and missions are as already described, with the addition of the term *unstable peace* to describe the range of situations in which peace enforcement is needed. Clearly, the peace is increasingly stable as one moves away from war and toward the consensus that peace is most desirable. The figure also shows the kinds of military skills required in various stages of the operation. When war is ongoing and peace must be imposed, the need is clearly for combat soldiers with all the equipment and other wherewithal necessary for providing self-protection and for imposing its will on a hostile enemy by brute force. When stable, self-sustaining peace is achieved, the monitoring function is largely a police function: the peacekeepers essentially make sure the "law" represented by the terms of the ceasefire is obeyed. The tools of their trade are light sidearms and aids to observation like binoculars. Combat soldiers may or may not be proficient at policing; police officers are typically not prepared for all-out combat.

The problem, of course, lies in the hybrid situation of unstable peace, which is the condition into which most outsider forces are in fact interposed (occasionally after imposing the peace in the first place) and in which they are likely to be called upon to perform in the future. Clearly, when peace is fragile and fighting could easily resume, both combat and policing skills are needed—and in varying mixes as the situation requires. When the experience of war is still fresh, combat soldiers will still be needed to intimidate and coerce the parties not to resume fighting among themselves or not to attack the peacekeepers. That role may provide a kind of shield behind which other, more positive and reconciling activities can take place, but in that role, soldiers do not contribute to the positive attainment of peace.

Ideally, the same people can fulfill both the combat and the policing roles, adapting chameleon-like to changing conditions and adapting their behaviors accordingly. Unfortunately, the character and skills that make a good combat soldier generally are not the same as those for a good police officer, and developing the second set of skills may degrade the primary skill: the soldier-cop becomes a less lethal soldier, and the cop-soldier becomes a less compassionate, more ruthless cop. This dynamic is explored in the caricature contained in Amplification 13.2. The bottom line is that real peacekeeping in the contemporary world includes a variety of roles that shift over time, suggesting the need to alter and fine-tune the composition of the force across time and as progress is attained.

Amplification 13.2

THE TALK–SHOOT RELATIONSHIP IN PEACEKEEPING

The kind of troops that should be employed in peacekeeping has been a matter of disagreement since the United States began participating in these enterprises and is an especially difficult matter in situations where duties go beyond simple observation and monitoring to actual or potential combat operations. Should peacekeepers be lightly and defensively armed observers on the model of military police? Should they be fully armed combat troops ready to respond to any situation? Or should the same peacekeepers be used to fill both functions?

The official position of the American military is that regular combat forces can be trained to be peacekeepers as well as combatants, and the frequent assertion by official military sources is that "any good soldier can do peacekeeping." But is that assertion true?

One way to look at the roles of passive peacekeeper/police officer and combat soldier/peace imposer or enforcer is what can be called the "talk–shoot relationship." For the policeman confronted with a potentially dangerous situation, the procedure is to try to resolve the situation peacefully and to fire only as a last resort in self-defense (talk first, then shoot). For a combat soldier, the failure to attack in a dangerous situation may put his or her life in peril, and the appropriate response is to defend one's self (shoot first, then ask questions). The peacekeeper who fires first may be a murderer; the soldier who fails to shoot first may be dead.

Can the same personnel perform both functions, making the right decision in contrasting stressful situations? What does the combat soldier on patrol do when he sees someone about to throw something at him, not knowing if the object is a rotten tomato or a grenade? The decision is particularly difficult if the assailant is a child, as is increasingly the case and for which the military has few developed procedures (see the Singer article, listed in the "Selected Bibliography," for an assessment of this aspect of the problem). Also, can soldiers effectively make the transition back and forth from one role to another? If involvement in other people's internal conflicts is to become a common part of the future, answers to these kinds of questions must be found.

Even when the complexities of these situations are recognized and addressed, they speak only to part of the problem. Almost all the conditions that peacekeepers contribute to fall within the category of conflict suppression. As the situation moves toward the peace end of the continuum, the peacekeepers as police may make some positive contributions to restoring public confidence in the criminal justice system, but this will mostly occur when they are handing off their duties to natives recruited to replace them.

Moving the situation to one of stable peace requires restoring (or creating) confidence in and loyalty to the existing order in the country itself. The changing roles assigned to peacekeepers may contribute to that goal and even be a necessary condition for success. Peacekeepers cannot create the conditions necessary to build a stable political system and economic prospects of prosperity. Doing those things is the province of individuals and organizations engaged in state building.

State Building

The rationale for state building is a logical extension of the justification for conflict suppression. A state intervenes in the internal affairs of another for one of two reasons: either because the target state is engaged in a civil disagreement that it seems incapable of solving itself and that manifests itself in great suffering (the humanitarian argument) or because the intervening state has some interest in a particular outcome (the realist argument). The first justification underlay American involvement in places like Bosnia, Kosovo, and earlier Somalia. The second justification formed the basis for American involvement in Afghanistan and Iraq and may be extended to other places as part of the expanded "war" on global terrorism in the future.

State building is a logical part of these motives because simple conflict suppression will not by itself solve the root problems from which the violence has arisen in the first place—the conditions of the swamp. Somalia in the 1990s and even today illustrates this problem. The roots of Somali anarchy lay in clan divisions that were deep-seated and historical and that had been magnified by several years of drought and starvation. The international effort there, however, was limited and short-sighted, at least partly because it was the first time the international community, with the United States in the lead, had tried to save a failed state. The initial effort was limited to conflict suppression designed to reinstate the flow of food supplies donated by the international community until the end of the drought began to result in crops being harvested. It never progressed far beyond that stage.

The concept of state building was first applied in the abortive U.S.-led mission to Somalia, which ended with a U.S. withdrawal and the continuation of effective anarchy in the country to this day (demonstrated most dramatically by the relatively open operation of modern pirates from Somali territory). After Somalia, the idea of state building went into disrepute, enshrouded as a form of hated mission creep (incremental, unplanned expansion of the mission that distorts its original intent) that had led to American failure in that campaign. The charge was always misinformed. The United States failed to produce a stable situation in Somalia not because of what it did but because of what it did not do, which was attempt to engage in meaningful state building. The effort might have failed anyway, in which case the United States would *truly* have failed. State building was not revived until the end of the 1990s, when the United States decided to try again, declaring the building of a stable state the goal in Kosovo, a promise reiterated for Afghanistan in 2001 and, at least implicitly, for Iraq in 2003.

Can state building turn a failed, noncompetitive state into a stable, contributing member of the international community? The answer is fundamentally unknown because the United States has never systematically tried to do so in the kinds of countries where attempts at state building are likely to occur in the present and future. It is sometimes suggested that state building was implemented in Germany and Japan after World War II, but the problems were not the same. In the former Axis countries, the problem was clearing the rubble and rebuilding the physical infrastructure. The price exacted was acceptance of democratic constitutions, the success of which was made highly likely with the generous influx of cash. If there is any parallel to the present, it may be the Republic of Korea, which became a priority after the Korean War. In Korea, resources were provided proportionately far in excess of the amounts that will be available in contemporary failed states.

The inability confidently to predict success, combined with the frank admission that it will be a long, expensive, and difficult process, makes selling state building difficult. Moreover, the places for which it is proposed are simultaneously the most in need and, by definition, the most unprepared for the process.

Having said all that, the last two American presidents (Clinton in Kosovo, Bush in Afghanistan and Iraq) committed the United States to engage in state building, and the Obama administration seems committed to a similar course. To help assess what lies ahead for these efforts, the author borrows three questions originally asked in *When America Fights* around which to organize the discussion: Where to go? What to do? How to do it?

Where to Go? For the immediate future, that question has largely been answered. The United States is the lead actor and committed to state-building efforts in Afghanistan and Iraq. If one includes the Clinton precedent in Kosovo, the "sample" has the virtue of representing the two motivations underlying intervention: humanitarianism in Kosovo and realism and geopolitics in Afghanistan and Iraq. The countries also represent the various levels of desperation state builders will encounter: Kosovo, as a province within European Yugoslavia, is much more developed than Afghanistan, whereas Iraq lies somewhere in between in developmental terms. At the same time, the outcome in Kosovo does not have the same urgency and thus priority that Afghanistan and Iraq have by virtue of being subsumed in the category of the war against terrorism.

Which countries become the subjects of intervention and state building is only partially a matter of choice. There may be some other places like Afghanistan, where an apparent deployment of necessity leads to a state-building mission of apparently equal necessity, or Iraq, where American initiatives trigger the need. More opportunities are likely to present themselves in states where failure and noncompetitiveness have their primary, even whole, negative impact on the citizens of the country itself and where involvement and subsequent state building must be justified on humanitarian grounds, deployments and missions of choice (Sudan). What they will all share is the enormous, even daunting, problems that state builders will encounter.

Recognizing how difficult circumstances are likely to be is crucial to determining whether to engage in state building. In most instances, there will be no government that has the loyalty of any sizable portion of the population. Instead, there are likely to be competing groups eager to ingratiate themselves with the state builders to benefit themselves but unable to cooperate or uninterested in cooperating among themselves (the internal political bickering in Iraq). Institutions are likely to be in ruin where they exist at all, and basic service providers are likely to be in short supply (during the Serb ethnic cleansing in Kosovo, public servants such as clerks and mail carriers were systematically targeted and killed to break down the Kosovars' ability to self-govern, for instance). Moreover, no single regime or group is likely to have legitimacy in the eyes of the general population, a problem likely exacerbated by atrocities committed during the violent stage of the civil unrest or, in places like Iraq, afterward. Sometimes these problems will be structural and historical, as in the tribal, clan-based warlord systems in Afghanistan and Somalia; sometimes they will be the result of the excesses of the civil conflict, as in Bosnia and Sierra Leone. Other problems, like those in Iraq, may be the result of regime change that threatens the established ethnic power order.

Economic travail is likely to be present as well. It is generally true that political peace and stability accompany prosperity and economic improvement, and not poverty and misery, and that misery coincides with and contributes to instability. Infrastructures are either nonexistent or destroyed by years of war (a central problem in Afghanistan) and neglect (Iraq) and must be built or rebuilt before other services can be addressed. In cold climates (Kosovo and Afghanistan) where winter is a problem and many homes have been destroyed, simply providing a warm space in which to live may be a top priority. In hot places like Iraq, turning the air conditioning back on is equally important.

What to Do? Although the generalized goals of state building are easy to articulate, getting there is difficult and is made more difficult by two problems, one discussed in this section, the other in the next. The first is what exactly needs to be accomplished and is made more difficult by the absence of any comprehensive list of goals and needs or plan for achieving them. The second is a general lack of detailed outsider knowledge about local conditions and people, creating a difficulty in knowing with whom to deal and how. Both were clearly present in Phase IV planning in Iraq.

Building or rebuilding an internal war–ravaged country requires action on at least four dimensions, all of which must be accompanied by and must reinforce efforts by peacekeepers. The first dimension is *political*, somehow bringing a sense of order and eventually legitimacy into a setting that probably lacks both. Within this category, the first and most vital task is the simple establishment of order and security, creating the condition where citizens can expect peace and the absence of crime or politically based violence or intimidation in their daily lives. Initially, this role will likely be assigned to peacekeepers, but their participation must be temporary if the mission is ultimately to succeed. Ultimately, security must be provided by indigenous forces, which must be developed and must gradually become viewed as trustworthy, effective, and legitimate.

A major first task is thus the recruitment of a police force, initially internationally and later from within the population. While this task seems obvious, it is not necessarily easy. Finding foreign police willing to serve in war zones is not easy; a force of thirteen thousand was authorized for Kosovo in 1999 and was never achieved, even at premium salaries of over $90,000 for a one-year tour. Finding locals may also be hard; when the United States recruited a gendarmerie for Haiti in the mid-1990s, it turned out that many of the officers hired were former members of the terrorist *tonton macoutes* who wanted to be police so they could extract bribes from drug traffickers operating in the country. In Iraq, the resistance has targeted police recruits for assassination as a way to discourage volunteerism. At the same time, the criminal justice system must be revamped so that people view it as fair, and other governmental institutions must be created or restructured and personnel recruited to operate them. Simultaneously, preparations for turning governance over to citizens must be undertaken. In many cases, this entails helping to draft constitutional documents and finding the appropriate people to engage in a constitutional convention in a situation in which outsiders know relatively little about the candidates and there is a long and well-established tradition of mistrust and noncooperation between groups in the political arena.

The second dimension of the problem is *economic*. When state-building efforts are considered, they likely occur where wretched economic conditions reflect the destruction of the economy or the absence of developed economic structures. In some cases, what little economic activity does exist may be criminal, as in Afghan poppy and heroin production. In virtually all cases, conditions are likely to be sufficiently chaotic and unappealing that foreign investors are almost certain to be unwilling to come in, limiting the prospects of help from the private sector.

The first task is basic infrastructure development and rehabilitation. Where they exist at all, roads and railroad tracks are in disrepair, bridges have been damaged or destroyed, and airfields have been pockmarked or mined or both. All need attention for normal activities, including commerce, to resume. At the same time, electricity and water supplies have probably been disrupted; schools, hospitals, and other public buildings burned or bombed; stores looted; and private homes and apartments damaged. Until basic conditions of survival and living can be secured and the most basic services necessary for commerce and economic activity reinstated, little progress can be made on other fronts.

Military personnel attached to peacekeeping can be useful in alleviating some of these miseries. Just as soldiers (and especially military police) can help establish order and civic affairs units can aid in institution building, so, too, can soldiers and military engineers repair and secure runways, roads, and bridges. These personnel are unlikely to be available in sufficient numbers or for long enough periods of time to make more than a dent in the problems (many of the American service personnel with the requisite skills are reservists whose long-term availability is controversial), but they can contribute to getting the process started. Private contractors have represented one alternative, but protecting them has been an added burden in Iraq, and charges of corruption and bribery in the awarding of some contracts and other misdeeds have tarnished that option.

Longer-term economic success almost certainly requires attracting outside capital in the forms of foreign direct investment, location of manufacturing facilities, and the like in the target country. In order for this to occur, however, the target country must make itself attractive to investors. In addition to overcoming a likely unsavory reputation from the past, this means the development of policies and laws friendly to investors, of financial and educational institutions to support business, and of a condition of tranquility and peace to reassure potential investors that their investments will not literally blow up in their faces.

The third dimension is *social*. In most of the likely target states, there is a social cleavage within the population that may be racial (Haiti), ethnic (Iraq and Sri Lanka), clan or tribal (Afghanistan and Somalia), religious (Indonesia), or some combination of those (Bosnia and Kosovo), wherein identification with one group and the targeting of one or more of the other groups has been the basis for violence. The result of violence, often aimed at innocent noncombatants, inflames hatreds already present, leaving a postwar condition of animosity, distrust, and desire for revenge that must be overcome. Doing so is usually easier said than done.

These emotions often run very deep, especially in countries where there was physical mixing of communities before the conflict. When the violence pits neighbor against neighbor, reconciliation after the fact can be especially difficult to accomplish. In Rwanda, for instance, Hutu tribal members identified their Tutsi neighbors for slaughter. In Bosnia, after marauding "militias" had driven particular ethnic groups out of villages, members of the offending group would occupy or destroy their homes. The Bosnian government and international peacekeepers spent years trying to return the dispossessed to their former homes. How Iraqi Sunnis, Shiites, and Kurds will finally reconcile is an ongoing question.

The residue of hatred and distrust in these communities will linger, in some cases for a generation or more. In some instances, it may be possible to partition the states in ways that leave ethnic or other groups together and secure. Cyprus is an example. In most cases, however, the partition solution is impossible or is more traumatic than not separating groups. In a country like Afghanistan, for instance, the commingling of population groups and the absence of natural physical boundaries (wide rivers, for instance) to create secure separation mean there are no easy ways to partition the country. At any rate, such solutions almost certainly involve uprooting and moving people to create ethnically pure communities. The history of such forced migrations does not commend partition as a method for broader application. The aftermath of partition of the Asian Subcontinent in 1947—when eight to ten million Muslims and Hindus were uprooted and forced to flee to countries where they were in the majority—is stark testimony to this problem.

The fourth dimension is *psychological*. Although many assessments of state building ignore or play down this dimension, it is clear that the atrocious conduct of many of these wars scars many of the survivors, often for life. People, especially children, see acts of gruesome violence committed before their eyes. When it is personalized—a child watching the gory execution of a parent—the result can be deeply traumatizing and require considerable counseling to assimilate. Even hardened soldiers experience debilitating mental problems, as has become increasingly apparent among Americans returning from Iraq and Afghanistan.

It is almost universally true that in the countries that experience these traumas, there is an absolutely inadequate supply of doctors and psychologists to deal with the problem. It is also usually the case that the health care systems in these countries are among the first victims of war. Since the health care systems typically were fairly primitive before the violence, the result is that a bad situation becomes even worse. An ABC television report on January 17, 2002, for instance, revealed there were only *eight* psychiatrists and three mental health wards in all of Afghanistan to treat the psychologically disabled there. The ward in Kandahar was little more than an open courtyard in which patients were chained so they could not harm others. Hopefully, the situation has improved; it probably has not been eliminated altogether.

How to Do It? The preceding discussion has touched on only the tip of the iceberg of substantive problems with which state builders must contend. This formidable list of tasks must be carried out in a situation in which multiple actors with very different perspectives and affiliations must cooperate with local officials in a place with which the state builders are only generally familiar. The environment is likely to be competitive and chaotic, and not all of the groups providing services will trust either one another or the target groups that they are trying to assist. To add to the problem, there is no "guidebook" on organizing such operations, and the international system lacks enough experience to suggest comprehensive useful precedents.

The first concerted state-building exercise identified as such was mounted for Kosovo. As Amplification 13.3 indicates, it is not a model one would necessarily impose on other situations, such as the efforts in Afghanistan and Iraq. Creating a monolithic effort wherein all helping groups are operating together in a spirit of cooperation and working toward commonly accepted goals is the obvious purpose. Accomplishing these goals is far from easy.

At a minimum, state building will have two different groups performing different tasks. On the one hand, there will be a military element engaged in peace enforcement or peacekeeping. The primary task of the military is, of course, keeping order and preventing the recurrence of violence, effectively acting as a shield behind which state building can move forward. The military's secondary mission, which is sometimes ignored by those planning or executing these missions, is self-protection, making sure its own members are not subject to lethal attacks from groups that suffer because of their presence.

The military component cannot be considered a single, monolithic entity, and it may have very different priorities than others. In most cases, the peacekeeping force will be a coalition of forces drawn from several countries under the auspices of either the United Nations or another organization, such as NATO. These countries will be present for a variety of reasons. Some have a philosophical commitment to this kind of mission (Canada and Norway as peacekeepers, for instance), while others will be there to collect the per diem allowance provided by the United Nations (Ghana and Bangladesh, for example). While a commander will be identified for the mission, the individual country contingents generally report to their own governments, which instruct them on which orders from the command structure to carry out and which to ignore. When national and international orders contradict one another, national priorities prevail.

Amplification 13.3

KFOR and UNMIK

At the end of the campaign to drive the Serbs out of Kosovo in 1999, the United Nations announced that the goal of the effort would be to build a stable, prosperous order in that province that could decide either to unite within a newly constituted Yugoslavia or to become independent. The mission is thus state building. The structure announced to implement the goal shows clearly the complexity and difficulty this kind of operation entails.

Although the entire effort is officially under U.N. control, this is not entirely the case in fact. Indeed, there are two separate entities operating in Kosovo, each part of a different command structure. The military peacekeeping element is the Kosovo Force (KFOR), which is a NATO force commanded by a NATO general and reporting to NATO headquarters. The state-building element of the operation is the United Nations Interim Mission in Kosovo (UNMIK), which is headed by the special representative of the secretary general (SRSG) of the United Nations, and he or she reports to the United Nations. The SRSG, in turn, oversees the operations of four activities that constitute the major emphases of the state-building enterprise. Designated the four pillars, each function is administered by a different international organization. Civil administration is the responsibility of the United Nations itself, the development of political institutions is handled by the Organization of Security and Cooperation in Europe (OSCE), economic development is the job of the European Union (EU), and refugees are dealt with by the United Nations High Commission on Refugees (UNHCR). Each of these organizations has somewhat different memberships and reporting requirements. The relationship between KFOR and UNMIK is informal, based upon the personal ability of the KFOR commander and the SRSG to cooperate.

The United States has a unique position in all these efforts. As the world's remaining superpower, the United States will almost certainly be involved at some level, usually including the provision of some troops. American presence is often at the insistence of the target government, and it may be the sine qua non for acceptance of a mission by the host country, as was the case in Bosnia. That participation will generally be somewhat reluctant and come with at least two conditions. One is a maximum participation by other states to demonstrate that the United States is not shouldering a disproportionate share of the burden. It will also insist that its forces remain under American command to avoid being placed in unnecessarily risky situations where casualties may occur. Often, the Americans are called upon to provide logistical support, such as getting supplies and personnel to the locale (which means, at a minimum, some American soldiers will be on the ground to protect airfields and ports), and to provide satellite and other signal intelligence that only the United States has the physical capability to provide. When the United

States is not present in such efforts, the mission is often compromised. The Darfur effort in Sudan and Chad is a prime example.

National control of peacekeeping forces and the mandate to limit exposure to danger mean the military side of the operation will be difficult and also virtually guarantee some level of friction between the peacekeepers and the civilian state builders. The civilian element will also be a hodgepodge of different groups with different priorities. Representatives of governments providing developmental assistance will be on the scene identifying projects and making sure that the private contractors with whom they do business are fulfilling their obligations. Representatives from whatever international body is in charge of the state-building enterprise must try to coordinate national efforts to be certain that the process is orderly and that vital priorities are being addressed. In addition, a multitude of nongovernmental organizations (NGOs) will be on the scene, either caregivers such as *Medicins sans Frontieres*/Doctors Without Borders ministering to medical needs or monitors such as Amnesty International or Human Rights Watch on the lookout for human rights violations. The media will also be present, at least in the early stages while the mission is still "news."

The ingredients for organizational chaos are clearly present and are made worse by two other factors. The first is dealing with the citizens of the country, who are the supposed beneficiaries of the effort. Who are their legitimate representatives? What do they want, and why? Will international efforts benefit one formerly warring group at the expense of others, thereby making things potentially worse rather than better? Do the state builders know enough about the country and its people to make valid independent judgments on any of these problems? The answers to these questions are often less than absolutely clear to the state builders.

The U.S. effort in Iraq does not precisely reflect these circumstances (the U.S. government, for instance, has no real decision-making competitors), but the tasks and the difficulties of achieving them are not dissimilar (problems reflected in Afghanistan as well, as the *Challenge!* box explores). In the Iraq case, most of the fissures have been internal—disagreement between the State Department and CIA and the Department of Defense over how to proceed, for instance—and have been complicated by the level of operational responsibility assigned to private contractors. At the same time, the fractiousness of internal elements within Iraq is quite similar to that encountered in more conventional state building missions.

Challenge!

WHAT SHOULD THE UNITED STATES DO IN AFGHANISTAN?

The removal of the Taliban government from power and its replacement by the Karzai government—supported by American and other foreign forces—represented the original conflict-suppression phase of the international effort in Afghanistan (Phase I). With the election of a permanent government in 2004 and the beginnings of international efforts to build and rebuild that war-torn country, an international state-building campaign began. The situation has been complicated by the return of the Taliban and a civil war since 2003 that arguably returns the situation to a peace imposition basis.

There has been clear rhetorical support for draining the Afghan "swamp" and building a stable country that will resist terrorist appeals and join the antiterrorism coalition in the future. That rhetoric had not translated into the massive assistance program that most agreed was necessary to produce a stable and hopefully democratic Afghanistan.

All four dimensions of state building need attention. Progress in the military dimension is questionable, as an Afghan armed force and constabulary have been initiated but have yet to be proven effective; partly, this is because the effort runs afoul of traditional Afghan tribal rivalries (Pashtuns, for instance, are apparently underrepresented). The Taliban now effectively rule a good deal of the countryside. The outcome of the civil war remains very much in doubt.

The economic dimension has hardly been addressed at all. There is wide agreement that massive amounts of money are necessary to build the Afghan economic infrastructure and to rebuild the country after so many years of war. Beyond more-or-less vague promises of assistance, the flow of resources has been slow to come, and Afghan patience is being tested. The social and psychological dimensions likewise suffer from years of privation and violence. Exacerbating the situation is official government repression of the one major cash crop that could pump money into the economy: heroin-producing poppies. Prior to the Taliban regime, nearly 70 percent of the world's heroin was grown in Afghanistan from poppies, and after the Taliban were overthrown, peasant farmers planted new crops that had been forbidden by the Taliban. At the prodding of Western governments, those crops were destroyed (with compensation) in 2002, but record crops have been harvested since. Afghanistan remains the source of most of the world's heroin (over 90 percent), and without the cash its sale provides, the economy would be virtually nonexistent.

What should the United States do for Afghanistan? How many American tax dollars should be spent on rebuilding the Afghan infrastructure and in building a prosperous society—especially since the results cannot be guaranteed? It is one thing to call for making an antiterrorist bulwark out of Afghanistan, but what budgetary sacrifices should Americans be forced to endure to produce such a state? Also, the degree to which the country responds to Afghanistan's plight will create a precedent for what other states may expect from the United States in the future. How seriously committed are Americans *in fact* to the continuing campaign against terrorism as it threatens to "attack" American wallets? If Americans are not serious about state building in Afghanistan, will anyone believe Americans are any more serious about neoconservative dreams to build a stable, democratic Iraq that will act as a regional role model? What do you think?

CONCLUSION: THE FUTURE OF TERRORISM, PEACEKEEPING AND STATE BUILDING

Contemporary military employments are very much unlike wars of the past. Traditional, symmetrical wars were more clear-cut and determinant, conforming to a *peace–war–peace* model that the present author described in *When America Fights* in 2000: "war is an interruption of peace, which is the normal and preferable condition. The function of military force is to repair a broken peace by going to war, subduing those who had breached the peace, and then returning to the normal condition, which is peace." The last truly clear example of that model in action was World War II. Terrorism and Iraqi-style Phase IV/peacekeeping and state-building considerations are far different because the end of formal hostilities does not automatically usher in the reinstitution of peace and order. Had Iraq conformed to the peace–war–peace model, it would have been an unquestioned success. But it did not because the model does not fit contemporary war. Dealing with terrorism conforms even more poorly to the model.

In modern, asymmetrical warfare, the period after what the Bush administration called "major combat operations"—Phase IV—is easily as vital to the eventual outcome as are traditional military operations. Not only must the main body of the enemy—where it has one—be subdued, but also all active groups in the target society must be convinced to embrace the peace. Force has a role in nurturing that embrace, but it also entails the multiple dynamics described here as peacekeeping and state building. As the discussion has sought to convey, these tasks are far more formidable and problematical than overcoming organized armed forces (particularly given the tremendous weight of American conventional forces). Although the United States may not botch peacekeeping/state-building operations in the future as spectacularly as it has in Iraq, there is clearly no proven American approach to peacekeeping, and especially to state building.

The requisites of peacekeeping and state building, in one form or another, will be part of the operational environment the United States will encounter when it contemplates the use of force in the post-Iraq world and the continuing campaign against terror. It is a chastening realization because factoring in these needs makes the planning and execution more complex and the prospects of success decidedly more difficult to project and achieve. In Iraq, these entirely predictable dynamics were ignored by those who made the decision to go to war, and the results are clear. If decision makers ignore this lesson and blithely proceed on the implicit assumption that the peace–war–peace model will hold, the results in Afghanistan and elsewhere could be similar to those in Iraq. If one assumes, however, that peacekeeping and state building are integral parts of modern *war making* in the modern world, some decisions may be quite different in the future.

STUDY/DISCUSSION QUESTIONS

1. What three characteristics are shared by modern wars? How do these affect how to think about involvement in modern wars?

2. How is terrorism a unique problem for those who want to suppress it? Why do common conceptualizations of war not fit it well? What may be the objectives of a terrorist-suppression strategy? Discuss.
3. Discuss the terrorism-suppression problem in terms of forms, focuses, and objectives. What conclusions do you draw about the nature and problem of dealing with terrorists?
4. What are peacekeeping and state building? What forms of activity can be included under the broad rubric of peacekeeping? Apply the distinctions to Iraq.
5. What was the original concept of peacekeeping? How has it been extended to deal with contemporary conflicts? Why? Explain the continuum from war to peace and the idea of unstable peace.
6. Briefly discuss the nature of state building and how it has evolved. Using the three questions posed in the text, discuss the nature and dictates of state building.
7. Why is an understanding of peacekeeping and state building critical to understanding the future of modern warfare?

SELECTED BIBLIOGRAPHY

Atwood, J. Brian. "The Development Imperative: Creating the Preconditions for Peace." *Journal of International Affairs* 55 (Spring 2002): 333–349.

Bates, Robert H. *Prosperity and Violence: The Political Economy of Development.* New York: W. W. Norton, 2001.

Boutros-Ghali, Boutros. *An Agenda for Peace: Preventive Diplomacy, Peacemaking, and Peace-Keeping.* New York: United Nations, 1992.

Bynam, Daniel. "Talking with Insurgents: A Guide for the Perplexed." *Washington Quarterly* 32, no. 2 (April 2009): 125–138.

Chandrasekaran, Rajiv. *Imperial Life in the Emerald City: Inside Iraq's Green Zone.* New York: Alfred A. Knopf, 2007.

Christia, Fotini, and Michael Semple. "Flipping the Taliban." *Foreign Affairs* 88, no. 4 (July/August 2009): 34–45.

Cordesman, Anthony H. *The Iraq War: Strategy, Tactics, and Military Lessons.* Washington, DC: Center for Strategic and International Studies, 2003.

Cronin, Audrey Kurth. "Sources of Contemporary Terrorism." In Cronin, Audrey Kurth, and James M. Ludes, eds. *Modern Terrorism: Elements of a Grand Strategy.* Washington, DC: Georgetown University Press, 2004.

Diamond, Larry. *Squandered Victory: The American Occupation and the Bungled Effort to Bring Democracy to Iraq.* New York: Times Books (Henry Holt and Company), 2005.

Durch, William, ed. *The Evolution of UN Peacekeeping: Case Studies and Comparative Analysis.* New York: St. Martin's Press, 1993.

Eisenstat, Stuart, John Edward Porter, and Jerry Weinstein. "Rebuilding Weak States." *Foreign Affairs* 84, no. 1 (January/February 2005): 134–146.

Glantz, Aaron. *How America Lost Iraq.* New York: Jeremy P. Tarcher/Penguin, 2005.

Goldstone, Jack A., and Jay Ulfelder. "How to Construct Stable Democracies." *Washington Quarterly* 28, no. 1 (Winter 2004–2005): 9–20.

Gurr, Ted Robert. *Why Men Rebel.* Princeton, NJ: Princeton University Press, 1973.

Hanson, Victor Davis. *Between War and Peace: Lessons from Afghanistan and Iraq.* New York: Random House, 2004.

Hulsman, John. *Lawrence of Arabia and the Perils of State Building: Heritage Lecture #900.* Washington, DC: Heritage Foundation, 2005.

Jones, Seth G. *In the Graveyard of Empires: America's War in Afghanistan.* New York: W. W. Norton, 2009.

Kemp, Geoffrey. "Losing the Peace?" *National Interest* 76 (Summer 2004): 46–48.

Kilcullen, David. *The Accidental Guerrilla: Fighting Small Wars in the Midst of a Big One.* Oxford, England: Oxford University Press, 2009.

Mueller, John. *Remnants of War.* Ithaca, NY: Cornell University Press, 2003.

Odom, William E. "Retreating in Good Order." *National Interest* 76 (Summer 2004): 33–36.

O'Hanlon, Michael. "Toward Reconciliation in Afghanistan." *Washington Quarterly* 32, no. 2 (April 2009): 139–149.

Pillar, Paul D. "Counterterroriam after Al Qaeda." *Washington Quarterly* 27, no. 3 (Summer 2004), 101–113.

Price, David G. "Global Democracy Promotion: Seven Lessons for the New Administration." *Washington Quarterly* 32, no. 1 (January 2009): 159–170.

Rachman, Gideon. "Democracy: The Case for Opportunistic Idealism." *Washington Quarterly* 32, no. 1 (January 2009): 119–128.

Rashid, Ahmed. *Descent into Chaos: The U.S. and the Disaster in Pakistan, Afghanistan, and Central Asia.* New York: Penguin Books, 2009.

Record, Jeffrey. *Dark Victory: America's Second War Against Iraq.* Annapolis, MD: Naval Institute Press, 2004.

Ricks, Thomas E. *Fiasco: The American Military Adventure in Iraq.* New York: Penguin Press, 2006.

Sachs, Jeffrey D. "The Development Challenge." *Foreign Affairs* 84, no. 2 (March/April 2005): 78–90.

Singer, P. W. "Caution: Children at War." *Parameters* 31, no. 4 (Winter 2001–2002): 40–56.

Snow, Donald M. *When America Fights: The Uses of U.S. Military Force.* Washington, DC: CQ Press, 2000.

——— and Eugene Brown. *International Relations. The Changing Contours of Power.* New York: Longman, (2000).

Tripp, Charles. *A History of Iraq.* 2nd ed. Cambridge, England: Cambridge University Press, 2001.

CHAPTER 14

Extending Security Under Obama

PREVIEW

While the environment in which national security policy is formulated will not necessarily change dramatically in the post-9/11 world inherited by the Obama administration, the way the United States views and interacts with that environment may well be different. One likely change will be in the degree of American military activism after the wars in Afghanistan and Iraq are concluded. Another is the likely extension of thinking about national security to include areas that do not have a heavy military content and that have not traditionally been thought of in national security terms. This chapter explores four of these policy areas that extend ideas of security in distinctly different ways: border security, natural resources security, environmental security, and health security. All are areas that have received priority commitment by the Obama administration. The chapter concludes with some discussion about how these extended applications will affect thinking about American national security in the future.

The environment in which national security policy is honed and in which threats to that security are mounted will not change completely after the Afghanistan and Iraq Wars are over. The Middle East will, for instance, continue to be the most troublesome, unstable part of the world, with places like Iran and Pakistan moving toward the center stage of concern. In addition, the continuing dependence of the United States on Persian Gulf petroleum will assure that American interests in the region will be sufficiently engaged to prevent total American disengagement from regional matters. The most spectacular aspect of that region's volatility will almost certainly continue to be international religious terrorism, the countering of which will remain a major focus of American security policy, although possibly having a different focus and employing different means. The most troubling potential problems in the Middle East will include ongoing internal volatility in Iran and concern over its nuclear program. Continuing Taliban and Al Qaeda activity could lead to the destabilization of a major ally such as Pakistan, with frightening possibilities.

Although projecting into the future is an inherently risky and speculative business, at least two major trends are likely to become prominent as the United States confronts the security environment of the next five to ten years. The first, resulting directly from the Iraq War experience, will almost certainly be a lesser inclination toward military activism manifested in a reluctance to commit large-scale American military assets except under the most unambiguous conditions of need (a war of necessity). Large-scale, costly deployments of choice will be difficult to sell to a wary, war-weary public and to a depleted, rebuilding military, which would have to implement such a deployment. Arguments that particular situations constitute deployments of necessity rather than choice will be subject to much greater scrutiny than they were before Iraq, which was arguably a deployment of choice defended as one of necessity. The reluctance to translate a "get tough" stance toward Iran into possible military action testifies to this legacy of post-9/11 bounds on activism. Moreover, the opportunities to employ force will be in new variations of asymmetrical warfare situations of which both the American military and its civilian leadership have become appropriately wary. After the Iraq lesson that deployments against asymmetrical opponents are likely to result in frustrating and inconclusive outcomes, they will be difficult to justify or gain support for, despite the efforts of military leaders like General David Petraeus and civilian leaders like Secretary of Defense Gates to better prepare the military for these kinds of situations.

The second trend is likely to be a broadening of the matters on the national security agenda to include more concerns that either lack or do not prominently feature a traditional military component. Chapter 8 specifically indicated some of these concerns and hinted at but did not discuss such contingencies in detail. One such dimension is *economic security*, and in a world of increasing U.S. indebtedness to the rest of the world and the shadow of the economic crisis that began in 2008, as well as growing dependence on foreign manufactures and capital, economic security can only increase in salience. At the same time, international religious terrorism will continue to represent a semimilitary threat wherein the traditional tools of national security policy play an important, varying, but not determinant role.

These are not the only areas of concern that will likely be added to the security agenda in the upcoming years. To some extent, the list will expand because the Afghanistan and Iraq experiences will discourage conceptualizing the world in terms of militarized situations and responses. At the same time, an expanded list will reflect a more complicated, variegated world where the real problems with which policy makers must deal can less and less be pigeonholed into traditional security and nonsecurity categories. Raising these concerns in a national security setting will be uncomfortable, even incongruous for many with a conventional view of national security. The contention here is that the failure to include these new areas within national security leaves an incomplete picture of the security environment of the future, and it is for that reason that this last chapter is devoted to these nontra-ditional security concerns that indeed extend thinking about national security.

There is no universal agreement about what a list of these concerns would con-tain or not contain, and there will be disagreement about the inclusion or exclusion of different concerns depending on individual interests and assessments: no list will please everyone. With no claims to inclusiveness, the author has chosen four areas for illustrative purposes. They all share the common characteristics of making Americans safe or feel safe (the heart of the definition of security) and of having both some conventional and some unconventional security aspects. They are pre-sented in descending order of conventional (i.e., military) content.

The four areas are border security, natural resource security, environmental se-curity, and health security. Problems associated with each—borders breached by ter-rorists, interruptions in the flow of oil, environmental catastrophes, the incursion of foreign deadly diseases—pose a threat to Americans (and everyone else), but each is unique in the threat it poses and how its risk can be reduced or eliminated. Border security seems the most obviously security-related issue, but it is a more complex is-sue than simply sanitizing or sealing the borders. Americans would clearly feel and be threatened by an interruption in the supply of natural resources to the country, but it is not clear whether or how, in different situations, the instrumentalities of national security apply to securing those resources. Environmental catastrophes of various kinds could represent the ultimate threats to security, even existence, but they lack obvious immediacy and thus tend to be consigned to future consideration even when current actions can accentuate or attenuate the threat. Although there have been both historical and contemporary examples where disease transmission has posed a threat to individual and national well-being, this prospect also tends to be consigned a lower order of priority until some apparent, proximate threat like the swine flu outbreak galvanizes public attention.

The list is not, of course, comprehensive, and other issues will arise that will act as occasional flash points of concern. The issue of piracy is an example. While the practice of committing crimes on the high seas (the core of all definitions of piracy) is certainly not new, the *Maersk Alabama* incident of 2009 brought piracy into the public spotlight for the brief period until the crisis was resolved. When that pirate attack was not immediately followed by additional instances, however, the persist-ent but low-profile pattern of international piracy and responses to it off Asian and African shores slid back down the public agenda. Piracy may resurface periodically, and other transient threats will undoubtedly dot the horizon but with equally ephemeral impacts on the overall thrust and direction of security concerns.

BORDER SECURITY

In some important ways, the security of national borders is the oldest and most fun-damental of all national security issues. Protecting and defending national, sover-eign territory is, arguably, the most important and vital priority and task of government. National (or homeland) security is, at its most elemental level, about protecting the citizenry from hostile others who might breach those borders and do harm to the citizens. As noted in Chapter 4, preparing to repel armed, hostile hordes has not been a prominent part of the American experience, but the task remains a fundamental part of the charge to government; it can be and often is argued that a government that cannot protect its borders from hostile invasion can serve no other useful function.

The contemporary border security issue facing the United States is not as basic or dramatic as that. There is no equivalent, except in the most allegorical sense, of Genghis Khan's Golden Horde gathering on the country's boundaries. Thus, the answer to the question "Protection from what threat arising from an arguably insecure border?" is neither simple nor obvious, and the issue of border security also demonstrates the extremely diffuse, even loose, way in which the underlying concept of security is employed in describing the problem. Framing the border security problem and determining its security content require examining border security from two vantage points. These are the physical extent and dimensions of American borders and the nature and locales of threats to those borders.

The Physical Problem

The territorial boundaries of the United States are among the most extensive, complex, and difficult to secure of any country in the world. They can be divided into land and sea borders, each of which poses different priorities and problems that can be described in varying security terms. The land borders of the United States are shared with two contiguous neighbors, Canada and Mexico. The land border between Canada and the United States is slightly more than 5,500 miles long (the boundary between Canada and the contiguous 48 states is 3,987 miles, and that between Canada and Alaska is 1,538 miles). The border between Mexico and the United States is 1,933 miles long. Thus, the land borders of the United States and its foreign neighbors total 7,458 miles. Even this formidable total pales in comparison to that of Russia, the world's largest country, which is twice as big as the United States and has land borders with fourteen countries that are approximately two-thirds longer than those of the United States.

Clearly, maintaining the absolute and inviolable sanctity of borders this long is physically impossible and would, for the most part, seem unnecessary. Which parts of which borders will be secured (i.e., made inviolate) is a matter of risk assessment and risk reduction: what are the threats posed by permeable borders at different locations? Admitting that the principle of sovereignty suggests all borders should be secure, what priorities should be attached to making which borders more or less impermeable? Some of the answers are relatively simple: there is little reason, for instance, to expend major resources securing most of the border between remote areas of Canada and Alaska because little threat is posed by allowing transit back and forth (which could probably not be prevented under any circumstances). Large urban crossings and the long border between the United States and Mexico may be different matters, however.

The sea borders of the United States are an even more daunting physical problem. Two measures are used to describe these dimensions: coastline and shoreline.

The coastline refers generally to a line drawn along the intersection of the coast and the ocean, not allowing for bays, inlets, and other water features, whereas the shoreline measures the total topography of the coast, including the shores of bodies of water emptying into the oceans and seas. Using figures provided by the National Oceanic and Atmospheric Administration (U.S. Department of Commerce), the coastline of the United States is 12,383 miles, and the shoreline is 88,633 miles.

As with the land borders of the country, sealing access to American territory along the seas is a daunting task, probably beyond the physically possible. Once again, the problem is differential. Almost 42 percent (5,580 of the 12,383 miles) of coastline is between Alaska and the various bodies of water that touch it (the Pacific and Arctic Oceans, the Bering and Beaufort Seas), and 35 percent (31,383 of the 88,633 miles) of shoreline is Alaskan. Parts of the Alaskan coast were important during the Cold War, and the 1,350 miles of Florida's coastline and 8,426 miles of its shoreline have long been a source of concern regarding both drug (and other) smuggling and illegal immigration.

The solution to the border security problem is thus a good bit more complicated than an atavistic call to "seal the borders." The physical dimensions of the problem are such that the task is probably impossible and certainly impracticable in terms of the resources necessary even to attempt it, and sealing great parts of the border would accomplish little toward achieving justifiable national priorities (most of the Alaska–Canada border and the Canada–United States border across much of the Great Plains and West).

These physical dimensions create enormous physical difficulties in trying to secure the country's borders. Clearly, continuously patrolling every inch of either the land or the sea borders goes beyond the capabilities of the various agencies assigned border protection tasks. The U.S. Coast Guard, for instance, is the agency primarily given the task of protecting the coastline and shoreline from unwanted foreign incursion, but it clearly lacks the number or quality of seacraft to prevent all intrusions that might be mounted. Preventing all intrusions would require a vast expansion of its capabilities (both sea- and air-based) that would go beyond any reasonable political expectations, and thus to announce that the entire coastline and shoreline will be sealed amounts to declaring a "paper blockade" of the coast. Similarly, the Border Patrol, which has comparable responsibilities for the land borders, cannot possibly seal every inch of the borders between the United States and Canada and the United States and Mexico. In both cases, it may be possible to provide a blanket protection of certain *parts* of the border or against particular intruders and intrusions (or both), but the attempt to guard comprehensively is feckless.

A couple of real examples may help clarify the magnitude of the problem of comprehensive border protection. According to Stephen Flynn, one of the country's leading experts in border and port security issues, in 2000 "489 million people, 127 million passenger vehicles, 11 million trucks, 2.2 million railroad cars, 829,000 planes, and 211,000 vessels passed through American border inspection systems." Given the limited resources available to border guards, it is physically impossible to inspect in any detail all of these entrants, and although most undoubtedly enter for legitimate and unimpeachable reasons, it is impossible to ensure that all undesirable people or things cannot enter. In addition, the border between the western extremity of Lake Superior and Boundary Bay, Washington, is monitored only at major crossing points; anyone who wants to walk across the border from Saskatchewan to Montana or North Dakota where there are no roads can do so with a high likelihood of success. To make matters more complicated, Flynn adds that one-third of all the trucks (almost 4 million) entering the United States annually cross over one of four bridges from Canada into Michigan or New York State. If a real attempt to monitor the movement of goods across these bridges were attempted (as was briefly tried on the Ambassador Bridge between Detroit and Windsor, Ontario), the result would be massive gridlock. In one actual attempt to do so, a number of Chrysler automobile assembly plants in the United States that depended on parts from Canada had to be shut down until the inspections were rescinded and normalcy returned. The problem is easily as great regarding the movement of vessels into the country's ports, where only a minuscule percentage of incoming freight is or can be inspected. Advanced technology is improving both these situations, but there remain barriers to an inviolable border.

To add to this problem, it is by no means obvious that essentially sealing the border from outside intrusion is desirable. A truly effective system of screening people and goods and services entering the country would, among other things, impede the flow of people, ideas, and goods across the border into the United States, a direct challenge to the dictates of globalization and free trade. In summer 2007, for instance, the Bush administration found itself in the incongruous position (although it did not admit the incongruity) of simultaneously promoting additional trade within the NAFTA trade area (which meant the increased flow of goods across the country's borders with Canada and Mexico) and arguing for increased border security that would have the effect of slowing and impeding, rather than facilitating, the very trade it was promoting. Which priority was thus to be served so that following one or the other did not have unintended consequences?

Border Threats

The question of border security must thus be made more specific, basically specifying who and what it is important to exclude from American soil and where that effort should be concentrated. An auxiliary question is to what agencies of the government different responsibilities should be assigned. This latter question is more complicated than it would seem on the surface, as the discussion will reveal. Moreover, attempts to create greater security may have undesirable, unintended consequences that must be taken into consideration when deciding the answers to any of these questions.

Because the United States is historically a country that has opened its borders to immigrants from around the world, the idea of secure borders in the sense of impermeable barriers to entry (or exit) from the country has not always dominated this aspect of the national security agenda. At the same time, it has also been true that the United States has always tried to keep what it viewed as undesirable people and unwanted things out of the country. The content of what or who is desirable and undesirable has changed across time: during Prohibition, for instance, it was a national priority to exclude alcoholic beverages from the country; at different times, the same exclusiveness has been aimed at different nationalities seeking to immigrate to this country (the Irish during the 1840s, for instance).

The current concern over border security must be placed in this context. Who and what does the United States seek to exclude from its sovereign territory? And how important is it that this exclusion succeed? In the current context, border security has come to be associated with the 1,933-mile United States–Mexico land border, and the political cry has been to seal that border from undesired and presumably undesirable intruders. Even narrowing the problem to that level (thereby excluding the Canadian-American land borders and the protection of the coastline and shoreline), the problem is daunting and requires further elaboration.

The major question is against what threat border security is aimed. As Payan points out, there are three aspects to the United States–Mexico border issue, and each poses a different kind of problem, a different priority, and a threat of differing security content. These three aspects are illegal immigration, drug trafficking, and terrorist penetration. Although they overlap some of the time (illegal immigrants may, for instance, carry drugs into the country, or they may also be terrorists), they are also distinct problems. Drug trafficking and illegal immigration may be primarily United States–Mexico border issues, but the penetration of the United States by terrorists can occur anywhere along the borders.

Immigration. The illegal immigration issue has become the political hot-button topic because of the flood of Mexican citizens entering the country since the middle 1990s and the institution of NAFTA (for an explanation, see Snow, *Cases in International Relations*, 3rd edition, Chapter 9). Although figures regarding illegal immigration are by definition unknown and unreliable, the number of Mexican citizens who are living in the United States but who have not entered the country through prescribed means of immigration has risen from about 1.5–2 million before NAFTA to 12–14 million today (some estimates are as high as 20 million).

What kind of problem does illegal immigration pose? That it violates the sanctity of the border is true by definition, but in and of itself, that raises the question, So what? Do illegal immigrants pose a security threat beyond the fact that they implicitly flaunt the sanctity of the border? Most of the arguments to staunch and reverse the flow are not made on traditional national security grounds (they pose no military threat, for instance), but on grounds such as the fact that these immigrants place additional demands on social services, they do not pay taxes, and they deprive American citizens of jobs. Regardless of the truth of these assertions (which are disputed), placing these problems under the heading of "security" may have the implicit (or intentional) effect of elevating its perceived importance in the pantheon of national priorities, but it is not clearly a part of the national security agenda at all.

Drugs. The second aspect of the border security problem is drug trafficking. Once again, precise determinations about the physical extent of the problem are probably unreliable, but Michael Shifter maintains, "Mexico is the transit route for roughly

70 to 90 percent of the illegal drugs entering the United States. . . . Along the U.S.–Mexico border, the kidnapping trade, clearly tied to the drug trade, is flourishing." Since the illicit drugs entering the United States have an impact on the criminal justice system designed to interrupt that commerce and to punish those who engage in it, it is also a domestic political problem rather than a national security problem on the face of it. It does, however, have strong indirect security implications: the deleterious effect of drug usage on Americans, and thus American society, and the political devastation to other countries (especially in but not limited to Mexico) created by the actions of drug traffickers.

The damaging effects of illicit drug usage on the United States have been sufficiently alarming that the Reagan administration declared it a national emergency during the 1980s (Nancy Reagan's "Just say no to drugs"), and George H. W. Bush upgraded the national effort to the "War on Drugs" during his term in office. The "war" analogy was always more symbolic than real, but it did include significant use of, for instance, military resources from the U.S. Southern Command (the military command whose mission covers Latin America) for identifying and destroying sources of drugs and processing facilities in South America and from the U.S. Air Force and Coast Guard for preventing transshipment of processed drugs through and over Central America and the Caribbean. While much of that effort has been scaled back, the interruption of drugs flowing into the United States, principally but not exclusively from Latin America, remains a high priority of the federal government.

Is the drug trade a national security problem? The argument that it is focuses on the negative impact that drugs have on the United States and Americans. Drugs are at the base of much crime (especially in inner-city areas), strain the criminal justice and penal systems, incapacitate and render socially less useful those Americans who use and abuse drugs, and even cripple the government's ability to conduct its business by denying it significant tax revenue from the illicit drug commerce. The contention is that the country would be stronger if drug use were sharply curtailed or eliminated.

If an argument can be made that drugs weaken the United States and thus are a legitimate national security concern, what solutions are there for the scourge they represent? Broadly speaking, there are two answers: demand side and supply side. Demand-side solutions are aimed at reducing demand for drugs so that the drug trade becomes progressively less lucrative and thus less appealing. Education is a prime example: teaching and convincing people that drugs are bad for them and should be avoided (the analogy with antismoking campaigns is often made). Supply-side efforts aim at reducing the availability of drugs for people. Such efforts include destruction of drugs at their source (the so-called Andean Initiative to destroy coca crops—the source of cocaine—and to destroy processing plants, mostly in Colombia) and interdiction of processed drugs coming into the country. As already noted, this latter effort has focused on the Mexican border, across which most of the drugs transit.

The transit of drugs through Mexico and across the border creates tremendous difficulties and strains in U.S.-Mexican relations. Drug smuggling is a big and very lucrative business, and it is very difficult to interrupt successfully. Peter Andreas, for instance, contends that "the amount of cocaine necessary to satisfy US customers for one year can be transported in just nine of the thousands of large tractor-trailers that cross the border every day." Given that the amount of commerce across the border—largely by trucks—is supposed to increase as the NAFTA-led integration of North American economies continues, monitoring this trade becomes increasingly difficult. At the same time, drug smuggling becomes intertwined with illegal immigration, as those seeking to enter the country illegally are recruited by drug smugglers to bring contraband across the border or, more insidiously, are required by agents who assist in illegal entry to engage in drug smuggling as part of the fee for assistance entering the United States. Efforts to interrupt the flow of immigrants and drugs has an unintended effect here, as Andreas describes it: "adding thousands of new Border Patrol agents has had the perverse effect of enriching smugglers rather than deterring immigrants since the problem of breaching the border is more difficult" and requires help for some immigrants. Moreover, the dual goals of immigrant and drug interdiction bring both the Drug Enforcement Agency and the Border Patrol to the border with differing and occasionally conflicting priorities, hampering enforcement. The poverty of interdiction efforts is suggested by the fact that the street price of cocaine in the United States has dropped in recent years, indicating either that demand has dropped significantly or that supply has increased beyond past demand.

The drugs that enter the United States across the border must first transit across Mexico, and the result has been to corrode and corrupt the Mexican political process. Shifter lays out some of these problems. Governmental corruption is an endemic problem in Mexico, and "the astronomical revenues generated by the drug trade fuel the rampant corruption that eats away at already fragile institutions." Drug money to bribe officials to, at a minimum, ignore drug trafficking has attacked the system from top to bottom. At the local level, "the police are thoroughly corrupt, unreliable, and ill-equipped to handle increasingly violent traffickers," and the taint has extended to the top levels of the military and central government. The great danger is a general destabilization of the entire Mexican political system; Mexico in the throes of revolution would clearly pose a national security threat to the United States. At a minimum, it would almost certainly result in a flood of additional illegal immigrants across the border.

The resulting destabiliziation of Mexican politics has added another danger with potential national security implications for the United States. In 2009, drug-related violence spiked to the point that it became unsafe to walk the streets of many Mexican cities, especially border towns, because of armed attacks by Mexican drug lords against one another. This posed two problems. One was that the violence might spill across the border into the United States. The other was that the violence would drive an already unstable Mexican political system closer to chaos and civil war. The problem was made worse because much of the violence was being committed with weapons bought in the United States with drug-generated profits from sales to American consumers.

Terrorism. The third aspect of the problem is the penetration of the border by terrorists. This is clearly a problem that affects both the United States–Mexico and the United States–Canada borders, although one can argue that since it is more difficult to enter Canada from elsewhere than it is Mexico, the problem is more severe along the Mexican border. Conversely, it is easier for a potential terrorist to cross the Canadian border than the Mexican border into the United States.

This terrorist aspect of the problem has the clearest national security content of any of the border issues. The difficulty is that border solutions to the terrorist entry problem are the most difficult to implement comprehensively. Current efforts by agencies like the Border Patrol and Immigration and Customs Enforcement (ICE) are necessarily concentrated at the points of greatest transit of goods and services—major crossing points on the borders and international airports and ports, for instance—and are totally inadequate to control or seal the entire border. Had, for instance, the terrorists who sought to attack Los Angeles International Airport in 2005 not tried to cross into the United States at the busy and well-controlled border crossing at Vancouver but instead had walked across the border into North Dakota, the chances are they would not have been identified or apprehended at that point. Moreover, the proposed (and congressionally authorized) 700-mile fence along the Mexican-American border will leave over 1,200 miles of border unfenced, including vast stretches along the Mexican border with Texas.

The border security issue is thus much more complicated and complex than is often argued in the general political debate. In the abstract, one can talk about the sanctity of the border as a general political value, but in an applied sense, the matter is by no means so simple. One must start with an observation similar to framing the terrorism problem in Chapter 13: what is the goal? In the terrorism case, the goal can be either elimination or control/reduction of the problem, with elimination as the ideal and reduction as the practical and attainable goal. The same is true of border security. It may, in an abstract sense, be desirable to make American borders impermeable to all undesirable outside intrusions, but the land and sea borders are simply too extensive for that to be practical. If one could construct an absolutely impenetrable boundary, it would greatly reduce or eliminate the movement of unauthorized immigrants, illegal drugs, and terrorists across the frontier, but such a restriction is almost certainly not possible. Moreover, it is not at all clear that building such a border would be desirable, a possibility explored in Amplification 14.1: An Impenetrable Border?

NATURAL RESOURCES SECURITY

All countries are, to varying degrees, dependent on natural resources that do not exist in adequate supply within their own territory for their well-being and, in the most extreme cases, for their national existence. As pointed out in Chapter 4, resource dependency has not been a historic American problem because of the natural physical endowment of the North American continent. For most of American history—at least up to the end of World War II—the United States was essentially resource independent, and the problem of resource scarcity was largely an abstract concern that affected other countries. Three factors have changed that. First, adequate supplies of some resources at economic costs for extraction have been depleted, making foreign sourcing

Amplification 14.1

AN IMPENETRABLE BORDER?

If it were possible, would sealing the border be desirable for the United States? Certainly, it would solve the problems of border penetration. But it might cause other problems that would be as bad or worse. First, it would be enormously expensive both to construct and to maintain. Electronic means of surveillance that might reduce human observation needs notwithstanding, such a system would require a large and expensive manpower commitment, and ironically, the less manpower intensive the system might be to operate, the more expensive it would be to build. Are Americans really willing to incur such costs, given other national priorities?

Second, such a system would, as already suggested, interrupt the flow of goods and services coming into the United States. In the most direct sense, the movement toward more secure borders runs directly counter to the greater globalization built into the full implementation of NAFTA, as described in its provisions. NAFTA may be controversial, but if it is, it should be addressed specifically on its own merits. Increased border security is an indirect assault on NAFTA—and other aspects of globalization.

Third, there is the symbolism of greater border security. The United States has a long tradition of encouraging migration to this country, and relatively easy access is a part of that tradition. Fortifying the border—turning the Mexican-American border into something resembling the Great Wall of China, for instance—has symbolic importance. Does the United States still adhere to the Statue of Liberty's invitation to "give me your tired, your poor, your huddled masses yearning to breathe free," or does it prefer to build a wall to keep the barbarians out?

either necessary or economically preferable. Petroleum is the primary example. Second, modern technology requires some resources that are not present in adequate supply or at all on or under American soil. Titanium, which is necessary for, among other things, jet engines, is an example. Third, Americans now desire and demand some commodities that are not indigenous to the United States and that must be imported. Spices and exotic fruits and vegetables are examples.

Not all of the resources in inadequate supply for Americans (and others) are equally vital and thus the subject of security concerns. Americans, for instance, might not like being deprived of cinnamon from Southeast Asia, but the country would not collapse if cinnamon became unavailable. On the other hand, there are resources that are going to be clearly scarce and strategically important for the United States and much of the rest of the world. Some of these scarcities will (and do) have a direct impact on the United States: petroleum is the obvious example. Others will not affect the United States directly in the sense of creating shortages from which Americans will suffer but will affect the United States indirectly if the competition for those resources causes conflicts among countries and in regions of interest to the United States; water is the obvious example. Each will be explored as exemplary of the resource problem and how it is a concern of American security policy. Like border security, neither the statement of the problem nor its solutions is entirely and unambiguously part of the traditional domain of national security.

Petroleum Energy Security

For the United States, the continuing availability of reasonably priced petroleum from the international community is, and will continue to be, a highly salient national security concern. The problem is not, however, exclusively American; it is part of a larger concern with energy security of which petroleum is one, if the largest, consideration, and its solution is only partly a matter of traditional national security. It is a dramatic and poignant security area both because of the heavy dependence of the American transportation system (including privately owned and operated vehicles) on petroleum and because of the obvious connection between petroleum and other, more volatile aspects of national security policy, notably policy toward the Middle East. It becomes an emotional issue because it gets wrapped up in the overall debate over energy policy and thus the heated disagreement between energy producers and conservationists over expansion of energy sources and uses. Moreover, petroleum is at the heart of President Obama's emphasis on energy security and the environment.

The American petroleum problem is part of the global dilemma over the adequacy of this form of energy. The origins of the global problem go back to the end of World War II, when those rebuilding the ravages of the war made the dual decisions to reorient the rebuilding economies of Europe and elsewhere around petroleum as the primary energy source and to count on controllably affordable supplies from the Middle East—primarily the Persian Gulf littoral. When these decisions were made, there was a geographically limited level of demand, and the supplies were controlled by western interests whose purpose was to keep the oil flowing at favorable prices. Subsequent events—the expansion of markets for petroleum and the nationalization of oil supplies—have changed that calculation.

The global oil situation is easy to describe, if not to manipulate. Global production is at about 85 million barrels of petroleum per day, with at least fourteen countries producing 2 million barrels per day according to 2004 figures. This production figure is balanced by demands for oil of approximately 83 million barrels per day, of which the United States consumes about 11 million barrels per day of imported oil. This makes the petroleum market "tight" because demand and supply are so close that even marginal change in either supply or demand can upset the balance. As Leonardo Maugeri points out, this has been the result of a twenty-year trend: "Between 1986 and 2005, the world's spare oil production (the amount produced beyond current demand) dropped from about 15 percent to between 2 and 3 percent of global demand." The result is clearly a seller's market, as witnessed by the rising costs of petroleum exemplified most dramatically by the cost of gasoline at the pump in the United States and elsewhere.

This problem could get considerably worse in the future, for two reasons. The first is increases in global demand. The chief sources of increased demand are China and India. According to *Infoplease* data, China currently produces about 3.62 million barrels per day but consumes 6.5 million, meaning it must import about 45 percent of its production. According to David Zwieg and Bi Jianhai, China "accounted for 31 percent of global growth in oil demand" in 2004. The Chinese government has adopted a policy of greatly expanded automobile production for Chinese citizens, meaning the demand for petroleum will continue to increase. The Indian example is slightly less dramatic but nonetheless significant: India currently imports about 1.5 million barrels per day, and even though Indian production is supposed to reach about 3 million barrels per day by 2010, it will continue to be an increasing importer as the country undergoes growing economic development and enters the world automobile market.

The other side of the problem is supply. With a spare production capacity of only 2 million barrels per day and fourteen separate countries producing at least that amount, there are multiple countries that could, by suspending production, drive supply and demand into a tailspin. This provides the producing countries with enormous leverage in their relations with the oil consumers, creating phenomena like "petrolist" politics, identified by Friedman earlier, and the rise in power and influence of exporting states like Russia. In addition, it makes countries like the United States extraordinarily sensitive to those parts of the world where petroleum is in great supply and creates interests in those regions that would probably not otherwise exist (or at least not be as intense). As suggested earlier, American interests in Iraq might be quite different if that country did not sit in the middle of the largest confirmed oil reserves in the world.

What constitutes a satisfactory situation in these circumstances? There are two possible goals, with differing political appeal and feasibility. One is *energy (petroleum) independence*, where the United State produces all the energy it requires and is thus independent of foreign sources of supply. Such a solution would be highly politically desirable—imagine its effect on American policy in the Middle East, for instance. Currently, however, such an approach is not feasible because of the worldwide distribution of petroleum reserves, the costs of extracting remaining U.S. reserves, and levels of demand. Only a revolutionary reduction in level of demand makes such a goal even conceivable.

The alternative is *energy (petroleum) security*: the reasonable guarantee of access to adequate amounts of energy at reasonable, acceptable costs. The definition contains three variable elements: access, adequacy of supply, and cost. All three elements can change and be manipulated to affect the suitability of the supply availability. Most critical is the guarantee of access, which is, of course, not a problem in the situation of energy independence. Until circumstances of supply and demand change radically enough to make it possible to think about independence, the less satisfactory, but more troublesome alternative of energy security appears the only realistic goal.

Operationally, solutions to the petroleum energy security problem can be thought of as discrete—how does the country guarantee the continuing flow of economical petroleum in adequate supply?—or as a supply-side problem. This approach to the problem is the easiest to couch in traditional security terms because it falls within the geopolitical paradigm of threats to security for which military solutions seem applicable. Thus, one way to solve the problem of reasonable access to Middle East petroleum is to have a military presence in the region that can assure physically that the oil continues to flow. That paradigm has arguably been dominant since President Jimmy Carter issued the so-called Carter Doctrine as part of his 1980 State of the Union address, declaring that continuing access to Persian Gulf oil was a vital American interest. American leadership in the Persian Gulf War effort to expel Iraq from Kuwait, the continued presence of American military forces in the region after 1991, and the Iraq War can all be thought of as actions consistent with that approach.

The second way to look at the issue is as part of a broader energy policy, an orientation that brings both elements of supply and demand into the equation. Framing the question in the broader context of energy policy broadens the concern and moves it beyond the more conventional bounds of national security consideration because unlike petroleum, alternative sources of energy are neither controlled overseas (solar or wind energy, for instance) nor subject to determination on national security grounds (whether the country invests in additional nuclear plants to produce electricity, for instance, is not at heart a national security issue). Much of the thrust of moving toward alternate energy sources reflects this position.

Subsuming the petroleum security question as part of energy policy opens additional strategic alternatives from both the supply and the demand sides of the energy equation. From the supply side, for instance, overall energy policy can view alternatives to imported petroleum as solutions to needs currently serviced by imported oil. These can include alternate sources of petroleum such as recovering hard-to-access petroleum in historical American oil fields, opening new domestic sources (the Alaskan wildlife reserves, for instance), tapping alternate sources of petroleum-based energy (Western oil shale or Canadian tar pits, for example), developing entirely different sources of fuel (corn-based ethanol), or moving to new energy sources (wind or geothermal). There are arguments, based largely in resource adequacy or cost, against each of these alternatives, but they are at least potential ways to reduce foreign petroleum dependency and the additional costs (e.g., military actions) that current policy entails. A supply-side approach also looks at alternative sources of energy, from wind power to thermal energy to "clean" coal to nuclear power as strategic alternatives. All are aimed at reducing dependency on foreign oil and the baggage such dependency carries; all of them are also nontraditional approaches to a national security problem.

The other side is demand, and the key element in these approaches is conservation of energy. Clearly, for instance, if the United States burned less gasoline (or fuel oil), there would be the need for less imported petroleum. Reductions can be achieved by switching to alternate ways to power automobiles—electricity or ethanol, for instance—or by demanding higher efficiency in existing or new automobiles—increases in the Corporate Average Fuel economy (CAFE) ratings such as those mandated in 2009 by the federal government.

This whole area evokes strong emotions when the question is expanded beyond petroleum to encompass broader energy policy, and especially when continued

Challenge!

OIL AND TERROR

There is an "urban legend" (a story said to be true but arguably not based in fact) that a group of Americans, armed with bumper stickers that say "I support Al Qaeda: Let Me Show You How," goes through Eastern urban areas placing those stickers on large, fuel-inefficient vehicles (e.g., Hummers, other large sport-utility vehicles). The message is intended to assert two things. First, it argues that terrorist groups do receive part of their funding indirectly from gasoline purchases in the United States. Thus, the United States buys oil from Saudi Arabia, some of that revenue ends up in the hands of private Saudi citizens, and some of them make contributions to Al Qaeda (no one seriously disputes that this happens at some level). Second, it asserts that people who drive fuel-inefficient vehicles disproportionately contribute to the problem because they end up spending more on gasoline that trickles back in larger amounts to fund Al Qaeda than do those who drive less-gas-guzzling models. Thus, driving such a vehicle can be argued to provide more indirect support to Al Qaeda than driving a vehicle that gets higher gas mileage. Taken to its extreme, one can even argue that it is more patriotic to drive a gas "sipper" than a gas "guzzler" if patriotism and refusal to provide support—however indirect—for terrorism are equated.

What do you think of this argument? Does it reflect a deeper relationship between energy security and the larger issue of national security?

petroleum dependency is viewed as a *cause* of national security problems. The current Middle Eastern, including Iraqi, situation offers the clearest example. One can argue that the United States would have no reason for a major presence in or commitment to the Persian Gulf region in the absence of a need for secure access to the petroleum it contains. What would American policy in the region look like if the United States did not need *any* oil from there? From that assessment, it can further be argued that an obvious way to get the United States out of the harm's way, which a visible presence in that volatile region entails, would be to reduce, and preferably eliminate, that dependence, since it would remove the need particularly for a military role in regional politics. A chance for the reader to assess his or her feelings about this controversy is contained in *Challenge!* Oil and Terror.

Water Security

Energy security has a direct and obvious impact on the United States that the question of water security lacks. It is, however, a pressing concern in at least one part of the world in which the United States is clearly entwined—once again, the Middle East. In that basically arid part of the world, water is in insufficient supply for current consumption in some areas both because the region is arid and because what water there is tends to be unevenly distributed. Water is in short supply in most of the region, and the problem is getting worse because the area has a growing population that will place even greater demands on the water supply in the future. This same dynamic can be projected in the future to other parts of the world; China is a particularly vexing prospect.

Water shortages are different than supplies of petroleum, in several ways. First, the problem of oil is not a matter of inadequate supply (although that will become a problem sometime in the future) but rather a matter of distribution and availability at acceptable cost. The problem of water supply results from finite amounts of the commodity where it is needed, and there are generally no feasible alternative sources of supply (a matter touched on below). Second, demands for water are inelastic in economic terms: the level of demand is based on what is required for human survival wherever scarcity occurs, and that demand cannot be greatly manipulated. Conservation is not as available a strategy as it is with petroleum, although it may be a partial solution in some cases (as the Turks argue with regard to the Tigris–Euphrates system). Third, there are no alternative sources of potable water as there are with energy. The only alternatives to unpolluted fresh (potable) water are salt water and polluted fresh water, and these are only very limited alternatives. Salt water from the world's oceans and seas is certainly abundant, but economically viable methods of desalination have not been found despite decades of concerted effort; removing pollutants from otherwise potable water solves only a small part of the problem in selected areas that are least threatened by water shortages (e.g., part of formerly Communist Europe). Fourth, there are no means to import enough water from water-rich to water-deficient areas for that to be a remedy, despite very inventive proposals (e.g., using boats to drag icebergs from the Arctic area to the Middle East).

The vitality and inelasticity of potable water supplies make access to water a particularly powerful source of conflict where scarcities are present. The two most obvious examples are in the Middle East and center around the two major river systems in that area (see Snow, *Cases in International Relations*, 3rd edition, Chapter 14, for an overview). One involves the Tigris–Euphrates system that rises in Turkey and flows through Syria and Iraq (the Euphrates River) and directly into Iraq (the Tigris River) before joining and forming the Shatt al-Arab and flowing into the Persian Gulf. Both Syria and Iraq are water deficient and rely on water from the system for survival; Turkey is water independent, although it uses water from the system to assist development in its eastern, poor, and rebellious Kurdish region (notably the Greater Anatolia Project, GAP). Because it controls the headwaters of the rivers, Turkey also controls the flow of water to the downstream riparian countries, who demand that more of the water be released for their use. The Turks claim that they do allow adequate supplies to flow but that the Syrians and Iraqis waste water by using inefficient irrigation methods (letting water move through open trenches so that much of it evaporates) or by growing crops that require an excessive amount of water (cotton, for instance). Turkey has overwhelming leverage in this situation, both because the rivers begin within its territory and because Syria and Iraq lack the military or other power to compel Turkey to provide them with additional supplies.

The other dispute is over the water from the Jordan River, which flows out of the Sea of Galilee and is a major source of water for Syria, Lebanon, Jordan, and Israel. It becomes a matter of strategic concern depending on what country controls the headwaters of the river where it leaves the Sea of Galilee and begins its southward journey. The eastern bank of the river runs along the Golan Heights, a strategic part of the Israeli-Syrian border that was seized by Israel during the Six Days War of 1967. One reason that occupied territory has not been returned to Syria is that it historically provided high ground (the heights are low mountains) from which Syria launched artillery attacks on northern Israel; the other reason is that the Israelis fear that if Syria controlled the region, it might find a way to deprive Israel of Jordan River water on which the country depends.

These disputes fall generally below the international radar of major conflict problems, but that does not mean they can be ignored, for at least two reasons. One is that these particular problems are only going to get worse, due to skyrocketing population growth rates in the Middle East that can only make a serious problem critical. Once (or if) normalcy is reinstated in Iraq, for instance, the water question must be addressed; Turkey knows it holds all the cards in discussions, making negotiations difficult and conflict potential great.

The other reason is that these same kinds of problems may be visited in other parts of the world that are more significant in an immediate, geopolitical sense. The most obvious case is China, where, according to a recent article by Elizabeth Economy in *Foreign Affairs*, "skyrocketing demand, overuse, inefficiencies, pollution, and uneven distribution have produced a situation in which two-thirds of China's approximately 660 cities have less water than they need and 110 of them suffer from severe shortages." This situation, part of a broader environmental crisis that China faces, has strong implications for the future of Chinese economic productivity, upon which the United States is heavily dependent in the consumer-products sector.

These examples of water scarcity, particularly when combined with the problem of petroleum energy security, demonstrate how resource scarcities are or can become an American security issue. The case of petroleum access is direct and compelling as long as the United States is dependent on foreign sources of petroleum to fuel its economy. The prospect of petroleum scarcity (however immediate or distant) will require an American effort to ensure that petroleum access is continual and that interruptions can be avoided or corrected. In the immediate case, this means the United States will almost certainly have to maintain a physical, including military, presence in the Persian Gulf region for the foreseeable future, whether it wants to or not.

The water scarcity problem is more indirect, but each of the three instances cited demonstrates it cannot be ignored altogether. Regardless of how the United States finally extricates itself from Iraq, it will retain a residual interest in the condition of that country; to the extent the dispute over the Tigris–Euphrates system affects Iraq's future, it will represent an American concern as well. The United States' close relations with Israel and the American commitment to Israel's survival (at least an implicit pillar of American foreign policy) mean that the United States shares with the Israelis an interest in continued Israeli access to and control over water from the Jordan River basin. The economic interdependence of the United States and

China creates an interest in assuring conditions in China that, in turn, assure the continuation of mutually beneficial economic relations and that do not force the Chinese to look outward—in a possibly antagonistic way—for alternative water sources. In combination, petroleum and water demonstrate the direct and indirect ways in which resource security affects the United States.

ENVIRONMENTAL SECURITY

The determination of what aspects of the physical environment contribute to safety or a sense of safety can be more abstract than either border or natural resource security and is thus more difficult to conceptualize within the normal structure of national security thinking. Partly, the reason is that the threat is more indirect: by and large, environmental catastrophes that could endanger people are either far into the future (projections about global warming, for instance) or the result of natural phenomena such as hurricanes or tornadoes over which there is little control. Environmental dangers lack immediacy, controllability, or both (who can know for sure, for instance, when the widely predicted massive earthquake will hit southern California?). Although environmentalists argue that many of the environmental threats faced by mankind are the result of human actions that are either creating future hazards or making them worse (global warming and the intensity of weather changes, for example), these are not clearly purposive acts of malevolent others that can be identified and their actions somehow stifled or reversed in the way that a physical invasion can be repulsed or terrorists frustrated or brought to justice. Moreover, environmental issues are not easy to specify in traditional national security terms—specifying who or what poses a physical *threat*, for instance—and their solutions are not within the obvious realm of traditional national security solutions.

Yet the term *environmental security* has entered the lexicon of applications of the term *security*, and the question is whether the designation is legitimate or whether it is more akin to the overextension and overuse of the term *war* to describe efforts aimed at phenomena as diverse as poverty, drugs, and terrorism. Environmental security is simply not a subject covered in most traditional treatments of national security. So why add environmental security to the present endeavor?

Beyond the attempt to broaden horizons about what constitutes security, two reasons will be suggested here. The first is that environmental factors, including those that may have consequences in a more-or-less nebulous future, do indeed have direct implications for the safety and well-being of people. If, for instance, the consequences of global warming are anything like those predicted by environmental scientists, they will have a major impact on the commodiousness and conditions of life for future generations, and thus, actions or inactions today will make future generations more or less secure. The second is that some of these impacts are already present, and although it has not been customary to think about them in national security terms, it might be helpful to do so. The clear and compelling example in this regard is the impact of Hurricane Katrina.

To explore the notion of environmental security, two examples just suggested will be explored. The first is the question of global warming, a topic that is widely discussed and debated but rarely as a security issue. The second is Hurricane Katrina as an emblem for the kinds of threats to safety and security caused by natural disasters and as a symbol around which to explore whether it would be helpful to think of such occurrences and responses to them in security policy terms. Certainly, the Obama administration's emphasis on environmental problems has elevated their place on the national agenda. The point of raising them is to explore whether it is helpful to think of either as a security problem.

Global Warming

Few issues in the contemporary political scene evoke as much emotion and disagreement as does global warming. The emotions tend to center around the severe environmental consequences of unchecked carbon dioxide release (the source of most global warming along with several other gases like methane).

If the trends projected by that part of the scientific community issuing warnings about global warming are (or will prove to be) true, the results could be cataclysmic across a range of environmental concerns. The disagreement centers on the accuracy of these projected dynamics. Although the vast majority of scientists who have studied the problem of global warming concur generally in issuing strong, even dire, warnings about the failure to curb the practices leading to global warming, a politically well-connected minority of scientists and others question the scientific bases of these dire projections and the policy implications that follow from those predictions. The disagreements are difficult to overcome because almost all the phenomena in question and all the predictions are in the future and thus not subject to current scientific observation and validation. The debate also tends to remain abstract and at the peripheries of the political debate because most people are not *currently* experiencing consequences that they attribute to global warming and thus demanding reform.

To make matters more politically difficult, proposed remedies for global warming center on potentially vast reductions in carbon dioxide emissions. The overwhelming majority of the carbon dioxide excess (that amount above the ability of the environment naturally to absorb and dissipate) comes from the burning of fossil fuels that provide most of the energy used for transportation and industry in the world. Thus, conservation efforts intended to reduce carbon dioxide emissions are aimed at practices that are at the heart of the productivity of societies.

More perversely, if all members of the international system do not participate equitably in reducing these emissions, those who do not potentially can gain economic and possibly other advantages because their industrial and transportation bases are not tethered by environmental restrictions. This fear is most often expressed with regard to China, which, as Economy points out, is fast becoming one of the world's leading carbon polluters and was a major part of the Bush administration's objections to the Kyoto Protocol of 1997, which aim at carbon dioxide reductions but exclude China from reduction quotas, an apparent inequity being negotiated in follow-on discussions to Kyoto in Copenhagen. The United States is the only major industrialized country in the world that is not party to the Kyoto Protocol but is an active partner in its successor, a position examined in Amplification 14.2: The United States, Kyoto, and Copenhagen.

Amplification 14.2

THE UNITED STATES, KYOTO, AND COPENHAGEN

As noted, the United States is the major nonmember of the Kyoto Protocol of 1997 among major industrialized countries. The Clinton administration had negotiated participation but had not submitted the treaty to the U.S. Senate for ratification before leaving office. On March 13, 2001, the Bush administration announced that it did not favor the treaty and would not transmit it to the Senate, thereby killing American participation.

The Bush administration stated two bases for its rejection of Kyoto. The first was that the United States would have to bear an unfair burden in implementing its provisions, since the United States was deemed the greatest contributor to greenhouse gas emissions (about 25 percent of all affected gases and 36 percent of carbon dioxide emissions worldwide) and would thus have to cut the most. Since U.S. compliance would require reduced fossil fuel burning beyond similar restrictions on other countries, the administration argued that participation would harm the American economy disproportionately and unfairly. Second, the Kyoto Protocol excluded from its provisions developing countries that had hitherto not made sizable contributions to the problem, even if those countries were becoming polluters or were projected to do so in the future. As noted, the chief culprit was China, with India as a potential troublemaker as well.

These American objections, which have been rejected by most of the participating members, mean that implementation of the Kyoto Protocol is less effective, since over one-third of the emissions are not regulated by the treaty's provisions. Fred Krupp, executive director of Environmental Defense, a private advocacy group, summarizes the concern: "It is bad for America's interests for the United States to be seen as a rogue nation of greenhouse gas pollution. By simply opposing the Kyoto Protocol, rather than seeking to improve it, the administration would have effectively blocked the only binding international agreement for fighting global warming, while offering no alternative path to protect the planet." The American position is, however, changing. The United States participated in the 2007 follow-up meeting to Kyoto in Bali, Indonesia, and endorsed a series of general principles agreed to by the participants (the so-called Bali Road Map) to be negotiated in Copenhagen, Denmark, scheduled to start in late 2009. The Obama administration has been an enthusiastic participant in these initiatives, sponsoring legislation in the U.S. Congress to set carbon dioxide reduction standards compatible with the Copenhagen guidelines and requirements. In so doing, the U.S. position on global warming has come full circle from enthusiastic advocacy to intransigent opposition to largely unconditional support. These steps by the United States should ameliorate much of the international dissent.

Is global warming, as the leading emblem of worldwide environmental concerns, a legitimate national security issue that should be considered along with other, more conventional national security matters? With no claim to inclusiveness or exhaustiveness, three perspectives can be examined to help formulate the answer.

One way to think about the question is in terms of *threat*, since that is the normal framework within which national security problems are measured. Does global warming threaten Americans (or citizens of the world in general)? Answering that question is complicated because the question is too simply put. Part of the answer is a matter of timing: global warming may pose some disquieting and inconveniencing short-term consequences (hotter summers, prolonged drought or rain-producing seasons, more violent weather generally), but it does not pose direct threats that people associate with the phenomenon. In the aftermath of unsettled weather that results in tornadoes ripping through the countryside, victims do not, after all, say, "If we had burned less gasoline in our cars, this tornado would not have happened." The longer-range consequence—the permanent flooding of low-lying coastal areas, making them uninhabitable—certainly affects the security of people who either live or want to live in those areas, but this consequence has not been experienced and lies somewhere in the future. Thought of in threat terms, global warming poses more of a *potential* than an immediate threat. (Global warming scientists would, of course, argue the consequences of that assessment, which can lead to inaction and thus make the long-term consequences worse than they would be if action were taken now.)

The security *consequences* of global warming are more difficult to specify, and thus, it is more difficult to know who to punish or how to punish them. It is, for instance, very hard to specify how people will suffer specifically because of the consequences of global warming and, most importantly, to *personalize* the quality and nature of that future suffering in a way that motivates current actions that involve personal and societal sacrifice. If one could demonstrate that reducing the weight of automobiles by a certain number of hundreds of pounds would result in fuel savings (and consequent carbon dioxide emissions) that would mean that ocean levels would rise a concomitant number of feet less than without that reduction in automobile weight and thus not inundate a predictable amount of coastline (preferably including a part on which people live) within the lifetime of those people, the plea might be quite effective. It is not possible responsibly to articulate such a threat, and thus, the question of consequences tends to become more abstract and, as a result, less actionable.

If one moves to the identification of *solutions* to global warming, the issue becomes both more contentious and more directly security oriented. All solutions to global warming hinge on carbon dioxide reduction, which, in turn, includes less burning of fossil fuels (principally petroleum). Proposals for such reductions activate opposition on traditional national security grounds: reduced energy production and its impact on economic productivity, the enormous dependency of modern military forces on petroleum for operational purposes, and the strategic leverage of petroleum possessors over those with dependencies, for instance. The impact is to bifurcate the argument into an either/or proposition: one can support traditional security *or* remedies to global warming, but since their consequences are incompatible (at least in the short run), one cannot support both.

The question remains, Is global warming a national security problem? (Alternatively, is it a national problem that can usefully be considered within the framework of national security?) The answer is not unambiguous. On one hand, categorizing global warming in these terms elevates its visibility and the extent to which it is taken seriously within the political process: the designation of national security, for better or worse, endows an issue with greater gravity in some circles than it possesses without it. Since those who are most interested in the global warming issue tend not to be participants in the traditional national security process, categorizing global warming as a national security issue probably raises its prominence and certainly broadens its audience. On the other hand, inclusion of global warming on the broader national security agenda can result in dilution of its consideration (global warming as one of many problems) or in the presentation of contrary arguments not directly relevant to the issue (global warming is important, but other concerns like economic disadvantages are more important). The audience may broaden, but it will include more hostile voices.

Hurricane Katrina

Where does one place natural disasters within the priorities of national security? Clearly, natural disasters affect the security of those subject to them and are thus important national concerns. Formal federal jurisdiction over such incidents resides with the Federal Emergency Management Agency (FEMA), created by President Carter in 1979, and implementation of the Homeland Security Act of 2002 placed FEMA (however reluctantly) under the auspices of the new Department of Homeland Security (DHS), thus implicitly according it national security status. The federal response to Hurricanes Katrina and Rita, however, raised serious concern about the actual priority assigned to this function, and the unavailability of National Guard units to aid in recovery efforts from subsequent natural disasters (because the units have been on active duty in Iraq) has only added to this concern.

The ongoing response (or lack thereof) to Hurricane Katrina by the federal government has become something of a symbol for those critical of federal priorities. In terms of human devastation, for instance, official statistics indicate that as of August 2006, 1,464 people had lost their lives as a result of the impact of Katrina on New Orleans and the Gulf Coast (in parts of Louisiana and Mississippi and, to a lesser extent, Alabama), nearly half the number of people who lost their lives in the September 11 attacks. Much rhetoric has surrounded federal efforts to respond to the human and physical suffering that centered on New Orleans, but even four years later, large parts of the city (notably the Ninth Ward) remained uninhabited and uninhabitable, and the same was true all along the affected Gulf Coast (principally in Mississippi). Emergency supplemental funding for the area has been slow to get to the places where it is most needed, and the inevitable question of what priority disaster relief has in fact is routinely raised.

Should responses to natural disasters like Katrina be part of the national security equation? If so, where should they be placed in the hierarchy of national security concerns? Is, for instance, planning for and funding programs against the possibility of a major earthquake in southern California more or less important than continuing funding for the military effort in Iraq or for a missile defense system in Europe or elsewhere? Or are these areas of concern so unrelated that they cannot and should not fall under the same umbrella of consideration?

As noted, the federal government has implicitly elevated environmental disaster response to a national security concern by placing FEMA under the DHS, thereby making it difficult for the government to argue disaster relief is *not* part of national security, and the states concur in this judgment by placing National Guard contingents under their control among the prominent first responders to national disasters within their jurisdictions. Yet National Guard units have been assigned to extended (and repeated) deployments to Iraq without apparent detailed regard to the effects of their absence from the resources available to deal with natural disasters, and FEMA resources originally intended for natural disaster relief have been diverted to priorities arising from the global war on terrorism (GWOT) (some of the first responses to terrorist attacks resemble similar responses to natural disasters).

Would the response to Hurricane Katrina have been different if it had been considered a threat to national security rather than a response to a horrific but naturally caused disaster? Unlike global warming, it is difficult to assign human blame for the occurrence of Katrina. (An argument can be made that global warming has resulted in higher water temperatures in the Gulf of Mexico, making the hurricane *worse* than it would otherwise have been, but that effect is marginal.) The fact that there was no identifiable human enemy who caused Katrina did not make its effects any less severe to those who suffered them, yet patterns of response were noticeably slower and less intense (and certainly less effective) than they might have been had the event been viewed as a traditional national security disaster.

Where should priorities lie in the future? If the global warming theorists are substantially correct in their projections, one of the major impacts of continued neglect of global warming will be an intensification of weather patterns, including the severity of storms and their impact, and Hurricane Katrina may be the harbinger of things to come. At the same time, seismologists and other geologists maintain that a major shift in the Earth's crust is inevitable in southern California in the upcoming years. Depending on exactly how the resulting earthquake is centered and directed (at the Los Angeles basin or southward toward Mexico), the resulting devastation could make Hurricane Katrina or September 11 pale in terms of human and property losses. Is that a matter of high national priority on a plane with threats in the Middle East or elsewhere? Should these possibilities be thought of separately or together? What national priorities should attach to each prospect, and should they compete for national security resources? The answers are not simple, straightforward, or necessarily obvious.

HEALTH/DISEASE SECURITY

In 2000, the Clinton administration declared the acquired immunodeficiency syndrome (AIDS) pandemic in Africa a national security priority for the United States. The basis for this assertion was that AIDS was effectively decimating the African

Continent of a generation of young men and women who will not be available to assume leadership positions in their countries in the future, with the consequence that many countries may become dangerously destabilized and thus troublesome and one reaction may be a massive migration of people from Africa to Europe and North America. This problem was discussed several years ago by Robert D. Kaplan in the more general sense of migration caused by human misery generally—hardly anyone paid attention.

In January 2001, a Congolese woman entered Canada on a commercial airplane. She was coughing uncontrollably during the flight, and after she had deplaned and disappeared, a concern was raised that she might have the incredibly deadly Ebola hemorrhagic fever, that she might have communicated the extremely contagious disease to other passengers in the enclosed (and almost ideal) incubating space of the flight, and that those passengers could further spread the disease (for which there is no known treatment) to others. When she was found, it turned out the woman was not infected, and the concern passed.

Is the threat of diseases a matter of national security concern? The recent pattern of outbreaks of diseases with the potential to spread misery and death broadly among populations (AIDS, Ebola, sudden acute respiratory syndrome, and avian and swine flu, for instance) has raised the national consciousness on such matters, and there are historical precedents as well. The "black death" of bubonic plague raged through Europe in the 1300s and claimed nearly one-fourth of the population as victims. At the end of World War I, American forces returning to the United States were exposed to the so-called Spanish flu (so named because the first cases were observed in Spain), and the result was an epidemic in which 675,000 (out of 105 million) Americans died. Are there similar prospects in the future, and what can or should be done about them?

There are two ways to think about the dangers of diseases as a national security matter. One is to think about the possible spread of diseases that originate elsewhere to the United States, where Americans could be infected and suffer or die. In the past several years, there have been numerous warnings about this possibility, normally associated with some form of influenza. The most recent threats came with the outbreak in China in February 2003 of sudden acute respiratory syndrome (SARS), which killed 8,098 people worldwide before it was declared eradicated in 2005 by the World Health Organization; the avian or bird flu (technically H5N1 avian flu), which appeared in various parts of Asia in 2005; and the swine (H1N1) flu first identified in 2009. In these cases, the U.S. government issued warnings about the possibility the diseases could spread to the United States, and the Centers for Disease Control issued guidelines about the diseases but admitted that vaccines against them were either nonexistent or available in grossly inadequate supply. Like the Canadian Ebola incident, these dangers have not materialized on a large scale (although the eventual death toll of swine flu is unknown at this writing), but that does not mean there are not others (particularly virulent and drug-resistant strains of tuberculosis, for instance) that will emerge as real threats on the scale of the Spanish flu (with today's population, that would result in about 2 million deaths) or even greater. One tantalizingly dire possibility comes from global warming scientists. Many of the most dangerous diseases come from the world's subtropical climates, and as global warming occurs, temperatures will rise enough that some of them can spread to places that formerly were too cold for them to survive and where the populations have not evolved immunities to them.

The second problem is the impact the existence or spread of diseases can have on other parts of the world. The most obvious case in point, as suggested in the introduction to this section, surrounds the impact of AIDS. Its most devastating effects have been and continue to grow in Africa and have been the subject of at least a handful of recent analyses (De Waal, Iliffe, and Patterson, for instance). Beyond the human tragedy associated with the loss of literally millions of victims, the shortening of life expectancies below forty years of age in several countries, and the prospects of continued ravages from more and more deaths, there are enormous geopolitical consequences that are moderated for the most developed countries only by the marginalization of Africa generally in world politics.

The AIDS problem is not, however, entirely isolated to Africa. Indeed, in recent years there have been reports of increased infection rates in China and India, to cite the most prominent cases. While neither country wants widely to publicize these outbreaks or their frequency (in some cases because they do not know, as they tend to occur in rural, outlying regions), a health crisis arising from an epidemic or pandemic could be severely taxing to the health care systems of these two aspirants to major-power status and could form another layer of obstacles to a country like China that is already struggling with an environmental crisis, as noted earlier.

Protecting the public health is an obviously major obligation of the government, and protecting the populace from the intrusion of disease seeping across the country's borders is arguably a priority on a par with preventing other forms of alien invasion of American soil. In this sense, one can easily think of health and disease security as a form of national security, although one for which traditional national security instruments and strategies are inappropriate or irrelevant. Yet in times other than apparent or potential crisis like the potential swine flu epidemic, there is little concerted public attention to these matters—and certainly nothing parallel, for instance, to the emphasis on terrorism or illegal immigration. Why not?

There are, of course, numerous possible explanations for this lack of emphasis, and three have been borrowed from the author's *Cases in International Relations* (Chapter 15) for mention. The first is the *seriousness and immediacy of the problem*. Despite the potential for catastrophic consequences from an outbreak of a hemorrhagic disease like Ebola in a large, metropolitan area or the spread of AIDS in the 1980s in this country, there have not been actual cases of a major disease-related national emergency since the Spanish flu over ninety years ago. As a result, the prospects remain at a lower level of consciousness, and thus demand for action remains weaker than that regarding more conventional threats. Having said that, the consequences of a disease for which there is no known cure or for which the supplies of curative medicines are in very short supply (and would thus have to be rationed) absolutely dwarf the consequences of the largest terrorist attack in human history (the September 11 attacks). It is sometimes suggested that terrorists might seek to attack the United States with pathogens in ways similar to the alleged provision of smallpox-infected blankets to American Indians during the 1800s: would some credible evidence of such an intention raise awareness and concern?

The second problem is *lack of personalization* of the problems. The African AIDS pandemic is, after all, thousands of miles away, and even attempts to publicize it by people like former Secretary of State Colin Powell and countless entertainers have not driven home the suffering that occurs where diseases like AIDS wrack the human condition. President George W. Bush announced what he called a major initiative in his 2003 State of the Union address to help alleviate African AIDS, the President's Emergency Plan for AIDS Relief, but it has languished at least in part because the general public has not demanded its implementation in the face of other priorities. Will it require thousands of Americans dying hideous deaths from some incurable disease to make these problems seem real enough to attract concerted attention?

The third problem stems from the first two: *low prioritization of the problem*. There is, after all, no shortage of demands upon national resources and energies, and not all of them can have an equally high priority. That, after all, is the nature of risk management: to choose those areas where one will move to reduce and eliminate risk and to ignore, either by specific action or implicitly, the others and accept whatever risk that entails. Concerns receive higher or lower priority depending on calculations of their immediacy and the consequences of inattention: which matters *must* be dealt with, and which can be deferred? To date, dealing with the prospects of major diseases intruding in the United States has not been assigned a particularly high priority in the scheme of security concerns. As long as there is no national crisis arising from the outbreak of some deadly disease, the decision remains a viable one. But what if a new and deadly disease suddenly appears and the country is unprepared for it? Will national security be served?

CONCLUSION: EXPANDED SECURITY HORIZONS

The end of the Iraq War will, among other things, release some of the resources and energies that have been devoted to that endeavor for other purposes. It will probably not bring a "peace dividend" like that unfulfilled promise of the end of the Cold War (where it was predicted that resources previously spent on the military competition with the Soviets could be redirected to other priorities). The reason is that the war has been conducted almost entirely "off budget" (through supplemental appropriations that will simply disappear after that spending ends, with no visible impact on the shape or priorities of the federal budget). Rather, since most of these supplemental appropriations have been financed through borrowing—particularly from foreign sources—the major effect will be that the country will decrease its rate of indebtedness to places like China. The expenditures are not inconsequential: the Bush administration had, by late August 2007, requested nearly $200 billion in supplemental appropriations for the upcoming 2008 fiscal year. Such appropriations never appeared as part of the federal budget, so their discontinuance will reduce neither the budget nor the deficit that past appropriations represent. If anything, there will be budgetary demands for additional funds to rebuild the armed forces to remedy their depletion in Iraq. There will not be any noticeable amount of resources "freed up" for alternate spending.

There will, however, be the release of some intellectual energy, both inside and outside of government. A central argument of this book has been that a post-9/11 United States will turn its attention to concerns in addition to those national security problems for which military force is a solution because there will be a reluctance—at least for a time—to employ military force to solve national problems. Iran is a prime example. Periodic saber rattling by the Bush administration demonstrated that the use of the military will be proposed, but with the current and post-Iraq condition of the military, it is difficult to imagine how the United States could or why it would engage in another large-scale deployment of choice for the next few years. After the post-Iranian election controversy of 2009 receded, the idea of using force against Iran has virtually disappeared.

Rather, militarized or semimilitarized efforts will likely be concentrated on the problem of terrorism, possibly conceptualized as something other than the GWOT. Government agencies not completely submerged in the terrorism campaign (the State Department, for instance) and analysts outside government will turn to other concerns that have been on the conceptual back burner since 2003, including the issues raised in this chapter and in Chapter 8.

Will these kinds of issues become a permanent part of the national security agenda? There is reason to believe both that they will and that they will not. Certainly, the kinds of problems discussed are likely to be enduring: global warming, natural disasters, infectious disease epidemics, petroleum dependency, and control of the country's borders are long-term problems that will not disappear in the short or mid-term, and emphasizing them is a way to move the spotlight away from the military realm of national security. At the same time, there will be resistance to thinking about these issues in national security terms. To some traditionalists steeped in the equation of security and military affairs, these nontraditional issues are "soft" in a geopolitical sense, important in their own right but not on a par with the military threats to national existence. In their view, elevating environmental security, as an example, to national security status thus diverts attention from what is truly important. At the same time, those people most concerned with the kinds of nontraditional issues discussed here are generally not sympathetic to more traditional, militarily oriented analysts (and vice versa), and it will take more than a little time and energy to bring both groups to the same conceptual page.

Will the center of national security concern move from its traditional military mooring toward nontraditional considerations? Probably, almost certainly, it will not. While there may be an interlude after the Afghanistan and Iraq Wars are over in which the United States is more reluctant to commit military forces to distant lands than before, the world will remain a dangerous place in which it would be imprudent to let down the country's guard. At the same time, the world environment is becoming more complex, and one clear manifestation of that complexity is the rise of troubling national and international concerns for which traditional national security solutions are inappropriate or ineffective. The result is a fuller and more diverse national security agenda.

Study/Discussion Questions

1. Why does the text maintain that nontraditional security concerns could become more prominent in the next five to ten years? Do you agree?

2. Define the border security problem in historical perspective. Why has maintaining a secure border been simultaneously so difficult and of such low priority historically for the United States?

3. Define the various aspects of the country's current border security problem. Briefly describe each aspect and the extent to which it is or is not a national security problem. Is an impenetrable border a feasible or desirable goal (or both, or neither)?

4. Why is resource dependency a national security problem? Using petroleum as an example, define what problem that dependency creates for the United States, what the consequences of that dependency are, and what can be done about the problem.

5. Why is the availability of adequate potable water a national problem or a potential national problem for some states of the world? Use examples.

6. Define *environmental security*. Is it legitimate and/or helpful to think of environmental concerns like global warming and natural disasters like Hurricane Katrina in national security terms? Why or why not?

7. What kind of threat does the prospect of the intrusion of deadly diseases present to Americans? Should it be thought of as a national security problem? If not, what kind of problem is it?

8. Should the future national security agenda of the United States be expanded to include nontraditional concerns like those discussed in the text? Why or why not?

Selected Bibliography

Andeas, Peter. "Politics on Edge: Managing the U.S.–Mexico Border." *Current History* 105, no. 695 (February 2006): 64–68.

Boot, Max. "Pirates, Then and Now." *Foreign Affairs* 88, no. 4 (July/August 2009): 94–107.

Browne, John. "Beyond Kyoto." *Foreign Affairs* 83, no. 4 (July/August 2004): 20–32.

Cashell, Brian W., and Marc Labonte. *The Macroeconomic Effects of Hurricane Katrina.* Washington, DC: Congressional Research Service, September 13, 2005.

Das, Gurcharan. "The Indian Model." *Foreign Affairs* 85, no. 4 (July/August 2006): 2–16.

De Waal, Alex. *AIDS and Power: Why There Is No Political Crisis—Yet.* Amsterdam, Netherlands: Zed Books, 2006.

Diehl, Paul R., and Niles Peter Gleditsch, eds. *Environmental Conflict.* Boulder, CO: Westview Press, 2001.

Ebola. (http://nyu.edu/educational/mindsinmotion/ebola/htm)

Economy, Elizabeth C. "The Great Leap Backward." *Foreign Affairs* 86, no. 5 (September/October 2007): 38–59.

Elhance, A. *Hydropolitics and the Third World: Conflict and Cooperation in International River Basins.* Washington, DC: United States Institute of Peace Press, 1999.

Flynn, Stephen E. *America the Vulnerable: How Our Government Is Failing to Protect Us from Terrorism.* New York: Harper Perennials, 2005.

Garrett, Laurie. "The Lessons of HIV/AIDS." *Foreign Affairs* 84, no. 4 (July/August 2005): 51–64.

———. "The Next Pandemic?" *Foreign Affairs* 84, no. 4 (July/August 2005): 3–23.

Iliffe, John. *The African AIDS Epidemic: A History.* Athens: Ohio University Press, 2006.

Kaplan, Robert D. *The Coming Anarchy: Shattering the Dreams of the Post Cold War.* New York: Random House, 2000.

Kim, Richard. "The People Versus AIDS." *The Nation* 283, no. 2 (July 10, 2006): 5–6.

Klare, Michael. "Navigating the Energy Transition." *Current History* 108, no. 714 (January 2009): 26–32.

Krauze, Enrique. "Furthering Democracy in Mexico." *Foreign Affairs* 85, no. 1 (January/February 2006): 54–65.

Krupp, Fred."Statement of Environmental Defense Fund President Fred Krupp. March 31, 2009 (http://www.edf.org/pressrelease.cfm?contentID=9474)

Maugeri, Leonardo. "Two Cheers for Expensive Oil." *Foreign Affairs* 85, no. 2 (March/April 2006): 149–160.

O'Neil, Shannon. "The Real War in Mexico." *Foreign Affairs* 88, no. 4 (July/August 2009): 66–77.

Patterson, Amy S. *The Politics of AIDS in Africa.* Boulder, CO: Lynne Reinner, 2006.

Payan, Terry. *The Three U.S.–Mexico Border Wars: Drugs, Immigration, and Homeland Security.* Westport, CT: Greenwood, 2006.

Pirages, Dennis C., and Theresa Manley DeGeest. *Ecological Security: An Evolutionary Perspective on Globalization.* New York: Rowman and Littlefield, 2004.

Podesta, John, and Peter Ogden. "The Security Implications of Climate Change." *Washington Quarterly* 31, no. 1 (Winter 2007–08): 115–138.

Roberts, Paul. "The Seven Myths of Energy Independence." *Mother Jones* 33, no. 3 (May/June 2008): 31–37.

Rockenbach, Leslie J. *The Mexican-American Border: NAFTA and Global Linkages.* Abingdon, England: Routledge, 2001.

Rozenthal, Andres. "The Other Side of Immigration." *Current History* 106, no. 697 (February 2007): 89–90.

Shifter, Michael. "Latin America's Drug Problem." *Current History* 106, no. 697 (February 2007): 58–63.

Snow, Donald M. *Cases in International Relations: Portraits of the Future.* 3rd ed. New York: Pearson Longman, 2008.

Stern, Todd, and William Antholis. "A Changing Climate: The Road Ahead for the United States." *Washington Quarterly* 31, no. 1 (Winter 2007–08): 175–187.

Victor, David G. *Climate Change: Debating America's Options.* New York: Council on Foreign Relations, 2004.

Yergin, Daniel. "Ensuring Energy Security." *Foreign Affairs* 85, no. 2 (March/April 2006): 69–82.

Zweig, David, and Bi Jianhai. "China's Global Hunt for Energy." *Foreign Affairs* 84, no. 5 (September/October 2005): 18–24.

Index

9/11 Commission, 98
9/11, legacies of, 211–41
　fault line of, 211
　terrorism, role of, 211–12
　principal, 228
1990s. *See also Cold War, end of;
　Globalization*
　characteristics of, 293–94
　circle of market democracies, 138
　globalization and, 131, 138
　new internal wars (NIWs), 273,
　　287, 292–93

The Absolute Weapon (Brodie), 248
Abu Ghraib prison, in Iraq, 87, 230
Afghan National Security Forces
　(ANSF), 311
Afghanistan, 41, 47, 48, 49, 142, 143,
　150, 164, 172, 173, 195. *See
　also Taliban government*
　American military
　　Afghan National Security Forces
　　　(ANSF), expansion of, 311
　　American involvement in,
　　　302, 307
　　asymmetrical warfare, 10–11, 275,
　　　284–85
　　charge of diverted attention of
　　　united states, 311–12
　　conventional force, use of, 12
　　ending the war, 314–15
　　funds earmarked for, 115
　　global war on terror (GWOT)
　　　campaign, 284
　　legacies of war in Iraq and, 327–35
　　　military, 329–30
　　　political, 328–29
　　mission feasibility
　　　Afghan National Army (ANA),
　　　　310
　　　ISAF military activity, 310
　　　military objective, 310–11
　　　Pashtuns, conversion of, 309
　　Operation Anaconda, 311
　　Pakistan, and Al Qaeda, 315
　　Pashtuns and, 308–9
　　Persian Gulf War, 1990–1991, 329
　　removal of Taliban government,
　　　362–63
　　similarities with Iraq, 312
　　unresolved dilemmas in war
　　　American attacks, reasons for,
　　　　305
　　　U.S. campaign against Al
　　　　Qaeda, 304, 306
　　　U.S. civil war for the control of,
　　　　304, 306
　　　U.S. commitments in, 302
　　vital and less-than-vital interests,
　　　60
Afghanization, 314

African embassy, attacks of 1998, 61,
　118
Against All Enemies (Clarke), 117
AIDS pandemic, 389, 391
Al Jazeera, 87
Al Qaeda, 4, 9, 41, 47, 49, 142, 144,
　151, 176, 212, 213, 215, 217,
　220, 221, 227, 228, 302,
　334, 381
Al-Bashir, Omar Hassan Ahmad, 40
Albright, Madeleine, 58
Allison, Graham T., Jr., 8, 130
Allison's tectonic plates analogy, 9
All-Volunteer Force (AVF), 88, 264
American Declaration of Indepen-
　dence and Constitution, 52
American economy, weakness of the,
　17–18
American experience. *See also Na-
　tional security; United States*
　ahistoricism
　　Europe and Asia, 69, 70
　　native Americans, 70–71
　　optimism resulting from, 71
　Anglo-Saxon heritage, 73–75
　　army on home soil, aversion to,
　　　73–74
　geography
　　diminishing advantages, 73
　　oil dependence on foreign, 73, 74
　　physical vulnerability,
　　　1814–1857, 72
　　telecommunications and trans-
　　　portation advances, 73
American military tradition. *See also
　Cold War; National security;
　United States*
　Cold war, 1945–1989
　　Cold Warriors, 83
　　involuntary draft system, 83
　　military prestige and respect, 83
　　military, as permanent part of
　　　peacetime life, 83
　　national conscription system, 83
　　permanent state of mobilization,
　　　83, 84
　　public support and opinion,
　　　86–88
　　thermonuclear weapons, expan-
　　　sion of, 83
　contemporary Period, 1989 to
　　Present
　　as formative and Cold War
　　　hybrid, 89–90
　　Cold war, collapse of, 89
　　formative period, 1789–1945
　　　"can do" syndrome, 79
　　　citizen-soldier, 78–79
　　　French revolutions, 81
　　　government overthrow, as
　　　　purpose, 82

Industrial Revolution innova-
　tions, 80
　invincibility, myth of, 79
　mobilization and demobilization,
　　80
　total war preference, 80–82
media, role of
　access to military operations, 86
　cable television news networks,
　　86
　imbedded reporters, 87
　instant analyses of events, 86
　worsening relationship, 85, 86
American Revolution, 71, 73, 76, 77,
　130, 279, 295
American tradition, conditioning
　factors in, 70–75
American views of geopolitics, 22
Amin Dada, Idi, 32
Amnesty International, 142
Anti-Americanism, 239
Antiterrorism, 238, 344–46
Argentina, 140, 197
Aristide, Jean-Bertrand, 348
Armed Services Committees, 111
Army of the Republic of Vietnam
　(ARVN), 279
The Art of War (Tzu), 278
Asia–Pacific Economic Cooperation
　(APEC), 196
Aspin, Les, 266
Atlantic Monthly, 134
Attacking Terrorism (Cronin), 214
Axis of evil, 144, 157
Azerbaijan, 176

Balkans, 137, 293, 339
Ballistic Missile Defense (BMD), 248
Basayev, Shamil, 216
Berlin Wall, 131, 163, 174
Bernanke, Ben, 199
Bi Jianhai, 379
Biden, Joe, 132
Bin Laden, Usama, 4–5, 202, 215,
　217, 267, 286, 291, 313, 343
　fatwa, 215
　pre-September 11 period, 6
　Saudi Arabia, U.S. presence in, 74
　terrorist acts of, 61–62
Bipolarity and multipolarity, 147
Blitzkrieg tactics, 283, 288
Bodin, Jean, 26, 35
Bonaparte, Napoleon, 175
Borden, William Liscum, 248
Border Patrol, 206, 371, 376
Border Protection, Antiterrorism, and
　Illegal Immigration Control
　Act, 206
Border security, 204–6, 369–76
　drug trafficking, 205
　illegal immigration, 205